**PSYCHOLOGY
AND SOCIAL
BEHAVIOR**

Under the Editorship
of Wayne H. Holtzman

PSYCHOLOGY AND SOCIAL BEHAVIOR

JOHN W. McDAVID
Georgia State University

HERBERT HARARI
San Diego State University

HARPER & ROW, PUBLISHERS
New York Evanston San Francisco London

Sponsoring Editor: George A. Middendorf
Project Editor: Alice M. Solomon
Designer: Emily Harste
Production Supervisor: Bernice Krawczyk

Library of Congress Cataloging in Publication Data
McDavid, John W.
     Psychology and social behavior.

     "Portions of this book appeared in Social psychology:
individuals, groups, societies, copyright 1968 by John
W. McDavid and Herbert Harari."
     Bibliography: p.
     1. Social psychology. I. Harari, Herbert, joint
author. II. Title
HM251.M16   301.1   73–16541
ISBN 0–06–044146–1

CONTENTS

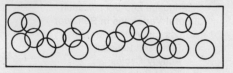

ILLUSTRATIVE RESEARCH EXAMPLES

ix

PREFACE

Man is a curious animal!

Apparently he has always been eager to analyze and understand himself and the social world he lives in. Even the oldest records of civilization evidence man's speculation about himself and his relationships with others.

But times change, and the context of man's curiosity about himself changes. Historically, we have seen the social sciences evolve from vague philosophical speculations about human relations into mature and methodical scientific ventures. And now, more recently, we have seen the nature of the student-scholar change very rapidly.

Less than a decade ago we prepared a textbook, *Social Psychology*, from an academic point of view. This book was aimed at arousing the reader's scholarly curiosity about this very interesting and still somewhat novel intellectual discipline. Its tone and content were geared to that purpose. It spoke in academic tones to the intellectually curious, describing social psychology as an end in itself.

Today's students are very different from those who led us to write the first book. They are more than intellectually curious; they are involved. They are concerned about social problems, overwhelmed by their range and complexity, and dismayed by the failure of prior generations to confront them and seek solutions to them.

This book is not merely a revision of the earlier book. It proceeds from a new point of departure and presents the domain of social psychology within a new frame of reference. It approaches social psychology as a tool contributing to the solution of overwhelming social problems with which today's student generation must deal effectively in the years to come. It does not claim to offer quick and easy solutions; instead, it merely points the way toward solutions yet to be attained. It presents social psychology as a field whose potential is yet to be realized. Although there has indeed been a vast and visible increase in everyday practical applications of social psychology during recent years, more is yet to come.

The applied orientation of this book is reflected in its definition of social psychology and its point of departure in Section I. Here, the reader is introduced to social psychology. In a brief academic excursion, he is acquainted with the science of social psychology in terms of its methods of research and theoretical frameworks. Chapter 3 is a departure from the mainstream of the text, because it includes considerable detail about specific methodological procedures. For this reason it is a chapter the reader may wish to browse through only very casually, continuing immediately on to Chapter 4. In this case he can use Chapter 3 as a reference source, referring back to it from time to time to amplify and clarify research procedures mentioned in later chapters. (A reader more seriously interested in the nature of psychological research will want to read Chapter 3 more carefully.)

The remainder of the book progresses through a review of the applicable content of accumulated research in social psychology. Section II examines the influences of the social world upon the individual's behavior and experience. Section III concerns diadic person-to-person social interaction. Section IV describes the qualities of organized interaction in social groups. And Section V deals with unorganized or loosely organized collective social situations.

The format in which the book presents this information was carefully planned and designed to facilitate the reader's understanding of what he is reading. Acknowledging that psychology tends toward excessive use of technical jargon, new concepts of a technical nature are italicized upon their first introduction. For this reason a review of the italicized words in each chapter can serve as a kind of glossary for the reader. The table of contents at the beginning of the book is amplified with subtitle listings, thus outlining in some detail what the reader may expect to find within each chapter. This chapter framework, repeated at the beginning of each chapter, serves as a set of instructional objectives to guide the reader's attention as he reads. Furthermore, at the end of each chapter there is a section labeled *Review,* which enumerates very briefly and concisely the major content of ideas in that chapter.

Near the end of each of the chapters describing the content of psychological research (Sections II through IV, or Chapters 4 through 13), there is a section labeled *Relevance and Application.* These are brief descriptions of the more direct applications of social psychology to significant social problems. In each chapter the content of social psychological research is reviewed in the context of the social issues to which it most directly relates. Some of these applications are obvious, others obscure or surprising.

Within each chapter are *illustrative research examples*—particular research studies or human events that are used as illustrations of the ideas outlined in the main body of the text. These are word-pictures, and they amplify the text by citing concrete examples of research findings and applications.

Finally, an *Instructor's Manual* and a *Study Guide* are available for use with the text.

As with any project of this kind, many people helped in many ways. Our gratitude cannot be measured, but we acknowledge to all of these our appreciation of their needed assistance along the way: Jim Applefield, Becky Boone, Frances Breitenbucher, Linda Carter, Gray Garwood, Phyllis Johnson, Andre Joseph, Barbara Kibler, Ruth McVay, Fred Munoz, Gretchen Murphy, Stephanie Ragsdale, Chris Smith, Judy Spector, Carol Sweeney, Doris Townsend, Marva Jo West. We are especially grateful for the untiring efforts and generous advice offered by Alice M. Solomon, Project Editor for this book.

John W. McDavid
Herbert Harari

SOCIAL PSYCHOLOGY

Social psychology is a member of the family of modern social sciences; it is the study of man's behavior in the social and cultural space surrounding him. Social psychology is both old (in content) and new (in method). The oldest records of civilization reveal man's continuing eagerness to understand himself and the universe around him. But it was only a century ago that man began to apply the methods of empirical science to his quest to understand relationships among the people who share this universe.

This book guides its reader on a tour of this domain of social science as viewed from the perspective of a particular kind of social scientist: the *psychologist*. This complex phenomenon of man in a social context can be approached from different points of view, using different methods of study, and drawing attention to different details of the overall pattern. All of the *social sciences*—anthropology, economics, political science, psychology, and sociology—share a common interest in studying relationships among people, but they use different methods to examine different details of these relationships. In many ways, man is a self-centered creature. This is not to say that he is selfish, but merely that he is interested in himself. Throughout history, man's self-reflective curiosity has been revealed through conjectures and speculations about "human nature." Modern psychology derives from man's inclination to place himself at the center of the universe and to begin his inquiry about the world with an inquiry into himself.

This book introduces the reader to *social psychology—the scientific study of the relationship of individuals to one another individually, in groups, and in society*. Social psychology is a very practical social science. It deals with one of the most exciting facets of human existence: human relationships. And it offers ideas that contribute significantly to the improvement of the quality of human existence. The scope and tone of modern social psychology have been shaped by the currents of American life; in turn, social psychology offers knowledge to shape the quality of American life in directions that prove more rewarding and more beneficial to human beings both individually and collectively.

Within this first Section, Chapter 1 describes the contemporary complexion of social psychology and the everyday social matrix within which it flourishes, as well as the historical-philosophical roots from which it grew. Chapter 2 outlines the general characteristics of an empirical-scientific approach to the study of social behavior; and Chapter 3 guides the reader through a digressive side trip into greater detail about the methods of scientific procedure employed by the modern social psychologist. The reader whose interests in social psychology turn to questions of "What has been discovered?" rather than "How has it been discovered?" may wish to skip Chapter 3 and proceed directly from Chapter 2 to Section II. For such a reader, Chapter 3 may be later read as a reference source on specific issues as they arise in other chapters.

1

PERSPECTIVES ON SOCIAL BEHAVIOR

In order to understand social psychology, it is necessary to recognize not only the *scope* of the issues with which it deals, but also its *perspectives* on these issues. The scope of social psychology is indicated by the definition offered earlier—the scientific study of the relationship of individuals to each other individually, in groups, and in society. But understanding the point of view and perspective from which social psychologists work requires a fuller examination of their context.

Social psychology is largely an American intellectual development. It has flourished within American psychology because it is compatible with the basic values and traditions that have shaped American thought generally. It is appealing because it satisfies several deeply ingrained values espoused by most Americans: pragmatism, respect for the scientific method as practiced in the natural sciences, and profound concern for the dignity of the individual in collective social systems. An appropriate place to begin one's orientation to modern social psychology is to examine the range of social issues to which it is addressed.

SOCIAL PSYCHOLOGY AND SOCIAL PROBLEMS

Social psychology deals with immediate, everyday social problems. It cannot find solutions for all of these problems, but in many ways it contributes useful guidance toward possible ways of understanding and working with these problems. As in any young and developing science, some research efforts may appear to be trivial and inconsequential. Yet these efforts are often necessary and vital to the continued accumulation of important scientific information. What seems trivial today may prove to be an important link to something of vast practical significance tomorrow.

Social psychology is so relevant to important social problems that there are often premature and excessive demands for application of partial or incomplete scientific knowledge. When this occurs, social psychology may be embarrassed by failure to provide adequate or lasting solutions to these problems. On the other hand, excessive caution and skepticism about applying psychological knowledge to practical problems earns no public acclaim either. Thus, social psychologists willingly apply their knowledge and theories to everyday social problems, but occasionally with a word of caution about gaps or ambiguities in areas that have not been thoroughly investigated. The third quarter of the twentieth century especially has been an era of increasing public awareness of the applicability of social psychology to important social issues.

Social Psychology in Education

Education is essentially a process of social learning, in which an individual attempts to communicate his skills and ideas to others. A teacher provides a model for imitative or observational learning, and he manipulates rewards and punishments contingent upon the student's behavior. Research concerning the functions of parents and authority figures in social learning may be applied to questions on teaching techniques and teacher training (Chapter 6).

American public education through practical necessity requires each teacher to deal with many students simultaneously rather than on a one-to-one tutorial basis. The teacher must use verbal communication in attempting to shape attitudes, opinions, and values of students. In this context, findings from research on communication and attitude change, persuasion, and propaganda are applicable to educational issues (Chapter 5). Teacher-student perception about one another can lead to expectations that affect classroom behavior and academic performance (Chapter 8).

APPLIED SOCIAL PSYCHOLOGY

In many areas of everyday human activity, research findings from social psychology have direct practical applications. Following are several concrete examples of such applications.

Military. Will a very efficient officer in charge of a group of bomber interception pilots show the same degree of efficiency if he is assigned to another military task involving other groups, such as infantry patrol? In other words, is a good officer always a good officer, in any military situation? (Research says the answer is NO.)

Industry. Will the participation of factory workers in setting their group's own production goals affect the rate at which they actually produce manufactured articles? (Research says the answer is YES.)

Politics. Are personality factors, such as values for conformity, related to the way a person votes in political elections? (Research says the answer is YES.)

Propaganda and Public Information. Does lack of valid and reliable information always lead to the circulation of untrue rumors? (Research says the answer is NO.)

Advertising. Can the content of an advertisement, the person who delivers it, and the manner of delivery affect the success of the advertisement in making people buy a product? (Research says the answer is YES.)

Education. Do American students work more effectively in a permissive classroom situation (no grades, no tests, and passive participation of the instructor) than in a strictly controlled classroom situation (formal grades, examinations, and firm control by the instructor)? (Research says the answer is NO.)

Mental Health. Are the kinds of personal problems that make people unhappy, psychologically disturbed, or neurotic related to their occupations and social class levels? (Research says the answer is YES.)

Because their interaction is continued over extended periods through a succession of purposes and activities, classroom groups eventually show many properties of organized groups. Thus educational research has directed its attention to the psychological study of group dynamics. The style of behavior of a teacher in the leadership role in the classroom tends to establish a well-defined group atmosphere. Practical circumstances require that the teacher exert some degree of control over students, with firm maintenance of disciplinary norms; consequently, most classroom atmospheres tend to be somewhat autocratic. This tendency is augmented by the fact that public school teachers are likely to show authoritarian tendencies in their personality structures. Several experimental investigations have actually compared such autocratic (teacher-centered) atmospheres with more democratic (learner-centered) ones. In general these studies suggest the superiority of nondirective, democratic, student-centered classroom atmospheres because they are associated with greater productivity as well as with greater satisfaction and higher morale among the students. However, there are exceptions to every rule: some students prefer more autocratic schoolroom atmospheres, and some teaching situations bog down under democratic atmospheres (Chapters 11, 12).

Social Psychology and Mental Health

Another significant area of applied psychology is that of mental health and psychotherapy. Clinical psychology has gradually become accepted as a member of the family of the "healing arts." As a branch of the behavioral sciences it attempts to apply basic psychological knowledge to both the prevention and the cure of individual behavioral disorders that threaten the smooth functioning, happiness, or security of either the individual or the society in which he lives .

From the very roots of the efforts of contemporary psychology to understand the makeup of human personality, it has been clear that the organization of behavior and experience is related to the social matrix. Sigmund Freud, in some of his later writings, spoke explicitly about the relationship between the individual's manner of handling his motivational impulses and his need for belongingness in his participation in groups and social systems. Many later theorists who embraced the core of Freud's ideas added further emphasis to the importance of interpersonal relationships and social influences in shaping both the healthy and the unhealthy personality (Chapter 6). Traditional methods of psychotherapy focused essentially upon a one-to-one relationship between the therapist and his patient. However, this patient-therapist relationship is a diadic interaction in which the therapist serves both as a model for the behavior of his patient as well as a manipulator of rewards and punishments for the patient's actions. Certain approaches to psychotherapy (called "directive" or "didactic") are formulated upon premises concerning the therapist's social control of the behavior of his patient through direct reinforcement and nonreinforcement (Chapter 6).

There have also been efforts to enlist the forces of group dynamics to contribute to the therapeutic process. Pioneering attempts in group psychotherapy initially met with hostile resistance from hospitals, clinics, and private psychotherapists. However, the growing demand for professional psychotherapeutic service to large numbers of patients eventually brought about a change of attitude. With World War II, the military, the Veterans Administration, and community mental health and child guidance clinics faced increasing pressure from waiting lists of clients in need of professional treatment. Thus in a sense the rapid development of group psychotherapy during the past 20 years occurred for a very poor (but nevertheless important) reason: it was conceived merely as a stop-gap measure aimed at attaining better patient-therapist ratios in the face of extreme shortages of trained psychotherapists. On the other hand, a number of clinical psychologists and psychotherapists have argued persistently for the expansion of group therapeutic techniques on the more logical premise that group forces may contribute directly to the therapeutic process itself. The therapeutic group is a miniature society in which the patient may enact new roles on a trial basis to gauge the reactions of others to his new behavior patterns. It becomes a source of collective reward and punishment through acceptance or rejection of each patient-member's actions. The group erects norms that guide and control the actions of each of its members; and quite importantly, it provides a shelter of collective support for the insecure patient as he works his way toward better adjustment to the less sensitive social world outside. Group therapy is not merely cheaper, but is a genuinely better way of accomplishing certain goals of psychotherapy (Chapters 10, 11, 12).

The Tavistock Clinic in England has become recognized as an outpost of strength in a movement called *social psychiatry* within the past two decades. This center has not only successfully amalgamated social psychology with applied clinical practice, but it has further brought about a reevaluation of concepts of the hospital or clinic as a therapeutic setting. The hospital, for example, is conceived as a closed community that includes not only psychotherapists and patients, but such auxiliary personnel as nurses, aides, clerks, supervisors, and volunteers. As a miniature society, the hospital may evolve its own culture, including customs and traditions that are transmitted through "generations" of rotating patients. In a sense, the entire hospital setting may be utilized as an enlarged psychotherapeutic group. In fact, the concept of the therapeutic community provides the basis for development of insulated communities for such purposes. The Hartford Institute for Living and other modern sanitarium-type hospitals are founded on such concepts. In effect, the patient in such a community profits from all of the benefits of enlisting social and group forces to aid in his own psychotherapy, but on a less miniaturized scale than the therapeutic group.

Interest in and support for a concept of *community psychology* has increased remarkably during the past decade. As an analog to preventive medicine, this concept argues that mental disease may be averted by early preventive measures. By providing facilities on a community basis, large numbers of individuals may be able to secure attention before the need becomes sufficiently great to cripple their daily lives and require hospitalization. The current temper of planning for public health services in the U.S. federal government includes considerable interest in the formation of community mental health clinics that would utilize discussion groups in a preventive rather than a therapeutic sense. Such clinics will presumably not only alleviate individual mental and behavior disorders, but would also aid in the solution of community problems and intergroup relations (Chapter 13).

Social Psychology and Crime and Delinquency

Although the problem of crime and juvenile delinquency is still met socially by traditional arguments for stringent police authority and punitive treatment of offenders, alternative approaches have been considered increasingly during the period since World War II. The fact that adolescents are especially prone to be "joiners" who participate in closely knit peer groups tends to insulate them from effective relationships with adult authorities. Especially in urban communities, juvenile delinquency is likely to occur in organized gangs that erect norms that override the individual youth's own personal standards of conduct. The identification of social status and acceptance within the peer group with such socially unacceptable acts as theft, rape, or excessive aggression induces widespread delinquent offense against organized society. Procedures patterned along the lines of group psychotherapy may be utilized to realign these adolescent group forces, so that they are more in accord with recognized dominant social standards. One such approach is that of the "street club worker," who gains the acceptance of an already organized adolescent group and thereby enters the group as an inconspicuous therapeutic force. Instead of "coming on strong" as a crusading reformer from outside, the street club worker gains access to the group from within and allows the group to utilize its own dynamics and gradually reorient itself into more constructive channels. Effective work in this capacity requires both sensitivity and skill on the part of the worker and full acceptance of the worker by the group. Slow and patient efforts to work with the group rather than "against" it have resulted in significant gains in relieving community pressures from organized juvenile crime (Chapters 10, 11, 12).

Social Psychology in Business and Industry

Economically significant applications of social psychology occur in the field of marketing and advertising. Under the free enterprise system, distribution of goods and services depends on making the consumer aware of their availability and persuading him to buy from one vendor rather than another. The advertiser must cultivate favorable attitudes toward his product. Large sums are spent annually by manufacturers to ascertain prevailing public attitudes in the market through large-scale survey research methods. Findings are translated into policy decisions involving the naming of products and stores, their packaging, location, and appearance, and their advertisement through mass media. Without several decades of research on the social psychology of attitudes (Chapters 4, 5) there would be no contemporary legend of Madison Avenue.

Another significant application of social psychology in business and industry derives from psychological research on the structure and function of small groups. Most industrial operations and business administrations involve complex social organizations. These may range from small groups of workers who interact to produce consumer goods along assembly lines, to administrative boards or committees at the managerial level. To some extent business firms represent miniature societies comprised of many interdependent subgroups, and they tend to evolve company norms and standards, customs, and traditions that constitute a "company culture" that is transmitted to new workers as they are "socialized" into the company. The applicability of psychological research findings on both the socialization process as well as group dynamics has given rise to what is now called *organizational psychology* (Chapters 12, 13).

The origins of organizational psychology coincide with pioneer studies in group dynamics. But as industrial social psychology has evolved from the 1930s into the organizational psychology of the 1960s, many other areas of applicability of social psychological research have been discovered. Although it appears that the typical American worker is highly task-oriented while on the job, there is evidence that his production rate and task performance are influenced to some extent by group norms and conventions. Job performance is also related to morale and job satisfaction. Managerial practices that cultivate the worker's identification with the business as a social community generally tend not only to make the worker better satisfied, but also to increase his productivity. Status and power within the industrial community are also generally related to one another. However, the manner in which power and social control are exerted within the organization may affect both worker satisfaction and productivity. In general it appears that American workers prefer relatively permissive supervision. Supervisors who rely exclusively on their power to grant or deny rewards (reward and coercive power) tend to be less effective than those who use their power to foster harmony and cooperation within the work group. In this context findings from research on organized social behavior shed considerable light on contemporary practices in business and industry (Chapters 10, 11, 12).

Social Psychology in Community and National Affairs

Social psychology and its research findings are broadly applicable to human affairs at community, national, and international levels. Preventive concepts of psychiatry and mental health encompass principles of group dynamics (Chapters 10, 11, 12) and of public opinion and attitude change (Chapter 5) in providing early support and assistance to people suffering from preneurotic conflicts.

Techniques similar to group therapy can be utilized to deal with general social problems involving group relations. Group therapy is sometimes used to alleviate racial and ethnic tensions. In business organizations similar techniques have been used to ease management-worker relations. At the community level "town hall meetings" operated along the lines of therapeutic groups have been able to expand the social awareness of the total community and to reduce detrimental selfish views that impede harmony within the community (Chapters 10, 11, 12, 13).

One of the most visible efforts to use principles of social psychology for the betterment of community and industrial relations has been represented by the programs of the National Training Laboratories since its inception at Bethel, Maine, in 1947. Through workshops designed to train key community leaders toward increased sensitivity to interpersonal relationships and awareness of the nature of groups and social systems, this program has had far-reaching effects. These workshops utilize a set of techniques that have come to be called *T-group* (training-group) approaches, and the change they propose to bring about in their participants is called *sensitivity train-*

ing. During the 1960s this movement gained momentum with the rediscovery and broader application of these approaches to community problems and mental health. Public interest in participating in these kinds of experiences led to a boom in encounter groups, which were designed to bring one into social confrontation with himself and others, utilizing methods derived from the early work at National Training Laboratories (Chapters 7, 9, 13).

A parallel to commercial market research and advertising exists in voter surveys and political campaigning. The presidential campaign platforms of the major political parties are produced under the influence of data from public opinion surveys of political attitudes and the advice of professionals in planning effective presentation of the platform and persuasion of the voter. Candidates depend on feedback from voter surveys to plan their speeches and maximize appeal to many disparate subgroups of voters while minimizing offense to any. In effect, political candidates are dealt with like consumer goods: what is in the package appears to matter less than the manner of packaging and presentation. Both the candidate and the voter are increasingly concerned with the image presented by the candidate. Conceding the impossibility of presenting a man candidly, fully, and directly to 70 million voters, the alternative becomes one of developing a legend as effectively as possible. The basic devices used in commercial advertising or any other kind of audience persuasion, then, become the tools of the trade for political campaigning (Chapter 5).

Many social psychologists have attempted to draw the attention of the public and key public officials to the potential contributions of psychological research at the level of international affairs. Isolated attempts to deal with the psychological sources of international tension and wars between nations have also been made from time to time in a speculative manner by anthropologists, economists, and historians (Chapters 9, 13).

Although America has been receptive to and supportive of the development of scientific social psychology, it appears that social psychological research has not yet made its full impact on everyday affairs. Nevertheless, the rapid increase in contingency between the pure science and theory side of social psychology on the one hand and human relations in education, business, industry, advertising, community affairs, mental health, and international relations on the other hand gives rise to optimism about the future utilization of social psychological knowledge for practical purposes. One must not dream at this stage of development that social psychology can solve all of the world's problems, but it is clear that it can at least contribute in significant ways to the betterment of the individual's existence in his social context.

PHILOSOPHICAL AND HISTORICAL ORIGINS OF SOCIAL PSYCHOLOGY

To argue that social psychology, as we know it now in the late twentieth century, is a relatively new emergent in scholarly activity is not to argue that it deals with novel and original problems and questions. It is merely to say that a new approach to old and enduring questions has evolved. Only recently have the social problems described earlier in this chapter been removed from the realm of metaphysics and philosophical speculation and translated into a context of empiricism and modern science. The historical roots of modern social *psychology* lie in the *philosophy* of the previous nineteen centuries and, perhaps, in centuries preceding them.

The basic questions confronting modern social psychology appear to have plagued human beings for as long as our records of history permit us to explore man's intellectual activity. The tenets of the Old Testament prophets suggest preoccupation with the importance of reciprocity in human interaction. There are variations of the "Do unto others as you would have them do unto you" precept, not only in most of the world's religious systems but even in such ancient codes as Hammurabi's "eye for an eye, and tooth for a tooth." Although Rousseau developed the concept much more articulately, it is fair to say that these ancient fundamentals are the essence of the *social contract* as the basis for organized social systems among men.

Throughout the intellectual history of Western civilization, a recurrent question has often been raised by philosophers: how and why did organized social systems among men arise? The opinions and points of view have been manifold. Plato, more than three centuries before the time of Christ, suggested in *The Republic* that states originate because man, the individual, is not self-sufficient. Plato argued that each man, in order to satisfy his own essential goals, needs the conjoint effort of others. Thus his proposed answer to the question is a utilitarian one: man is committed to be a social organism because of pragmatic, presumably reasonable, voluntary entry into cooperative organization.

In contrast to Plato, Aristotle (also four centuries before Christ) in his *Politics* posited an instinctual basis for man's entry into social organization. Like Plato, Aristotle saw man as clearly committed to social participation. But he suggested that man is bound by his nature to be gregarious and affiliative with others. Aristotle's arguments (like many that have followed, even into the twentieth century) unfortunately dismissed the most provocative aspect of the question by ascribing the basis of man's participation in societies to "human nature."

Recovery from the intellectual stagnation of the "dark" Middle Ages led eventually to a late-Renaissance burst of intellectual and philosophical concern with the same old problems. The seventeenth century was a peak of focus on social and political questions. A number of philosophers who have profoundly influenced the evolution of Western political and social thought wrote during this period. And perhaps not merely by coincidence, several crucial social movements followed within the century: the Reformation, the French Revolution, the settlement of the New World, and the origin of new forms of government in the New World. All of these carried the dominant theme of the *dignity of the individual* within the framework of a social system. Jean-Jacques Rousseau, in the middle of the eighteenth century, wrote *The Social Contract* as an exposition and extended development of the *utilitarian* notion that man's entry into organized social systems was essentially an act of compromise for his own eventual benefit. Rousseau's name is usually associated by historians with the social contract notion, but he is by no means its original author. The essentials of the concept are reflected in Plato, if not earlier. Rousseau's *Emile,* a treatise on education and the socialization process, further develops the same line of thought.

John Locke, during the latter part of the seventeenth century, anticipated much of Rousseau's point of view, stressing man's rationality. Locke, with rather strong convictions about the dominance of man's intellect over his emotions, focused his attention on the argument that man is basically a rational and logical creature, and that his intellect underlies his practical and utilitarian decision to participate in social organizations.

Also during the seventeenth century, Thomas Hobbes wrote an intellectual fantasy about the origins of a hypothetical state, the *Leviathan,* which is essentially congruent with the ideas of Locke and Rousseau in arguing that man voluntarily enters into social organization and thus evolves complex social systems. Although the many interpreters of Rousseau have difficulty in selecting their quotations to determine exactly how "good" or "bad" he thought society was for man, there is little doubt that Hobbes conceived of social systems as highly ameliorative and ennobling. Rousseau referred to "the noble savage," implying that man in his preorganized state was essentially a noble and beneficent creature, and also to the fact that social organization was sometimes a set of "shackles" in which man is "enchained." Thus there is some reason to argue that Rousseau regarded social organization as a compromise at best—and as a "necessary evil" at worst. (However, there are other parts of Rousseau's writings, especially in *Emile,* that reflect a somewhat more optimistic evaluation of social organizations.)

Hobbes, in contrast, characterized the natural and presocial state of man as solitary, crude, and savage, and argued that it is through social organization that he is able to rise to something better. Locke, more of a neutralist in the matter, simply held that man is reasonable, and that he arrived at the logical conclusion that social organization is to his advantage. Jeremy Bentham stressed collective practicality and implied that man realizes, rationally, that societies provide "the greatest good for the greatest number."

PRESCIENTIFIC NOTIONS OF MAN AND HIS FELLOW MAN

Different views, different interpretations; the same basic question: "What is the basis of social interaction?"

520 B.C.—CONFUCIUS, *The Analects*
The word *shu* serves as the principle of life . . . [it means] do not do unto others what you do not want others to do to you. (Social contract)

360 B.C.—PLATO, *The Republic*
A state arises out of the needs of mankind. No one is self-sufficing, but all of us have many wants. (Utilitarianism)

350 B.C.—ARISTOTLE, *Politics*
To live alone, one must be either an animal or a god. (Gregarious instinct)

100 A.D.—MATTHEW, The New Testament
As ye would that men should do to you, do ye also to them likewise. (Social contract)

1378 A.D.—IBN-KHALDUN, *Prolegomena*
It is evident that men are by nature in contact with and tied to each other. Such contact may produce solidarity nearly as powerful as that produced by kinship. (Gregarious instinct)

1651 A.D.—HOBBES, *Leviathan*
Without social interaction, the life of man is solitary, poor, nasty, brutish, and short. (Beneficial social contract)

1689 A.D.—LOCKE, *Essay on Human Understanding*
For God having joined virtue and public happiness together, and made the practice thereof necessary to the preservation of society, it is no wonder that everyone should not only allow, but recommend and magnify those rules to others, from whose observance of them he is sure to reap advantage to himself. (Rational social contract)

1762 A.D.—ROUSSEAU, *The Social Contract*
All men are created free. Society takes from man his native individual powers and equips him with other [powers], which he cannot use without the assistance of other [men]. (Compromising social contract)

1789 A.D.—BENTHAM, *Introduction to Principles of Morals and Legislation*
[Social interaction] is guided by the principle of utility: the greatest possible amount of happiness for the greatest possible number of members [of society]. (Utilitarianism)

Arguments as to whether society is "good" or "bad" for man, however, are essentially more appropriate questions for philosophy than for psychology. In its commitment to the scientific method, psychology rules out *evaluative* questions of ethics and morals and adopts as its objective the goal of *understanding.* Thus these philosophical antecedents of modern social psychology are significant, not because of their ethical conclusions but because of their assumptions about the *purposive* nature of man's entry into social organization. Hobbes, Rousseau, and Locke all suggest that man participates in organized social systems voluntarily and presumably for some purposive end.

Another set of ideas, developed during the latter part of the nineteenth century, had a profound effect upon virtually all of the life sciences: Charles Darwin's theory of evolution and the survival of better-adapted forms of life. Although Darwin's theories were primarily addressed to biological evolution and accounted for the apparent phylogenetic continuity of the world's variety of living organisms, they contained implications for social adaptation as well. Herbert Spencer (1855) and Lecomte de Nuoy (1947) articulated these implications in the argument that social evolution also seemed to proceed as though a principle of "survival of the fittest" were in operation. Just as biologically well-adapted forms of life were more likely to survive and reproduce, so also were socially well-adapted organisms more likely to survive and perpetuate their forms of social adaptation (Moreno, 1934). Thus the utilitarian aspects of man's purposive entry into organized social systems were further emphasized by the claim that social organization has survival value and contributes directly to the maintenance of man as a socially participating organism.

THE VALUE CONTEXT OF SOCIAL PSYCHOLOGY: THREE PERSPECTIVES

It is not an accident that social psychology evolved rapidly in the United States. A variety of intellectual, political, philosophical, and even economic climates steered this course of development. Several of these are so clearly reflected in the tenor of contemporary social psychology that they are readily recognizable.

The Natural Science Perspective

The tendency to emulate the natural sciences, both physical and biological, and to expect a recapitulation of the pattern of their development in the social sciences has been apparent in American psychology virtually from its inception. Wilhelm Wundt's introduction of psychological phenomena into the laboratory in Germany in 1879 was pursued actively in the United States by Edward Titchener and others in the early twentieth century. By 1930, the divergence of American and European psychology was suggested. After World War II, the clear and open domination of American psychology by the laboratory method and demands for a sound empirical basis were firmly established. Between 1945 and 1960 this divergence became even more patently defined—not only in social psychology, but in other areas such as educational and developmental psychology. In Europe the emphasis on exploration of the biological and physiological foundations of behavior was perhaps stronger than in America, but in America the social emphasis was dominant. In European psychology the study of social problems and man's social behavior was slower to pull away from its philosophical roots. As a result the empiricist tradition of the natural sciences was more strongly reflected in social psychology in America than in Europe. Thus one of the most clearly evident characteristics of modern American social psychology is its adoption of the scientific method: the demand for rigor in definition of basic concepts, the demand for refinement in the methods of observation that provide the basic data

of the science, and the concern for ordered integration of observations into theories
and scientific laws. These characteristics are described in detail in Chapter 2.

13

Perspectives on
Social Behavior

The Democratic-Humanistic Perspective

A political context of intense concern for the dignity of man and for the integrity of
the individual as a unit within the social system has characterized American thought
from the very political origins of this nation. This ideological background is also reflected in the tone of contemporary American social psychology. The American psychologist has pressed beyond the raising of questions about the nature and operation
of social systems and social phenomena, and has directed his attention particularly
to questions about the individual's relationships to social systems. Thus a more
meaningful distinction between sociology and social psychology has evolved within
American psychology.

The antecedents of this democratic ideological atmosphere are manifest in several
social movements about the time of the political birth of the American nation. One
such movement was the French Revolution, which was a direct reaction to the
subjection of the individual to collective and organizational abuse. And the same
currents of thought have presented themselves again and again in the political
history of this nation: in the antislavery movements of the nineteenth century, in
the rise of Jeffersonian concepts of democracy in the nineteenth century and their
revival in strong feelings about states' rights and anti-Federalism in the twentieth century, in the labor reforms of the early twentieth century, and in the civil rights movements of the mid-twentieth century. Quite naturally such a political and ideological
milieu has come to be reflected in the development of scientific approaches to the
study of social organizations. American social psychology consequently is characterized by its focus on the *individual* as the basic unit of analysis in exploring and understanding the operation of social phenomena.

A strong resurgence of this tradition in American psychology in the 1960s and
1970s has exerted other forces to reshape modern social psychology. The humanistic
values of the "human resource" movement are built upon the concept of the dignity
of the individual. Between 1930 and 1960 the strength of the "natural science" tradition in American behavioral science produced an extreme swing of the pendulum
toward a dehumanized view of man as an object of rigorous scientific study. The
perspective of the natural sciences did not differentiate man from any other scientific
object. But the humanistic tradition has tempered this with a counterpressure toward
emphasis on the distinctly human qualities of man: his feelings and emotions, his
sense of self, and his awareness of his relatedness to others.

The humanistic perspective does not argue with the *methods* of the natural science
perspective, but only with its *values*. Thus the two perspectives are not necessarily
contradictory. Social psychology in the 1970s will probably reflect the reconciliation of
these two perspectives, merging toward an approach that blends the values of hu-
manism with the methods of natural science.

The Utilitarian Perspective

A third perspective, economic in nature, is also strongly reflected in the general tone
of modern social psychology. Practical, utilitarian value systems typify American
thought. The impact of these values has perhaps been felt more directly in technological areas, in which the applied aspects of a science have supported the development of basic or purely theoretical aspects of the science. For example, the practical
and applied value of engineering fields has tended to carry forward the development
of the related "pure" sciences. Enthusiasm for the contributions of industrial chemis-

try has supported rapid development of basic theoretical chemistry. Americans are traditionally interested in science not just for its own sake, but for its application to issues and problems of immediate practical relevance. There is a tendency to weigh the worthiness of intellectual pursuits in terms of fairly immediate economic payoff.

As this tradition has been reflected in the development of American psychology, those aspects of psychology that promise immediate applicability have received intensive investigation, leaving gaps in basic theoretical knowledge. For example, the general state of basic personality theory lags somewhat behind the current state of refinement of psychological measurement and diagnostic procedures (especially those that are useful in job selection and placement, academic placement, and the prediction of individual success in particular functions). In conceiving of psychology as a profession, the public tends to think first of the practicing clinical psychologist as a diagnostician and a therapist, rather than of the psychologist as a basic scientist or researcher in the sense of the biologist, the chemist, or the physicist.

In social psychology this uneven development is reflected in the accumulation of extensive descriptive knowledge of organized small groups, attitude assessment, and the bases of interpersonal perception and attraction, but with little articulated theory. At the same time, despite their important social consequences, difficulties in conducting appropriate research have resulted in a serious lack of knowledge of such phenomena as large social movements, unorganized crowds and mobs, and complex political systems.

Although psychological research has tended to delve first and most deeply into problem areas of direct practical interest, it would be inaccurate to suggest that psychologists have set aside their interest in basic theory. But the result of these circumstances has been that psychological theory is largely made up of isolated hypotheses and circumscribed theoretical models designed to deal with a particular phenomenon or narrow range of phenomena, rather than of highly integrated and comprehensive theoretical systems.

Modern social psychology fits directly into the matrix of contemporary American life. It grapples with problems of vast social significance and, despite its youth, occasionally offers worthwhile knowledge to contribute to the solution of social problems.

REVIEW

1. The study of social behavior originated in philosophical speculation, but it has evolved toward commitment to the methods of empirical science. This is *social psychology—the scientific study of the relationship of individuals to one another individually, in groups, and in society.*

2. Social psychology is addressed to many kinds of social problems—in *education, mental health, crime and delinquency, business and industry,* and *community and national affairs.* These areas of relevant application anchor the significance of social psychology in contemporary American life. They are reviewed here generally, to introduce the scope and content of social psychology, and they are related in greater detail to the content of social psychology at the end of each chapter in Sections II, III, IV, and V of this book.

3. Prescientific Western European and American philosophical notions about man's relation to society suggest that man enters voluntarily into a *social contract* with others for both individual and collective benefit, and that organized societies evolve out of such contracts. There are several points of view as to *why* man enters such implicit contracts, but modern social psychology assumes that this is a complex learned behavioral adjustment of man to the social world around him.

4. Modern social science, including social psychology, has been shaped by several important *value traditions* in Western thought. These traditional values, in turn, give rise to different *perspectives* in viewing man's social behavior: a *natural science* perspective (which treats man as a scientific object); a *democratic-humanistic* perspective (which emphasizes the uniquely "human" qualities of man—his feelings, his awareness of himself, and his relation to others—and the dignity of the individual); and a *utilitarian tradition* (which stresses pragmatic values and demands that social psychology be relevant and applicable to the solution of social problems).

2
THE SCIENCE OF SOCIAL BEHAVIOR

The most essential characteristic of modern social psychology is its commitment to the *scientific method* of understanding man's social behavior through direct observation. This commitment, which is known as *empiricism,* involves systematic and detailed attempts to establish orderly comprehension out of an array of many kinds of observations. This includes three basic operations: the careful collection of observations or data (methodology), the ordered integration of these observations into hypotheses and scientific laws (theory building), and tests of the adequacy of these theoretical laws in terms of whether they can successfully predict future observations (scientific experimentation and application).

SCIENCE AND EMPIRICAL OBSERVATION

The term used by scientists to refer to their basic observations is *data,* from the Latin for "given." The singular form (datum) refers to an isolated observation that is accepted as a fact.

Science is a public affair in that it must be communicated among scientists who develop theories as well as among users of these theories who apply them to practical affairs in everyday life. Consequently the observational data from which a science is built must be observable by any and all scientists. This way of thinking about science rules out as inappropriate all kinds of observation that are limited to only one scientist—for example, reflections upon his own experience. Acceptable scientific data include only phenomena that can be observed by any scientist who repeats the conditions of observation used by any other scientist. Such convictions about proper scientific procedure have important implications for psychology as a science: they imply directly that subjective experience cannot be accepted as observational data in psychology, and that only overtly observable behavior can provide the scientific data from which psychological theories are built. Indeed, this philosophy of science (*logical positivism,* or *scientific empiricism*) was at first embraced only by behavioristic theorists in psychology, who wished to discard any reference to subjective phenomena. As scientific psychology has matured, more temperate positions have evolved. In contemporary behavioral science almost all conventionally accepted theory is derived from publicly observable data, but these observations may reflect private experience or feelings. For example, a person's dream world is not directly observable by others, but his verbal descriptions of it are. His feelings and mood are private, but his posture, expressions, words, and choices that reflect this mood are public. In many cases such inferences about subjective *experience* are drawn from observation of overt *behavior*.

Psychologists tend to be self-conscious about the status of their field as a science. They are highly aware of its youth and immaturity. But the general temper of modern American psychology remains one of dedication to the aspiration that psychology can indeed establish itself as a science. Frequently psychologists appear to be more concerned about questions of the underlying philosophy of science than are their colleagues in the physical and biological sciences, who are more comfortable in taking many issues for granted. Although all of the sciences are traditionally self-critical with respect to issues of *methodology* and of *theory,* psychology may appear to be supersensitive about these issues. But this apparent excessive concern for theory and methodology, which leads to qualifications and guardedness in stating laws and principles of human behavior, may be understood by recognizing the fact that psychology is still an immature science.

Reliability and Validity

The empirical scientist is concerned with two kinds of "truth" in evaluating his methodology. One, *reliability,* involves the extent to which the scientist can place confidence in his data as accurate and stable observations. The other, *validity,* concerns the degree to which his *interpretations* of what he observes are sound and meaningful representations of the universe.

The concept of reliability includes several kinds of evaluations used to assess the dependability of scientific observations. High levels of reliability mean that one may expect to observe essentially the same thing on repeated occasions under the same circumstances. The most conventional assessment of reliability involves observation of the same phenomenon on several occasions, known as *repeated measurement* (or test-retest) reliability. If measured phenomena occur once and only once, there is no possibility for repeated measurement. In such cases, other means of assessing reliability must be used. If a set of observations are made simultaneously (for example, a set of test items), they may be divided randomly into smaller sets and compared; this procedure is known as *split-half* reliability. A similar procedure may be used to evaluate reliability of a set of test items by comparing each item with the total score from all the items; this procedure provides a *part-whole* reliability estimate. It is the basis of *item analysis,* a procedure for determining which items within a test are most useful in securing a stable and reliable total test score. In other cases, measurement may be based on one observation of a unique event, permitting neither repeated measurements nor part-whole estimates of reliability. In such cases, *interobserver* reliability estimates may be used to evaluate the dependability of observations. That is, if two observers independently witnessing a phenomenon at the same time record the same kind of observation, some assurance is provided that each one's record is probably dependable.

Finally, one additional procedure for taking account of the reliability of observations may be incorporated into the statistical handling of empirical data when interpretations are made and conclusions are drawn: an estimate of the *error of measurement* may be determined. If a set of repeated observations (either of similar phenomena in the behavior of one person, or of the same phenomenon in the behavior of a sample of similar people) consists of measures that are highly variable and different from one another, the estimated error of measurement is large; on the other hand, if these repeated observations are very similar to one another, the estimated error of measurement is small. Statistical handling of estimates of variability and error in measurement may thus take account of the degree of unreliability of observations and discourage the scientist from drawing improper conclusions from interpretations of his observations. Regardless of the method used, the question of reliability of observations is basic and crucial in an empirical science. Chapter 3 describes a number of methods widely used in social psychology and discusses ways of evaluating the reliability of observations.

The problem of validity in scientific data is related to the interpretation of observations (theory) rather than to the observations themselves (methodology). A valid interpretation is one that allows logical integration of all data already observed, but also allows prediction of future observations. An interpretation must tie together all available observations without apparent contradiction. For example, observation may show that the number of babies born in certain regions is closely related to the number of storks' nests in those regions. To conclude that storks bring babies would be invalid if one could also produce evidence that babies are born in regions where storks do not exist at all. Furthermore, if one doubted the hypothesis that storks bring babies, but had no evidence to the contrary, he could set out to make a future set of observations to test the hypothesis. He could go to another area and collect new observations of birthrate and stork population.

A variety of procedures are utilized to assess validity. The most straightforward involves checking the interpretation of one set of observations against another more familiar kind of observation. In psychological testing, for example, if a new test is constructed to measure intelligence, a direct way to judge whether scores on this new test are in fact good measures is to compare them to scores made by the same people on a test already known to measure intelligence. This procedure is known as *criterion validation* (checking validity by referring to a known criterion). When no trustworthy known criterion is available, other estimates of validity are required. In such cases an approach known as *content validation* may be employed, by checking to see whether interpretation of a set of observations is congruent with particular predicted implications of that observation. For example, if a new intelligence test is constructed, the new test scores should be related to all the other kinds of behavior with which intelligence is associated. If intelligent people ordinarily solve more puzzles in a given time than unintelligent people, then one expects that high-scorers on the new test would solve more puzzles than low-scorers. Sometimes content validation procedures may be elaborated into an exploration of relationships of several logically related measures (for example, puzzle solution, reading speed and comprehension, vocabulary, spelling ability, and perhaps even grades in school). When related observations show systematic relationships that focus on one kind of interpretation, the soundness of this interpretation is evaluated by *construct validation.* A risky and sometimes misleading kind of validation may be argued when a scientist makes a subjective "obvious" interpretation of his data. This argument on the basis of obviousness is referred to as *face validity*. For example, if a scientist wishes to study a person's social acceptance of others by observing whether they speak to one another when they enter a room, his interpretation of an exchange of greetings as a measure of social acceptance may be invalid for people who have been taught that greetings are customary whether or not one likes another person. In many cases, face validation of a set of observations may be appropriate, but it is often inappropriate in empirical science because what one scientist regards as obvious may not be at all obvious to another, and he may inaccurately project his own personality into his interpretation of his observations.

Causality and Correlation

When two kinds of observations are observed empirically to be closely related, a scientist may still have considerable difficulty in deciding whether one variable (i.e., one set of observations) causes the second. Two variables that are related are said to be correlated (co-related), but correlation does not necessarily imply causation. Because human beings are accustomed to understanding causation in terms of sequential time relationships, scientists may attempt to establish causality by demonstrating that variations in one set of observations are associated with observations at a later time. But simply to measure two variables at different points does not mean that the cause and effect relationship is conclusive. If one makes observations of school grade in September, and then comes back in December to make observations of chronological age, he certainly could not conclude that being promoted from one grade to the next in school "causes" a person to age one year. The evaluation of cause and effect relationships is very elusive in empirical science, and in general scientists are rather cautious about making unqualified statements about one variable's causal effects on another.

THE SOCIAL PSYCHOLOGY OF SCIENCE

As a scientist, the psychologist sets for himself a very difficult task: he attempts to use the same tool (himself, a human being) as an instrument for observing his target (his subject, another human being). Thus the human factor in social psychology as an empirical science is critical. Important personal and interpersonal factors may confound the process of observing behavior. Some of these originate within the experimenter-observer (E), others within the subject (S), and others from the situation in which E and S interact while observations are being made.

The Experimenter-Observer

The personality and mannerisms of the experimenter-observer sometimes produce different effects on the behavior of subjects he is observing; these are called *experimenter-attribute* effects (Rosenthal, 1963; Sattler, 1970; J. Jung, 1971). For example, the *sex* of the experimenter has been found to be important in such situations as studies of social reinforcement and social control of behavior, conducting clinical interviews, and administering projective tests. *Racial or ethnic* characteristics of the experimenter are likely to influence the expression of religious, racial, and ethnic attitudes in behavior. In fact, racial and ethnic factors have even been found to influence a child's performance on tests and learning tasks (Strickland, 1972). *Personal mannerisms* (friendliness, warmth, calmness, and the like) also influence the observations made by an experimenter, even affecting such measures as intelligence test performance, clinical evidence of hostility and fantasy, performance on learning tasks, and compliance with the experimenter's instructions.

The experimenter-observer's own biases and expectations about what he is observing can exert important influences on the data collected in psychological experimentation. Rosenthal (1966) particularly called attention to gross errors of observation when different observers collect data from comparable groups of subjects. He has summarized some common kinds of experimenter-observer-bias effects:

1. E's expectations determine the nature of the data he obtains.
2. E's awareness of his own motivation to obtain certain kinds of data may reverse the E-bias effect, making him seem to bend over backword to counteract bias.
3. Es who obtain "good" data at the beginning of data collection obtain even better subsequent data; Es who obtain "bad" data at first obtain even worse data.
4. Cheating, falsification of data, or unfair prodding of Ss cannot account for the evidence of E-bias observed; rather, it appears that E subtly, even without awareness, reinforces particular kinds of behavior by means of verbal conditioning and implicit rewards to Ss for displaying the desired or expected behavior.
5. E-bias may be mediated by verbal cues such as voice inflection and tone, and E-bias is increased by visual cues when E and S are visible to one another during the experiment.
6. E-bias is greater in Es who show strong needs for approval, inclination to use physical gestures, and friendly and interested behavior when dealing with the Ss.
7. E-bias is greater when E and S are well acquainted.
8. E-bias is greater for female Es than for male Es.

Rosenthal's demonstrations of dramatic bias effects in experimentation have been challenged by critics of his methods as well as his statistical analyses (Barber & Silver, 1968). However, the failure of Rosenthal's critics—who expect his findings to be in error—to replicate his findings ironically may reflect the very kind of nondeliberate experimenter-bias effects that Rosenthal suggests!

The Observed Subject

The subject under psychological observation is an active participant, not merely a passive object, in psychological research. His characteristics, like those of the observer, may introduce many sources of error into the collection of data.

THE ROSENTHAL EFFECT: EXAMPLES OF EXPERIMENTER-BIAS

Rosenthal has demonstrated dramatic nondeliberate, unintentional effects of an observer's personal biases on the observations he makes. These are honest errors of
observation, not deliberate attempts to falsify or misrepresent data. Two sets of
experiments were conducted with over 200 "experimenter-observers" recruited from
advanced undergraduate and graduate students in psychology, education, and the
humanities. In the first set of studies each E conducted an experiment with a sample
of Ss who were requested to rate photos in terms of the "success" or "failure" of
the person photographed—ostensibly an experiment in empathy. Some Es were told
that their Ss would probably give above-average ratings in appraising the photos;
other Es were told that their Ss would probably give below-average ratings. A third
group of Es were told nothing about their Ss. In the second set of studies each E
conducted an experiment with rats; some were told that their rats were bred for
brightness, some that their rats were bred for dullness, and some were told nothing.
In both studies the effects of E-bias were dramatic: the lowest mean rating reported
by any E instructed to expect high ratings on the photographs was higher than the
highest mean rating obtained by Es expecting low ratings; similarly, Es believing
that their rats were bred for brightness obtained better learning from their rats than
did Es who believed their rats were dull. Yet in both cases each respective subject
sample was homogeneous and drawn from the same population.

ROSENTHAL (1966)

Orne (1962) suggested that subjects respond alertly to cues about the purpose or
intention of the observational situation and develop assumptions called the *demand
characteristics* of the experiment. In responding to these, some choose to be "good
subjects" and try to please the observer. Such a *willing subject* may perform utterly
asinine boring tasks for long periods of time, all the while generating far-reaching
speculations to justify the importance of what he is doing (Orne, 1962). Others are
apprehensive subjects, whose fear of being evaluated make them anxious and eager
to appear in the best possible light (Rosenberg, 1965). *Faithful subjects* unquestion-
ingly try to carry out the experimenter's desires as a demonstration of their faith and
loyalty (Fillenbaum, 1966). The *transparent subject* cooperates with the experimenter
by stripping himself emotionally, baring his personal feelings for observation (Hood &
Back, 1971). The *selfish subject* cooperates with the experimenter only to the extent
that the experimenter's purposes coincide with the subject's purposes, including
preservation of his self-image and self-esteem (Sigall, Aronson, & VanHoose, 1970).

Most subjects in psychological research willingly allow themselves to be observed
for scientific purposes—they are *volunteer subjects*. College sophomores enrolled in
introductory courses in psychology have traditionally constituted a vast reservoir of
human subjects. Sometimes these subjects truly volunteer, but more often they are
drafted for service as part of a course requirement or bribed by promise of grade
credit (McDavid, 1965a; Ora, 1965; Rosenthal & Rosnow, 1969; Rosnow & Rosenthal,
1970; J. Jung, 1971).

The *suspicious subject* (and most subjects are at least slightly suspicious of psychological observation) attempts to mask his behavior and hide parts of himself from
the observer. There is a dimension of self-disclosure (Jourard, 1964; Rotter, 1967)
running from extreme suspicion and distrust to exhibitionist transparency (Hood &
Back, 1971). The mode for most well-adjusted people is at a moderately "open" level
along this continuum; excessive suspicion and guardedness is associated with
paranoia, but excessive openness and transparency—like a kind of nudity—is regarded as socially distasteful in our culture.

THE VOLUNTEER SUBJECT

Examination of characteristics of people who volunteer to be subjects in psychological experiments has shown that these people are especially likely to

1. perceive volunteering as a socially desirable act
2. be influenced by seeing others volunteer as Ss
3. engage in "arousal-seeking" habits such as the use of pep pills, smoking, and coffee
4. seek social approval
5. be intrapunitive and moody
6. be introverted
7. be more intelligent
8. show strong needs to belong to an "elite"
9. show strong needs for affiliation
10. show strong needs for achievement
11. be the first born child in the family
12. show symptoms of general neuroticism
13. be of higher occupational status

MCDAVID (1965a), ORA (1965)
ROSENTHAL AND ROSNOW (1969)
ROSNOW AND ROSENTHAL (1970), J. JUNG (1971)

Ethics in Psychological Research

In order to cope with the problem of reluctance to disclose behavior for observation, psychologists must sometimes resort to deception of the subject about the true purposes of the experimental observation. In some kinds of research "blinds" are necessary, because awareness of the actual purposes of observation would produce serious distortions of data. For example, in drug research, the behavioral effects of a drug are often largely in the mind and expectations of the subject. These imagined effects (which result from suggestion) are called *placebo effects;* a sugar-pill (placebo) may appear to produce imagined calming effects comparable to a dose of tranquilizer. In a *single-blind* experiment, the subject is kept uninformed or deceived about the true purposes of observation and the experimenter's expectations. A more complete effort to mask the effects of expectations held by both subject and observer is the *double-blind* experiment, in which both the observed subject and the observer are kept uninformed of which subject is receiving which kind of treatment.

Many psychologists regard these deceptions of the subject as dishonest and unethical (Kelman, 1967), but others regard them as necessary (Seeman, 1969). The question of ethics in protection of the rights and privacy of subjects in psychological research is so important and controversial that the American Psychological Association instituted the Ad Hoc Committee on Ethical Standards in Psychological Research in 1965. Among the membership of APA, many varied opinions were represented (Ring, 1963; McGuire, 1969; Seeman, 1969; Silverman, 1970). These were polled and reviewed by the committee, and finally in 1973 a manual of ethical principles was published (APA, 1973). These principles focus primarily upon protection of the legal rights, health, safety, welfare, and privacy of the subject. It was decided that the ultimate determinant of ethics is redeeming social benefit. In psychological research, deceit of the subject is not to be practiced unless it can be fully justified by the social benefits gained from the research.

THE CONTEXT OF PSYCHOLOGICAL RESEARCH

Whether the researcher conducts his investigation in the broad setting of natural conditions or within the confines of his laboratory, his ability to observe is subject to various limitations. It is impossible to observe every act of every human being about which the psychologist might wish to make scientific statements. Thus the process of scientific observation normally involves only a sample of human activity. Only a portion of the behavior of selected individuals can be observed directly, and if the scientist wishes to make interpretative statements that apply to all of the behavior of all people, he must assure himself that the sample he has observed is truly typical and representative of all of the behavior and all of the people he wishes to describe. The degree to which observations of a sample of behavior are applicable to an entire population is called the degree of generalizability of findings.

Sampling

A set of conventions has been evolved to maximize proper generalization from sampled observations; these conventions are called *sampling procedures.* A scientist who makes an improper general statement about a population on the basis of his observation of a sample that does not truly represent that population is said to have committed a *sampling error.* Sampling errors may be best avoided by explicit definition of the sample on which observations were based (thereby defining the kind of population about which generalized statements may legitimately be made), and by elaborate care to insure that the observed sample is as representative as possible of the population about which scientific statements are to be made.

A *random sample* can be truly representative of a given population from which it is drawn only if three important criteria are met. First, the total population to be represented must be carefully and fully defined; that is, the investigator must offer comprehensive information about the size, location, limits, and other relevant dimensions of the population about which generalized statements are to be made and from which the sample is to be selected. Second, every individual in the population must have an equal chance of being selected in the sample. Third, the selection of any individual must in no way be tied to the selection of any other. That is, every individual in the population must be equally "available" for selection, and the selection of one must not automatically determine that another particular one will be selected. For example, husband-wife pairs must be neither systematically selected nor systematically avoided. A variety of procedures may be employed to maximize the operation of nonsystematic laws of probability and random chance. Lottery procedures might be utilized, or tables of random numbers (which are specially prepared from lotterylike procedures) may be used. Strict adherence to these rules is necessary in order to draw a truly random sample. Of course, in order to make certain that these criteria can be met, the researcher is forced to know a great deal about possible sources of systematic bias, and must be empowered to rule aside such biases. For this reason simple random sampling often may be accompanied by certain kinds of extensions to control sampling biases.

One such procedure is that of *stratified sampling.* When the investigator has some reason to assume that certain predefined variables (such as age, sex, location, or other descriptive attributes) might systematically bias the sample with respect to the population he wishes to study, he may subdivide the total population into categories and sample randomly within each specific predefined category. Such a combination of systematic selection and random sampling is known as *stratified random sampling.* Another procedure often used to control for systematic bias is known as *quota sampling.* Such predefined biasing variables as those mentioned may be used to define categories within the total population, and a quota for the number of individuals to be drawn within each category may be prescribed. For example, to draw a representative sample of American adults, an investigator might consult such sources as census records to determine the proper ratios for selection of men and women, whites and blacks, Jews and gentiles, Catholics and Protestants, or professional people and laborers. Quota sampling represents only a mechanical simplification of stratified random sampling by designating a specified number of individuals to be selected from each specified category within the population. Another procedure used in the selection of stratified random samples is that of *area sampling*. Instead of identifying particular subpopulation categories to which each individual belongs, geographical locations may be characterized on the basis of population dimensions. For example, a particular neighborhood may be identified as predominantly Protestant, black, low-income; a second identified as predominantly Jewish, white, middle-income; a third as predominantly Catholic, white, upper-income; and so on. Each "area," then, may be utilized to define a quota category, with random sampling of individuals within the area. Area sampling is often useful in selecting samples to represent a large and heterogeneous population, as in large-scale surveys. But population shifts and heterogeneity of population within particular neighborhoods often introduce error in such procedures. Quota sampling procedures maintain their accuracy somewhat better. Such procedures as these are useful in selecting samples if the statistical sources utilized for determining quotas are accurate and reliable and if the sampling of individuals within each quota category is appropriately random.

Settings for Psychological Research

Human behavior is highly dependent on the context in which it occurs. Such factors as the time, location, and physical attributes of the setting in which observations are made are very important in psychological research. In fact, one approach to the study of human behavior, *behavioral ecology,* involves the careful descriptive cataloging of a person's behavior as he moves among various natural environments in his everyday life (Schoggen, 1951; Barker & Wright, 1954). Such catalogs are called "ecological records."

One of the most difficult problems to overcome in psychological research is the effect of the fact of observation itself. That is, human beings often behave atypically simply when they become aware that they are under observation. This effect, commonly referred to by psychologists as the *Hawthorne effect* because it was first discussed extensively by a group of investigators studying the behavior of workers in the Hawthorne, Illinois, plant of the Western Electric Company (Roethlisberger & Dickson, 1939), poses a serious problem in any research in which an individual knows that his behavior is under scrutiny. It is, of course, especially associated with investigations in laboratory settings. The normal ongoing behavior of a sample of people may be critically disrupted by the fact of observation itself, such disruption making the sample of observations no longer representative of the behavior of the people observed and thus no longer representative of the population they represent. The very fact of being brought into a laboratory may arouse a "laboratory-set" in which the individual assumes that his every act may be observed, which produces a similar Hawthorne effect. Although this problem in the collection of scientific observations presents a number of difficulties, it does not require that all procedures be discarded. A variety of arguments may be used to defend the utility of laboratory studies, especially when explicit attempts are made to evaluate the extent to which Hawthorne effects may occur.

Different kinds of settings for the collection of data are used for different purposes by psychologists, and each has advantages and disadvantages. The observations of behavior that provide basic research data are assumed to be consequences of the total context in which they occur, including personality factors and individual differences within each individual present; factors in the past experience, either recent or remote, of each individual; factors associated with the presence of others; and factors associated with the physical surroundings. Thus the observations are called *dependent variables,* referring to the fact that they are dependent on the conditions of observation. In scientific research the major purpose of an experimental investigation ordinarily is to determine the manner in which the observed dependent variables are affected or influenced by specific conditions within the situational context, including the kinds of factors just mentioned. These variables are called *independent variables,* referring to the fact that they comprise the starting point for investigation. In order to identify and describe specific relationships between independent and dependent variables (especially in attempting to determine whether changes in conditions of an independent variable actually cause an effected change in a dependent variable), experimentation involves the manipulation of changes in independent variables while dependent variables are under observation.

Field Studies.   Observations that are carried out for the purpose of studying social interaction without attempting to manipulate or influence the individuals under observation are called *field studies.* Great care is usually taken to insure that the investigator's presence has as little effect as possible upon the observed behavior. An investigation of interpersonal attraction among residents of a housing project (Festinger, Schachter, & Back, 1950) is typical of this type of research. The major advantage of the field study is its natural setting and "real-life" atmosphere, and its corresponding relative freedom from Hawthorne effects. Of course, not all field studies are free of Hawthorne effects because individual subjects may necessarily become aware that they are being studied as soon as polls are taken or interviews are arranged. Unfortunately it is often difficult to obtain adequately representative samples in field studies. A group of individuals who under natural conditions are available for study in the same place at the same time may be likely to be systematically homogeneous in ways that make them unrepresentative of the total population. Furthermore, because no experimental manipulation of independent variables is undertaken, it is rarely possible to interpret the direction of causal relationships in field studies. Under most circumstances field studies are particularly useful either at the very early stages of investigation of a particular issue (in order to evaluate the kinds of variables most likely to be related to the dependent variable under study, and thus most appropriate for further research) or at very late stages of investigation, when a great amount of specific knowledge about a particular kind of behavior has been accumulated and it has become desirable to test particular hypotheses or theories in natural contexts.

Natural Experiments.   A natural experiment is essentially only a field study in which nature and circumstance cooperated by the occurrence of a critical manipulative event. The natural occasion of a certain event may produce a change in conditions that serves the purpose of a manipulated independent variable. Natural experiments are rare and fortuitous combinations of circumstance. A researcher, knowing that some critical event is to take place, may execute field studies to coincide with the occurrence of the critical event, thereby providing data comparable to an experiment in which he himself brought about a manipulated change of conditions. S. Lieberman (1956), for example, studied the opinions and attitudes of workers before and after an already scheduled change in which some workers were promoted to foremen and others to union stewards. The greatest disadvantage of natural experiments is their rarity. Often it is impossible to anticipate appropriate kinds of critical events for experimental study of an issue before they have actually occurred. Furthermore, it is often difficult to establish proper controls to rule aside the effects of changes other than the critical event. Because manipulation of an independent variable occurs in this kind of experimentation, it is possible to make some interpretation of causal relationships. Otherwise, however, the characteristics, merits, and flaws of the natural experiment are identical to those of the field study.

Field Experiments. To overcome the problems of inadequate control and manipulation that characterize field studies and natural experiments, while preserving their advantage of naturalness, a research approach known as the field experiment was widely employed by Lewin (1951). Rather than wait for the natural occurrence of a critical change in natural conditions, an investigator may intrude into a natural situation and cause some event to occur in order to manipulate a particular independent variable for the purpose of studying its effects on the behavior under observation. A study of production rates and attitudes of workers in a factory under three pre-planned conditions of change in worker assignments (Coch & French, 1948) exemplified the field experiment. This form of experimentation is especially useful in social psychology. It preserves all of the advantages of the naturalistic field approaches as well as some of the refinement of laboratory control and manipulation. However, the ideal conditions for proper field experimentation are not always available. It is not always possible to bring about appropriate changes to manipulate independent variables in natural settings, either because it is beyond the experimenter's control, or because it would be unethical or improper to do so. One especially important ethical consideration in the case of field experiments is the fact that the effects of the manipulation occur in natural settings, affording greater likelihood of their generalized overflow outside the experimental setting. The investigator cannot afterwards relieve his subjects by explaining that "it was only a game." Because the consequences of experimentation occur in natural settings, this kind of research is called "action research." Whether the "real-life" effects of the manipulation were intended (as in the case of the advertising campaigns) or were by-products of a theoretical investigation (as in many studies of changes of worker attitudes in connection with management policies and practices), the investigator must be prepared to assume ethical responsibility for these consequences. Unfortunately, the greater the experimenter's efforts to insure that his subjects are aware that his manipulations are only experimental, the greater the likelihood of Hawthorne effects, and consequently the greater the loss of the advantages of the natural setting.

Laboratory Experiments. The confines of the laboratory offer the experimenter maximum control over the independent variables that may affect his observations, for he is permitted to control and manipulate any and all conditions within the range of his physical ability and ethical responsibility. However, in order to achieve this degree of control, he must forego the real-life quality of natural conditions. Laboratory behavior is not unreal, for a human being's behavior in the laboratory is just as real as his behavior anywhere else. But the laboratory often intentionally restricts the kinds of behavior an individual may display, especially for the purpose of forcing him into specially contrived choices or decisions. He may never encounter exactly such conditions outside the laboratory. However, if the laboratory investigation has been successful in pinpointing the relevant independent variables that control behavior, the investigator may be able to anticipate exactly what kind of behavior will occur when a certain crucial condition is encountered outside the laboratory. Laboratory studies are generally most appropriately used at a stage of investigation when the experimenter is well acquainted with the major independent variables that govern the behavior he wishes to study and when he is prepared to control these variables by manipulating the ones whose effects he wishes to investigate and holding constant those that are outside his focus of exploration. It may be possible to test integrative hypotheses and theories in the laboratory to determine their soundness under relatively sterile conditions before returning to natural settings to test the hypotheses under somewhat greater contamination and lack of control of interfering variables.

Simulation Experiments. It is sometimes impossible or impractical to duplicate natural conditions in the laboratory. In such cases procedures may be designed to reproduce only the most essential features of a natural situation in a stylized or abstract way. Such procedures are called *simulation*. The most serious limitation on the generalizability of findings from this kind of research is the accuracy with which the truly essential features of conditions outside the laboratory have been identified and reproduced. If only irrelevant and nonessential features have been omitted, then the simulation may be generalized easily to other situations. But if the simulation is inadequate and omits critical conditions that influence behavior or fails to identify them clearly, simulated approaches may be quite limited in generalization to nonlaboratory conditions.

One kind of simulation commonly employed, especially for reasons of economics when time, resources, or the subject population is limited, is the simulated presence of other people by means of tape recordings, films on closed-circuit television, or "faked" messages. It appears that in general people do react to such simulations as though other people were actually present, and hence that the simulation procedures are adequate.

Another kind of simulation is involved when laboratory tasks are intended to reproduce the essential features of everyday real-life tasks outside the laboratory. In this kind of procedure, stylized tasks are developed by abstracting the basic elements of everyday activities for presentation as tasks to be executed in the laboratory. The *gaming* procedures used in current research on decision making, conflict, and strategy planning represent this kind of simulation. For example, war games, in which the individuals function as the heads of committees in charge of the international affairs of a hypothetical nation, have been developed to study human behavior in international affairs. Similarly, banking games have been used to study psychological factors in economic strategy decision making, and other aspects of organizational psychology in business (Tuckman, 1963). Simpler games have been employed in studies of individual conflicts, cooperation, and competition. Such simulations are particularly useful in the study of the effects of conditional manipulations, which would otherwise be too costly, complex, or otherwise impractical to permit experimentation and scientific investigation. Several kinds of games used in research on bargaining and decision making in social situations are described in detail in Chapter 3 (pages 60–63), and the results of studies using these procedures are summarized in Chapter 9 (pages 242–244).

Cross-cultural Research

Social psychologists often conduct research involving comparisons among various societies and their members. Such cross-cultural investigations, like any other kind of research, are beset by problems of sampling, reliability of observation, and validity of interpretation. Often, however, these problems are made more acute by the investigator's lack of familiarity with societies other than his own. This fact of being "culture-bound" within the beliefs, values, and ideologies of one's own culture may lead to further errors by the investigator, not only in making his observations but also in interpreting them.

The danger of personal bias on the part of the observer is inherent in any kind of data collecting, but cross-cultural studies carry an additional peril in that the observer may apply the values and frame of reference of his own culture, sometimes inappropriately, to his observation of members of other cultures. For example, in our society it is practically self-evident that a child's biological father is normally one of the primary agents in the child's socialization. However, Malinowski (1927) has shown that in some societies this does not hold, for the maternal uncle may fulfill this role. Failure to be aware of such differences may jeopardize the accuracy of both observations and interpretations in cross-cultural research.

The confounding effects of an observer's theoretical biases on his observations present serious problems in any kind of data collection, but such problems are particularly important in cross-cultural studies. Such biases often govern the selection of variables to be observed, perhaps even blinding the investigator to the importance of other variables. As Hilgard (1962) has commented, one might wonder whether variables related to aspects of child-rearing such as toilet training and weaning would have been such frequent choices for investigation in cross-cultural research were it not for the fact that theoretical orientations derived largely within our own Western culture emphasize the importance of these variables in the socialization of western Europeans and Americans.

Linguistic differences among societies may also lead to serious problems of semantic misunderstanding. In cross-cultural research, errors in communication through language and translations are often critical. Not only have psychological measures of variables such as intelligence (Klineberg, 1964) and memory (Bartlett, 1932; Harari & McDavid, 1966) been found to be subject to confounding cultural factors, but even the interpretation of such unstructured projective tests as the Rorschach inkblots appears to be similarly affected by cultural differences (Bleuler & Bleuler, 1935). One authority on psychological testing procedures (Buros, 1959) has concluded from an appraisal of traditionally used tests in cross-cultural studies that there is no such thing as a "culture-free" test (i.e., free of any effects of cultural context). Instead, he suggests, the best one might argue is that certain procedures are "culture-fair" in that they are not systematically oriented to favor members of one culture over members of another culture with which comparisons are to be made.

THE NATURE AND PURPOSE OF THEORIES

The role of theory in an empirical science is crucial. The second stage of the scientific process (theorizing) is concerned with ordering and integrating observations that have been made. Scientific theories are designed to provide pictures of the orderly, logical arrangement of the universe, as reflected in collected observations or data. A *hypothesis* represents a general statement of a logical or systematic relationship embracing a set of observations. For a given limited set of observations, there may be more than one way of ordering them reasonably. There may be more than one form that a statement about their basic order and interrelatedness may take. Hypotheses are therefore essentially tentative. Inasmuch as all the data (all possible observations that might ever be made) are never "in" and assembled at any given time, a final and ultimate hypothesis is not conceivable. Consequently, science tests the value of its hypotheses in two ways: by the adequacy of their "fit" to all available observations already made, and by their success in "fitting" observations made subsequent to formulation of the hypotheses. A hypothesis that does not successfully stand both tests is discarded or reformulated until it survives both tests. A hypothesis that meets such standards is retained.

A hypothesis is only as good as the observations on which it is based. If the observations have been carelessly made, or if crucial kinds of observations have been ignored, one cannot expect great predictive value from the theory. Certain kinds of observations may be inappropriate starting points for building scientific theories. Science is a public affair, and the theories that meet criteria of acceptability in science must necessarily be public ones. They must state explicitly the assumptions that enter them, and they must specify openly the nature of the observations on which they are based. For example, an individual may experience certain ideas or feelings about a particular event, but these are not directly available to another individual. Because these are private data, or subjective observations, and are not equally accessible to others, they therefore do not constitute appropriate scientific observations. However, an individual's verbal comments about his experiences, or even the gestures or postures or facial expressions that accompany his experiences, are indeed in the public domain of science. These may be observed directly and become a common part of the experience of other observers. One way scientists attempt to assure the public nature of their observations is to specify very carefully the conditions under which observations are made and the methods of observation employed, even, if necessary, by giving a brief recipe for reproducing all of the conditions that give rise to a particular event to be observed (*operational definitions*).

Everyone, in his daily activity, makes use of hypotheses. For example, the decision whether or not to wear one's raincoat on a cloudy day involves theory. If one has in the past observed that a cloudy sky typically precedes rain later in the day, it could be said that one has formed a "cloudy sky-rainy day" hypothesis. But theories, whether of this sort or of the more elaborate kind employed in science, are highly dependent on the kinds of observations on which they are developed. If the observations have been incomplete, the theory may not successfully predict future events. For example, it may be useful to differentiate scattered fleecy white clouds from dense, dark clouds in making predictions about rain; it may also be useful to take into account other variables such as wind direction and velocity. (The refined meteorological theories utilized by the weather bureau, of course, do precisely this.) If a prediction of rain were based on pain and stiffness in one's rheumatic left knee, someone else who cannot experience that particular quality of pain could not possibly make use of such a "stiff knee-rainy day" hypothesis.

The term "theory" is normally applied to the higher-order integration of hypotheses into systematic networks that attempt to describe and predict broader ranges of events by allowing one hypothesis to qualify another or to specify the conditions under which another will be appropriate. Psychology currently has relatively few systems of hypotheses that merit the label theory. Most of its hypotheses and tentative prototheories deal only with limited aspects of behavior and experience. At the present stage of development of social psychology as a science, there is no single theoretical system that clearly excels others in either the adequacy with which all accumulated observations are integrated or the accuracy with which future observations may be predicted. Some theoretical frameworks are more useful in dealing with particular kinds of phenomena than others, and some theoretical systems have been more widely explored and utilized in social psychology than others. But it would be inaccurate to claim at this time that one theoretical system is superior. As a young science, psychology is still characterized by *eclecticism,* the use of different theories for different purposes. Many theoretical systems have influenced the development of social psychology, and several are still reflected clearly in the general complexion of the field. There are many criteria for comparative evaluation of different theoretical systems. But among the many kinds of theory employed in modern psychology, none emerges as distinctly superior to others on all of the criteria.

THEORETICAL CONCEPTIONS OF MAN

In the early years of the twentieth century, when social psychology first emerged, psychology was less concerned with the process of theory-building than it has been during the past few decades. The early theoretical models used to conceive of man and his nature were very crude and unsophisticated. But as more and more empirical observations have been collected to acquaint us with man's nature, different models have evolved.

Early psychology tended to be rather uncritical of its sources of data, and the method of *introspection* (requesting an individual to "inventory" his own subjective experience and to report it verbally) provided the most commonly utilized source of observations. William MacDougall's writings (including his 1908 textbook in social psychology) are typical of this era. The major concern was with the enumeration of the *sentiments* (dispositions) that guide human behavior, such as instincts of imitation, gregariousness, suggestion, dominance, and the like. Eventually, skepticism arose as to whether such enumerations actually provided fruitful leads toward understanding behavior. By the 1920s a rather strong and clearly defined "anti-instinct" movement had taken shape within psychology, and there were demands for reevaluation of these older notions of human behavior. More rigorous definitions of the concept of *instinct* were demanded, and specific criteria were suggested as basic attributes of an instinct. The result was a rather thoroughgoing discard of these older notions. Early primitive theories were treated as intellectual curiosities, and for decades the very term "instinct" was an off-color word not admitted into polite discussion in scientific psychology. However, in recent developments in physiological psychology, comparative psychology, and ethology there is a respectable reentry of this concept into psychological theory.

Among the theoretical systems that have contributed most directly to the development of social psychology, four are especially important: *psychoanalytic, cognitive, behavioristic,* and *humanistic.* Within each of these categories there are many variations, but each defines a family of related theoretical systems that adopt a common conception of man's nature. It is in terms of these conceptual models of man that the families of theory can be most easily distinguished. A descriptive framework proposed by Luchins (1964) can be extended and modified to describe these four kinds of conceptions of man, using Latin phrases to denote the essence of each model. The *Homo volens* ("man of will") model stresses that man is primarily a creature of strivings and emotions, guided by blind and unconscious inner urges. This is the basic model of man in psychoanalytic theory. The *Homo sapiens* ("man of knowledge") model stresses man as a cognitive creature, capable of grasping the meaning of a situation and guiding his behavior according to his understanding of the situation. This is the predominant model of man for cognitive theory. The *Homo mechanicus* ("mechanical man") model views man as a machine, more or less like a complex computer programmed to link input information to output behavior. This model is characteristic of modern behavioristic theory. Finally, the *Homo ludens* ("man of play") model stresses a man as a creature who encounters his world as a game, trying to cope with his world and the people in it with a variety of strategies, and enjoying or suffering while the game is played out. This is the conception of man that underlies humanistic theory.

Each of these models alone is probably insufficient: man is a synthesis of all four. There are ways in which he is a creature of blind striving, but there are other ways in which he is a creature of meaning and understanding. If we are to understand and predict man's behavior scientifically, we must also view him as an orderly machine. Yet, with all these, his most human qualities are reflected in his joy and grief as he engages in the game of living. When social psychology ultimately evolves an adequate model for understanding man's behavior, it will no doubt include some elements of all four of these conceptions of man (see Table 2–1).

Psychoanalytic Conceptions of Man

Despite the fact that psychoanalytic theory has influenced social psychology by calling attention to issues or factors that seem to merit particular investigation and exploration, none of the psychoanalytic writers has been a good theorist in the sense of developing and expounding very explicit, articulated, and testable hypotheses.

Theory	Conceptual Model of Man	Major Representatives in Social Psychology	Areas of Contribution to Social Psychology
Psychoanalytic	*Homo volens* ("man of will")	Freud, Jung, Adler, Abraham, Fromm, Horney, Bion	Personality development Socialization Aggression identification Culture and behavior
Cognitive	*Homo sapiens* ("man of knowledge")	Lewin, Heider, Festinger, Piaget, Kohlberg	Attitudes Language and thought Group dynamics Propaganda Interpersonal perception Self-concept
Behavioristic	*Homo mechanicus* ("mechanical man")	Hull, Miller & Dollard, Rotter, Sears, Skinner, Bandura	Experimental and theoretical rigor Socialization Social control Social rewards and punishments
Humanistic	*Homo ludens* ("man of play")	Rogers, Combs & Snygg, Maslow, May, Satir, Perls	Self-concept Interpersonal transactions Society and the individual

The fact is, however, that Freudian and other psychoanalytic ideas have often been translated into the language of other theories, and in that form submitted to empirical test. Newcomb (1950) has translated psychoanalytic notions into concepts dealing with social and behavioral roles. Miller and Dollard (1941), Dollard and Miller (1950), and Sears (1944), among others, have translated psychoanalytic theory into the concepts of behaviorism and reinforcement theory. In this sense, even "weak" theory may make useful contributions to the development of a science. But as theory per se, psychoanalytic theory is weak when judged according to modern criteria for evaluating the usefulness of scientific theories.

Cognitive Conceptions of Man

Cognitive theory is more widely represented in contemporary social psychological research than are other kinds of theories. Although there are no elaborately comprehensive cognitive theories addressed to the entire range of human activity, there are many segmented theoretical models that deal with particular circumscribed phenomena. For example, there are cognitive theories of attitude change and development (Katz & Stotland, 1959), of interpersonal perception and attraction (Heider, 1958; Newcomb, 1961), and of social influences on perception, memory, and cognition (Helson, 1947; Festinger, 1954, 1957). During the 1930s and 1940s especially, cognitive theory (particularly Lewin's field theory) had the virtue of being highly instructive and productive of new ideas and lines of investigation. The cognitive theories were pioneering, unafraid to embark upon new areas of research. Willing to accept temporary crudity of theory, they made headway in attacking new problems in research. Furthermore, their richness as descriptive devices has served to generate significant exploratory research.

Behavioristic Conceptions of Man

The newer forms of behaviorism have been highly responsive to early criticisms of classic behaviorism. The influence of Gestalt theory and field theory has exerted pressure on behaviorism to deal with larger units of analysis and with more complex conceptions of the elaborate stimulus configurations that determine behavior. Behaviorism's concepts of both discriminative stimuli (cues that serve as signals that elicit behavior) and reinforcing stimuli (consequent conditions that serve to reward or punish behavior) have become increasingly molar and less molecular. These concepts now deal with larger configurations rather than merely oversimplified portions of the environmental context. Behavioristic concepts of motivation are to some extent translations and revisions of psychoanalytic concepts. The canalization of libido is analogous to the direction of generalized drive along specific habitual channels of behavior or toward certain goals that have acquired reward value. Although staunchly adhering to its conviction that observable behavior must be the starting point for erecting a theory, behaviorism has conceded to cognitive theory the importance of the individual's experience.

Kenneth Spence, one of the most ardent enthusiasts for revised and extended forms of Clark Hull's behavioristic theory, has commented that behaviorism as a school of thought no longer exists, and that some of its early emphases are ubiquitous (Spence, 1948). Even the contemporary forms of cognitive theory, although emphasizing conscious experience, concede that science must work with concepts that have observable referents. Bronfenbrenner (1953) has suggested that the real point of current dissension has to do with the immediacy of the need for operational definitions: whether to start there right now and work out, or to start with the vaguely defined and circle in on the·concept. Behaviorists prefer to start with the explicit operational definitions and gradually work toward theories that can cope with more complex and elaborate phenomena in behavior, whereas cognitivists prefer to start with the obvious complexities of human behavior and work gradually toward adequately precise definitions. There is encouraging evidence in contemporary psychology that the rapprochement of these diverse preferences is near.

Humanistic Conceptions of Man

The humanistic movement in the behavioral sciences gained momentum rapidly during the 1960s. Prior to the mid-sixties, the humanistic protests against the "dehumanization" of man by science represented merely a set of values, and not a theoretical approach to the study of man. But the humanistic point of view has gained stature as its proponents have begun to articulate their theoretical concepts of man and evolve them into hypotheses and scientific statements about behavior (Rogers, 1951; Maslow, 1954, 1968; May, 1969a, 1969b). This emerging body of theory reintegrates the cognitive and the affective components of man's makeup, and takes a fresh approach to the recognition of the *phenomenological* ("first-person") point of view. That is, this approach emphasizes the need for the scientist to understand his subject by trying to understand how that person feels and experiences the world.

Humanistic approaches are often subject to criticism for being excessively subjective and mentalistic. However, like psychoanalytic theory, they make use of the individual's verbal behavior (to describe and report his subjective experiences) and the reflections of his values and feelings in the choices he makes, and the expressions he reveals in his face and body—which are overt and observable behaviors.

Humanistic conceptions of man occur most frequently in research concerned with the study of values and motivation in social contexts, explorations of the self-concept and man's awareness of his social relationships with others, studies of diadic interpersonal transactions, and analysis of the individual in a complex social structure. As the humanistic point of view matures into articulated theory, it is likely that its contributions to social psychology will increase even further.

All four of these theoretical conceptions of man are reflected in the research conducted by social psychologists. Despite some very important differences among them, it is perhaps more important to emphasize the fact that in the final analysis the major conclusions and inferences drawn from observations within all four frameworks are highly congruent. Their similarities are perhaps more significant than their differences. Yet it is the differences among the points of view that provide the most persuasive argument in favor of an *eclectic* approach: one that uses particular theories or models for analysis of the particular facets of human behavior for which they are best suited.

REVIEW

1. The *scientific method* includes three basic operations: the careful collection of observations or data (*methodology*), the ordered integration of these observations into hypotheses or scientific laws (*theory building*), and tests of the adequacy of these theoretical laws in terms of whether they can successfully predict future observations (scientific *experimentation* and *application*).

2. *Empiricism* in science is a commitment to understand the universe through direct observation of events. The basic observations of science are called *data*. The philosophy of science that demands that all data be publicly observable by any scientist is *logical positivism* or *scientific empiricism*. Overt actions or *behavior* are observable, but information about subjective *experience* must be inferred indirectly from observable actions.

3. *Reliability* is the extent to which a scientist can place confidence in his data as accurate and stable observations. Reliability can be assessed through *repeated measurement, split-half* comparisons, or *part-whole* comparisons, including *item analysis. Error of measurement* is a statistical estimate of reliability.

4. *Validity* concerns the degree to which a scientist's interpretations of what he observes are sound and meaningful representations of the universe. Validity can be assessed through *criterion* validation, *content* validation, or *construct* validation.

5. *Correlation* demonstrates a parallel relationship between two measures, but *causation* requires considerably more information in order to reach conclusions about the direct of cause and effect or antecedent-consequent relationship.

6. Scientific observation in social psychology requires interaction between one person as the *experimenter-observer* and another as the *subject* being observed. Both may contribute human factors, which introduce errors into the scientific process. Among those associated with the experimenter-observer are his *sex, racial* or *ethnic* qualities, *personal mannerisms,* and *expectations* or *biases*. Subjects in scientific observation usually form ideas about the purposes of the study called *demand characteristics* of the experiment. Among the problems of observation associated with the subject are the fact that he may be *willing* to be too agreeable, *apprehensive* about being observed, *faithful* with blind loyalty to the experimenter, *transparent* or exhibitionistic in wanting to strip naked emotionally, *selfish* in trying to serve his own interests in the experiment, *suspicious* of the experimenter's purposes, or motivated to *volunteer* to be observed for reasons which distort his behavior.

7. Sampling procedures attempt to maximize the range of generalization of observations from the original research to other areas of application. Improper generalizations from a limited set of observations are called *sampling errors*. Attempts to control such error include *random* sampling, *stratified* sampling, *area* sampling, and *quota* sampling.

8. The setting in which observations are made in research influence the behavior being observed. *Behavioral ecology* is an approach that describes a person's behavior as he moves among natural environmental contexts in his daily life. The *Haw-*

thorne effect describes the distortion of behavior from the simple fact of being observed.

9. *Field studies* involve observations made in natural settings with no intervention or manipulation of conditions. *Natural experiments* involve observations made in natural settings, with only natural accident intervening to change or manipulate conditions. *Field experiments* involve observations made in natural settings when the observer intervenes to manipulate conditions. *Laboratory experiments* involve observations made in carefully controlled settings under maximum control of the observer to remove extraneous influences. *Simulation experiments* involve observations made with procedures which reproduce critical determinants of behavior in abstract and stylized forms.

10. *Cross-cultural* research involves observations made in different cultural contexts for purposes of descriptive comparison.

11. *Theories* are sets of related *hypotheses*, which are statements of logical systematic relationships among observations. The most appropriate way to define concepts within a theory is through *operational definitions* (outlines for reproducing the conditions for observing the event to which the concept refers).

12. Among the theoretical systems that have contributed most directly to social psychology are *psychoanalytic, cognitive, behavioristic*, and *humanistic* theories. Each of these adopts a slightly different conception of the nature of man. Psychoanalytic theory stresses a *Homo volens* ("man of will") creature driven by inner strivings and urges. Cognitive theory stresses a *Homo sapiens* ("man of knowledge") creature capable of grasping the meaning of a situation and guiding his behavior accordingly. Behavioristic theory uses a *Homo mechanicus* ("mechanical man"), which views man as a machine-like computer linking input information to output behavior. Humanistic theory views man as a *Homo ludens* ("man of play") creature who encounters his world as a game, trying to cope with the world and the people in it with a variety of strategies, enjoying or suffering as the game is played out.

13. All of these theoretical conceptions of man are represented in modern social psychology and its theories. Their similarities are more important than their differences, but each kind of model is suited for the analysis of different facets of man's social behavior. An *eclectic* approach in science uses different theories for different purposes.

3
METHODS OF STUDYING SOCIAL BEHAVIOR

If you are more interested in *what* has been discovered in social psychology than in *how* it has been discovered, you may disregard this chapter and proceed to Chapter 4. This chapter is concerned primarily with methodological problems of collecting, reducing, and interpreting data that are commonly encountered by social psychologists. You may, however, find Chapter 3 helpful as a reference source on specific issues that arise in other chapters.

METHODS OF DIRECT OBSERVATION
Chronograph Records
Bales' Interaction Process Analysis
Coded Observations of Educational Interaction

METHODS OF CONTENT ANALYSIS

METHODS OF SUBJECTIVE REPORT
Response Set
Social Desirability
The Dimension of Structure
The Dimension of Disguise
The Interview

ATTITUDE ASSESSMENT
Unstructured-Undisguised Techniques
Unstructured-Disguised Techniques
Structured-Disguised Techniques
Structured-Undisguised Techniques
    Bogardus Social Distance Scale
    Method of Cumulative Scaling (Guttman)
    Method of Equal-Appearing Intervals (Thurstone)
    Summated Ratings Method of Scaling (Likert)
    Semantic Differential

36

Social
Psychology

SOCIOMETRIC ASSESSMENT
Sociograms
Numerical Sociometric Indices
Tagiuri's Relational Analysis
Field Sociometry
The Reliability and Validity of Sociometric Data

GAMING AND SIMULATION
Zero-Sum Games
Nonzero-Sum Games
Complex Simulations

Review

The earmark of modern social psychology is *empiricism,* an approach based on careful observations of behavior by reliable and impartial observers. Chapter 2 outlined the characteristics of scientific inquiry and described the basic commitment of social psychology to empirical methods of study. Chapter 3 is a further excursion into greater detail about the specific procedures commonly used by social psychologists to investigate man's social behavior. In this sense, it is a digression from the main course of this book, and this chapter may be used from time to time as a reference source in connection with reading subsequent chapters.

Probably the most straightforward approach to studying social behavior would be simply to stand in a public place and watch people in situations where the behavior under scrutiny is expected to occur. In the absence of actual opportunities to do that, an investigator may refer to records of such behavior that has occurred in the past, or he may ask someone to tell about his behavior in situations in which the investigator is interested. With any of these approaches, it would still be necessary for the observer to plan carefully the manner in which his observations will be made and recorded in order to ensure that they are objective, unbiased, and unambiguous. He would want to maximize their reliability (precision in observation) as well as their validity (accuracy of interpretation).

The empirical-scientific process includes potential problems at three levels of operation. At the level of *data collection,* one must consider possible error and bias in the actual process of watching, listening, or recording. In most cases, the raw data (observations) thus collected are transformed through scoring, coding, or sorting, into scores and indices; this is the process of *data reduction.* Bias and inaccuracy may also be introduced in errors at this level. Finally, at a third level, reduced data must be examined for meaning and interpreted by the observer; this is the level of *data interpretation.* Questions of *reliability* apply to errors at the first two levels (data-collection and data reduction), whereas questions of *validity* are concerned with errors at the third level (data interpretation).

Before proceeding further to describe the content of psychological research into man's social behavior, Chapter 3 offers a general evaluation of methodological problems of collecting, reducing, and interpreting data that are commonly encountered by social psychologists. A variety of typical procedures employed in social psychology are described in three broad categories: direct naturalistic observation, subjective reports of behavior and experience, and content analysis of records of behavior. Other special techniques that combine elements of these three categories are also oulined and decribed: attitude assessment, sociometry, and experimental gaming.

METHODS OF DIRECT OBSERVATION

Direct observation of ongoing behavior by the investigator is perhaps the least intrusive procedure for collecting research data, especially if the observations can be made while the observer is concealed behind one-way glass, or through closed circuit television or hidden movie cameras. By such means, the effects of the presence of an observer (and consequent Hawthorne effects) may be minimized (see Chapter 2).

The most critical problem in direct observation procedures is that of defining the unit of observation. Of course, there are mechanical devices for recording the entire flow of behavior (sound recorders, TV tapes, or movie films), but these devices merely preserve the record of behavior for future use by an investigator. He would subsequently be faced with something analogous to the content analysis of behavioral records, and the problems of converting these records to scientifically useful observations would be much the same as if he were observing ongoing behavior directly. The basic task of the investigator in using direct observation as a method of research is to convert the continuous flow of observed activity into coded units. Unfortunately, there is no simple and specific definition of an act of behavior. The purposes of the investigator determine the unit that will be most useful to his research. In the case of verbal behavior, a simple sentence (which, by definition, expresses one complete thought) offers a convenient unit for observation. Similarly, compound sentences, as well as some complex sentences would ordinarily be coded as multiple units. But nonverbal behavior, which represents a more continuous flow, does not lend itself to such arbitrary conventions. Time intervals provide a possible solution to this problem: a period of 1 minute of head scratching might be coded as one unit of "deep thought"; while 2 minutes of the same activity could be coded as two units in the same category. But such conventions are arbitrary, and before coded records of observed behavior can be properly used as research data, it is necessary for the investigator to insure that he (and any other observer who wished access to the same kind of data) is able to adopt the same conventions consistently and explicitly.

Coded behavioral data may be handled as a simple descriptive record, or it may be evaluated. Categorical coding is the simplest nonevaluative way of handling behavioral observations: an observer simply utilizes a predetermined set of definitions to sort into designated categories the units of behavior he observes. Bales' method of Interaction Process Analysis, described later in this chapter, represents such a nonevaluative descriptive coding system. However, observers may go further than simply labeling each observed unit of behavior—they may rate each unit evaluatively according to some predefined scale. For example, certain units of behavior may be assigned to a general category labeled "aggression," but then be subsequently rated by the observer along a scale from "mildly aggressive" to "violently aggressive." Because evaluative coding demands more judgment than descriptive coding, the accuracy of coding, as estimated by the degree of agreement among different observers coding the same behavior or by measures of an observer's consistency over time, is usually greater for descriptive coding than for evaluative coding.

Because individual differences in the personalities and abilities of different observers are quite variable, direct observation procedures often suffer from inconsistencies from one observer to the next. A variety of procedures may be used to combat such inconsistency, including the preparation of explicit manuals that provide instructions for defining units of behavior and each of the categories to which a coded unit might be assigned. Furthermore, extensive training of observers, with full discussion of uncertainties and disagreements in coding, can enhance interrater agreement considerably. The disruptive interference of the mechanical task of tallying records may be at least partially alleviated by providing the observer with mechanical devices to facilitate recording. Most of the conventionally used procedures for direct observation of social behavior described here make use of all of these means of increasing the accuracy of observation.

Chronograph Records

In Chapple's (1940) system of recording direct observation, the observer merely indicates the beginning, duration, and end of verbal interpersonal behavior. Concerned primarily with the timing of interpersonal behavior and ignoring its content, this procedure is relatively free of contamination by subjective observer judgment. Because the direction in which recorded behavior is addressed is not recorded, such observational records are more useful in studies of diadic (two-person) situations than of larger groups. The Interaction Chronograph is a device with a continuous sheet of moving paper with keys to mark records in ten channels: the observer makes a record simply by pushing a button in the channel corresponding to the individual being observed and holds it down until interaction terminates. The interrater relia-

bility with this method is quite high, but the procedure has limited utility because it
ignores the content of coded interaction. Among the variables that may conveniently
be explored by this procedure are frequency of activity, duration of activity, relative
amounts of inactivity, frequency of interruption, and response to interruption.

Bales' Interaction Process Analysis

The most widely used system for coding direct observations of social behavior is
that developed by Bales (1950). It is intended to be comprehensive of all kinds of
interpersonal behavior, and mechanical devices facilitate the mechanics of recording
codes. Bales defines the basic unit of observation as "the smallest discriminable
segment of verbal or nonverbal behavior to which the observer using the present set
of categories after proper training, can assign a classification under conditions of
continuous serial scoring" (Bales, 1950, p. 37). The observer is instructed to act as
"the generalized other"; that is, he classifies the observed behavior in terms of its
presumed significance for the observed person. Subjective inferences are minimized
by instructing the observer to interpret an act in terms of the act that immediately pre-
ceded it. The system defines twelve discrete categories that are subsumed within four
broad categories as indicated in Table 3–1. The extreme categories (A, positive reac-

Table 3–1 Bales' Interaction Process Analysis

Social-Emotional Area: Positive	A	SEEMS FRIENDLY 1 (shows solidarity, raises other's status, gives help or reward) DRAMATIZES 2 (shows tension release, jokes, laughs, shows satisfaction) AGREES 3 (shows passive acceptance, understands, concurs, complies)
Task Area: Neutral	B	GIVES SUGGESTION 4 (direction, implying autonomy for other) GIVES OPINION 5 (evaluation, analysis, expresses feeling or wish) GIVES INFORMATION 6 (orientation, repeats, clarifies, confirms)
	C	ASKS FOR INFORMATION 7 (seeks orientation, repetition, confirmation) ASKS FOR OPINION 8 (seeks evaluation, analysis, expression of feeling) ASKS FOR SUGGESTION 9 (seeks direction, possible ways of acting)
Social-Emotional Area: Negative	D	DISAGREES 10 (shows passive rejection, formality, withholds help) SHOWS TENSION 11 (asks for help, withdraws out of field) SEEMS UNFRIENDLY 12 (shows antagonism, deflates other's status, defends or asserts self)

A = Positive reactions
B = Attempted answers
C = Questions
D = Negative reactions

Source: Adapted from Robert F. Bales, *Interaction Process Analysis: A Method for the Study of Small
Groups,* Addison-Wesley, 1950.

tions and D, negative reactions) describe social-emotional behavior patterns that deal with the organization of the group and involve problems of personal tension management, maintenance of harmony, and group integration. The middle categories (B, attempted answers and C, questions) are emotionally neutral and are geared to carrying out the task confronting the group; they include activities concerned with definition of the task situation, development of common value systems within the group, attempts of individuals to control or influence one another, and progress toward final decisions in connection with the task. Observations may be converted to quantitative measures by computing the frequencies of acts in each of the twelve categories to yield a profile for either an individual or a group. These profiles may then be interpreted to characterize the degree of harmony within a group, the extent of a group's orientation to its central tasks, or the amount of interpersonal tension within a group, for example. With respect to individuals, profiles may be used to evaluate their investment in the group's task, their efforts to maintain harmony within the group, or their manner of handling their own tension in the group. Because Bales has provided an elaborate manual for coding, with concrete examples of each category, as well as explicit instructions for the training of observers, the system is one that can fairly readily be employed by other investigators. Thus it has become a rather commonly used procedure in research in social psychology.

Coded Observations of Educational Interaction

The paradigm of Bales has been adopted by other investigators for a variety of specific purposes. These techniques have proved especially useful in educational research for the study of classroom interaction of pupils and teachers, as well as for the empirical study of curriculum in terms of interactions among teachers, learners, and materials. Flanders and Amidon (Amidon & Flanders, 1963; Flanders, 1970) standardized a derivative from the Bales Interaction Process Analysis for describing classroom interaction, emphasizing verbal behaviors. Subsequently, Ober, Bentley, and Miller (1971) developed two similar systems: the *Reciprocal Categories System* (covering both verbal and nonverbal behavior) and the *Equivalent Talk Categories* (emphasizing verbal interaction). Similar schemes have been modified for elementary and preschool classroom interaction, including Medley's (1969) OSCAR (Observation of School Classroom Activities Record) and PROSE (Pupil Record of School Experiences) (Medley, Qiurk, Schluck, & Ames, 1971) and Stern and Kiesler's (1968) OSCI (Observation System for Classroom Interaction).

METHODS OF CONTENT ANALYSIS

When there is no opportunity for direct observation of behavior as it occurs, an investigator may utilize records of behavior that has already occurred as a basis for his research data. In some cases, especially when records are virtually complete, as in the case of tape recordings, TV transcriptions, or movies, the problems of converting these continuous observations into coded usable forms are essentially identical to those of the direct observation procedures already described. In other cases the records that are analyzed are themselves selective and specific, and special procedures must be employed in using them as data sources.

The term "content analysis" is conventionally applied to the analysis of the manifest content of communications. Berelson (1954) has been most closely identified with the development of standardized procedures for content analysis, and he construes

	Definition	Example
Uses	Trends in communication patterns	Change in textbook content
	International differences in communication content	Semantic differences between Americans and Russians
	Coding of qualitative research material	Virtually all verbal illustrations in this textbook
	The exposure of propaganda techniques	Conventional "tricks of the trade"
	Variations in stylistic expressions within or among societies	Acting styles
	The reflection of "cultural patterns" (attitude, interests, and values) of population groups	Folklore interpretation
	The assessment of mass-media effects	Popular family-type magazine content
Units of Analysis	*Word:* the smallest unit	Term or concept
	Theme: a larger unit about which an inference is made	Projective TAT measures
	Character: fictional or real persons around which narrative is woven	Comic-strip characters
	Item: the whole unit, as employed by the producers of symbolic material	A complete news story on a particular topic (with minimum within-category variation)
	Space-and-Time Measure: a physical separation of communication content	Pages, column inches, film footage, minutes of radio listening or TV viewing
Content Categories	*Direction: pro* and *con*	Approval-disapproval
	Standards: the basis for the direction taken	Moral or legalistic reasoning
	Values: general goals and motives	Affiliation or achievement, through wealth or prestige
	Traits: ordinary descriptive personal characteristics	Fat, shy, loyal, old, etc.
	Actors: action initiators	Pilots, Germans, Jews, Teachers, etc.
	Authority: source of communication	In whose name was communication made?
	Origin: location of source	The place where the communication originated
	Target: to whom the communication is directed	Pilots, Germans, Jews, Teachers, etc.
Form	*Type* of communication	Newspaper or magazine, verbal or pictorial
	Form of communication	Grammatical, syntactical, factual, evaluative, etc.
	Intensity of communication	Variations in emotional expressions of anger, love, hostility, etc.

the term "communication" in this context to refer to a body of meaning conveyed in symbolic form. Because meaning may be conveyed by a variety of kinds of symbols (e.g., verbal, musical, plastic, graphic, or gestural), content analysis may be applicable to almost any kind of behavioral product, including records of everyday conversations, literature, and various forms of art. The manner of analysis used depends upon the investigator's purpose. For example, the plays of Shakespeare might be analyzed to determine the extent to which his phraseology has become an integral part of contemporary spoken and written English, or they might be analyzed to ascertain a description of Shakespeare's personality, including his interests, values, feelings, or habits. In social psychological research, content analysis is especially useful in the exploration of consensual beliefs and values of organized societies, and the cultural products that are most frequently subjected to content analysis are the news media, periodical literature and books, folklore, and legends, and arts and crafts. Table 3–2 outlines a comprehensive description of content analysis as applied to verbal communication records according to Berelson (1952).

Other techniques of content analysis have been applied to various kinds of behavioral products. Some of these resemble the categorical observation systems described earlier, in that they systematically code verbal units into predefined categories. The method of *conversational analysis* (Landis, 1924) was an early precursor of modern techniques for coding verbal interaction. This family of related techniques may be used on spontaneous free verbal samples drawn from natural conversation. Psycholinguists also make use of methods of content analysis to study freely occurring verbal behavior. Markle's (1969) *descriptive linguistic analysis* is an example of this kind of methodology.

Problems of sampling are especially important in content analysis. When cultural products are thus analyzed, the investigator must be concerned that the sample he analyzes is truly representative of the products of the individual or the society he wishes to characterize. For example, one could argue that it would seem rather presumptuous to infer national characteristics of the American public from the content of successful stage plays because these plays may reflect only the taste of the sophisticated urbanite, or, worse still, the taste of a handful of powerful drama critics in New York. Similarly, the New York tabloid newspapers would be representative of the reading tastes and habits of a different segment of the population from that represented by the *New York Times* or the *Wall Street Journal.* Within either kind of newspaper, selected samples would differ according to space, page location, size of type, and the like. In other mass media, such as radio and television, the time slot, length, and whether the analyzed sample was shown in color or black-and-white would be related to the content of the communication.

As in the direct observation of behavior, the reliability and validity of data obtained by content analysis are dependent on the definition of the basic unit of analysis. Reliability generally increases with simpler categories and units, with more complete and precise rules for coding, with experienced and well-trained coders, and with more frequent or larger samples. The validity of interpretation of such data is enhanced by procedures that minimize the role of subjective judgments of the coder in interpreting coded units.

METHODS OF SUBJECTIVE REPORT

The greater portion, by far, of all psychological research data is derived from observations of a person's report of his own behavior. Interview data, as well as most data obtained through psychological tests, fall into this category. A psychological test is merely a device for precipitating the occurrence of a particular kind of behavior or report of behavior. Thus in order to understand and interpret observations obtained by this method, an investigator must necessarily take into account the procedures he uses to precipitate the observed behavior.

Response Set

One of the most crucial problems encountered in the method of subjective report is that of response sets or biases on the part of the respondent. When a person is presented a set of materials that are intended to elicit a judgment or other selective response, the form and content of the test materials themselves often induce systematic response tendencies that may obscure his true response. For example, the so-called acquiescent response set is a generally observed tendency among individuals to agree with any statement offered by an investigator in an interview or a test. That is, in a true-false test, regardless of the content of the statements offered, there is an underlying tendency for most people to lean toward true answers rather than false answers. This tendency has been found to hold true generally in the testing of American adults, with the result that test scores derived from counting the frequency of agreement with verbal statements are artificially inflated, and scores based on frequencies of disagreement are artificially reduced. A rather interesting converse "deviation hypothesis" has been offered by Berg (Berg & Bass, 1961), who has proposed that certain kinds of individuals may be systematically inclined toward a form of contrary deviation from convention and acquiescence, so that they systematically avoid agreement and prefer disagreement. Although there is limited evidence in support of this hypothesis, at least with respect to individuals who already deviate from the general population in some way (such as neurotics, criminals, and the like), there is no evidence that it is a pronounced general kind of response set in the average test-taker.

Social Desirability

Another factor that may tend to obscure a person's true response on a subjective report test is the likelihood that test responses will be systematically distorted in the direction of reflecting what the respondent assumes to be socially desirable or socially accepted responses. To the extent that conventional norms apply to all members of a society or group to define what is socially desirable, this factor may induce systematic distortions in test responses. However, these tendencies in test-taking are not entirely predictable, not only because conventional standards of social desirability may fluctuate from time to time with respect to particular kinds of behavior, but also because different individuals may hold different concepts of what they think is regarded as socially desirable in their psychological reference group. Certain steps may be taken to control and compensate for culturally defined standards of social desirability—when cultural norms for desirability on a given issue are known, they may be applied to discount or weigh a subject's subjective report. However, idiosyncratic individual codes of social desirability are difficult to anticipate and ascertain; hence it is extremely difficult to control or take account of their effects upon a person's responses in interviews and questionnaires.

The Dimension of Structure

The procedures used by an investigator to precipitate responses on the part of his subjects may be described in terms of the dimension of *structure*. This dimension concerns the extent to which the devices used to precipitate behavior limit the kinds of behavior that may occur. Of course, any verbal device for precipitating behavior has a certain degree of structure in that it is designed to elicit a verbal response. But beyond this minimum, an unstructured device would be one that affords the greatest latitude for variety of response by the subject; at the other extreme, a highly structured device would be one that limits the subject's response to one or two categories.

Probably the most unstructured self-report method used in the collection of psychological data is that of free association. With this method, the subject is instructed to verbalize each and every thought that passes through his awareness in the continuous stream of experience. No doubt, the physical surroundings in the room, and even the presence of the investigator himself, provides cues that narrow the range of likely behavior. In contrast, among the most highly structured devices used in data collection by the subjective report method are tests such as attitude scales that restrict the subject's response to "Yes or No" or "Agree or Disagree" answers. As a rule, the greater the degree of structure in the test or interview situation, the greater the reliability of the data obtained, although exceptions may occur if the test is so highly structured that it restricts the subject's response to categories that are all unacceptable in his judgment. However, in the very early stages of investigation of a particular issue, an investigator often lacks sufficient knowledge to prepare appropriate devices to structure the response of his subjects, and he must begin his task of investigation with relatively open and unstructured procedures.

The Dimension of Disguise

Another dimension along which testing and interviewing procedures may vary is that of *disguise.* This dimension concerns the extent to which the investigator's procedures conceal from the subject the particular area of self-report or behavior in which he is actually interested. Various misleading devices may be employed to distract the respondent's attention from the focus of investigation. Disguised techniques are particularly appropriate when the investigator has reason to believe that his subjects may be inclined to distort their responses under the influence of such factors as social desirability, embarrassment, or desire to please the investigator.

The Interview

One of the simplest and most convenient procedures for obtaining subjective report data is for the investigator simply to ask his subjects direct questions. Interviews may be either *unstructured* (open-ended questions that no not lead the respondent into particular channels of response) or *structured* (specific questions that lead the respondent progressively into increasingly narrow channels of response). Interviews ordinarily involve face-to-face verbal encounters between an investigator and a respondent, but in essence, a psychological test may simply be a written interview— especially if the investigator is present while the subject responds to the questions.

A properly planned interview includes prior critical appraisal of all the procedures to be employed in collecting data, including specification of the content and form of questions to be used, predetermination of the manner in which responses are to be coded and recorded (which involves anticipation of the methodological problems described earlier in connection with direct observation and content analysis techniques), and consideration of the relationship between the interviewer and the respondent.

An interview should avoid questions that unintentionally rest upon prior assumptions that the respondent may reject. For example, the old question, "Have you stopped beating your wife?" rests upon an implicit assumption that may confuse the respondent. Does an answer of "No" mean "No, I am still beating my wife," or "No, I haven't stopped because I never started"? In some cases the investigator may intentionally wish to catch the subject off guard by asking such questions, anticipating their effect and coding responses accordingly. Such questions can induce the respondent to talk about areas he might otherwise conceal or distort.

To standardize an interview so that it is repeated in the same manner with each subject observed, it may be necessary to be very rigid about asking each subject each question in a specified order, regardless of the trend of the conversation. Unstandardized interviews that vary flexibly according to the tenor of the conversation may be more comfortable for both interviewer and respondent, but they sacrifice consistency from one subject to the next, resulting in corresponding losses in the reliability of the data.

Table 3–3 summarizes a variety of methodological problems in the preparation of interview questions (Maccoby & Maccoby, 1954).

Just as in the case of direct observation procedures, mechanical devices may be employed to facilitate the interviewer's task. By recording the interview, he may go back later, under more convenient circumstances, to convert the recorded verbal behavior into more usable coded form. However, he is forced to depend upon his memory for details of accompanying gestures or contextual events.

In using interview methods of data collection, sampling problems are often inflated. Interviews require the respondent's participation in a close face-to-face interaction with a stranger, and many people are unwilling to cooperate under the more anonymous conditions of a written questionnaire administered in a group. In large-scale surveys, in which interviewers are designated to go into the homes of respondents, a subject may be caught at an inopportune time, or he may not wish to receive the interviewer as a caller. Thus the selective factors associated with volunteering may become especially critical. Furthermore, if the interview is conducted at an inoppor-

Table 3–3 Problems in Phrasing Interview Questions

Phrasing Problem	Example
Connotative meaning	*"Are you a fair reader?"* Poor reader? Impartial reader?
Brevity and clarity	*"Do you believe that no Negro should be deprived of a franchise except for reasons which would disenfranchise a white man, regardless of whether this occurs south or north of the Mason-Dixon line?"* Most likely to be incomprehensible.
Projection	*"What do most people think of the United Nations?"* What does the respondent think about the United Nations? What does the respondent think other people think about the United Nations?
Specification	*"How did you feel about this issue when you were young?"* In your childhood? In your teens? During the first year of marriage? *"Are promotions in your office based on merit?"* Are favoritism or seniority to be ignored if answer is positive?
Especially important in sensitive issues demanding reduction of personal defensiveness:	
Unfamiliar vocabulary or jargon	*"Do you believe that autistic children should be continuously reinforced?"*
Social desirability	*"Do you think that children should be taught not to fight with each other?"* Is this socially acceptable? How do others feel about it? Better phrasing: "Some parents feel it's terribly important to teach a child not to fight with other children. Others feel that in some circumstances, a child must learn to fight. How do you feel about this?"
Euphemisms	*"What are your methods for punishing your children?"* Substitute: "disciplining" for "punishing."
Partiality-Impartiality	*"What do you like least about your boss?"* should be preceded by "What do you like best about your boss?"
Face-saving	*"Before leaving Russia, were you a Communist?"* if asked of a Russian refugee will not elicit a positive response as easily as "Before leaving Russia, were you able to keep out of the Communist Party?"

tune time, the sample behavior obtained may not be at all representative of the respondent's ordinary behavior. Thus, just as individuals may be sampled from a population of people, likewise, selected behavioral samples may be drawn from the total behavioral continuity of a person's lifespan.

ATTITUDE ASSESSMENT

Whereas interviews represent face-to-face encounters between an observer and his subject, other similar techniques standardize the request for self-report in written forms called *questionnaires* or *inventories.* The interview affords greater opportunity to observe and record a wide range of behaviors (facial expressions; postures; tangential, irrelevant remarks and acts), it also affords greater opportunity for the intrusion of errors and biases through the social interaction of the observer and his subject. Written questionnaires and inventories reverse this; they are more limited and restrictive in the behavior recorded, but the role of the human factor is somewhat better controlled.

The concept of *attitude* is discussed in detail in Chapter 5. An attitude is a relatively stable system of organization of one's behavior and experience related to a particular object or event, and it includes a basic cognitive component (an idea or belief), an affective component (value), and a behavioral component (predispositions or inclinations in a behavioral direction). Attitude-assessment procedures include a variety of ways of measuring the ideas, values, and actions that reflect any kind of attitude.

The dimensions of structure and disguise, discussed earlier in connection with methods of subjective report and interviews, are applicable to the variety of procedures used in attitude assessment. Highly structured devices are those that restrict the range of the subject's expressed judgments; unstructured devices include those that permit him to express a rather large variety of judgments. Disguised techniques are those that attempt to conceal from the respondent the particular kind of attitudes being investigated; undisguised techniques include those that openly indicate the kinds of attitudes being studied. Table 3–4 summarizes four categories of approach to attitude assessment, with examples of commonly used procedures in each category.

In general, unstructured techniques are necessary in early stages of investigation of a particular attitude because the investigator may initially lack sufficient information to permit the construction of highly structured techniques that narrow the range of response down to a few highly pertinent kinds of judgment. Eventually, with suffi-

Table 3–4 Some Common Measures of Attitudes
(Classified According to Disguise and Structure)

	Structured	**Unstructured**
Disguised	Error-choice technique (Hammond) Syllogistic reasoning (Thistlethwaite) Lost-letter technique (Milgram) Wrong-number technique (Gaertner)	Projective techniques Rorschach Inkblot Test Thematic Apperception Test (Murray; McClelland)
Undisguised	Social distance scale (Bogardus) Method of cumulative scaling (Guttman) Method of equal-appearing intervals (Thurstone) Method of summated ratings (Likert) Semantic differential (Osgood)	Open-ended interviews Sentence completion tests Open-ended questionnaires Biographical statements

cient information about the most relevant kinds of judgment determined by the particular attitude in question, the investigator may be able to use more economical and efficient structured techniques. The greatest advantage of disguised techniques is that they permit the assessment of attitudes concerning issues about which the respondent may be sensitive and reluctant to express himself. Because disguised techniques usually involve a certain amount of beating around the bush, they are ordinarily less efficient or economical than undisguised techniques. Consequently, in the assessment of attitudes on nonsensitive issues about which people are willing to express themselves, the procedure that secures from the respondent the greatest amount of information in the least time is that of the structured and undisguised techniques. This category of procedures includes the family of conventional attitude scaling procedures that have been highly refined during the past 30 years by such psychometricians as L. Guttman, L. L. Thurstone, and Rensis Likert.

Unstructured-Undisguised Techniques

This category of attitude assessment procedures represents the most direct and common-sense approach to attitude measurement. Individuals are simply asked in a straightforward manner to express judgments about a particular object or issue. Open-ended interviews are representative of this approach. For example, an individual might be asked, "How do you feel about labor unions?" Another approach, which imposes slightly more structure upon the subject's response, but which nevertheless permits expression of a wide range of judgments, is the sentence completion technique. This method presents to the respondent a set of phrases that he is asked to complete to make full, reasonable sentences. The stems might include such phrases as "Jews are . . ." or "Labor unions . . ." Space is provided for completion of a short sentence. In either procedure the investigator must subsequently analyze and code the content of his subjects' responses. Open-ended written questionnaires are like open-ended interviews in that they are direct and to the point, yet do not restrict the subject's response. In practice, however, they are restrictive in that they require skills of verbal composition; space limitations of the paper itself confine the response. Sometimes *biographical statements* may be requested: the subject is asked to write a free and unrestricted statement on a particular topic. This method also represents an unstructured and undisguised procedure.

The methods of content analysis described earlier are applicable to data of this type. By using standardized procedures, the investigator can convert the content of the subject's interview answers of sentence completions into usable form for further analysis.

The major advantage of the undisguised and unstructured techniques is that they are straightforward and direct, and thus inexpensive to construct and administer. However, they often elicit responses that afford little information about the attitude being studied. They permit the respondent to stall and even to avoid the issue if he is skillful and elusive. Because they are undisguised, they maximize effects of psychological set, social desirability, and other confounding factors. Finally, they require time-consuming and often subjective coding in order to convert them to usable forms for further handling of the data.

Unstructured-Disguised Techniques

In assessing attitudes about which an individual is reluctant to express candid and undistorted judgments, it may be necessary to disguise the intention of the attitude scale and to distract the respondent from the attitude being measured. A number of techniques of psychological diagnosis are properly identified in this category because diagnosis involves at least in part the assessment of an individual's attitudes and feelings about certain crucial people or events in his life. Thus projective personality tests, such as the Rorschach inkblots or the story constructions of the Thematic Apperception Test, may be used to secure observations related to an individual's attitudes. In their customary form, these standard techniques would be rather uneconomical for the assessment of a particular single attitude because they are so unstructured that they permit too much latitude of response. However, they may be modified to increase the "pull" of the stimulus materials for particular categories of response. For example, inkblots that are selected because they are highly suggestive of black-face caricatures might tend to elicit responses that reflect the individual's attitude toward blacks. Proshansky (1943), in fact, used a variation of Murray's Thematic Apperception Test to assess attitudes toward organized labor. By presenting the respondents ill-defined pictures, and asking them to identify the people in the picture, tell what they were doing, what had led up to the current situation, and what would follow in consequence, Proshansky elicited a set of verbal responses from which attitudes could be inferred. By selecting appropriate picture materials he was able to increase the frequency with which the subjects' responses reflected their attitudes toward the particular issue being studied.

In general, unstructured and disguised assessment techniques are wasteful in that much of the subject's response may be irrelevant to the particular attitude under investigation. The only circumstances under which this approach to attitude measurement might be particularly useful are cases in which the experimenter wishes to undertake research into attitudes about which people are relatively sensitive and about which he lacks sufficient information to construct a more highly structured assessment device.

Structured-Disguised Techniques

A set of rather contrived procedures for assessing attitudes can be developed by combining camouflage procedures with high degrees of structure that limit the subject's judgmental responses. One such approach, Hammond's error-choice technique (Hammond, 1948), disguises the intent to measure attitudes by presenting the subject with a supposed "test of general information." In fact, however, both answers are factually wrong, and the respondent's choice is assumed to reflect his attitude toward the issue with which the supposedly factual question is concerned. For example, one item might state: "The number of man-days lost because of strikes by organized labor between January and June of last year was (a) 34.5 million or (b) 98.6 million." Both answers would be chosen as equally in error from the correct answer, 66.5 million. Presumably, the individual's choice of wrong answers would reflect systematic bias in line with his attitudes; prolabor individuals would underestimate the harmful economic consequences of strikes, whereas antilabor individuals would choose the overestimated answer. The error-choice technique assumes that the respondent will be basically ignorant of the correct answers to the questions, or at least that he will not be well informed over the entire series of questions. As in the case of any psychological test, one response to a single item is ordinarily of little value, but a consistent pattern of responses over a series of items gives evidence of systematic organization of behavior, which is considerably more meaningful. A similar approach has been utilized by Thistlethwaite (1950), with a test of syllogistic reasoning. The subject is presented a series of syllogisms, in the form "If A is true and B is true, then deduction C follows," some of which involve faulty reasoning. He is requested to find the flaws in the syllogisms, and it is assumed that tendencies to overlook faults in reasoning where they do occur, as well as to report faults where they do not occur, will be systematically linked to the person's underlying attitudes.

Because they are rather contrived, some of these procedures bring protest and rejection from subjects. Nevertheless, for efficiency in gaining quick and easily evaluated data about attitudes on sensitive issues, they are very useful.

Naturalistic settings permit much more effective use of structured and disguised experimental techniques. Several clever procedures in this family have been used in recent research. The *lost-letter technique,* used by Milgram (1970), provides a reflection of attitudes by confronting people with a dilemma that demands a choice of actions in a natural setting. Preaddressed and prestamped letters are "lost" in highly visible settings where subjects are bound to find them. Certain letters might bear the return address of, for example, a well-known extremely conservative party (the John Birch Society), and others the return address of a known radical group (the Black Panthers). The finder of the letter is faced with a choice: he can place it in a mailbox, leave it, or dispose of it. If he mails it, it might be assumed that his attitudes are relatively supportive of the group that "lost" the letter; if he refuses to mail it, the opposite could be assumed. By simply counting the number of letters of each type (conservative or radical), the investigator can gain a measure of attitudes along that dimension.

A very similar technique involving use of the telephone has been used by Gaertner (1970). In the *wrong-number technique,* the investigator telephones a subject and outlines a hypothetical sob story about a crisis: he is stranded on the highway with his car broken down, and he has used his last dime to telephone his garage mechanic to make repairs. Having reached the wrong number, and unable to make another call, he asks the person on the telephone if he would call the garage for him to report his plight. Presumably, a person sympathetic to the caller would be glad to do so; a person antagonistic to the caller would not. By introducing salient clues as to characteristics of the caller (name, dialect, identification of geographical area or place of residence, and the like), this technique can be used to study racial and ethnic attitudes. Although both are cleverly disguised techniques that permit fairly concrete assessment of attitudes, the lost-letter and wrong-number techniques share a common disadvantage: it is difficult to maintain specific records of the behavior of a specific respondent. Both procedures are most easily used when the investigator merely wants a survey of attitudes among a given population rather than diagnostic data about a particular individual. In the latter case, it would be necessary for the investigator to be able to identify each subject's "lost" letter or to make quite sure that the particular story told in the wrong-number technique is plausible to the subject in every detail.

Structured-Undisguised Techniques

This category of techniques represents the most widely used approach to the measurement of attitudes, and during the past 30 years considerable effort has been directed toward the refinement of these methods. Highly sophisticated quantitative techniques have been developed for the participation and evaluation of undisguised structured scales for the efficient measurement of attitudes with high degrees of reliability and precision. In general, the attitude scales that comprise this category of techniques involve the presentation of written statements with which the respondent is asked to express agreement or disagreement. Each item in the scale is carefully evaluated in terms of its relationship to other items. Each must describe a particular position along the hypothetical underlying continuum of the attitude from "favorable" to "unfavorable." The items must be stated so that they are understandable and interpreted in essentially the same way by each subject. Statements that are too obvious or loaded may elicit only socially desirable responses, whereas items that are too subtle, complex, or bland may elicit random and irrelevant responses. A properly constructed scale contains a sufficient number of items to encompass the full range of judgments related to the attitude under investigation, but it must not be so long that the respondent becomes fatigued. The items must be discriminative, so that people who hold different attitudinal positions will respond differently to them, and this discriminative value must hold for all positions along the continuum from "extremely favorable" to "extremely unfavorable."

The distinction between two of the most commonly employed kinds of attitude scales, that typified by Thurstone's method of scale construction and that typified by Guttman's procedures, rests upon the distinction between two forms of individual items within the scales. One type (monotone item) is stated in a manner that describes a point along the attitude continuum so that all individuals who hold less favorable attitudes will respond in one direction (e.g., "disagree"), whereas all individuals who hold more favorable attitudes will respond in a different direction (e.g., "agree"). In contrast, the other type of item (nonmonotone) is stated in a manner that describes a particular point along the continuum so that only individuals who hold attitudes at or near that point on the continuum will agree with it, and all others (with either more or less favorable attitudes) will disagree with it. This distinction, crucial to understanding the differences among attitude scales, may appear more difficult and subtle than is actually the case.

An example stated in terms of a more familiar dimension, that of one's height, may serve to clarify the distinction between monotone and nonmonotone items (see Table 3–5). Suppose a scale to measure an individual's height by means of expressed judgments is to be developed, using items that can be answered yes or no. A monotone item for such a scale would be "Are you taller than 6 feet?" All people who are more than 6 feet tall (including those who are 6'1" as well as those who are 10-foot giants) would answer yes, whereas all who are less than 6 feet tall (including those who are 5'11" as well as those who are 3-foot midgets) would answer no. A similar nonmonotone item for such a scale would be "Are you between 5'9" and 6'3" tall?" To this item, only people who are in the neighborhood of 6 feet tall would answer yes. People who are 5'8" or less and people who are 6'4" or more would answer no. Table 3–5 shows the pattern of responses to items on each kind of scale by two individuals, Mr. Tall who is 6'2" and Ms. Short, who is 5'4". (The other columns and figures in the table are explained below to illustrate further differences between Thurstone-type scales and Guttman-type scales.) With this basic description of item characteristics, one can now understand the following descriptions of several conventional procedures in attitude scaling.

Table 3–5 An Illustration of Items Comprising a Guttman (Monotone) Scale and a Thurstone (Nonmonotone) Scale of Height

Guttman Scale			Thurstone Scale			
	Responses of				Responses of	
Item (monotone)	Ms. Short	Mr. Tall	Item (nonmontone)	Scale Value	Ms. Short	Mr. Tall
I am more than 4'6" tall	Yes	Yes	I am between 4'3" and 4'9" tall	1.0	No	No
I am more than 5'0" tall	Yes	Yes	I am between 4'9" and 5'3" tall	2.0	No	No
I am more than 5'6" tall	No	Yes	I am between 5'3" and 5'9" tall	3.0	Yes	No
I am more than 6'0" tall	No	Yes	I am between 5'9" and 6'3" tall	4.0	No	Yes
I am more than 6'6" tall	No	No	I am between 6'3" and 6'9" tall	5.0	No	No
No. of affirmative answers	2	4			1	1
Scale score	2.0	4.0			3.0	4.0

Bogardus Social Distance Scale. One of the earliest attempts to scale attitudes was by means of a social distance scale developed by E. S. Bogardus in 1925. The original scale consisted of seven monotone items designed to measure expressions of social distance (and its inverse, social acceptance) in attitudes toward members of various national or ethnic groups. The respondent was asked to indicate his willingness to admit members of a particular group to each of seven levels of social closeness, ranging from very near to very remote, as follows:

1. To close kinship by marriage
2. To my club as personal chums
3. To my street as neighbors
4. To employment in my occupation in my country
5. To citizenship in my country
6. As visitors to my country
7. Would exclude from my country

The items are monotonic in form because it can be assumed that a person who agrees with item 5 would also agree with items 6 and 7, or that a person who disagrees with item 4 would also disagree with items 1, 2, and 3. This scaling procedure illustrates the nature of monotonic items in attitude scale construction, and it has historical interest as an antecedent of later, more sophisticated cumulative scaling techniques.

Method of Cumulative Scaling (Guttman). A scale containing monotone items that can be arranged in order so that a respondent who answers affirmatively to any particular item will also answer affirmatively to all items of lower rank order is known as a cumulative scale. Such scales are often called Guttman scales, because of his association with the development of this type of attitude scaling procedure (Guttman, 1944, 1950). The scale in the first column of Table 3–5 is a Guttman scale, and the patterns of response of Ms. Short and Mr. Tall represent orderly responses to such a scale. In a perfect cumulative Guttman scale it is possible to reconstruct the entire pattern of responses by a given individual knowing only the number of items he answered affirmatively. For example, if we know that Ms. Short received a score of 2 on the scale in Table 3–5, we can reproduce her pattern of responses as shown in the table. Similarly, we could reproduce Mr. Tall's responses, knowing only that his score was 4. The more complex items used in the somewhat longer scales for measuring attitudes by the method of cumulative scaling often afford something less than perfect reproduction of individual patterns of response from scale scores. However, a statistical index of the accuracy of reconstruction of individual patterns of response may be used to evaluate the scale itself; this index is known as the coefficient of reproducibility. In well-constructed cumulative scales the coefficient of reliability ordinarily exceeds .90 (i.e., 90 percent accuracy of reconstruction), but rarely reaches 1.00.

Method of Equal-Appearing Intervals (Thurstone). One of the earliest sophisticated techniques for assessing attitudes was developed by Thurstone (1929, 1931) and Thurstone and Chave (1929). This is known as the method of equal-appearing intervals, in reference to the way the scale is constructed rather than to the way a respondent uses it. This procedure uses nonmonotonic items (such as those in the right half of Table 3–5), each of which is assigned a particular quantitative scale value through elaborate preliminary procedures. In constructing the scale, a large number of statements of opinion or attitude are presented to a panel of judges who are requested to sort the statements into eleven groups separated by intervals, or steps, that appear to be equally separated along the attitude continuum from "favorable" to "unfavorable." The judges are ordinarily instructed that the first category should represent the most "favorable" attitudes, the sixth category should represent "neutral" attitudes, and the eleventh category should represent "unfavorable" attitudes. A large number of judges are employed in this judging process, and items whose classification they do not generally agree on are discarded, with the assumption that they must be ambiguous, irrelevant, or poorly framed. Items on which the judges generally agree are selected to represent positions all along the continuum from the first category to the eleventh, and these items are assigned scale values corresponding to the median value of the category to which each item was assigned by the judges. These scale values are then utilized to score the test.

Because the items in Thurstone-type scales are nonmonotonic, respondents are expected to agree only with a limited number of items that correspond very closely to their own attitudinal positions. Thus the scale cannot be scored simply by counting the frequency of affirmative responses. It is important to know not merely how many items the respondent agreed with, but which items he answered affirmatively. His score on the scale is then computed as the medial scale value of the items with which he agreed. In the illustration in Table 3–5, only a five-point scale is described. Assuming that the judges were unanimous on assignment of items to each of five categories, the appropriate scale values are entered beside the items. Ms. Short and Mr. Tall each agreed with only one item (that of each one's own height), and their scores on the scale are thus computed according to the scale value of the item with which each agreed.

Thurstone scales and Guttman scales represent the two most commonly employed procedures in current attitude scaling. Thurstone scales have the advantage of affording a higher order of quantification, for a clearly defined region of neutrality may be defined. Because the items in a Guttman scale can be evaluated only with respect to their rank-order relationships, it is impossible to determine an absolute neutral point on them. The Thurstone-type scale, however, has the disadvantage of an additional intermediate step in construction requiring a set of judges and a time-consuming sorting process. Not only does this complicate the process of constructing such a scale, but there is also evidence to suggest that this judging process may introduce additional systematic errors of measurement. Several studies (Hovland & Sherif, 1952) have shown that bias resulting from the attitudes of the preliminary judges themselves may affect the determination of scale values. Extremely biased judges may tend to contrast statements that differ from their own attitudinal positions, assigning them to scale value categories more remote from their own position. Thus it becomes important that the panel of judges used in the preliminary construction of the scale correspond generally to the population with which the scale is to be used. Furthermore, if biased judges produce biased scale values, the definition of neutral regions on the scale must be considered to be relative to any bias on the part of the original judges.

An additional limitation of Thurstone scales, which does not apply to Guttman scales, is the fact that Thurstone-type items must have face validity: the attitudinal position they describe must be openly recognizable by the preliminary judges, and therefore presumably recognizable by the person tested. On the other hand, the items comprising a Guttman scale are rank-ordered empirically only on the basis of the frequency with which a set of respondents agree with them, using special procedures such as a scalogram analysis (B. F. Green, 1954). Thus it is possible to include within a Guttman scale blind items that are not visibly identifiable with respect to the attitude being measured, so long as they can be reliably rank-ordered in the array of items comprising the scale.

Summated Ratings Method of Scaling (Likert). The method of summated ratings was employed by Likert (1932) a few years after Thurstone's initial efforts at attitude scaling. Likert's major innovation was to enable the respondent to express degrees of agreement or disagreement with attitudinal statements, in contrast to the all-or-nothing response categories provided in other techniques. Conventionally, a Likert-type scale resembles the Guttman cumulative scales in using monotone form items. However, the respondent is allowed to express degrees of agreement or disagreement, usually in five or six categories ranging from "complete and unqualified agreement" to "complete and unqualified disagreement." With an odd number of response categories a neutral response is possible, permitting the subject to "duck out" of an answer; however, with an even number of categories, the respondent is induced to climb off the fence and commit himself.

Customary scoring procedures for Likert scales simply involve the assignment of an integer value to each of the categories of response, in a consistent direction, so that scores can be estimated not merely by counting frequency of agreements with items but by summation of the agreement ratings he assigns to each item. A maximum score is achieved by the strongest degree of agreement with the greatest number of items. In selecting items for the construction of a Likert-type scale, the relationship between agreement ratings on each item and total score on the scale is evaluated. Only items that show strong correlations with total scores are retained. This method of item analysis, then, allows for the inclusion of blind items, which are not identifiable at face value with particular attitudes so long as agreement with them is correlated with the total score on the scale.

The construction and evaluation of the internal properties of a Likert-type scale is easier than for Thurstone-type scales, and less elaborate analysis of individual response patterns is necessary. Furthermore, the procedures for constructing a Likert-type scale, like those utilized in building a Guttman-type scale, permit the inclusion of blind items whose relevance to the attitude being measured is not recognizable at face value by the respondent so long as the respondent's answer to the item is consistent with his total score on the entire set of items. These attributes make the Likert procedure particularly attractive to investigators who wish to develop fairly reliable procedures for assessing attitudes with a minimum of expense and effort. It has the further advantage of appealing to respondents because of the latitude of judgmental response it allows them.

Semantic Differential.　An entirely useful technique for measuring attitudes in terms of the values associated with verbal concepts was developed by Osgood (1952). This technique had its origin in research on *synesthesia,* the association of a particular object or symbol with specific images in another dimension or sensory modality. This is common in language: we speak of being in high or low spirits, or of white hopes or black despair. The subject is given a variety of bipolar paired adjectives representing many dimensions and sensory modalities, and is asked to evaluate a specified verbal concept. He is provided a framework of bipolar items defining the end of a continuum separated by seven intervals, and is asked to check a point along this continuum to represent his judgment of the relation between the specified verbal concept and the dimension represented by the bipolar adjectives. Figure 3–1 illustrates a typical semantic differential response. Here the concept in question is the term "polite." Profiles for two groups of twenty subjects are shown, revealing the consensus and uniformity of connotations associated with this term. The ten bipolar adjective pairs shown in Figure 3–1 are typical. Using factor analysis statistical techniques, three underlying dimensions of response have been identified: an *evaluative* factor (good-bad), an *activity* factor (active-passive), and a *potency* factor (strong-weak). Any object, person, idea, or event that can be represented by a symbol—usually verbal, but not necessarily—can be assessed with the semantic differential. The technique has acceptable reliability estimates and has been validated in several contexts. Among its advantages are sensitivity (in ferreting out nuances of meaning

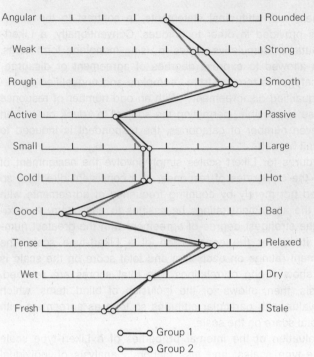

Figure 3-1 lines connecting scale positions for the concept, with legend:
○——○ Group 1
○——○ Group 2

Figure 3-1 Osgood's semantic differential: median responses from two groups of twenty subjects each for the concept "polite." (Redrawn from *Introduction to Psychology,* 3rd Edition, by Ernest R. Hilgard, copyright, ©, 1962 by Harcourt Brace Jovanovich and reproduced with their permission. Originally appeared in C. E. Osgood, "The Nature and Measurement of Meaning," *Psychological Bulletin,* 1952, **49,** 197–237.)

and value that are hard to verbalize), comparability (across individuals, groups, or various concepts), and utility (for establishing semantic norms, assessment of individual attitudes and values, description of cultural values and norms, quantification of subjective language data, and application to problems of cross-cultural communication).

SOCIOMETRIC ASSESSMENT

There is one form of scientific observation that is virtually unique to social psychology and sociology: *sociometry.* In its literal definition (social measurement), this term embraces all techniques for measuring interpersonal relationships, but in practice it is usually applied specifically to techniques evolved from those developed by J. L. Moreno in the early 1930s. These are essentially subjective report methods, but like attitude assessment procedures, they involve the expression of judgments and choices by the respondent rather than a mere verbal account of his experience.

The most frequently investigated sociometric dimension is that of liking, or simple interpersonal attraction. However, the same kinds of procedures may be used in the study of power relationships (interpersonal influence) or respect and admiration. Although the applicability of sociometry is by no means restricted only to these three dimensions of interpersonal relationship, these variables account for the majority of research investigations that have used sociometric techniques.

In standard sociometric procedures a verbal statement is provided to describe the particular dimension of interpersonal relationship to be investigated. This statement is called the *sociometric criterion.* Although it might appear that such dimensions

should be easily described, one of the greatest difficulties in the collection of sociometric data is the statement of the sociometric criterion. From his experience in using

sociometric procedures, J. L. Moreno has suggested that concrete, rather than abstract, statements yield the most meaningful sociometric data. For example, it is
wiser to define interpersonal attraction by a concrete criterion statement such as "a
person with whom you would like to work," than by an abstract statement such as
"a person whom you like very much." Abstract descriptions using such loose terms
as "like," may have different meanings for different individuals. Furthermore, Moreno
suggested that the most appropriate criterion statements are those that are meaningful for the respondent and that have real and direct consequences for him. For example, the usefulness of a criterion such as "a person with whom you would like to
work" in sociometric measurement can be enhanced if it is possible to assure the individual that actual work assignments will be based on his reply to questions about
his criterion in the sociometric questionnaire.

It is often easy to define one pole of a sociometric dimension, but difficult to define its opposite. For example, one might question whether the opposite of liking
(positive attraction between two people) is dislike or indifference. In some investigations a negative sociometric criterion may be provided to define the opposite pole
of the dimension being studied. However, factors such as social desirability or fear
of disapproval often make the respondent reluctant to express such negative sociometric judgments of others. It may be necessary to employ euphemisms and circuitous descriptions to minimize such effects. For instance, instead of requesting that
a subject name people whom he "dislikes," the sociometric questionnaire may ask
him to name people whom he "likes less than others in the group."

In the sociometric questionnaire itself, the respondent is asked to judge other individuals with whom he interacts according to the degree to which the stated criterion
is applicable to his relationship with them. Normally the nominations method is the
simplest and most straightforward procedure for securing these judgments. In this
method the respondent is asked merely to name one or more people who best fit
the relationship described in the sociometric criterion. He may be requested to name
one person or a limited number of people in ranked order. Or he may be asked to
name as many people as he wishes, which would enable the investigator to obtain
additional useful information about the expansiveness of an individual's judgments
of his relationships with others. Whether the respondent is allowed to name people
from his entire array of acquaintances or whether he is confined to naming people
from within a specified group depends on the purposes of the investigator. In studying interpersonal relationships within very large groups, a list of names of members
of the group may be provided to boost the respondent's memory, but normally, sociometric procedures do not use such rosters because it is assumed that individuals
whom the respondent might forget are people to whom he is more or less indifferent.

When the experimenter wishes to obtain more extensive or precise sociometric
assessments, he may request more elaborate judgments from the respondent than
simple nominations. The respondent may be asked to rank-order all members of a particular group according to the degree to which the sociometric criterion is applicable,
or even to use a rating scale to indicate quantitatively the degree of applicability of
the criterion to his relationship with each person in his group. Exhaustive procedures
such as the method of paired comparisons (in which each possible pair of individuals
within a group are compared to ascertain which best fits the sociometric criterion)
are rarely used because they are likely to become boring and tedious for the respondent, especially if the group studied is very large.

In most cases sociometric data are obtained by means of written questionnaires.
However, with young subjects who cannot read or write well, oral interviews may be
used. In some cases (such as investigations of interpersonal relationships among

preschool children) pictures may be used, requiring merely that the respondent point to a photograph of the person or persons whose relationship to him fits the sociometric criterion being studied.

The most distinctive quality of sociometric data is that they represent measures of relationships between individuals rather than assessments of individual attributes. A liked person is liked only with reference to someone who likes him; and a powerful person is powerful only with reference to someone over whom he exerts influence. Investigators (as well as nonpsychologists) often fall into the trap of automatically assuming that such variables as popularity or leadership are attributes of an individual's personality. However, these are variables that describe relationships among people, and it is important in psychological research to interpret them as such.

Empirical observations collected by the sociometric procedures described may be subjected to several kinds of analysis. They may be represented in graphic form, or they may be converted to various numerical indices. Several kinds of standard methods of handling the analysis of sociometric data have been developed.

Sociograms

The graphic representation of sociometric observations is called a *sociogram*. In the sense that "one picture is worth a thousand words," a sociogram may serve to condense a vast amount of information about interpersonal relationships within a group. Conventional sociograms represent individual people by small circles, from which arrows are drawn to designate each individual's expressed sociometric choices or rejections. The actual preparation of a sociogram is to some extent a matter of trial and error in attempting to achieve the most comprehensible graphic display of data. Ordinarily the vertical dimension is used to indicate quantitatively each individual's choice status on the investigated dimension, with those individuals who receive the greatest number of choices represented highest in the space of the sociogram. Efforts are made to minimize the number of choice lines that cross one another, as well as to make the choice lines as short as possible.

Figure 3–2 shows a typical sociogram representing the choice status and sociometric choices of eleven people in a group derived from an investigation of interpersonal attraction. An individual who receives a large number of sociometric choices is called a star (Person A). An isolate is one who receives no sociometric choices at all, despite the fact that he is nominally a member of the group (Persons F, G, H, I, J, and K). An isolate is not necessarily a rejectee (one who receives many rejections and few positive choices) but is sometimes referred to as a neglectee, because he is

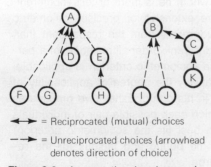

◄—► = Reciprocated (mutual) choices

- - ► = Unreciprocated choices (arrowhead
denotes direction of choice)

Figure 3-2 A conventional sociogram depicting interpersonal attractions expressed in a sociometric assessment of a group of eleven children.

ignored by other members of his group. In contrast, a rejectee is recognized by other members, but in a negative manner. (Figure 3–2 shows no rejectee because negative choices or rejections were not obtained in the sociometric assessment illustrated.) Vertical relationships within the sociogram in Figure 3–2 show that Person A occupies a position of highest popularity status, followed by B and C, with six members of the group left as isolates at the bottom of the sociogram.

Not only can a sociogram display information about individuals within a group, it may also provide a descriptive picture of the structure of the group itself. For example, cliques or subgroups may be apparent. (Figure 3–2 shows cleavage between two subgroups, A-D-E-F-G-H and B-C-I-J-K, for there are no choice lines connecting these two sets of individuals.) Mutuality of choice of individuals is displayed directly (Persons A and D, and B and C). The number of mutual attractions and subgroup cleavages within a group may provide clues about its cohesiveness and stability, for a well-organized group would be expected to show a maximum number of reciprocated attractions and little evidence of clear cleavage.

Cleavage within a group sometimes is based on significant variables characterizing individuals within it. For example, if a group of grade school children includes both boys and girls at two age levels, subgroup cleavages may be systematically associated with age and sex differences. A modified procedure for preparing sociograms on a circular grid, the target sociogram, was developed by Northway (1940). Concentric circles are used to designate choice status, with the center of the "target" representing highest choice status. The field of the target may then be divided into sectors corresponding to differential characteristics of members of the group. Figure 3–3 shows a target sociogram prepared from the data in Figure 3–2. This method of displaying the data affords immediate interpretation of the cleavage within the group:

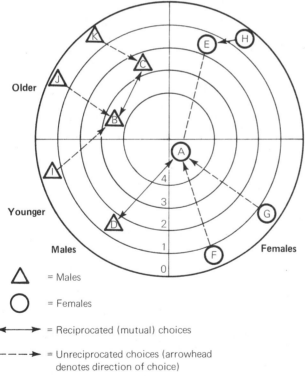

△ = Males

◯ = Females

◄————► = Reciprocated (mutual) choices

———► = Unreciprocated choices (arrowhead
      denotes direction of choice)

Figure 3-3 A target sociogram depicting interpersonal attractions expressed in a sociometric assessment of a group of eleven children.

there are clusters within age levels as well as within sex groups, with the two major subgroups identified as older males and younger females.

Numerical Sociometric Indices

Sociometric data may be converted to numerical form and organized to provide indices of measurement that represent particular qualities of an individual's position within a group or of the group itself. The simplest kind of numerical index is an absolute number representing the frequency of choices or rejections received by an individual. Other information about an individual's sociometric status might be represented by subtracting the number of rejections received from the number of positive choices received, or by dividing choices by rejections to derive a choice-rejection ratio (Proctor & Loomis, 1951). The number of choices expressed by an individual when the sociometric questionnaire permits him to name as many choices as he wishes may serve as an index of what Moreno (1934) has called "social expansiveness."

An integrative analysis of an individual's status within a group may be derived through what Jennings (1943) has described as sociometric profile analysis, using six numerical indices simultaneously:

1. choices expressed
2. choices received
3. positive reciprocations (mutual choices)
4. rejections expressed
5. rejections received
6. negative reciprocations (mutual rejections)

The first three items comprise the individual's "choice pattern" and the last three his "rejection pattern." By assigning each item a value of + (if it is above the mean frequency for the group) or − (if it is below the group mean), a coded profile can be derived. For example, a profile reading +, +, +, +, −, − would reveal that the person tends to reject a large number of individuals within his group, but this fact does not seem to affect his popularity within the group, and his rejection of others is largely unreciprocated.

Indices may also be computed to characterize the group itself. For example, the number of mutual choices or the inverse of the number of isolates in the group would provide quantitative measures of the cohesiveness and integrated organization of the group. Such absolute numbers, however, have limited meaning because their values depend on the number of people in the group and the number of choices expressed. Indices that permit comparison of groups of varying size may be computed by means of ratios that divide the frequency of a particular kind of choice by the total number of such choices that might be possible for a group of a given size. The number of observed mutual (reciprocated) choices divided by the number of possible choices provides a "compatability index" (McKinney, 1948); similarly, the number of mutual pairs divided by the number of possible pairs yields a related kind of "group cohesion index" (Proctor & Loomis, 1951). An almost infinite variety of descriptive numerical indices could be computed in such manner.

A few investigators have also attempted to make use of matrix algebra in handling sociometric data, but because of their complexity such techniques have not been frequently used in handling sociometric data.

Tagiuri's Relational Analysis

Basically sociometry is concerned with the observation of an individual's subjective judgments about his relationships to others. However, investigators frequently wish

to secure information about an individual's perception of how other people feel **59**
toward him. Tagiuri (1952) developed a method of analysis for this purpose known Methods of
as *relational analysis.* In addition to standard sociometric judgments, the respondent Studying Social
Behavior
is further requested to make guesses about which people in his group will choose or
reject him. Eight categories of response are thus derived:

1. whom the subject chooses
2. who chooses the subject
3. whom the subject rejects
4. who rejects the subject
5. who guessed that the subject would choose him
6. whom the subject guessed would choose him
7. who guessed that the subject would reject him
8. whom the subject guessed would reject him

The major value of Tagiuri's relational analysis is that it permits comprehensive
evaluation of an individual's social position in terms of both actual and perceived
relationships with others. It is especially useful for the investigation of variables such
as social sensitivity and accuracy of perception of interpersonal relationships.

Field Sociometry

Sociometric methods have been as widely used in sociology as in psychology, especially to study social organization and social structure. When applied broadly in
naturalistic settings, special techniques for "field sociometry" may be required. One
example of such methods is the *Small-World Technique* used by Milgram (1970) to
study social distance in broad natural settings. This procedure involves the transmission of a message from some remote location to a particular target person. It is required that the original sender does not know the ultimate receiver, but the message
must be transmitted between persons directly acquainted with each other. That is,
no one may transmit the message to a complete stranger. Thus, the number of separate steps of transmission required for the message to travel from sender to receiver
is a measure of the social distance between them. Amazingly, Milgram found that for
any two people in the United States, even thousands of miles apart, the average number of steps required in this procedure was six! It is a small world indeed!

The Reliability and Validity of Sociometric Data

The concept of reliability must be interpreted cautiously in evaluating the quality of
sociometric observations. Most customary practices for evaluating the reliability of
measurements are based on the stability of repeated measurements of the same
variable. However, by virtue of the very fact that groups are fluid and changing structures with continuously changing interpersonal relationships within them, a certain
amount of instability in sociometric measurement is to be expected. Consequently,
test-retest reliability measures provide only a limited evaluation of the quality of
sociometric data. If the test-retest interval is very short, high reliability coefficients
(correlations between the two measures) may result from sheer memory of previous
choices. On the other hand, if the interval is long, the fluid nature of people in groups
may result in changes in patterns of interpersonal relationships.

Furthermore, the quality of sociometric measures may be evaluated in terms of
either choices expressed or choices received. It is possible, for example, for an
individual to maintain a particular level of popularity within a group, even though
there are shifts in individual choices within the group. That is, in a class of twenty
children, a particular child may receive eight choices as "best friend" on one occasion, and in a reassessment by the same group still receive eight choices, but from

eight different people. Thus the stability of sociometric data over time may be evaluated either by indices of the percentage of overlap between choices expressed by each individual on two different occasions or by indices of the correlation between the number of choices received on two different occasions.

In evaluating sociometric measures or the extent to which they measure what the investigator intended to measure, it is virtually impossible to define a single criterion against which validity may be checked. Sociometric measures are more or less unique, and there are few other methods of assessing interpersonal relationships. It is possible to compare sociometric data to direct observations of the frequency of particular kinds of interaction between individuals, but because sociometry is based on subjective judgments, and direct observation techniques deal with overt behavior, some discrepancy may be expected, for they measure two different kinds of phenomena. In most cases, sociometric data are accepted at face value if they are found to be reliably measured, and construct validation approaches are used to interpret their meaning by investigating their systematic relationships with a variety of other kinds of measurement of the individuals or groups studied.

GAMING AND SIMULATION

Laboratory procedures have been developed in recent social psychological research to study negotiation, bargaining, and conflicts of interest between individuals or groups. These make use of several kinds of simple games, modified for laboratory use. Experimental situations may be designed to permit controlled interaction between players as they select strategies in playing a game, thereby enabling the investigator to produce situations that are analogous to everyday interpersonal relationships, competitive endeavors in business, or wars and coalitions in international affairs. The essential characteristics of these games permit each player to adopt a strategy in advance of his action, but not to know what plan his opponent has adopted. The joint outcome for particular combinations of strategies by opposed players can be determined and manipulated by the experimenter in terms of specific payoffs or winnings in the game. Such game situations may be described verbally to the players or presented in abstract form in the context of a matrix such as those shown in Table 3–6.

In most psychological research studies the matrix form is used, graphically presenting to each player a set of rows and columns representing the strategies available and indicating the payoffs associated with each combination of strategies. The game is then played repeatedly, with each player permitted to reevaluate and stabilize his strategies as he wishes. Certain kinds of game matrices are particularly useful for studying cognitive processes within the individual as he learns to select winning strategies, but others are more appropriate for investigating interpersonal and social relationships.

Zero-Sum Games

The zero-sum game is arranged so that one player (a person or a team) plays against another in direct opposition. The payoffs to each of the players for any strategy combination sum to zero: that is, one player wins the exact amount the other loses on any given play. Only competitive strategies are possible in games of this sort because one player's winnings always mean equivalent losses to the other. In such games there is no provision for profitable cooperative coalitions between the two players. The familiar parlor game scissors-paper-rock is an example of a zero-sum game that permits no single dominant or rational strategy that can be adopted as a sure way of consistently

A. "Scissors-Paper-Rock": A Zero-Sum Game in Matrix Form

		Player B		
		Scissors	Paper	Rock
Player A	Scissors	A wins 0 B wins 0	A wins 1 B loses 1	A loses 1 B wins 1
	Paper	A loses 1 B wins 1	A wins 0 B wins 0	A wins 1 B loses 1
	Rock	A wins 1 B loses 1	A loses 1 B wins 1	A wins 0 B wins 0

In this parlor game, each player's winnings equal the other's losses, and no single strategy can be selected by either player with certainty of maximizing his own gains. Hence it is said to be a zero-sum game with no rational solution.

B. A Rationally Solvable Zero-Sum Game in Matrix Form

		Player B	
		Red	Black
Player A	Red	A wins 6 B loses 6	A wins 5 B loses 5
	Black	A wins 5 B loses 5	A wins 4 B loses 4

In this game, each player's winnings equal the other's losses, but there is a strategy by which A can maximize his winnings and B can minimize his losses. Rationally, Player A should select the "red" strategy, since his minimum win, regardless of what the other player does, is greater there; likewise, Player B should select the "black" strategy, since his maximum loss, regardless of what the other player does, is less there. The intersection of these strategies in the upper-right quadrant defines the saddle point of this rationally solvable game, although the game is, overall, quite unfair to Player B, who can never win.

C. The Prisoner's Dilemma: A Nonzero-Sum Game in Matrix Form

		Prisoner B	
		Not Confess	Confess
Prisoner A	Not Confess	X: 5 years (C) Y: 5 years (C)	X: 20 years (S) Y: 1 year (T)
	Confess	X: 1 year (T) Y: 20 years (S)	X: 15 years (P) Y: 15 years (P)

For cooperation in refusing to confess to a crime, two prisoners can be sentenced to 5 years for another less serious offense. If one confesses to implicate the other, he will receive only a one-year sentence, whereas his partner receives 20 years. However, if both confess, each is sentenced to 15 years. (C) represents a cooperative payoff, (T) represents the temptation strategy, (S) depicts the "sucker" strategy, and (P) is the punishment payoff.

winning. In this game, scissors cut (wins over) paper, paper covers (wins over) rock, and rock breaks (wins over) scissors. The three-strategy matrix for two players shown in Table 3–6(A) describes this game in matrix form.

Although the scissors-paper-rock game does not permit a player to adopt a rational sure-to-win strategy, there are other types of zero-sum games that do permit rational solutions. The matrix in Table 3–6(B) describes such a game. Two strategies are available to each player: he may bet on red or on black. As the matrix shows, the game is slightly unfair to Player B because he can never come out ahead, and the best he can hope for is to minimize his losses. But from Player A's point of view, he may maximize his winnings by adopting the strategy that affords the greatest possible gain. Player B may minimize his losses by adopting the strategy that affords the minimum loss. By assuming the most damaging possible countermove by his opponent, each player can choose the strategy that is to his own advantage. If the game is arranged as a zero-sum game with a rational solution, this solution turns out to be the one affording the greatest possible gain and the least possible loss, and is termed a minimax solution. To discover this rational solution, each player must search the matrix to determine which strategy has the largest minimum payoff and which the smallest maximum loss. If these occur in the same strategic combination, that combination is called a saddle point. Any game matrix that offers a saddle point affords a rational minimax solution so that a player can maximize his gains and minimize his losses.

B. Lieberman (1962) found that players normally tend to adopt such rational strategies consistently as they play the game over and over, at least with relatively simple and easily understood matrices. If the matrices are made more complex and harder to analyze or comprehend, rational strategy choices are made less frequently (Steele, 1966). Games of this sort permit investigation of the rationality and cognitive function of individuals, but they are of relatively little direct interest to the social psychologist in his study of interpersonal relationships.

Nonzero-Sum Games

The nonzero-sum game is arranged so that although one side plays against the other, they may also play "against the house." The payoffs in the game matrix are such that the winnings of one player do not exactly equal the losses of the other. These games are of particular interest to the social psychologist because they afford variability in the selection of strategies. A player may elect to compete with the other player, as in zero-sum games, but it is also possible for two players to enter into cooperative coalitions against "fate" or "the house." Games that afford no single rational solution, but instead permit the player to elect various strategies according to his own interests in his relationship with his opponent, are called mixed-motive games. Research has shown that even when the game matrix offers a dominant solution whereby a player who assumes a few basic laws of probability may optimize his own gains over a series of plays, people nevertheless often play such games irrationally (Luce & Raiffa, 1957).

A particular type of nonzero-sum game that has been widely used in social psychological research is the so-called prisoner's dilemma. This game is built on the analogy of two people who are simultaneously arrested and charged with a crime, although their captors lack sufficient evidence to convict either of them unless at least one confesses. Both are told that if neither confesses, each will, at worst, receive a light sentence for a much less serious legal offense. However, each is encouraged to confess by promising that if one "turns state's evidence" and confesses to implicate the other, the confessor will be rewarded with a minimum penalty, whereas his partner will receive a severe sentence. At the same time though, there is some risk that both captives will confess, giving the authorities all the evidence they need to convict both and impose relatively severe sentences.

In experimental studies the prisoner's dilemma is framed as a game in which a matrix describes the severity of the sentence associated with each strategy. Table 3–6(C) illustrates such a matrix. The nonzero-sum game shown in Table 3–6(B) is an abstract game that has the essential properties of the prisoner's dilemma. In Table 3–6(C) the letters in each cell describe the consequences of each strategy from the point of view of each player. The upper-left cell represents the logically secure combination of strategies in which each prisoner resists the temptation to confess, and both cooperate in holding out. From a purely logical viewpoint, this is a rational solution. However, the temptation to risk confession on the chance of gaining a lighter sentence at the expense of a severer penalty for his partner may make one prisoner elect to confess. The upper-right cell describes the combination of strategies in which prisoner X is the "sucker" (S) who holds out, whereas his partner, Y, succumbs to the temptation (T) to defect to the authorities and confess. The lower-left cell represents the reverse situation, in which X is tempted and Y is the sucker. The lower-right cell describes the combination of simultaneous confessions, in which both prisoners are severely punished (P). Thus, for each player in a Prisoner's Dilemma game, the rational overall strategy of cooperation, although it minimizes losses, carries a certain amount of risk that the other player may be tempted to defect.

Complex Simulations

Much more complex laboratory confrontations have evolved. With the assistance of computers to store programmed information and select branched alternatives dependent upon the behavior of players, extremely complex representations of everyday natural situations may be generated in the laboratory. This procedure is called *simulation*. For example, a complete stock market and banking situation has been simulated, permitting groups of players to buy and sell stocks and bonds, borrow and lend money, and otherwise participate in capitalistic business transactions (Lupfer, 1964; Streufert et al., 1965). Likewise, the inter-nation simulation (Guetzkow et al., 1963) represents in the laboratory a miniature governmental process in which players adopting the role of national decision-makers confront economic crises, formulate policies in response to public opinion and international pressures, and even declare limited or nuclear war.

The experimental methodology of game studies affords a useful means by which social psychologists can investigate many kinds of interpersonal and intergroup behavior. Although game theory was first evolved by mathematicians who assumed that human beings are always rational and logical, psychologists have found that human beings are sometimes very irrational and illogical when they play these games. This kind of investigation is still relatively new, and psychologists must continue to be cautious in interpreting and generalizing from these findings. A number of factors may govern the individual player's selection of strategies: factors associated with the situation in which he plays the game, with his personality, and with his perception of his adversary. There is still insufficient research to answer such questions. Furthermore, care must be taken that the operational definitions of such variables as cooperation, competition, risk, trust, and the like have equivalent meanings in the game situation and in other kinds of more naturalistic interpersonal situations. As yet, very little research has connected the behavior observed in playing laboratory games to everyday interpersonal behavior. Unfortunately, game-playing is characterized by an "as if" quality that permits the player to behave differently from the way he might act outside the laboratory.

1. The earmark of modern social psychology is *empiricism,* an approach based on careful observations of behavior by reliable and impartial observers.

2. Error or bias in observation may occur at any of three levels: *data collection* (watching, listening, or recording), *data reduction* (scoring, coding, or sorting), or *data interpretation.*

3. Questions of *reliability* concern potential error or bias in data collection and data reduction; questions of *validity* concern errors or biases in data interpretation.

4. Methods of *direct observation* permit the collection of data in everyday situations as well as in the laboratory. The most crucial problem with use of these methods is that of defining the basic *unit* of behavior to be observed and recorded. Standard *coding* systems (e.g., Chapple's chronographic method, Bales's Interaction Process Analysis, and others) are often used to standardize such definitions.

5. *Content analysis* refers to the coding, counting, or sorting of the manifest content of any behavioral sample. However, the term is especially used with reference to coding verbal communications (speeches, letters, literary products, etc.).

6. Methods of *subjective report* are based on an individual's report (usually verbal) of his own experience and behavior. Among the most critical problems associated with these methods are: *response set*—habits of response that systematically bias self-report, such as acquiescence to suggestion or rebellious denial; and *social desirability*—the general tendency of most people to distort their self-descriptions and self-reports toward what they consider desirable and attractive to others.

7. Subjective report methods vary in the manner of request directed toward the subject. The dimension of *structure* refers to the extent to which the methodological procedure restricts the variety of appropriate behavioral responses that may be displayed and recorded. For example, a true-false test is a *structured* method because it limits scorable response alternatives; an essay test is an *unstructured* method because it opens a much broader array of possible scorable responses.

8. The dimension of *disguise* refers to the extent to which the observer tries to veil or conceal the true intent of his request from the subject under observation. Disguised techniques are used when subjects are expected to try to distort or conceal their true feelings and behavior.

9. *Interviews* are face-to-face requests for subjective reports. As such, they afford the advantage of richer opportunity for recording a wider range of behaviors, but they suffer the disadvantage of greater difficulty in controlling the intrusion of human factors in the observer-subject interaction. Written *questionnaires* and *inventories* reverse these advantages and disadvantages.

10. *Attitude assessment* embraces a wide variety of psychometric measurement procedures, including many kinds of personality tests, inventories, and questionnaires.

11. *Projective* techniques include unstructured, disguised methods of attitude assessment.

12. *Attitude scales* include structured, undisguised methods of attitude assessment.

13. A *Thurstone-type attitude scale* is constructed by the *method of equal-appearing intervals.* This procedure requires that a panel of judges predetermine a *scale value* to be assigned each item and used in scoring the scale. Since *nonmonotone* items (describing a specified range of attitude along the attitude dimension) are used, the procedures in constructing and scoring a Thurstone-type scale are relatively tedious. But they have the advantage of producing a higher order of scaling (an *interval* scale) and defining a hypothetical point of neutrality of attitude.

14. A *Guttman-type attitude scale* is constructed by the *method of cumulative scaling.* This procedure uses *monotone* items (describing a turning-point of attitude shift

along the attitude dimension), and therefore requires less tedious procedures in construction. Statistical analysis can replace the preliminary judgments required in a Thurstone-type procedure. Although Guttman scales produce a lower order of scaling (an *ordinal* scale) and define no point of neutrality of attitude, they are more easily constructed and scored than Thurstone scales. Whereas the items comprising a Thurstone-type scale must necessarily have *face validity,* this is not a requirement for a Guttman-type scale.

15. The *summated ratings method* broadens the choice alternatives available to the respondent on an attitude scale by affording him opportunity to qualify his response by shading his degree of agreement or disagreement with an item statement.

16. The *semantic differential* is a method of assessment that simultaneously measures cognitive and affective components of an attitude; it is therefore a particularly useful tool for studying *values.*

17. *Sociometry* refers to the measurement of *interpersonal* dimensions of relationship between people (in contrast to *psychometry,* which refers to measurement of *intrapersonal* dimensions within a person).

18. A *sociogram* is a graphic representation of a set of sociometric data.

19. *Field sociometry* is an extension of ordinary sociometric methods into naturalistic field settings by combining methods of direct observation and experimentation with sociometric procedure.

20. *Simulation* refers to the creation of controlled environmental situations in a laboratory setting to approximate or represent specified conditions outside the laboratory. The elaborateness of simulations in psychological research has expanded dramatically with the advent of computer technology.

21. *Gaming* represents a particular kind of simulation, in which observed subjects participate in game-like situations. In a *zero-sum game,* there is always a winner and a loser; the winnings of one player directly offset the losses of the other. In a *nonzero-sum game,* the "house" may take a cut or even win, so that one player's winnings are not in direct balance with the other's losses.

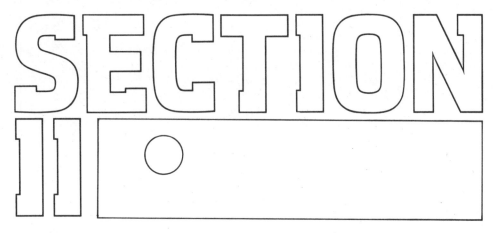

INDIVIDUAL SOCIAL BEHAVIOR

Social psychology includes the study of an individual's relations with other people—individually, in groups, or in societies. In order to understand social interaction at any of these levels, it is first necessary to consider the broad social context in which man exists. This includes the framework of his culture, his society, his community, his friends, and his family. In order for us to fully describe and analyze this social matrix, many kinds of social scientists must cooperate in interdisciplinary effort. Just as in the legend of the blind men and the elephant (each touched only the trunk, the tail, a leg, a tusk, or the belly, and none got a total notion of what an elephant is like), each of the social sciences examines a portion of man's social context from a particular point of view.

Section II of this book examines man's individual behavior as it normally occurs in a sociocultural context. Taking the point of view of the psychologist, the focus is upon individual behavior and experience. But before we examine man's interaction with other people individually and collectively, we will first consider how society shapes thinking processes and language (Chapter 4) as well as man's beliefs, values, and attitudes (Chapter 5); how man is assimilated into his culture through socialization (Chapter 6); and how man evolves a sense of identity within a society (Chapter 7).

4

SOCIAL COGNITION: THOUGHT AND LANGUAGE

The process of perception—the experience and awareness of events—is one of the most widely explored aspects of human psychology. In fact, the initial emergence of psychology as an experimental science was a consequence of Wilhelm Wundt's curiosity about this process. At first, psychology considered perception in terms of psychophysics, the immediate response of the organism to the impingement of energy on his specialized sense organs—the eyes, ears, taste buds, olfactory receptors, and specialized skin and muscle senses. With increasing knowledge, psychologists eventually found it useful to distinguish the simple process of *sensation* from the more complex processes of "making sense" out of sensations. Thus the term *cognition* has come to label the many processes of assimilating experiences and relating them to previous experiences, of attaching meaning and value to them, and of ordering them into organized patterns of knowledge and feeling.

COGNITION AND THOUGHT

During the 1950s the psychological study of perception and cognition was very much influenced by a new approach formulated by Bruner and his colleagues at Harvard University (Bruner & Goodman, 1947; Bruner, 1957). This "new look," as other psychologists later tagged it, emphasized two important characteristics of cognition: the fact that perception is selectively organized, so that new experiences are assimilated selectively and incorporated with prior experiences into ordered conceptual categories that are meaningful and functionally useful to the individual; and the fact that cognitive processes operate to minimize surprise, so that new experiences are assimilated more readily when they fit congruently with past experiences than when they are incongruent. Thus the "new look" emphasized both functional utility (relevance to the goals and purposes of the experiencing person) and dependence on the accumulation of past experience (relevance to learned expectations and anticipations).

In the decade that followed, the influence of the Swiss psychologist Jean Piaget on American explorations of cognition was sudden and dramatic. Although Piaget began his work in the early 1930s, he had little impact upon American psychologists until the 1950s. But his ideas were congruent with other new approaches to perception, and his analysis of the structural and functional properties of cognition were readily accepted and adopted as theoretical formulations rich in both scientific and practical implications. As a theorist, Piaget has tended to focus on the rational facet of man, keeping his attention primarily on knowledge and logic and their development. He has not been especially concerned with feeling, value, or purpose. Thus his theoretical formulations are more useful in studying the purely rational side of man's cognition than in exploring values, feelings, or motives.

Concept Formation

Modern cognitive theory, emphasizing the orderly arrangement of new experiences alongside previous ones, has described several mechanisms that underlie this grouping process. The chief of these is *concept formation*. At its simplest level, this involves the recognition of repeated identical events. Or it may require recognition of shared characteristics within a set of events (*stimulus generalization*), or reciprocally, the recognition of shared differences (*stimulus discrimination*). In some cases, the essence of similarity may be some functional property that must be distilled out as an *abstraction* that defines the nature of a particular conceptual category. (Automobiles, airplanes, ships, and roller skates do not resemble each other physically; but they are functionally similar as means of transportation.) These processes define a

complex operation known as *classification,* which proceeds developmentally from
the simple to the complex. At first, a child is capable of only very simple, concrete,
one-dimensional concepts. But as he grows older, his conceptual capacity becomes
more complex, more abstract, and more multidimensional (Piaget, 1952). Most of the
events with which social psychology is concerned are complex, abstract, and multidimensional, in that they may be characterized by several attributes or dimensions
simultaneously, thus affording many possible ways of sorting them into conceptual
categories.

Attention

The relative "openness" of a conceptual category for assimilation of new perceptual
input as similar to the prior content of that concept is termed *perceptual readiness.*
In this sense, perception, concept formation, and classification are very active cognitive processes. Cognitively, the individual is much more than a passive sponge absorbing sensory input. The "grouping" mechanisms (described above) that underlie
concept formation simply determine where to sort and file away new experiences as
they occur, according to their content. But another set of "gating" mechanisms operate to determine the readiness of existing conceptual structures to admit new experiences of sensory input.

There are two major determinants of perceptual readiness: *probabilistic expectancies* evolved out of accumulated past experiences according to the frequency
of their occurrence and their redundancy in certain patterns, sequences, or contextual associations; and *purposive orientations* derived from the needs, values, or
goals of the person. These processes in operation give rise to what is commonly
called *attention.*

These mechanisms of attention sometimes operate so strongly that they generate
selective filtration and screen the admission of certain kinds of input into cognitive
experience. Extreme readiness may lead to *perceptual vigilance,* a state of alertness
(especially in anticipation or desire of a particular kind of event) that results in admission into an especially receptive cognitive category even experienced events that
ordinarily would not be placed there. The ringing of a familiar doorbell may be mis-
taken for the telephone when one awaits an important call. Or when one reads a passage of familiar printed material, misspelled words and typographical errors may be
overlooked.

Perceptual vigilance ("overreadiness") may in turn make other perceptual categories less than ordinarily accessible to new stimulus input. The resulting inaccessi-
bility ("underreadiness"), *perceptual defense,* bars the admission of certain kinds of
input into appropriate categories of cognitive experience. For example, individuals
shown a picture of a black man and a white man conversing while the white man
holds an open straight razor in his hand (Figure 4–1) may differ widely in their later
recollection and description of the picture. People who hold unfavorable prejudices
about blacks, expecting the black man to be associated with violence and aggression, tend to perceive and recall inaccurately that the black man held the razor (Allport & Postman, 1947).

Perceptual defense and perceptual vigilance lead individuals, even without conscious intent, to direct their attention very selectively toward some of the events that
occur around them, while selectively ignoring others. A man who has just witnessed
a collision between his wife's car and another car may selectively recall that she
entered the intersection first at a slow speed, and the other driver entered later at a
greater speed. But he may ignore the fact that the traffic signal was red in her direction but green in the other driver's direction. Because of such effects upon cognitive
experience, all witnesses are not equally reliable in a courtroom. Even the most

Figure 4-1 The details of this illustration are perceived, remembered, and related to others differently by different people, according to their prejudices, intentions, values, and past experiences. One person might describe it as a picture of "a woman and a Negro who has a razor in his hand," whereas another might describe it simply as a picture of "one man giving directions to another on a subway train." (From *The Psychology of Rumor* by Gordon W. Allport and Leo Postman. Drawings by Charles Wadsworth. Copyright 1947 by Holt, Rinehart and Winston, Inc. Reproduced by permission of Holt, Rinehart and Winston, Inc.)

scrupulously honest and ethical person may not escape the selectivity of perceptual experience generated by these gating mechanisms. As President Nixon pointed out during the 1973 Senate "Watergate" Hearings, he was reluctant to release the tape recordings of telephone conversations with the White House staff because the interpretation of the literal words recorded there might vary considerably from one listener to the next, according to his intentions and purposes.

Frames of Reference

In recognizing that perceptual experience is steered actively by expectations and desires, psychologists utilize a descriptive concept, *frame of reference*. This term denotes the overall context within which behavioral response to an experienced event is organized. It includes the past experiences of the person (his learned expectancies, his acquired values, his perceptual sets, and even his momentary states of perceptual readiness and attention), as well as the simultaneous patterns of events that occur in the periphery of his attention (other people, things, and events that are associated in space or time as a "background" to the perceived event). Although this concept originally evolved from studies of psychophysical judgments (Wever & Zener, 1928), it has been useful in analyzing the perception of social objects as well (Helson, 1947, 1959). Certainly a small elephant is larger than a gigantic flea. The same concept applies as well to judgments of social objects and events. McGarvey (1943) found that judgments of the prestige status of a particular occupation varied, depending on the kinds of occupations with which it was compared. An annual income of $13,000 might signify success for a newly graduated Ph.D. in English, but failure for one in aeronautical engineering. The concept of frame of reference accounts very

SHORT AND TALL FRAMES OF REFERENCE

A sample of 160 college men was divided into two groups according to height: tall (6' and over) and short (5' 8" and less). In judging the height of others, short subjects judged others as taller more often than tall subjects judged others as shorter. The short subjects, presumably unable to perceive themselves as "neutral" in their subjective ratings, accepted as their point of reference a social convention that favors men being tall.

HINCKLEY AND ROETHLINGSHAFER (1951)

well for the old adage "one man's meat is another man's poison." Psychologists have found the concept very useful in exploring cognition and judgment because it incorporates both antecedent sources and immediate sources of expectations and desires that affect the interpretation of perceptual experience and the organization of behavior.

Cognitive Dissonance

During the 1950s, the many new demonstrations on and theories in perception set the stage for emphasis on the tendency toward order, congruence, and organization in cognition and behavior. Subsequently, both neuropsychological theories and cognitive-behavioral theories of perception have proceeded in this direction. Attention is drawn to the fact that specific acts of behavior (judgments, preferences, choices, and other actions) may be predicted from information about states of *consonance* (balance, order, congruence, and internal consistency) or *dissonance* (imbalance, disorder, incongruence, and internal inconsistency) within a person's cognitive systems. The cognitive categories that comprise the total "file" of an individual's experience are not discrete and unrelated; they are interconnected with one another. Just as there is a tendency toward organized consistency within each conceptual classification, so is there also a tendency toward organized consistency among the various conceptual categories within the total framework of one's personality.

Leon Festinger outlined the implications of these tendencies toward organizational consonance in a *theory of cognitive dissonance* (1957). Two basic notions subsume the essence of this theory. The existence of dissonance in a cognitive system is psychologically uncomfortable and motivates the individual (1) to try to reduce dissonance and achieve consonance, and (2) to avoid situations and information that would increase the dissonance. Thus not only may perceptual selection and distortion operate to reduce dissonance (or at least prevent its increase), but behavioral actions may even occur in the attempt to change the situation that induces dissonance.

Although this conception of dissonance reduction provides a very useful device for understanding and predicting behavior, several important issues with respect to the theory must be recognized. First, it describes dissonance as a subjective variable. That is, dissonance is not defined by the external conditions of the environment, but in terms of the experiencing individual's internal experience. Inconsistencies that are apparent to one individual may, through perceptual selection and distortion, be perceived as consistent and consonant by another. This fact makes the theory of cognitive dissonance more useful as an after-the-fact descriptive device than as a model from which precise predictions about behavior may be generated. This shortcoming is common to many cognitive theories dealing with inferred constructs (such as cognitive organizations) that are not themselves directly observable (see Chapter 2).

A THEORY OF COGNITIVE DISSONANCE

In his book *A Theory of Cognitive Dissonance*, Leon Festinger outlined a theory that human behavior is directed by a tendency to achieve *consonance* (consistency) and to avoid *dissonance* (inconsistency) in the organization of cognitive experience. The following examples illustrate the major elements of this theory.

Sources of Dissonance

New Information (momentary dissonance). A person plans to go on a picnic, confident of good weather. Just before he leaves, it begins to rain. This new knowledge is dissonant with his previous confidence.

Uncontrollable Circumstances. A person deciding how to invest his money knows that the outcome of his investment depends on economic conditions beyond his control.

Logical Inconsistency. A person believes that man will land on the moon in the near future, but he also believes that man is incapable of building a device to sustain life outside the earth's atmosphere.

Cultural Mores. A person at a formal dinner uses his fingers to eat a piece of chicken, but knows that this practice violates proper etiquette.

Inclusion of a Specific Attitude in a More General Attitude. A person is a loyal Democrat, but in a particular election prefers a Republican candidate.

Inconsistency with Past Experience. A person enters a self-service elevator, pushes the button marked "U," and feels a sensation of descending.

Means of Reducing Dissonance

Changing Behavior. If a person starts to go on a picnic and it rains, he goes home.

Changing Conditions of the Environment. The arrival of an unexpected guest upsets a hostess' carefully planned seating arrangements for dinner, so she serves buffet style.

Adding New Cognitive Input. A habitual smoker who reads a report of research showing an association between lung cancer and smoking goes to a medical library to seek out reviews that criticize the methods of research and point out inadequacies of the report that smoking is associated with lung cancer.

Conditions Under Which Dissonance Is Tolerated

Dissonance Reduction May Be Painful or Costly. A person spends a great deal of money to purchase a new home but later finds a house for sale that he likes much better. However, buying the preferred house would necessitate the discomfort of moving as well as possible financial loss in selling the first house, so he keeps the home that he no longer prefers.

Dissonance May Be Accompanied by Other Conditions That Are Highly Satisfying. A person might continue to have lunch at a certain restaurant even though it serves poor food, if most of his friends eat lunch there regularly.

Dissonance Reduction May Be Impossible Because of Circumstances. A father may be unable to change his inappropriate behavior toward his children simply because he knows no other ways of behaving.

FESTINGER (1957)

Source: Abstracted from Leon Festinger, *A Theory of Cognitive Dissonance* (New York, Harper & Row, 1957).

Another important characteristic of the dissonance model, somewhat related to the point just made, is the fact that it suggests that the consequences of cognitive dissonance are directly carried out also at the cognitive level. That is, dissonance produces pressures toward consonance. The achievement of consonance at the unobservable level of individual experience may be reflected in observable behavior in a variety of ways. Consequently it is difficult to utilize the dissonance model to predict the specific kinds of actions that an individual may undertake to restore consonance in his cognitive experience.

Finally, it is also important to recognize that the theory of cognitive dissonance does not argue that all of an individual's cognitive organization is at all times in a state of complete consonance. It states merely that there is a tendency in the direction of reduced dissonance. The state of minimum dissonance (or maximum consonance) is an objective toward which behavior and perceptual organization are addressed, but not necessarily an objective that is always achieved fully. Any novel experience may create at least momentary dissonance in cognition until it is assimilated into some portion of the organization of cognitive experience. Furthermore it is only when two or more dissonant elements of cognitive structure are brought into focus simultaneously by a particular set of environmental conditions (a *conflict* situation) that the pressures toward consonance bring about active attempts to reduce dissonance or restore consonance.

These characteristics of Festinger's dissonance theory have brought sharp criticism. For example, Chapanis and Chapanis (1964) made a careful evaluation of the empirical evidence cited in support of the dissonance theory and found that in almost all cases it was impossible to be confident that the particular experimental manipulations used to arouse cognitive dissonance had in fact done so. In most cases the behavioral activity that Festinger and his colleagues interpreted as evidence of dissonance reduction could be explained and interpreted in other ways as well. Furthermore in most of the studies there was no real assurance that these manipulations actually provoked incongruity or dissonance in the cognitive experience of the subjects themselves. Nevertheless Festinger's dissonance model has facilitated the study of several issues in social psychology both directly and indirectly. It has been directly applied to studies of attitude change, described in detail in Chapter 5, and has contributed to the extension of two widely used schematic frameworks for analyzing interpersonal perception and attraction (Newcomb, 1953; Heider, 1958), described in detail in Chapters 7 and 8.

A very similar schematic framework, the *congruity model,* was developed almost simultaneously by Osgood and Tannenbaum (1955). This model is somewhat more circumscribed, and it is stated in behavioristic terminology, but its major implications are parallel to those of Festinger's dissonance theory. Another outgrowth of dissonance theory is *reactance* theory, which suggests that if a person's freedom of choice is restricted, he will put a great deal of effort into trying to regain that choice. To reduce his dissonance he may, in fact, have a more favorable attitude toward that choice than he had before it was suddenly restricted (Brehm, 1966, 1972).

Cognitive Styles

People differ from one another, in terms of the specific details of their cognitive functions, according to the nature of their accumulated cognitive experience and the conceptual habits they have developed. These differences are sometimes referred to as *cognitive styles.* Several different kinds of cognitive styles have been described and classified. For example, Piaget (1952) has distinguished four developmental periods, progressing from the primitive to the mature. These are the *Sensorimotor Period* (reflex and simple unmediated sensory input/motor output linkages); the *Pre-*

REACTANCE AROUSAL: THE ROMEO AND JULIET EFFECT

Married and unmarried (dating) couples were studied over a period of up to 10 months on their degree of expressed romantic love and parental interference. Parental interference was defined as the perception that the parents are a bad influence, are hurting the couple's relationship, take advantage of her, do not accept him, try to make him look bad, and so on. In both married and unmarried couples parental interference was positively and significantly related to mutual feelings of love. Moreover, this relationship grew progressively stronger over time, akin to the classic Romeo and Juliet situation, in which parental opposition only served to strengthen the love relationship. In terms of reactance theory, parental interference in love relationships is a direct threat to a couple's freedom to act on feelings of love for each other, resulting in "reactance arousal" and subsequent intensification of feelings of romantic love among couples.

DRISCOLL, DAVIS, AND LIPETZ (1972)

operational Period (during which symbolic mediation and language skills evolve); the Period of Concrete Operations (when the school-age child begins to understand concrete empirical logic); and the Period of Formal Operations (the highest level of abstract formal rationality). Two basic processes underlie this developmental progression: assimilation, the process of shaping the perception of each new experience to fit into the existing conceptual frameworks of the present stage of cognitive development; and accommodation, the process of modifying and reforming conceptual frameworks as they accept each new experience. These continuing processes account for continuity in the spiral development of cognitive processes, but the developmental levels outlined above are descriptive of the particular characteristics of cognition at any given developmental level.

In a similar way, Harvey, Hunt, and Schroder (1961) have described developmental progression from simplex, one-dimensional, concrete levels of cognitive function in infancy to complex, multidimensional, abstract, interdependent levels in maturity. Whereas Piaget's central concern is the description of developmental levels of progression, Harvey, Hunt, and Schroder use their framework to describe individual differences in cognitive style at any age.

Another approach to differences in cognitive style is that of Witkin (Witkin et al., 1962), describing people as primarily field-dependent (global) or field-independent (analytical) in cognitive-style habits. The former are inclined to handle cognitive experiences in a global way, incorporating both background and focal figure into one complex event perceived as a unit. The latter are inclined to select or abstract specific components of each cognitive experience, decomposing the whole into each of its separate elements.

Kagan (1965) has described another dimension of cognitive style—that of impulsivity (inclination toward quick and often simplistic processing of information from experiences) versus reflectivity (inclination toward slower, more cautious and filtered processing of information). Like Witkin, Kagan has focused upon the description of individual differences and the investigation of their developmental origins.

Still other psychologists have concerned themselves with the capacity to shift flexibly from one conceptual structure to another, or to maintain a large number of operative concepts simultaneously. Early studies of the reluctance of some people to modify and update old concepts or to shift to newer conceptual structures with new experiences termed this quality perceptual rigidity (Luchins, 1945), or intolerance of ambiguity (Adorno et al., 1950). More recent formulations have broadened their scope to consider *dogmatism*—the degree of "openness" (or "closedness") of the cognitive system in assimilating new experiences (Rokeach, 1960).

LANGUAGE

The most significant difference between man and the subhuman animals is probably the fact that the human being makes use of elaborate symbolic systems to organize his cognitive experience and, thus, his behavior. Empirical research on the learning process in lower animals reveals that many animals have remarkable capacities for adapting their behavior in organized ways to their experience of changing conditions in the world around them. But there is no doubt that this capacity is considerably greater in the human being than in even the highest of the subhuman species, such as the anthropoid apes and perhaps the dolphin. In general, research suggests that a great deal of the advantage in complexity of human learning and behavioral organization is a consequence of the human capacity for using symbolic language systems.

What Is a Language?

A language is a system of social conventions that specify particular relationships between a set of symbols and a set of ideas. A particular set of symbols, *verbal symbols,* are of special interest in studying the role of language in human behavior. These include both utterances (spoken *speech*) and graphic patterns (the alphabet and printed or written *words*). But many other kinds of symbols besides letters and numbers may serve to represent ideas; artists use the languages of form, color, and texture to represent ideas abstractly. In human interaction, facial expressions, gestures, and even postures also may symbolize particular ideas and feelings. The scientific study of symbolic activity in human thought and behavior is known as *psycholinguistics.* This specialty area within psychology has developed rapidly during the past two decades.

Psycholinguists (e.g., G. A. Miller, 1951) point out that the particular relationship between a given concept and a given symbol is largely "a matter of social coincidence." Yet this coincidence is not randomly determined; it is a product of the social evolution of rules and conventions for these symbolic relationships as a cultural product over ages of human interaction. Thus a language system includes a set of conventional rules about relationships between particular symbols and the particular ideas they represent (*semantics*) as well as conventional rules about the assembly of several symbols together to represent more elaborate ideas (*syntax*). In other words, the study of word meanings falls within the realm of semantics, and the study of grammar falls within the realm of syntax.

Verbal symbols are used by the individual as labels for organized sets of cognitive experiences; hence there is an intimate relationship between language and thought within the individual. However, the verbal symbolic habits of the individual are not unique to him; common conventions for representing abstract ideas by verbal symbols are adopted within a society, allowing individual members of the society to communicate their ideas and experiences to one another. Thus there are also important relationships between the linguistic and symbolic habits of an individual and the society to which he belongs. In this chapter, the role of language in the cognitive activity of the individual is discussed. The relationships between language systems and other aspects of a society are considered in Chapter 6.

Many explorations of human learning have shown the functional significance of language in facilitating the individual's capacity to learn. Verbally meaningful material is ordinarily learned more rapidly and remembered longer than nonsense material. Mnemonic devices that relate unfamiliar or meaningless material to familiar verbal concepts also facilitate learning and memory (Bartlett, 1932; Carmichael, Hogan, & Walter, 1932). Students who must memorize the order of the twelve cranial nerves commonly use a seemingly stupid rhyme to organize this unfamiliar information—"On old Olympus' towering top, a Finn and Greek viewed some hops!" This is a great deal easier to remember than the unfamiliar "olfactory, optic, oculomotor, trochlear, trigeminal, abducens, facial, auditory, glossopharyngeal, vagus, spinal accessory, hypoglossal." However, the relation of a particular familiar verbal label with an unfamiliar or abstract concept often influences the conceptual interpretation of the unfamiliar concept, and this influence may be reflected later in remembering the less familiar concept. For example, the use of verbal labels to characterize geographic shapes (that is, the "boot" of Italy, or the "panhandles" of various states) may lead to highly distorted maps drawn from memory. Similarly, the student who uses the mnemonic couplet described to learn his neuronanatomy may be lost indeed in a discussion of the eighth cranial nerve (auditory) by its Latin name, the vestibulocochlearis. The influence of verbal labels upon perception and memory has been explored experimentally, and the implications of such influences with respect to the verbal transmission of information and rumors have also been investigated (Allport & Postman, 1947).

Verbal Meditation and Abstractions

It has been suggested that the process of *verbal mediation* accounts for many of the complex "higher mental processes" that characterize human learning (Dollard & Miller, 1950). Through the attachment of verbal labels to concepts that represent categories of related experiences (*abstraction*), efficient shortcuts in the learning process may be achieved. Although the primary stimulus or cue qualities of a set of experiences may be quite dissimilar, they may be functionally related to similar kinds of behavioral response. For example, boiling water, the flame of a match, and the coils of an electric kitchen range may appear very unalike to a young child. Yet their functional relationship (in the sense that all would burn if touched) can be represented by the verbal label "hot."

The process of extracting functional similarities under appropriate verbal labels is the basis of abstraction. On later occasions, the association of an old verbal label with a new experience may elicit appropriate behavior: the association of the verbal label "hot" with a sidewalk that has been in the blazing sun all day may avert the catastrophe of a pair of blistered feet for a tenderfooted child. Instead of learning through painful trial and error that sunny sidewalks may also burn, the verbally labeled abstraction "hot" affords a shortcut to efficient learning. Included in the notion of *verbal mediation* are both *mediated generalization* (the use of verbal labels to conceptualize abstracted functional similarities) and *mediated discrimination* (the use of verbal labels to conceptualize abstracted functional differences). The role of verbal mediation in human learning, especially in young children, has been studied experimentally in considerable detail (e.g., Razran, 1939). These processes of mediation and abstraction provide the basis for the psychological concept of meaning.

Cognition and Meaning

The processes of concept formation and verbal mediation described in the preceding paragraphs account for the most basic kinds of meaning in cognition. Experiences are grouped together in conceptual categories on the basis of essential similarities in terms of some specified abstracted characteristic or set of characteristics. Hunt and Hovland (1960) have distinguished among conjunctive, relational, and disjunctive concepts. *Conjunctive* concepts are those embracing a class of objects that share common perceptual qualities; for example, rubies are all hard, red, and translucent. *Relational* concepts embrace a set of objects that do not necessarily show common perceptual characteristics, but share some fixed relationship to one another; for example, the legs of an isosceles triangle are equal in length, but they can be of any length and have any size angle between them. *Disjunctive* concepts embrace members that are associated within a class because they possess one of two or more basically different characteristics; for example, in the game of baseball the concept of strike includes either a pitched ball at which a batter swings and misses or a pitched ball that crosses the plate between the batter's knees and shoulders, even though he may not swing at it.

Conceptual meanings may vary in the difficulty with which they can be recognized, grasped, or understood by their users. Experimental studies have shown that disjunctive concepts are somewhat more difficult to recognize than conjunctive or relational ones (Hunt & Hovland, 1960). Other studies have found that even relational concepts may vary considerably in difficulty; for human subjects, simple relational concepts embracing similar concrete objects are most easily recognized, with spatial forms, colors, and quantities (numbers) increasing in difficulty (Heidbreder, Bensley, & Ivy, 1948; Grant, 1951).

Psychologists have found it difficult to agree on one interpretation of meaning, perhaps because this term embraces so many different kinds of links that integrate various aspects of behavior (Humphrey, 1951). One may speak of the *meaning* of certain symbols that show characteristics of properties of the objects they represent, as in the case of psychoanalytic interpretations of the snake as a penis symbol in dreams and myths (Freud, 1913; C. G. Jung, 1923). Or meaning may imply a common linkage of two signs or symbols with a common third abstract symbol, as in the case of Osgood's studies of meaning and value through the semantic differential (Osgood, 1952; Osgood, Tannenbaum, & Suci, 1957). Still a third interpretation is the association of two or more symbolic signs with a common behavioral response, as in the studies of verbal mediation in discrimination learning (Kendler, 1962). Thus psychologists have attached a variety of different meanings to the verbal concept "meaning."

When the abstracted qualities that delineate a verbal concept can be made fairly explicit, the concept can be defined specifically. An operational definition of a verbal concept is one that specifies exactly what procedures are required to observe the essential perceivable and experiential qualities that delineate the concept. These properties determine the concept's *denotative* meaning. However, the different experiences within a common conceptual category may possess other less directly noted characteristics that differentiate them from one another. These may be only vaguely noted, and they may involve subjective feelings and attitudes. They are not a part of the explicit reference of the concept, but a surplus of implicit attributes that generate an appended halo of *connotative* meaning.

For example, the adjectives "nude" and "naked" denote essentially the same thing; however, their connotations differ very slightly—enough to make one choose one or the other according to the context of his conversation and thoughts. The concept "mother" may be defined explicitly according to its denotation of the female parent, but the connotation of this concept involves different feelings and attitudes for different people. It is the connotative meaning of a concept that gives rise to the affective and evaluative properties of an attitude. These properties of attitudes, which constitute what psychologists conventionally call *value,* will be described later. Often differences in connotations attached to a particular concept interfere with effective communication between individuals or between members of different societies (see Chapter 6).

Word Associations. One of the most straightforward ways of exploring the meaning and value of verbal concepts is through word association. The tendency of the individual to relate one verbal label to another often gives clues to the connotative meanings he attaches to each. Experimental studies of meaning using this approach were undertaken very early in the psychological exploration of human learning, and word-association techniques have also been used widely in psychological diagnosis and the study of personality (Kent & Rosanoff, 1910; Woodworth, 1938; Goodenough, 1942). A number of flaws, however, limit the usefulness of superficial word associations in investigations of meaning. Often associations represent nothing more than clichés from conventional language habits and common idiomatic phrases. For example, "chair" is usually associated with "table," and "salt" with "pepper." Furthermore, certain conventional sequences account for many common associations such as "foot" and "ball."

THE WORD ASSOCIATION GAME

In a typical word-association study, an experimenter facing a subject's back reads aloud words from a list and asks the subject to respond by giving the first word that occurs to him (other than the stimulus word). Over time, certain uniformities in responses have been observed. For example, the three major responses to "chair" are "table," "seat," and "sit," and the overwhelming response to "lamp" is "light." Children rarely respond with the opposite of the stimulus word, but tend to respond with concrete-type words that somehow extend or enlarge the stimulus word, as for example, table-eat, dark-night, man-work, or mountain-high. Adults tend to respond with related but parallel words or with opposite words, as for example, table-chair, dark-light, man-woman, or mountain-hill. Sex differences occur in words that are connotative of sex-appropriate behavior. For example, the word "bow" rarely, if ever, elicits any references in males to hair or ribbon, but does so very often in females. Similarly, the stimulus word "file" elicits in females significantly more references to fingernails or manicuring and fewer references to wood or metals, than the same stimulus word elicits in males.

KENT AND ROSANOFF (1910)
WOODWORTH (1938)
GOODENOUGH (1942)

Measurement of Meaning. A somewhat more elaborate approach to the experimental study of meaning and value has been developed by Osgood (Osgood, 1952; Osgood, Tannenbaum, & Suci, 1957). The *semantic-differential* technique affords a method of standardizing assessment of meaning that permits comparison of the connotative meanings of different concepts for a given individual as well as comparison of connotative meaning of a given concept from one individual to another. By having a person rate a particular verbal concept on a standard set of bipolar scales (such as "good-bad," "active-passive," and "strong-weak"), connotative meanings may be objectified and quantified. Although some of the bipolar dimensions used in the standard semantic differential may not strike one as logically applicable to the particular concept being investigated, most people respond stably and reliably to the task. Furthermore, typical patterns of response imply that connotative meanings show some consistency among members of the same society or subgroup. The semantic-differential method, then, is a particularly useful tool for studying both individual differences and intercultural differences in meaning and value. The fact that

THE MEASUREMENT OF MEANING

A comprehensive attempt to find new ways to deal with the complex and "philosophically hazy" concept of *meaning* was presented in 1952 by Charles Osgood of the University of Illinois.

One of the problems in studying meaning is a self-evident fact: stimulus signs and stimulus objects are never identical. The *sign* (word) "hammer," for example, is not the same thing as the *object* hammer. The problem, therefore, is to find the conditions under which something that is not an object becomes a sign for that object.

Osgood's early research focused on *synesthesia,* a condition in which the perception of certain type of object or sign is regularly linked with another sensory mode (also reflected in metaphors such as "high" or "low" feelings). Osgood's major achievement, however, was the introduction of a technique to measure meanings. The *semantic differential* (fully described on pp. 53–54) is a series of scales measuring the meaning of a given stimulus word by asking the test-taker to relate the word to *evaluative factors* (concepts) such as good and bad, *potency factors* such as strong and weak, and *activity factors* such as active and passive.

Osgood's technique gets at the *connotative* rather than the *denotative* meaning of words. The word "hammer," for example, may be connotatively interpreted as heavy, cold, strong, or threatening rather than by the denotative, dictionary-like definition: "an instrument for driving nails, etc." That different individuals or groups tend to attach their unique connotative meanings to words has been known all along, but Osgood succeeded in measuring these meanings by "the objective method of scientific inquiry." As early as 1941 he assessed the connotative meaning of such loaded words as "pacifist," "Russian," "dictator," and "neutrality" (probably just as loaded as the contemporary concepts of motherhood, apple pie, flag, and law and order).

OSGOOD (1952)

particular linguistic systems tend to generate similar connotative meanings for concepts among individual users of a common language contributes to the development of uniformity of values and beliefs among members of a society, thus reflecting another avenue through which socialization prepares the individual for assimilation into his society.

RELEVANCE AND APPLICATION

The logical beginning of social psychology is in the analysis of social and cultural influences on the individual's basic processes of thinking and organizing his experience in a social world. Even the most basic processes of cognition take place within a social matrix. The most basic concepts used to classify and arrange perceived experiences are derived in part from the culture in which one lives and the people who have made that culture. One's society, neighborhood, family, and friends all contribute to the frame of reference one employs in interpreting and judging the world he experiences. Consequently, it is almost impossible to analyze and understand human thought and learning processes without giving some consideration to the sociocultural matrix in which they occur.

The quest for logical order in understanding the experienced world is so pervasive that it sometimes becomes an important basis of the driving motivation in human behavior. People often put forth considerable energy and effort to maintain and protect an orderly understanding of the world about them. This fact in many cases affords the only plausible explanation of the goals or purposes of behavior that otherwise seems pointless and directionless.

Language systems are tangible evidence of the close relationship between society and basic thought processes. Languages are cultural products generated by people in social interaction. In fact, language is probably one of the most important tools man has ever produced; without it, the learning process would be much slower, more laborious, and less efficient, and communication of ideas and accomplishments would be severely hampered. For this reason, the study of language and its social origins is one of the most essential first steps toward understanding human learning and education.

In *forensic psychology* (applications of psychological knowledge to law and court-room practice), a great deal of importance is attached to the sociocultural factors that influence perception and recall. The selection of jurors likely to respond sympathetically (or at least objectively) to one's arguments may be an important factor in the outcome of a trial, and the attorney who selects carefully by analyzing probabilities related to cognition and perception may develop an advantage. Likewise, the selection and handling of witnesses during questioning may also capitalize on predictable factors in cognition to benefit the argument of the case.

Educational practice has profited considerably from the broadened theoretical approaches to perception and cognition that have evolved during the last few decades. Instructional technology has begun to capitalize on psychological analysis of attentional processes and conceptual organization to develop better, more comfortable, and more efficient systems of instruction. Explorations of individual differences among learners (including analysis of cognitive styles) have suggested ways of adapting instructional procedures to suit the cognitive style of the learner.

In business, industry, and marketing, these analyses of perception, cognition, experience, and memory have all been brought to bear upon planning advertising campaigns and marketing products. Political campaigning has followed the same route; the most successful candidate, like the most successful salesman, is one who capitalizes on understanding of the basic ways in which people think and act in a social context.

REVIEW

1. *Cognition* refers to the process of assimilating experiences, relating them to one another, and attaching meaning and value to them.

2. *Cognitive processes* include many kinds of mechanisms for ordering one's experiences. Among these mechanisms are *concept formation* (sorting and grouping of experiences according to similarities and differences) and *attention* (selective screening of experience according to one's purposes and expectations).

3. *Frames of reference* provide the background against which each focal event in one's experience is evaluated and interpreted. These incorporate past experience as well as present background conditions into the interpretation of each new event experienced. They are a function not only of physical contexts, but of social contexts as well.

4. The theory of *cognitive dissonance* describes a general tendency for a person to attempt to find order and congruity in his experiences—if necessary, even by shaping his interpretation of events to make them seem compatible with past related experiences.

5. Individual people differ from one another in their conceptual habits of ordering, arranging, and processing the stream of experiences they encounter. These differences are described as *cognitive styles.*

6. *Language* is an important element in cognitive organization, especially from a sociocultural point of view. A language is a system of social conventions that relate a set of symbols to a set of ideas or experiences.

7. The use of word symbols to represent categories of experiences (concepts) is called *verbal mediation.* This process facilitates conceptual *abstraction* as a means of representing qualities of similarity in otherwise different single experiences. In turn, this abstraction of relevant dimensions of similarity and difference among events or conditions in the world enables one to take shortcuts in learning, affording more complex mental activity in the human being.

8. The study of relationships between symbols and ideas includes the exploration of *meaning.* Psychologists examine two kinds of meaning: *denotative meaning* (the literal and specific defining referents of a symbolic concept) and *connotative meaning* (the additional overflow of subjective feeling and attitude that may be attached to a symbolic concept by the individual).

5

ATTITUDE DEVELOPMENT AND CHANGE

One of the most useful concepts that psychologists have evolved to deal with the organization of experience and behavior is *attitude.* Like many other similar concepts in psychology, attitude is a hypothetical construct; it refers to something that cannot itself be directly observed. Nevertheless, attitudes can be inferred indirectly from their effects on behavioral actions (such as judgments and choices), which are directly observable. A more familiar hypothetical construct, *temperature,* illustrates the same qualities. Temperature is not directly observable, but can be inferred from its effects on observable phenomena (high temperatures melt objects, burn fingers, or evaporate liquids; low temperatures freeze liquids into solids and condense gases). Likewise, attitudes are not directly observable, but their effects are certainly observable and measureable.

An attitude may be defined as *a relatively stable system of organization of experience and behavior related to a particular object or event.* At the core of every attitude is a rational, *cognitive concept* (like those described in Chapter 4), classifying a set of related cognitive experiences. In addition to this, an attitude also includes a range of associated *affective* values, feelings, and emotions. Finally, these rational ideas and affective values are in turn associated with a specific range of *behavioral* tendencies, which may be revealed as overt choices, judgments, or actions. So every attitude includes three components: a cognitive core (*belief* or *idea*), affective *values,* and behavioral action tendencies (*predispositions*).

In measuring attitudes, the psychologist must infer them from his examination of the choices and other actions that reflect them. He may search for patterns of agreement or disagreement expressed by a person with respect to a variety of statements about an object (an attitude scale). He may evaluate a person's voluntary remarks about an object, or the frequency with which a person chooses one object rather than another. Because attitude is such a useful and pervasive construct in psychology, a considerable amount of effort has been invested in refining methods for measuring attitudes as precisely as possible. In Chapter 3, several conventional procedures that psychologists use to measure attitudes were described.

The Cognitive Element in Attitudes: Beliefs and Ideas

The rational core of an attitude is the conceptual category of objects or events to which the attitude is addressed. This concept defines the *object* of the attitude. Thus, in psychology, the term attitude is always used in reference to an object; it makes no sense to say that a person has "a positive attitude." It is necessary to specify "attitude toward *what?*" This question specifies which objects (or people or events) are included within the range of the attitude, and it defines the range of the feelings or values and behavioral predispositions embraced by the attitude. This range may be very specific (such as a particular dish of ice cream on which a fly has just landed), or it may be more general (such as all forms and varieties of ice cream, whether real or imagined). It may be an intangible abstraction (such as motherhood, sin, or honesty). The object of an attitude may be a particular person (one's wife, one's father, or one's employer, for example), members of a class or group of people (such as blacks, Jews, or people who voted Republican in the last election), or even social institutions (such as labor unions, political organizations, or the federal government). Although tradition has associated the study of attitudes with social psychology, the usefulness of this concept is by no means limited to that field. In fact, many of the descriptive dimensions used to characterize individual differences in personality by clinical psychologists are actually attitudes. Attitudes are of interest in practically all areas of psychological research, but social psychology is most directly interested in those with social objects—attitudes toward people, groups, and cultural elements.

The cognitive concept that defines an attitude is often referred to as an *idea* or a *belief*. This rational component may be investigated and described in itself, like any other kind of concept. Ordinarily, however, psychologists are equally interested in the values and behaviors that accompany a belief or an idea.

The Affective Element in Attitudes: Values

Every attitude also includes an affective component (feelings and emotions) accompanying the core idea or belief. These feelings comprise what psychologists refer to as *value*. An important basic idea in analyzing the forces that direct man's behavior is *hedonism*. The quest for comfort and pleasure (and its reciprocal, the avoidance of pain and discomfort) is predominant in the writings of Aristotle (pre-Christian), in those of Descartes, Hobbes, Smith, and Bentham (all philosophers of the seventeenth and eighteenth centuries), and even in the ideas of Freud, Hull, Skinner, and the other giants of twentieth-century psychology. Modern hedonistic views suggest that even behavior that appears superficially to be self-sacrificing and painful may nevertheless, at a deeper level, be instrumental to the attainment of alternative or subsequent states of pleasure for the individual.

The essence of psychological value is *hedonic tone*. In simple terms, this refers to the general overall positive or negative feeling-tone associated with an attitude. If the attitude embraces generally positive, favorable, and pleasureable feelings, it is considered to be a positive attitude. Obversely, a negative attitude is one embracing predominantly negative, unfavorable, and painful feelings.

The Behavioral Element in Attitudes: Predispositions

The affective quality of an attitude is rather directly linked to tendencies toward action. Positive feelings usually generate tendencies directed toward bringing the person into closer contact and prolonged experience with the object of the attitude (*approach* tendencies). Similarly, negative feelings usually involve *escape* or *avoidance* tendencies (directed toward increasing distance between the person and the object of the attitude for terminating experience with that object). For this reason, attitudes have strong motivational properties that direct the individual's behavior. The object of a positive attitude would be said to have positive value for a person, and it would thus be expected to be a sought-after goal-object the attainment of which should serve as a rewarding state of affairs for the person. In the same way, the object of a negative attitude has negative value for a person, and enforced contact with that object is expected to provide a punishing state of affairs. Conceived in this fashion, attitudes are closely related to the psychology of motivation, goal seeking, and purposive behavior.

But attitudes are not always directly and simply linked to specific behavioral actions. Many attitudes may interact in complex combinations to determine one's specific course of action. Moreover, their effects may be tempered by situational circumstances. Because a perfect one-to-one correspondence between a single attitude and a specific act is rarely expected, the motivational directions involved in an attitude are best called behavioral *predispositions*—general inclinations toward action in a predicted direction. Although a given attitude may be inferred from an observed pattern of behavioral acts, prediction of actions from attitudes is usually general rather than specific (Wicker, 1969, 1971; Ajzen & Fishbein, 1970; Fishbein, 1972).

A review of forty-six studies in which verbal and behavioral responses to objects of particular attitudes were compared suggested an unstable relationship between the two variables (Wicker, 1969). People may *say* that they would not reject a member of a minority group or that they would attend an important meeting or that they would

DO AS I SAY, NOT AS I DO

Shortly before the 1968 presidential election campaign, observers were stationed throughout Davidson County, Tennessee, for the purpose of ascertaining (1) whether motorists had complied with a law that they purchase and display an automobile tax sticker, and (2) the type of bumper sticker (if any) on the automobile, to indicate its owner's presumed political preference. The results showed that automobiles with pro-Wallace stickers carried significantly fewer tax stickers than did the automobiles carrying pro-Nixon or pro-Humphrey stickers. The possibility that pro-Wallace supporters were poorer and hence could not afford to buy the tax sticker was discounted in view of the fact that the number of late-model automobiles bearing pro-Wallace stickers did not differ significantly from those bearing other political stickers (or no stickers). It was concluded that pro-Wallace supporters—whose main political issue throughout the campaign had been "law and order"—subscribed to it less than did other citizens.

WRIGHTSMAN (1969)

not cheat on an examination—because all of these things are socially desirable. But they do not necessarily *act* accordingly. On the other hand, there are many demonstrations of remarkably good prediction from paper-and-pencil verbal measures of attitudes to actual willingness to engage in interracial activities or work for civil rights causes (Fendrich, 1967; Green, 1969).

Attitudes, Values, and Motivation

In human behavior, attitudes, values, and motives are all part of the same process. From the early twentieth century, psychologists have agreed that man's behavior is purposive and goal directed. But there have been many approaches to describing the ways in which psychological energy is channeled into action. The early instinct theories have proven inadequate for understanding the variations of motivated behavior associated with different cultural backgrounds and different learning experiences. Modern psychological theory generally accepts a notion of a generalized energy source within the person, which through learning comes to be directed toward particular goals in particular ways. Freudian theorists refer to this general energy concept as *libido* (Freud, 1913). Modern behaviorists entertain a very similar notion of *general drive* (Hull, 1943, 1952; Dollard & Miller, 1950; Skinner, 1971). Cognitive theorists, stressing the rationality of man, consider the general motivational properties of states of *cognitive disparity, dissonance,* or *incongruity* (Festinger, 1957; Harvey, 1963). Those who hold the newer, humanistic positions (like the cognitivists, stressing the subjective experience of goal-directedness) emphasize the operation of inherent forces impelling each person to want to "become" or "realize" himself (Rogers, 1959). Maslow (1954) calls this process *self-actualization*—the acme of a hierarchy of needs ranging from primitive physiological needs through intermediate needs for personal safety, love and belongingness, and esteem, to the highest needs for self-fulfillment and actualization.

A certain set of predispositional motives stem from unlearned biological properties of the organism. These are called *biogenic* (of biological origin) or *primary* motives, and they include hunger, thirst, sex, and the need for oxygen, for example. These motives do not necessarily include specific neuromuscular mechanisms that define action; they merely specify a need for a particular kind of goal object or goal state. Another set of predispositional motives derives from learning and accumulated experience. These are called *sociogenic* (of social origin), or secondary or derived motives. It is with this set of predispositions that psychology is most directly concerned in the study of attitudes and values. The concept of attitude does not ordinarily include *tropisms* (unlearned orientations toward or against certain objects), although in a strict sense tropisms show some of the properties of attitudes. Positive thermotropism (attraction to heat) or phototropism (toward light) may be observed in moths, or even in plants. Unlike these, the attitudes, values, and predispositions that psychologists examine as sociogenic motives have been found to: vary considerably from one individual to the next, despite biological similarity; vary systematically from one culture to another; and be manipulated fairly easily by controlling the experience of the individual, even over brief periods of time.

Delay of Gratification. Freud introduced an important notion into hedonistic psychology by proposing that man has the capacity to delay gratification of his desires; he pointed out that on certain occasions, one may endure discomfort or even suffering temporarily in order to later attain some desired state. This notion of "psychological delay" is basic to modern psychological theory of personality. The capacity to await delayed goals—the *delayed-gratification syndrome* (DGS)—is learned through early socialization (Mischel, 1958; Aronfreed, 1968). Individuals, even in maturity, may differ a great deal with respect to their preferences for immediate or delayed goals and their tolerance for delay of gratification. The roots of this capacity are twofold. First, a rational capacity for understanding the logic of antecedent-consequent causal relationships is necessary in order to understand action-goal contingencies. Second, an interpersonal-trust relationship between the person and the one who controls the dispensation of his rewards must be cultivated (Mischel, 1958).

Aversive Motivation. A special negative quality in some attitudes involves the direction of behavior away from, rather than toward, particular consequences. For a particular behavioral action, it may sometimes be difficult to ascertain with confidence whether its motivational origin was primarily *aversive* (avoiding undesired consequences) or *appetitive* (seeking desired consequences). Action often stems from a combination of both. The most basic kind of aversive motivation is pain itself. Very intense stimulation of almost any of the sensory channels in the human being produces discomfort and negative feelings, usually followed by efforts to reduce the pain by escaping its source. From experimental studies of both human beings and animals, psychologists have concluded that pain arouses a basic emotional (and motivational) state called *fear,* which tends to instigate various kinds of *escape* behavior. Withdrawal of one's hand from contact with a "live" electric wire, putting one's hands over one's ears to reduce the intensity of jet noise at an airport, or running from intense heat in a fire are all cases of fear-motivated escape behavior. A very closely related kind of aversive motivation can be learned. Events or objects that are initially neutral and inoffensive may, through association with the arousal of fear, eventually become sources of a similar learned state resembling fear, which has been called *anxiety.* Like fear, anxiety tends to instigate behavior that will remove the individual from the conditions that arouse the anxiety. Such behavior is parallel to the escape behavior that accompanies fear, but because it occurs prior to the occurrence of any direct pain to the organism, it is called *avoidance* rather than escape.

Superstitious Attitudes. Many kinds of behavior that we might call "superstitious" in the human being actually represent cases of anxiety-based avoidance. A youngster who sincerely believes that if he steps on a crack in the sidewalk, his mother will break her back (as the old rhyme goes) is extremely reluctant to test his belief. The distress of the anxiety evoked by his belief in the rhyme is so painful that the avoidant superstition perpetuates itself; avoidance of cracks reduces anxiety and alleviates its distress. Dollard and Miller (1950) referred to the apparent "stupidity" of the neurotic person who continues to display unreasonable symptoms because they alleviate learned anxieties. Mowrer (1950) has described the "neurotic paradox" that tends to perpetuate maladaptive avoidant behavior in the neurotic patient. Because his anxiety-motivated avoidant behavior removes him from situations that would permit discovery that his anxieties are unfounded and his avoidances unnecessary, the neurotic falls into a vicious circle of inappropriate behavior.

Conflict. The fact that attitudinal systems rarely operate in isolation (one at a time) occasionally produces conflicts in the direction of behavior. When two attitudes predispose the person in the same general behavioral direction, their compatibility produces no distress. But when two attitudes simultaneously predispose the person in incompatible directions, psychological *conflict* occurs. When two appetitive attitudes are in conflict (as, for example, when one cannot choose between going to a concert or to a play when both are scheduled for the same evening), the situation is described as an *approach-approach conflict.* When two sets of aversive circumstances occur simultaneously, so that one is motivated to escape or avoid both, the situation is called an *avoidance-avoidance conflict.* In the latter case, the conflict is usually readily resolved, because one can ordinarily find a third alternative in behavior that averts both undesired circumstances. A third type of conflict, especially important in the motivation of social behavior, is the *approach-avoidance conflict.* This occurs when appetitive and aversive attitudinal systems are directly in opposition with respect to the same direction of behavior. A child who wants a piece of cake before dinner but fears that his mother will punish him if he takes it suffers such conflict. Approach-avoidance conflicts occur frequently in social situations when a person wishes to do something he fears may be disapproved of by people whom he likes and wants to like him.

The socialization of attitudes and goal-directed behavior occurs within a complex social framework described further in Chapter 6.

PUBLIC OPINION, PROPAGANDA, AND ATTITUDE CHANGE

For several decades, the assessment and manipulation of the attitudes of large audiences have comprised an important venture—socially, politically, and economically—in American life. Much time, effort, and skill have been applied toward refinement of methods of sampling large populations to gauge public opinion and collective attitudes (see Chapter 3). Within a society, a subculture, a social class, or any other social system, opinions and attitudes show characteristic general homogeneity just as do overt behavioral habits (see Chapter 6).

The term *propaganda* is applied generally to any kind of effort to manipulate the attitudes of an audience. The word is derived from Pope Urban VIII's creation of an institution in the seventeenth century (the "College of Propaganda") to train priests for missionary work in the propagation of the Christian faith. Although the term has come to imply conniving falsehoods or half-truths, this connotation is not literally accurate. Any attempt to influence the development or change of attitudes may be properly called propaganda. Education itself is a form of propaganda, as are commercial advertising and political campaigning.

Although attitudes may be shaped or changed in many ways (including exertion of the kinds of social influence and social power described in Chapter 9), the term "propaganda" is usually applied to communication that intentionally attempts to persuade the listener. Lazarsfeld, Berelson, and Gaudet (1944) describe the basic function of propaganda as one of activation, that is, of shaping a latent attitude and converting it into manifest behavior such as buying, voting, or choosing. The effects of propaganda in this activation process include four processes: arousal of the interest and attention of the audience to the attitudinal issue in question, exposure of the audience to new information and ideas, selective guidance of the audience's attention toward a certain range of information or ideas, and crystallization of action related to the attitude in question.

Audience Arousal

The first task in any propaganda attempt necessarily involves the attraction of the audience's attention. That is, the audience must become polarized toward the communicator who wishes to build or change attitudes. In printed publications, splashes of color, large letters conveying shocking messages, or elaborate borders may be used in the hard-sell tradition to gain a reader's attention; or novelty and humor may be used more subtly but just as effectively. A soft-sell approach of dramatic understatement, satire, or even irrelevant humor may stand out and snag the reader's attention. Radio advertising usually relies upon loud and splashy auditory appeals; television utilizes both sight and sound to gain audience attention.

Psychologists who have studied the effects of attention and distraction on attitude change have come up with some interesting findings. Earlier studies had unexpectedly shown that audience distraction actually *increased* the persuasive impact of a communication. One possible explanation for this effect is "audience sensitization," that is, the subjects listening to the communication were distracted enough to lessen the chance that they could form counterarguments to it (McGuire & Papageorgis, 1962; Festinger & Maccoby, 1964). Subsequent studies, however, showed that whether a communication becomes more potent depends on the affective nature of the distraction. Zimbardo, Ebbesen, and Fraser (1968) presented subjects with a persuasive communication while being "positively" distracted (watching sexually provoking slides). The subjects changed their attitude in the direction of the communication more often than when they were "neutrally" distracted (watching innocuous slides of scenery); but when they were "negatively" distracted (watching medical slides of dismembered limbs and third-degree burns), they changed their attitude less than under the other forms of distraction. The implication for propagandists is quite clear: pleasant distractions will increase the potency of your message, unpleasant distraction will decrease it.

There is some isolated evidence that propaganda may sometimes be successful without gaining the conscious attention of an audience. *Subliminal* (i.e., below the threshold of conscious perceptual awareness) advertising has attempted experi-

---

THE CONDITIONING OF ATTITUDES: EATING WHILE READING

Even though most studies on attitude change are couched in cognitive terms, several studies have used the traditional concept of reinforcement. In one study, subjects read persuasive communications either while eating desirable food (peanuts and Pepsi-Cola) or without the presence of food. The donor of the food (the experimenter) disassociated himself from the content of the communication, thus ensuring that the reinforcement (the food) was not to be cognitively associated with him. The subjects in the reading-while-eating condition showed greater attitude change in the direction favoring the communications than did those who merely read them. In a similar way, the introduction of an unpleasant odor (butyric acid) while reading a persuasive communication lessened the chance for its acceptance.

JANIS, KAYE, AND KIRSCHNER (1965)

SUBLIMINAL PERSUASION

Each of two groups of viewers were presented with a 16-minute movie on the psychology of learning. One group saw the movie with the word "beef" superimposed every 7 seconds at the speed of 1/200 second (below the threshold of average conscious perceptual awareness), and the other group watched the movie without any changes. At the conclusion of each session the subjects filled out various questionnaires and checklists about their food preferences in sandwiches (beef, steak, hamburger, tuna, or cheese) and their hunger state at that time. There was no difference between the groups in their preference for a particular type of sandwich, but the viewers who had watched the movie with the superimposed word expressed significantly more hunger.

BYRNE (1959)

mentally to induce changed attitudes and behavior by communicating to the audience at a subconscious level. Whether these attempts are truly successful remains to be evaluated accurately, but there is at least some possibility that a new realm of propaganda and attitude change may be opened through the use of subliminal communication. Even so, it will remain the task of successful advertisers to engage the subconscious, if not the conscious, attention of the audience.

Apparently, attitudes can be conditioned rather easily with only minimal awareness of the persuasion going on. Scott (1958, 1959) showed that when groups systematically reward an individual member for expressing attitudes counter to his own, the member begins to change subtly in the direction of the expressed attitudes. Insko (1965) demonstrated how reinforcement in the form of verbal approval can condition attitudes, and Bem (1970) showed that an individual's overall cognitive structure is affected by the way he perceives his own behavioral actions.

Although the devices used to gain audience attention are most patent in commercial advertising, similar devices must be employed in other kinds of propaganda. In political campaigning, a candidate's speeches and public appearances must secure his audience's attention before the task of shifting voting habits can be begun. In education, the successful teacher must often resort to gimmicks and tricks to seduce his students into allowing themselves to be educated.

Reason and Emotion

Because attitudes involve both rational (cognitive) and emotional (affective) components, either avenue may be used effectively to carry out propaganda. *Rational* propaganda attempts to persuade the audience that the advocated attitude is reasonable and logically sound. For example, certain toothpastes have been endorsed by dentists as successfully combating tooth decay, providing an advantageous rational appeal in the advertising of those toothpaste manufacturers.

Often, pseudorational approaches are developed in advertising to delude the audience into assuming that the propaganda offers logically sound information. Such double-talk as "nasograph demonstrations" of antihistimine effectiveness and animated cartoons of "B" tablets chasing "A" tablets through a maze of pipes purported to represent a stomach are intended to imply to the audience a factual basis for the intended change in buying behavior. Even in political campaigning, a candidate may capitalize on the naiveté of his audience with double-talk. In a backwoods community of poorly educated voters, a candidate might gain a number of votes by accusing his opponent of having practiced "celibacy" when he was an adolescent and pointing out that his opponent has advocated the use of the United Nations as a forum for "open social intercourse."

Emotional propaganda may be based on attempts to persuade an audience in the absence of pertinent facts. A variety of devices may be employed to achieve this kind of change. *Prestige identification* of the intended attitude with a highly regarded reference group or public figure may be gained directly (e.g., "Thinking men smoke Viceroy cigarettes" or "Joe Namath wears Hanes underwear") or indirectly (e.g., by photographing a middle-priced automobile in front of a well-known luxury hotel). *Sympathetic identification* may provide leverage for persuasion by inducing the audience to feel sorry for the persuader, or at least to feel a close and sympathetic relationship with him. In the business of renting automobiles, Avis keeps "trying harder" because it is merely number two in the business, but behind the efforts to become number one, it remains just a shade closer to the audience in its number two status. In political campaigns there is somewhat more virtue in having been born in a log cabin than in having been reared in a wealthy and aristocratic family, at least to many voters. Political advantage is usually gained by the candidate who appears to be just like the folks next door, as long as he can emphasize that he, by his own brilliance and diligence, has accomplished just a shade more.

A rather widely used basis of emotional propaganda is the *fear appeal.* In advertising, threats that failure to use a certain toothpaste will result in aching cavities, or that use of the wrong brand of coffee will wreck marriages, are used to gain attitude change in the absence of convincing rational information. In political campaigns the opposition party is almost always the "war party" or the "tax party," regardless of its record. Propaganda attempts are often outlined on the premise of reducing anxiety or perceived threat; and in some cases there even may be intentional attempts to create or elevate the anxiety whose relief is promised (Janis & Feshbach, 1953).

The use of fear does not guarantee successful persuasion. When communications become too frightening, they may lose their effectiveness. A severe threat may arouse so much fear and anxiety in individuals that they may defensively avoid the communication (Janis & Feshbach, 1953; Nunally & Bobren, 1959; Janis & Terwillinger, 1962). Other studies, however, have found that the higher the induced fear level of a communication, the greater its acceptance (Niles, 1964; Leventhal & Singer, 1966; Leventhal, 1967). Much of the confusion is probably due to the fact that what one experimenter perceives as extremely frightening may be only moderately fear-arousing to another. It is also possible that intense threats may be ineffective because

---

FEAR APPEAL

An illustrated lecture to high school students on the topic of dental hygiene was presented at three different intensities of fear-arousing threat to three matched groups of students. Acquiescence to the message of the lecture (better oral hygiene) was inversely related to threat intensity. Mild threat ("pain from toothaches") produced 37 percent net attitude change in the desired direction; moderately intense threat ("having cavities filled," or "sore, swollen, inflamed gums") produced 22 percent change, and extremely intense threat ("cancer, paralysis, or blindness," or "having teeth pulled") produced only 8 percent change. Resistance to subsequently presented counterpropaganda showed similar relationships: the mild-threat group was most resistant; the moderate-threat group was less resistant; and the intense-threat group was least resistant. Perhaps the ineffectiveness of extreme threat in producing attitude change is due to defensive hostility toward the communicator, leading to rejection of his arguments.

JANIS AND FESHBACH (1953)

they are perceived as implausible and therefore ignored by the listener. Most likely the relationship between fear arousal and attitude change is, as suggested by McGuire (1966), curvilinear: up to a certain point, the more fear-inducing a message is, the more attitude change will it evoke; after that point, its effectiveness will decline.

As an attention-getting device, *prior* to presentation of factual information, the intentional evocation of fear (up to a point) seems to increase the effectiveness of propaganda. In contrast, however, the presentation of emotional fear-evoking appeals *after* the factual argument has been offered seems to have little or no effect on the success of the propaganda attempt (Cohen, 1957). The "fear-fact" approach is an effective one, but the "fact-fear" approach is not. The implication is that effective propaganda may utilize emotional appeals to create chaos into which persuasive information may then be rushed.

Presentation of Arguments

Even when propaganda is planned on an honest factual basis, the manner of presentation of arguments may influence the persuasive impact on the audience's attitudes. Several aspects of presentation have been explored experimentally to determine their relationship to propaganda effectiveness.

Drawing Conclusions. Among lawyers, the phrase *res ipsa loquitur* is used to describe an argument in which the facts appear to speak for themselves, needing no further interpretation or elaboration. Empirical studies of propaganda, however, suggest that there are few cases in which facts do indeed speak for themselves. The same facts may speak a different language to each listener, and the conclusion drawn by one may differ vastly from that drawn by another. The effectiveness of the same argument (presented by the same source to similar audiences) may vary according to how clearly the communicator states his intended interpretation and conclusions (Hovland & Mandell, 1952; Fine, 1957; Weiss & Steenbock, 1965). The effective propagandist stands to gain by explicitly pointing out the conclusions he wishes to have drawn from his message, no matter how obviously he may think the facts speak for themselves (Haskins, 1966).

FACTS DO NOT SPEAK FOR THEMSELVES

A taped speech on devaluation of currency was presented to audiences under either of two conditions: with the conclusion that it is desirable to devaluate currency explicitly drawn by the speaker, or leaving it to each individual in the audience to draw his own conclusions. Pre- and postexperimental measures showed greater agreement with the speaker's position when the latter drew the conclusion (51.2 percent) than when the individuals in the audience drew their own conclusions (30.7 percent). Similarly, when the individuals in the audience drew their own conclusions, there was greater opposition to the speaker's position (11.4 percent) than when the speaker himself drew the conclusions (3.3 percent).

HOVLAND AND MANDELL (1952)

Order Effects. Among the general public there is some conviction that there is an advantage in presenting one's argument first, before the opposition has a chance to reach the audience (a primacy effect), but there is also wide belief that some advantage may be gained by having the last word (a recency effect). Several studies of how individuals organize information as they form an impression of the personality of a stranger have shown that, at least in the perception of strangers, primacy effects are quite pronounced unless the perceiver is warned of the dangers of first impressions or unless there is a considerable gap of interspersed irrelevant activity between first impressions and later impressions (see Chapter 7).

Early studies of primacy and recency effects in the presentation of persuasive arguments to an audience suggested that primacy effects were dominant, with first arguments being more persuasive than later ones (Lund, 1925). However, other studies found that the issue was not so simply resolved. For example, when public commitment in expressing one's attitude on an issue is necessary, primacy effects do tend to occur (Hovland, Campbell, & Brock, 1957). First arguments tend to be more effective in propaganda when members of the audience must take a public stand on the issue: having once expressed an attitude publicly, an individual may thereafter be more resistant to subsequent shifts or changes. On the other hand, when the individual is free to make up his mind but to avoid a public expression of his attitude, primacy effects tend to be obscured. Even though the listener may have made up his mind to some degree on hearing an initial argument, if he has not expressed himself openly, a subsequent argument may induce him to change his mind.

In general, recency effects tend to operate when the audience is relatively unfamiliar with the issue of the propaganda message, and when the subject matter of the latter is of relatively little interest to the listener. Under such circumstances, the propagandist who has the last word may be more successful than the one who speaks first to argue his position. But with controversial, interesting, and highly familiar issues primacy effects are dominant, and thus one's best bet is to present his case first (Rosnow & Robinson, 1967).

One-sided and Two-sided Arguments. The sincere and dedicated believer may feel that his argument would be enhanced by attempts to be fair and impartial in presenting both sides of an issue, confining his persuasive effort to pointing out the advantages of his position over the alternative position. In studies comparing the effectiveness of one-sided and two-sided propaganda presentations, there appears to be no clear immediate advantage of the two-sided argument. A few studies have suggested a slight advantage of the two-sided argument under certain specific conditions, but the difference is not an appreciable one (Hovland, Lumsdaine, & Sheffield, 1949). However, there is evidence that latent gains may be made that can become important later. When subsequent attempts are made by other propagandists to change attitudes, an audience that has previously heard a two-sided presentation may prove more resistant to later attempts to change their attitudes in a direction opposed to that of the initial propaganda attempt. Audiences that originally heard only a one-sided argument appear more susceptible to subsequent attempts to change their attitudes in the other direction (Lumsdaine & Janis, 1953).

Thus the order in which a propagandist gains access to his audience may determine the relative effectiveness of one-sided and two-sided arguments. For one who makes an initial attempt to persuade an audience, he stands to gain by presenting both sides of the issue, outlining the kinds of counterarguments likely to be used by his opposition, but drawing conclusions that make a pitch for his side of the issue. For one who comes later to attempt to persuade the same audience, there is little advantage to be gained by reviewing the original counterargument. In fact, such a two-sided review may merely invite debate and comparison of the two arguments.

Counterpropaganda and Immunization

A strong case for the relative effectiveness of two-sided arguments in combating counterpropaganda has been made by McGuire and Papageorgis (1961, 1962). A common-sense approach might suggest that a propagandist should "let sleeping dogs lie" and not do his enemy's work for him. There ought to be power in a positive, one-sided approach that attempts to sell one's own views or product but ignores the opposition. According to McGuire and Papageorgis, the gains for the propagandist using this one-sided approach are at best short-lived. In presenting their case for the effectiveness of two-sided arguments, they draw an analogy from medicine. Many diseases are contracted by individuals because at a given point their resistance happens to be low. It is therefore sound practice to engage in preventative steps by prescribing supportive therapy such as exercise, proper diet, or rest. But it is even better to immunize a person by inoculating him with a weak virus of the very disease he may contract, because it will help him to mobilize his defenses. A two-sided argument that outlines the most likely counterargument of the opposition thus "inoculates" a person and induces in him resistance to subsequent counterpropaganda attempts.

Immunization against subsequent propaganda may also be achieved through derision and derogation of the source of later arguments. Direct attempts to reduce a speaker's prestige and credibility may induce an audience to give little attention to him and to discount his message (Allyn & Festinger, 1961). "Afterwarnings" that advise an audience that they have already heard an attempt to change their attitudes appear to be of little immunizing value; it is only when warnings are stated in advance of the attempt that resistance to propaganda is achieved (Kiesler & Kiesler, 1964). After the maiden has been seduced, it is too late to warn her that her suitor is a cad.

INOCULATION FOR COUNTERPROPAGANDA

"Cultural truisms" express widely shared beliefs that are not likely to be opposed. After listening to four such truisms (e.g., "everyone should brush his teeth after every meal if at all possible"), subjects underwent the following experimental conditions. (1) *Supportive defense:* one-sided arguments were presented favoring the position stated in the truism (e.g., brushing teeth improves appearance, prevents decay). (2) *Refutational defense:* two-sided arguments were presented, a weak one against the position stated in the truism (e.g., brushing teeth sometimes injures gums, toothpastes have harsh abrasives), and a strong one for it (e.g., brushing teeth prevents decay, stimulation improves gum conditions, harsh abrasives are eliminated by the Food and Drug Administration). (3) *No defense:* the truism was presented without arguments.

Two days later the subjects met again and faced a strong attack on the position stated in the truisms (counterpropaganda). The subjects in the no-defense condition were most vulnerable (least resistant) to this attack, whereas the least vulnerable subjects were in the refutational-defense condition. Suggesting a medical analogy, the results imply that the best way to combat counterpropaganda (the disease) is by using two-sided arguments, one of them being a weak countermessage (the virus) aimed at helping the individual to mobilize his defenses against future attacks.

MC GUIRE AND PAPAGEORGIS (1961)

Sources of Propaganda

The source of a communication that attempts to influence the attitudes of an audience may be an important determinant of the success of the attempt at persuasion. Individuals who attempt to persuade others, as well as groups whose norms operate to influence the attitudes of others, may be reacted to differently by different people. Groups and individuals who a person respects or admires or to whom he is attracted tend to be particularly effective in influencing his attitudes and behavior (see

Chapter 9). In some cases a reference group or individual influencer may be rejected directly, resulting in inverted shifts in attitudes or behavior called "boomerang" effects. Every act of communication involves both a source (one who communicates to another) and a message (an idea comprising the content of communication). Thus every propaganda attempt is characterized by certain attributes of its content and certain attributes of its source.

Source Credibility. The credibility of a source of propaganda may vary considerably. If he is regarded as an authority who is well qualified to speak on the issue, and one whose judgment about the issue is to be respected, his propaganda attempts are likely to be successful. On the other hand, if he is regarded as poorly qualified to speak on the issue, or as patently biased and thus not trustworthy, his arguments may be rejected. In experimental studies, arguments attributed to a respected and highly credible source have been found to be more effective in influencing an audience's attitudes than identical arguments attributed to a noncredible source (Hovland & Weiss, 1951; Zagora & Harter, 1966). During election campaigns, strict party adherents and voters who make up their minds early in the campaign may tend to accept without question the arguments of their chosen candidate, rejecting wholesale the arguments of his opponent. For much of the American public, attribution of a controversial item of opinion or information to the Soviet News Bureau TASS or to *Pravda* is the kiss of death to its credibility.

HOW TO GAIN AND MAINTAIN CREDIBILITY

Groups of college students were presented separately with an identical communication citing the effects of smoking on health, from the following alleged sources: The Surgeon General's Report on Smoking and Health (high-credibility source); a *Life* magazine article (moderate-credibility source); and an advertisement by the American Tobacco Company (low-credibility source). With increased credibility, there was greater agreement with the information contained in the communication.

In a similar way, subjects were exposed to arguments about "How much power should Portuguese prosecutors and police possess in dealing with criminals?" The arguments, advocating more or less power, were presented by either a prosecuting attorney (high-prestige source) or by a criminal, "Joe the Shoulder" (low-prestige source). Regardless of their respective prestige, both sources gained equal credibility when they advocated positions opposed to their own interests.

The third communication dealt with the tripling of truck-license fees. When the subjects were told that this speech had been given to a group of railwaymen, they agreed less with the communicator than when they were told that the speech had been given to long-haul truck drivers. The implication is that there is less suspicion about the motives of a communicator about to embark on an unpopular course; or he may be admired merely for his courage. In either case, his credibility and effectiveness as a persuader increase considerably.

ZAGORA AND HARTER (1966)
WALSTER, ARONSON, AND ABRAHAMS (1966)
MILLS AND JELLISON (1967)

Source Attractiveness. More subjective and personal attributes of the source of a persuasive argument may also affect its influence upon an audience's attitudes. Admiration, personal attraction, and identification with a source of communication may tend to make an audience more receptive to his arguments, regardless of his actual credibility. Much contemporary advertising is based on prestige identification of the

product with admired and liked public figures. Sports heroes whose sophistication with respect to detailed merits of various razor blades, cigarettes, medications, or foods may be highly limited are nevertheless wooed elaborately by advertisers to gain their endorsement of products. California political candidates who have been movie stars themselves have capitalized on that image to solicit voter support. Thus personal attractiveness of a source of propaganda may enable him to be more effective both in gaining the attention of an audience as well as in communicating a persuasive argument successfully.

The bulk of the experimental evidence suggests that there is indeed an increased persuasive impact when the communicator is perceived by people as attractive, or as similar to themselves—and hence attractive (Tannenbaum, 1956; Cohn, Yee, & Brown, 1961; Newcomb, 1961; Stotland, Zander, & Natsoulas, 1961; Dabbs, 1964; Brock, 1965; Mills & Jellison, 1968). On occasions, however, there are situational factors that can overcome the impact of the communicator's perceived attractiveness. A person may listen to a communicator and then decide to comply with the latter's request. If he volunteers to comply he may also experience cognitive dissonance because he now finds himself committed due to his own "fault." To reduce this dissonance, he can adopt a more favorable attitude toward the communicator, the communication, or both. In general, the change is toward greater acceptance of the communication. Because dissonance is presumably greater when one complies with a request by an unattractive rather than by an attractive communicator, the attitude change induced by the former is greater than that by the latter. For example, college students and Army reservists who were persuaded to eat unattractive food (grasshoppers) and complied with the request showed a more favorable attitude toward eating grasshoppers when the persuader was unattractive, than when he was attractive (Zimbardo, Weisenberg, Firestone, & Levy, 1965).

"Sourceless" Communications. The American public often reacts to the somewhat impersonal printed media as "sourceless" communications, accepting newspaper information as free of contaminating bias from human intervention in reporting, editing, or copy layout. Some readers may draw sharp distinctions between the credibility of items on the editorial page or under the by-line of a syndicated columnist, as compared to front page unsigned news items, but many do not. Radio and television, as more immediate communication media, are especially subject to the influence of source characteristics on their effectiveness as propaganda channels. During World War II the radio voice of H. V. Kaltenborn inspired the trust and confidence of millions—even without visual presence—and gained their susceptibility to his influence in presenting not only information but opinion as well. With added visual presence, TV also evolved its "heroes of information" (Huntley, Brinkley, Cronkite, and others), but in general it appears that the viewing and listening public have become far more cynical about the integrity and credibility of the heroes of the mass media in the 1970s.

In mass audiences public opinion is often shaped through chained series of successive influences. Katz and Lazarsfeld (1955) have described a *two-step hypothesis* of opinion flow that suggests that mass media exert their greatest influence on the public indirectly. The mass media sources themselves influence the opinion of key individuals in each community subsegment of the population (step one), who in turn function as opinion leaders and exert influence on the opinions of their friends, colleagues, and admirers (step two). These community opinion leaders are generally people of high status, and their presence as familiar figures at local levels of social organization permits them to be more effective in shaping audience opinion than the relatively impersonal mass media sources could otherwise be.

Assimilation, Contrast, and Intensity

The investigations of a number of psychologists have shown that the same objective event may not be perceived by all people in the same way. The perception and interpretation of events may depend on what is going on in the background (described earlier in this chapter). During the 1950s the attention of several investigators became focused on the role of such factors in propaganda. Several studies found that a middle-of-the-road argument may be perceived as an extremely pro argument if one has just listened to a contrasting anti argument, or vice versa. People tend to exaggerate the difference between their own attitudinal position and that of others communicating with them when there is considerable discrepancy between their positions (*contrast effect*); on the other hand, people often minimize perceived differences between their own position and that of others when their positions are initially similar to one another (*assimilation effect*).

Obviously, propaganda arguments that are very near to an individual's original attitudinal position will produce relatively little shift in his attitude because assimilation effects obviate any need for change. More discrepant arguments may produce greater shifts in attitude. However, great discrepancies that produce strong contrast effects may lead the recipient to reject the persuasive argument as so extreme and far-fetched as to be completely incredible, resulting in failure of the propaganda attempt (Hovland & Pritzker, 1957). Highly discrepant attitudes may lead the recipient of propaganda to reject the source of an argument personally, thereby destroying the effectiveness of the influence attempt. Because the frames of reference and adaptation levels that anchor the attitudes of individuals are varied and unpredictable, there can be no truly objectively defined middle-of-the-road argument. Everyone tends to see the middle in a slightly different place.

Although the intensity characteristics of attitudes are difficult to study scientifically, there is general evidence that the relationship between attitudinal position and attitudinal intensity is U-shaped. Extremeness in any direction, either pro or con, tends to be associated with more intense feeling and conviction about the issue. In general, moderate attitudes and middle-of-the-road positions tend to be held with much less tenacity. Of course this relationship is not necessarily true of all attitudinal dimensions. For example, on a continuum of racial attitudes ranging from extreme "white supremacy" to extreme "black supremacy," many individuals may hold with great intensity and conviction to the opinion that egalitarian black-white social relationships are more desirable. In general, however, middle-of-the-road positions often characterize individuals who are either uninformed about or uninterested in the particular attitudinal issue being considered. Thus people who hold moderate positions are normally more susceptible to propaganda attempts in either direction than are people with extreme attitudes. And regardless of the content characteristics of the attitude, greater intensity of conviction is associated with greater resistance to propaganda (Tannenbaum, 1956). Artificial limits are also placed on individuals who hold extreme attitudes: a dedicated member of the Ku Klux Klan is unlikely to shift his attitude much in response to racist propaganda urging attitudes of white supremacy because his attitude may already be about as far in that direction as it can go. These limits, of course, represent merely methodological artifacts as a consequence of the ways attitudes are measured.

Boomerang Effects

Occasionally, persuasive communications induce an unexpected reversal in attitude shift in a direction opposite to that intended (*boomerang effect*). These backlashes are especially likely to occur when individuals are coerced by external forces into direct contact with the object of a negative attitude (Mussen, 1950) or when attempts are made to produce sudden and dramatic changes in extreme attitudes. Great discrepancies between an attitudinal position presented in propaganda and that of the audience may produce contrast effects and subsequent rejection of both the source and the content of the argument (Whittaker, 1965b). Extremely negative reactions to the source of a persuasive communication, whether in terms of rejecting his credibility, or in terms of distaste and negative identification may also be associated with boomerang effects.

Sleeper Effects

Although the effects of a direct propaganda attempt in changing an audience's opinion are often immediately apparent and measurable, there are some circumstances under which evidence of the intended attitude change may not appear until later. Such delayed effects are termed *sleeper effects.* This delay occurs frequently in propaganda, but it is difficult to analyze its sources specifically. Hovland and Weiss (1951) suggested that with the passage of time the recipient of propaganda tends to forget the source more rapidly than the content of an argument. It is possible that the sleeper effect may be due to the slow and gradual assimilation of information contained in the original argument. However, it is also possible that the effect is more superficial. Sleeper effects are especially likely to occur when an individual must renege upon an earlier public expression of his attitudinal position: his own personal attitude change may occur somewhat earlier than he is willing to express publicly, especially if he feels that his associates have not yet shifted.

THE SLEEPER EFFECT: WHO SAID WHAT, AND WHEN

College students were given communications attributed to either trustworthy or untrustworthy sources. The communications, presented either as for or against a certain issue, used essentially the same factual material. The immediate effect was that 23 percent of the subjects changed their opinion along the lines advocated by the purported trustworthy source, whereas only 7 percent were changed by the untrustworthy source. However, a "sleeper effect" occurred after 4 weeks: there was a decrease in agreement with the trustworthy source and increased agreement with the untrustworthy source. The results suggest that with the passage of time, people tend to forget *who* presented the argument (the source) more rapidly than *what* the argument (the content) was all about.

HOVLAND AND WEISS (1951)

PERSUASIBILITY AND ATTITUDE CHANGE

The basic dynamics of social influence and power (described in Chapter 8) are applicable to analyzing propaganda and attitude change. Persuasive communication is merely a special case of the operation of interpersonal and group influence processes. However, there are several other ways besides verbal propaganda whereby attitudes may be influenced or reshaped.

Attitude Change Through Direct Experience

Because attitudes are in some measure generated through direct social learning as a consequence of experience with the object of the attitude, this process is also a reasonable route through which attitudes may later be shifted. An individual's attitudes often are modified simply through further experience with the object in question.

For example, it can be argued that individuals with negative attitudes toward blacks would adopt more benevolent attitudes if they had greater opportunity to interact socially with them. From this argument it should follow that school desegregation in the South ought to bring about improved interracial attitudes. Unfortunately, this result does not always occur, especially when attitudes are strongly aversive. As in the case of learned fears (see Chapter 6), avoidance involves the conditioned association of unpleasant anxiety responses to otherwise harmless cues, and forced confrontation of the avoidant individual with the source of this anxiety serves merely to accentuate the unpleasant anxiety response. Thus learned fear and avoidance may merely be intensified.

In the case of prejudicial negative attitudes, an individual is likely to be selectively attentive to events that corroborate his original attitudes and selectively blind to the contradictory new experiences that should bring about a change in his attitudes. Under such circumstances, direct confrontation with the object of a negative attitude may merely consolidate the old attitude rather than produce a change. Such effects have been observed in studies of attempts to improve interracial attitudes through forced integration of races (Janis & King, 1954). For many whites, of course, the opportunity to interact with blacks does bring about more favorable attitudes. Especially in cases in which negative attitudes are based on stereotypes derived from limited information and experience, exposure to black colleagues with common interests and values can prove to be a very effective means of bringing about a desired social change.

In general, when the issue is one in which the goal of a propaganda attempt is to produce a general mass effect, so that failures to produce the change in a few isolated individuals are unimportant, direct experience with the object of a negative attitude may be an effective persuasion procedure. But when the occasional individual failures are expensive, in the sense of producing a hardened core of resistance or a vocal and restless minority, this procedure can be costly.

Attitude Change Through Vicarious Experience

Attitude change may also occur through indirect or vicarious experience. Remarkable shifts in an individual's attitudes often occur if he can be induced to behave as if he held attitudes different from his own. Through playing the role of a person with

---

ATTITUDE CHANGE THROUGH ROLE PLAYING

College students were asked to argue, through role playing, for an opinion differing from their own actual beliefs. Subsequent measures showed a greater change in the direction of the argument (counter to own attitude) among the role players than among a control group of passive listeners to propaganda. A further experiment investigated the extent that such changes result from insight and information gained during improvisation of the assigned role. Under one condition the subjects were asked to develop and play roles themselves, whereas in the other condition they simply had to read a counterargument aloud from a prepared script. A persuasive message suggesting that students should be drafted within 1 year of their graduation and for 3 (rather than 2) years produced greater shifts of attitude under the improvisation condition than under the script-reading condition.

JANIS AND KING (1954)
KING AND JANIS (1956)

a particularly defined set of attitudes, one may often find that his own attitudes have undergone a shift in that direction. For example, taking a certain position for the purposes of debate (even when that position is not one's own) tends to induce a shift of attitude toward the position argued, especially if the argument is regarded as a good and convincing one (Scott, 1957). The effect is more pronounced when individuals are asked to develop and improvise their own arguments for the "as if" position than when they merely read a prepared script passively; Janis and King (1954) have referred to this effect in their improvisation hypothesis. In fact, this kind of procedure has even been used as a technique of psychological therapy, especially in connection with modifying a poorly adjusted individual's attitudes toward himself and his close associates (Kelly, 1955). Presumably the shifts in attitudes that occur under these conditions are due to a combination of factors that include exposure to new information as attention is redirected as well as a reorganization of the individual's own cognitive structure.

Persuasion and Cognitive Organization

Dissonance Reduction.   Because attitudes are basically patterns of cognitive organization, attempts to shift an individual's attitudes are attempts to reorganize his cognitive structure. Because the overall pattern of an individual's cognitive interpretation of the world around him is normally well organized, he will experience cognitive dissonance when disruption and deviation from that pattern occur (see cognitive dissonance theory, discussed in Chapter 4). Such dissonance is especially prevalent when the individual finds himself doing something that he really does not like. One of the earliest studies in cognitive dissonance showed that subjects engaged in a boring and repetitive task for a relatively small reward were more willing to say that they enjoyed the task than those who performed the same task for a large reward. Evidently the only way that the subjects could solve the dissonance caused by the fact that they were doing something unpleasant for a paltry reward was to state that they liked that task more. This change of attitude did not extend to subjects who received large rewards because they experienced relatively little dissonance in doing a boring, but well-paid task (Festinger & Carlsmith, 1959). The critical issue, of course, is whether the subjects were forced to comply with the experimenter's request. If they volunteered for the disagreeable task (as in the previously described grasshopper study by Zimbardo et al.), cognitive dissonance is likely to be high; if they were forced to comply, cognitive dissonance is likely to be low because the subjects can always shift the blame for their predicament to the enforcers.

Because propaganda often involves situations in which individuals are induced to express attitudes or opinions that are different from their private beliefs, it is not too surprising that many psychologists became interested in the issue of *forced compliance*. During the past decade a substantial number of studies have been conducted in this area. They usually involve the assessment of attitude change in subjects who had previously been induced to engage in counterattitudinal behavior, such as writing essays that strongly advocate an attitude they do not share, or eating unpleasant food. The results of these studies are far from clear-cut, but it seems that substantial attitude change is most likely to occur when a person realizes that he is personally responsible for the aversive consequences of his counterattitudinal activities. For example, when subjects were induced to write an essay suggesting that toothbrushing is dangerous *and* were led to believe that their arguments might result in the abandonment of a successfully operating program in dental hygiene, they subsequently changed their own attitudes by indicating that toothbrushing is indeed less healthy and that toothpastes are unhealthy (Hoyt, Henley, & Collins, 1972).

DISSONANCE REDUCTION OR HOW TO JUSTIFY ONE'S OWN BEHAVIOR

For the past 2 decades the literature and lore of psychology have abounded with attitude studies based on the theory of cognitive dissonance (see Chapter 4). These studies demonstrate that people will reduce dissonance (cognitive inconsistency) by going to great lengths to bring their attitudes into line with their current or antici- pated behavior. A major aspect of these studies is the issue of volition and commit- ment. People who commit themselves voluntarily to behavior inconsistent with their beliefs are likely to experience a great deal of dissonance—after all, they can only blame themselves for their predicament. On the other hand, people who were forced to comply under these circumstances are expected to experience relatively little dissonance—they can always shift the blame to the enforcer.

The following findings cover diverse topics, but they comprise merely a small sampling in research on the avoidance or reduction of cognitive dissonance.

Working. Workers who voluntarily accept a paltry sum for performing a bor- ing task like it more than workers who are paid well for the same task (Festinger & Carlsmith, 1959; Brehm & Cohen, 1962).

Playing. Horseplayers committed to betting on a certain horse attribute to it increasingly higher qualities (Knox & Inkster, 1968).

Studying. Students who have made an irrevocable choice between taking essay or objective examinations subsequently choose to seek out arguments in support of their choice (Mills, Aronson, & Robinson, 1959).

Shopping. New car owners avoid reading advertisements of similar cars by an- other manufacturer lest they may encounter features that are missing in their own car (Ehrlich, Gutterman, Schonbach, & Mills, 1957). Shoppers discovering that their brand product costs more nevertheless continue buying it because of its presumed superior quality (Doob, Carlsmith, Freedman, Landauer, & Tom, 1969).

Socializing. Prospective group members attribute the greatest liking to the group that puts forth the most obstacles to their joining (Aronson & Mills, 1959; Gerard & Mathewson, 1966).

Marrying. Young men with a negative attitude toward marriage who become subsequently engaged increase their expressed affection toward their fiancées (Brehm & Cohn, 1962).

Eating. Children induced to eat disliked food (which they usually refuse at home) increase their liking for the food when told that their parents will be in- formed (Brehm, 1959).

Smoking. Heavy smokers show the greatest amount of skepticism about the validity of reports that smoking is a health hazard (Festinger, 1957; Pervin & Yatko, 1965; Johnson, 1968).

Rumor and Brainwashing. Successful propaganda attempts often include active efforts to disorient an audience and to dislodge whatever cognitive order exists. Rumor, of course, thrives in times of crisis and disorientation. The widespread sus- ceptibility of individuals to illogical stories, unverified information, and embroidered fragments of fact that exceed the proportions of reason is accentuated under condi- tions that produce cognitive disorder (Allport & Postman, 1947). Extreme propaganda attempts often occur in wartime, especially when military prisoners constitute captive audiences toward whom intensive propaganda may be directed. Such severe propa- ganda campaigns are often referred to as brainwashing. By calling upon the array of principles of cognitive organization described in Chapter 4 and in this chapter, a frightening degree of success in total reorganization of an individual's basic attitudes may be possible. Schein (1957) has described a number of ways in which the Chinese Communists achieved this end. In general, security may be enhanced by familiarity of both physical and social surroundings; consequently, an individual may be made more susceptible to propaganda by removing him from contact with familiar people or familiar surroundings. Unfortunately the chaotic disorder associated with natural disasters such as floods, hurricanes, earthquakes, and the like tends to produce conditions that enhance susceptibility to rumor, hence adding to other kinds of social disorganization that cause increased death, injury, and damage.

Persuasion and Personality

Because the process of persuasion is basically a particular category of social influence, the determinants of an individual's susceptibility to propaganda or other attempts to persuade him to modify his attitudes or behavior are essentially those described in Chapter 9. Social influence on the individual is enhanced by social conditions that create ambiguous and unstructured situations or cognitive disorientation; respect for the influencer as a reliable source of knowledge or useful information; admiration for the influencer and desire to be like him in either values or behavior; and personality characteristics in the individual that contribute to lack of confidence in one's own ability or judgment, fears of social disapproval and marginality, or strong needs to be recognized and accepted by others. An individual's expressed attitudes and opinions may be influenced through the operation of several kinds of social power (described in Chapters 8 and 9). Reward and coercive power, as forms of fate or outcome control, enable a communicator to influence his audience's opinions, at least at the level of overt expression if not at the more basic level of implicit attitude. Expert power affords informational social influence on cognitive attitudes and opinions, whereas referent power affords similar normative influences. The large body of research literature concerning individual susceptibility to social influence contributes directly to understanding the attributes of people who are especially susceptible to propaganda and the circumstances under which this susceptibility is accentuated.

The transmission of rumor through an audience, with pervasive shifts in attitudes or beliefs as the rumor spreads, appears to thrive under conditions of perceptual ambiguity and arousal of motives such as fear, hostility and aggression, hope and wish, or simply curiosity (Allport & Postman, 1947).

Research on personality correlates of persuasibility suggests that certain kinds of susceptibility to propaganda are "content-bound," "communicator-bound," or "media-bound," in the sense that they are specific to influence on certain issues, or from certain sources, or through certain channels of communication (Janis & Field, 1959). However, there appears to remain a residual of general susceptibility, which might be termed "unbound persuasibility" in that it cuts across specific situations. With respect to this kind of general susceptibility, several stable personality correlates have been demonstrated. In our society, females are generally more persuasible than males (Janis & Field, 1959; Scheidel, 1963). Persuasibility is associated with authoritarian attitudes, especially with respect to feeling that it is proper to be respectfully submissive to any authority figure. High levels of self-esteem and regard for one's own abilities are associated with nonpersuasibility and resistance to propaganda (Janis, 1954, 1955) and so are high levels of intelligence (Carmet, Miles, & Cervin, 1965). Among children persuasibility is associated with nonaggressiveness and social isolation, at least for boys (Lesser & Abelson, 1959).

There also is evidence that the patterns of socialization and parent-child interaction in the developmental backgrounds of persuasible people differ from those of nonper-suasible people. Among boys parental domination is associated with persuasibility. For both boys and girls extensive parental use of physical punishment and deprivation of privileges in order to control and train the child appears to contribute to increased persuasibility (King, 1959).

RELEVANCE AND APPLICATION

In human behavior, cognition (thought), affect (feelings), and behavioral actions are interwoven and inseparable. For this reason, the concept of attitude is applicable to analysis of almost any facet of man's existence. The concept of *personality* is the psychologist's way of dealing with two basic psychological qualities of the human being: (1) the organization of behavior and experience within the individual, and (2) the uniqueness of each individual as compared to any other. The assessment of human personality relies heavily upon the concept of attitude, because many of the basic dimensions used to characterize personality are in fact attitudinal systems. Personality scales that measure such variables as aggressiveness, dependency, self-esteem, and masculinity/femininity (to mention only a few examples) are, in fact, measures of attitudes. Such measures are important tools in the study of both the normal personality and its development (personality theory) and the abnormal or pathological personality (clinical psychology). Exploration of value systems and their relationship to behavioral predispositions (especially those which involve anxiety and avoidant behavior) also contributes directly to the development of more effective techniques of psychotherapy and preventive mental health.

The manipulation of attitudes provides an immensely powerful means of controlling human behavior. Thus, the technology of attitude development and change affords a weapon the potential strength of which is almost immeasurable. For this reason, the study of attitudes and their manipulation was one of the first applied focuses of early social psychology. The manipulation of worker attitudes in factories was an important element in early industrial social psychology (Mayo, 1933; Homans, 1950), and atti-tude control was the key to worker morale and satisfaction as well as industrial pro-ductivity. In marketing, the manipulation of consumer attitudes controls the buying behavior of the public, exerting vast and far-reaching economic forces. Producers create products not only to suit the tastes of the public; they even create tastes for their products when necessary to boost a market (Packard, 1957). Political elections are no longer left to the untended preferences of the voter; preferences are created and manipulated with great skill through expensive campaigns that represent the most refined technology of attitude manipulation available to the candidates (White, 1960, 1973). Education—the dissemination of knowledge, ideas, and values through institutionalized practices—is one of the nobler forms of propaganda. Good educa-tional practice can be derived directly through application of principles of effective propaganda and attitude change (Getzels, 1969). Likewise, in legal practice, the courtroom lawyer may plan his strategies of argument and presentation as cam-paigns of persuasion directed at the jury. Even governmental agencies have entered the field of attitude control and manipulation, dealing with propaganda as a tool of war to undermine and destroy enemy populations while strengthening and consoli-dating domestic support.

REVIEW

1. An *attitude* is a relatively stable system of organization of experience and behavior related to a particular object or event. Attitudes include a *cognitive* core (rational

ideas or *beliefs*), an *affective* component (*values*), and general *behavioral* inclinations (*predispositions*).

2. *Hedonism* (the pleasure-pain principle) is the basis of analysis of the affective component of attitudes (values). If an attitude embraces generally positive and pleasurable *hedonic feeling tone*, it usually predisposes one to *approach* the object of the attitude, and it is said to be *appetitive.* If an attitude embraces generally negative and unpleasant feelings, it predisposes one to *escape* or *avoid* the object of the attitude, and it is said to be *aversive.*

3. Attitudes are *hypothetical constructs,* inferred from observed patterns of behavioral action rather than directly observed themselves. Prediction of actions from attitudes is usually general rather than specific; precise acts may not be predictable, but the general direction of one's course of action is predictable.

4. Attitudes, values, and motivation are closely interrelated in human behavior. Modern psychological theory recognizes a general concept of psychological energy that is channeled into particular behavioral directions through learned attitudes and predispositions. Freudian theory describes psychological energy as *libido;* behaviorism utilizes a similar concept of *general drive;* cognitive theory attributes general motivating properties to *cognitive dissonance;* and humanistic positions recognize the same qualities in the drive for *self-actualization.*

5. Some motivational predispositions are unlearned and biological in origin (*biogenic motives*), whereas others are learned and experiential in origin (*sociogenic motives*).

6. An important quality of human motivation is the capacity for *psychological delay* —the *delay of gratification syndrome* (*DGS*). This refers to the ability to suspend immediate gratification and await more remote delayed goals.

7. *Pain* arouses a basic affective state called *fear* and instigates *escape* behavior through direct *unlearned* mechanisms. A parallel exists in *learned* behavior; originally neutral objects and events, when associated with pain and distress, may come to evoke a fear-like affective state called *anxiety,* which in turn instigates *avoidance.* Avoidant behavior resists elimination through further learning because it supports itself through the reinforcement of reducing the anxiety that instigated it.

8. *Conflict* results when incompatible attitudinal systems operate at the same time. *Approach-approach* conflict occurs when two appetitive systems are incompatible; *avoidance-avoidance* conflict occurs when two aversive systems are incompatible. An *approach-avoidance* conflict occurs when an appetitive attitude and an aversive attitude simultaneously embrace the same behavioral action.

9. *Propaganda* is a term used to describe any effort to manipulate and control attitudes.

10. Successful propaganda depends first upon the *arousal* of the target audience, and it may use techniques that play on *reason, emotion,* or both together.

11. The effectiveness of a propaganda campaign depends on whether or not clear *conclusions* are drawn for the listener, whether the argument is *one-sided* or *two-sided,* and the order in which various arguments are heard by the listener.

12. The *source* of propaganda is an important factor in whether attitudes will be changed successfully. Both *rational credibility* as well as *personal attractiveness* may influence one's success as an agent of propaganda.

13. Sometimes propaganda effects fail to produce desired outcomes; a *boomerang effect* is a backlash of counterreaction in the direction opposite the propaganda attempt.

14. Under some circumstances, the intended effects of attitude change may remain dormant for some time, revealing themselves at a later time; this is called a *sleeper effect.*

15. Sometimes clever early propaganda can "immunize" a listener against possible later attempts by other propagandists; this is called *counterpropaganda.*

16. Attitudes may be developed and changed either through *direct* or through *vicarious* experience.

17. *Persuasibility* refers to the individual personality characteristic of susceptibility to propaganda. It is related to one's state of cognitive organization, relationship to the source of propaganda, self concept, and socialization history.

6

CULTURE AND SOCIALIZATION

Every group, society, or social system controls the behavior of its members through standards, norms, and "rules of conduct." Their purpose is to maintain continued stable existence of the social system. Many of these controls produce uniformity among members of the society, but some maintain appropriate diversity, as in the case of differing standards for males and females. These control functions become vital to the continued existence of the society, and there are several means of enforcing them.

Socialization represents the society's way of achieving this control over the individual. The practices involved in the social training of the individual as he is assimilated into a social system are articulated and interwoven. Socialization is basically a conservative process (in that it encourages uniformity and discourages innovation or change from the traditional), but it is not a static process. Societies are dynamic systems that change with time. The relationship between the individual and his society is one of give and take; and it is variation in the behavior of individual members that eventually produces changes in a society. But the general direction of socialization within any society tends toward the conservation and maintenance of that social system.

There is hardly an area of the individual's behavior and experience that escapes at least some degree of social control. The values and goals that direct his behavior are in many cases socially learned, and the kinds of behavior that he comes to adopt habitually as ways of satisfying needs and attaining goals are largely shaped by socialization (Chapter 4). The manner in which he organizes his conceptual experience and understanding of his world, and the symbols of language he uses to represent his ideas and to communicate them to others are taught to him through socialization (Chapter 4). Even his recognition and evaluation of himself are socialized (Chapter 7).

The integrated set of standards and conventions that define socialization within a particular society essentially summarizes its *culture.* These standards vary considerably from one society to another. Certain standards of behavior accepted by the majority of members of a society may be explicit and formal; others, however, may remain implicit and informal. *Laws* or statutes are formalized standards that provide for punishment for acts that violate the society's best interests. Other standards, however, remain informal and implicit as *customs, traditions,* or *folkways.* These standardized rules of conduct, both formal and informal, are called *social sanctions.* They include standards for reward of socially condoned behavior (positive sanctions) as well as for punishment of socially unacceptable behavior (negative sanctions). The term *taboo* is used by anthropologists to describe rather stringently enforced negative sanctions, usually those that have to do with activities that are especially threatening to the stability of the society.

Cultural anthropologists and psychologists both study socialization and culture. Anthropologists usually focus on the culture, describing and comparing different cultures. In contrast, psychologists usually focus on the individual, describing the processes of learning and adaptation that go on in socialization. As in many other areas of investigation, collaboration among different kinds of social scientists is particularly useful. Exchanges of data and ideas among disciplines such as sociology, anthropology, psychology, and even history and political science, enable each discipline to see its own problems in better perspective. But these interdisciplinary efforts do not necessarily obscure the fact that the particular interests of each discipline are different.

Scientific study of the socialization process is not as easy as one might think at first glance. Any reasonably well-adjusted adult (and most scientists do fit that description) is likely to take his own socialization and that of his associates for granted. He is likely to assume that uniformities of behavior among the people he knows are simply inherent natural characteristics of man. However, even casual ex-

posure to members of other cultures quickly brings into focus the fact that different **109**
cultures produce different kinds of typical adults. For this reason, the cross-cultural
Culture and
Socialization
approach to psychological investigation is especially well suited for the study of
socialization.

Another approach to the study of socialization might be to compare the characteristics of man before and after he is socialized. Practically, however, this is impossible. In human development socialization is embedded in a matrix of physiological maturation (changes in behavior that are a function of growth rather than of learning), which complicates the study of social learning as such. Furthermore, cases of physically mature individuals who have not been at least partially socialized simply do not occur. On several occasions, investigators have been led to believe that reported cases of *feral men* (unsocialized savages) might provide keys to the essential nature of man without the effects of socialization. But such reports have usually proved to be hoaxes. The legend of Romulus and Remus, the founders of Rome, who were reared from infancy by a wolf, as well as the many other stories of savage children reared by jungle animals, remain only legends. However, from time to time, abnormal conditions that distort or impede normal socialization do occur. For example, K. Davis (1947) reported in detail the case of a little girl named Isabelle who was discovered after having been reared in isolation by a deaf-mute mother for the first 6 years of her life. Although such cases do not directly reveal the state of wholly unsocialized man, they are like cross-cultural investigations in that they permit the comparison of normal patterns of socialization with unusual or atypical ones.

Thus, because the ideal conditions for studying socialization simply do not occur, the methods of investigation that have been utilized to gain psychological knowledge of this aspect of human behavior are derived primarily from three sources: comparative studies of the behavior of members of different cultures, studies of the normal patterns of psychological development within a particular culture, and studies of individual cases of abnormal or impeded socialization.

SOCIALIZATION: LEARNING AND CONTROL

The term *socialization* refers to the sequence of social learning experiences that result in the integration of the individual into a society. One might describe and analyze the socialization process with respect to an individual's assimilation into a particular group. For example, the introduction of a child to a new group of playmates when he enters a new school, or the entry of a new member into a group that has already begun its work. But the term "socialization" is also used to describe the long and complex process of social learning through which an infant, during his progression toward adulthood, is assimilated into his society. Thus a major portion of the child-rearing process involves socialization, and the exploration of this area of interest represents a point of intersection between social psychology and developmental psychology.

Social Learning

The key to the socialization process is *social learning*. Psychology defines *learning* as any modification of behavior resulting from experience in the environment, particularly those modifications shaped by contingent rewards or punishments. The kind of learning with which social psychology is particularly concerned is any learning that occurs in connection with social elements in the environment: other people, groups, or cultural products and institutions.

Most learning is evidenced directly in behavior. Although a certain amount of learning involves cognition, conceptual organization, attitudes, and values, these changes in the private realm of experience readily reveal themselves in behavioral actions. Hence, we usually infer that learning has probably occurred whenever overt behavior changes.

Inasmuch as modern psychologists generally assume that human behavior is purposive and goal-directed, we usually assume that learning involves goal-directed changes in behavior. Thus the learning process rests on motivation and value: we assume that one must be motivated to attain some goal in order to make the behavioral adjustments and changes we call learning. Accordingly, psychologists assume that the consequences of a particular behavioral change (in terms of whether goal attainment is facilitated or hindered) are critical in steering the course of the learning process. This assumption is the basis of *reinforcement theory* in the psychological analysis of learning. It leads to emphasis on the reward and punishment consequences of action as an approach to understanding the learning process.

In simple terms, there are three kinds of consequences that can occur following any behavioral action: the action can bring the person nearer to his goals and facilitate goal attainment (*reward*); the action can put the person in a painful or distressing position that interferes with or is incompatible with his goals (*punishment*); or the action can produce no appreciable change and neither facilitate nor interfere with goal attainment (*non-reward*). These contingencies are represented schematically in Table 6–1.

Reward consolidates the behavior that led to the attainment of positive conditions or facilitated goal achievement. That is, reward makes a particular action more likely to occur again in similar situations in the future. Furthermore, it accrues value and positive attitudes on the part of the learner, and these positive attitudes tend to spread to the entire learning situation. Thus reward not only directs the course of accumulation of habits in the individual, but it is also the critical basis of many of his attitudes, values, and the situations he learns to enjoy.

Punishment deters the behavior that led to the occurrence of stressful or painful conditions incompatible with goal attainment. Thus punishment makes a particular action less likely to occur again. Furthermore, it makes the individual apprehensive about such situations in the future. This learned fear is called *anxiety*. Even though it comes simply from the occurrence of punishment in an otherwise harmless and

Table 6–1 The Reinforcement Contingencies of Behavioral Action and Their Implications

Action	Reinforcement Contingencies	Consequences in Learning	By-Products
Any New Response or Modification of Previous Behavior	*Reward:* Goal attainment or approach to goals (greater or more positive than expected)	Learning Habit Consolidation Increased Probability of Future Occurrence	Positive attitudes Positive emotional feelings Comfort in the situation
	Non-reward: (No change in status with respect to goal attainment or goal approach)	No learning Continued efforts to attain goals Continued exploration of alternative actions	No change in attitude or feelings No change in perception of the learning situation
	Punishment: Stress, pain, or displeasure; increased distance or incompatible situation with respect to goals (more negative than expected)	Avoidance learning Suppression of behavior that led to punishment Termination of efforts along related lines	Negative attitudes and emotional feelings Anxiety and distress Avoidance of the learning situation

innocuous situation, it may sometimes be so strong that the individual will go to considerable trouble to avoid risking repetition of the punishment. He may display *avoidant behavior* and refuse even to enter similar situations in the future. These particular qualities of anxiety and avoidance that are associated with punishment introduce a paradox of avoidant learning: punishment tends to cut the individual off from further learning attempts or goal pursuit along the lines he had been following. When punishment is intense enough to produce anxiety-based avoidance, the learner becomes so fearful of the original learning situation that he refuses to enter similar situations in the future. The very fact of entering them sets off the anxiety (including negative attitudes, feelings, emotions, and even internal stress states and such symptoms as nausea, sweating, or trembling) learned in the punishing situation. For this reason avoidant behavior that has been learned through punishment and anxiety is very difficult to extinguish and "unlearn" later.

Non-reward (absence of either punishment or reward following a behavioral action) tends to leave the individual in his original status quo with respect to goal-directed efforts. Being neither nearer nor farther from his goals, the learner continues his efforts along other lines, trying other behavioral alternatives. The nonproductive unrewarded behavior is abandoned, but the behavioral situation remains as attractive as before.

Differences among these various contingencies in the learning process have important implications for the management of the learning process in socialization. Obviously the reward of socially desirable behavior encourages members of a society to act in ways that maintain the stability of the cultural order. But the consequences of punishment are very different from those of non-reward. When behavior is ignored or treated with indifference (non-reward), the individual tends to drop those actions in favor of ones more likely to gain reward. But he associates neither positive nor negative attitudes with the occasion, accrues no anxiety, and shows no signs of becoming aversive to the situation. In contrast, when punishment occurs, the individual is likely not only to suppress the behavior that led to it, but to leave the situation completely and terminate his efforts or activities in that situation. If he is forced by circumstances to remain in the situation, he may become so fearful and anxious that he is emotionally crippled for all practical purposes.

To define what constitutes reward or punishment for a particular person in a particular situation is not as easy as one might think. The old saying that one man's meat is another man's poison is true. What is pleasure for one may be disappointment for another. Probably the most critical variable determining the difference between reward and punishment is *expectation*. The level of consequences that one expects to occur following his actions is the threshold between reward and punishment. If the consequences are greater (more positive) than expected, one experiences reward; if they are a great deal less (more negative) than expected, one experiences punishment. Thus, if one experiences pain when he expected pleasure, he will view that as punishment. But if he experiences pain when he expects pain, this may be viewed as nonreward. Moreover, if he experiences the termination or lessening of pain when he expected it to continue, he may view this as reward. Expectations are generated out of one's level of past experience, and they are very important in analyzing what constitutes pain or pleasure, or punishment or reward, for a person.

Agents of Socialization

Social sanctions may be enforced in a variety of ways. Certain sources of social control remain *external* to the individual and steer his behavior by means of rewards and punishments administered by others to induce him to adhere to conventional standards. Such direct rewards and punishments may be given either individually by parents, teachers, or other authority figures who function as agents of the culture. Or they may be administered collectively, as approval and acceptance (or disapproval and rejection) by one's associates and peers.

In some cases control is exercised through the promise of reward and threat of punishment from supernatural forces or in a life after death. Although these consequences do not become real within the individual's lifetime, if they are promised convincingly enough, anticipation or apprehension can operate very effectively to manipulate and control behavior.

Other sources of social control induce the person to accept and incorporate society's standards as his own personal standards, so that he controls his own behavior by administering rewards and punishments to himself. These *internal* sources of control include the entire process of learning motives, values, and attitudes (as described in Chapter 4), as well as the internalized desire to adhere to cultural standards of social acceptability and the exercise of personal pride and guilt through one's conscience. In general these internalized sources of social control are derivatives from experience with direct external controls. External controls are incorporated into the individual as his own internal standards.

In human socialization the most important external sources of social control are specific *agents of the society,* who relay to him its values, beliefs, and conventional standards, preparing him for assimilation into the adult society. The child's earliest encounters with other members of his society normally involve his parents, and they are the first significant agents in his experience. The child's interactions with his parents usually cut the pattern for all of his later encounters with other people, so early parent-child interactions are especially important. As the child grows older, he moves under the influence of other socializing agents (teachers and other adult authorities, as well as older children) outside the home.

These agents of the society provide two important kinds of training for the young person. First, they manipulate and shape behavior through direct *reinforcement* and contingency management (including reward, non-reward, or punishment). Second, they provide *models* or examples that demonstrate to the child the appropriate or conventional behavior expected of him by society.

Mechanisms of Socialization

Reinforcement of Behavior. The management of reinforcement contingencies by socializing agents is a very important force in the early behavioral development of the child, especially in terms of his later adjustment to his society. An agent who does not represent the dominant culture fairly accurately may reward and encourage patterns of behavior that deviate from social norms and conventions. But for the most part, parents, teachers, and the other critical agents of socialization have been trained to incorporate standard social values and beliefs, and to pass them on to the children they socialize.

Social Approval. Rewards and punishments for behavior may sometimes be administered collectively in the form of social acceptance or rejection. In our culture children are at first controlled primarily by parents, then later by teachers and specific authority figures. Then in middle childhood, the peer group comes to be a powerful source of collective control of behavior by providing models for everything from personal appearance and language to beliefs, ideologies, and values.

The derivation of approval-seeking motivation from early infantile dependency is an extended process in human socialization. In infancy, dependency is necessary at first (instrumental dependency), but may later come to be a valued end in itself (emotional dependency). Just being loved and cared for is its own reward. Thus merely being accepted by another person or group eventually comes to hold a certain value.

SOCIAL MANIPULATION

The "isolate" behavior of a preschool girl was manipulated by means of systematic use of social reinforcement principles. The positive reinforcer, teacher's attention, was given upon interaction with peers, and withheld upon solitary play or interaction with adults. Results showed increased social behavior through the rest of the school year.

ALLEN, HART, BUELL, HARRIS, AND WOLF (1964)

As affiliation with others becomes increasingly valued as the child grows older, the promise of acceptance is valued as a reward and the threat of rejection is feared as a punishment. Acceptance of a person by a group is contingent upon his adherence to the group's norms and standards (see Chapter 10). Thus social acceptance and rejection become very powerful tools of social control that enable a society to control the behavior of its individual members.

As one learns, through socialization, to become sensitive to the approval and acceptance of his peers, he gradually recognizes and incorporates their standards for approval and disapproval into a code of his own. This code becomes his criterion for self-approval or self-disapproval. In the same way, this code is related to another basis of social control: *social desirability codes*. These codes, which deal with society's standards for acceptable behavior, are rarely stated formally and explicitly. They nevertheless constitute a powerful incentive for the exercise of self-control and development of morality (see Chapter 7).

In some cases, when the child exhibits behavior that is not socially desired or acceptable, he may be ignored; he may gain favor and attention only by doing something that is culturally valued. Thus, a combination of reward and non-reward may be used to achieve socialization (especially in such areas as language learning, eating behavior and manners, or dress and appearance). In other cases, socially undesirable behavior may be the subject of strong social taboos, and may be met not with indifference, but with social hostility and punishment. The child's misbehavior may be punished physically, verbally, or symbolically, leading him to suppress the unacceptable behavior and experience anxiety and aversion about its future occurrence. Thus a combination of reward and punishment may be used to achieve socialization (especially in such areas as toilet training, and possibly dependency in boys and aggression in girls). In some cases, merely punishment for "wrong" behavior with no demonstration or reference to "right" behavior may occur (as in the case of sexual behavior for most children in our own culture). In those areas of socialization with which punishment is customarily associated, it is reasonable to expect a great deal of later conflict and anxiety in the same areas of adult life. It is certainly true that, in our culture at least, sexuality, male dependency, and female aggressiveness are all common areas of neurotic conflict.

Aronfreed (1968) has differentiated two categorical techniques of socialization according to the aforementioned distinctions. *Induction* techniques of socialization rest heavily on the occurrence of reward for desirable behavior, with non-reward (indifference) for undesirable behavior. Clear models demonstrating the desirable behavior are provided, and the occurrence of punishment is minimized. Socialization by induction cultivates a close relationship and positive affect between the learner and his agent of socialization, optimizes his feelings of security in the situation, and facilitates internalization of the agent's values by the learner. In contrast to this, *sensitization* techniques of socialization rest heavily on the occurrence of punishment for undesirable behavior. The desired behavior is treated as the expected minimal standard, deserving no special recognition. The models for defining and demonstrating desirable behavior may be ambiguous or even absent. Socialization by sensitization threatens the relationship between the learner and his agent of socialization, because negative affect, fear, and anxiety are all associated with the punishing agent. The agent, as well as all his values and beliefs, may come to be feared and avoided. Thus, internalization of the values of the agent by the learner is hindered and discouraged.

Aronfreed has suggested that in our culture the masculine role is generally taught by sensitization (i.e., little boys are taught to avoid being feminine), whereas the feminine role is taught by induction (i.e., little girls are taught to be like their mothers). This is consistent with general cultural observations that masculinity is highly stereotyped in our culture, whereas femininity is more ambiguous and variable. Moreover, adult males are more likely to experience anxiety and conflict about threat to masculinity, but adult females rarely complain of threats to impairment of their femininity.

Sears, Maccoby, and Levin (1957), analyzing styles of parent-child interaction in toddlers and preschoolers, described another distinction of styles of socialization. They described love-oriented techniques as those that revolve around interpersonal affective warmth, emphasizing closeness and interpersonal acceptance in much the same way as induction techniques do. In contrast, they described object-oriented techniques as those that are depersonalized, revolving around nonpersonal bribes and tangible rewards as well as physical punishment and impersonal deprivation of privileges to punish socially undesirable behavior.

The effectiveness of interpersonal approval as a reinforcer to manipulate human learning has been found to vary as a function of characteristics of both the one who gives approval and the one who is approved. The individual who is especially sensitive to this kind of social control is typically kind and succorant to others, nurturance-seeking, humble, and self-abasing (McDavid, 1959). He is likely to display chronically high levels of anxiety (Crowe & Marlowe, 1964; McDavid, 1965a). He is also likely to have been reared by parents who emphasized interpersonal or love-oriented disciplinary techniques (Sears, Maccoby, & Levin, 1957; Aronfreed, 1968).

Rather consistently, children (and even college students) have been found to be particularly sensitive to social reinforcement from members of the opposite sex. That is, approval by men affects the performance of girls more than of boys, and approval by women affects the performance of boys more than of girls (Stevenson, 1961). In some cases it has appeared that this sex difference is more pronounced for boys than for girls, perhaps because certain factors obscure the cross-sex relationship in girls. The role of the mother (at least in our culture) is especially characterized by nurturant warmth, enhancing the effectiveness of her approval as a reward for children of either sex; furthermore, in our educational system, most of the teachers who act as agents of the society during early childhood are women. These factors would enhance the cross-sex effect in boys but would obscure it in girls. More specific characteristics of individuals whose approval is particularly effective in manipulating the behavior of others have been identified by Stevenson.

The effects of parent-child interaction on the socialization of the child, especially in terms of the reward and punishment of the child's behavior by the parent, have been explored at length by developmental psychologists. Extensive interviews of mothers of 5-year-olds explored by Sears, Maccoby, and Levin (1957) and the longitudinal studies of a set of children and their parents from the child's birth to his adulthood conducted at the Fels Research Institute (Kagan & Moss, 1960; see Behavior from Birth to Maturity, pp. 115–116), represent two of the most elaborate studies of the socialization of the child by parents as agents of the society. The specific effects of such adult control upon particular kinds of behavior in the child have also been explored (Miller & Swanson, 1958; Kagan & Moss, 1960).

BEHAVIOR FROM BIRTH TO MATURITY

A research team at the Fels Research Institute studied seventy-one children longitudinally, at regular intervals from birth to the age of 14, and again as adults. The investigation was thorough and carefully executed, using direct observations of behavior, interviews, and personality tests. Parent-child interaction patterns were assessed in the home by trained observers, and testing and interviewing of the subjects as adults were conducted by experimenters who had no knowledge of the subjects' earlier behavior as children. Of special interest was the stability from childhood to maturity of behavior that in our society is frequently associated with motivational conflicts: dependency, aggression, achievement, sexuality, and social interaction.

Dependency

Dependent relationships with a loved person were stable from childhood to adulthood in the female, but not in the male. Presumably because males are rewarded rather early for sex-appropriate inhibition of dependency, they experience greater conflict about being dependent on loved ones; in contrast, females are relatively free of such conflicts and they tend to remain dependent on ones they love.

Dependent relationships with peers and friends were stable for males, but not for females. For males adult peer-dependency appears to be an instrumental problem-solving mode of behavior rather than a consequence of need for affection. For females it appears that extreme dependency within the family during childhood satisfies the girl's needs for nurturance, reducing the likelihood that she will form dependent attachment outside the family.

The overall results indicated that patterns of instability in dependency behavior were more pronounced in males.

Aggression

Boys' aggressiveness toward their mothers and their dominance of peers were related to displays of adult aggressive behavior in the male. Aggressiveness in girls did not show such stability; in fact, girls who had displayed strong aggressiveness during childhood showed considerable "femininity" and lack of aggressiveness as adults. Presumably, such girls were subjected to conflict-producing demands for sex-appropriate behavior (the "well-mannered young lady" code), which in adulthood was expressed in acquiescence to the traditional sex-role code.

Boys' aggression toward peers in childhood seemed to reflect nothing more than a desire to practice the male role, but it also served as a good predictor of competitiveness as adults.

The results here showed a trend in a direction opposite to that of dependency behavior: patterns of instability in aggressive behavior were more pronounced in females than in males.

Achievement

Unlike dependency and aggression, achievement behavior during childhood was equally stable for both sexes throughout adulthood. Most subjects came from middle-class families where differences in traditional sex-role standards are markedly blurred when applied to achievement behavior. Nevertheless adult males displayed more withdrawal behavior and greater fear of failure than did adult females, presumably because boys and male adolescents are generally subject to greater parental pressure with respect to an achievement-related area—the choice of an occupation.

Two factors seemed to contribute to the high stability of achievement behavior: it is socially approved for both sexes and it frequently leads to status, acceptance, and personal satisfaction.

(Continued on p. 116)

Sexuality

Boys who showed opposite-sex-typed interests (e.g., cooking) and who failed to adopt effective heterosexual interaction patterns during adolescence showed strong inhibitions in their adult premarital heterosexual erotic behavior and high degrees of sex anxiety. Sexuality in childhood and adolescence was, however, a poor predictor for sexuality in the adult female. Opposite-sex-typed interests in girls (e.g., athletics) are less frowned upon than in boys. Among girls, too, effective heterosexual interaction patterns during adolescence, such as dating behavior, is a matter of opportunity rather than an expression of persistent needs. Moreover, heterosexual interaction during adolescence for girls is generally so anxiety-producing that frequently repression occurs.

It seems that in the adult male the adoption of *traditional masculine roles* in childhood is the best predictor for adequate premarital heterosexual interaction. In the adult female, childhood sexuality is of little consequence, and her sexual interests seemed to be primarily the function of her desire and opportunity to establish a love relationship with a man.

Social Interaction

Social anxiety in adults was related to feelings of inhibition and lack of spontaneity in childhood. The *high stability of social interaction* patterns for both sexes clearly demonstrated that *people* comprise a particularly relevant set of stimulus objects to which individuals react.

The researchers concluded that "when a behavior is congruent with the traditional definition of sex-appropriate behavior, it is likely to be predictive of . . . similar-appearing behavior in adulthood," and "when [such behavior] conflicts with the traditional sex-role standards, the relevant motive is more likely to find behavioral expression in . . . substitute responses that are socially more acceptable."

KAGAN AND MOSS (1962)

Supernatural Control. Standards of socially acceptable behavior in some cases are formalized by a society as ethical and moral principles thought to be enforceable by superhuman beings. Usually these are interwoven with the religious beliefs and practices of the society. But the effectiveness of these controls rests heavily on the individual's capacity to delay gratification. The *delay of gratification* syndrome includes two important components: the capacity to extend one's concept of personal time from the past into the remote future and trust in the reliability of those agents who promise reward at some later time. For a society to exert effective supernatural control over its members, it must generate both of these: extended belief about the state of the individual in the past and future, even including past and future states of being in "other worlds"; and unquestioning belief in the existence and reliability of the supernatural. Such "superstitious" behavior has an interesting quality similar to that of phobic avoidance behavior: it is self-sustaining. One who is anxious about a particular situation (for example, taking an examination) proves his belief that the situation is threatening (by actually becoming uncomfortable, queasy, and shaky when he goes to take the test), and thus reinforces his belief that test situations are terrible. Likewise, a person who has been taught to expect benevolence from the gods when he behaves according to their desires is set to interpret good fortune accordingly. When good circumstances follow the behavior he thinks the gods desire, he interprets that as benevolent reinforcement delivered from the gods. In the same way, of course, fear or dread of the threatened punishment of the gods may be even more powerful as a punishing social control. Not only may coincidental misfortune corroborate anxiety-based superstitions, but the very state of anxiety itself is distressing and

---

COALITION WITH GOD

A comprehensive study of 367 families revealed that social control via parental "coalition with God" (that is, a parent tells the child that God will punish him if he misbehaves) occurs quite frequently. Such "coalitions" were found to be employed by parents who were "clearly ineffectual and somewhat powerless persons within the family and the world at large" and who hoped to gain some means of indirect control over their children.

NUNN (1964)

---

punishing to the individual. It is consistent with this observation about human motivation, then, that most of the supernatural means of social control observed in various societies are more dependent on threatened punishment for misdeeds than upon promised reward for good deeds.

Anthropologists have described many kinds of sorcery-based means of social control in primitive societies, ranging from beliefs that particular individuals may succeed in placing a hex on one who commits an unacceptable act to beliefs that deities may visit misfortune upon one who violates a taboo (Schneider, 1957; Lambert, Triandis, & Wolf, 1959). It should not go unnoticed that even the religious beliefs of "advanced" societies often incorporate these same elements of supernatural social control. Fundamentalist Christian traditions promise fire and damnation for those who violate the standards of proper conduct. However, unlike primitive religions that depend almost exclusively on anxiety and threatened punishment in the hereafter for effective social control, the religious beliefs of the more "advanced" societies are more likely to emphasize the internalization of religious, ethical, and moral principles as standards for one's own experience of pride (self-reward) and guilt (self-punishment) (see Chapter 7). The *Protestant ethic* in our own culture, with its emphasis on personal guilt and the sense of sin, represents an internalized conscience-based source of social control rather than a supernatural threat of punishment.

Models for Behavior. In addition to directly rewarding and punishing the child's behavior according to socially defined standards mediated and filtered through their own personal standards, parents also provide models that children are encouraged to emulate. The child is urged both directly and indirectly, by several kinds of pressure, to adopt the same kinds of behavioral patterns displayed by his parents, teach-

---

SIN, SORCERY, AND SOCIAL CONTROL

Studies of devices for social control in various cultures show that early seduction and severe punishment for childhood sex results in fear of others, controlled by using *sorcery*. Early childhood neglect followed by severe punishment for aggression produces fear of punishing gods, controlled by capitalizing on a person's feeling of *sin*. Socialization practices that emphasize father-child rivalry for mother's nurturance produces personal guilt, controlled by appealing to a person's *superego* (conscience). Belief in *malevolence* of the supernatural is related to punitive practices in child-rearing because the child's perception of an aggressive god is compatible with his anticipation to be hurt (which reduces anxiety somewhat). Nurturant child-rearing practices are related to belief in *benevolence* of the supernatural, providing nurturant gods for identification and imitation.

LAMBERT, TRIANDIS, AND WOLF (1959)
WHITING (1959)

MODELS FOR SUCCESS

Black high school students were asked to interact with several adult blacks who were former slum-dwellers but had become successful despite the many adversities encountered on the way. Because of their similar background to the students, the successful adults (including a teacher, a lawyer, and an engineer) served as credible models for the students. The models were not only emulated but also provided the imitators with increased self-esteem.

D. A. SMITH (1967)

MODELS FOR VIOLENCE

A group of elementary school children viewed aggressive, action-oriented scenes from an actual TV crime show (*The Untouchables*) while another group of children viewed action-oriented, but nonaggressive scenes (track and field competitions). Subsequent observations showed that the children who had been exposed to the aggressive TV scenes showed a greater disposition to physically harm another child than the children who had viewed the nonaggressive TV fare.

LIEBERT AND BARON (1971)

ers, and other adults. Because much of psychology's scientific understanding of the learning process has been derived from studies of relatively simple kinds of behavior in subhuman animals, the details of such observational learning were not widely explored until relatively recently. (Chapter 9 discusses the mechanics of imitation and observational learning in greater detail.)

Children vary in the degree to which they are inclined to model their own behavior after adults whom they observe, and several recent investigations have attempted to identify the particular conditions of child-rearing and parent-child interaction that enhance this tendency.

Skinner (1953) has developed an analysis of operant conditioning that suggests that during the course of learning a brand new way of behaving, an individual's behavior is gradually "shaped up" by successive approximations that bring it to a level of maximum efficiency. However, Skinner's analysis of learning does not directly consider the role of models or examples as criteria toward which behavior is shaped. Miller and Dollard (1941) and Dollard and Miller (1950) stressed the importance of imitation and observational learning in the socialization process, but their investigations dealt primarily with the process involved in learning *to* imitate another person rather than with learning *through* imitation. Several psychologists have extended their analysis of learning to include the function of imitated models in shaping complex learned behavior, as well as attitudes and values (for example, Bandura, Ross, & Ross, 1961, 1963; Bandura & Walters, 1963; Berkowitz & Daniels, 1964). Such learning through imitation provides an important route for insuring the continuity of behavior within a society.

Although parents function as primary agents of socialization, the important role of teachers and other adults outside the home, as well as peers, must also be recognized. Especially during adolescence, older youths may come to be idolized as heroes and serve as agents of socialization. They provide models to be emulated, and their approval constitutes highly valued reward for the younger child. Furthermore, popular heroes, both real and fictional, may provide models for behavior that influence the youngster (D. A. Smith, 1967; Liebert & Baron, 1971; Eron, et al., 1972; Holden, 1972). For this reason, parents, educators, professionals, and even politicians, have expressed concern about the influence of television and movie heroes on the socialization of young people in our society, especially with respect to violence and

MOVIE MODELS

To study the impact of movies and movie heroes on seventh grade children, excerpts from a movie (*Junior G-man*), which included an upper-middle-class youth and a lower-class youth as central figures, were shown. Boys tended to like best and to identify most directly with the figure compatible with their own social class, whereas girls tended to like best the upper-class figure regardless of their own social class. The socioeconomic class to which a girl aspired to belong proved more closely related to this preference than was the class to which she actually belonged. Boys remembered more of the activity of male heroes (especially such sex-typed activity as aggression), whereas girls remembered more of the activity of female heroines.

MACCOBY AND WILSON (1957)

aggression. The evidence on this point is inconclusive, but at least there is a logical basis for assuming that the child's attitudes, values, and behavior may be influenced by the implied acceptability of the behaviors he sees displayed by acclaimed heroes. When these idolized heroes of the entertainment world provide models for behavior that are inappropriate for the child's own circumstances, the resulting socialization influences are neither adaptive nor appropriate. On the other hand, the same psychological forces probably operate in many cases to foster conventional socialization.

Deviation and Abnormal Socialization

An important consequence of social variations in beliefs, values, ideas, and behavior is the fact that concepts of what is normal and what is abnormal differ from one society to another. The behavioral scientist ordinarily is careful to remember that normality, like modality, is a statistical concept. It refers only to the "average" pivot point from which individual variations extend. In this pure sense, normality is an objectively descriptive term that should not be confused with standards of good and bad or right and wrong. However, any society (and perhaps especially our own) tends to regard deviations from its own standards of normality as undesirable in that they threaten to change the existing norms. In many cases, deviations from the average in one direction are considered less desirable than deviations in another direction. For example, the exceptionally bright, able, and creative person in our society is valued somewhat more than the dull, naive plodder. In any case, the concept of normality in one culture may often prove to be highly abnormal (or "nonaverage") in another society.

Despite the general tendency of the socialization process to produce uniformity of behavior among the members of a society, failures and distortions of socialization sometimes occur. The result of such failures is the production of an individual who is poorly adapted to his society. Certain kinds of maladaptation to societal standards may in the long run offer beneficial and constructive changes in the society. With respect to the example mentioned in the preceding paragraph, for example, highly creative and innovative individuals who, for one reason or another, are not socialized to accept the conventional standards of their society are sometimes able to bring about revisions of societal standards. Although there are many ways in which societies appear more tolerant of potentially beneficial deviations such as creativity and genius than of other kinds of deviation, the evaluation of benefit or damage to the society usually requires the test of extended time. Often it is difficult to recognize potential benefit when it first occurs.

Many journalists, and even some social scientists, have commented on our own contemporary society as one that cultivates mediocrity through mass conformism (e.g., Fromm, 1941; Riesman, 1950; Whyte, 1956). In the miniature society of the middle-class school, despite the rewards of teachers and parents for academic and scholarly distinction, students themselves may generate a code of mediocrity that decrees that the "gentleman's C" is a more socially desirable level of scholastic achievement than either failure or the distinction of an A. Despite these informal pressures, however, men of genius and exceptional ability nevertheless occur and are rewarded socially in other ways.

Behavioral deviations that are especially threatening to the society also occur through failures of socialization. There are, in any society, mechanisms for coping with failures of socialization such as crime and delinquency: formal systems of law and penal practice as well as informal standards of social desirability, respectability, and prestige. However, there are other, less socially threatening, failures of socialization that produce conflicts within the individual when he moves from one subculture to another.

Certain kinds of deviations from social conventions are sufficiently threatening to the stability of a society that formal devices to discourage such offenses may be instituted. Crime and delinquency fall into this category. In our culture, criminal offenses are punishable by fines, imprisonment, or, in extreme cases, death. Many psychologists and sociologists have proposed that crime and delinquency are best analyzed as failures of social control over the individual. However, one of the greatest problems in the psychological study of crime and delinquency has traditionally been the difficulty in defining these terms explicitly. One advantageous step toward clarifying the psychological origins of crime and delinquency would be to distinguish *asocial* behavior from *antisocial* behavior.

Asocial behavior refers to the individual's inability to control or inhibit impulses toward socially unacceptable acts that stem from otherwise relatively normal motivational bases. Such behavior is socially unacceptable, of course. It is a consequence of a breakdown in the socialization of the individual, resulting in his failure to learn or to accept socially defined standards for behavior. The individual fails to learn to regulate his behavior through the inhibition of socially unacceptable acts.

Excessively aggressive behavior may be considered as a case in point. Psychologists generally consider the impulse toward aggression as a fairly natural consequence of frustration (see Chapter 9). Every individual occasionally experiences frustrations of his efforts to attain his goals, but one objective of socialization in our culture is to inhibit direct aggressive assault upon the frustrator. Destruction of life and, in most cases, destruction of property are socially unacceptable in our culture. People are encouraged, through socialization, to inhibit this relatively normal impulse and to substitute in the place of direct aggressive assault more acceptable behavior such as verbal aggression (name-calling or insults), patient tolerance, or even sublimation of the aggressive urge into fantasy. But occasionally the socialization process fails to induce an individual to develop internalized personal standards or sensitivity to social approval and desirability that could inhibit direct aggression. Lacking internal controls, he can depend only on external controls to inhibit unacceptable impulses (Harari, 1971). The research on adolescent aggression conducted by Bandura and Walters (1963) revealed several ways in which breakdowns of normal patterns of parent-child interaction and other early socialization experiences result in excessive aggression among adolescent boys.

Antisocial behavior, on the other hand, refers to a direct and purposeful attack on society. This psychological basis of criminal behavior has been emphasized considerably by the psychoanalytic point of view in legal and criminal psychology (Aichorn, 1935; Bettelheim, 1950; Redl & Wineman, 1951). The individual who experiences frustration and sees it as a result of society's interference with his own personal objectives may be motivated to attack society directly. Or, in a more constricted

DELINQUENCY AND CONTROL

Delinquent and nondelinquent adolescent males were presented with a series of hypothetical situations that were potentially tension-inducing (dissonant). The perceived attributes of the other person in the situation were a significant factor in determining subsequent attempts by the youngster to reduce dissonance: delinquent boys responded to the other person's *power* to act, whereas nondelinquent boys responded to the other person's *moral obligation* to act.

Such differences reflect different standards, norms, and "rules of conduct" in the two groups' socialization process. For the delinquent adolescent seeking help, this suggests that therapists should act in terms of power and external control, using techniques that are directive, structured, and limit setting.

HARARI (1971)

sense, an individual adolescent may wish to express aggression against his father, and instead of doing so by means of direct assault, may carry out some act that he knows is socially unacceptable, with the intention of expressing vengeance against his father. The exaggerated rebellion against authority that is characteristic of many juvenile delinquent offenses may thus represent antisocial behavior. The adolescent "rebel without a cause" who steals cars, destroys property, participates in aggressive gang rumbles that involve bodily injury to others, all with no apparent purpose, may indeed have a "cause" that simply is not apparent at first observation: he may wish to prove to society that he is capable of intentionally violating its standards.

Although the distinction between asocial and antisocial psychological origins of crime is not conventionally made in court practices in our society, there is some evidence of gradual progression in this direction. The long-standing precedent for establishing legal culpability or responsibility for crime on the basis of the individual's ability to recognize right from wrong according to society's standards stems from an 1843 case in British law (M'Naghten's case). This convention, known as M'Naghten's rule, implicitly assumes that all crime is directly and intentionally motivated. However, a milestone in the progressive incorporation of psychological knowledge into legal practice occurred in 1924 when Clarence Darrow, in the Loeb-Leopold murder trial, argued that not only legal insanity (according to M'Naghten's rule) but even "mental disease" should relieve the individual of personal culpability for criminal behavior. Eventually courts began to recognize "irresistible impulse" as a basis for certain crimes. This kind of legal decision (for which there is now precedent in many states) recognizes the occurrence of some kinds of crime as a consequence of uncontrolled motivational impulses; in other words, asocial behavior. The "senselessness" of many adolescent crimes (petty theft, auto theft for brief joy rides rather than for resale, pointless vandalism, and the like) as well as the relative rarity of carefully planned crimes (forgery, extortion, or premeditated assault) among adolescents suggests strongly that the bulk of juvenile delinquent offenses may be asocial rather than antisocial in origin.

Delinquent or criminal behavior may also occur when an individual is socialized into a delinquent or criminal subculture. In the normal course of human development, both peer influence and peer reinforcement play directly constructive roles in the socialization process. The peer group functions as an agent of the culture or adult society, and many of the customs, traditions, and standards of the normal society are communicated to the youth through his contacts with peers. A healthy peer group contributes to the healthy socialization process.

However, in some cases socialization into an unassimilated social subsystem may prove incongruent with the majority or general social system. The youth who grows

---

DELINQUENCY AND THE COMMUNITY

Court records of 1100 white male juvenile delinquents provided information about social control, as measured by the success and failure of the delinquents' adjustment during probation. Failure on probation was associated with "dependent family" status (income from public welfare), one or two parents deceased, incompatibility between natural parents, parental techniques of child-rearing congruent with delinquent norms, and institutionalization during childhood. Community and institutional factors in failure on probation were: residence in high delinquency areas and commercial neighborhoods, truancy, and poor deportment in school.

REISS (1951)

---

up within a deviant minority society may learn an inappropriate set of values and standards, although the basic psychological dynamics of his social development do not themselves seem aberrant. The processes through which adolescent delinquent gangs operate are not themselves abnormal; they are simply distortions of normal group dynamics. Communication of skills occurs in almost all groups, whether this involves teaching the individual how to make a soapbox racer or a zip gun. The punishment of deviation from group norms occurs whether it involves ostracism and social rejection for cheating at a game, or rejection for "stooling to the cops." The rites of admission to the Boy Scouts or DeMolay involve relatively formal rituals that serve essentially the same dynamic purpose as the rituals of the urban street gang. Both may require the demonstration of prowess or achievement, whether this be through earning merit badges or achieving status by successful assault or rape. When the individual's peer-group society is not normally assimilated into the larger society, its influence in the socialization of the individual may eventually produce criminal or delinquent behavior (Reiss, 1951).

Lapses in the normal course of socialization and socialization into an abnormal subculture both may contribute to crime. In either case, criminal and delinquent behavior represents failures of normal socialization. It should be directly implied, then, that concepts of rehabilitative treatment of criminal offenders should focus on possible avenues of "resocialization," and that the appropriate means of crime prevention require exploration and manipulation of early socialization.

DELINQUENCY AND SOCIALIZATION

Over a 5-year period observations were made on the day-to-day behavior of 253 boys and their families. Twenty years later the criminal records of these boys were examined. Because all men were from relatively lower-class urban areas, a major factor in causation of crime (influence of delinquent subculture and tradition) was held constant. The effect of a criminal father on criminality in the son depended on other factors within the family: if the father was a criminal and the mother also was a deviant model, then regardless of the affection they bestowed on their son the chances of criminality were maximized; if, however, the father was criminal and the nondeviant mother was affectionate yet firm in disciplining her son, or if both the criminal father and the nondeviant mother were affectionate, the son's criminal tendencies were considerably reduced.

McCORD AND McCORD (1958)

In studying human behavior scientifically, psychologists have from the outset been particularly impressed by the fact that experience and behavior are highly organized within each individual. One's ideas, feelings, and behavior are all interrelated in orderly and systematic ways. The concept of personality is used to refer to the two major implications of this state of organization within the individual: that behavior and experience within each single person are orderly and coherently related, and that the particular pattern of organization within each person makes him unique.

This organized quality within each individual is to a great extent a product of socialization. The unique genetic makeup of each individual, as well as the unique sequence of learning experiences during the course of his development from birth to adulthood, generates a unique organization of his personality as an adult. At the same time, however, certain aspects of socialization are more or less uniform for all members of a particular society, with the result that the personality structures of most socialized adults within a society resemble one another closely.

Within a society, the socialization process involves a complex articulation of specific practices that systematically direct the individual's motives, goals, and values, as well as his habitual behavioral activity, toward conformity to the existing conventions of his society. As a rule, socialization is a conservative process, discouraging excessive deviation or innovation. The more tightly knit this articulated complex of training and control devices, the greater the tendency to shape all members of the society into the same mold. Such uniformity of behavior among members of the same society is typical at virtually all levels of social organization. Ordinarily, social scientists use the term *society* to refer to a very large and complex, yet organized, social system that embraces a large number of interrelated subsocieties, subgroups, and individuals, all of whom share a common body of beliefs, ideas, values, and practices. In the broadest sense, then, one would expect to find a certain degree of uniformity among members of such a large social system as, for example, Western civilization, perhaps in contrast to another system, such as Oriental civilization. At a slightly more restrictive level, even greater uniformity might be expected among members of the same national or political system. Similarly, subsocieties defined on bases of ethnic group membership, religious affiliation, socioeconomic class, and the like are also characterized by uniformities of individual behavior. At an extremely specific level, one could observe the uniformities of behavior among members of a particular Boy Scout troop in a particular part of a particular city. No matter what the level of social organization one might discuss, the same consequences of behavioral uniformity among individual members of the social system tend to occur.

Cultural Products

The term *culture* is often misused in everyday conversation to refer to the "fine" arts. To the behavioral scientist, the term culture embraces all of the products and by-products of man's activities. *Material culture* includes tangibles such as tools, structures, and other artifacts. *Nonmaterial culture* includes the abstract and intangible products of man's activities, such as his language, laws, customs, and traditions, as well as the design and artistic qualities (in contrast to the physical attributes) of his art, sculpture, music, architecture, and literature. The total array of cultural products of a society constitutes the social matrix in which man exists.

Cultural products preserve and perpetuate the society and are thus instrumental in the socialization process. By condensing ideas, beliefs, and values into symbolic form, culture affords transmission of these elements to its newer and younger members. The transmission of such ideas, beliefs, and values over time is described by the term *cultural tradition*. Similarly, the spread of these elements over a geographic

"KITSCH"

The German word *kitsch* describes the various forms of popular and commercial art and literature commonly referred to as "mass culture." *Kitsch* was perceived as a product of the industrial revolution that urbanized Western society, including the United States. Before the revolution, "culture" had been the prerogative of those who commanded leisure and comfort. However, when the upper-class monopoly of culture was broken by political democracy and mass education, the newly acquired reading and writing by the masses resulted in their putting up pressures to relieve boredom, resulting in *kitsch* cultural elements: vicarious experiences, faked sensations, spuriousness, and superficiality.

GREENBERG (1946)

THE VALUES OF ORPHAN ANNIE

A content analysis of over a hundred "Little Orphan Annie" comic strips showed that 50 percent of Annie's time is spent fighting for the preservation of capitalism in the struggle against communism, and in aiding small, honest, and decent business-men against young hoodlums. The other 50 percent of her time is devoted to helping the poor and the unfortunate with money from a vast treasure that had been acquired with the aid of a magic whistle. Annie's values were found to be identical to those approved or condemned by the upper and middle classes in America. Approved were capitalism, honest merchants, smart businessmen, people with "class" whether rich or poor, Santa Claus, providence, school, prosperity, peace, Horatio Alger, honesty, brains, going straight, curiosity, and equal opportunity. Disapproved were laziness, parental neglect of children, "bleeding hearts" who worry too much about the troubles of others, the belief that wealth is a sin, and those who become too concerned with great causes and crackpot schemes.

SHANNON (1954)

ACHTUNG! SHOWTIME!

A content analysis of forty-five of the most popular plays in both America and Germany during the relatively "normal" year of 1927 showed that the American plays were more concerned with love and personal morals, as opposed to social and political problems; their endings took place more frequently in contemporary rather than historical settings; they included greater flexibility and attitude change in the play's characters as the plot progressed; and they had a greater frequency of women playing the central role (who showed greater "femininity" behavior than the women who occupied central roles in the German plays). In general, individual virtue finally triumphed in American plays, whereas in German plays (where society rather than the individual was pictured as "responsible"), power and ruthlessness led to eventual success. It was suggested that the results reflect differences in "national character" between the two countries, and that the Germans' peculiar combination of politics and folk idealism was highly conducive to the eventual establishment of the Nazi regime.

McGRANAHAN AND WAYNE (1948)

area is referred to as *cultural diffusion*. In both ways, cultural products enhance the spread of a social system over both time and space.

The beliefs, values, and ideas of a given society often differ markedly from those of other societies. The reflection of such differences in cultural products results in identifiable characteristics of the culture of different societies or subsocieties. Even within our own American society, there are marked differences in the cultural products and tastes of members of different social classes. Because such differences constitute earmarks for the identification of one's membership in a particular social class, they tend to be recognized as symbols of status or prestige. This aspect of cultural variation has attracted a large amount of research interest during recent years as technological advances have made possible larger and larger audiences for the consumption of cultural products. (These implications of the mass media of communication are discussed more extensively in Chapter 13.) Such research has also furthered the understanding of the relationship between the attitudes, values, and behavior of the individual and the socialization system under which he was reared.

Ecology and Environment

Often the environmental conditions surrounding a particular social system operate to produce certain uniformities in the conditions of social learning and the kinds of experiences from which individual members of the society learn their values and behavioral habits. The nature of these relationships (behavioral ecology) has attracted the interest of cultural anthropologists for many years, and recently an increasing amount of experimental research in the behavioral sciences has been addressed to the study of ecological determinants of behavior. Members of cold-climate societies differ, apparently, from members of tropical societies; members of seacoast societies differ from members of inland societies; and members of agrarian societies differ from members of urban industrial societies.

An early descriptive study of a small town in Kansas (Barker & Wright, 1954) showed how physical and social environment are related to one's behavior. *Behavior settings* (describing the context of behavior in terms of time, place, and objects) include such situations as schools, stores, hotels, barbershops, hospitals, churches, theaters, or beauty salons. In each of these, specific patterns of behavior occur, regardless of the particular people interacting in those settings.

In the 1960s, man became increasingly aware of his remarkable adaptation to polluted air and water, dense overpopulation, cluttered living conditions, and excessive noise. The entire environment had become polluted with both people and things. Social psychology began to turn its attention more directly to studies of the relationship between behavior, cultural factors, and the physical environment. Sommer (1969), for example, steered psychologists toward the study of spatial boundary markers as determinants of behavior. Spatial arrangements were found to affect many kinds of behavior, including cooperation, competition, affiliation, communication, and both personal performance and satisfaction (Hare & Bales, 1955; Hall, 1960; Felipe & Sommer, 1966; Sommer & Becker, 1969; Aiello & Jones, 1971; Freedman, 1971).

ECOLOGY AND ACHIEVEMENT

Analyses of the content of educational textbooks and folktales in various societies served as cross-cultural indices for achievement motivation.

The economic growth of the countries was measured by various standard indices such as electrical output in kilowatt hours. Achievement motivation scores and economic indices of development in each of the countries were positively related, which suggests that achievement motivation is a factor in the economic development in a culture. Also, a greater amount of achievement motivation was found in societies where there was relatively little variation in cold weather (beginning with below 40° average temperature) than where there was relatively little variation in warm weather (beginning with 80° average temperature). In general, variation in temperatures was positively related to degrees of achievement motivation: societies that had average temperature variations between 40° and 60° showed the highest degree of achievement motivation.

McCLELLAND (1961)

PERSONAL SPACE

A study examining the effects of sitting too close to a person showed that people tend to perceive such behavior as an intrusion of their "personal space" to be met by such defensive postures as shifting positions, interpositioning barriers, moving farther away, or even flight (see Figure 6–1).

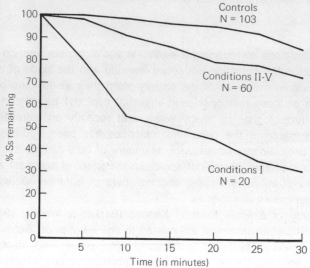

Figure 6–1 Flight! This figure shows what happened to "victims" in a study hall of a university library when an experimental confederate invaded their personal space. It shows the percentage of people remaining in the hall after condition 1 (maximum intrusion—confederate takes seat less than 15 inches from the victim), conditions 2 through 5 (four less intrusive arrangements), and control condition (no intrusion, observed person stays and leaves at will). (Redrawn from N. J. Felipe Russo and R. Sommer, "Invasions of Personal Space" *Social Problems,* 1966, 14, 206–214. By permission of the senior author and The Society for the Study of Social Problems.)

A study of U.S. Navy personnel in various degrees of isolation showed that the more isolated a group was, the less territorial marking of furniture occurred. Members of such groups showed a general maladaptive pattern and made increased use of their beds, displaying either withdrawal (amount of time spent in bed) or restlessness (frequency of getting on and off the bed).

Other studies have shown that cooperating pairs studying together prefer corner seating at a 90° orientation, whereas coacting pairs studying separately preferred opposite seating. The upper limit for comfortable conversation between North Americans was found to be 5½ feet, but Latin Americans prefer to stand much closer. Probably these preferences are acquired early in life and are carried into adulthood as facilitators or inhibitors of communication and social interaction. Studies of grade school children on school playgrounds have shown that middle-class white children stand farther apart than lower-class black and Puerto Rican children.

Sometimes a mere change of furniture arrangement can have a profound effect on people interacting in a particular setting. Observations of seating arrangements in homes, bus depots, theaters, hotel lobbies, hospital recreation rooms, and so on led to the surprising conclusion that much of the failure of these places to facilitate positive social interaction was due to faulty furniture arrangement. Among corrective measures adopted was the breakdown of large spaces into smaller, intimate ones (e.g., removing couches along the wall and replacing them with small tables around the room); the introduction of "conversation pieces" such as flowers and vases to create a homelike atmosphere; and the provision of storage place for books and magazines not in use. One study showed that the introduction of merely one conversation piece (abstract sculpture) greatly enhanced the amount of positive interaction among initially shy people congregated in a waiting room.

HALL (1960)
FELIPE AND SOMMER (1966)
SOMMER (1969)
SOMMER AND BECKER (1969)
AIELLO AND JONES (1971)
ALTMAN, TAYLOR, AND WHEELER (1971)
MEHRABIAN AND DIAMOND (1971)

The negative effects of polluted and overcrowded environments have also been shown. Sometimes these effects are rather harmful. Population density is related to death rate, infant mortality, suicide, venereal disease, illegitimacy, and crime (Schmitt, 1966). Urban living (as compared to rural) brings more hypertension (Scotch, 1960) and less politeness, trust, and altruism (Milgram, 1970). Yet some other studies suggest that crowding may not always be so seriously harmful (Freedman, 1971). Even pollution from excessive noise in the environment (from machines, aircraft, and automobile traffic) lowers frustration tolerance, impairs performance, induces illness, and upsets people (Glass, Singer, & Friedman, 1969; Reim, Glass, & Singer, 1971; Cameron, Robertson, & Zaks, 1972).

PEOPLE POLLUTION?

If groups in isolation are negatively affected, what about the behavior pattern of people crowded in relatively small areas? In view of the current controversy over the so-called population explosion, studies of the effects of crowding on the quality of social interaction have become increasingly important. A few investigators tend to take a relatively optimistic attitude as a result of their studies. One group of experimenters varied density by placing people in rooms of 160, 80, and 35 square feet. Groups of five to nine subjects were placed in the rooms and given various tasks (e.g., group discussion, crossing-out task, memory task). In the extreme density condition, where nine subjects were seated in chairs with a desk-type arm in the 35-square-foot room, there was just enough space for the subjects not to touch each other. Regardless of density, the productivity and quality of the output of the various groups did not differ significantly.

FREEDMAN (1971)
FREEDMAN, KLEVANSKY, AND EHRLICH (1971)

Language and Culture

The greatest social significance of language is that it affords a means by which ideas and experiences may be communicated from one individual to another. Through language, the experiences of one person may be transmitted into the experiences of another, thereby allowing the second to learn vicariously from the first without having to undergo the same experiences himself. Because languages provide symbols to represent conceptual ideas, they permit ideas to be *hypostasized*. This word means, figuratively, that ideas can be "placed out there." They can be brought out of the privacy of subjective experience, and in symbolic form they can be placed in a common domain where they are accessible to others. Verbal labels allow ideas to be communicated, at least to others who have adopted the same set of linguistic convictions as the speaker. This function of language permits the exchange of ideas between one individual and another, consequently facilitating the transmission of cultural ideas, beliefs, and values over both time and space. As a cultural product, then, language plays a crucial role in the perpetuation of cultural traditions over time, and in the spread of culture spatially through cultural diffusion.

Language and Communication. The term *communication,* in the psychological sense, refers to the exchange of ideas and experiences between individuals. However, communication between two individuals is possible only when both have adopted the same conventions for relating a particular graphic or spoken symbol to· a particular conceptual experience. Thus, in order for language to be a tool of communication, there must be *consensus* among individuals as to the semantic relationships between verbal symbols and the ideas they represent. The term *encoding* is used by psycholinguists to describe the process through which an individual converts an idea or concept into a verbal symbolic representation (a word); similarly, *decoding* refers to the process through which a verbal symbol is converted back to the concept or idea it represents. Thus, effective communication requires that the encoding process and decoding processes correspond. Whenever the same conventions for encoding and decoding are adopted by more than one person, they may use those conventions (language) to communicate with one another (Brown & Lenneberg, 1954; Lantz & Stefflre, 1964).

The essence of the complexity of human social interaction is the richness and flexibility of transmission of thoughts and ideas that man's highly elaborated language systems permit. Even the highest of the subhuman anthropoid apes do not utilize language systems that approach the complexity of human languages (Goodall, 1963). However, it appears that at least in principle, many subhuman animals do communicate. The terror cries and mating calls of birds, pack animals, and monkeys appear to communicate fairly specific ideas to other members of a species (Osgood, 1953; Zazzo, 1960). Among white-tailed deer, the lifted tail, exposing a highly visible tuft of white fur, communicates the idea of danger to other deer. There is some evidence that army ants may communicate unintentionally through means of odors from chemical substances they exude (Schneirla & Piel, 1948). One of the most elaborate language systems among lower animals, that of bees, has been extensively investigated by von Frisch (1950) and others, and there is evidence that fairly complex ideas with respect to nectar and pollen sources may be intentionally communicated from one bee to another through means of complex patterned "dances." Although such evidence establishes the fact that subhuman animals are capable of a considerable degree of communication, it does not necessarily justify the conclusion that the social behavior of the so-called social insects or the pack and herd mammals is fully analogous to that of human beings. The language systems utilized by civilized men are, without question, a great deal more elaborate and complex than those of lower animals. Thus, although behavioral science may look to study of the lower animals for suggestive leads about various aspects of human social organization, one must be cautious (and, indeed, such caution is warranted in all of comparative psychology) about making generalizations that involve direct extrapolation from lower organisms to human beings without full investigation of the comparative differences between the two.

Spoken and written languages provide the human being's most important tools of communication, but there are other ways people communicate their ideas and feel-

BODY LANGUAGE

The gestural behavior pattern of three groups—traditional Italians living in Little Italy, New York City; traditional Jews living on the Lower East Side, New York City (a Jewish neighborhood); and assimilated Italians and Jews living in "Americanized" environments—was systematically observed and recorded. The gestural patterns of the traditional Italians and Jews were found to be uniform but distinctive. On the other hand, such gestures were absent in both Italians and Jews belonging to the "assimilated" groups. The results supported the notion that expressive gestures that accompany speech have a cultural basis and do not reflect the basic "emotionality" of a person.

BOAS, EFRON, AND FOLEY (1936)

ings. Facial expressions, gestures of the hands, and bodily postures may all serve as avenues of communication (Boas, Efron, & Foley, 1936; LaBarren, 1947). A person's anger or joy or fear may be inferred from his facial expression and posture in large measure, although this "language" often communicates inaccurately and inefficiently (Pudovkin, 1954). One can make certain inferences about the mood and thoughts of a person who walks erect and holds his head high, but different ones about someone who walks in a slump with his chin on his chest. However, the postural droop and the long face may reflect either sadness and depression or fatigue.

Consensual meanings may also be associated with abstract symbols of many kinds. Most members of Western civilization comprehend the meaning of the cross, or the swastika, or the Star of David in more or less the same fashion. Flags are recognized conventionally as symbols of particular national or political groups. C. G. Jung (1939) stressed the communality of symbolic meaning for members of a common culture, and even proposed that certain kinds of symbolic meaning may be more or less universal among men. Most of the orthodox or "high church" Freudian psychoanalytic theorists subscribe to the notion that the symbolic meaning of various elements occurring in dreams and fantasies are fairly general across subcultural boundaries.

Furthermore, the arts provide elaborate media of communication. Painters attempt to communicate (through colors, forms, and textures) ideas that might actually be less effectively communicated through the more conventional vehicles of spoken or written formal language. In studying the psychology of esthetics, some psychologists have found that certain emotions and ideas are more or less uniformly associated with cer-

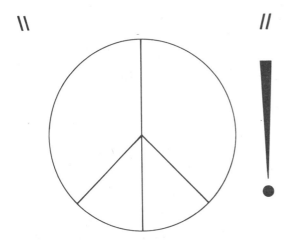

tain colors (Osgood, 1960; Winnick, 1964). In the same way, musical patterns, and even patterns of bodily movement (dance), may communicate moods and ideas effectively, at least among individuals who share a common cultural heritage.

Quite commonly, miniature socialization systems produce miniature language systems. That is, within an organized group, a private language may be evolved. Twins, who are reared in close association with each other and who interact with each other relatively more than with other individuals, may comprise a miniature society of two people. They are often observed to develop private languages of their own, permitting communication between them that is understood by no one else (Zazzo, 1960). Dialects represent miniature linguistic systems within a larger linguistic society. Occasionally, under conditions of social and cultural deprivation, isolated cultural pockets may develop, resulting in linguistic patterns that afford reasonably clear communication within the isolated system, but do not permit clear communication outside of that social system. For example, the middle-class schoolteacher with proper grammatical habits may simply fail to comprehend the dialect of the lower-class black child. Not only does the dialect of the American black differ from "the King's English" in its pronunciations and inflections, but there are certain ways in which unusual grammatical constructions are used conventionally (Baehr, 1965; Hess & Shipman, 1965).

Sometimes particular occupational groups evolve a jargon of their own that facilitates communication within that group, but sets the group apart from others (Elkin, 1945). The jargon of the American advertising industry and that of show business represent such restricted communication systems. Although the particular nature of their colloquial speech often changes rapidly, adolescents frequently set themselves apart from adults by means of delineated systems of slang and jargon. One particularly important function of the use of jargon and slang among members of specific age or occupational groups is that it serves to enhance the clarity of identification and membership in the particular subgroup. Esoteric and distinctive jargon, not fully comprehended by outsiders, is in many cases an important instrument for distinguishing the "ingroup" from the "outgroup." There are many ways in which speech habits may become important earmarks of membership in particular subgroups, and even, in some cases, earmarks of status levels within a social system.

Although linguistic conventions specify the proper encoding and decoding of words as symbols of ideas, they ordinarily focus on the specific denotative meanings of the words. The fringe of connotative meaning that includes subtle emotional and atti-

---

FRENCH OR ENGLISH LEAVE?

Idioms in various languages that reflect stereotypes were found to include American expressions such as "Dutch treat" (when each person pays his own way), "Dutch uncle" (one who gives instructions strictly and severely), "Double Dutch" (very incomprehensible), "fine Italian hand" (subtle and devious), "Chinese puzzle" (very complicated), "Jew him down" (bargain for a lower price), and "to take French leave" (to slip away quietly when no one is watching). The French expression for the latter behavior is *filer à l'anglaise* ("like the English"). The Italian expression *fare il portughese* ("do what the Portuguese do") is the equivalent of the American "gate-crashing," or otherwise "getting away with it." When a Frenchman prefaces his remarks with *Je suis un paysan du Danube* ("I am a peasant from the Danube"), he means that he is ignorant of the subject he is going to talk about. Chinese expressions of this sort are generally favorable, such as *mei kuo* ("beautiful country") for the United States, but the phrase *yang kuei tzu* ("ocean devils," or "foreign devils") for whites in general is still frequently used.

KLINEBERG (1964)

I AM ECCENTRIC, YOU ARE CRAZY!

I am sparkling; you are talkative; he is drunk.

I am beautiful; you have good features; she isn't bad looking.

I am fastidious; you are fussy; he is an old lady.

I have reconsidered; you have changed your mind; he has gone back on his word.

I have about me something of the subtle, haunting, mysterious fragrance of the Orient; you rather over-do it; she stinks.

READER'S DIGEST (1948)

---

tudinal overtones is often idiosyncratic (i.e., peculiar to the individual), and is not fully encoded into the word as a verbal symbol of the idea (see Chapter 4, Measurement of Meaning).

There is evidence that the connotations of words and idiomatic phrases are fairly uniform among homogeneous users of a language, but dialect groups may maintain differing connotations (Dennis, 1957; Bernstein, 1959; Klineberg, 1964). To convey particular moods or feelings, lyric poets and prose writers often depend more on connotative meaning than on denotative meaning. In fact, there are even uniformities of connotation associated with particular speech sounds (Williams, 1935; I. K. Taylor, 1963). Even in everyday conversation words are often chosen on the basis of their connotations to convey rather specific evaluative overtones. Whereas denotative meaning permits forthright communication, connotative meaning affords communication "between the lines." For example, when I am tired, I become "irritable," but when my wife is tired, she becomes "crabby."

The problems of translation from one linguistic system to another often bring into focus the importance of connotative meanings in determining an individual's response to information communicated to him. Transliteration permits direct substitution of the verbal symbol of one languge for the verbal symbol of another with respect to a given concept, but differences in subtle connotations often create misinterpretation of the idea being communicated. For example, the old adage, "The spirit is willing, but the flesh is weak," upon translation into German and back into English by individuals unfamiliar with the implications of this saying, might eventually become "The wine is excellent, but the meat is none too good." Such problems of translation quite clearly have serious implications in the conduct of international affairs and international diplomacy.

The interdependence of thought and language provides a reciprocal relationship between the individual's thought habits and the language conventions of his society. On one hand, his thought is shaped by the linguistic symbols he uses to label his grouped categories of experience; on the other hand, the conceptual habits of members of a particular culture give rise to the production of cultural conventions for labeling these experiences. The paradoxical reciprocal relationship between man and his culture is such that man simultaneously shapes his culture and is shaped by his culture. As an especially significant element of culture, language is related to the individual's cognition in the same reciprocal manner. Language is a product of man's cognitive habits, but at the same time, man's cognition is shaped by the language he uses.

Linguistic Determinism and Relativism. The thesis of *linguistic determinism* emphasizes one side of this reciprocal relationship. In short, this notion stresses the fact that *language determines cognition.* It holds that the concepts an individual learns to employ in organizing his experience are taught to him by his society as a part of the socialization process. Because of the stress placed on the relationship between lan-

IT SUFFERS IN TRANSLATION

Linguistic misinterpretations were found to have adverse effects on international negotiations among American, French, and Russian diplomats. The verb "to compromise" has two distinct meanings in both English and French, but the first meaning in one language is secondary in the other: in English, its primary meaning indicates agreement, accord, and adjustment and settlement of differences; its secondary meaning indicates exposure, embarrassment, losing one's reputation, or compromising someone. Because the order of meaning in French is reversed, "it is easy to understand the unpleasant reaction of the French when the suggestion was made 'to compromise.' " The frequently quoted remark by former Premier Khrushchev about America, "We will bury you," has been literally translated into "We will destroy you" or "We will conquer you," in the active sense of the English language, rather than as "We will outlive you," or "We will still be alive when you are dead," in the passive sense of the Russian language.

KLINEBERG (1964)

guage and thought by the distinguished linguist and anthropologist Benjamin Whorf (1940), this notion is often referred to as the Whorfian hypothesis.

Linguistic determinism is represented at one level by the fact that through socialization individuals learn to group their conceptual experiences into the verbal categories provided by the language conventions of their society. Innovative reclassifications according to other conceptual schemes become difficult, if not impossible, once one has adopted the linguistic habits of his own society. For example, the Indo-European languages (of which English is one) are constructed on a framework based on a primary distinction between objects (nouns) and action concepts (verbs). On occasions it has been suggested that this framework is quite appropriate for Newtonian concepts of matter and energy, but somewhat awkward in handling the concepts of modern Einsteinian relativity. Our language structure readily describes activities and states of being, but differs from certain other languages (for example, some American Indian languages) in dealing with states of transition or becoming. The effect of language upon thought is represented when verbal symbols give rise to a perceptual set or state of readiness that steers the interpretation of a perceived event (Carmichael, Hogan, & Walters, 1932; Kluckhohn & Leighton, 1946; Brown, 1958; Lander, Ervin, & Horowitz, 1960).

The reciprocal thesis, *linguistic relativism,* emphasizes the fact that *language is dependent on cognition.* Anthropologists frequently have observed, especially in the study of primitive language systems, that linguistic habits are closely related to a

LINGUISTIC DETERMINISM AND RELATIVISM

The contention that a language "is not merely a reproducing instrument for voicing ideas but rather itself a shaper of ideas" (the Whorfian hypothesis) was demonstrated by several examples. A comparison between the Hopi Indian language and English showed a relatively high degree of "timelessness" in the Hopi language in contrast to the "temporal" aspects of the English language: in English verbs are placed in different time duration categories such as past, present, and future, but in Hopi such distinctions are absent. The Hopi also call the words "insect," "airplane," and "aviator" by one word, a notion as surprising to us as our habit of combining "snow" into one class is to the Eskimos, who use a variety of terms for it.

WHORF (1940)

society's ecological and economic conditions. For example, Eskimos utilize a more refined set of differentiated verbal labels for snow and ice than do American Indians, who live in desert surroundings. The Masai tribe of central Africa is a primitive society whose existence is dominated by economic dependence on cattle, which provide food, clothing, shelter, and materials for medicinal and cosmetic uses. Congruent with the importance of cattle in the Masai experience, their language utilizes a wide array of different verbal labels for cattle, according to their condition and potential utility to the society (Merker, 1904). In the same manner, Arabs use a wide variety of terms for the camel (Thomas, 1937).

On a less elaborate scale, the language habits of various subgroups within our own linguistic community reflect the same relationship to the importance of particular kinds of experience. Among skiing enthusiasts, snow may be described by a variety of terms according to its appropriateness for a day of good skiing. Among racehorse breeders, the differences between a colt, a filly, a mare, a stallion, a horse, and a gelding are meaningful, although to one who is indifferent to horse racing, the single verbal symbol "horse" may suffice to encompass the entire equine world.

The dependence of language on thought is particularly reflected in examinations of the development of language habits, both within a society as it evolves a language as a cultural product and within the individual as he is socialized. Psycholinguists have conducted relatively little experimental research on the development of artificial languages (R. W. Brown, 1958). However, several studies of gradual changes in linguistic habits over time have demonstrated linguistic relativism, both in progressive changes in word usage that evolve as people use old words in new ways as well as in the introduction of new words into a language (Elkin, 1945; Ogden & Richards, 1947; Brown & Lenneberg, 1954). Although the phrase "hardtop convertible" was not in the vocabulary of American car buyers in 1945, the development of a new automobile body style brought the term "hardtop" into common usage a decade later. Although most Americans would recognize immediately the auto style to which this term refers, it is by no means "convertible" (to an open car), and the tops of virtually all American automobiles except convertibles are made of "hard" steel.

Because there are intimate relationships between language and other cultural products of a society, the impact of one culture's superimposition upon another is often reflected in changes in linguistic habits. As one society assimilates or rejects the culture of another society that has conquered it or diffused into it, it may either assimilate or reject linguistic conventions from the new culture. Following World War II, Japan was rapidly "Westernized" by the influx of the American conquerors, and there are many words and idiomatic phrases incorporated from English into the Japanese language. The conquest of the American Indians by the Spanish conquistadores brought about similar kinds of linguistic changes among the Indians (Dozier, 1956).

Despite the superficial implication that the hypotheses of linguistic relativism and linguistic determinism are exclusive alternatives in interpreting the relationship between language, cognition, and society, it would be unrealistic to discard either of the two. They are like two sides of a single coin in that each describes one direction of a reciprocal relationship. When one considers the relation between the cognitive habits of the individual and the linguistic habits of his society, the deterministic effects are most readily apparent because he is born into a society whose linguistic habits are already well established. These habits are imposed upon him through socialization, to some degree forcing him to "think like his society" and to organize his experiences into the conventional conceptual categories utilized by his society. On the other hand, when one considers language as a cultural product, the relative dependence of language structures and verbal habits on the experiences of users of the language becomes most salient. Language, cognition, and society are mutually interrelated, and in continuing interaction with one another.

PSYCHEDELIRIUM TREMENS

Remember when HIPPIE meant big in the hips and a TRIP involved travel in cars, planes and ships?

When POT was a vessel for cooking things in, and HOOKED was what Grandmother's rug might have been?

When FIX was a verb that meant mend or repair, and BE-IN meant existing somewhere?

When NEAT meant well organized, tidy and clean, and GRASS was a groundcover, normally green?

When lights and not people were SWITCHED ON AND OFF, and the PILL might have been what you took for a cough?

When CAMP meant to quarter outdoors in a tent, and POP was what the weasel went?

When GROOVY meant furrowed with channels and hollows, and BIRDS were winged creatures, like robins and swallows?

When FUZZ was a substance that's fluffy like lint, and BREAD came from bakeries, not from the mint?

When SQUARE meant a 90-degree angled form, and COOL was a temperature not quite warm?

When ROLL meant a bun, and ROCK was a stone, and HANG-UP was something you did to a phone?

When CHICKEN meant poultry, and BAG meant a sack, and JUNK trashy castoffs and old bric-a-brac?

When JAM was preserves that you spread on your bread, and CRAZY meant balmy, not right in the head?

When CAT was a feline, a kitten grown up, and TEA was a liquid you drank from a cup?

When SWINGER was someone who swung in a swing, and PAD was a soft sort of cushiony thing?

When WAY OUT meant distant and far, far away, and a man couldn't sue you for calling him GAY?

When DIG meant to shovel and spade in the dirt, and PUT-ON was what you would do with a skirt?

When TOUGH described meat too unyielding to chew, and MAKING A SCENE was a rude thing to do?

Words once so sensible, sober and serious are making the FREAK SCENE like PSYCHEDELIRIOUS.

It's GROOVY, MAN, GROOVY, but English it's not.

Methinks that the language has gone straight to POT.

CALIFORNIA FOLKLORE SOCIETY NEWSLETTER (1968)

Language and Socialization. As the individual is socially trained by agents of his society, his cognitive and linguistic habits are shaped, as are his motives, values, and goal-directed behavioral habits. The individual learns a language system as a part of his culture. At the same time, language provides an important tool for socialization, for without it, the complexity of a society's standards and conventions of complex behavior could hardly be taught to a young child during a single lifetime. Thus there is a paradoxical dual relationship between language and the socialization process: language is simultaneously both an instrument for and a product of socialization. This spiral relationship begins very early in the child's life as he begins to learn the language of his culture. Using linguistic tools, he is further socialized, learning greater skills in social living, including greater skills in the use of language.

The particular verbal symbols (including both the auditory symbols of uttered

speech and the visual symbols of a written alphabet or numerals) that become associated with cognitive concepts are for the most part taught to the individual systematically as a part of his socialization. In our linguistic society, objects that share the
common characteristic of supporting our weight when we rest in them are grouped
together under the verbal symbol "chair"; in the linguistic society of French-speaking
people, approximately the same conceptual category is related to the symbol "chaise";
and for German-speaking people, the symbol for essentially the same concept is
"stuhl." Although the structure of all three language systems is highly similar (all
are members of a linguistic group known as Indo-European languages) in that each
has a particular written and spoken symbol for this conceptual category, the specific
pattern of the symbol chosen to represent that concept is different in each. Linguis-
tically speaking, then, here are three language subcultures: the French child is socialized into the habit of utilizing the symbol "chaise," the German child into using
"stuhl," and the American child into using "chair" to represent this category of his
experience.

Studies of the development of language in individual children suggest that the first
concepts to be verbally labeled are those of greatest functional relevance to the individual. For most children, the first spoken word is likely to be either "mama" or
"dada." Thus there is evidence of an example of linguistic relativism in that the first
verbal labels are related to especially important or meaningful concepts for the child.
On the other hand, through socialization, the child is induced to modify his functional concept of "mama" as any nurturant, loving adult, and to accept the socially
prescribed differentiations of "Mom," or "Dad," or "Grandma," or "Nurse," or
"Maid." Eventually, he is induced to use the conventional words used by other members of his society to address or refer to these significant figures in his life.

Piaget (1926, 1952) has described the normative development of language in children and its related concomitants in their intellectual activity. He has pointed out
that the initial use of spoken language is largely *egocentric* in that the child speaks
without caring whether anyone listens, and until he is 5 or 6, much of his verbal behavior has little social significance. Gradually, however, the child's verbalization
becomes more *sociocentric,* or socially oriented. As he grows older, he is more concerned with using language to address a listener, to try to influence another person,
or to exchange ideas with others. Some psychologists (e.g., McCarthy, 1954) have
disagreed with Piaget's suggestion that egocentric speech is *predominant* in young
children. They argue that estimates of functionally egocentric speech in children
rarely go as high as 50 percent.

Inhelder and Piaget (1958) have described the intellectual development of the
child with reference to his verbal and symbolic activity. They point out that in early
stages of development, the child is inclined to confuse the verbal symbol with the
object, person, or event it represents. That is, very young children cannot recognize
a significant distinction between a thing itself and the abstract symbol that represents it in language. These authors propose that during the first 2 years of life (the
sensorimotor stage), the child displays minimal symbolic activity. Between the ages
of 2 and 7 (the *preconceptual* and *intuitive* stages), the child learns to label objects
and events, and his verbal concepts are concrete and are based on perceptual qualities of the thing itself. Between 7 and 11 (the stage of *concrete operations*), the child
begins to display logical intellectual activity, but it involves merely the application of
logical rules to concrete objects. Only during adolescence (the stage of *formal operations*) does the individual become capable of truly abstract thinking, which involves the manipulation of abstract symbols in thought and the capacity for deductive
reasoning and simultaneous manipulation of a number of related operations and
ideas.

Skinner's behavioristic analysis of the development of verbal behavior, which deals primarily with uttered speech and thus treats language as a set of behavioral responses, emphasizes that verbal habits of the child are shaped progressively by his experience in using them (Skinner, 1957). Systematic reinforcement, in connection with socialization, rewards certain forms of verbal behavior and extinguishes others. *Mands,* according to Skinner, are utterances that stem from the need of the speaker himself (commands, demands, and requests), and if they lead to reinforcement or the satisfaction of a related need, they tend to recur like any other rewarded habit. *Tacts* are utterances that refer simply to facts about the environment, and their reinforcement and recurrence depend on the reactions of others. Thus such agents of the society as parents, teachers, and peers are instrumental in manipulating the development of this group of verbal habits. In terms of Piaget's analysis of linguistic development, mands are more or less egocentric, whereas tacts involve more socially oriented speech. Because of the nature of his assumptions about theory-building and the nature of man (the *Homo mechanicus* model described in Chapter 2), Skinner offers little discussion of the relationships between language and the cognitive experience of the individual.

As is true of other aspects of socialization, the social training of linguistic habits is not carried out uniformly among all segments of our society. The verbal and linguistic development of boys and girls differs considerably. In general, linguistic skills appear to be somewhat more highly valued for girls than for boys, with greater reward provided for verbal accomplishment in girls (McCarthy, 1954). Unusual conditions (such as cultural, social, and educational deprivation) or handicaps (such as deafness) that limit the child's socialization produce clear retardation of verbal and linguistic development (Pettifor, 1964). On the other hand, enriched verbal and social interaction with adults, either through direct and intentional training, or as a by-product of membership in more privileged socioeconomic classes, may afford accelerated verbal and linguistic development (Irwin, 1960; Hess & Shipman, 1965).

Piaget's descriptions of language development have been criticized by some psychologists for their failure to direct attention to individual differences and variations in the socialization of language. Although Skinner's analyses of verbal development omit concern about the functional symbolic aspects of language, his work does direct attention to the effects of social learning on the development of verbal behavior.

Cultural Variations in Behavior

The fact that socialization produces behavioral uniformities enables the social scientist to utilize a concept to describe the typical product of a particular socialization system: *modal personality.* "Modal" means most frequently occurring. It is important to recognize this fact when utilizing such a descriptive concept. The term "modal personality" describes the typical member of a society, but does not necessarily apply literally to every individual member of the society. The socialization process is not "leakproof." Despite all its consistency, it still permits some range of individual variation. Although the concept of modal personality is highly useful for general descriptive purposes, it does not enable one to make very specific predictions about particular individuals. The concept of modal personality permits one to expect no more than this: if a single individual is drawn at random from a particular society, the odds are strong that he will conform in most aspects of his behavior to a descriptive picture of the modal, or typical, member of that society. It must not be surprising to discover that a few aspects of his behavior may be highly atypical of his society.

The concept of modal personality is closely related to the tendency of individuals to perceive one another in terms of social stereotypes, as described in Chapter 8.

People often make the erroneous conclusion that all members of a particular class or race or ethnic group are alike.

Furthermore, it is important to recognize that a description of modal personality does not *explain* behavior; it merely *describes* it. The psychoanalyst-anthropologist Kardiner (1939) utilized the term "basic personality structure" to describe the modal product of a particular system of socialization. Unfortunately other writers have occasionally used this concept as though it were explanatory. But to argue that a person behaves in a particular way because of his basic personality structure is to engage in the ridiculous circularity of arguing that a person behaves as he does because he behaves as he does.

The term *national character* is frequently used by behavioral scientists to refer to the modal personality of a given national society. That is, the socialization system producing a particular kind of uniformity is defined in terms of geographic and political boundaries. Quite often, of course, the actual limits of a social system may not conform to geopolitical boundaries: a society may spread across several nations, or a nation may embrace several subsocieties. Consequently, the term "national character" must be utilized cautiously. It is equally meaningful to investigate the modal personality characteristics of members of regional groups, occupational groups, or even groups defined according to their level of social and economic status within a larger society.

A number of anthropological investigations have yielded descriptions of the modal personality characteristics of members of particular national groups (LaBarre, 1946; Inkeles, Hanfmann, & Beier, 1958). Studies of the modal personality of the adult American are relatively infrequent, perhaps because of the complexity of American society and the fact that it is made up of a number of interrelated subsocieties. Despite the fact that the American society shares a core culture of generally similar ecological, political, and legal systems, there are great variations in the socialization practices and typical personality structures of different socioeconomic classes and religious and ethnic subgroups. It is rather difficult for the American behavioral scientist to assess the national character of his own society objectively because this would entail in part looking at a collective reflection of himself. Nevertheless, there are many ways in which behavioral scientists have contrasted various subgroups within our own complex society, affording information about the typical characteristics of individual members of these subgroups.

Cross-cultural Differences. The socialization process is instrumental in governing the particular behavioral habits an individual uses to satisfy his motives. For several

---

ADOLESCENTS IN INDIA AND AMERICA

High school student samples from northern India and western United States responded to statements covering a wide range of values. As expected from the clear authority structure in their families and society, the Indian adolescents attributed greater importance to deference, conformity, and response to external control. The American adolescents, as expected from the relative importance of their peer culture, valued sociability more highly. The Americans also scored higher on sensuous enjoyment, religiosity, and especially on self-reliance (often marked by a competitive fear of dependence and insecurity). No differences were found between the cultures in such areas as individuality, free will, and democratic values. In fact, both cultures showed four times as much commonness as divergence on the values under study.

SUNBERG, ROHILA, AND TYLER (1970)

SIX CULTURES

A group of social scientists from Harvard, Yale, and Cornell conducted a series of investigations on child-rearing practices, ecological background, economic systems, and political organizations in various cultures. Unlike previous studies that liberally employed secondhand reports, these investigations were carried out by highly trained on-the-spot observers who applied rigorous criteria to their findings. Six relatively unknown cultural samples were studied: New Englanders in Orchard Town, United States; the Gusii community of Nyasango, in eastern Kenya; the Rajputs of Khalapur, in northern India; the village of Taira, in northeastern

Table 6–2   Child-Rearing Attitudes and Practices in Six Societies

Child-Rearing Practices	Society					
	America	Kenya	India	Okinawa	Mexico	Philippines
Infancy: up to age 2 Parental view of infant	*potential for future development*	*instrumental to household*	*pure and holy* "God's gift"	*pitiable and helpless*	"*empty slate*" *no awareness*	*charming and helpless*
Parental response to infant's crying (hunger)	*demand feeding* (*most families*)	*demand feeding*	*demand feeding*	*demand feeding*	*demand feeding*	*demand feeding*
Parental response to infant's crying (discomfort)	*ignoring, regarded as inevitable,* "*good for character and lungs*"	*annoyance, threat, derision, physical punishment*	*pacification by distraction or use of opium*	*pacification by distraction or petting*	*annoyance, scolding, physical punishment*	*pacification by distraction or petting*
Infant's toilet training	*strict, praise or scolding*	*strict, physical punishment*	*lax*	*lax*	*lax*	*lax*
Early Childhood: ages 2 to 5 Availability of peers	*minimum*	*minimum*	*average*	*maximum*	*minimum*	*minimum*
Expected attitude toward adult	*politeness, no rudeness, no aggression*	*blandness, no aggression, no sex-play, little initiative*	*obedience*	*adequacy but without excelling*	*obedience*	*no demands no expectations*
Enforcement of socially desirable behavior	*strict, praise or scolding*	*strict, physical punishment*	*lax*	*lax*	*strict, physical punishment*	*lax*
Sex-appropriate behavior	*encouraged*	*discouraged*	*indifference*	*encouraged*	*indifference*	*encouraged*

Okinawa; the Mixtecan Indians of Juxthahuaca, in southwestern Mexico; and the Ilocos of Tarong, in the northern Philippines. Observations of child-rearing practices in each society (see Table 6–2) were compared to behavior patterns in the adult samples in order to support the investigators' hypothesis that "different patterns of child-rearing will lead to differences in the personality of children and thus to differences in adult personality."

Adult Attitudes and Practices

Social Control. Systematic observations in the area of social control yielded a rather uniform pattern: in all but the Kenyan sample, leadership was not identified with social control; apart from some outward signs in formal interactions, respect for leaders was solely on the basis of personal merit. Social control was manifest in group sanctions such as avoidance, exclusion, and similar indirect measures. The apparent reasons for adherence to group sanctions varied considerably from one sample to another, but showed a consistent relationship with the severity of rearing that members of each sample had experienced in their childhood.

In the American sample, where the enforcement of socially desirable behavior and toilet training had been strict, group sanctions were valued for their instrumentality: they punish deviant behavior such as lack of industriousness and lack of personal and home cleanliness. Adherence to group sanctions in the samples where enforcement of socially desirable behavior and toilet training had been rather lax (Okinawa, India, Philippines) was related to strong feelings of obligation and identification with one's group. In the Mexican sample, where toilet training had been lax in contrast to the strict enforcement of socially desirable behavior, adherence to group sanctions was related to strong fears of ostracism. Only in the severely reared Kenyan sample did leadership (rather than group sanctions) serve as social control: it had immense power and prestige, and its decisions were revered and regarded as ultimate.

Social Solidarity. Gregariousness, friendship, loyalty, and similar variables related to social solidarity were evident in all but the Kenyan sample. In the American sample, social solidarity was slightly more formally expressed than in the less strictly reared Okinawan, Indian, and Philippine samples. The permissively toilet-trained but otherwise severely reared Mexican sample showed a particular pattern of social solidarity: calculating, instrumentally oriented, and lacking in gregariousness. No signs of social solidarity were evident in the severely reared Kenyan sample; instead, its members consistently displayed insidious behavior such as suspicion, blame avoidance, and petty crime.

Religious Beliefs. Religiosity and statements of religious belief tended to be directly related to severity of child rearing. The Kenyan sample strongly believed in all-powerful supernaturals whose punishing intervention in one's personal life had to be pacified. In the less strictly reared American sample, religion expressed itself primarily in statements of belief in the infinite mercy of the supernaturals (God and Jesus), but statements concerning their intervention in one's personal life were only rarely encountered. In the permissively reared Okinawan, Indian, and Philippine samples, religious commitments (apart from some formal ritual of ancestor worship) were exceedingly casual. The Mexican sample showed a mixed pattern of formal adherence to Catholic rituals and lack of any religious beliefs.

WHITING (1966)

kinds of biologically based motivation, the mechanisms for their satisfaction are rather specific and automatic: breathing satisfies the need for oxygen and the elimination of dioxide, and the behavior involved in breathing is subject to limited voluntary individual control. For others, such as the elimination of waste materials from the body, the specific mechanisms are at first automatic, but social learning may induce the individual to inhibit these mechanisms temporarily, allowing them to operate only under specific socially defined circumstances, in acceptable places at acceptable times.

Food and Eating. Biologically based motivation directs behavior toward the maintenance of the living organism through ingestion of food and water. Under conditions of very extreme deprivation of specific nutritive substances, animals and men may unconsciously and automatically begin to show preferences for the missing substance. But in the normal flow of behavior in the adequately nourished individual, food preferences and food habits are largely products of socialization (C. W. Townsend, 1928; Blackwood, 1935).

For example, human flesh may be adequately nutritive, but most cultures forbid cannibalism under normal circumstances. Anthropological evidence suggests that even in the most primitive societies, the eating of human flesh is sanctioned only in connection with isolated magical ceremonial rites. Members of our own society are horrified by even the thought of consuming human flesh. Most people acquire a preference for cooked meat and a keen distaste for raw flesh of any kind. Although among gourmets, highly seasoned raw beef may constitute a delicacy known as steak tartare, the uninitiated individual (that is, one not yet socialized into the elite society of gourmets) may be nauseated by this dish. Fried ants, rattlesnake steaks, and snails may be regarded as delectable by one individual, but as repulsive by another. What Americans know as corn was once regarded by the English (who know it as maize) as more suitable for stock feed than for human consumption. The thoroughly assimilated member of a vegetarian cult may keep himself adequately nourished on foods of vegetable origin and experience genuine distaste for meats of all kinds. The orthodox Jew systematically eliminates pork from his diet, and the devout Roman Catholic may rigidly shun certain foods during Lent.

Human beings do not eat continuously, like grazing animals. The capacity of the stomach sets a limit on the amount that can be eaten at one time, and the time required for the digestive processes places limits on the interval before the motive will again become sufficiently intense to dominate the direction of behavior. But within these limits, considerable variation occurs. Most American families eat primarily during three fairly brief intervals each day. Some take a larger meal in the middle of the day and a smaller one at night, but the majority make a larger meal of dinner than of lunch. The old English custom of tea in the midafternoon, the Latin American custom of a late supper shortly before retiring, and the Jamaican custom of "elevensies" in mid-morning, all represent subcultural norms introducing an additional small meal into the 24-hour cycle.

The handling of eating utensils is also a product of socialization. Complex cultural prescriptions about "manners" (i.e., socially acceptable patterns) of eating behavior are imposed on the child. The nipple provides an entirely practical means of drinking, but infants in our culture are very early induced to use a cup or glass. As soon as possible, they are encouraged to supplement the milk diet with solid foods and to use a spoon. Later, the spoon is not a socially acceptable utensil for solid foods, so the child is coerced into using a fork, holding it between certain fingers, at a certain angle, in a certain hand. Eventually, he is taught to recognize certain foods as requiring the use of a fork, rather than a spoon.

Many of these complexities are very practical (ice cream might melt and run through the tines of a fork, but meat is conveniently speared by the same tines), but others are not (round peas roll off a fork more readily than they would from a spoon, and though the best part of a stew might be its gravy, the spoon must not be used). Europeans use the fork with the left hand, Americans with the right. Some foods may even be more practically and conveniently handled with the fingers than with utensils, but many subcultures are rigid about even this. In the southern United States, where fried chicken is prepared with a relatively ungreasy crust, it is permissible to use one's fingers for this food, but in Boston, where it is prepared in an oven (and therefore greasier) the use of one's fingers to eat fried chicken is considered gauche and unacceptable. But the Bostonian who has dry chicken or the Alabaman who has greasy chicken would be considered socially proper only if each adheres to the conventions with which he is socialized.

The complexity of our culture's social pronouncements about eating behavior is interrelated with social interactions. Mealtime is a social time, a time of convocation of family or friends. Because they serve also to satisfy affiliative social needs, the banquet, the ceremonial dinner, and the businessman's luncheon all serve more social than nutritional purposes.

Activity Cycles. In considering socialization of the need for rest and recovery of fatigued body tissue, it is difficult to separate these systems from socialized aspects of hunger and thirst. The cycles for intake of food are related to the cycles of activity and rest in the organism. Biologically, the optimum amount of rest and maximum inactivity (sleep) required for the human being appears to be about a quarter to a third of his time. In our own culture, the typical cyclical pattern is such that about 16 or 18 waking hours are followed by 6 or 8 hours of sleep. Some cultural groups, especially in tropical climates, adopt the habit of interrupting the activity phase of this cycle with a briefer period of rest or sleep. The siesta in Mexico is a social tradition that provides a rest period not used or even desired by Americans. The shops in Rome may close for several hours in the middle of the day for the noon meal and a period of rest or sleep, but American shops may do a roaring business during the same hours. Like eating cycles, sleeping and rest cycles are limited by biologically founded boundaries of variability. Yet within these boundaries, cultural and individual variations are quite marked.

The flexibility of eating and sleeping cycles under influences of social learning have been investigated in several ways. Marquis (1941) explored the early socialization of activity cycles in human infants and described generally the processes through which infants learn to modify their initially *polyphasic* cycling (six to eight sleep/rest cycles during each 24-hour period) to adapt to the prescribed adult *monophasic* pattern (one complete sleep/rest cycle per day). The usual adult pattern for sleep in our culture is monophasic, but the pattern for eating is polyphasic. Some of the cultures mentioned earlier whose members observe regular midday naps would be said to be diphasic with respect to sleep and rest (two cycles per day).

Explorations of sleep cycles in adults have yielded direct evidence of the flexibility of adult sleeping and eating cycles under artificial conditions that modify the normal cues for these cycles, such as the onset of darkness and evening temperature drops (Kleitman, 1952).

Toilet Behavior. In our culture, toilet functions comprise an area of socialization that is almost as elaborately complex as the socialization of eating behavior. The essential conditions that give rise to the motivational direction of behavior toward elimination of waste materials are biological: pressure in the bladder or the anal sphincter. In the unsocialized infant, the response to these conditions is automatic: he urinates and defecates irregularly as the need arises, whenever and wherever he happens to be. But very rapidly the infant is induced to begin to conform to social conventions about the times, places, and procedures involved in relieving these pressures. By his third year, the typical American child has been trained to urinate or defecate only a few times a day, in specific places, from specific postures (according to his sex), and frequently at prescribed times. For several decades, the advertising of California prune growers has implied that it is socially (if not necessarily medically) desirable to "join the regulars" in defecating once a day, and even further, that this should be at a particular time of day. Little boys may be subject to ridicule by their age-mates as well as their parents if they urinate from a sitting rather than a standing posture.

That our culture is highly specific in its pronouncements about toilet function is apparent in many ways. Cross-cultural studies have shown that our culture is more coercive than many others in the severity with which it trains the child in these functions. The average American, with an acute sense of modesty, tends to feel that moral values are directly involved with toilet functions. The *pissoirs* on the public streets of Paris may be offensive to a straitlaced midwesterner because they do not conceal their purpose. American colloquial speech is laden with euphemisms for toilet functions and toilets. There are restrooms and lounges with no facilities for resting or lounging, and bathrooms with no bathing facilities. (In fact, "toilet" itself is a euphemistic word.) In many parts of the world, urination may occur on public streets and highways with no more embarrassment than would be caused by sneezing or coughing. For most members of our culture, the elaborate socialization of toilet functions is so pervasive that the typical individual is highly aversive to excretory products, being disgusted or even nauseated by their sight and odor. Very uncomfortable conflicts sometimes occur when one is highly motivated to relieve himself (approach), but simultaneously reluctant to announce to a class or a group of people seated for dinner that he must "excuse" himself, for fear of social embarrassment (avoidance).

That members of our culture experience some anxiety about toilet functions is suggested by several approaches to the study of humor. It has been suggested that one function of humor is to ventilate and relieve anxiety about particular areas of behavior. Indeed, in our culture, many jokes have to do with sexual behavior, toilet functions, the expression of hostility and dependency, and even racial and ethnic prejudices. In some other cultures, however, such an area as eating behavior or aggression may be the focus of off-color jokes.

Sexual Behavior. Perhaps one reason for the elaborateness of socialization with respect to urination and defecation is that these functions are anatomically associated with another biogenic motive of considerably more direct social significance: sexual motivation. The introduction of morality, ethics, and other kinds of social control with respect to sexual behavior is socially important because of the reproductive aspects of sexual functions. Population is at least to some degree controlled through customs, traditions, and laws concerning marriage and the production of children.

That this area of human motivation and learning is cloaked with anxiety, conflicts, and taboos in our own society is abundantly clear. In fact, sexual behavior has until fairly recently been virtually inaccessible for scientific study. Until the middle of the twentieth century, behavioral scientists were much better acquainted with the varieties

---

FOOD, SEX, AND LAUGHS IN TWO CULTURES

A study of the Buka society in the Melanesian South Sea Islands yielded the following observations: (1) extreme parental laxness in toilet training of infants; (2) children's imitation of their parents' sex-play is regarded as natural; (3) stories and myths concerning sexual incidents are told without any special comments, are not joked about, and children's questions are always answered directly; (4) no shame or any particular taboo is associated with body exposure and waste elimination; (5) food taboos are more stringent than sex taboos, and in some cases people of the opposite sex may not eat in each other's presence, and are thus "precisely reversing the taboos observed among ourselves."

BLACKWOOD (1935)

CROSS-CULTURAL SEX

Cross-cultural studies of sexual behavior in over 200 societies showed that hetero-sexual behavior is universally favored, but there are almost as many societies that condone homosexual behavior as condemn it. In fact, in some societies homo-sexual behavior is not only approved, but males are singled out as peculiar if they engage exclusively in heterosexual behavior. On the other hand, in nearly all so-cieties masturbation is met with strong social disapproval, frequently in the form of ridicule. Sexual practices with animals are acceptable in some societies, ridiculed in others, and strongly condemned in still others. Stable partnerships are formed in all societies, but there are variations in degrees of sexual extramarital liaisons. How-ever, the pattern in American society that formally recognizes only one form of sexual partnership is atypical, found in only 16 percent of the societies under in-vestigation. Similarly, unless there are specific pressures against such behavior (as in our society), women were found to initiate sexual advances as often as did men.

FORD AND BEACH (1951)

of sexual behavior occurring in subhuman animals and members of primitive cul-tures than they were with the sexual behavior of American adults, other than them-selves. Kinsey, Pomeroy, and Martin (1948) achieved a major breakthrough (even then antagonizing a large moralistic segment of the population) when they utilized sur-vey techniques to catalog the varieties of American sexual behavior. The accuracy of Kinsey's data may be questionable, in view of the fact that the "typical" American adult will not, and perhaps cannot, because of the nature of his early socialization with respect to sexual attitudes, speak candidly about his sexual behavior. Thus Kinsey's data may reflect a rather atypical segment of the population. Nevertheless, these data are in most cases more complete than any alternative sources of informa-tion. In any case, Kinsey's data, as well as cross-cultural comparisons among various societies, provide strong evidence that although sexual motivation is biogenic in origin, the particular habits adopted by a person to achieve sexual gratification are socially learned (Ford & Beach, 1951; Christensen & Carpenter, 1962; Masters & Johnson, 1966).

In practically all cultures, incest is forbidden. The specific limitations of relationship must vary in relation to the particular kinship system in a particular culture, so the specific definition of incest may vary from one culture to another. In our own culture the boundary of acceptability is somewhere in the vicinity of the first-cousin relation-ship, so far as legal statutes concerning permissible marriages are concerned. Incest between parents and children, or between siblings, is punishable by law in the United States. Sexual relations between adults and young people below the age of legal maturity is usually punishable by law, and many states punish sexual behavior involv-ing two members of the same sex. All of these social controls of sexual behavior are at least indirectly related to the conservation of the social system, through attempting to assure controlled repopulation of the society. Rape is also punishable, no matter what the relationship between the parties involved. Most of these variations of sexual behavior outside the normally expected marital sexual activity of married couples are controlled through cultivated aversions (a product of socialization) as well as by law.

Through anxiety about anticipated social disapproval, or through guilt and self-disapproval, most individuals are deterred from such deviant sexual practices as in-cest, homosexuality, rape, or sexual activity with small children (pedophilia). However, there are other practices, such as extramarital activity and particularly masturbation, that are not openly socially condoned, but that appear to be practiced with some fre-quency even by otherwise reasonably well-socialized individuals. In some cases, so-

SEX AMERICAN STYLE

Over 20 years ago Alfred Kinsey and his associates studied the sexual behavior of about 12,000 American males and 8,000 American females by means of systematically conducted interviews. The following patterns were observed. (1) *Masturbatory behavior* was practiced by 93 percent of the males and 62 percent of the females; practice increases with level of education and urban living but decreases with religious devoutness; males often suffer accompanying feelings of guilt and worry, but females rarely do. (2) *Extramarital sexual relations* have been experienced by 50 percent of the males and 26 percent of the females by the time they reach the age of 40, but this pattern is less pronounced in Americans born prior to 1900 than in the younger generation. No particular social class differences were evident, but religious devoutness in females tends to inhibit this behavior; practice of extramarital relations by one's spouse is rated as ground for divorce by 51 percent of the males but by only 27 percent of the females. (3) *Homosexual behavior* in some form has been experienced by 50 percent of the males and 28 percent of the females by the age of 45, increasing with level of education in both sexes, and among single females. Most homosexuals of both sexes express no regret for their behavior, but males particularly tend to have feelings of worry and concern.

Nearly twenty years after Kinsey published his findings, William Masters and Virginia Johnson reported on the detailed *physiological* responses of 382 women and 312 men observed during masturbation and sexual intercourse. Direct observations were augmented by filming responses during excitation, orgasm, and the return to an unexcited state. Valuable medical information was made available concerning problems of infertility, contraception, and impotence. Three major myth-exploding findings were (1) *penis size* is not related to sexual performance, nor to the partner's satisfaction; (2) females do not experience clitoral and/or vaginal orgasms, but only *one* type of orgasm—*sexual orgasm;* and (3) *orgasm frequency* for females is not limited to one climactic orgasm to produce satiety, as in males.

KINSEY et al. (1948, 1953)
MASTERS AND JOHNSON (1966)

cial controls of deviant sexual behavior vary as a function of the sex of the individual, his age, or the social class to which he belongs (Kinsey et al., 1948, 1953).

Because the social control of sexual behavior in our culture usually involves the intentional cultivation of learned anxieties, approach-avoidance conflicts in this area of motivation are not unusual. Young girls are often induced to be fearful of premarital pregnancy, and some women experience difficulty in later overcoming these anxieties when they are married. Anxieties about homosexual relationships may induce panic in a young male following an exploratory sexual episode with a classmate. The clinical psychologist often encounters neurotically miserable adults suffering from sexual frigidity or impotence as a consequence of socially learned anxieties about sexual behavior. The accumulated evidence that the patterns of adult behavior used to attain sexual gratification are products of socialization thus has some important implications not only for the scientific understanding of personality development, but also for clinical and legal psychology and family and social welfare services.

Learned Values and Motives. Probably the greatest variations of behavior from one culture to another are those that involve socially learned values and their motivational consequences. These are described in greater detail in Chapter 7. The social learning history of each individual produces within him a unique combination of values and related behavioral traits in such areas as dependency, aggression, power-seeking, approval-seeking, achievement, and recognition-seeking. Thus, there are ranges of variation within any culture. However, within any given culture the range of socialization practices, traditional values, and cultural standards may be somewhat restricted. The result is that ranges of observed variation often do not overlap much. What is considered unusually aggressive in one culture may be considered mild and docile in another. Consequently there are general ranges of difference in the observed behavior of members of different cultures, and these are especially pronounced and visible in connection with socially learned motives.

Social Class Differences.   A society is comprised of many interrelated groups and social subsystems. The more complex the society, the greater the variety of interrelated social systems within it: communities, families, institutional organizations, or social classes, for example. Certain standards for conventional behavior are applicable to all members of a society, regardless of their affiliation with particular subsystems. Other conventions, however, differentiate members of one subsociety from members of others.

In organized groups, stabilized patterns of behavior define particular roles associated with particular positions in the social system. The term *position* is used by social scientists to describe the niche, or slot, occupied by the individual within a society, and the term *role* applies to the stabilized patterns of behavior associated with a position. In other words, a position refers to a particular set of circumstances or conditions that dictate a particular set of conventional expectations for behavior. In large groups and societies, roles and positions often are not recognized as unique to a single individual. Instead, a cluster of similar positions and roles may be perceived as a *class*. Thus similar behavioral patterns come to be expected from members of particular classes or subgroups within the larger society (see Chapter 13).

Within each subgroup, miniature systems of socialization occur. Although an overall systematic set of socialization practices may operate for the majority of members of a society, particular subsystems within the society may evolve specific patterns of socialization and social control of the individual's behavior. In either case, socialization is geared to prepare the individual for assimilation as an adult member of his own social subsystem. This is especially true of social class subgroups: just as princesses are reared to become queens, middle-class children are reared to become middle-class adults.

The basic values of the lower class and the middle class in our society differ in several important ways. McCandless (1961) has summarized these differences by pointing to the fact that the middle-class American typically places high values on personal cleanliness, the dominance of intellect over emotion, and the importance of education for its own sake. Furthermore, he is characterized by the values of Cal-

---

THE SHOPKEEPER'S SON AND THE BOOKKEEPER'S DAUGHTER

This study of occupational status and child-rearing practices used a representative sample of 582 mothers living in the Detroit area. The mothers came from families that had been designated as being either entrepreneurial or organizational. A family was considered entrepreneurial when the husband was self-employed in a small-scale organization and most of his income came from profits, fees, and commissions. In organizational families the father worked for wages in a company of moderate complexity (three or more supervisory levels). It was assumed that child-rearing practices in entrepeneurial families would reflect risk-taking and independence, and in organizational families, dependency and security. Observations showed that organizational families engaged more frequently in dependency-fostering practices such as immediate attention to the crying baby, demand feeding, and rare parental absence from home.

MILLER AND SWANSON (1958)

SOCIAL CLASS AND CHILD REARING

In the 1950s a comprehensive cross-sectional exploration of child rearing displayed by mothers of 5-year-olds was conducted in two suburbs of Boston, one of which was predominantly middle class and the other working class. Comparisons yielded the following findings.

Feeding and Eating. Social-class differences were unrelated to the mother's handling of infant feeding and childhood eating problems.

Toilet Training. Working-class mothers were more severe with toilet training and accomplished it more rapidly than did middle-class mothers. Working-class mothers used punishment and "shaming" more often.

Dependency Behavior. Working-class mothers were generally stricter than middle-class mothers in handling dependency, and were more inclined to be irritated by the child's dependency and to punish it directly.

Sexual Behavior. Sex training was much more severe among poorly educated working-class mothers. Middle-class mothers reacted to the child's sexuality with less intense emotion and anxiety.

Aggressive Behavior. Although aggression toward parents was generally disapproved, middle-class mothers were more likely to overlook and minimize such incidents than were working-class mothers, who were more directly punitive of the child's aggressiveness.

In the 1940s, however, investigators had attributed a high degree of permissiveness to the child-rearing practices of lower-class parents. A reappraisal of the controversial findings between investigators in the mid-forties and the mid-fifties showed both sides to be right: since the mid-forties a consistent shift toward permissiveness was typical of middle-class mothers who, compared to the lower-class mothers, had been more exposed (and responded more positively) to the general permissiveness that has been the prevailing theme of experts and authorities such as Dr. Benjamin Spock and *Infant Care,* a bulletin published by the U.S. Children's Bureau (an analysis of which reflected the trend from strictness to permissiveness during that decade). It was concluded that the trend in the early sixties to maximize achievement drives might have been an incentive for the future adoption of less permissive child-rearing practices.

HAVIGHURST, ROBINSON, AND DORR (1946)
SEARS, MACCOBY, AND LEVIN (1957)
BRONFENBRENNER (1958, 1961)

vinism (hard work, self-discipline, and perseverance) and the Protestant ethic (a personal sense of sin and guilt for wrongdoing). In contrast, these values are less pronounced among members of the lower classes. Because the middle class is the backbone of the society, representing the core culture to which the greater proportion of the population subscribes, its values tend to define our society's general standards of social desirability. It is this set of values that is imposed upon virtually all children through such formal agencies as our public school system, regardless of the individual student's social class origins.

Racial and Ethnic Differences. Although most people who are not behavioral scientists (and even occasionally a careless behavioral scientist) confuse the concepts of *racial* and *ethnic* classifications, the two are not parallel. Race is a biological concept, whereas ethnicity is a sociological concept. Racial identification is established by means of biological characteristics that are transmitted genetically. Ethnic identification is established by examining the society (including its customs, conventions, and socialization practices) of which the individual is a member. The fact that the concepts are often difficult to differentiate for purposes of research into racial or ethnic bases of behavior has resulted in limitation of our scientific knowledge of the contributions of race to the determination of human behavior.

Even when racial identification is clearly recognized to be biologically defined, it is often still difficult for the scientist to establish racial membership conclusively. Everyday conventions for defining race are far too inconsistent to be of any scientific use: in our society, for example, convention decrees that an individual who has one black great-grandparent (i.e., "one-eighth Negro" in common parlance) should be classified as Negro. On the contrary, the individual with one white great-grandparent is not classified as Caucasian.

Perhaps the greatest source of difficulty is the fact that the human species is highly hybridized and interbred. Relatively few individuals are of truly pure genetic stock, and it is almost impossible to trace specific strains. Furthermore, even biologists and physical anthropologists do not entirely agree on the proper criteria for biologically defining race. Skin color does not provide discrete categories for classification because shades may range from charcoal black to albino white. Moreover, skin shade is often modified through disease, diet, and environmental effects such as suntan. Eye color provides more discretely defined categories, but the range of classifications is too small to be scientifically useful; dark eyes characterize all racial classifications except the white-skinned Caucasian, who may have hazel or blue eyes. Blood group classifications have shown some promise as a basis for rigorous biological classification because frequencies of blood types have been found to be somewhat correlated with other racial characteristics such as skin and eye color. Unfortunately, however, if anthropologists did accept blood groups as the basic criterion for defining races, it would be necessary to discard virtually all of our other conventional criteria because none is perfectly correlated with blood classification.

A variety of anthropometric indices (measures of the physical form of the human body) may be used in racial classification: the size of the head, the size of the chest and trunk, the length of limbs, and various ratios among these measures. The amount, quantity, texture, and distribution of hair over the body have also been considered as possible indices of racial classification. Certain groups of human beings possess a great deal of body hair, and others possess almost none. And the texture and curliness of hair on the head varies considerably from one race to another. Certain specific races occasionally are characterized by more or less unique body characteristics: for example, the epicanthic fold (an inner upper eyelid) is characteristic of the Asiatic yellow races, but not of others.

From these examples one can readily see that efforts to establish reliable scientific criteria for defining the biological concept of race have proceeded in many directions. The conventions of contemporary anthropology are such that all of these criteria are pooled in making judgments of racial membership. The most conventional system of classification of races, arising from such pooled criteria, describes three major classes: the Mongoloids (yellow-skinned Asiatics), the Negroids (black-skinned Africans and Pacific groups), and the Caucasoids (white-skinned Europeans). These groupings are sufficiently coarse that a fourth "unclassified" category must be retained for leftovers. Certain anthropologists have argued that the history of known migrations cannot account for the geographic distribution of these categories over the earth, and have therefore proposed a minimum of eleven necessary racial classifications (Coon, Garn, & Birdsell, 1950).

Under any circumstances, the preceding paragraphs should be sufficient to indicate that everyday nonscientific concepts of race are far removed from refined scientific

RACE CLASSIFICATION

An extended method for classifying human society on the basis of groups or races that seem similar, rather than on the basis of race as such, yielded the following descriptions. (1) *Caucasoids:* approximately a billion people; skin color, head hair, and stature show great variations; narrow and projecting noses varying in size; relatively thick body hair and thin lips; almost impossible to divide into subraces; called the white race due to popular usage. (2) *Mongoloids:* about a billion people; average skin color light yellowish-brown; head hair usually black and sparse; lips of medium thickness; forward and laterally projected cheekbones; epicanthic folds over eyeballs. (3) *African Negroids:* 100 million people; skin variations from yellowish-brown to almost black; head hair curly or wooly; little body hair; wide noses varying in size; small ears; lips vary but tend to be fleshy. (4) *Melanesians:* about 2 million people living on islands from New Guinea to Fiji; Negroid in appearance but not racially related to African Negroids; greater variations in skin color and heavier browridges than in African Negroids. (5) *Micronesians-Polynesians:* about 400,000 people living north and east of Melanesia (Hawaii, New Zealand, etc.); skin color light; wavy hair; of unknown hybrid origin. (6) *Central African Pygmies:* about 100,000 people; genetic relationship with African Negroids doubtful; less dark than the latter; average stature less than 5 feet. (7) *Far Eastern Pygmies:* about 25,000 people, mostly in the Philippines; fairly thick lips; skin color very dark; average height 5 feet; woolly hair. (8) *Australoids:* about 40,000 people living in Australia; with exception of darker skin color, anatomical features resemble those of the Caucasoids. (9) *Bushmen-Hottentots:* about 20,000 people living in the African Kalahari desert; excessive fat on thighs and buttocks; some tendencies for epicanthic folds; Hottentots are taller than the 5-feet-tall Bushmen, and also have more frizzly hair. (10) *Ainus:* about 10,000 people in Northern Japan; feature resemblance somewhere between Australoids and Caucasoids; assumed to be the population of ancient Japan. (11) *Veddoids:* a remnant group living in Ceylon; anatomically intermediate between Caucasoids and Australoids, but displayed more delicate features than Ainus.

COON, GARN, AND BIRDSELL (1950)

criteria for defining biological and genetic strains. More often, what is implied by everyday notions of race is really a matter of ethnic classification. It is indeed possible to refer to descriptive characteristics of a particular society and to classify (at least crudely) individuals according to their social heritage in being members of a given social community. Throughout history geographically contiguous societies have tended to intermingle genetically, and consequently, biological lines have often blurred with social lines. Thus, if one speaks of the American Negro as a racial group (biologically defined), he is immediately immersed in a complex of scientific errors; however, if he speaks of the American black as an ethnic group (sociologically defined), he may be able to define a miniature society that is as coherent a social system as a social class or a national political system. Likewise, Jews do not constitute a biological race, but they do constitute a homogeneous society with a common social heritage of many centuries. Unfortunately, most current nonscientific notions of Jewishness are based on the society of the Jew in America, rather than on the true communality of the social heritage of Jews throughout the world in the Diaspora. And, of course, to speak of the Jews of Israel since 1947 is to speak of a third rather different society.

As in the case of explorations of social class differences, the investigation of ethnic group differences may permit the social scientist to identify specific characteristics of a social system (especially with reference to its socialization and social

MY SON THE DOCTOR

An analysis of the records of over 6000 liberal arts undergraduate freshmen students showed that Jewish students worked more nearly to the limit of their abilities in college than did non-Jewish students. (The experimental data were derived from intercorrelations of aptitude-test scores and grade-point ratios.) The streotyped notion of the highly academically achievement-oriented Jewish student was thus confirmed. Moreover, statistics on Jewish student enrollment in American colleges and universities in 1963 show that the Jewish college population amounted to 70 to 80 percent of all college-age Jews, whereas the percentage of college population for all American youth was 27.

E. L. CLARK (1949)
JOSPE (1964)

control practices) and in turn to identify modal personality characteristics among members of that ethnic group. But to do so is to say nothing whatever about a biological concept of race.

For this reason, current research on racial differences in behavior must be evaluated with extreme caution. Even when adequate provision is made to define racial membership according to explicit biological criteria that are not contaminated and confounded with social and ethnic characteristics, it is still necessary to distinguish direct from indirect consequences of racial origin. *Direct* consequences include behavioral attributes that can be ascribed directly to the biological qualities defining racial origin. *Indirect* (mediated) consequences include those that stem from the nature of the social matrix in which the racial group is embedded. For example, the religious and cultural traditions of the American black give rise to a more or less homogeneous society within the greater society, and like any subculture, the values, beliefs, and habits of this society are perpetuated through succeeding generations (at least until more or less complete assimilation of the subculture into the larger culture occurs).

Moreover, there are many differences in the way society treats blacks and whites. With unequal opportunities for employment, education, and social achievement, blacks are simply not subjected to the same kinds of experiences in socialization as are the dominant majority, the "right-side-of-the-fence" WASPs (white-Anglo-Saxon-Protestants). In American society, the black subculture is almost completely contained within the lower socioeconomic class subculture, and the two are often difficult to isolate (Herzog, 1969).

Considerable effort has been expended in the exploration of racial and ethnic differences in human behavior, but one must be extremely cautious in evaluating the soundness of these findings, in view of the inherent conceptual, methodological, and procedural difficulties encountered in conducting such research.

Race and Intelligence. One of the most hotly controversial issues of discussion in connection with racial and ethnic differences in behavior is that of intelligence. Unfortunately, this argument has gone on for nearly half a century, generating more heat and smoke than light and clarity. The issue regained the spotlight during the late 1960s, when arguments were polarized. One camp, typified by J. McVicker Hunt, held forth with emphasis that intelligence and experience were inextricably related, so that the child's intellectual capacity was so much a product of his early environment that genetic and environmental sources of variation could not be isolated (Hunt, 1961; Dreger & Miller, 1960, 1968). A counterposition, typified by Arthur Jensen, examined similar data in the light of statistical analyses of sources of variance and concluded that measured intelligence and intellectual performance of the child were highly heri-

RACE AND SPORTS

During socialization, whites are more likely than blacks to be exposed to self-paced activities where they are free, within limits, to respond to stimulus conditions when they so choose. Blacks are more likely not to have as much freedom to respond, and so must react to changes in stimulus conditions when those changes occur. In sports, whites would therefore tend to be more successful in areas demanding self-paced activities, and blacks in areas demanding reactive activities. To test this hypothesis, statistics were collected from professional baseball and basketball sources. In baseball, pitching is a self-paced activity, whereas hitting is reactive. Of the 429 American-born players on major baseball league rosters in 1969, 24 percent of the nonpitchers were black, but only 7 percent of the pitchers were black. In basketball, free-throw attempts are more self-paced than field-goal attempts. Of the players who played at least 1000 minutes during the National Basketball Association 1967–1968 season, 55 were black and 45 were white. After subtracting for each player the percentage of successful field-goal attempts from the percentage of successful free-throw attempts (a measure for self-paced activity), whites showed significantly higher scores than blacks.

WORTHY AND MARKLE (1970)

RACE AND SPEECH PATTERNS

A sample of black adolescents attending a Chicago public high school was selected on the basis of an intelligence score of 100 or better, membership in the lower class, birth and residence in Chicago, and parents born in the South. Tests were administered to the subjects in order to assess their achievement motivation and presence or absence of southern dialect. This was followed by a neutral (paralinguistic) situation in the form of a friendly conversation. Responses were recorded on tape and classified into eight categories of southern American pronunciations such as raising and lowering of vowels, drawl, loss of consonants, dissimilation, nasality, and the like. The intensity of southern pronunciation was determined by noting the frequency of occurrence. In the linguistic task, high-need-for-achievement boys consistently displayed less southern dialect than did the low-need-for-achievement boys, suggesting that the display of characteristics of middle-class speech patterns in the high-need-for-achievement boys was not part of their normal speech pattern; rather, it was conceived as part of their general achievement-orientation aimed at higher status and upward social mobility. The lack of identical patterns in females was explained in terms of role conflict (achievement motivation and intellectual, or women's role).

BAEHR (1965)

table. This latter position (sometimes referred to as Jensenism) uses the concept of heritability to refer to the proportion of observed variation in measures of intellect that can be accounted for by analysis of genetic factors (Shuey, 1966; Jensen, 1969).

Unfortunately this polarization does little to resolve the old nature-nurture argument about intelligence. To begin with, such extreme polarity obscures the more productive view that genetic forces *interact* with environmental forces to generate particular behavioral products, and that the variance arising from the interaction between the two may be considerably more important than the variance arising from either in isolation. Asking the question in either-or format is basically inappropriate.

Moreover, most of the studies on which these arguments have been based begin with somewhat inadequate definitions of race or genetic grouping. Statistical records in most segments of our society are actually *ethnic* rather than *racial*. Rarely is any kind of biological essay the basis for entering "black" or "Negro" (rather than "white" or "Caucasian") in a blank on a test form or a school registration card. Instead, this record is a sociocultural judgment derived from perception of skin color, or self-report, or even simply reputation. Only when research studies begin with biological racial differentiations can we legitimately discuss biological or genetic interpretations of them.

In addition, most sandardized intelligence tests are culturally limited in that (being standardized in a given culture with a given population) they are unfair to members of different cultures. Any test, on being translated, will tend to favor those who take the test in its original language and will pose a disadvantage for those who take the translated version, unless the translated test has been fully restandardized with the new population. The same thing is true of cultural or ethnic minorities. Unless they are a part of the standardization population, they are at a cultural disadvantage in taking the test. To demonstrate this fact, several investigators have purposely standardized tests that reflect the black American subculture, and using these tests, have "proven" that the white is intellectually inferior to the black. This is no more ridiculous than contrary demonstrations, using tests based on the white culture.

In summary, then, it is difficult at this point to make strong and definitive statements about racial and ethnic differences in intelligence and intellectual capacity. If we talk about *test scores* (performance itself), then data generally suggest that ethnic minorities are at a disadvantage on most of our currently used tests. But if we talk about *intellectual capacity* (the hypothetical variable underlying performance), we can be less certain, largely because of inadequacies and imperfections in our test procedures. Furthermore, if we are cautious and critical of our operational definitions of ethnic or racial classification, we cannot accept the inadequate definitions used in

---

THE CHITLIN' TEST

Arguing that all U.S. employment and IQ tests reflect the culture of white, middle-class America, black sociologist Adrian Dove, a program analyst for the U.S. Budget Bureau, devised his own quiz. Wryly known as the "Soul Folk Chitlings Test," it is cast with a black bias. Among the items:

1. Whom did "Stagger Lee" kill (in the famous blues legend)? (a) His mother, (b) Frankie, (c) Johnny, (d) His girl friend, (e) Billy.
2. If you throw the dice and seven is showing, what is facing down? (a) "Seven," (b) "Snake eyes," (c) "Boxcars," (d) "Little Joes," (e) "Eleven."
3. In *C.C. Rider,* what does "C.C." stand for? (a) Civil Service, (b) Church Council, (c) Country Circuit (Preacher), (d) Country Club, (e) "Cheatin' Charlie" (the "Boxer Gunsel").
4. Cheap chitlings (not the kind you purchase at a frozen food counter) will taste rubbery unless they are cooked long enough. How soon can you quit cooking them to eat and enjoy them? (a) 15 minutes, (b) 8 hours, (c) 24 hours, (d) 1 week (on a low flame), (e) 1 hour.
5. Hattie Mae Johnson is on the County. She has four children and her husband is now in jail for nonsupport, as he was unemployed and was not able to give her any money. Her welfare check is now $286 per month. Last night she went out with the biggest player in town. If she got pregnant, then 9 months from now, how much more will her welfare check be? (a) $80, (b) $2, (c) $35, (d) $150, (e) $100.
6. The "Hully Gully" came from (a) East Oakland, (b) Fillmore, (c) Watts, (d) Harlem, (e) Motor City.
7. Many people say that "Juneteenth" (June 19) should be made a legal holiday because this was the day when (a) The slaves were freed in the United States, (b) The slaves were freed in Texas, (c) The slaves were freed in Jamaico, (d) The slaves were freed in California, (e) Martin Luther King was born, (f) Booker T. Washington died.

Answers: 1(e), 2(a), 3(c), 4(c), 5(c), 6(c), 7(b).

DOVE (1968)

most studies of race and intelligence; more seriously, we cannot accept the careless leaps back and forth from ethnicity to genetics. All in all, those who claim to have answered questions of genetic bases of intelligence are most likely simply voicing their faith. In fact, one study has shown that the best predictor of the findings generated by a particular investigator or research reviewer on this controversial issue is knowledge of the biographical characteristics of the investigator himself (Sherwood & Nataupsky, 1968). A kind of chauvinistic ethnocentrism characterized those reviewers who voiced faith in the conclusion that blacks are inferior to whites; reviewers who were moderate, cautious, or middle-of-the-road in their interpretations tended also to be moderate and "middle-of-the-road" on basic descriptive biographical characteristics.

Sex Differences.   In our society, the roles associated with being male or female are rather sharply defined. The specific content of the masculine and feminine roles has varied considerably throughout history, and under the concentrated pressure of current social movements the social differentiation of male and female is very much on the wane. Nevertheless, the culture still maintains different expectations for males and females, and consequently the typical behavior of males and females still differs visibly. These differences are most apparent in such areas as aggression, dependency, and sexuality (Pope, 1953; Kagan & Moss, 1960; Maccoby, 1966).

As in the study of racial and ethnic effects on behavior, the issue is easily confused when one fails to distinguish between *direct* (biological) and *indirect* (sociocultural) effects of sex. In fact, a few contemporary psychologists suggest the use of two completely different words to refer to these differences: the word *sex* would be reserved to define biological identity as male or female and the word *gender* would refer to sociocultural notions of masculinity or femininity.

There are many well-documented differences in the everyday behavior of men and women in our culture. Men and boys typically are more aggressive and less dependent (Sears, Maccoby, & Levin, 1957; Kagan & Moss, 1960; Maccoby, 1966). Girls typically show faster verbal development, better school achievement in elementary and middle-school years, and better school adjustment (Maccoby, 1966). Boys show faster motor development, sometimes better school adjustment in later years (high school and college), and higher levels of career achievement than girls (Maccoby, 1966; Horner, 1969). But of course these are largely the results of differential practices in socialization associated with boys and girls from infancy on (Sears, Maccoby, & Levin, 1957; Kagan & Moss, 1960).

Thus, the culture has its own built-in mechanisms for creating self-fulfilling prophecies: *social expectations* generate *training practices* that produce *behavior* that vali-

---

MUY MACHO

A cross-cultural appraisal by a Mexican psychoanalyst suggests that American women's discontent must be bewildering to many of their Latin American sisters socialized in the *machismo* culture (a tradition that accords practically no choice to women). A woman is an object selected solely for a man's personal use (unless she belongs to another man), and she has no right to rebel. If, for example, she rebels by refusing the *macho's* invitation to dance, he has the inherent right to shoot her to atone for his injured pride. Exceptions to this kind of treatment are accorded only to two women in the *macho's* life: his mother (to whom he has been proving all along that he is a real man) and to the Virgin Mother (to acquit himself of all sins).

ARAMONI (1972)

EXPECTATIONS FOR BOYS AND GIRLS

Twelve-year-old children from different schools in different areas of a large city were divided into two socioeconomic status groups: high (essentially middle-class), and low. In both groups popularity was related to sex-typed behavior, but expressed in different ways. Among the lower-class children, popularity for boys was positively related to sociability, a sense of humor, and frequently, aggressiveness; for lower-class girls, popularity was positively related to tidiness, friendliness, and being a good student, *or* rowdiness, attention-getting, and aggressiveness. Studious and classroom-conforming boys were generally rejected as "sissies." For boys of higher socioeconomic status, popularity was positively related to friendliness, good looks, and scholastic achievement, whereas aggressiveness and untidiness were not. For the higher-class girls, popularity was positively related to good looks, friendliness, and tidiness, but not to rowdiness and aggressiveness.

POPE (1953)

WOMEN'S LIB BEGINS IN THE CRIB

Studies have shown that as early as 6 weeks after a baby's birth, parents respond differentially on the basis of the infant's sex. Girls are talked to more often than boys, and boys are handled more often than girls.

By the time children reach the age of 6, the results of the socialization practices can be assessed fairly accurately. First-grade children agreed, when shown pictures of "animals that are like you," that the tiger was appropriate for boys and the lamb was appropriate for girls. Adult men and women, too, agreed that males are stronger, more aggressive, and more daring than women. They also agreed on what does not necessarily follow from such comparisons, namely, that males are less inadequate, more mature, and more competent than females.

KAGAN, HOSKIN, AND WATSON (1961)
KAGAN (1971)

dates the *social expectations,* generation after generation. This is the vicious circle from which modern women wish to be liberated (Freidan, 1963; Millett, 1970; G. Greer, 1971; Call, 1972). The stereotyped perception of women and their expected roles in our culture is well defined and resistant to change because of this gyroscope-like self-perpetuation (Goldberg, 1968; Horner, 1969; Broverman et al., 1970; Hart, 1971; Pheterson, Kiesler, & Goldberg, 1971).

RELEVANCE AND APPLICATION

The study of socialization and cultural differences is the first step toward applying psychological knowledge to understanding and improving human relations at the societal level. Analysis of the communalities of beliefs, values, and actions within a group of people enables one to predict and understand their collective behavior, and in turn to deal effectively with it. Such analysis would be applicable to the study of geopolitical groups and their international encounters, ranging from alliances and mutual dependencies at the economic and political level, to their hostilities and warfare. It would be equally applicable to the study of internal domestic problems within a society, among its diverse subgroups of people. In either case, the betterment of human relations at collective levels demands knowledge of the mechanisms through which cultures are generated and perpetuated, and the devices through which individual people operate as part of greater cultures.

The analysis of individual social learning histories, including their reinforcement histories and the agents of socialization who steered the course of their preparation for adult society, affords some important clinical applications. Many neurotic maladjust-ments, conflicts, anxieties, and minor emotional disturbances that hinder optimum productivity and happiness in the otherwise normal adult are traceable to elements in early socialization. In a preventive sense, the frequency of such consequences can be reduced by enlightened education of parents in terms of broadened awareness of the implications and consequences of parent-child interaction patterns and the parental role as an agent of the society. These clinical implications are paralleled by similar implications for the understanding, prevention, and even rehabilitation of many kinds of criminal behavior.

Attention to the relationships between man's sociocultural style and his physical habi-tat has made us increasingly conscious of the need for care and conservation of the physical environment. Its profound influences on behavior are only beginning to be understood fully. But already it is clear that in order to maintain a planet on which man can flourish as man, he must be increasingly conscious of the reciprocal rela-tionship between behavior and environment: that the environment will govern and limit man's behavior, just as his actions will yield consequences that alter his future environment.

When one reflects his analysis of cultural determinants of behavior upon himself, he is enabled to become more acutely aware of himself and his role in his society. One's identity is a combined product of his sex, his racial origins, his ethnic affiliations, his educational, vocational, and economic identities, and the many other definitions of his location in cultural space. To understand himself and his relationships to others, one must begin by examining and understanding this identity.

REVIEW

1. *Socialization* represents a society's way of controlling the behavior of its individual members, through manipulation of social learning.

2. A *culture* can be defined as a bounded set of norms, standards, and beliefs among a group of people, resulting in common socialization practices and common patterns of behavior, belief, and values among members of that group.

3. Social learning is defined as a modification of behavior as a consequence of ex-perience in the social environment, including other people, groups, and cultural in-stitutions. This includes behavioral changes guided by *models* or examples for be-havior as well as management of *contingent consequences* of behavior.

4. Contingent consequences of behavior may include *reward* (conditions that facili-tate goal attainment), *non-reward* (conditions that do not change the status quo with respect to goals), or *punishment* (conditions that interfere with or are incompatible with goal attainment).

5. *Punishment* has certain particular qualities that may produce undesired conse-quences: it generates *anxiety* and *avoidance,* and may close the learner off from fur-ther attempts to learn in the punished situation.

6. Reward and punishment can be defined explicitly only with reference to the learner's *expectations:* conditions more positive than expectations will be viewed as rewards; conditions more negative than expectations will be viewed as punishment.

7. Socialization may be accomplished either through *external* controls (models and sources of reward or punishment outside the individual himself) or through *internal* controls (models, standards, and capacity for reward and punishment that the indi-vidual has internalized).

8. *Agents of socialization* carry out the socialization process. These include specific adults (such as parents, teachers, and authority figures), collective agencies (peer groups and organized institutions), and cultural codes (such as standards of social desirability and religious and ethical systems). In some cases even supernatural forces may be introduced into the socialization process, in the form of instructions and guidance from gods and deities and the promise of reward or retribution from them.

9. In our society, socialization styles may vary. In some cases socialization is accomplished through a mixture of reward and non-reward, or *induction* techniques. In other cases it is accomplished through a combination of punishment and non-reward, or *sensitization* techniques.

10. Socialization by deviant agents or subcultures may produce behavior that is not culturally appropriate or accepted, leading to criminal, neurotic, or delinquent behavior.

11. Because socialization practices are more or less homogeneous within a given culture, the typical behavior of adult members of that culture is also homogeneous. It is called *modal personality* style.

12. Cultural communality is a product of common *socialization* practices, common ecology (physical environments), and common cultural *products* that are both *material* (tools, artifacts, and the like) and *nonmaterial* (languages, beliefs, religions).

13. Language is reciprocally related to culture: it is at the same time a cultural product (*linguistic relativism*) as well as a factor in steering the socialization of new members of the culture (*linguistic determinism*).

14. Cultures may be compared with one another, and the typical behavior of members of different cultures may be described and compared. This is called *cross-cultural* study.

15. Within a broader culture, such groups as social classes, as well as sexual, racial, and ethnic groups, may generate homogeneous *subcultures,* with typical socialization practices and modal personality styles.

7
THE SOCIAL SELF

One of the most interesting social objects one may perceive and react to is *oneself*. That one perceives oneself in very much the same fashion that he perceives other people is by no means a novel idea: James (1890, 1902) wrote extensively about the self as an object of knowledge, and Cooley (1902) formulated several ideas about how the perception of oneself arose out of social origins. Cooley suggested that one perceives himself as he might perceive his image in a mirror and, in fact, he described this conception as the "looking-glass self." G. H. Mead (1934) later developed Cooley's early ideas in somewhat greater detail by proposing that one managed this reflexive look at oneself largely by taking the role of others. In thus stepping into the shoes of another person, one is able to look back upon himself much as he might regard any other person, as a social object.

These early ideas of Cooley and Mead were formulated in very general terms and were not submitted directly to empirical verification, but they provided a foundation for later expansion of scientific knowledge about self-perception. They place the process of self-perception within the framework of the general principles that govern the perception of people (see Chapter 8) and of role perception (see Chapter 11). Furthermore, they specify the importance of social and interpersonal origins of the self-concept by implying that, at least to some degree, "we see ourselves as (we think) others see us."

SOCIAL ORIGINS OF SELF-PERCEPTION

The concept of *self* has its origins in the prehistory of personality theory. One primary objective of scientific *personality* theory (as considered apart from general theories of *behavior*) is to account for the unique organization of behavior within the single individual. Sigmund Freud used the term *ego* to refer to this organized aspect of personality, and numerous other theorists have adhered to this usage. Others have used the term *self*. Regardless of terminology, almost all personality theories contain at least one construct that labels the unique organization of behavior within the single individual. In the discussion presented here, *self* is used consistently to label the totality of actions and behavior of the single individual. It represents the summation of what he "is" behaviorally, and thus it represents the object of perception that he is.

The term *self-concept* is used to refer to the organized cognitive structure derived from one's experience of one's own self. As personality theory has evolved, many theorists (especially those who stress a person's capacity to know and understand his world) wished to distinguish the self as a coherent organized system of behavior from the individual's perceptual recognition and evaluation of himself. It was recognized that a person might show certain misperceptions and distortions in his understanding of himself, just as he might misperceive or distort his perception of other people. For this reason the notion of self-concept was evolved.

The self-concept is a particular kind of attitudinal structure. The principles of perceptual organization described in Chapter 4 apply to self-perception just as they apply to the perception of others. The self-concept includes elements of sheer perceptual recognition, which do not necessarily always correspond fully to the "reality" of the self. Through such processes as selective attention, perceptual readiness and set, expectancies, and perceptual vigilance and defense, various distortions in self-perception may occur. For example, a person, after buying a box of Girl Scout cookies, may begin to see himself as a philanthropist. This isolated experience of himself has provided the basis for an inflated and exaggerated cognitive structure in his self-concept (perceptual vigilance). The same person may be completely ignoring the fact that he has on twenty-three previous occasions refused to donate to charities, buy gifts for his employees at Christmas, or support his college alumni association (perceptual defense).

Like other concepts, the self-concept is self-sustaining. Once evolved, it guides selectively the admission of new experiences or information into this conceptual category. In other words, the existing self-concept always provides a *frame of reference* for interpreting new experiences of oneself. Information that is compatible or congruent with the existing concept is readily admitted; but information that is incompatible or incongruent tends to be filtered out. The self-styled "philanthropist" probably is quick to recognize his generosity in buying his secretary a birthday present but blind to his short-tempered refusal to discuss the alumni fund with an old college classmate. These mechanisms maintain the cognitive stability of the self-concept. They govern the way a person reacts to new situations and new conditions. Thus they are responsible for the consistency of behavior one displays, and therefore provide a significant organizing aspect of personality.

The self-concept is a coherent and internally consistent cognitive system. From time to time new experiences necessitate adjustment and revision of the self-concept. The straight-A honor student may one day fail an examination and somehow have to reconcile this with his general conception of himself. The dimension of cognitive *rigidity* (or *flexibility*) thus may describe one aspect of the self-concept. An extremely rigid self-concept involves excessive use of defensive processes in perception at the expense of gross distortion of the self-concept as compared to the "real" self. Changing circumstances often force a reorganization of self-concept in a direction inconsistent with one's earlier conception of himself. Excessive rigidity prevents such realignment of the self-concept. This is not serviceable in meeting a changing world with changing demands on the individual, and it may generate difficulties in personal adjustment. On the other hand, an excessively flexible self-concept, which reshapes itself capriciously in the face of each new experience, is also of limited utility in achieving consistency in a changing world. The student who feels that he is a genius every time he earns an A and an idiot every time he fails a quiz is inconsistent; he lacks a stable and serviceable personal estimate of himself as a frame of reference for long-range planning and decision making. Such a condition contributes to what Freudian psychoanalytic psychologists have described as "low ego strength." Either excessive rigidity or excessive flexibility may produce pathological conditions in personality organization.

The development of the self-concept follows the same course that occurs with the development of other kinds of cognitive concepts. The first items of information that comprise the concept are associated because of similarity. At first these are very primitive and generalized; later they are very subtle and refined.

The most primitive aspect of the self-concept is the differentiation between experiences that concern what is "me" and those that concern what is "not-me." One essential component in this delineation of oneself involves the discovery that everything within the outer limits of the skin is a part of the self. This aspect of self-concept, perception of the physical self, is referred to as *body image*. Not only does this constitute the primitive core of the self-concept, but it continues to be a critical component of the self-concept even in maturity. Others perceive and react to a person, at least partially, in terms of his size, skin color, appearance, and physical makeup, so the individual's perception of himself reflects considerable attention to such features. Deformities and physical abnormalities may seriously affect one's perception of himself.

The self-concept includes much more than mere perception of one's physical form. It also includes cognitive awareness of one's behavior and interactions with other people and with the environment. In the beginnings of self-awareness, the self-concept is likely to be constituted largely of "me" elements: experiences in which the self is the object of actions on the part of others. Someone loves *me;* someone takes care of *me;* something frightens *me.* Later, with a developing sense of potency and capacity to manipulate and control the environmental world, "I" elements are incorporated: experiences in which the self is the agent or source of action. *I* can feed myself; *I* can play baseball; *I* can please or distress my parents. Eventually a periphery of identifications may be incorporated into the self-concept: I am a boy, I am a member of my family, I am like others who speak a particular language or have a particular skin color. Thus the self-concept includes also elements that are "mine": my family, my group, my race, my community, my nationality. James (1902) summarized the individual's self-concept as the "sum-total of all that he can call his."

Identification and the Self

The *identification* process (described in Chapter 6) is a means by which a person takes on the values, beliefs, and actions of other people. In socialization this is the way parents and other agents of the culture transmit beliefs and values to younger people being assimilated into the society. Because the self represents a particular set of beliefs (about oneself—self-concept) and values (for oneself—self-esteem), identification also provides an important basis for the development of the sense of self.

Identification is an important kind of social interaction. It involves role-taking ("playing the role" of another person by acting as if one were in his shoes), intro-jection (assimilating the values of another person as if they were one's own), and imitation (copying the actions and behaviors of another person). There are many bases of identification. Freud (1933) suggested that the identification process is par-tially unconscious. He proposed that people tend to want to incorporate the actions and ways of other people who are especially important to them. If the object of identification is a nurturant and rewarding loved one, a person is likely to identify with the *love object.* (Freud proposed that this wards off fear and anxiety about the grief of losing this loved one, and referred to the process as *anaclitic* identification.) Another basis of identification may occur when one attempts to assimilate the actions and ways of powerful or threatening figures. (Freud termed this identification with the *aggressor,* or defensive identification.)

Cooley (1902) and Mead (1934) were among the first to suggest that the self-concept arises in identification and interaction with others. One achieves a concept of himself by assuming the role of another person, stepping into his shoes, so to speak, to have a look back at himself. At first one views himself as he thinks he is viewed by others who are especially important or meaningful to him—parents, teach-ers, or other loved or respected figures. Mead described this process as assuming the role of the *significant other.* Later the individual develops a composite notion synthesized from his interactions with many people over a range of time, and evolves a highly generalized conception of others. This collective conception, representing another kind of role into which one might step for a look back at himself, Mead called the *generalized other.* Mead did not attempt to verify his ideas through empirical research, but other investigators have done so.

Social Interaction and the Self

In one study (Manis, 1955), previously unacquainted young men who lived together for a number of weeks were seen to revise their own conceptions of themselves in the direction of the collective impression of them held by their close associates. The closer their association, the greater the influence of each on the other's self-concept. *Liked* others served in the capacity of *significant* others. Principles of perceptual selection nevertheless operated in screening the information acquired in the form of feedback from others: these interpersonal influences were more effective in producing socially *desirable* changes in the self-concept than socially *undesirable* changes.

In the same way that individuals hold stereotyped generalized notions about other people as a function of their identification with a particular ethnic, national, racial, or social group, people also hold stereotypical notions of themselves. Common themes

---

THE SELF AND SOCIAL INTERACTION

Starting with the assumption that one's social interactions with others provide the basis for his perception of himself, this study arranged to assess the self-concepts of a number of young men both prior to and after a period of close interaction with a set of new acquaintances, and to compare each man's concept of himself with the general concept of him held by his associates. Subjects were 101 male freshmen at the University of Illinois, most of whom were between 17 and 19 years of age. They were assigned to 8-man groups that occupied suites of adjacent rooms in a dormitory.

Major Questions and Findings. By comparing each man's description of himself and of others on the two different testing occasions, several hypotheses about the social origins of the self-concept were tested.

1. Does the difference between a person's concept of himself and that held by others decrease after he interacts with them for a period of time?

There was considerable evidence that the self-concept and the average concept held by others in the dormitory group (a "generalized other") converged over time, so that the two were more similar after 6 weeks of interaction than they had originally been.

2. Does the convergence of self-concept and the concept held by others result from changes in one's concept of himself, or from changes in the others' concept of him?

The results showed rather consistently that the increased similarity of self-concept and the concept held by others after 6 weeks of interaction resulted primarily from revisions in the individual's description of himself.

3. Do these changes in one's self-concept involve both changes for the better as well as for the worse?

There was consistent evidence that men were more willing to revise their concepts of themselves in a favorable or socially desirable direction than in an unfavorable direction. The greatest amount of change occurred in cases in which the initial self-concept was less socially desirable than the initial concept held by others; that is, revision of the self-concept toward that of the generalized other occurred most frequently in a socially desirable direction.

4. Are the influences of friends ("significant others") and non-friends equally effective in bringing about revision of the self-concept?

Revisions of the self-concept toward the concept held by specific other individual associates were more pronounced in the case of pairs of friends than in the case of pairs of non-friends.

Summary. In general, this investigation provides direct evidence that a person's concept of himself is influenced by the way others perceive him. At the same time, there was no evidence that the individual's concept of himself appreciably influenced the way others perceived him.

MANIS (1955)

THE MAKING OF A DOCTOR

A survey of medical students showed variations in the degree to which the occupational term "doctor" was incorporated into the self-concept. Thirty-one percent of the first-year students indicated that while dealing with patients they thought of themselves as doctors rather than as students. In the fourth year, 85 percent thought of themselves as doctors. Students generally indicated that they were more likely to think of themselves as doctors while interacting with patients than in their interactions with nurses, faculty members, and their fellow students. The greater the belief that the patient thought of him as a doctor, the greater the tendency for the student to think of himself as a doctor.

HUNTINGTON (1957)

have been found to recur among the self-concepts of members of particular cultural or subcultural groups. Members of a group often tend to attribute to themselves characteristics they assume to be typical of groups to which they are strongly attracted and with which they wish to identify themselves. This is true of many professional groups and professional roles.

In most cases, members of minority groups that are clearly differentiated within a society are especially likely to perceive themselves as typical of the particular group to which they belong. However, in certain cases (especially very young children) the desire to be affiliated and identified with a powerful dominant majority may lead to perceptual distortions in the self-concept. For example, preschool black children have appeared to be so strongly attracted to identify themselves with the dominant white majority that they may even suppress their own recognition of skin color (Clark & Clark, 1957).

The socialization process (Chapter 6) fosters the development of particular qualities in the self-concept. For example, in our culture, training cultivates sex-role differentiation and induces even very young children to recognize their identification with one sex or the other and to perceive in themselves qualities that are associated with cultural expectations for the behavior of members of that sex (Kagan, 1971). A little girl is likely to be rather reluctant to recognize herself as tough or tomboyish, and a little boy reluctant to recognize himself as dainty or shy.

BLACK DOLLS ARE BEAUTIFUL NOW

During the 1940s, about 250 black children between the ages of 3 and 10 were presented 2 dolls that differed only in hair and skin color: a black doll and a white doll. They were asked to hand the experimenter the doll that was "nice," or "best for playing," and so on. The overall pattern revealed a consistent preference (67 percent) for the white doll. In response to the request to indicate the doll that "looks like you" (presumably in skin and hair color), very young children chose the white doll more often than the black one. In 1969 the study was replicated with 89 black children and 71 white children. This time the majority of the black children (70 percent) preferred the black dolls. Like the blacks, the majority of the white children preferred the doll of their own race. The race of the interviewer had no effect on the children's choices.

CLARK AND CLARK (1957)
HRABA AND GRANT (1970)

SOCIAL ORIGINS OF SELF-ESTEEM

Like any other attitudinal structure, the self-concept includes not only perceptual *recognition* but also *evaluative* components. Beyond the fact that a person may misperceive and distort his conception of himself, he either likes or dislikes what he does recognize about himself. This evaluative aspect of self-perception (the degree to which one likes himself) is referred to as self-regard or *self-esteem.* A person who generally regards himself favorably, has a general feeling of approval of what he perceives in himself, and thus "likes himself," would be said to have a high level of self-esteem.

The idealized cognitive structure that a person holds as the composite of all he wishes he were and would like to be is called the *ideal self,* the standards for which lie within culturally defined standards of social desirability. The notion of the ideal self should not be confused with the fact that standards of social desirability or social acceptability often lead to idealization or glamorous aggrandizement in one's concept of himself. Processes of perceptual defense and vigilance often give rise to inaccuracies in self-perception and distortions in the direction of greater social desirability. The personality theorist Horney (1950) was particularly specific in distinguishing the "ideal" self (a set of notions about what one would ideally like to be) from what she called the "idealized" self (the polished-up and selectively aggrandized notion that constitutes a distorted self-concept).

Social Standards and Self-esteem

The evaluative aspects of the self-concept depend on social origins. Culturally defined standards of social desirability provide the standard against which aspirations and ideals are framed and against which one gauges his regard for himself. One's direct experiences of success and failure in his various efforts, of course, underlie his evaluation of himself. However, even success and failure must be defined with respect to some standard. Festinger (1954) formulated a theory of social comparison processes, which holds that most people evolve their own standards for personal success and failure out of implicit comparisons of themselves with the performance of other people whom they regard as peers or equals. Several experimental investigations have shown evidence that such social comparisons are indeed an important basis of self-evaluation (Chapman & Volkman, 1939).

There are many ways in which the systematic organization of training and social learning within the socialization process (Chapter 6) govern the development of self-esteem. Cross-cultural investigations comparing self-concepts and self-regard of members of various cultural groups suggest several kinds of variability. One interesting consequence of such differences accounts for some of the difficulties that members of one culture often experience in trying to understand the behavior of members of other cultures. For example, the characteristic American concern for the dignity and worth of the individual and the importance of self-respect is congruent with a generally high level of self-regard. In contrast, the traditional religious and social convictions (and perhaps even economic conditions of overpopulation) of the Oriental often generate a sense of personal humility and worthlessness. Thus the typical American may conceive of the Oriental as excessively humble and self-effacing, with an almost pathological lack of self-respect; on the other hand, the typical Chinese may think of the American as excessively vain and self-satisfied, with a pathological degree of egotistical conceit (LaBarre, 1946).

Members of a common culture, who share common standards for what is socially acceptable and valued, generally hold similar conceptions of the ideal self. The norms and standards of groups or cultures to which the individual belongs may also influence the standards against which he evaluates himself.

AMERICAN AND VIETNAMESE SELF-CONCEPT

A comparison of the performance of American and Vietnamese children on a sentence completion task showed that different cultural values govern their respective self-concepts. The self-concepts of the Vietnamese children were heavily infused with aspects of work and family life, those of the American children with aspects of recreation and self-reliance.

LEICHTY (1963)

Other investigations within our own culture suggest that the position one occupies in the social hierarchy of his society is related to his conception of himself and his self-esteem. Individuals who rank higher on the social ladder typically express greater self-esteem and show less evidence of feelings of personal inadequacy than do individuals in the lower classes (Himmelweit, 1955). In the 1950s members of discriminated-against minority ethnic or religious groups typically showed low levels of self-esteem and feelings of inferiority. But in the 1970s these differences were no longer so evident (Lessing & Zagorin, 1972).

Other investigations have shown that popular and well-liked persons tend to hold higher levels of self-esteem than rejected and disliked persons, at least up to the point that extremely high levels of self-regard represent obnoxious conceit (Fey, 1955; Reese, 1961). It appears, then, that being liked and approved of by others provides one important basis for liking and approving of oneself.

Social standards are instrumental in defining the criteria one uses in evaluating

BODY AND SELF

A group of 17-year-old boys that included early-maturers (physically accelerated adolescents) and late-maturers (physically retarded adolescents) underwent a projective picture test. Late-maturers displayed significantly more "negative characteristic" responses (less favorable self-concept) than the early-maturers. Similar results were obtained in a population of early- and late-maturing 17-year-old girls. It was suggested that early-maturers are generally treated in a mature manner by their peers and by adults and are thus relatively free from the tenseness involved in striving for status, which affects the self-concept adversely.

MUSSEN AND JONES (1957)
JONES AND MUSSEN (1958)

"SOUL" AND SELF

Studies conducted in the 1950s and 1960s have shown many instances of self-depreciation among blacks. Black children low in self-acceptance tended to repudiate not only themselves and the out-group of white children, but also their own ethnic group. Blacks in segregated households also tended to show significantly lower degrees of self-esteem than those in desegregated households, suggesting that "the (segregated) black community depresses the self-esteem of its members." It appears, however, that the relatively new black power ideology has reversed this trend, at least among the young. College students of both races, scoring high on measures of black-power orientation, placed a lower evaluation on white persons and a higher evaluation on black persons than did those low in black-power belief.

TRENT (1957)
HAGGSTROM (1963)
LESSING AND ZAGORIN (1972)

himself, but one may also depend on the judgments of others when the criteria of success or failure are ambiguous. The content of the self-concept is derived from taking the role of others for a retrospective look at oneself, and one's measure of his own attractiveness may be derived in the same way. One is likely to approve of those aspects of himself that others approve, and to disapprove of those elements that others disapprove. Sears, Maccoby, and Levin (1957) have suggested that the origins of pride (self-approval) and shame (self-disapproval) derive from the early recognition of the standards used by others in expressing their approval and disapproval of one's behavior.

Of course, one is selective about the criteria against which he judges himself. One does not blindly accept all feedback from others with equal significance. The standards for self-evaluation depend on the content of one's self-concept. A professional psychologist does not evaluate his piano-playing ability by comparisons with Van Cliburn; likewise Van Cliburn does not evaluate his knowledge of psychology by comparison with the current president of the American Psychological Association. James (1890) described these selective mechanisms in screening feedback from others when evaluating oneself, and they are the basis of a descriptive theoretical model that Festinger (1954) calls the *theory of social comparison processes.*

Attractiveness to Others

The social origins of self-esteem include one's attractiveness to other people. The more a person feels that others find him attractive, the more he will regard himself well. Both Newcomb (1961) and Tagiuri (1957) found that people overestimate reciprocation of their attraction to others. That is, if Person A is attracted to Person B, he is inclined to overestimate the extent to which B is in turn attracted to A. Mutuality of attraction is certainly to be expected in friendships (especially if they occur in natural groups and are sustained over some period of time), and therefore actual

---

PERSONALITY OF A LOSER

Society's deviants—the genius, the idiot, the midget, the giant, the Klansman, the Weatherman, and so on—have at least one thing in common: during their socialization they frequently encounter rejection, persecution, or second-class citizenship. A series of laboratory studies was designed to "create" social deviants by giving subjects a series of personality scales to fill out, as well as the purported scores of 1000 similar subjects who had filled out the scales earlier. The subjects were then given their own scores for comparison, with the feedback for "deviants" showing their scores to be at or near the end of the scales. The "nondeviants" were given scores at the center of the scales. The procedure was repeated three times, with the deviants showing increasing worry. When given scores of others and asked to choose groups, deviants tended to seek out other deviants, following a real-life pattern (e.g., artists seek out artists, homosexuals seek out homosexuals). When deviance scores were either made public or remained confidential, the subjects in the latter category, when given the choice, preferred to work alone more than subjects in the other category. In real life this behavior is analogous to people hiding their backgrounds, Americanizing their names, and so on in order to keep their deviance undisclosed. Finally, when asked to help in a task of writing as many as fifty letters, twice as many deviants were willing to help as nondeviants (especially if the request for help came from the latter), presumably because such prosocial behavior tends to make deviance more palatable to others.

FREEDMAN AND DOOB (1968)

reciprocation of attraction is far greater than random or chance prediction. But subjective estimates of reciprocation usually even exceed the actual level of mutuality (Tagiuri, 1957), which suggests that a person tends to project his own liking for another to that other person, whether the other reciprocates this attraction or not.

Further studies have suggested that low-status, unpopular individuals tend to either exert considerable effort to ingratiate themselves with popular individuals (Freedman & Doob, 1968) or underestimate their own rejection by others, overestimating their attractiveness (Ausubel & Schiff, 1955; I. K. Taylor, 1956). However, very popular people may also sometimes overestimate their own popularity (Brandt, 1958). Evidence related to this question is varied, so that no single conclusion can be clearly drawn as to differences in the accuracy with which one's attractiveness to others is perceived from various vantage points in the status hierarchy. In one investigation people in an experimental discussion group overestimated their own attractiveness to high-status people, and underestimated their own attractiveness to low-status people (Hurwitz, Zander, & Hymowitch, 1960).

SELF-CONTROL

Social control and self-control are very closely related. The socialization process entails a tremendous exertion of social control forces over the individual's behavior. Not only through the manipulation of rewards and punishments, but also through control of the models and examples provided, one is very much controlled by his society. Moreover, socialization provides some insurance for stability and perpetuation of the society. Through identification and the emergent sense of self, one incorporates standards of self-control that are congruent with the interests of the society to which he belongs.

People differ with respect to the relative importance of internal and external controls in their lives. From a sociological point of view, Riesman (1950) characterized people as either *other-directed* (controlled by other people and group standards), *inner-directed* (controlled by internalized personal standards unique to each individual), or *tradition-directed* (controlled by traditional codes and standards of the society, incorporated as one's own). A related clinical approach to the study of such differences has been undertaken by Rotter (1966, 1967) and others (e.g., Chance, 1965). This involves the use of a diagnostic measure called the Locus of Control Scale, which is designed to measure the extent to which a person thinks of his behavior as controlled by fate, supernatural sources, or entrenched power structures (external locus of control) as compared to conscience, will, or free choice (internal locus of control). Of course, many people who think of themselves as internally controlled may be very well socialized, so that their behavior is congruent with the standards of their society.

Social Desirability

Recognition of a society's standards for acceptable behavior affords an important means through which social control of behavior may be internalized within the individual. The experience of personal satisfaction for adhering to those standards evolves out of the initial conditions of infantile dependency. From nurturance-seeking, one eventually comes to seek approval as an end in itself. Eventually, the quest for direct social acceptance and approval evolves into general efforts to insure the collective approval of other members of the society. The standards that determine society's approval or disapproval of behavior are recognized incorporated as internal standards that allow one to anticipate whether his behavior will gain approval.

SOCIAL DESIRABILITY AND THE APPROVAL MOTIVE

In the 1950s it became increasingly clear that a dimension of *social desirability* underlies all self-descriptive items of the sort used in psychological tests. One investigator (Edwards, 1954, 1957) used a battery of items from standard tests of psychopathology on which test takers usually displayed "faking" by responding in a socially desirable way, that is, describing themselves as cooperative, agreeable, objective, responsible, and the like. From these items he constructed a test that aimed to measure social desirability as a particular personality trait that is more pronounced in some individuals than in others.

In 1964 Douglas Crowne and David Marlowe extended these principles into a set of explorations designed to study the origins and nature of *approval-seeking* motivation. Although their original interest in conducting these studies centered on the tendency of people to describe themselves in socially desirable ways on personality tests, their research findings added considerably to the understanding of relationships between approval seeking and other areas of human behavior. The Marlowe-Crowne Social Desirability Scale measured approval seeking by the extent to which a person agreed with a set of statements describing himself in socially desirable ways and disagreed with socially undesirable descriptions. In this it differed from Edwards' measure because it contained no items describing undesirable pathological conditions and was thus confined to relatively "normal" ranges of behavior.

Need for Approval and Conformity. The experimenter, acting authoritatively and purportedly high in status and prestige, put a group of college students to a dull, boring, and repetitive task of spool-packing. High-need-for-approval subjects rated the task as more enjoyable than did low-need-for-approval subjects, in line with the experimenter's implied demand for conformity. High-need-for-approval subjects also showed greater suggestibility to group pressure and maintained this behavior even when group pressure was absent (as when subjects were asked to indicate whether they detected heat in an element that actually never warmed up).

Need for Approval and Language Behavior. A work association test was administered to subjects under varying conditions of speed and time limits, and their responses were analyzed in terms of "commonality scores" (extent to which a subject responded as he thought his peers would). High-need-for-approval subjects showed the greatest commonality.

Need for Approval and Verbal Conditioning. High-need-for-approval subjects, presumably showing greater sensitivity to the experimenter than low-need-for-approval subjects do, showed greater conditionability under verbal reinforcement, that is, a greater verbal output with experimenter approval and less output with experimenter disapproval.

Need for Approval and Risk-taking. The fact that high-need-for-approval subjects displayed more restricted and cautious choices in a dart-throwing task than did low-need-for-approval subjects was assumed to reflect their adherence to an implicit norm of American society: one should neither undertake a task too easy or show off by undertaking one too difficult.

Need for Approval and Attitude Change. Improvised role-playing in which subjects were required to rehearse, reformulate, and spontaneously present a persuasive communication counter to their own beliefs resulted in a greater attitude change toward the communicated idea in high-need-for-approval subjects than in low-need-for-approval subjects.

Edwards, and Crowne and Marlowe suggested that social desirability or the need for approval is a stable dimension of the individual personality itself. However, there is also evidence that certain classes or groups of people have unique codes of their own on what constitutes social desirability. When high school students were presented with a list of descriptive personality traits and asked to rate them for social desirability, female subjects gave higher ratings overall than male subjects. The same tendency for high rating was displayed by scholastic overachievers (presumably displaying an unrealistic, rose-colored view of the world). Subjects from higher socioeconomic backgrounds, as well as those with higher IQ levels (regardless of social class), varied little in their ratings, thus showing considerable certainty and agreement on what is socially desirable. Subjects with histories of discipline difficulties displayed higher ratings for negative or negatively toned traits, presumably displaying defensive defiance.

EDWARDS (1954, 1957)
CROWNE AND MARLOWE (1964)
STILLER, SCHWARTZ, AND COWEN (1965)

Standards of social desirability are rarely stated formally and explicitly, yet they are generally well known to individual members of any social system. By the age of 5, most American children are already keenly aware of the informal standards that distinguish the sexes. The threat of being called a sissy upsets any first-grade boy who has been relatively normally socialized. Adolescents are remarkably sensitive to their own group's standards of dress, hair style, and slang. Subcultures of the theater, the advertising industry, and even academic psychology, have their own habits of dress, conventions of social behavior, and codes of general conduct. To find a catalog defining these standards would be virtually impossible, yet every assimilated member of each of these subcultures knows its standards intuitively.

Standards of social desirability vary slightly from one individual to another, and they vary somewhat more from one subculture to another within a larger society (Edwards, 1957). Yet several researchers have found that these standards are well conventionalized even within complex social systems. Edwards (1957) first described the potency of social desirability in steering both normal and pathological human behavior. Later, Crowne and Marlowe (1964) extended his work into an exploration of "the approval motive" as a coordinating force in shaping personality. Under some circumstances, the approval motive may become pathologically strong, producing a type of person who values the acceptance of others so highly that he appears to have no standards of his own for self-acceptance. His behavior, then, is predominantly under the control of others rather than himself, and he is described by Riesman (1950) as the "other-directed person" and by Rotter (1966, 1967) and others as having an "external locus of control of behavior."

LOCUS OF CONTROL

To find out whether you are inclined toward internal or external control, simply add your choices on each side (left—internal, right—external).

Table 7–1   Locus of Control Scale

I more strongly believe that:	or
Promotions are earned through hard work and persistence.	Making a lot of money is largely a matter of getting the right breaks.
In my experience I have noticed that there is usually a direct connection between how hard I study and the grades I get.	Many times the reactions of teachers seem haphazard to me.

(Continued on p. 168)

The number of divorces indicates that more and more people are not trying to make their marriages work.	Marriage is largely a gamble.
When I am right I can convince others.	It is silly to think that one can really change another person's basic attitudes.
In our society a man's future earning power is dependent upon his ability.	Getting promoted is really a matter of being a little luckier than the next guy.
If one knows how to deal with people they are really quite easily led.	I have little influence over the way other people behave.
In my case the grades I make are the results of my own efforts; luck has little or nothing to do with it.	Sometimes I feel that I have little to do with the grades I get.
People like me can change the course of world affairs if we make ourselves heard.	It is only wishful thinking to believe that one can really influence what happens in society at large.
I am the master of my fate.	A great deal that happens to me is probably a matter of chance.
Getting along with people is a skill that must be practiced.	It is almost impossible to figure out how to please some people.

Source: Reprinted with permission of the author. These items were taken from an earlier, discarded form of the test and are not included in currently used measures.

ROTTER (1971)

Morality: Conscience, Pride, and Guilt

Among the most significant elements in Freud's early description of the structure of personality were the *superego* and the *ego-ideal*. The function of these aspects is to exercise control over the part that organizes behavior, the *ego*. Freud described the ego-ideal as the seat of personal satisfaction (pride) and dissatisfaction (guilt), and suggested that it has social origins in the child's identification with authority figures whose standards of conduct are assimilated as his own. This analysis evolved out of Freud's clinical experiences with neurotic Victorian upper-middle-class Europeans, but it is congruent with general analysis of the function and origins of *conscience* derived by empirical research from other theoretical points of view. Because Freud's description of the superego carried a number of surplus connotations beyond the functions of personal pride and guilt, many contemporary psychologists prefer the term *conscience* to refer specifically to the person's acquired capacity to control his own behavior through self-administered rewards (*pride*—self-approval and self-satisfaction) and punishments (*guilt*—self-disapproval and self-dissatisfaction).

The identification process is an important basis for the development of conscience. Through identification (described earlier in this chapter) one assimilates the values of other agents of the society. Socialization practices within the society attempt to foster this process as a means of preserving stability in the society. Certain kinds of practices in socialization cultivate conscience, and others retard it. (See Chapter 6

FINKING ON FRIENDS

From previous ratings made by members of four groups of adolescents, two high-status and two low-status members were selected to act as experimental confederates. In the experiment proper, each group witnessed a transgression against adult authority committed by one of the confederates. The manipulated transgressions were the theft of 75 cents from a teacher by either the high-status or the low-status confederate; or the erasure of an important tape left in the group leaders unattended recorder by either confederate. All subjects were subsequently interrogated by adult authority about the transgression, forcing them to make a decision between two contending principles: not to lie to adult authority, or not to "fink" on a peer. When interrogated alone, subjects showed little reluctance to report the transgression. When interrogated in pairs, they did not hesitate to "fink" on the low-status peers, but refused overwhelmingly to "fink" on the high-status peers.

HARARI AND McDAVID (1969)

for a broader discussion of variations in socialization practices). The child's early experience of approval and disapproval by others provides the foundation from which conscience grows. Sears, Maccoby, and Levin (1957) found that the same kind of "love-oriented" child-rearing practices (involving interpersonal warmth and its withdrawal) that accentuate the development of approval-seeking behavior also facilitate the early development of conscience. This poses an apparent paradox: approval-seeking (external control of behavior) and conscience (internal control of behavior)

Table 7–2 Kohlberg's Six Stages of Conscience Development

Stage	Characteristics	Example
Preconventional		
1. Punishment and obedience	Physical consequences of action determine morality. Avoidance of punishment and deference to power guide conscience.	Renfield, Dracula's assistant, who did all that his master commanded.
2. Instrumental relativism	Personal needs, primarily one's own, but occasionally those of others, determine morality. Reciprocity of satisfaction guides conscience.	Tom Sawyer, the self-centered pragmatist.
Conventional		
3. Interpersonal concordance	Approval-seeking determines morality. The "good boy/nice girl" concept guides conscience.	Mary Poppins and her representation of all that is nice and good and lovable.
4. Authority orientation	Duty, respect, and maintenance of social order determine morality. Rules of conduct guide conscience.	Colonel Saito (in *Bridge on the River Kwai*), or "the captain who goes down with his sinking ship."
Postconventional		
5. Social contract	Utilitarian values, combined with procedural rules, determine conduct. Rules of conduct—viewed as means to ends, not ends in themselves—guide conscience.	Captain Vere (in *Billy Budd*) or writers of the U.S. Constitution; the "official morality" of the U.S. government.
6. Universal ethics	Abstract universal principles of justice and human rights determine morality. Respect for the dignity of human beings guides conscience.	Joan of Arc; the martyr who transcends this world and manifests universal principles.

STATUS AND STEALERS

The status of an experimental confederate was varied by having him wear either a suit and tie (higher status) or work clothes (lower status). On 276 occasions he entered specified public phone booths at Grand Central Station and Kennedy Airport in New York, pretended to engage in a brief telephone conversation, deliberately left a dime on the shelf in front of the telephone, and then made his exit. Two minutes after another person occupied the booth, the confederate returned and asked that person whether he had found the dime left there earlier by the confederate. When appearing to be of high status, the confederate got his dime back 77 percent of the time, but when he appeared to be of lower status, he got it back only 38 percent of the time. When college students were asked to predict what they thought would happen under such circumstances, they predicted a money return of about 70 percent of the time, regardless of the loser's status (but they predicted a return rate of about 95 percent for themselves if approached by the loser).

BICKMAN (1971)

arise out of the same kinds of early experiences and parent-child interactions. But this paradox is resolved with the recognition that internal controls are nothing more than external controls that have been absorbed and internalized.

Socialization practices that emphasize reward for "good" behavior and non-reward for "bad" behavior have been described by Aronfreed (1968) as *induction* techniques. These techniques foster attraction between the trainer and the learner and increase the likelihood that identification will occur and that the learner will adopt the values of the trainer. In contrast, practices that emphasize punishment of "bad" behavior and indifference to "good" behavior have been described as *sensitization* techniques (Aronfreed, 1968). These rest upon anxiety and aversive learning, and they interrupt identification of the learner with the trainer, discouraging internalization of the trainer's values. Consequently, induction techniques tend to facilitate the early development of conscience, while sensitization techniques retard it.

Piaget (1952) described the development of the child's sense of *morality* and the concept of justice from a cognitive point of view. He outlined steps in the development of conscience: first, blind obedience to authority; second, recognition of social standards of right and wrong; and third, incorporation of these standards into the experience of guilt. According to Piaget, the child's concept of justice progresses gradually from *moral realism* (absolutism) to *moral relativism*. Up to age 7 or 8 the child conceives of justice within rigid and inflexible standards of right and wrong. Between 8 and 11 he becomes increasingly concerned with equalitarianism, and eventually his concept of justice is tempered with notions of equity and fairness, with the realization that circumstances may justify exceptions to certain moral rules. For example, Piaget asked very young children, "Why shouldn't you lie?" Very young children regarded lying as bad, regardless of circumstances. But older children showed recognition of "white lies" and special conditions that justified a "fib" (Harari & McDavid, 1969).

Kohlberg (1969) has extended Piaget's early analysis into a more detailed description of the progression of moral development. Kohlberg describes three general levels of moral thinking: *preconventional* (based on the perception of power to manipulate reward and punishment consequences of behavior), *conventional* (based on conformity to expectations of others and maintenance of social stability), and *postconventional* (based on autonomous moral principles with universal validity and applicability) (see Table 7–2).

RIPPING-OFF THE BOOKSTORE

Shoppers were observed while browsing in the paperback book section of a college bookstore. All of the 129 male and 111 female shoppers were white and approximately 18 to 30 years of age. When a shopper was observed alone in a particular section of the store (i.e., no other shoppers within 50 to 60 feet), an experimental confederate approached the spot and staged a theft in full view of the observed subject: the "thief" reached in front of the observed subject, picked up a book, and placed it inside his (or her) shirt, and then retreated to another area of the store. Another confederate, acting and dressed as a bookstore employee then moved within 3 to 4 feet of the subject, either waiting for the subject's report or (if none was forthcoming) questioning him (or her) about the theft. The four accomplice "thieves" were played by black male, black female, white male, and white female undergraduate students dressed neither outlandishly nor overly conservatively.

As expected, there was a significant difference between reporting the crime spontaneously (without prompting) or confirming it (prompted by questioning). In either case, however, the rate was extremely low: no subject spontaneously reported the theft, and only 6.7 percent did so upon prompting. Evidently the institution of the campus bookstore is generally regarded as a "rip-off" (having an excessive profit margin)—to be ripped-off. Shoplifters were not reported differentially as a function of their sex, but female observers tended to report thefts more often than did males. Thefts committed by black shoplifters were confirmed more frequently than those by white shoplifters. If reporting and/or confirming is viewed as a punitive act, then the differential rates represent a manifestation of racial prejudice.

DERTKE, PENNER, AND ULRICH (1972)

Conscience is an extended form of social control. It represents the transmission of culturally defined standards for behavior to the individual. Once this capacity is acquired, one may exercise self-control in place of control by others. Standards of social desirability become one's own standards. Taboos, social sanctions, and moral codes are incorporated as personal standards. Ultimately the experience of personal guilt is more powerful in controlling behavior than any threat of retribution, whether in the form of legal punishment, witchcraft and the supernatural, or eternity in hell.

SELF AND SOCIETY

The organization of behavior into a coherent personality within each individual under the influence of his culture was described in Chapter 6. But this chapter is concerned with the individual's awareness of himself and his conscious relationship to his society. The interplay between self and society is at the heart of social psychology. Each concept gives validity to the other: *society* has meaning because it is comprised of many unique and individually different selves; conversely, *self* has meaning because it is embedded in a social matrix. There are many ways in which a person's experience of himself and his related experience of his society are closely linked.

Values, Goals, and the Self

The humanistic point of view in modern psychology represents a set of values, rather than an organized theoretical structure (May, 1953; Maslow, 1968; Hamacheck, 1971). These values emphasize each person's expression of himself as an individual. Maslow (1968) has described this kind of expression as an impulse to improve oneself, to actualize one's potentialities, and to move in the direction of human fulfillment—and

A HIERARCHY OF NEEDS

Abraham Maslow, a widely read spokesman for the humanistic point of view in modern psychology, has outlined a hierarchy of basic human needs, arranged from the most potent to the least potent, as follows:

1. The physiological needs (hunger and thirst)
2. The safety needs (security)
3. The love and belongingness needs (security and affection)
4. The esteem needs (affection and regard)
5. The self-actualization needs (self-fulfillment)

Maslow has further described the features that characterize people who achieve the ability to function at the highest reaches of this hierarchy. By studying such self-actualized figures as Lincoln, Jefferson, Whitman, Beethoven, William James, Franklin Roosevelt, Einstein, Eleanor Roosevelt, and Schweitzer, Maslow concluded that all of these

were realistically oriented
accepted themselves and others
were spontaneous in thoughts, feelings, and actions
were task-centered more than self-centered
had a need for occasional privacy
were autonomous and independent
were continually awed by simple basic beauty
had frequent "mystic" or "oceanic" (not necessarily religious) experiences
felt a sense of identification with mankind as a whole
had intensely profound relationships with a few loved people
were democratic and equalitarian with respect to people of various races, beliefs, or
    positions
were highly creative
possessed a highly developed sense of ethics
possessed a good sense of humor
resisted cultural conformity

MASLOW (1943, 1954, 1968)

has labeled it *self-actualization.* In Maslow's schematic representation, a hierarchy of needs progresses from the most basic and animalistic (physiological) needs to the most human need (self-actualization).

Social psychologists have also been concerned with the expression of these kinds of values in human behavior, especially as they are related to their social context. Although there is considerable evidence (outlined earlier, and discussed further in Chapter 9) that the dependency of the human infant induces him to learn to value nurturance by others, it is also true that as he matures he comes to value his ability to master and control his environment. Through personal success in coping with the world—as well as through direct training to become independent—autonomy and independence come to be valued objectives. The successful manipulation of events and people in order to satisfy desires and reach goals may become an end in itself. Adler's (1925) interpretation of personality development stresses the importance of the "struggle for power" and the effort to overcome "inferiority" (forced dependency). It is clear that *mastery*—the desire to manipulate and control the environment—plays an important part in growth and development. Both animals and human infants can be observed to sit for long periods manipulating various kinds of gadgetry with no further incentive than the play itself (Harlow, Harlow, & Meyer, 1950; Butler, 1953; Berlyne, 1955). Children's play (and probably adult recreation too)

seems to be driven by its own rewards (Piaget, 1951; L'Abate & L'Abate, 1973). In
fact, much of man's exploratory behavior in both work and play is difficult to account
for without assuming that he must experience some kind of satisfaction from merely
exploring and mastering his environment (Piaget, 1952; Berlyne, 1958; Elkind &
Flavell, 1969).

Such "curiosity" motivation probably also induces man to attempt to complicate
and enliven his environment (by decoration and innovation) when it becomes sterile
and boring (Hebb, 1955). *Creative* behavior (as opposed to merely *intelligent* behavior) also represents a socially useful form of curiosity and exploration. Intelligent behavior reflects the ability to *solve* problems, whereas creative behavior reflects the
ability to formulate or *make* problems as well as to solve them (Getzels & Jackson,
1954). Psychologists are still undecided as to the specific origins of curiosity motivation, but it is probably closely related to direct independence training in socialization
and to the fact that manipulative control of the environment is usually a prelude to
the achievement of many other kinds of goals and objectives.

Social power represents the manipulation and control of the social aspect of one's
environment—other people. This facet of human motivation has been termed *Machiavellianism* (Geis & Christie, 1970; Christie & Geis, 1970). Niccolò Machiavelli, the
Renaissance statesman, is remembered for his cynical views on the successful
manipulation of others. Christie and Geis (1970) have used simple paper and pencil
tests to measure Machiavellian attitudes. People who like to manipulate others
("Machiavellians") are more likely to be among males, to come from urban backgrounds, and to be relatively young members of the society (who grew up in the
context of a newer set of social ideas than the older generation). Machiavellians are
likely to be in professions that involve manipulating people (psychiatrists as opposed
to surgeons; social psychologists as opposed to physicists) (Geis & Christie, 1970).
They are able to cheat on tests and then deny it and stare the accuser coolly in the
eye. The Machiavellian is cool and detached, resistant to social pressures, rational,
and logical; in contrast the non-Machiavellian is a "soft touch," empathizes with others, is warm, and gets caught up in human interaction (Christie & Geis, 1970).

Social power of adults over children (but not the reverse) is the accepted social
pattern in our culture. To a limited extent tradition has endorsed the dominance of
male over female. This fact underlies the discontent of women in our culture and the
frustration they experience in their pursuit of autonomy, power, and control (Horney,
1939; Komarovsky, 1946; de Beauvoir, 1953; Friedan, 1963; G. Greer, 1971).

The motivation that induces people to strive for *prestige* is closely related to social
power and social manipulation. A position of high social status implies the ability to
dominate and control others. But this capacity is related to many other aspects of
social interaction. Prestige is partially dependent on gaining the acceptance and approval of one's peers. Furthermore, the symbols of one's social status are in many
cases material ones, so that the attainment of high status in a society may involve the
acquisition of particular goods or the control of resources (capital). All of these are
usually closely intertwined in our culture. However, under special circumstances it
is possible to dissociate them. For example, one may be wealthy but have neither
social power nor prestige (if he is a miser who hoards his fortune in secret, or an
embezzler who must hide his riches); or one may exercise social power without either
wealth or prestige (in a military system); or one may accrue prestige without either
wealth or power (deposed royalty, unseated nobility, or distinguished scholars or
scientists in nonlucrative fields).

The symbolic value of property as evidence of social power and prestige is very
strong in our culture. Many people fall into the trap of judging their own personal
worth in terms of material acquisitions, and they believe that others also judge them
by the same standards. In some cases, *acquisitive* motivation (to amass tokens and

Table 7–3 Are You a Machiavellian?

	Disagree		Neutral	Agree	
	A lot	A little		A lot	A little
1. The best way to handle people is to tell them what they want to hear.	1	2	3	4	5
2. When you ask someone to do something for you, it is best to give the real reasons rather than giving reasons that might carry more weight.	5	4	3	2	1
3. Anyone who completely trusts anyone else is asking for trouble.	1	2	3	4	5
4. It is hard to get ahead without cutting corners here and there.	1	2	3	4	5
5. It is safest to assume that all people have a vicious streak and it will come out when they are given a chance.	1	2	3	4	5
6. One should take action only when sure it is morally right.	5	4	3	2	1
7. Most people are basically good and kind.	5	4	3	2	1
8. There is no excuse for lying to someone.	5	4	3	2	1
9. Most men forget more easily the death of their fathers than the loss of their property.	1	2	3	4	5
10. Generally speaking, men won't work hard unless they're forced to.	1	2	3	4	5

Check the point on the scale that most closely represents your attitude. To find your Mach score, add the numbers that you have checked in each column. The National Opinion Research Center, which used a form very similar to this in a random sample of American adults, found that the national average was 25.

Source: Reprinted from *Psychology Today*. Adapted from Richard Christie and Florence L. Geis, *Studies in Machiavellianism* (New York: Academic Press, 1970). © 1970 by Academic Press.

CHRISTIE (1970)
CHRISTIE AND GEIS (1970)
GEIS AND CHRISTIE (1970)

symbols of wealth) does not end with the hoarding and retention of goods, but extends even to their ostentatious use and *conspicuous consumption*. Veblen (1899) wrote of the "leisure class" in society and the importance of using up consumable goods as a symbol of high social status. Many aspects of our culture tend to support this, although in the final analysis, one who cannot dissociate his own sense of personal worth from the goods he has amassed has a distorted sense of self. A self-concept and self-esteem founded on such values is neither durable nor stable.

A certain amount of acquisitive motivation derives logically from experience. Many objects that are associated with mastery and control of the environment become instruments of satisfaction of needs, and thus accrue value. If these objects are recognized culturally as symbols of esteem and prestige, their value is even further enhanced. But extremely high levels of acquisitive motivation (greed or miserliness)

> **THE STATUS-SEEKERS**
>
> Observations showed that conspicuous consumption, depending on the product, can either reinforce or elevate the consumer's status. Purchasing a Buick or an Oldsmobile indicated the consumer's way of showing he was going upward, but not enough, at this stage, for a Cadillac. Sterling silver was praised for its craftsmanship, and pipes and ball points (at $50 each) for their durability, but were bought for their upper-class appeal. Regardless of one's personal preferences, dresses and curtains were bought in line with what magazines described as fashionable.
>
> PACKARD (1957)

are not usually regarded as socially desirable. However, they are rarely discouraged or punished in our society. But the type of collectivist society envisioned by Marx (Marx & Engels, 1847) would abolish private ownership of property and socially discourage acquisitive motivation.

In a series of studies of attitudes toward personal property, children and adults living in a *kibbutz* in Israel were questioned (Spiro, 1958). The children expressed much greater interest in personal property than did their elders. The authors concluded that extended socialization in the kibbutz gradually extinguished the early acquisitive motivation of the youngsters. However, another plausible explanation might also be considered: the adults of the kibbutz had been taught that open expressions of interest in personal property are socially unacceptable, making them less willing to express any interest in private ownership to a visiting interviewer. (Yet at night, the same adults very likely retired to listen to their own transistor radios, hidden carefully beneath their pillows.)

Environmental mastery, curiosity, material acquisitiveness, and social prestige are all components in what psychologists call *achievement* motivation (Berlyne, 1955; Maw & Maw, 1965). In a way it would be useful to make a clearer distinction between achievement motivation and achievement behavior, for there are many possible motivations and values that underlie and produce achieving behavior in a person. Some approaches to the study of achievement behavior focus on persistence in the face of obstacles and frustrations as one strives to master his environment (McClelland et al., 1953), whereas others focus on competitive standards of excellence and public recognition of achievement (Edwards, 1954). Both, of course, are components in achievement. Some investigators have further proposed a distinction between a positive component of achievement striving—*hope for success* (high aspirations and

> **HOPE FOR SUCCESS AND FEAR OF FAILURE**
>
> Subjects in an experiment were asked first what they realistically expected to score on an exam, and then were asked to indicate the grade they would settle for. People who indicated willingness to settle for a grade very near the upper limit of their expectations were described as "hopeful of success," whereas those who indicated willingness to settle for a grade near the lower range of their expectations were described as "fearful of failure." These two groups were characterized by lower levels of achievement motivation than the middle-range group. The findings were interpreted as evidence that people who have very strong needs for achievement are likely to prefer moderate risks and moderate goal levels, and to avoid setting either very low or very high goals for themselves.
>
> CLARK, TEEVAN, AND RICCIUTI (1956)

high expectation to succeed)—and a negative component—*fear of failure* (high aspirations and low expectation to succeed) (Bieri, 1953; Clark, Teevan & Ricciuti, 1956).
The description of these varieties of motivation under a single label is useful in considering the overt activities that serve these needs (because they all tend to converge upon the goal of personal success); but to analyze and understand the many
sources from which achievement stems, it is misleading to simplify achievement
under one broad label (Ausubel, 1968).

Socialization practices (especially those associated with early independence training) vary considerably among the many subcultures within our society. Consequently,
research has discovered many intriguing kinds of variation in achievement motivation and behavior. In general, firstborn children display relatively strong achievement
motivation and outstanding records of achievement (Schachter, 1963). Furthermore,
achievement is more characteristically associated with the male role than with the
female role in our school systems (Chance, 1965; McCandless, 1967). In fact, to
some extent females are even taught an aversive "fear of success" (Horner, 1969).
Areas of differential expectation for achievement are culturally defined; females are
expected to (and do) achieve more in verbal areas and reading, whereas males excel
in quantitative areas and mathematics (Maccoby, 1966). There is also considerable
evidence that membership in a culturally disadvantaged minority group subject to
bigotry and prejudice interferes with achievement motivation and behavior (Pettigrew, 1964; Baehr, 1965). However, certain ethnic groups less subject to bigoted
suppression—notably Jews (Jospe, 1964) and Japanese (DeVos, 1961; Caudill & Lin,
1967)—show unusually strong aspirations and expectations for achievement. Typically, the lower socioeconomic classes in our culture are less achievement-oriented:
parents do not hold high expectations for their children, and their socialization practices do not emphasize achievement. In turn, the children hold lower evaluations of
their capacity to achieve and set lower goals for themselves (B. C. Rosen, 1955).

HOW TO SUCCEED IN BUSINESS

Over a hundred executives from various types of business establishments were
tested and personally interviewed. A history of continuous promotion, a high degree
of future promotability, great responsibility, and a high salary level were the criteria
for "success"; converse patterns indicated "failure." The successful business executive was found to reflect many of the attitudes and values generally accepted by
middle-class American society: a desire for achievement, a strong mobility drive, a
view that authority is controlling but helpful rather than destructive, a well-defined
self-structure (knowing what one is and what one wants), and "positive" aggression
(not destructive, but channeled into work or struggle for status). However, such
individuals also pay a price for upholding these values and profiting from them:
uncertainty, constant activity, continual fear of losing ground, inability to be in-
trospectively leisurely, and artificial limitations to their emotionalized interpersonal
relations.

HENRY (1949)

Social Mobility and Alienation

Under many circumstances—especially when there is social upheaval and instability
—one's sense of self and one's relationship to society may be disturbed. Socialization
practices within a given society or subsociety operate to produce uniformities of behavior and to prepare the person for assimilation into his society. But sometimes a

person who is socialized in one society may seek to gain entry into another and find that he is unprepared for it. This difficulty of social adjustment is especially true in our own culture when a person moves from one social class into another. In a caste-based social structure (where lines of class distinction are rigid and impermeable, regardless of what the person achieves or does with his life), such social mobility or migration into new subcultures cannot occur. But our society is a fluid one, permitting rather free social mobility. Despite fairly clear implicit demarcations of social classes according to income, educaton, tastes, manners, and habits, society permits (and even encourages) one to migrate upward to higher class levels on the basis of individual initiative and achievement. This is called *upward social mobility*. Its consequences for the individual are manifold. The person who is effectively socialized within the lower class, assimilating its values and standards, may experience some difficulty when he later seeks to be assimilated into an upper-middle-class subculture when he has achieved wealth, prestige, and status because of his accomplishments or alliances. The disdain of the "old guard aristocracy" for the "nouveau riche arriviste" typifies such difficulties in social assimilation.

The very fact of upward social mobility implies a kind of failure of socialization: the individual who is hypothetically fully socialized at the lower levels of the society normally would not be expected to develop aspirations toward higher levels of social function. Several sociological and psychological analyses of poverty (for example, Harrington, 1962) describe the stultifying effects of lower-class socialization on the aspirations and achievement motivation of lower-class individuals. But our culture's middle-class values encourage every man to rise to the highest level of achievement of which he is capable. This concept produced the notion of the "white man's burden" to lift primitive societies to higher levels, as well as Galbraith's argument, in *The Affluent Society* (1961), that the American middle class is morally obligated to encourage the upward mobility of the impoverished lower classes. The difference between the welfare programs of the 1930s and those of the "Great Society" of the 1960s was that the latter were addressed to the socialization process itself. They sought to manipulate the conditions of socialization that perpetuate poverty, rather than simply to manipulate the resultant symptoms of poverty superficially. In some situations upwardly mobile people may anticipate their migration to higher status levels and assume the values and habits of the social position to which they aspire. This is called *anticipatory socialization* (Merton & Kitt, 1950).

In general, research shows that upward social mobility engenders problems of personal adjustment, producing anxiety symptoms and even psychosomatic disorders (Hollingshead & Redlich, 1958; Scotch, 1960). But people who are successful in rising to higher status levels comfortably are found to be more than ordinarily resourceful, and better able to withstand personal conflicts (Douvan & Adelson, 1958).

Another kind of social disorganization may occur gradually and progressively over time. Social critics occasionally analyze our own society as "sick." References are made to the behavior of individuals during the decline and fall of Greek and Roman civilizations. Unfortunately, such progressive social disorganization is difficult, if not impossible, to identify from within while it is actually occurring. Consequently investigations of the reversal of socialization under such conditions is highly speculative. The concept of *anomie* refers to the loss of one's sense of identity in connection with social decay and disorganization. The concept of *alienation* discussed by modern existential psychologists describes a similar condition in which the individual loses his sense of identification with and assimilation into his society (Dean, 1961; Ransford, 1968).

WHO IS ALIENATED?

A measuring device designed to assess the concept of *alienation* included three major components: *powerlessness*—a feeling of inability to understand or to influence life events occurring in the mass societies of the twentieth century; *normlessness*—lack of purpose and direction to life; and *social isolation*—feelings of separation from society and its standards. Subsequent administration of the test to randomly selected individuals from various precincts in a large midwestern city showed increased alienation with advancing age; and decreased alienation with higher levels of occupational prestige, education, and income.

DEAN (1961)

ALIENATION AND MARIJUANA

It is generally assumed that marijuana users operate within a "hang loose" ethic that rejects commonly accepted social norms. A study of 168 college students sorted them into four categories; nonusers, experimenters, recreational users, and potheads. Alienation from conventional social standards was directly associated with degree of marijuana usage. But this collective alienation from socially accepted goals and standards (*societal alienation*) is not the same as *personal alienation*, which is marked by individual feelings of isolation, remoteness, cynicism, distrust, and apathy. Such personal alienation was unrelated to marijuana usage. The student who uses marijuana frequently does not necessarily view himself as different from the nonuser, nor does he feel any more personally estranged and isolated; indeed, he may be closely identified with a group or subculture that collectively rejects conventional social norms (the counterculture).

KNIGHT, SHEPOSH, AND BRYSON (1973)

ALIENATION AND VIOLENCE

In order to investigate the effects of alienation (isolation, powerlessness, and dissatisfaction) on participation in violence, 312 black males between the ages of 18 and 35 responded to an interview schedule administered by black interviewers. The results showed a direct relationship between feelings of alienation and viewing violence as necessary for racial justice. Unlike the more optimistic, middle-class blacks who participate in organized civil rights protest, the population in this study (65 percent of which fell into the "highly alienated" category) seemed to have lost faith in their leaders and to have little hope for improvement through organized protest.

RANSFORD (1968)

Marginality and Role Conflicts

Demands are placed on an individual by the position he occupies in a society, and he tends to adopt a stable pattern of behavior in response to these demands. This response to the expectations of others is called a *social role*. Normally, people participate in a large number of different kinds of groups. Even a child in school is a member of a family, a school, a neighborhood play group, perhaps a church group, and so on. He may be psychologically identified with ethnic, racial, or national groups as well, and he is likely to have a clear recognition of his identification with his own sex group and social class. Membership in only one group is almost inconceivable in a complex organized society, so *multiple group membership* is almost inevitable. When an individual is caught in the no man's land between these group identifications, under conflicting demands from his varied memberships, he is said to be a *marginal man* (Stonequist, 1937). (The concept of role and its relationship to human behavior in organized groups is described more fully in Section IV, especially Chapter 11.)

179
The Social Self

Many kinds of neurotic conflicts in our society derive from marginality and role conflicts. Fortunately, under normal circumstances such conflicts are minimized by a number of factors. For one thing, most people control their voluntary participation in groups so that their identifications remain congruent and coherent. Women who are active in the League of Women Voters (which involves expectations of rather liberal political and economic views) tend not to be active in the Daughters of the American Revolution (with expectations of somewhat less than liberal views). Men who belong to the Knights of Columbus, a Catholic organization, are not likely to become participants in the Planned Parenthood League, which advocates contraception and birth control. Furthermore, participation in various kinds of groups tends to be successive rather than simultaneous. An individual may move from one social situation to another fairly rapidly, but ordinarily he is actively engaged in only one group at a time. Consequently only one set of positional demands is dominant at one time.

Despite these conditions, which normally minimize role conflicts, the individual who is multiply associated with a variety of organized groups may now and then find himself in positions of conflict. Such situations, in which the demands of two kinds of positions are simultaneously imposed on him, are described as *marginal* positions. In a complex society, women who pursue careers in business or professions often encounter such conflicts, and because our society is characterized by fairly clear delineation of ethnic, racial, and social-class groups, individuals who are identified with racial or ethnic minorities, or ones who climb rapidly from one social class to another, are often subjected to role conflicts. Similar conflicts, which stem from sex-related roles, differ somewhat for men and women in our society. Because the feminine role is somewhat more ambiguously defined than the masculine role, women often encounter role conflicts as the result of uncertainty about the demands of their position; for men, the masculine role is so highly stereotyped that the conflicts concerning masculinity are likely to be ones in which the male has difficulty reconciling particular activities with the cultural stereotype of masculinity, making him doubt or question his virility.

Rigidity, Dogmatism, and Ethnocentrism

The psychological study of cognitive processes includes examining how people organize their experiences into concepts (see Chapter 4). One dimension used to describe this process is *rigidity,* the degree to which a person resists modifying his conceptual systems when he encounters new experiences. A rigid person is inclined to ignore or distort new experiences that disturb his existing concepts, whereas a flexible person alters his concepts to fit each new event he encounters. The dimension of rigidity also applies to descriptions of self-concept. Some people are very rigid and never change their opinions of themselves, regardless of what happens; others flutter with the wind, and change their self-concepts with every success or failure.

One's perception of himself and his role in society is particularly sensitive to changing patterns of relationship with others, changing social expectations and demands, and changing needs of the individual himself. But some people are especially rigid and unchanging in their relationships to society. Rokeach (1960) has described this as a dimension of "open and closed minds." The term *dogmatism* is applied to the measure of this kind of rigidity. A dogmatic person is one who is rigidly closed-minded about changing his concepts of himself and society. He may be a dogmatic right-winger or a dogmatic left-winger, but in either case, so long as

THE OPEN AND CLOSED MIND

"Ideological dogmatism" refers to a relatively rigid outlook on life and intolerance toward those with opposing beliefs. High scores on the *Dogmatism Scale* display closedness of mind, lack of flexibility, and authoritarianism—regardless of espoused social or political ideology. For example, high scorers included authoritarian left-of-center groups (Communists and religious nonbelievers) *and* authoritarian right-of-center groups (Catholics).

The dogmatic individual tends to accentuate differences between belief and disbelief:

The United States and Russia have just about nothing in common.

Within his belief system, the dogmatic individual tolerates coexistence of contradictions:

Even though freedom of speech for all groups is a worthwhile goal, unfortunately it is necessary to restrict the freedom of certain political groups.

The dogmatic person displays feelings of aloneness, fear of the future, and need for martyrdom:

Most people just don't give a damn for others.
It is only natural for a person to be rather fearful of the future.
It is better to be a dead hero than a live coward.

Self-aggrandizement, self-proselytization, and a paranoid outlook on life serve as defenses against the dogmatic person's self-inadequacy:

If I had to choose between happiness and greatness, I'd choose greatness.
Once I get wound up in a heated discussion I just can't stop.
I have often felt that strangers are looking at me critically.

The dogmatic person is uncompromising in his beliefs and intolerant of others:

To compromise with our political opponents is dangerous because it usually leads to the betrayal of our own side.
When it comes to differences of opinion in religion we must be careful not to compromise with those who believe differently from the way we do.
It's all too true that people just won't practice what they preach.
There are two kinds of people in the world: those who are for the truth and those who are against the truth.

ROKEACH (1960)

he is closed-minded in his commitment, he would be considered dogmatic. The original meaning of the word "liberal" (before everyday use contaminated it to imply "leftist" thinking) denoted "free-thinking" or open-mindedness in the sense of non-dogmatism. Research on this attribute of personality has shown that dogmatism is not exclusively aligned with political or economic ideologies on the left or right, and that it is associated with general perceptual rigidity (Rokeach, 1960).

An earlier, but similar, exploration of closedness of the self-concept was carried out by a group of social scientists working to describe the personality characteristics associated with *ethnocentrism* (the tendency to center oneself in one's own group and to distrust outsiders). This typical ethnocentric personality was described in *The Authoritarian Personality* (Adorno, et al., 1950). The authoritarian tends toward fascistic political beliefs, does not tolerate ambiguity very well, is conceptually rigid, and is generally antidemocratic. He is also inclined toward submission to authority, prefers autocratic styles of leadership, and conforms to convention readily (Haythorn, et al., 1956; Nadler, 1959; Wright & Harvey, 1965).

THE AUTHORITARIAN PERSONALITY

In 1950 a group of psychologists at the University of California, headed by T. W. Adorno, published *The Authoritarian Personality,* a comprehensive study of college students, public school teachers, public health nurses, prison inmates, mental patients, veterans groups, members of labor unions, and members of the Kiwanis club. These subjects were chosen for what was initially intended to be a study of the psychological roots of anti-Semitism. One common characteristic of the subjects was that they were white, non-Jewish, native born, and from an essentially middle-class background. During the study it became increasingly evident that extreme anti-Semitic attitudes did not exist in isolation: a constellation of ethnocentrism, political and economical conservatism, and implicit antidemocratic ideology was found to surround anti-Semitism.

The profile of the authoritarian can best be described by the kind of statements that he tended to endorse consistently, and by the interpretation of his responses to interview and projective-type questions.

Anti-Semitism

The authoritarian's basic premise seems to be that Jews can and should be stereotyped. Hence, he gives unqualified endorsement to these statements:

There may be a few exceptions, but in general Jews are pretty much alike. No matter how Americanized a Jew may seem to be, there is always something different and strange, something basically Jewish underneath.

A particularly intriguing aspect of the authoritarian's personality is his "consistent inconsistency": he tends to endorse the most irrational and contradictory statements as long as they are compatible with his overall prejudicial views. Thus he regards Jews as rich and powerful but also as poor and dirty. Jews are "foreign," clannish, and underassimilated into the American culture, but they are also intrusive, over-assimilated, and hiding their Jewishness. The best way to deal with Jews is by avoiding them but also by attacking them directly.

Ethnocentrism

The authoritarian does not limit his antagonism to Jews. He is equally as antagonistic to such out-group members as Negroes, "Japs," "Okies," members of small political parties, intellectuals, criminals, subnormals, or members of juvenile "cult-groups" (at that time "zootsuiters"). Thus, he suggests that

Negroes have their rights, but it is best to keep them in their own districts and schools and to prevent too much contact with whites.
Zootsuiters prove that when people of their type have too much money and freedom, they just take advantage and cause trouble.
The businessman and the manufacturer are much more important to society than the artist and the professor.

At the same time, however, the authoritarian's professed patriotism seems to be boundless:

Certain religious sects that refuse to salute the flag should be forced to conform to such patriotic action, or else be abolished.
America may not be perfect, but the American Way has brought us as close as human beings can get to a perfect society.

Political and Economic Conservatism

Indices of political and economic conservatism were less consistent in their co-variations with the general trend. Some professed liberals were also highly anti-Semitic and ethnocentric, even though to a markedly lesser extent than the professed conservatives. One reason was that the conservatism of the authoritarian is not the traditional laissez-faire type of conserving things as they are. Rather, it is a

(Continued on p. 182)

pseudoconservatism, which frequently seems to threaten the very institutions or beliefs with which the authoritarian tends to identify. For example, despite his endorsement of extremism with respect to minorities, in the context of socioeconomic ideology he endorses the following statement:

The best way to solve social problems is to stick close to the middle of the road, to move slowly, and to avoid extremes.

At the same time, however, he also endorses the traditional tenets of conservatism:

In general, full economic security is harmful; most men wouldn't work if they did not need the money for eating and living.

Thus, the following statement is consistently rejected:

The only way to provide adequate medical care for the entire population is through some program of socialized medicine.

Authoritarianism

The consistent overall endorsement of certain statements reflects the essentially antidemocratic attitude of the authoritarian. His attitudes are rigidly conforming to conventional American middle-class values:

Obedience and respect for authority are the most important virtues children should learn.

The authoritarian's inability or unwillingness to criticize or rebel against conventional ingroup ideals and moral values is reflected in endorsement of such statements as

Young people sometimes get rebellious ideas, but as they grow up they ought to get over them and settle down.
Every person should have complete faith in some supernatural power whose decisions he obeys without question.

The authoritarian seems to avoid insight and reflection:

When a person has a problem or worry, it is best for him not to think about it but to keep busy with more cheerful things.

To the authoritarian, the world seems a threatening place, against which one has to be on guard in order to defend himself:

Nowadays when so many different kinds of people move around and mix together so much, a person has to protect himself especially carefully against catching an infection or disease from them.
Most people don't realize how much our lives are controlled by plots hatched in secret places.

The authoritarian adheres to particular forms of pessimistic or optimistic superstition:

Wars and social troubles may someday be ended by an earthquake or flood that will destroy the whole world.
Someday it will probably be seen that astrology can explain a lot of things.

The rigid, "clear-cut" attitude of the authoritarian on power, sex, and human nature in general is reflected in the following endorsements:

People are divided into two distinct classes: the weak and the strong.
Homosexuals are hardly better than criminals and ought to be severely punished.
The wild sex life of the old Greeks and Romans was tame compared to some of the goings-on in this country, even in places where people might least expect it.

As a rule the authoritarian was subjected to harsh parental discipline in his childhood, which made parental love contingent on displays of approved behavior.

Compared to non-authoritarians, who did not hesitate to criticize their parents on several issues, the authoritarian showed far less criticism of his parents, presumably displacing his ambivalent feelings to outside objectives.

The authoritarian female tends to be power-oriented, although she sometimes has to resort to apparent submission to her husband in return for concrete benefits in the marital situation. She is less interested in companionship and sexual love than in her partner's deference and "thoughtfulness" toward her. She tends to be highly moralistic and condemning rather than permissive, and she generally conceptualizes human nature as two types of people: "clean and dirty."

ADORNO, FRENKEL-BRUNSWIK,
LEVINSON, AND SANFORD (1950)

RELEVANCE AND APPLICATION

The understanding of most social problems begins with analysis of the individuals who make up a society. Consequently, applications of social psychology over the full range of social problems rest on the ideas described in Chapter 7. It would be impossible to isolate the remainder of this book from the notions of self described here.

Perhaps the most significant area of application of explorations of the relationship between self and society are in the domain of mental health. There are several important social consequences that follow from particular kinds of variation in self-perception and self-regard, with significant implications for psychological health. The "accuracy of self-perception" (indexed by the degree of correspondence between self-concept and the actual self) supplies useful diagnostic information to the clinical psychologist. Exaggerated discrepancies between the perceived self and the actual self are associated with personal maladjustment (Calvin & Holtzman, 1953; Hamachek, 1971). Of course, just as it is difficult to assess the accuracy of interpersonal perception (see Chapter 8), it is also difficult to assess the accuracy of self-perception because of difficulty in defining the "real" self. A commonly used approximation of reality in both cases is the consensus of collective judgment by a number of people well-acquainted with the person being studied.

Another aspect of self-perception with considerable clinical diagnostic utility is the general level of self-esteem. People generally distort their perceptions of themselves slightly, exaggerating their socially desirable qualities and minimizing the undesirable ones (Brassard, 1964). It is unusual for a person to regard himself less favorably than his friends and associates do. Consequently unusually low levels as well as inflated levels of self-esteem suggest pathological conditions within the personality.

Many psychotherapists and counselors, especially those who adhere to the theoretical framework and techniques developed by Rogers (1951), consider the major objective of therapy to be the reshaping of the individual's conception of himself. This includes the newer humanistic therapies as well (Satir, 1968; Fagan & Shepherd, 1970; Hamachek, 1971). Disturbances of self-perception and self-evaluation provide the source of many kinds of minor neurotic conflicts—especially those derived from role conflict, marginality, and social disorganization—and if they become severe enough, they may produce dramatic deteriorations of personality such as schizophrenia.

An extended form of self-awareness is represented in the attempt to contemplate one's cosmic position in the universe. This transcends the conventional structures that define "self" in terms of one's primary group and social identifications. *Yoga* (the "gateway to higher self-realization through cosmic consciousness"), *transcendental meditation* ("chanting a specially designed sacred syllable—mantra—over and over during meditation"), and *zen* ("suspended thoughts during meditation, as a doorway to the superconsciousness") all represent these extended notions of the self (Criswell & Peterson, 1972).

Humanistic approaches to the study of self-awareness and self-regard have also made significant contributions to educational practice. These ideas have been incorporated directly into teacher training and indirectly into curriculum planning and the development of educational materials. By matching educational purpose and objectives to the self-conception, self-evaluation, aspirations, and expectations of the learner, the entire learning process can be expedited (Bracht, 1970).

REVIEW

1. The *self* is the organized total of a person's actions and behavior. *Self-concept* refers to the organized cognitive structure derived from one's experience of his own self. *Body image* is the physical aspect of self-concept, including everything within the body limits.

2. *Identification* is the process through which a person incorporates the values, beliefs, and actions of others. *Anaclitic* identification occurs when one identifies with a nurturant or rewarding *love object*. Defensive identification occurs when one identifies with a powerful or threatening *aggressor*.

3. Social interaction and reflective feedback from others provides an important basis for development of the self-concept.

4. *Self-esteem* is the evaluative component of self-perception, the extent to which one likes himself. Cultural standards of social desirability and awareness of one's attractiveness to others influence self-esteem.

5. *Self-control* is internalized social control. People differ in terms of their perception of whether the *locus of control* of the rewards that guide their behavior is external or internal.

6. Standards of social desirability may be defined generally by a culture, but these in turn are internalized by each individual as his own idiosyncratic code of social desirability.

7. *Conscience* refers to a person's acquired capacity to control his own behavior through self-administered rewards. *Pride* is self-approval and self-satisfaction; *guilt* is self-disapproval and self-dissatisfaction.

8. *Morality* (the sense of justice) progresses from blind obedience to authority, through recognition of social standards of right and wrong, to internalized personal standards of justice and equity. This can be described as progression from *moral realism* (absolute standards of right and wrong) to *moral relativism* (qualified and flexible standards of justice).

9. *Self-actualization* is a higher-order human need to improve oneself, to actualize potentialities, and to move in the direction of fulfillment.

10. *Mastery* is the desire to manipulate and control the environment, either as a means to an end or as an end in itself.

11. *Social power* represents manipulation and control of the social aspect of one's environment: other people. *Machiavellianism* is a measure of this desire and ability.

12. *Prestige* is the recognition, respect, and admiration by one's peers.

13. *Acquisitive* motivation is the desire to amass tokens and symbols of wealth, or to hoard and retain goods and resources. The ostentatious use of goods is called *conspicuous consumption*.

14. *Achievement* motivation and behavior include both *hope for success* (high aspirations and high expectations) and *fear of failure* (high aspirations and low expectations).

15. *Social mobility* is the freedom to move from one social position to another. *Anticipatory socialization* involves assuming the values, beliefs, and habits of another group or culture that one hopes or expects to enter.

16. *Anomie* is the loss of identity or sense of self that accompanies social disorder or social deterioration.

17. *Multiple group membership* occurs when one belongs to several subsocieties at the same time; it is almost inevitable in a complex society. Within a society, demands and expectations placed on the individual cause him to adopt a stable pattern of behavioral responses called the *social role*. When a person is caught between conflicting memberships and social roles, he is said to be a *marginal man*.

18. *Rigidity* is the degree to which a person resists modifying his conceptual systems when he encounters new experiences. *Dogmatism* is a measure of rigidity or closed-mindedness in perceiving one's relationship to society. *Ethnocentrism* is the tendency to center oneself in one's own group and to distrust outsiders. The "authoritarian personality" is a composite description of the kind of person who shows all of these kinds of rigidity.

19. The concept of self has particular relevance for the understanding and solution of social problems. It is particularly critical in mental health and psychotherapy.

SECTION III

INTERPERSONAL SOCIAL BEHAVIOR

In contrast to Section II (concerned with the behavior of the *individual* in social settings), Section III is concerned with the behavior of two people in mutual *interpersonal social behavior.*

The basic unit of interpersonal interaction is the *diad,* a set of two people whose behavior has significant impact on each other. Each is aware of the other's presence, and the actions of each generate reactions in the other. One of the most important qualities of diadic interpersonal behavior is that it is *continuously emergent:* the actions of one person stimulate behavioral reaction in the other, and these reactions in turn stimulate further reaction in the first. This sequence of social action and reaction is ongoing and continuously changing.

In some ways the diadic unit is the basic building block for higher levels of social behavior and social organization. Thus analysis of the simplest forms of relationship between two people is a starting point for approaching the analysis of more complex forms of social organization and collective behavior. However, there are some important differences between simple one-to-one social interaction and the broader generalizations that are involved in the individual's relationship to complex social systems and cultures (the latter are considered in Section IV).

Chapter 8 describes the basic psychological processes involved in *interpersonal perception* and *interpersonal attraction* (including popularity, friendship, and love). Chapter 9 describes some of the most basic forms of patterned interpersonal interaction in diads, including prosocial helping behavior (*dependency* and *nurturance*), social power (including *compliant* behavior and social *manipulation*), *imitation, observational learning, behavioral contagion, negotiation* and *bargaining,* and *aggression* and *violence.*

8

INTERPERSONAL PERCEPTION AND ATTRACTION

The term *social perception* has broad implications. Social psychology has learned that a number of social factors (such as interpersonal influence, cultural values and beliefs, and socially learned expectations) influence one's perception of both social and nonsocial objects and events.

Modern theories of perception stress the reciprocity of the "transaction" between the perceiver and the perceived object. In exploring the perception of people, it has become possible to integrate many observations of applied social psychology concerning prejudice and the stereotyped perception of people with basic principles of perception. Sociometric procedures, permitting measurement of the relationships between individuals (Chapter 3), facilitate the investigation of ways individuals experience the presence of others and develop attitudes and feelings about them. Studies of the behavior of individuals in organized groups (Section IV) expand evidence of the importance of roles (stabilized patterns of displayed behavior that are related to others' expectations about the behavior of an individual in a group) as determinants of behavior. One of the most active areas of recent scientific investigation in social psychology has been the study of interpersonal perception and attraction.

In analyzing the perception of social objects, two approaches may be distinguished. One is addressed to the study of the *content* of interpersonal perception (the dimensions that characterize people as perceived objects, and the particular properties of social objects) and the other to the *processes* of perceptual organization that operate in the perception of other people and groups. These two approaches are intertwined and mutually dependent.

The basic principles or laws governing perception are the same, regardless of the nature of the object perceived. But social objects (people, groups, and cultures) have several properties that are unlike nonsocial objects. Person perception entails a *double* interaction because the perceiver, through his own presence and behavior in the perceptual situation of the other, may alter the characteristics of the person he is perceiving.

FORMING IMPRESSIONS OF PEOPLE

Psychological studies of the basic processes involved in perceiving people and in being attracted to them often have failed to distinguish clearly between first impressions and deeper familiarity. Although it may be reasonable to assume that somewhat the same general fundamental processes may operate in both cases, the relative importance of several particular factors differs from one case to the other.

Several investigations have probed into the means by which people form initial impressions of one another. Generalizations from past experience usually offer a starting point. When one first encounters a stranger, his initial reactions are likely to be governed largely by attempts to extend his previous experiences with similar individuals: people of the same skin color, people from the same region of the country, people in the same social or vocational roles, or even someone who physically resembles the stranger. To some extent, even latent associations based on similarities between the newly encountered stranger and people known in the past, of which the perceiver himself may not be fully aware, may enter into initial impressions of a stranger's personality.

Attribution Theory

One significant aspect of social perception is the tendency to attribute *causal* ability to people. When a person is closely associated to some event, one tends to attribute the causation of that event to that person. Often the bases for such attribution are very tenuous and farfetched. Heider (1944) illustrates this point by referring to an experiment conducted by Zillig (1928). Two groups of children, one well liked and the other disliked, performed calisthenic exercises before their classmates. Although the liked children intentionally made mistakes in their performance, and the disliked children performed perfectly, the audience later remembered the liked group as having performed well and the disliked group as having performed poorly. Thus, as Heider pointed out, "bad" acts were attributed to "bad" people.

Other investigations have shown that this tendency to attribute causality also occurs when people anthropomorphize inanimate objects. That is, people may interpret inanimate nonsocial objects as though they were people and to attribute causation to them in the same way. Heider and Simmel (1944) designed an animated cartoon in which geometric forms moved around within a framework of lines, appearing to bump one another and push one another around. When subjects were asked to describe the cartoon, they tended to use anthropomorphic terms to describe the geometric forms. They attributed "aggressiveness" to a large triangle that "bullied" a smaller one, and they described their interactions as "rivalry" over a smaller circle that was described as a "shy, timid female."

Michotte (1954) extended this kind of exploration further as he attempted to define the particular kinds of stimulus conditions that might be associated with the perception of causality. In stylized animated drawings, the speed and direction of movement of geometric forms governed the subject's perception of causation and consequences. Small rectangles moving toward or away from each other were viewed under varying conditions of speed, direction, and distance. Judgments of the viewers indicated that even in perceiving nonsocial stimuli, attribution of causation occurred: one rectangle moving at high speed toward the other was perceived as "striking" the latter, whereas at low speed merely as "touching it"; if after contact there was a short pause, the movement was perceived as friendly "getting together," whereas if there was no pause after the first rectangle approached the second one with an increasing rate of speed, the latter was perceived as being "forcibly" carried off by the former.

An elaborate theory of attribution in interpersonal perception has been outlined by Jones and Davis (1966) and amplified by Kelley (1972a, 1972b). People tend to want to know the causes of and the sources of responsibility for the everyday events that take place around them. Attribution theory distinguishes two kinds of perceived causation. *Environmental* causation involves attribution of responsibility for events to circumstances and forces of nature outside the people participating in those events. This kind of perceived causation is associated with philosophies of behavioristic determinism. *Personal* causation involves attribution of responsibility for events to one or more of the people involved. This kind of causation involves philosophies of freedom of will and volitional choice of the individual. It appears to be more typical in everyday human behavior, and attribution theory is more directly concerned with the analysis of this kind of perceived causation.

According to Jones and Davis (1966), one's perception of personal causation steers one's predispositional intents and actions toward others. Three factors influence such dispositions: social desirability—the surrounding context of conventions and expectations held by others; hedonic relevance—the balance of costs (pains) and benefits (pleasures) involved in the activity, and their importance to the person; and personalism—the specific details of the relationship between the perceiver and the other person as they bear upon influence and responsibility for the other's action.

Kelley (1972a, 1972b) has extended attribution theory further into the realms of forming perceptual impressions of people and of the analysis of the individual's attribution of causation in his own behavior to internal or external sources. Kelley points to three major variables influencing these processes: distinctiveness—perceived

---

INSOMNIA AND THE ATTRIBUTION PROCESS

Insomniac subjects were given placebo pills to take a few minutes before going to bed. After being assured that the drug was harmless, some subjects were told that it would arouse them (increase body temperature, heart rate, etc.), and some were told that it would relax them (lower body temperature, heart rate, etc.). Contrary to expectations, the subjects who were told that the drug would relax them had a more difficult time getting to sleep than usual, whereas the subjects who were told that the drug would arouse them got to sleep faster than on the nights when they took no pills. The results were explained in terms of attribution theory. When the insomniac begins his usual tossing and turning after taking the "arousal" pill, he attributes his sleeplessness to external causes (the pill), which alleviates a great deal of anxiety and thus facilitates eventual sleep. On the other hand, experiencing the discomfort of sleeplessness despite the fact that he took a relaxation pill makes him attribute his discomfort to internal causes (himself), which in turn increases his anxiety and insomnia. The findings suggest the feasibility of therapy based on a reattribution of symptoms, and calls for the modification of traditional suggesting procedures using placebos.

STORMS AND NISBETT (1970)

---

uniqueness or circumscription of the object, event, or person judged; consistency— the durability of perceived qualities over time or over different dimensions of the judged object, event, or person; and consensus—the validation of one's perceptions and judgments against those of other people. For example, suppose A perceives B as a "dog lover." Attribution of this perception to B is greatest if B's fondness is limited to dogs and no other pets (distinctiveness), if B's feeling extends to all breeds and types of dogs over a long period of time (consistency), and if other people who display kindness toward dogs are generally perceived as dog lovers (consensus). Under these conditions, A is likely to interpret a particular episode in which B stoops to pet a stray dog by attributing the label "dog lover" to B. Under reversed conditions (B is kind to all animals, not just dogs, but his kindness depends on his mood and the situation, and he seems no more interested in dogs than anyone else), then A is likely to interpret the same episode by attributing the causation to the dog ("This dog is hungry and wants a handout"). These theoretical formulations have generated considerable research in social psychology including such diverse areas as persuasion, impression formation, and moral development (Collins, 1969; Kelley, 1971; Himmelfarb, 1972).

The perception of people involves much more than simple physical dimensions. At a basic level, our impressions of others are influenced by physical qualities (whether they are tall or short, broad or thin, white or black, and so on); but our perception is enriched by information about their behavioral characteristics (whether they are stingy or generous, hostile or benevolent, jolly or dour, and so on). Furthermore, impressions are influenced by our specific interactions with others (whether they depend on us, influence us, like us, admire us, and so on). Thus, person-perception includes three kinds of dimensions: *physical*—color, size, shape; *behavioral*—traits of action; and *interactional*—interpersonal relationships.

Stereotyping and Prejudice

An extremely important by-product of the tendency of human beings to try to classify their experiences by integrating them into organized conceptual systems is the fact that objects and events must often be judged and interpreted on the basis of limited information. Rarely does one know all that could possibly be known about an object or event as he experiences it. However, one ordinarily does not become greatly concerned about this lack of information if the object or event being experienced displays even a few familiar characteristics.

According to cognitive theorists, new experiences are sorted into conceptual categories on the basis of their similarity to previous experiences. On the basis of such similarity, one may reasonably expect the new experiences to continue to show other properties in common with familiar past experiences. A student who enters a lecture hall three times a week for a semester may sit in a different seat each time he goes there. But because all the seats appear to be the same, he expects each to support him reliably when he sits down. But one day he may come in and start to sit in a broken chair and fall to the floor. By prejudging this particular chair on the basis of direct extension of past experience with similar chairs, it seemed reasonable to expect the chair to support him. Yet this is not always the case, for many rules have exceptions.

This tendency to act on the basis of partial information is an integral part of basic processes of concept formation, as described in Chapter 4. It is the beginning of what social psychologists call *prejudice* at a more complex level. An excessively generalized concept based on very incomplete or ambiguous information is called a *stereotype*. Very rarely in human experience are *all* pertinent facts available, so our expectancies about the things we perceive very rarely reach the level of 100 percent certainty of accuracy. In some cases, our conceptual generalizations are so well founded in sound information that our expectations are reliably borne out. But in other cases people hold concepts that are overgeneralized and inaccurate, and expectations based on them are ineffective and full of error.

Such inaccurate and overgeneralized concepts generate superstitious fallacies called stereotype prejudices. The basic cognitive processes that underlie them are normal and reasonable; consequently, their accuracy is to some degree a matter of subjective interpretation. Some psychologists simply use the term stereotype to refer to generalizations that are considered unjustified by the person who affixes such a label to them (Brigham, 1971). What appears to one person as an accurate and reasonable belief may appear to another as an unwarranted and overgeneralized stereotype. In any event, the social psychologist is not usually concerned with changing or eliminating these basic cognitive processes. Instead, it is more accurate to say that his objective is to sharpen these processes by educating people and encouraging them to base their conceptual generalizations on the most comprehensive and accurate information available to them.

That people are very much inclined toward prejudice and stereotyping in the perception of individuals and groups is quite clear. Early investigations found that teachers, businessmen, and college students were all quite consistent in expressing the degrees of social intimacy with which they were willing to admit members of particular ethnic, national, racial, or religious groups (Bogardus, 1925; Thurstone, 1928; Guilford, 1931). Such classifications as "Canadian" or "English" were rather uniformly regarded as admissible to such close relationships as kinship through marriage and personal friendship, whereas such classifications as "Hindus" or "Turks" were uniformly regarded as admissible only to very distant kinds of relationships, such as admission to the country only as visitors. The consistency of such judgments suggested to other investigators that people do indeed have rather stereotyped and generalized concepts of members of such groups.

Katz and Braley (1933) asked Princeton students to use an adjective checklist to describe a number of different national groups, and they found a surprising degree of consistency among students in their characterizations. The widely believed stereotype of the American Negro, for example, as "superstitious, lazy, happy-go-lucky, ignorant, musical, and ostentatious" emerged clearly in these descriptions. However, the same kind of investigation was repeated 20 and again 40 years later with comparable groups of students (Gilbert, 1951; Karling, Coffman, & Walters, 1969), and although students were less willing to express consistent generalizations about members of various ethnic or national groups (during the intervening years social norms had arisen to make the expression of such stereotypes socially unacceptable), there was still evidence that stereotyping is an important component in the perception of people. Furthermore, other studies reveal that people are quite willing to exercise stereotypes in judging members of other kinds of groups about which there is less sense of "social conscience." For example, Wells, Goi, and Seader (1958) found that people were quite willing to stereotype the drivers of various makes of automobiles.

Thus, despite evidence that social values and conventions about the public expression of stereotypes and prejudices may change over time, the evidence seems to remain that stereotyping is still a basic and integral part of the process of perceiving social objects. The poorly educated, unambitious black person encountered by the provincial white citizen of a small town in Mississippi still provides the basis of the latter's overgeneralized perception of all blacks, and the distinguished black public figure is ignored as the exception to the rule. Unfortunately, in many cases, loud and bigoted white supremacist leaders may provide the basis for equally inappropriate stereotyping of the community leaders and political figures of the governments of southern American cities and states, with the more reasonable but less vocal moderates ignored as exceptions to that rule of stereotyping.

Nevertheless it is important to recognize that stereotyping and prejudgment represent a basic process of perceptual organization: generalization of expectations based on experience into new situations that resemble the old ones. Without exercising such processes, the individual would be immobilized because the world in which he functions is an ever-changing series of new experiences. Even with respect to the perception of people, there is some evidence that certain commonly held stereotypes of ethnic groups are related to at least partial substantiation in fact. For example, the popular stereotype of the American Jew as ambitious and highly motivated toward achievement and upward social mobility has been corroborated by empirical research

---

THREE GENERATIONS OF STEREOTYPES

In 1933 Princeton students were given an adjective checklist to describe a number of different national, racial, and ethnic groups. A considerable degree of consistency was shown in the way students characterized members of each group. Negroes were generally perceived as "lazy," Jews as "shrewd," Italians as "impulsive," and Americans as "progressive." The study was repeated in 1951 and showed a marked decline in definitiveness of certain stereotypes, especially in traits usually associated with bigotry (perhaps because it was less "socially desirable" in 1951 than in 1933 to adhere to such stereotyped notions). The study was repeated for the third time in 1969 and the same drop in traits associated with bigotry occurred. The apparent fading of stereotyping in 1951, however, was not upheld in 1969. Stereotyping was in fact fully restored, except that this time it was in line with the increasing "liberal" norms on campus. This new view of blacks focused on such traits as "musical" and "pleasure-loving" instead of "superstitious" or "lazy" and the previously held Jewish stereotype of "ambitious" and "materialistic" was now attributed to the American stereotype.

KATZ AND BRALY (1933)
GILBERT (1951)
KARLING, COFFMAN, AND WALTERS (1969)

WHAT'S IN A NAME?

Like surnames, first names are often associated with particular stereotypes—over-generalized notions perhaps fed by novels, stories, and comic strips in which the heroes are always "Steven and Elizabeth" while the villains and fall guys are always "Elmer and Bertha." These implicit stereotypes also lead to differential expectations of people who bear particular names.

One way in which such expectations may lead to nondeliberate bias in judging others was demonstrated in a study of blind grading of essays by fifth grade teachers. Experienced teachers were asked to evaluate a set of short essays, which were linked to supposed fifth grade authors by first name only. The same essays were randomly associated with four names stereotyped by teachers as attractive and favorable (David, Michael, Karen, and Lisa) and four regarded as unattractive and unfavorable (Elmer, Hubert, Bertha, and Adelle). Even though the same essays were associated with different names for different teachers, those reported to be authored by "favorable" names were graded a full letter grade higher than those reported to be authored by "unfavorable" names. The effect was stronger with boys' names than with girls' names. In a parallel study of college sophomores in teacher training, these differential stereotypes were much less pronounced than in experienced teachers.

HARARI AND McDAVID (1973)

A ROSE BY ANY OTHER NAME

College students were asked to rank photographs of thirty girls on beauty, intelligence, character, ambition, and general likeability. Two months later the procedure was repeated, but the photographs also showed some purported surnames: Jewish (e.g., Rabinowitz, Finkelstein), Italian (e.g., Scarano, Grisolia), and "old American" Anglo-Saxon (e.g., Adams, Clark). The addition of Jewish and Italian surnames caused a considerable drop in rating of likeability, and to a lesser degree, in beauty and character. In the case of the Jewish surnames, there was also an increase in the attributed characteristic of ambition.

RAZRAN (1950)

that reveals that Jewish students are more frequently "academic overachievers" in that they earn better grades in school than would be predicted from intelligence test scores, and that a greater proportion of young people from Jewish families go to college than do young people from non-Jewish families (Clark, 1949; Jospe, 1964).

The fact that particular cultural and subcultural groups show certain threads of consistency of behavior among individual members constitutes the basis of the concept of *national character* or *modal personality* (discussed in Chapter 6). The fact that the social environment that surrounds each member of a given cultural group and shapes the course of his socialization and social learning may be fairly homogeneous within that group would be expected to result in some degree of consistency of behavioral characteristics among adult members of such groups. In this sense, to the extent that the cultural context does in fact contribute to the personality structure and typical behavior of an individual, the concept of modal personality is the seed of truth in every stereotype. Furthermore, as Pettigrew (1964) has suggested, there is a quality of self-fulfilling prophecy in stereotypes that are rigidly and popularly held. The effects of the discriminatory practices that have occurred in the United States as a function of widely believed stereotypes about black inferiority may have produced an inferior subculture into which blacks continue to be socialized and assimilated. It is clear that in terms of social consequences, it is very harmful for stereotyped generalizations to be over-extended.

PYGMALION: BLACK AND WHITE

How stereotypes about black inferiority are perpetuated, even in the face of evidence to the contrary, has been demonstrated in a study involving sixty-six white female teachers-in-training. Prior to interacting with their students (264 junior high school students in a midwestern city), each subject was given a description of the students labeling them as "gifted" (selected from the school's gifted program) or "nongifted" (selected from the school's regular track). All the descriptions were, in fact, contrived and randomly assigned to students. Teachers' expectations concerning both color and giftedness influenced their behavior toward students; black students were given less attention, ignored more, praised less, and criticized more, than their white counterparts. White "gifted" students received the most favorable preferential treatment of all. Most surprising and disturbing was the fact that black "gifted" students received even *less* preferential treatment than black "nongifted" students, even though (or perhaps *because*) their description did not fit the conventional negative stereotype of the black student.

RUBOVITS AND MAEHR (1973)

Most of what we traditionally catalog as sex differences (see Chapter 6) are much less biological than social in origin. There are few direct, *unmediated* biological differences between male and female, and these have to do largely with physiological attributes. But the indirect, *mediated* sex differences that are due to the differing social roles accorded male and female and the expectations that accompany each role are far greater in both number and scope so far as social behavior is concerned. And these role expectations, in turn, are largely the product of stereotypes that have become consolidated and entrenched over the years. It is from these stereotypes and rigid role expectations that groups such as the National Organization for Women (NOW) wish to liberate the American female.

Overgeneralized stereotypes occur most frequently in the absence of adequate knowledge or information. Many stereotypes in the perception of people operate at the level of relatively insignificant and unimportant dimensions of interpersonal perception: skin color, facial features, the sound of one's name, and the like (Razran, 1950; Lambert, Hodgson, Gardner, & Fillenbaum, 1960; McDavid & Harari, 1966; Harari & McDavid, 1973). But when attention to these details precludes a closer and more accurate evaluation of someone's actual behavior, interpersonal relationships are crippled. If one's perceptions of others are based on their behavior—or even more than that, on interaction with them—overgeneralized stereotypes usually recede and more effective interpersonal perception is possible.

Sometimes extremely rigid stereotypes are strong enough to prohibit any opportunity for close encounters with the objects of the stereotype. Thus revised perceptions and expectations are impossible. For this reason even direct encounter and physical proximity of members of groups that hold strong prejudices toward one another do

BUT YOU DO LOOK JEWISH

Gentile and Jewish college students were presented with a series of unlabeled photographs of adult males and asked to label them as "Jewish" or "non-Jewish." Anti-Semitic subjects tended to label most photographs as "Jewish" indiscriminately, which cast doubts on their actual accuracy in perceiving Jews.

SCODEL AND AUSTRIN (1957)

STEREOTYPES FOR FEMALE ACHIEVEMENT

The implications of contemporary stereotyping practices for women have been described in a series of studies. Although some competitive sports such as swimming or tennis are "acceptable" for women competing against each other, women competing against men in such sports tend to remember that "a girl may win the game but lose the boy." The plight of the woman athlete was also cited: even at the time when it was fashionable for women's hair to be short, female athletes refused to cut theirs for fear that it would only strengthen their stereotyped image of excessive masculinity.

Women tend to alleviate stereotype-anxiety by a motivation to avoid success. Males and females were administered a standard achievement measure in which a student called John in one case, and Anne in another, each finds himself or herself at the top of the class in medical school. When asked about Anne's situation, a majority of females (65 percent) said that Anne would be worried about her loss of femininity, and that she would experience social rejection. Some of the females actually denied that a girl could really have been that successful in the first place (only 10 percent of the males voiced similar views about John).

Little wonder, then, that women develop a prejudice against their own sex. Even clinical descriptions (by males *and* females) of the mentally healthy adult were found to resemble more closely that of a mentally healthy male than that of a female. Pictures for entry in an art show were judged by females as being of higher quality when the presumed artist was a male. In another study a group of females was shown a series of purportedly published journal articles by male authors on linguistics, law, art, history, dietetics, education, and city planning. Another group of females was shown the identical articles, but supposedly authored by females. The "male-authored" articles were rated higher in quality than the "female-authored" ones.

GOLDBERG (1968)
HORNER (1969)
BROVERMAN, BROVERMAN, CLARKSON, ROCENKRANTZ,
AND VOGEL (1970)
HART (1971)
PHETERSON, KIESLER, AND GOLDBERG (1971)

not always prove successful in reducing prejudiced stereotypes. The study of propaganda, persuasion, and attitude change has analyzed many of the factors that operate in reducing interpersonal prejudice and stereotypes (see Chapter 5).

Prejudice is a perceptual process in which objects or people are prejudged on the basis of rather meager and limited information. When individuals belong to highly organized groups or societies, they are likely to be restricted in their interactions with members of other societies or social subgroups, and thus their interpersonal relations are likely to be based on prejudices more than on accurate and reliable information and direct experience. By-products of group organization, such as competitive conflict with other groups, redirection of hostility toward outsiders through scapegoating, and insulation from interaction with outsiders, all tend to foster unpleasant feelings and attitudes toward members of alien groups. Scapegoating is likely to lead to tendencies to project unacceptable personal attributes onto members of other groups, generating negative feelings and dislike toward them. Furthermore, norms within an organized social group by definition favor adherents to those norms; outsiders are judged as deviant and unacceptable. It is unfortunate that social organization often fosters prejudice and poor intergroup relations. Superordinate societies are possible only when the many interlocked groups within them coalesce from time to time and share certain dominant norms, values, and goals.

RACE AND BELIEF

White junior high school students answered a questionnaire about teenage attitudes toward minority groups. Two months later each student was presented with the purported answers of four other students from "other parts of the country." One of the purported answers was identical to the subject's own, and the other three were varied to avoid any suspicion on his part. "Information" about the others' academic success, school programming, and race was also added. By manipulating the latter three variables, it was shown that the major differentiating factors in judgment of the other was belief in similarity (e.g., higher positive ranking if the other was described as of similar academic status or having similar interests) rather than race as such. Only when information about belief was lacking, race emerged as the major differentiating factor, presumably because the subject was forced to fall back on partial information supplied by racial stereotyping.

STEIN, HARDYCK, AND SMITH (1965)

That human beings judge one another in terms of stereotypes and prejudices has been amply demonstrated both in recorded history and current events, as well as in experimental investigations. Citizens of the United States tend to hold rather stereotyped notions of citizens of other countries even when they have learned that it is socially undesirable to express such prejudices openly. Many Europeans express stereotyped prejudices toward the American tourist. The same tendency often occurs among subgroups within a society.

The expression of interpersonal prejudice among members of various subgroups has been investigated in many ways. Bogardus (1925) developed a means of measuring the "social distance" that separates individuals who belong to different social subgroups (see p. 51). G. W. Allport (1958) explored prejudice in many forms and concluded that there were two important sources of prejudice. An individual may be personally prejudiced toward others who represent a threat to his security or comfort. Thus many lower-class white Americans are strongly prejudiced toward blacks because they fear for their job security if desegregation permitted blacks to compete freely for all kinds of jobs. Another type of prejudice may occur because of the individual's adherence to the norms of his group, and not because he personally is compelled toward prejudice and negative feeling (Pettigrew, 1958). There is a great deal of evidence that much antiblack prejudice in the United States occurs in this way. In communities where respected white civic leaders (the "community power structure") have spoken out to make desegregation and the elimination of discrimination socially desirable values, the process of legal desegregation has proceeded relatively smoothly.

PREJUDICE AND SOCIAL CLASS

Observations in a racially mixed Baptist church in Chicago showed the same frequency of initiated conversations by members of each race to one another (about 50 percent). Although there was some tendency for the blacks and whites to sit apart from each other during church services, this was not the case during the more socially oriented Wednesday night suppers. The writer considered this to be a "rewarding finding" on the effectiveness of integration, but pointed out that similar attempts in Chicago churches with a lower-class membership had been unsuccessful.

PARKER (1968)

Because discrimination in the perception of individuals and patterns of direct inter-personal attraction appear to be more or less inevitable qualities in human behavior, it is important to recognize the difference between legal desegregation and everyday social integration. The removal of formal legal barriers to opportunities for whites and blacks to become directly acquainted with one another and in some cases to partici-pate collaboratively in some endeavors may eventually bring about the realignment of many kinds of social boundaries. However, other boundaries based on delineations of groups with common interests, values, and characteristics are likely to continue to exist. Legal segregation of various racial and ethnic groups is an unfair practice that restricts their freedom of movement and social participation; moreover, it is an un-necessary practice that wastes manpower and human resources. At the same time, practical everyday segregation of homogeneous groups of people in their informal social activities may continue forever. When the latter is based on actual experience unfettered by legalistic boundaries, rather than on artificial prejudices supported by formal insulation between members of various groups, it does not necessarily consti-tute a social evil.

Certain people are particularly inclined to center their attitudes within their own social group and express exaggerated prejudices against alien groups. These people are said to be *ethnocentric,* or centered in their own *ethos* (tribe). The stereotyped image of the white Anglo-Saxon Protestant American (WASP) is typically ethnocentric in that he is expected to be antiblack, anti-Semitic, anti-Catholic, antiforeigner, and anti-everything-except-other-WASPs. The vast body of research on authoritarianism that has accumulated since 1950 demonstrates the social significance of this aspect of personality. The authoritarian personality shows exaggerated tendencies toward ethnocentric orientation and suspicious rejection of outsiders (Adorno, et al., 1950), as described in Chapter 6.

NO VACANCY

Discrimination in apartment rentals was studied in New York and southern Cali-fornia, by having white, black, and Mexican-American couples of college students pose as prospective tenants for advertised apartments for rent. In New York, land-lords displayed no discrimination in their willingness to show the apartment or in quoting the amount of rent, but when it came to willingness to rent the apartment, white couples obtained apartments more readily than black couples. In California, blacks were discriminated against more often than Mexican-Americans, who in turn were more discriminated against than whites. Overall, not only was the least number of apartments available to blacks, but blacks were also quoted the highest rental and miscellaneous fees. Over 75 percent of the apartment house managers dis-played some overt indication of racial discrimination.

McGREW (1967)
JOHNSON, PORTER, AND MATELJAN (1971)

Cognitive Integration

Several studies have succeeded in isolating other factors that influence first impres-sions of people. Asch (1946) read a list of characteristics of an unknown person to a group of college students and asked them to write a brief personality sketch. The characteristics were made as simple and discrete as possible, for example, "ener-getic," "cold," or "inquisitive." The resulting descriptions of the perceived stranger indicated that these adjectives were organized into meaningful conceptual structures

PREJUDICE WITHOUT AUTHORITARIANISM

A study of attitudes toward South African natives was conducted among 600 white South African college students. Scores on various personality measures indicated extremely strong feelings of prejudice, especially among white Afrikaners as compared to the Anglo-Saxon whites. Yet authoritarianism among the Afrikaners was no higher than among the Anglo-Saxon whites, and the total South African sample was equal in authoritarianism to a similar sample of American college students. Prejudice in one country (due to its political structure and prevailing norms) was thus higher than in the other, although there was no difference between them in authoritarianism.

Another study, conducted in four southern and four northern communities in the United States, showed similar results. Unfavorable, prejudicial responses were more prevalent among southern respondents, yet both samples did not differ in authoritarianism. In the southern sample conformity to the prevailing norm, as expressed by the highly prejudiced responses (apart from authoritarianism), was higher for females than males, for churchgoers than nonchurchgoers, for nonveterans than veterans, and for the less educated than the more educated. In the northern sample, churchgoing and expressions of prejudice were negatively related.

PETTIGREW (1958)

by the perceiver. Some students even introduced wholly new attributes that had not even been mentioned in the original description, merely in order to complete a pattern of cognitive organization. From these observations, Asch described several processes contributing to these organizing patterns.

The fact that perceptual events tend to be integrated into organized conceptual structures implies that when one judges another person, he will attempt to fit isolated experiences into a larger and more comprehensive framework. For example, when Asch introduced the adjective "warm" into the context of "intelligent-skillful-industrious-determined-practical-cautious," he elicited a completely different overall impression of personality than when he introduced the word "cold" into the same context. This change of only one descriptive word out of seven was sufficient to produce different interpretations of the other six. When the list contained the word "warm," the person was characterized as rather benevolent and dedicated to his work; but when the word "cold" was substituted, the person was characterized as snobbish, unsympathetic, and egotistical. In the perception of people, as in the perception of nonsocial objects, the discrete elements of sensory input are assimilated into organized cognitive patterns. The frame of reference (described in Chapter 4) provides one theoretical model to account for cognitive integration. More recent models (e.g., Fishbein, 1963; Anderson, 1968; S. Feldman, 1968; Wyer, 1970) have focused their attention on complex cognitive processes in impression formation.

In perceiving others, people often make use of their own miniature "implicit theories of personality." That is, without necessarily realizing it, they make assumptions about certain kinds of supposed orderly associations and relationships in human behavior (Thornton, 1944). For example, they may assume that all people who are fat with round faces and pink complexions must also be jolly, kind, and generous. Or they may assume that people who are honest must also always be kind, or that people who are aggressive must also always be untrustworthy. They may assume that men are more practical than women, or that women are poorer drivers. Certain kinds of systematic associations may be factually accurate (otherwise there would be no merit in scientific psychological theories of personality), but the average person may be very unsophisticated as to the actual kinds of lawful associations that occur in

COGNITIVE PROCESSES IN IMPRESSION FORMATION

In a typical experimental investigation of impression formation, subjects are presented with a descriptive set of adjectives or other bits of information and asked to make an evaluation of a hypothetical target person. In the present study, college students were given redundant (related to the same dimension) and nonredundant (not related to the same dimension) sets of adjectives. For example, when a person is perceived as "sociable," he may also be judged as "warm," or "friendly," even though these descriptions may convey somewhat different impressions. If the person is described as "unsociable," or "unfriendly," or "cold," another set of impressions is conveyed. Yet all these descriptions are redundant to a certain extent, because they belong to the same basic dimension of "sociability." On the other hand, if the "sociable" person is also described as "responsible," or "unreliable," the latter impressions are considered to be nonredundant, or relatively independent of the dimension of sociability.

The results of subjects' evaluations suggested that cognitive processes in impression formation are largely governed by the nature of the incoming initial information. When the initial judgment is acceptable, or considered likely to be true, people tend to rely on nonredundant information in forming their impressions, presumably because of their desire to know more about new and different aspects of the target person (e.g., "He is sociable. Is he also reliable?"). However, when the initial judgment is considered doubtful or unlikely, people tend to seek out redundant information to add support for their initial judgment (e.g., "He may be unsociable. Is he also unfriendly and cold?").

BRYSON (1973)

personality and behavior. His implicit theories of personality may be based on stereotypes, superstitions, or old wives' tales. They may represent highly inaccurate assumptions. Asch's study suggested that people do make use of such assumptions, without questioning their accuracy or validity, and that they trust such assumptions when asked to elaborate on a description of another person about whom they know very little.

Halo Effects

A particular kind of generalization about associated attributes of personality may be labeled the *halo effect.* This describes the tendency to blur one characteristic into another, especially in speculative kinds of associations among various attributes of personality. For example, the display of a few socially desirable or valued characteristics may lead a perceiver to assume that a person generally displays favorable or liked attributes. A person who has been described as kind and generous may then be attributed with characteristics such as trustworthiness, good humor, and intellectual brilliance. A generally favorable impression of another person tends to spread into one's judgments of all that person's attributes, and a generally unfavorable impression may sour one's judgments or guesses about unknown characteristics of the person. The halo effect in impression formation appears to be most pronounced when the perceiver has a minimum of information about the perceived person, when the perceiver's judgment of another concerns moral evaluation, or when the perceiver is unfamiliar with the traits or attributes he is judging in another (Symonds, 1925).

Gollin (1954) extended Asch's investigations of impressions of personality a step further by intentionally making it difficult for the perceiver to develop a coherently organized impression of the stranger. He prepared a short motion picture in which a young woman was portrayed in several different scenes. Two of these scenes showed kind and considerate behavior on her part; two others, however, suggested that she was sexually promiscuous; the fifth was a neutral scene. When students were later asked to write brief personality descriptions of the young woman, about half the subjects mentioned only one of the two major kinds of behavior shown in the movie, but did not attempt to integrate both into one coherent impression. A quarter of the students mentioned both kinds of behavior, but were unable to integrate them, and only a quarter were able to develop an integrated reconciliation of the two partially contradictory exposures to the young woman in the movie. Thus Gollin's experiment questions Asch's suggestion that discretely perceived characteristics of another person will be integrated into an orderly and coherent overall impression. By providing incompatible samples of the other person's behavior, Gollin made it difficult for the perceiver to organize his overall impression of personality.

Order Effects: Primacy and Recency

Luchins (1957a) identified at least one factor that accounts for selective emphasis on particular discrete and incompatible attributes when the perceiver attempts to develop an overall impression of another person. He found that the order in which a perceiver is exposed to particular characteristics of another person determines his overall impression. Four groups of subjects were used, each receiving a description of a stranger named Jim. The description presented to the first group portrayed Jim as an extroverted person; that presented to the second group portrayed him as introverted, shy, and withdrawn. The remaining two groups were presented with descriptions that combined introversion and extroversion, but in reversed orders: the third group was presented with the extroverted character description first, followed by the introverted description; and the fourth group was presented with the introverted description first and then the extroverted description. The subsequent character sketches of Jim written by each of the four groups were then compared. As expected, the first two groups provided rather different descriptions of Jim. However, the latter two groups also generated rather different impressions of him, depending on the order in which they had been exposed to conflicting descriptions: in both these groups, the first description dominated the second. It appeared indeed that first impressions are lasting ones. This dominance and durability of initial impression is described as a *primacy effect,* and it appears to occur in the development of many kinds of attitudes. However, when a person is generally familiar with another person but later encounters an array of new information about that person, *recency* effects often occur: the most recent information encountered tends to occupy a dominant position in cognitive organization.

Although the primacy effect in formation of impressions of personality was very clear in Luchins' experiments, he found in other studies (e.g., Luchins, 1957b) that it might be reduced in several ways. By forewarning the perceiver about the fallacies of first impressions and the likelihood that initial impressions can be quite misleading, the degree of primacy was considerably reduced. Furthermore he found that when contradictory descriptions of the person were separated by unrelated activities (rather than placed immediately after one another in time sequence), the primacy effect was also reduced, and in fact, a recency effect occurred.

INTERPERSONAL PERCEPTION

In the kinds of experimental studies just described, the investigations were not focused on whether the impressions of people were *accurate.* However, psychologists have explored this issue in other studies. It appears, at least superficially, that effective interpersonal relationships might depend in part on the ability of one person to understand accurately the behavior and experience of another. Although basic physical attributes of others are ordinarily perceived reasonably accurately, under certain extreme conditions even size judgments of people may be distorted (Wittreich, 1952) (see Figure 8–1). There is ample evidence in everyday experience that inferences from physical features as to the racial origins of another person are often inaccurate. In their research on these matters, however, psychologists have generally been more interested in the accuracy of other kinds of judgments about others: judgments of their emotional characteristics, of their attitudes or values, of their behavioral traits, or other psychological characteristics. In early social psychology, the capacity to make accurate judgments of this sort about others was included in the concept of empathy, although this term is less frequently used in contemporary psychology.

The kinds of behavioral attributes appropriate for the study of accuracy in interpersonal perception are, of course, limited to those for which some reliable measure of "reality," or veridicality, is possible. Often it is difficult to measure precisely what a person is "really like"; consequently, studies of accuracy of judgment of others are sometimes focused merely on comparisons of one person's description of another with the latter's own description of himself, or with a consensual judgment from a pool of people about the characteristics of that other person. It should be recognized, of course, that both of these kinds of measures provide only an approximation of reality against which accuracy of judgment may be gauged.

There are four essential sources that may contribute to the perceiver's overall perception and judgment of another: variables associated with the perceiver himself, variables associated with the person being perceived and judged, variables associated with the psychological relationship between the judge and the person judged, and the situational context in which the perceptual judgment is made.

Characteristics of the Perceiver

Although several studies have attempted to define psychological attributes associated with the ability to judge other people accurately, the results have generally indicated

---

BLACK AND WHITE PERCEPTION

Pictures of professional actors (ten white, ten black; five females and five males of each race) portraying different emotions (anger, happiness, surprise, fear, disgust, pain, and sadness) were presented for judgment to college students (eighty white and eighty black; forty males and forty females of each race). Responses were analyzed in terms of patterns of correctly perceived emotions or incorrectly perceived emotions (emotions were in fact perceived, but the perceivers did not judge them correctly). Blacks were more accurate in their perception than whites, but the sex of the perceiver was not a significant factor. In all cases, females were more frequently judged correctly than males, and males were more frequently judged incorrectly than females. The suggested explanation for the findings was that females are more suitable than males as expressers of emotions (even though they are no more accurate perceivers than males) because of the sex-role relationship, which sanctions such behavior in females. The fact that blacks were more accurate than whites as perceivers was presumed to be a function of their cultural sensitivity to emotional nuances developed during their history of subservience in the United States.

BLACK (1969)

little or no stability of this capacity. There is little evidence to support the notion that "ability to read character" is a stable measurable attribute of an individual. A person who accurately describes someone today may not be equally able to describe someone else tomorrow. Considerable evidence has accumulated to suggest that if, indeed, there is such a thing as a skill of accurate interpersonal perception, the skill is not a general one. Studies have found that in some cases such skills appear to be confined to particular attributes or dimensions of personality, and in other cases confined to particular populations of people judged. One investigation, however (Cline & Richards, 1960), which argues that there may be some stability in interpersonal judgment skills, suggested two kinds of abilities in judging others: one related to stereotypes and accurate perception of people in general (i.e., accurate guesses about attributes true of most people belonging to a particular class or group), and the other related to specific accuracy in perceiving individuals as different from one another. Because only ten selected people were judged in this study, however, this is only very tentative evidence of any general ability to judge all kinds of other people accurately.

In clinical psychology one often assumes that the good clinician and diagnostician must be particularly sensitive in judging others. This attribute of successful interpersonal relations is particularly stressed by the humanistic tradition and proponents of Gestalt therapy and transactional analysis (e.g., Perls, 1969a, b; Fagan & Shepherd, 1970). Nevertheless, whether it be called "sensitivity" or "empathy," this quality is very elusive. It is difficult to assess. Probably the most widely used method of measurement of such interpersonal sensitivity is the "Carkhuff Scales" (Carkhuff, 1969, 1971), a set of judgmental criteria for gauging the degree or level of insight in interpersonal perception. There is limited evidence that emotionally healthy people show greater sensitivity on these scales than unhealthy ones, and that during the course of successful therapy, sensitivity increases somewhat (Carkhuff, 1967, 1969; Truax & Carkhuff, 1967).

This evidence is by no means unequivocal and uncontested. Other studies suggest that accuracy of interpersonal perception is not a quality that can be readily cultivated or acquired through training or therapy. Apart from their technological skills in utilizing certain specific diagnostic tests and procedures, professional psychologists and graduate students in psychology are not highly distinguishable from untrained college students so far as the ability to judge everyday nonpathological attributes of personality is concerned (Kremers, 1960). In fact, some have gone so far as to suggest that certain kinds of "overtraining" may lead to decreased general accuracy of

---

TRAINING FOR SENSITIVITY

Subjects were presented with twenty-five hypothetical situations and asked how they would react to them. At the same time, their close friends indicated their expectations of how these individuals would react. Respondents who showed the greatest consistency in their replies and whose friends judged them most accurately were chosen as object persons. Judging these object persons were undergraduate and graduate students majoring in psychology, classics, and the natural sciences. Their task was to predict the object persons' responses to the hypothetical situations after hearing them give a 10-minute speech about labor relations. Accuracy of prediction was assessed by counting the number of a judge's predictions agreeing with the responses of the object person. Relatively high perception accuracy was displayed by only 14 percent of the judges. Moreover, no differences were found between the accuracy scores of undergraduates and graduate students or among the three types of majors.

KREMERS (1960)

interpersonal perception by directing undue attention to details of individual differences, causing a student to lose sight of the overall composite of the total personality (Crow, 1957).

Several aspects of personality and personal adjustment have been identified as contributing to one's ability to judge others accurately. Through the mechanism of *projection* (unconsciously externalizing a subjective experience) one sometimes attributes to others characteristics he dislikes (either consciously or unconsciously) in himself, a process that appears to interrupt interpersonal perception (Sears, 1936). Indeed, a certain amount of projection is typical in everyone from time to time, but its consistent and excessive occurrence is associated with neurosis and emotional maladjustment. Of course one who exercises a great amount of projection is a rather inaccurate judge of others because he is inclined to confuse the picture by attributing to others his own qualities, regardless of his actual experience with them. People who generally accept themselves the way they are and who possess accurate insight about their own make-up tend to judge others more accurately (Norman, 1953; Omwake, 1954; Baker & Block, 1957). Secure, outgoing, sociable people are particularly benevolent in their judgment of others, and they tend to credit others excessively with warmth, sociability, and other desirable characteristics (Bossom & Maslow, 1957). This "benevolent generosity" in judging others has been described as a *leniency effect.*

There is no convincing evidence that intelligence as such has a strong correlate of accuracy in interpersonal perception. Intellectually dull individuals tend to judge others inaccurately, but intellectual brilliance is no guarantee of accurate judgment (Taft, 1955). A capacity that may be related to intelligence, as well as to emotional maturity, has been found to be related to accuracy of interpersonal judgment in studies of the basic cognitive ability to use complex multiphasic conceptual schemes or frameworks in perceiving people (Leventhal, 1957; Harvey, Hunt, & Schroder, 1961).

Characteristics of the Perceived Person

On the other side of the interpersonal relation, other studies have explored the capacity to be judged by others accurately. The question raised is whether there may be particular kinds of people who are especially "transparent" and thus easily judged accurately by others, as opposed to some who might be relatively obscure and difficult to judge. Here again, the research evidence is meager and inconclusive.

Perhaps the most important variable concerning this question is the *willingness* of the individual to expose himself to others. This variable, of special interest in clinical psychology, has been referred to as "self-disclosure" (Jourard, 1964). Certain people (and perhaps everyone, under certain circumstances) are inclined to be unwilling to expose themselves for judgment by others, and they attempt to veil or hide them-

---

BENEVOLENT PERCEPTION

On the basis of various measures of security, friendliness, and sociability, a sample of 44 college students was divided into a "very secure" group, and a "very insecure" group. They were then presented with 200 photographs of persons and asked to indicate whether the latter were "very warm," or "warm" (positive rating), or "very cold," or "cold" (negative rating). The "very secure" group made considerably more positive judgments than did the "very insecure" group (a "leniency effect").

BOSSOM AND MASLOW (1957)

selves in various ways. Others take the other extreme and display themselves almost exhibitionistically, hiding no secrets at all. The underlying variable of greatest importance in self-disclosure seems to be *anxiety,* involving perceived threat or fear that the consequences of judgment by others might be painful or unpleasant. It is associated with clinical anxiety, threat, neurosis, and emotional maladjustment (Himelstein & Kimbrough, 1963; Jourard, 1964; Rotter, 1967).

Transparency to others may also be associated with *extremeness* of particular characteristics. That is, certain kinds of dominant attributes (especially those of great interpersonal relevance, such as friendliness, hostility, or dependency) may become salient even in very limited interaction with others if they are strongly pronounced. People who display such qualities at extreme levels thus may be judged more readily and more accurately than people who show such qualities only rarely or moderately.

Another kind of transparency may be associated with what has been called "stereotype accuracy." Individuals who are typical of a particular highly stereotyped group to which they belong or with which they may be identified by others may tend to be judged more accurately than people who are atypical and do not conform to stereotypes. Inasmuch as ethnic identification, social roles, and group identifications provide supplementary cues to a perceiver when he judges another person, an individual who is typical of the stereotypes that others are likely to apply to him will be judged more accurately than a person who is atypical. This, of course, represents a kind of accidental or coincidental accuracy of judgment.

One person's judgments of another may be considerably affected by the judge's knowledge of the other person's position in the complex framework of social institutions within which human beings live. Individuals who occupy particular kinds of social positions may be expected to display particular kinds of attitudes. In studying the behavior of individuals in formally organized social systems (see Section IV), psychologists have developed a useful set of concepts relating to the roles and positions occupied by individuals in the complex social system (Linton, 1945; Newcomb, 1950). The term *position* is used to denote the structural niche in a social system that designates a particular kind of expected function. Examples of commonly encountered positions include age groups, sex groups, family kinship groups (such as "mother," "father"), occupational groups, social status groups, and other similar terms that define a functional category or "bloc" within a social system. Associated with a position is a particular set of assumptions about that position as well as a particular set of expectations about the behavior of people who occupy such a position. The term *role* refers to the dynamic aspects of a position: the actual behavior displayed by individuals who occupy the position. As such, roles are models by means of which the attitudes and behavior of a person become predictable for other individuals who participate in the same social system. By knowing something about the position a person occupies in a group or society, others can perceive and predict his behavior more stably and accurately (Harvey, 1956; Abravanel, 1962).

VISIBLE TRANSPARENCY

Navy enlisted personnel were divided into groups that worked and lived together aboard ship for at least 2 months. They were subsequently asked to indicate their choices for a companion for a 72-hour liberty, as well as to guess the choices of the other subjects. The most accurate guesses were obtained when certain attributes of the perceived person were highly visible or "transparent" (e.g., excessive cleanliness, or excessive reserve).

TAGIURI, KOGAN, AND BRUNER (1955)

A MAN IS 10 FEET TALL

In a study designed to assess the effects of status on perception accuracy, the same individual was introduced to college students at various times as a student, as an assistant, as a lecturer, or as a professor at Cambridge University. After the individual's departure the students were asked to estimate his height. With increased status, there was a corresponding increase in overestimation of height.

P. R. WILSON (1968)

It is relatively easy to identify a variety of positions in a formally organized social system, but positions in an informal organization are often rather vague. Although Argyle (1959) has argued that the concept of position cannot appropriately be applied in the study of casual informal groups, stable patterns of behavior (roles) do in fact evolve rather rapidly in even short-lived informal groups (Benne & Sheats, 1948; Bales, 1950; P. Slater, 1955). All participants in a social system do not behave identically, and as they interact, distinctive behavior comes to be expected of different members of the system. Thus despite the vagueness of positional definitions in informal groups, role differentiations do emerge. Roles and their relationship to group structure are discussed further in Chapter 11.

Relationship Between Perceiver and Perceived Person

One of the factors most clearly associated with accuracy of interpersonal perception is the degree of propinquity (physical nearness) or frequency of association between the perceiver and the perceived person. Individuals who belong to and participate in the same kinds of informal social groups tend to perceive one another more accurately than they perceive outsiders (Altman & McGinnies, 1960). The most obvious interpretation of these findings is that closer association results in increased exposure of one person to another, permitting more accurate judgments. However, psychologists have been careful to recognize that other factors may contribute to such observations. The fact that individuals who are in close social association are likely to be homogeneous with respect to many attributes, interests, and attitudes must be considered. Such processes as projections of one's own attributes to others, as well as stereotypical generalizations about members identified within a given group, would tend to enhance, rather than to detract from, accuracy of judgment. Thus a kind of coincidental accuracy (the "stereotype accuracy" described earlier) may occur in interpersonal judgments within a particular social group. However, it has also been found that close associates and friends are sometimes inclined to overestimate their similarity to one another, a fact that occasionally may lead to inaccuracies in interpersonal judgment. It has been demonstrated in a variety of situations that following group interaction, members come to perceive their partners and associates as more similar to themselves than had been the case prior to interaction (Gage, 1952; Bieri, 1953).

There is further evidence that individuals who occupy positions of high status or popularity in a given social group are able to judge other members of their own group more accurately than individuals in low-status or low-popularity positions (Chowdry & Newcomb, 1952; Gage, 1956).

Investigations have shown several interesting kinds of distortion in perceiving and judging highly familiar people. The transactional point of view emphasizes the importance of familiarity and value in the perception of both nonsocial objects and events as well as of people and groups. Its proponents have demonstrated, for

PSYCHOTHERAPEUTIC ENCOUNTER

A review of black-white encounters in therapeutic settings (involving therapists, counselors, caseworkers, and their patients or clients) summarized the following findings.

White Therapist–Black Client. The white, middle-class therapist who values verbal facility will often label the black client as uncommunicative; he tends to feel guilty about his own racial and class identity and allow these feelings to intrude on the therapeutic relationship; he is tempted to turn to social issues that are important but therapeutically irrelevant; and he is often viewed by the black client as a patronizing reinforcer of "Uncle Tom" manners.

Black Therapist–White Client. The black therapist tends either to vent his hostility by being unsympathetic or punitive toward the white client or to be too permissive toward him because of his anxiety and overidentification with whites.

Black Therapist–Black Client. The black therapist is trained primarily in a white milieu and like his white counterpart is often above the client's level; he is perceived as a "collaborator" with the white enemy; and he is frequently inept because he has been hired solely for being black.

SATTLER (1970)

example, that assumptions about the meaning of a visual pattern affect one's judgments of its size and its distance from the viewer (Wittreich, 1952). Figure 8-1 shows a specially constructed distorted room arranged from trapezoidal shapes to provide the same image on the viewer's retina that an ordinary rectangular room would provide. Such a room produces a variety of extreme distortions in the viewer's perceptions and judgments as a result of his efforts to interpret what he sees in the distorted room within the context of his assumptions about familiar rectangular rooms. Marbles rolling along a trough that is actually inclined downward, but that appears (in the context of assumed rectangularity) to be inclined upward, seem to roll uphill.

INTERNATIONAL PERCEPTION

Social encounters were experimentally manipulated with over 3000 citizens of Boston, Paris, and Athens. In each city the typical encounter involved either a fellow citizen or a foreigner who asked the local citizen for directions or to mail a letter, or gave him the opportunity to cheat in commercial transactions (e.g., a local storeowner was overpaid and thus given a chance to cheat the compatriot or the foreigner; observations were made on taxicab charges to either compatriot or foreigner). The foreigners or fellow citizens were confederates of the experimenter; their apparent socioeconomic class was varied by having local social scientists determine the type of clothes they should wear. The socioeconomic class of the accosted local citizens were also determined by the types of clothes they wore. In general, Parisians tended to treat the compatriot better than the American foreigner, especially as the demands of the accosting stranger increased. They also cheated the foreigner more than the compatriot. The Athenians, on the other hand, treated the American foreigner far better than their fellow citizen, presumably because of traditional norms of hospitality to foreigners and deeply ingrained distrust of their own people. The Bostonians made little or no distinction in their treatment of foreigner and fellow citizen, but they tended to give preferential treatment along socioeconomic in-group considerations.

R. A. FELDMAN (1968)

Figure 8–1 A distorted room demonstration. These three men are actually the same size! (William Vandivert)

Strangers who stand in a corner of the room at the short dimensions of its rear trapezoidal wall appear to be giants, whereas strangers appear to be midgets when they move to the long dimensions of the trapezoidal rear wall. Thus the demonstration shows clearly that the perception of people—even the perception of their physical size—may be subject to distortions in the perceiver's efforts to fit them into a familiar contextual frame of reference.

However, an interesting exception to this kind of distortion, the "Honi Phenomenon," was discovered by Wittreich (1952) when the experimenter viewed his wife's face through the windows of the distorted room. Ordinarily a stranger's face seems relatively smaller when it appears in a window at the large end of the rear trapezoidal wall, but relatively larger when it appears in the actually smaller (but apparently identical) window at the small end of that wall. Wittreich found, however, that the familiar—and presumably highly valued—face of his wife was not subject to such distortion, and that in fact, the room appeared to distort around her face, while the perceived size of her face remained relatively stable. A series of explorations with other viewers revealed that familiarity with people viewed in the room often overrides assumptions about the rectangularity of the distorted room. Thus when highly familiar people are perceived and judged, it is possible that the perception of the context in which they appear may undergo distortion in efforts to maintain stability in perception of the familiar person. The distorted room demonstrations are dramatic in that they show the occurrence of distortions of judgments of very basic physical attributes of another person or the context in which he is judged.

Less dramatically, of course, such distortions occur widely in judging behavioral attributes and personality characteristics of others. The father of an adolescent boy arrested for stealing an automobile may disbelieve the reports of police or trustworthy eyewitnesses or the implications of clear and unchallengeable evidence in his efforts to maintain his stable judgment of his son as an honest, well-behaved youth. Conversely, he may wish to condemn a stranger accused of stealing his own car even on the basis of doubtful evidence and despite the testimony of character witnesses who vouch for the honesty of the accused. The demonstrations represent rather elaborate examples of the role of frames of reference in guiding perceptual judgments of both people and their physical surroundings.

Situational Context in Person Perception

There is abundant evidence that the more one knows about the context in which he attempts to judge another person, the more accurate will be his perception of that person. On the surface it seems that judgments of emotions being experienced by another person might be made easily and accurately if one could see his facial expression. However, the evidence from psychological studies of such judgments is highly inconsistent and contradictory. Several early explorations yielded evidence that people can accurately judge emotions, but others have found that accuracy of judgment appears no greater than chance or random accident would predict. Many of these studies are rather crude ones, lacking methodological refinement, so it is difficult to analyze them and to attempt explanation of their different findings.

It has been suggested that the judgment of emotions from facial expressions may be little more than a consequence of accepting the conventions of the theater and dramatics. Studies in which actors have posed the facial display of certain prescribed emotions (e.g., Hulin & Katz, 1935) have usually yielded more evidence of accuracy in judgment of emotion from facial expression than have studies using real photographs of people actually experiencing certain emotions (e.g., Landis, 1924, who used photographs of subjects in a laboratory watching such gruesome procedures as cutting off the head of a rat, or Munn, 1940, who clipped candid photographs from magazines). Pudovkin (1954), however, found that even judgments of photographs posed by an actor varied as a function of the context in which the actor was photographed. In any case, there is considerable evidence of variation from one individual to the next with respect to the facial expression of emotion.

Moreover, there is evidence of variation among cultures in the expression of emotion. During World War II, the Japanese soldier was widely characterized to the American public as an apparently demented, sadistic individual who met the gruesome experience of direct combat and watching his enemy die with a wide grin exposing pearly white teeth between upturned lips. Students of the Oriental personality and those well acquainted with the Japanese people, however, were aware that this particular expression (which, to the Westerner, is associated with glee and pleasure) is a typical expression of grim determination for the Oriental. Many Japanese regard the typical American's facial expression to be generally dour and scowling, whereas Americans often regard the Japanese as insincere because of their

---

FIXED FACES

A simple, passive facial close-up of a well-known actor was joined to three different strips of films that introduced varying backgrounds: a bowl of soup, a dead woman in a coffin, and a little girl playing with a toy bear. The viewers judged the actor's facial expressions in terms of the situational contexts (pensive, sad, or happy), although in all three cases the facial expression remained exactly the same.

PUDOVKIN (1954)

habitual smiles (Hearn, 1894). Thus even our theatrical stereotypes of the facial expression of emotion may themselves be culture-bound, restricting accurate judgments of experienced emotion from theatrical expressions only to members of a common culture.

The accuracy of judgment of emotions from facial expressions increases considerably when the judge is aware of the situational context in which the expression occurs. In studies using facial photographs from popular news magazines, the surrounding photographic contexts provided sufficient contextual anchoring to increase the precision of judgments of emotion considerably (Munn, 1940; Pudovkin, 1954).

INTERPERSONAL ATTRACTION

The study of interpersonal perception is only the beginning of the analysis of interpersonal relationships. Evaluative attitudes of attraction or repulsion tend to play an even more important role in the perception of people than in the perception of nonsocial objects. During the 1930s and 1940s, sociometric methods were developed to permit scientific exploration of the complex processes of interpersonal attraction and rejection. These methods afford direct measurement of the degree to which individuals are attracted to one another, both through subjective reports from the individual himself (standard sociometric methods) as well as through the patterns of his overt behavior in social interactions (direct observation methods) (see Chapter 3).

Friendship is psychologically more complex than might at first be apparent. It is particularly important to recognize that popularity and personal attractiveness are not simple attributes or characteristics of an individual in the usual sense of beauty, strength, or honesty. They are truly *interpersonal* variables inasmuch as they involve interrelationships with other people. That is to say, to be *liked,* one must be *liked by someone;* to be *popular,* one must be regarded collectively as attractive *by the members of some group.* Thus the social psychologist cannot comprehensively attempt to analyze interpersonal attraction without being concerned both with the popularity or attractiveness of a given individual and with the person or people to whom he is attractive.

Furthermore it is important to distinguish *popularity* (general or collective attractiveness to others) from specific *friendships* (diadic interpersonal attractions between individuals). The psychological variables associated with one may not necessarily be associated with the other. In 1937 F. W. Burkes compared a measure of a person's "social prestige" (popularity) with a measure of his "ability to inspire affection" (individual attractiveness to others) and suggested that although the two measures were closely related, they were not identical. Naegele (1958) discussed this issue further, pointing out that popular people may have many admirers but few friends. He even suggested that being singled out for admiration may actually tend to isolate a person from close personal relationships, especially if the qualities of accomplishment that earn admiration are envied by others who lack those qualities. Blau (1962) suggested another distinction between popularity and individual friendship, by proposing that the two be dichotomized with reference to whether the interpersonal relationship between two people is basically an *evaluative* one (admiration or popularity) or an *interactive* one (friendship).

In addition, attraction to another person on first encounter is not necessarily to be accounted for by the same psychological factors that account for continued friendships and sustained loyalties. Often in psychological research these two kinds of interpersonal attraction have been confused, and interpretations of the results of research investigations have not directly considered the possibility of important differences between them.

Popularity

Popular people generally tend to exhibit what psychologists refer to as *socially desirable* characteristics. Although this statement sounds circular (and indeed it is, conceptually), research methods can independently assess them separately. Individuals may be asked directly to evaluate traits or descriptive adjectives according to the degree to which they feel the described attributes are generally desirable characteristics in a person (Edwards, 1957). Apart from this, the actual personal characteristics of people who are regarded as popular and attractive may be assessed by a wide variety of psychological inventories, self-descriptive tests, or attitude and need surveys. Few studies have directly attempted to demonstrate that attributes that people regard as socially desirable are in fact associated with particular people regarded as popular or attractive, for the inherent circularity of this proposition would describe one measure simply as a validation of the other. However, there is ample indirect and anecdotal evidence to convince one that these variables are the same (Gronlund & Anderson, 1957). In general, the entire array of personal characteristics found to be associated with popularity, at least with respect to studies of Americans, would be regarded by most members of our culture as socially desirable personal characteristics.

Among children as well as adults, socioeconomic status has been found to be generally correlated with popularity. Individuals who occupy relatively higher positions in the socioeconomic hierarchy (usually defined by such measures as annual income, amount of education, occupation of the head of the household to which the individual belongs, or some combination of such indices) are generally relatively popular among their colleagues (Loomis & Proctor, 1950).

Similarly, various measures of intelligence and scholastic achievement have been found to be correlated with popularity status. Individuals who are popular among their colleagues have generally been found to be brighter in terms of assessments of basic intelligence (Grossman & Wrighter, 1948), as well as in terms of school grades and other indices of intellectual achievement (J. A. Davis, 1957). However, it must be remembered that intellectual capacity is only one of many kinds of socially attractive personal characteristics. As Grossman and Wrighter (1948) and Bonney (1955) have pointed out, brilliance alone may not be sufficient to earn popularity, but more clearly, intellectual dullness seems to stand in the way of popularity among one's colleagues, as least among American children and adolescents, whose social groups are often closely related to scholastic settings (R. W. Brown, 1954).

Good physical and mental health also seem to be closely related to popularity status. Popular individuals appear relatively healthy (French, 1951). Other studies show that popularity is associated with personal security (Bonney, Hoblit & Dreyer, 1953), healthier self-concept and self-regard (Reese, 1961), and freedom from problems of personal adjustment (Kuhlen & Bretsch, 1947). The relationship between popularity and healthy psychological adjustment may in part be a circular one. Social

---

STATUS AND POPULARITY

Interpersonal choices of agricultural county agents and librarians who were participating in a university workshop served as the basis for a popularity index, and their annual incomes served as a measure of socioeconomic status. The two measures were found to be positively related: the more popular the person, the higher was his income.

LOOMIS AND PROCTOR (1950)

MALADJUSTMENT AND POPULARITY

The self-concept and socioeconomic status of 400 elementary and junior high school pupils were assessed by means of various rating scales. The relationship between self-acceptance and popularity was curvilinear: those with a moderate degree of self-acceptance (and presumably also the most adjusted) were found to be most popular; those with high self-concepts were less popular; and those with low self-concepts were least popular.

REESE (1961)

rejection and isolation may precipitate personal insecurity, low self-esteem, and poor regard for oneself, especially because one major source of the information that constitutes one's conception of himself (see Chapter 6) rests with what others think of the individual and the feedback he receives from them about himself. Nevertheless, the reverse conjecture—that poor personal adjustment interferes with the attainment of popularity—is consistent with the general fact that socially desirable characteristics are associated with popularity, for certainly the display of neuroticism and psychological maladjustment is generally regarded as socially undesirable behavior in our culture (Reese, 1961).

In the same vein are several studies that reveal that, at least in industrial settings, popularity is inversely related to accident proneness (Speroff & Kerr, 1952). That is, individuals who have poor accident records tend to be unpopular among their co-workers.

It may be that the frequency with which research studies have confirmed the importance of intelligence, scholastic achievement, and socioeconomic factors as determinants of popularity status is related to the kinds of social groups that have been studied. Without question, a disproportionate number of these investigations have been conducted in public school settings. Within the context of the school, one might reasonably expect intelligence and academic achievement to be regarded as particularly desirable attributes. Similarly, one might expect freedom from accidents to be particularly regarded as a virtue in industrial or military settings. Thus it may be wise to exercise caution about generalization of these demonstrated relationships to all kinds of social groups. The correlates of popularity in one setting may not necessarily be associated with popularity in another group in another context with different standards for desirable behavior.

Several kinds of evidence suggest that certain correlates of popularity may indeed be more or less unique to the particular kind of group in which popularity is studied (Bretsch, 1952). In physical education classes, athletic skills were associated with popularity (Breck, 1950). Somewhat similarly, personal attributes associated with popularity in girls include appropriate sex-typed behavior such as docility, demureness, and such "feminine" characteristics; among boys, however, aggressiveness and assertiveness are associated with popularity (Pope, 1953). Although there is gen-

ACCIDENT-PRONENESS AND POPULARITY

Steel workers with low sociometric status had more industrial accidents than those with high status. It was suggested that sociometric "reassignment" can reduce the frequency of industrial accidents in workers who are demonstrably low in social choice.

SPEROFF AND KERR (1952)

eral evidence that in racially and ethnically mixed groups, individuals tend to be popular among members of their own group (Raths & Schweikert, 1946), there is some indirect evidence from other studies suggesting that even minority groups may sometimes subscribe to the values of a dominant majority group. Thus among certain Negro groups studies have yielded evidence that higher status may be accorded to individuals who show fewer "Negroid" and more "Caucasoid" characteristics in facial features, skin shade, and the like (Martin, 1964). Even possessing a first name that is regarded as attractive by one's colleagues is associated with personal popularity in some settings (McDavid & Harari, 1966).

In summary, then, it appears that the values of a particular group will determine the desirability or attractiveness of personal attributes and characteristics, and that individuals who display the valued characteristics will be accorded popularity by their associates. Because popularity is inherently a dimension of *relationships* among people, rather than of characteristics of an individual, it is unlikely that research studies will reveal much evidence of stable correlations between popularity and personal attributes without considering explicitly the nature of the values and standards of the group in which popularity is considered.

NAMES AND POPULARITY

Grade school children indicated how much they liked names from a given list (e.g., David and Karen were rated high, Sanford and Adelle were rated low). The popularity status for each child was obtained and found to correlate with the likeability of the rated names. Whether or not the raters were acquainted with the particular child bearing a given name made no difference in the findings. This evidence suggests that not only do children hold stereotypes about names, but that these stereotypes may influence a child's popularity among his classmates.

McDAVID AND HARARI (1966)

Friendship

The label "friendship" is conventionally used to designate interpersonal association ranging from passing attractions to deep and long-lasting mutual relationships. In either case, psychologists have found it necessary to distinguish individual friendship from the concept of popularity just discussed. As Naegele (1958) argued, popularity and collective admiration may be accompanied by envy on the part of others. Blau (1962), in differentiating popularity and individual attraction, not only described popularity as an evaluative relationship and friendship as an interactive one, but he further pointed out that friendship may be instrumental to an individual's attainment of particular goals or satisfaction of particular needs or desires. That is, individual friendship pairings may represent instrumental interactions in which one person's attraction to another may be contingent upon the other's behavior and its instrumental value to the first person in pursuit of his goals and interests.

Speculations such as these about the origins of interpersonal attraction thus generate at least two fairly plausible hypotheses. On one hand, *similarity* of attitudes, values, and goals might be expected to contribute to individual attractiveness: people who perceive one another as colleagues "in the same boat," sharing the same goals and interests and possessing similar abilities, capacities, and attitudes, might be expected to be attracted to one another. This hypothesis is reflected in the old saying, "Birds of a feather flock together." Indeed, several elaborate investigations of interpersonal attraction have produced convincing evidence to support this hypothesis.

On the other hand, it is also reasonable to expect that *complementarity* of needs might contribute to individual attraction. An individual with a particular kind of need-system should be attracted to those whose requirements and behavior are instrumental to the satisfaction of his needs. For example, one might expect that highly dependent people (who evidence strong needs to be helped, encouraged, and supported) should be particularly attracted to those who are highly nurturant (evidencing strong needs to help, encourage, and support others). This hypothesis reflects the idea behind another old adage, "Opposites attract." There is also a certain amount of evidence from research that this hypothesis is tenable and that instrumental complementarity of needs is a basis of at least certain kinds of interpersonal attraction.

Propinquity.   Perhaps the most fundamental prerequisite for the establishment of any kind of direct interpersonal relationship is propinquity. There must be opportunity for two people to come into contact and interact before any kind of attraction can be established. (Of course, psychological interaction may be achieved through many different forms of communication, including written correspondence, telephone, radio, or television, but ordinarily friendships evolve out of direct face-to-face interpersonal contact.) Consequently most research investigations show rather clearly that physical proximity is closely related to the formation of individual friendships. Individuals who live close to one another are more likely to be become friends than individuals who live some distance apart (Lundberg, Hertzler, & Dickson, 1949; Festinger, Schachter, & Back, 1950; DeVault, 1957), and people who interact frequently are more likely to become friends than people who interact rarely. Opportunity for extended interaction, then, is vital to the formation of friendships, and all other things being equal, people who are psychologically near to one another (in close communication and interaction) are considerably more likely to become friends than people who are psychologically distant from one another.

THE NEARNESS OF YOU

Families living in two university housing projects (at M.I.T.) were observed for their choice of friends. The greatest number of friendship choices were made from those living closest to the chooser's home, progressively declining as that distance increased (although the total distance was never larger than 180 feet).

FESTINGER, SCHACHTER, AND BACK (1950)

Attitudinal Similarity.   There is abundant evidence that people of similar interests are especially likely to become friends. Consistently, psychological studies of the attraction of individuals to strangers at initial encounter, as well as of friendship bonds sustained over longer periods of time, have shown that similarity of attitudes and interests is correlated with interpersonal attraction. Several investigations have revealed that among school children, friendships between members of the same sex occur more frequently than friendships across sexes, even among young children whose activities are not sharply differentiated by sex (Hollingshead, 1949). Similarly, in racially and ethnically mixed groups, minority group members tend to show considerable homogeneity of "within-own-group" choices in their expressed preferences for close friends (Criswell, 1939; Goodnow & Tagiuri, 1952). Furthermore, other studies have shown that homogeneity of basic values (Richardson, 1940), similarity of vocational career preferences (Bonney, 1946), and similarity of religious affiliation (Goodnow & Tagiuri, 1952) and of status (Berkowitz & Macauley, 1961) are all correlated with individual friendship choices. Similarity of socioeconomic status and occupation

BIRDS OF A FEATHER

A 1-hour group task consisting of thinking up questions for a college admissions interview was given to various 9-person groups of college students. The composition of each group was determined on the basis of previously obtained biographical material including information about subjects' academic achievement, parental support, parental leniency, socioeconomic status, scientific interest, religious background, and personal adjustment. At the completion of the task, group members were asked to rank others within the group according to how much they liked them and how similar they felt to each other. The results showed that both similar background and perceived similarity were related to greater liking for the other person.

BOWDITCH AND KING (1970)

have also been found to be associated with friendship (Hollingshead, 1949; Udry, 1960). At virtually all levels, from preschool children to adult housewives, similarity of age has been found related to choice of friends.

Much of this evidence that similarity of personal characteristics underlies interpersonal attraction must be interpreted with caution because it does not imply unequivocally that interpersonal attraction follows directly as a consequence of similarity. However, people who participate in the same kinds of activities and informal social groups are indeed likely from the outset to share similar characteristics, especially with respect to their attitudes and interests. Thus much of the observed similarity between pairs of friends may be directly related to factors that brought them into social interaction in the first place, and may thus reflect the issue of propinquity discussed earlier rather than simple attitudinal similarity as such. Furthermore, Schachter's (1959) studies of the "psychology of affiliation" also suggest another way in which similarity may be an indirect, rather than a direct, source of interpersonal attraction. In line with his hypothesis that social affiliation may serve to reduce anxiety, he found that when individuals were given a choice of groups with whom they wished to await a dreaded experience, they preferred to wait with others who were "in the same boat" in sharing anticipation of the dreaded event. In other words, "misery loves miserable company." Walster and Walster (1963) have suggested that fear of being disliked by dissimilar strangers may underlie the strong tendency of people to express greater attraction to people they perceive as similar to themselves than to people they perceive as dissimilar.

Several investigations have attempted to resolve these questions about the isolation of effects of propinquity and opportunity for interaction among people of similar interests from more direct effects of attitudinal similarity as a basis of individual attraction. Comparisons have been made of the individual's assumptions and beliefs about his similarity to his friends as opposed to the degree of real or actual similarity between them. Studies of initial attraction to strangers in laboratory settings, as well as studies of actual friendships in natural groups, have demonstrated clearly that *perceived similarity* is more closely associated with friendship choice than is *actual similarity* (Davitz, 1955; Smucker, 1960). On the whole it appears that the belief that another person is similar to oneself is a more significant determinant of one's attraction to that person than is actual similarity.

Newcomb (1961), on the basis of close observations of the actual processes of acquaintance among college men in a natural situation, found evidence that perceived similarity of attitudes and values contributes directly to the formation of personal attractions particularly in connection with topics or values that are of considerable importance to the persons concerned. This hypothesis is certainly plausible,

NEEDS AND AFFILIATION

The nature of motivation to seek the company of others was investigated by Stanley Schachter at the University of Minnesota in 1959. Subjects for Schachter's studies were students taking courses in psychology who were given extra credit for taking part in the experiments. They were strangers to one another, and every effort was made to prevent them from becoming well acquainted prior to their participation in an experiment. Different procedures were utilized to study several variables associated with affiliative behavior.

Stress, Anxiety, and Affiliation

In one study women were divided into two groups that received different treatments. One group (high-anxiety) was met by a serious-looking gentleman wearing a white laboratory coat and surrounded by formidable-looking electrical equipment. He introduced himself as Dr. Gregor Zilstein of the Medical School's Department of Neurology and Psychiatry, and he told the subjects of his intention to use them in an experiment in electroshock therapy, which would be a painful, although not permanently damaging, experience. A second group (low-anxiety) entered a similar situation, but were introduced to Dr. Zilstein without the array of equipment and without identification of his affiliations or purposes. They were told that the experiment would be enjoyable, with no painful effects. Subjects in each group were then told that a 10-minute wait would be necessary, and that they had the choice of waiting either alone or with a group of other girls. The choices they expressed showed evidence that the arousal of anxiety, through anticipation of a painful and unpleasant experience, was associated with affiliative preferences (Table 8–1).

Table 8–1 Anxiety and Affiliation

	Expressed Preferences		
Anxiety Level	Wait with Others	Don't Care	Wait Alone
High Anxiety	20	9	3
Low Anxiety	10	18	3

Early Socialization and Affiliative Motivation

In connection with the studies of affiliative preferences under anxiety aroused by threat of pain, further analyses revealed differences in affiliative preference that were systematically associated with the order of the individual's birth in his family. Firstborn and only children showed the greatest evidence of preference to await the dreaded experiment in the company of others; later-born children showed considerably less. In this sense, the only child or oldest child in a family appears to be more dependent on others and more driven by "affiliative needs" than later-born children (Table 8–2).

Table 8–2 Stress, Anxiety, and Affiliation

	Expressed Preferences	
Birth Order	Together	Don't Care and Alone
Firstborn	32	8
Later-born	11	25

Source: *The Psychology of Affiliation* by Stanley Schachter. Tables 8–1 and 8–2 reprinted with the permission of the publishers, Stanford University Press © 1959 by the Board of Trustees of the Leland Stanford Junior University.

(Continued on
p. 218)

The Specificity of Affiliative Motivation

Another extension of the studies of affiliative preferences under the threat of pain revealed that the anxious subjects preferred the company of the other girls who were "in the same boat." In a study using the same procedures outlined earlier for the arousal of anxiety, the girls were given the choice of waiting alone or with other girls who were awaiting the same dreaded experiment. None of the girls in this study chose to wait alone, and the majority preferred to wait with others who shared their anxiety.

Misery Loves Miserable Company

Other studies of affiliation support Schachter's findings, especially about the strong affiliative tendencies of firstborns. The subjects' affiliation needs are selective: they prefer to stay with other (presumably anxious) subjects waiting to participate in the experiment rather than to wait with those who already had participated, or with an unrelated group of people. Thus it is not enough to say "misery loves company"; it is more accurate to say "misery loves miserable company." The underlying motivation of this kind of affiliative behavior, however, has not been clearly established. Whether threat of electric shocks, hunger, altered glucose level of blood, or intense auditory stimulation really induces anxiety is debatable. Possibly subjects affiliate merely for the sake of curiosity, or to fulfill the experimenter's expectations.

SCHACHTER (1959, 1963)
WRIGHTSMAN (1960)
CAPRA AND DITTES (1962)
ZIMBARDO AND FORMICA (1963)
RING, LIPINSKI, AND BRAGINSKI (1965)
MACDONALD (1970)

but empirical research evidence as to whether the importance of the area of similarity is critical in the generation of friendship bonds is contradictory and inconclusive (Byrne, 1961; Newcomb, 1961; Byrne & Nelson, 1964).

The notion of attitudinal similarity as a basis of interpersonal attraction provides an important fundamental element in the theoretical models of the interpersonal perception and attraction processes proposed by Newcomb (1961), Heider (1958), and others. These models are based on the principles of cognitive organization discussed in Chapter 4. The theory of cognitive dissonance assumes that the process of cognitive organization generates pressures that induce one to make overt efforts (either in one's behavior or in distortions of perceptual experience or both) to achieve states of maximum consistency, or consonance, among the elements in a cognitive structure (and conversely, to avoid states of dissonance or disharmony). Attribution theory, described earlier in this chapter, suggests a number of ways in which the characteristics attributed to a person are associated with one's interpretation of the causation of events with which he is associated. From these starting assumptions, several theoretical models for analyzing interpersonal attraction have been extrapolated; notable among these are Newcomb's A-B-X model and Heider's balance theory.

Newcomb's A-B-X Model. To describe interpersonal interaction, Newcomb (1961) represents three basic elements in the interaction situation: A, the perceiver; B, the other person; and X, some issue or event with which both are concerned. Newcomb's model is addressed to the problem of representing A's cognitive experience of the interaction situation, regardless of whether this experience corresponds with "reality." According to the model, the basis of consonance in A's experience of interaction with B is A's perception of similarity between his and B's attitudes toward X. Perception of attitudinal similarity should generate liking or attraction between A and B, whereas perception of dissimilarity should generate dislike and rejection.

THE ACQUAINTANCE PROCESS

A series of studies conducted at the University of Michigan investigated the process through which strangers become acquainted with one another in a natural setting. On each of two occasions, seventeen men who were strangers to one another accepted invitations to live rent-free in a cooperative house in return for devoting several hours each week to providing experimental data throughout a full semester. All subjects were males and all were transferring to Michigan as sophomores or juniors. None had yet chosen a major, and they were evenly distributed between enrollment in the College of Arts and Sciences and the College of Engineering. They were all native-born Americans, and the group included eight Protestants, four Catholics and five Jews. All were white, and their average age was 20. Each subject supplied data from Measures of Interpersonal Attraction, attitudinal similarity, and various personality patterns.

The program of research was particularly concerned with the relationship between attitudinal similarity and interpersonal attraction, but other incidental observations were reported as well. The questions discussed here summarize these findings.

1. Is interpersonal attraction systematically related to similarity of attitudes between two people?

There is consistent evidence that attitudinal similarity in the preacquaintance period serves as a good predictor of later attraction between people. Table 8–3 shows the number of pairs of friends during both years of the study according to whether their level of attraction was very high or not high, and whether their level of initial similarity was very high or not high.

Table 8–3   Attraction and Attitudinal Similarity

Level of Final Attraction	Preacquaintance Attitudinal Similarity		
	High	Not high	Total
High	25	57	82
Not high	18	172	190
Total	43	229	272

Source: *The Acquaintance Process* by Theodore M. Newcomb. Copyright © 1961 by Holt, Rinehart and Winston, Inc. Reprinted by permission of Holt, Rinehart and Winston, Inc.

2. Is the relationship between interpersonal attraction and attitudinal similarity a stable one?

The following figure shows that the degree of relationship (average correlation coefficient) between the level of interpersonal attraction and the level of attitudinal

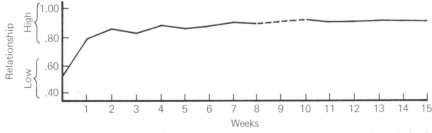

Figure 8–2   The relationship between interpersonal attraction and attitudinal similarity, over time. (Redrawn from *The Acquaintance Process* by Theodore M. Newcomb. Copyright © 1961 by Holt, Rinehart and Winston, Inc. Reprinted by permission of Holt, Rinehart and Winston, Inc.)

(Continued on p. 220)

agreement within pairs of subjects remained quite stable after the second week of acquaintance.

3. Is it likely that variables other than attitudinal similarity account for these patterns of interpersonal attraction?

Other than attitudinal similarity, the two most likely variables underlying attractions were personality factors and physical proximity.

4. How accurate were the subjects' perceptions of attitudinal similarity to others?

In general, individuals who were strongly attracted to one another tended to overestimate their similarity. Accuracy tended to increase generally with extended length of acquaintance, but individuals differed widely in the accuracy of their estimates of others. On the whole, perceived or assumed similarity was more closely related to interpersonal attraction than was real or actual similarity.

5. What is the nature of the functional relationship between interpersonal attraction and attitudinal similarity?

During the first 2 weeks of acquaintance the relationship between attitudinal similarity and interpersonal attraction was unstable, and it is difficult to determine whether each subject simply assumed that the people to whom he was attracted were similar to him, or whether the people he assumed to be similar then became attractive to him. With extended acquaintance, it is likely that the latter holds true: that attraction follows as a consequence of perceived similarity as individuals become better acquainted with each other.

NEWCOMB (1961)

Newcomb makes the initial assumptions that accurate communication (dependent on some opportunity for interaction, of course) between A and B will produce some increase of attitudinal similarity toward X; attitudinal similarity of this sort is a desired and rewarding state of affairs for A because it achieves consonance within his overall cognitive experience of the situation; and even if it requires strain and effort, A will continue to strive to maintain attitudinal similarity of this sort so long as he maintains his interaction with B. Thus the model implies that any perceived discrepancy between the attitudes of A and B toward X will induce efforts on A's part either to change his own attitude to make it more congruent with B's, or to change his perception of B's attitude to make it more congruent with his own. The third alternative in this pursuit of cognitive consonance, of course, would be for A to terminate his interaction with B—to reduce his attraction to B and thus reject him. Newcomb's model successfully incorporates the accumulated evidence that attitudinal similarity is an important basis of interpersonal attraction, and because it is focused on the perceiver's subjective experience of phenomenal similarity, it is addressed to issues of assumed rather than actual similarity.

As an example, suppose that A, a young businessman, and his wife, B, sit down to discuss his desire to buy an expensive boat, X. A is an ardent fisherman who enjoys water-skiing, and he would like very much to have his own boat. B, however, dislikes all water sports and argues that the boat would be a ridiculous extravagance. Yet, A and B in other respects enjoy each other's company a great deal and are very happily married. The state of cognitive dissonance generated by this situation for A, represented schematically in Figure 8–3(a), poses an impasse that must be resolved. A's attraction to his wife (A + B) precludes divorce or separation, a consonant resolution depicted in Figure 8–3(b). A solution might be attained if he gave up his desire to buy the boat (A + X) and convinced himself that the whole idea was an

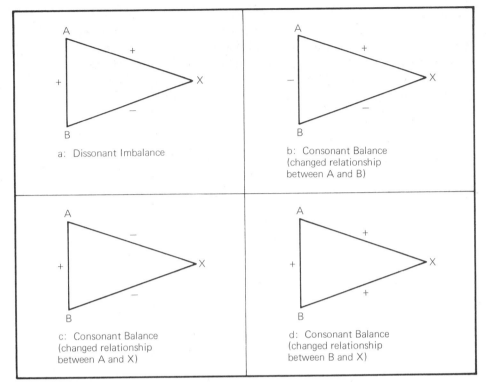

Figure 8–3 Newcomb's A-B-X Model of interpersonal perception and attraction.

extravagant fantasy (A − X), as represented in Figure 8–3(c). But he wants the boat too badly to give up easily, and he is particularly skeptical of allowing himself to become henpecked by his wife. So he considers the alternative of changing his wife's attitude toward buying the boat (B − X). In fact he might successfully persuade her to change her mind and become favorably disposed toward the idea of owning a boat (B + X), a solution attained through modifying her attitude and behavior, as shown in Figure 8–3(d).

However, according to Newcomb's model, which is concerned with the attainment of cognitive consonance, not with reality, another resolution is possible: A may attain the resolution depicted in Figure 8–3(d) by believing that his wife does not really object to buying a boat, and that she only expresses reservation about its extravagance in order to maintain his image of her as a thrifty and practical housewife. Thus, A may escape the cognitive dissonance induced by the original impasse by means of cognitive distortion. Of course this resolution, if it results in the actual behavior of buying the boat, may generate subsequent dissonant interactions with his wife that may be somewhat more difficult to resolve.

A very similar model, the *congruity* model, proposed by Osgood and Tannenbaum (1955) and elaborated and extended by R. W. Brown (1965), offers an analysis of interpersonal perception and attraction that is almost identical to Newcomb's A-B-X model.

Heider's p-o-x *Model.* The model that Heider (1958) formulated for the analysis of social interaction is very similar to Newcomb's, but somewhat more complex in its elaboration of the variety of ways individuals may be related to one another as well as to objects and events. Heider's approach is based on what he calls "common sense psychology": the process through which *Homo sapiens,* the thinking man, "puts two and two together" to make logical sense. According to Heider, the cognitive field of the perceiver in an event of social interaction contains three cardinal elements: p, the perceiver; o, the perceived other person; and x, a third person, object, or event to which both p and o are somehow related psychologically. The relationships among these parts of the cognitive unit are conceived as interdependent. They may be based on either of two qualities: *affection* (a person's regard for or attraction to the other person, object, or event) or *cognitive unit formation* (a cognitive logical basis of association between persons, objects, or events). Affection refers essentially to the like-dislike dimension, whereas cognitive unit formation occurs through similarity, proximity, causation, or the association of "belonging."

An elaborate system of notation may be utilized to describe a vast array of possible kinds of affection and cognitive relationships. For example, pLo denotes that the perceiver likes the other person, whereas p — Lo denotes that the perceiver does not like the other. Similarly, pLx and p — Lx denote, respectively, that the perceiver does or does not like some third person, object, or event with which both he and another person are involved. The notation oCx indicates that the o is perceived as the cause of event x. Like Newcomb, Heider assumes from the principles of cognitive organization that the perceiver will seek to achieve, maintain, or restore cognitive order or *balance* in his perceptual structure. Unless *only one* or *all three* of the three relationships of the p-o-x cognitive unit are "positive" (the perception of affective attraction or cognitive relationship), the perceiver's cognitive system is considered to be in a state of "imbalance."

Table 8–4 represents the analysis of several possible p-o-x situations according to Heider's balance theory. Situations I through IV represent common-sense balanced situations, which are cognitively comfortable for the perceiver. Situations V through VIII represent "imbalanced" situations that presumably generate cognitive tension in the perceiver, inducing him to attempt to restore a comfortable balance. Heider's balance theory postulates that there is a tendency for cognitive structures to achieve balance states; if no cognitive balance exists, forces toward its attainment will arise; and if no balance is attained, the residual state of imbalance will produce tension and

Table 8–4 Heider's p-o-x Interpersonal Situations

Situation	p-o-x pattern	Description
Type I balanced	pLo, oCx, pLx	Perceiver (p) likes other person (o) who causes what perceiver likes (x).
Type II balanced	pLo, o-Cx, p-Lx	Perceiver (p) likes other person (o) who does not cause what perceiver dislikes (x).
Type III balanced	p-Lo, oCx, p-Lx	Perceiver (p) dislikes other person (o) who causes what perceiver dislikes (x).
Type IV balanced	p-Lo, o-Cx, pLx	Perceiver (p) dislikes other person (o) who does not cause what perceiver likes (x).
Type V imbalanced	pLo, oCx, p-Lx	Perceiver (p) likes other person (o) who causes what perceiver dislikes (x).
Type VI imbalanced	pLo, o-Cx, pLx	Perceiver (p) likes other person (o) who does not cause what perceiver likes (x).
Type VII imbalanced	p-Lo, oCx, pLx	Perceiver (p) dislikes other person (o) who causes what perceiver likes (x).
Type VIII imbalanced	p-Lo, o-Cx, p-Lx	Perceiver (p) dislikes other person (o) who does not cause what perceiver dislikes (x).

p = perceiver
o = perceived other
x = any object or event
C = causes
L = likes

discomfort. Like Festinger's cognitive dissonance theory (Chapter 4), Heider's balance theory implies that motivational forces arise from the tendency toward ordered cognitive experience. The example of the man, his wife, and the purchase of a boat, used earlier to illustrate Newcomb's A-B-X model, also illustrates Heider's model. The original state of affairs, in which the man likes his wife, the man likes the boat, and the wife dislikes the boat, is similar to the imbalanced situation depicted in Type VI (changing "causation" to "liking"). The resolution achieved through his cognitive distortion of his wife's true relationship to the idea of buying the boat represents the state of balance similar to Type I.

Empirical observations consistent with both of these models have been provided through several investigations of diadic interaction and attitude change (Davitz, 1935; Jordan, 1953; Burdick & Burnes, 1958; Sampson & Insko, 1964). Recent investigations (Harari, 1967, 1971) of the cognitive reactions of several hundred adolescents to verbally described diadic interaction situations explored several previously uninvestigated aspects of Heider's balance theory. In general, these subjects displayed clear tendencies to attempt to restore cognitive balance in imbalanced situations, even through distortions of the described situation. However, the extent to which such efforts occurred appeared to be a function both of personality characteristics of the perceiver, as well as of more detailed circumstances of the interaction situation. On the whole it appeared that the kinds of people whose experience and behavior are best described by Heider's model are independent, unemotional, intelligent, and socially detached. Others, including people who reflected strong values for conformity, interpersonal support, and benevolence toward others, showed less evidence of the efforts toward attainment of cognitive balance that Heider's theory predicts. These studies, then, suggest that Heider's balance model provides a useful starting point for the analysis of interpersonal perception and attraction, but that it may not be equally applicable to all kinds of human beings, nor equally applicable to all of the complex kinds of interaction situations that occur among people.

Although psychological research has only tapped the surface of complete understanding of the complex relationships between attitudinal similarity and interpersonal attraction, the evidence yielded thus far shows convincingly that such similarity does at least contribute to the attraction of one person to another.

Need Satisfaction. The second hypothesis about the bases of interpersonal attraction, described earlier, suggests that a particular kind of dissimilarity between two individuals may contribute to their attraction to each other. If their needs and goals are different, and especially if they interlock so that one person's needs tend to satisfy the needs of the other, two individuals may be highly attracted to each other. This type of interpersonal attraction, in which one person is instrumental to the other's satisfaction, has been discussed theoretically by Blau (1962), Jones and Thibaut (1958), Ktsanes (1955), and Winch, Ktsanes, and Ktsanes (1954). Winch's hypothesis of "need complementarity" proposes that interpersonal attraction may result from interlocked reciprocation of needs that complement one another. Thus highly dependent people may be attracted to highly nurturant people, or very dominant people may be attracted to very submissive people.

One source of ambiguity in connection with this hypothesis, however, is the difficulty of defining actual reciprocation of need systems and their satisfaction. Winch, Ktsanes, and Ktsanes (1954) distinguished two types of need complementarity: type I, in which the needs of one person differ in *intensity* from those of the other, and type II, in which the needs of one person differ in *kind* from those of the other. Furthermore, psychological concepts of the dimensions along which needs are measured are often difficult to interpret in terms of complementarity or reciprocation. One might assume that a very dominant person would find interaction with a nondominant person satisfying if it can be assumed that the nondominant person allows the other to dominate him freely. However, the nondominant person might not find being dominated by the other highly satisfying unless his submission actually involves a "need to be dominated." Thus a reciprocal difference in kind of needs (dominance versus submission, in this case) may enable one person to be highly rewarded in his interactions with the other. However, a difference in intensity of needs (high versus low dominance, in this case) might at least allow the highly dominant person to exercise and satisfy his need without being thwarted or frustrated by the other.

Perhaps largely because of such conceptual difficulties, empirical evidence in support of the need-complementarity hypothesis is still somewhat inconclusive. Most of the evidence that corroborates the hypothesis is derived from studies of extremely close and long-lasting diadic relationships such as marriage (Winch, Ktsanes, & Ktsanes, 1954; Ktsanes, 1955; Kerckhoff & Davis, 1962). Other studies, however, have failed to confirm the hypothesis (Altrocchi, 1959; Katz, Glucksberg & Krauss, 1960; Murstein, 1961). At present, the most that can be said is that, although the hypothesis of need complementarity offers a plausible basis for one kind of interpersonal attraction, research evidence has not yet convincingly supported it. It may be that conceptual difficulties in framing proper research to test the hypothesis, rather than fault with the hypothesis itself, underlie this failure. In any case, what little evidence there is to support the need-complementarity hypothesis is largely based on studies of marital relationships, a particular type of very intimate and closely bound interpersonal attraction.

Although it might appear that the hypothesis of attitudinal similarity and the hypothesis of need complementarity offer mutually contradictory accounts of the bases of interpersonal attraction, this is not necessarily the case. In the formulation of their hypothesis of complementarity, Winch, Ktsanes, and Ktsanes (1954) point out directly that the evidence for complementarity of needs occurred in the company of overt similarity of other "social characteristics." Furthermore, Newcomb (1956) has commented that his model, which postulates that attraction results from attitudinal similarity, is not necessarily in opposition to Winch's hypothesis. Instead, he regards the thesis of complementarity as a special case of similarity, shifting his level of analysis of the problem. He suggests that the apparent complementarity between one "assertive" and one "receptive" partner in a marriage actually represents a case of similarity of attitudes toward the notion, either conscious or unconscious, that one of them should be assertive and the other receptive. The X in the A-B-X model of such a situation would be the notion that the marital roles should be thus interlocked, a point on which the two partners agree.

Love, Dating, and Marriage

It is surprising that despite its significance in all kinds of human social behavior, love relationships have been studied very little by psychologists. Perhaps this is due in part to the fact that (at least in our culture) love traditionally has been considered an extremely private relationship, and as such has been protected from scientific intrusion. However, the "flower people" and their followers in the youth counterculture of the 1960s brought it into the open. They viewed this intense and rewarding relationship as real, acceptable, and respectable—in contrast to the Victorian concept of love as ethereal, unmentionable, and separated from sin only by a thin line drawn by the angels. Fortunately, this element of the counterculture has found its way into the dominant core culture as a reform in our dominant value system. We now speak more openly about love and the human behaviors that express it, including not only sexuality, but simple touching and body contact in the form of handshakes, embraces, and the like. The reforms in moral outlook sought by such groups as the Gay Liberation Front do not focus on sexuality as such, but they are more broadly concerned with seeking recognition of the validity of love relationships among members of the same sex. The humanistic movement in clinical psychology and education is also seriously concerned with drawing more attention to the love relationship as one of the most basically human qualities that set man apart from the lower animals. These changes in value structure are very recent in our culture, and there has not yet been time for accumulation of much empirical scientific research to reflect this release of the taboos that have cloaked the study of love relationships.

The concept of love has eluded scientific definition largely because it cannot easily be defined operationally. The behaviors that express it are many and varied. Standard expressions differ among cultures (especially in such areas as the touching, kissing, or embracing actions associated with greetings or departures from loved ones); yet these behaviors are also highly variable within a culture and include very private and idiosyncratic kinds of expression between lovers. Love may be expressed in words, gestures, facial expressions, touching, giving to the other, or accepting from the other. Sexual behavior is only one expression of love (under some circumstances abstinence and celibacy may express genuine love and concern for another); nor does all sexual behavior express love (rape clearly does not). Moreover, even within sexuality, the expression of love ranges from tenderness and gentleness to the aggressive dominance of the sadist and the submissive acceptance of pain by the masochist. Kinsey et al. (1948, 1953) documented the variability of human sexual behavior, and Masters and Johnson (1968) have further described the bridge between sexual expression, emotionality, and personal adjustment.

Clear and precise definitions of love are few in theoretical psychology. But many psychologists have pointed particularly to the *unselfish* quality of love, as distinguished from other interpersonal relationships (Fromm, 1947; May, 1964; Perls, 1964; L'Abate & L'Abate, 1973). The humanistic position especially has stressed that love encompasses the acceptance of "the bitter with the better," so that the sadness and grief of the loved one are accepted as readily as the gladness and joy (May, 1958). It has also stressed the *giving* qualities of love along with the *taking* qualities, including the assumption of responsibility, care, and concern for the loved one (L'Abate & L'Abate, 1973). It has been suggested that the capacity for loving another presupposes the capacity to love oneself (Fromm, 1947). That is, full acceptance of another rests upon similar acceptance of oneself. From these kinds of statements, then, one might approach a definition of love as *the most intense and encompassing form of interpersonal attraction,* involving an extension of the self to incorporate the other and an internalization of the other into the self.

The less intense forms of interpersonal attraction discussed earlier in this chapter —popularity and friendship—are more selfish in that they are derived considerably from personal needs and satisfactions. The research of Winch, Ktsanes, and Ktsanes (1954) suggests that mutual need satisfaction is a critical element in the durability of lasting relationships such as love, dating, and marriage. However, empirical support for the simple need-complementarity hypothesis has been equivocal and incomplete; perhaps the critical element in this hypothesis is that of *mutuality.* Although unstressed in the statement of the hypothesis, it is probably the unselfish *reciprocation* of need satisfaction, the combined giving and taking, that contributes most to the durability of these relationships.

The progression of immature early friendships, through dating behavior in adolescence, and finally into adult love, involves an advancing decentralization of the selfish basis of interpersonal attractions. Friendships among young children are best predicted along simple lines of attitudinal and interest similarity, and mutual entertainment and amusement. With adolescence, the nature of cross-sexed interpersonal relationships changes. At first physical attractiveness (related to personal gratification, either fantasied or actual) is important in dating relationships (Walster, Aronson, Abrahams, & Rottman, 1966; Stroebe et al., 1971). Eventually both sexes approach dating with increased regard for *mutual* fulfillment of each other's needs, including not only sexual, but emotional, social, and even political needs (Vreeland, 1972). Finally, adult maturity brings the capacity for expanded mutuality and reciprocation that is required for a durable love relationship.

THE DATING GAME

Three male photographs and three female photographs were chosen to represent three levels of attractiveness (high, medium, and low) on the basis of ratings by a sample of male and female college students. The photographs were subsequently presented to a larger sample of students (100 males and 100 females) who were asked to rate the photographs on general liking, preference for working, and—in the case of opposite sex—willingness to date, and consideration for marriage. The judges' own level of attractiveness was established by experimenter ratings and by self-ratings. In addition, attitudinal similarity was manipulated by having the person in the picture appear similar to the judge on the basis of the latter's responses to a previously administered attitude questionnaire. The results showed that both males and females felt more attracted to physically attractive than unattractive opposite-sex others, with males displaying this behavior more often. On the other hand, females were more affected than males by similarity to others in their liking or preference for them as co-workers. Attitudinal similarity had no effect on dating or marriage choices. These two choices, however, differed significantly from the judges' self-rated level of attractiveness. Compared to judges who perceived themselves as attractive, judges who perceived themselves as unattractive were not very choosy and were more willing to date unattractive others. In the marriage consideration, however, judges who perceived themselves as unattractive also considered dating attractive others, presumably because given other good qualities an unattractive person may not be very desirable as a date, but still have good prospects as a marriage candidate.

STROEBE, INSKO, THOMPSON, AND LAYTON (1971)

GAME PLAN: HOW TO CATCH A MAN

Masculine folklore suggests that the woman who is hard to get is a more desirable catch than the eager, desperate-for-a-date woman who threatens a man's cherished independence. Yet men are ambivalent in their perception of both kinds of women. Those who play hard to get have certain perceived assets (they are "selective," "desirable," "discriminating") as well as liabilities (they are "cold," "frigid," "unfriendly"). Those who are easy to get also share assets (they are "friendly," "warm," "popular") and liabilities (they are "indiscriminate," "desperate," "unpopular").

In a set of experiments, male college students were invited to a dating center to choose potential dates. They were given folders on three fictitious women showing their choice of males from computer profile descriptions. One woman was described as uniformly hard-to-get (willing to date the men described by the computer profiles, but unenthusiastic and reserved about it). Another was described as uniformly easy to get (enthusiastic and eager to date anybody, regardless of their computer profile). A third woman was presented as easy for the particular subject to get, but hard for anyone else to get (enthusiastic about the subject's particular profile, but cool toward others). The most popular date-choice was the woman who was hard to get for others, but easy to get for the subject. This selective attention to the subject induces him to perceive her as possessing all of the assets and none of the liabilities of the otherwise hard-to-get or easy-to-get women.

WALSTER, WALSTER, PILIAVIN, AND SCHMIDT (1973)

THE COMPUTER DANCE

A "computer dance" for 376 male and 376 female incoming University of Minnesota freshmen was promoted for the purpose of this study. The students were told that in exchange for some information about their personalities and interests they would be matched by a computer with a suitable date. They were also rated on physical attractiveness by 2 male and 2 female college sophomores who acted as ticket salesmen and computer specialists. The more attractive males and females were, the greater was their tendency to like their partner less. Individuals did *not* best like dates similar in attractiveness to themselves. Actual attempts by males to ask a girl out again depended, in fact, on how attractive she was: the most attractive girls were most often asked out, regardless of the attractiveness of the men asking for the date.

WALSTER, ARONSON, ABRAHAMS, AND ROTTMAN (1966)

RELEVANCE AND APPLICATION

The psychological study of interpersonal attraction began as a theoretical exercise impelled largely by scientific curiosity. But with changes in our value system during the 1960s and 1970s, there emerged a great demand for better scientific understanding of the emotional bases of interpersonal relationships. As a culture and a civilization we are more concerned than ever before with the human side of international affairs, and with the foundations of war and peace at personal and interpersonal levels.

The implicit attitudes of ethnocentrism and racism were a part of the informal values and the formal law of our society for several centuries. Slavery was abolished only a little more than a century ago, and even more recently, formalized law provided for equal educational and employment opportunities for all human beings, regardless of ethnic or racial origin. Despite such changes in our formal legal system, attitudinal bases of behavior at the personal and interpersonal levels still prohibit true freedom and equality of opportunity for members of ethnic and racial minority groups. Now society is becoming even more aware of other forms of chauvinism and group-centeredness as it confronts demands for liberation voiced not only by blacks, but by women, homosexuals, and other "minorities." Psychological analyses of the basis of stereotyping, prejudice, and ethnocentrism developed during the 1930s and 1940s have more relevance than ever before. Yet there is still a need for further expansion of our scientific knowledge for understanding the bridge between attitudes and action, and between action at the individual interpersonal level and at the collective level of society.

Interpersonal attraction ranges from the minimal level of interpersonal *acceptance,* or the ability for people to live, work, and play side by side without interfering with one another, to increasingly intense levels of interpersonal attraction and satisfaction. The legal rights of minorities demand only the minimal level of human relationship (acceptance), but the qualities that are truly "human" involve the emergence of more intense levels of attraction. The psychological bases of *friendship* are reasonably well understood, and there is sufficient technical knowledge to afford control of conditions facilitating the emergence of friendships. But largely because of the Victorian value system that dominated our culture until the 1960s, more intense levels of interpersonal attraction were veiled in secrecy and taboos that shielded them from scientific exploration. Only recently has scientific psychology approached the study of *love.* Consequently, in spite of its clear relevance and applicability, there is a lack of accumulated research on human love relationships and their behavioral expression.

Nevertheless it is already clear that the solutions to many serious contemporary social problems—including school desegregation, public housing, equality of employment and educational opportunity, mental health of minority group members, racial and ethnic conflicts, minority and individual rights, and even national and international conflicts—all rest on expanded scientific analysis of interpersonal perception and attraction, and on expanded application of the knowledge base already acquired.

REVIEW

1. Basic principles of perception of nonsocial objects also apply to the perception of *social* objects (people and groups). But the most important difference is that social objects respond to the perceiver and are changeable, whereas nonsocial objects usually are not.

2. *Attribution theory* deals with analysis of the tendency for people to attribute causal powers to people in connection with the events in which they participate. *Environmental* causation (like behavioristic determinism) attributes responsibility for events to circumstances and forces of nature outside the people involved; *personal* causation attributes this responsibility to the people involved in events.

3. A *stereotype* is an overgeneralized cognitive concept based on inaccurate or incomplete information. Expectations based on such inaccurate generalizations give rise to *prejudice.*

4. *Ethnocentrism* refers to the tendency for members of a particular cultural group to insulate themselves from members of other groups. It generates cultural isolation, hostility, fear, and distrust of outsiders.

5. In perceiving strangers, one tries to organize information into an overall, integrated impression of personality. Sometimes the order in which one is exposed to different items of information about others will shape the overall impression formed.

6. In perceiving particular people, one's relationship to the perceived person may be very important. One may *project* one's own characteristics to the other person, judging him more leniently if he is like oneself. When one perceives a highly familiar person, he may distort his perception of objects or events surrounding the familiar person in the effort to preserve one's image of that person.

7. In perceiving others, one's perception of the motivational intent of the other is a critical factor. One is likely to attribute benevolent motives to a familiar and liked person; vice versa, one is likely to be attracted to a person to whom he attributes benevolent motives. Among the many models for predicting interpersonal attraction and perception from analysis of perceived causation are *Heider's balance theory* and *Newcomb's A-B-X model.*

8. *Popularity* is the simplest collective form of interpersonal attraction in a group. It is the manifestation of a group's standards for socially desirable behavior.

9. *Friendship* is the simplest diadic form of interpersonal attraction between two people. It usually rests on the *nearness* or availability of companions, *attitudinal similarity* and parallel interests and values, and *need satisfaction* and mutual personal gratification.

10. *Love* is the most intense and encompassing form of interpersonal attraction, involving outward extension of the self to the other and internalization of the other into the self. Love, more than popularity or friendship, is based on unselfish acceptance to the other person, including both positive and negative qualities. The most significant qualities of love are mutuality and reciprocation.

9

INTERACTION WITH OTHERS

In a sense the entire field of social psychology is the study of social interaction, so the phrase "interaction with others" is somewhat ambiguous. However, there are certain patterns of social interaction that are essentially *diadic*—two people are involved in a specific kind of reciprocal relationship. This chapter is concerned with some special categories of social behavior that involve face-to-face confrontation of two people who enter into reciprocal social interaction with each other.

RECIPROCITY, EXCHANGE, AND EQUITY: ECONOMIC THEORIES

A very powerful belief system called the *norm of reciprocity* underlies behavior in practically all aspects of social interaction (Gouldner, 1960). The assumption that people "do unto others as others do unto them" underlies several theoretical formulations which analyze the psychological economics of social interaction. *Exchange theory* proposes that interpersonal confrontations involve an exchange of costs and benefits, or expenditures of behavioral energies invested against the return of possible outcome (J. S. Adams, 1963). Thibaut and Kelley (1959) used a similar kind of exchange analysis. Similarly, *equity theory* combines the notion of mutuality inherent in Gouldner's norm of reciprocity with the economic analysis of Adams' exchange theory, and holds that interpersonal confrontations and transactions are ultimately determined by arriving at a point of equity between the parties involved in the transaction (Homans, 1961).

Most studies on people's quest for equity have been of interest to industrial psychologists because they deal with problems connected with work: wage inequity can

---

THE QUEST FOR EQUITY

Profitable Inequity. A group of college men were hired through a referral agency to work as interviewers at a pay rate of $3.50 per hour. Half of the men were subsequently told that the referral agency had made a mistake in hiring them and that they lacked the qualifications for the job. They were also told that they would be hired anyway at the original pay rate, even though $3.50 was too much to pay them. The other half of the men were told that they qualified for the jobs as interviewers and that $3.50 was the standard pay rate for such work. The men who believed that they were overpaid "regained equity" by interviewing an average of forty people per interviewer, as opposed to the twenty-eight people per interviewer in the adequately paid group.

Unprofitable Inequity. Two-man teams worked on an arithmetic problem for $1.40 reward. One of the team members, an experimental confederate, was given the task of allocating the payoff at will. In some cases, inequity was kept moderately high: the confederate gave the subject $.40 and kept $1.00 for himself; in other cases, the inequity was very high, since the confederate gave the subject a nickel and kept $1.35 for himself. When the subjects were given the opportunity to further reduce their own reward, none in the moderately high-inequity condition chose to do so, whereas one-fourth of the subjects in the high-inequity condition chose that course of action. Post-experimental questioning revealed that this behavior was aimed at embarrassing the allocator for his gross unfairness in distributing the reward. In another study, however, allocators who were not experimental confederates tended to reward maximum performance by low-aptitude workers more often than below-maximum performance by high-aptitude workers.

ADAMS (1963)
LEVENTHAL AND BERGMAN (1969)
LEVENTHAL AND WHITESIDE (1973)

result in overproductivity, underproductivity, and sometimes even in a deliberate choice of reduction of one's wages to embarrass the inequitable payoff source (J. S. Adams, 1963; Lawler, 1968; Leventhal & Bergman, 1969). But it is obvious that this belief that people will reciprocate action also contributes to the occurrence of altruistic nurturance and benevolent prosocial behavior, to compliance and obedience, and even to the inhibition of aggressive behavior. The reciprocity norm also involves the ability to take the role of another person, projecting upon him the likelihood that he would act as the role-taker would in a given situation. In summary, behavioral reciprocation carries two very important implications for social organization: it provides a stabilizing force toward equilibrium in groups and societies, and it also provides a rationale for the initiation of action in social situations.

PROSOCIAL BEHAVIOR

One of the most important kinds of interaction is the benevolent exchange of help and goodwill. Psychologists have used the term *prosocial behavior* to refer to this broad category of activities, but the most common kinds of prosocial behavior are dependency (care-seeking) and nurturance (care-giving).

Dependency and Help-seeking

Dependent behavior is one of the most common forms of human activity. Of all the mammals, the human infant at birth is the most poorly equipped for independent survival. He cannot feed himself; he cannot move his body effectively to escape harm or shelter himself from threat; he cannot maintain his body warmth; his neuromuscular systems are poorly related to his body mass and proportions. In summary, he is dependent on others for his survival.

It is helpful to clarify a distinction between dependent behavior (which may serve as a means of attaining a variety of motivational goals) and dependency motivation (the need or desire for dependency in itself). *Dependent* behavior is care-seeking behavior (including help-seeking, attention-seeking, and affection-seeking). Such behavior can occur sometimes as a means of achieving goals such as satisfying hunger, attaining physical comfort, or securing something beyond one's independent abilities: in this case it is called *instrumental dependency.* In other situations, the attention or nurturance sought is a luxury rather than a necessity, sought simply as a pleasurable end in itself: in this case, it is called *emotional* dependency. The child who asks his mother to tie his shoes when he lacks the dexterity to do it himself is showing instrumental dependency; the child who is fully skilled in tying his shoes, but nevertheless asks his mother to tie them for him because he enjoys her attention and warmth, displays emotional dependency.

From birth, the satisfaction of one's basic needs is associated with dependency on the nurturant care of another person. This association is the root for development of sociogenic or learned motivational systems (as described in Chapter 6). Thus emotional dependency motivation represents a learned sociogenic value system. The infant comes to value being cared for and attended as an end in itself, even when it is no longer required for the satisfaction of his basic needs for survival (Dollard & Miller, 1950; Sears, Maccoby, & Levin, 1957). In general, child-rearing practices and other conditions during socialization that connect care-taking and interpersonal attention with other rewards (or withdrawal of nurturant care and attention with frustration and punishment) usually result in intensified emotional dependency motivation (Sears, Maccoby, & Levin, 1957; Kagan & Moss, 1960).

Another point of view is that some components of dependency and nurturance-seeking are unlearned. The fact that it is observed in very early infancy does not contradict the hypothesis that it is a learned motive, however, because the conditions for its learning occur very soon after birth. The fact that deprivation of nurturant care often leads to severe physiological symptoms has also been suggested as evidence that dependency motivation is unlearned. The *marasmus* sometimes observed in maternally deprived infants (Spitz, 1945, 1946) involves genuine physiological deterioration (lethargy, loss of appetite, weight loss, and deterioration of muscle tone), but its effects follow logically from disturbances in the feeding situation and general understimulation of the infant (loss of interest in food in the absence of accompanying nurturance and social satisfactions). Comprehensive reviews of research on the effects of maternal deprivation (Caster, 1961; Schafer & Emerson, 1964) have concluded that the most serious need of the infant during his first few months of life is varied stimulation (from either social or nonsocial sources) and that the deterioration shown by maternally deprived infants is more directly an effect of understimulation than of lack of nurturance, love, or interpersonal warmth.

An interesting set of studies of maternal nurturance and infant dependency in chimpanzees suggested some evidence contradictory to the notion that dependency is a learned motivational system (Harlow, 1958; Harlow & Zimmerman, 1959). After separation of infant chimps from their mothers shortly after birth, the crucial biological needs of the infants were met through a "surrogate mother," an elaborate apparatus containing a thermostatically controlled heater and a nippled bottle of milk. These infant chimps were never allowed contact with a natural mother, and they survived infancy with little difficulty. Some of the monkeys, however, were provided with two surrogate mothers: one that was nurturant (in supplying warmth and food) but made of wire hardware cloth, and another that was nonnurturant (no heater, no milk) but covered with a furry terry-cloth material. These infants secured food and warmth from the nurturant surrogate mother, but seemed to develop considerable more "affection" for the terry-cloth mother. They spent most of their time hovering about and hugging the terry-cloth mother, and they retreated to it when threatened or frightened. From these observations, Harlow concluded that "contact comfort" is a very basic component in the development of affection, and even suggested that this phenomenon might be specific within various species so that although chimpanzees seemed to prefer furry textures, hippopotami might prefer hippopotamus hide (Harlow, 1958).

In subsequent studies of these same chimpanzees as they matured, a variety of disturbances in their patterns of interpersonal behavior became apparent. Allowing them to have extended contact with other young monkeys produced some constructive modification of their behavior toward the patterns shown by normally reared chimpanzees (Seay, Alexander, & Harlow, 1954). Even at maturity, other effects were noted, particularly a lack of interest in sexual activity. These studies clearly imply that sensory (at least tactile) stimulation is crucial during infancy. Although they offer no support for the notion that dependency motivation is learned, they do not contradict the idea that affection and value come to be attached to figures that are instrumental in gaining other satisfactions, whether these figures are made of living flesh or of wire and wood.

Dependent or nurturance-seeking motivation is significant as the first step in a chained sequence of associations that eventually give rise to some of the bases of affiliative motivation and the quest for social acceptance and approval. Human nurturance is normally a phenomenon of social interaction: basic needs are satisfied almost altogether in the presence of another person, and the presence of others becomes generally rewarding. The sounds, sights, and other concomitants of interpersonal warmth and affection acquire reward value. In our culture, the typical patterns of parent-child interaction tie these signs of affection to approved and acceptable behavior. The child who behaves as his parents wish and approve receives affection and warmth, but these qualities are withdrawn following disapproved behavior. This chain of related associations ties the origins of dependency motivation to later motivation to seek and retain the approval and acceptance of others—not only parents, but other adults and peers as well. This outgrowth of dependency motivation, the "approval motive," comprises an essential basis of the social control of the individual's behavior, discussed more extensively in Chapters 6 and 7.

The variety of behavioral patterns motivated by the quest for nurturance are subject to complex training in socialization. Dependent behavior is age-governed in our culture. As the child grows older, emotional dependency (dependency for its own sake) is regarded as less acceptable. Although instrumental dependency remains socially acceptable, as the individual approaches maturity he is increasingly capable of achieving his goals without help from others, and the occasions that prompt instrumental dependency become fewer. Certain kinds of prosocial dependency, however, remain acceptable even in adulthood: what is often called "cooperativeness" often involves the acceptance of mutually dependent relationships with others. The need for security that often motivates one to seek employment by the firm offering the greatest assurance of security in old age, illness, or other kinds of distress represents a dependency on an institution rather than on another individual. Fromm's (1941) analysis of the individual's desire to escape the loneliness of freedom because it involves autonomous responsibility represents another kind of dependent motivation that, he suggests, may induce some individuals to acquiesce to a dictator who will promise to protect and shelter them (such as the submission of the German people to Hitler) and others to acquiesce to collective security in the crowd (which, he suggests, occurs in the mass conformism of America).

In our culture, dependent behavior is also sex-related. The American girl is permitted, and even encouraged, to be far more dependent than the American boy, and

---

HELP!

Female undergraduate students listened to a series of tapes featuring spontaneous conversations between two graduate students. Each subject was asked to rate on a 9-point scale how neurotic the conversations were. They were also told that they could be aided by guidelines (provided in a manila envelope), but only if necessary. Some subjects' instructions were intended to threaten their self-concept: they indicated that inability to identify neurotic interactions could reflect a rater's own neurotic state. Other subjects received instructions that were of only peripheral importance to their self-concept: it was indicated that failure on the task had little to do with the rater's mental health. In some cases subjects were also allowed to explain any anticipated failure "externally"; that is, they were told that as a rule a majority of raters (65 percent) tend to seek help from guidelines. In another condition, instructions were more "internally" oriented, indicating that only a negligible number of raters (10 percent) use the guidelines. Finally, all subjects took a battery of personality measures. The frequency with which the guidelines were consulted was the measure for help-seeking behavior. Help-seeking was most prevalent in subjects low in achievement motivation, and when the responsibility for failure could be attributed externally. Compared to subjects high in self-esteem, subjects low in self-esteem sought help more frequently when there was a major threat to their self-concept. The findings were seen as particularly relevant to persuasive messages aimed at overcoming peoples' reluctance to seek help. To be maximally effective, such messages should minimize threats to one's self-concept, offer external justification for possible failure, and imply that help-seeking is not necessarily an admission of failure.

TESSLER AND SCHWARTZ (1972)

this differentiation continues rather stably into adulthood (Kagan & Moss, 1960). Other cultures do not make such sharp sex-related distinctions, and still others reverse the differentiations made in our culture (Mead, 1935).

The term *independence training* describes the socialization practices through which a child is taught the distinctions between acceptable and unacceptable forms of dependency, and the specific conditions under which dependent behavior is socially condoned. Such training involves the intentional cultivation of personal anxiety about dependency through such devices as threatened disapproval. Young boys are usually taught that excessive dependency is "unmasculine" and thus undesirable. Independence, autonomy, and self-sufficiency are praised and rewarded as mature, desirable, "manly" attributes. As in the socialization of sexual behavior, however, such anxieties often enter into motivational conflicts. The conditions of infancy and the patterns of the child's early social interactions with adults tend to enhance the value of nurturance-seeking and dependent motivation. Later, the process of independence training works to cultivate aversive anxieties and approach-avoidance conflicts about certain kinds of dependency. For example, excessively nurturant parental care during infancy may induce the child to be highly motivated toward dependency, but excessively punitive discouragement of dependency in the older boy may later make him very anxious about displaying such behavior (Kagan & Moss, 1960). This conflict may be the seed of problems of personal and social adjustment in later life.

Nurturance and Altruism

The other side of the reciprocal relationship in dependency is nurturance—caregiving behavior (including help-giving, attention-giving, and affection-giving). The motivational forces behind altruistic nurturance are related (but not identical) to those of dependency motivation. The dependent condition of the human infant works directly to enhance his selfish value of dependency; but the same circumstances work indirectly to attach value to the nurturant role he recognizes in others who

---

WHO HELPS?

The effects of models in eliciting altruistic behavior was studied in various natural settings. In one study a young female was put in a situation that implied the need for help: she was stationed by a 1964 Ford Mustang with a flat left rear tire and an inflated tire leaning on the left side of her car. The model situation consisted of a 1965 Oldsmobile located about 400 yards behind the first car, raised by a jack, and a girl watching a man changing a flat tire. Of 4000 cars that passed, only 93 stopped to help (virtually all males). There were, however, almost twice as many offers of help from those who had passed the Oldsmobile than when it was absent.

Around Christmas Salvation Army kettles were placed on the sidewalk in various shopping centers. The solicitors were two females who rang the Salvation Army bell at regular intervals but did not engage in verbal pleas or eye contact with the shoppers. Once every minute, a male dressed as a white-collar worker approached the kettle from within the store and contributed a nickel. The 20-second period following the model's return to the store was designated as the observation time for the number of people who made a donation. In 112 times out of 365, donations were made, with about twice as many donations made when the model was present than when he was absent. Subsequent studies that varied the sex and race of both solicitor and model produced essentially the same results, except for a tendency for black solicitors to elicit a lower percentage of donors than did the whites.

BRYAN AND TEST (1967)

I DON'T WANT TO GET INVOLVED

In a series of studies, bystanders were observed to see if they intervened in a variety of experimentally controlled "emergency" situations (smoke trickling into a waiting room, an epileptic seizure being experienced, or a fall being suffered). Some were observed alone, and some in the company of others. The old adage that there is "safety in numbers" did not necessarily hold true. Knowledge or the assumption that others were *also* aware of the emergency situation inhibited bystander intervention. Evidently, when the bystander was alone in a crowd, he was reluctant to assume sole responsibility for his intervention, or, he assumed that others would intervene. He was more likely to intervene when in the company of friends than with strangers. The conclusion was that "if you are involved in an emergency, the most helpful number of bystanders is *one*."

DARLEY AND LATANÉ (1968)
LATANÉ AND DARLEY (1968)
LATANÉ AND RODIN (1969)

satisfy his dependency needs. As the sense of self emerges (as described in Chapter 7), the capacity for recognizing and taking the role of others develops more fully. The humanistic view of man suggests that these factors contribute to the emergence of the capacity for loving, in the broad sense of willingness to express concern and care for others (May, 1953, 1969a, 1969b; Maslow, 1954, 1968).

Many factors affect prosocial altruism, but generally the circumstances in which help is given appear to be more important than inherent attributes of the person offering help. Research in naturalistic settings has proved to be an effective way of studying this kind of behavior. Milgram's (1970) "lost letter" studies, described in Chapter 3, confront people with a dilemma demanding a choice between helping (by mailing a preaddressed and prestamped letter that appears to have been misplaced by its sender) or refusing help (ignoring or destroying the letter). Gaertner (1970) has used a similar naturalistic technique in his studies of the responses of people to telephone pleas for help, also described in Chapter 3.

WHY ONE HELPS

Personality tests were administered to students in college introductory psychology courses. This was followed by a 50-item multiple-choice test in psychology, purportedly serving as a self-improvement program for those courses. Each subject was assured that the test would not affect his course grade unless he made a very high score. In half the cases an experimental confederate posing as a student who had already taken the test gave each subject the chance to cheat by disclosing that most of the correct answers were "B" (which in fact they were not). Half the subjects were also given bogus feedback designed to bolster their self-image: as the subject was about to conclude his test, he was given a written interpretation of his performance on the personality test which was highly complimentary (e.g., "poised, self-assured, resourceful, flexible"). In all conditions, each subject was then asked to comply with a request for help that involved the scoring of a stack of about 500 tests. The highest rate of compliance was displayed by subjects who cheated but had received no bogus feedback. The offered explanation was that a person's act of cheating is inconsistent with his positive self-image, and by complying with a request he can restore that image. The subjects who prior to the request for help received the bogus feedback had their positive self-image restored that way and thus did not feel the need to comply.

McMILLEN (1971)

THE GOOD SAMARITAN

About 4450 men and women who traveled on a New York subway during a 9-week period were observed in this study. The particular train was chosen because it typically carried a composition of riders that was 55 percent white and 45 percent black. On different occasions each of four informally dressed young men (three whites and one black) simulated emergency situations that called for help. About a minute after the train passed the first station, the "victim" staggered forward, collapsed, and remained supine on the floor looking at the ceiling. To simulate the effect of intoxication, he smelled of liquor and carried a liquor bottle tightly wrapped in a brown paper bag. On other occasions illness was simulated by having the victim carry a cane. On several occasions each of four young white men acted as models who administered immediate or delayed help. Observers noted the race, sex, and location of every person who helped the victim, of every person who was in an adjacent area to the victim, and in all cases tried to elicit comments from these people. Helping behavior occurred with rather high frequency (about 60 percent), mostly by males, with a same-race tendency to help when the victim appeared drunk. The victim who appeared ill received help more frequently than the one who appeared drunk. The number of bystanders had little effect on the speed of helping, and the major impact of models dissipated the longer the emergency lasted without help being offered. The experimenters concluded that the extent of given help can best be measured by the anticipated result for the helper: praise, censure, self-blame, effort, embarrassment, disgust, possible physical harm, and so on. The major implication of this view is that positive "altruistic" behavior is largely governed by a selfish desire to rid oneself of unpleasant emotions.

PILIAVIN, RODIN, AND PILIAVIN (1969)

The presence of people who set an example of giving help will induce others to help too (Bryan & Test, 1967), but if others refuse to give help, altruism is discouraged (Darley & Latané, 1968; Latané & Rodin, 1969).

To some extent utilitarian values determine whether one will show benevolent altruism. If one is placed in a situation where benevolence can atone for misdeeds or "buy" another person's good will, one is likely to offer help and nurturance willingly (Piliavin, Rodin, & Piliavin, 1969; McMillen, 1971).

SORRY, WRONG NUMBER

Two groups of New York registered voters, 230 Liberal Party members and 217 Conservative Party members, were individually matched as well as possible on their election districts and type of dwelling unit. Each subject received an apparently wrong number telephone call in which the caller (a male or a female posing as a stranded motorist) asked for help in easily identifiable white or black accent. The caller asked for Ralph's Garage and immediately informed the subject that he was stuck on the parkway. Upon being informed that he had the wrong number, the caller then indicated that he was out of change to make an additional call and asked the subject to relay the message to the garage. The frequency of calls to the number provided by the stranded motorist (actually to a telephone manned by the experimenter) served as the measure for helping behavior. Males tended to render assistance more frequently than females did, but females were not assisted more frequently than were males. In all cases, whites received more help than blacks, but the extent to which blacks were helped less than whites was greater among conservatives than among liberals.

GAERTNER (1970)

Finally, the characteristics of the dependent person needing or seeking help also determine whether or not altruistic behavior will occur. When the relationship between two people is one of respect and mutual acceptance, benevolent help-giving is much more likely to occur than when the relationship involves dislike, distrust, or prejudice (Gaertner, 1970; Milgram, 1970).

AGGRESSION AND VIOLENCE

A malevolent counterpart of benevolent prosocial behavior is *aggression*—behavior the intent of which is to injure or destroy. A certain amount of aggressive behavior probably results from adaptive responses to frustration—the effort to overcome and remove obstacles that hinder one's pursuit of his goals. In other situations, however, aggression seems to be an end in itself, driven by hostile feelings and hatred that seem to have no purpose or cause.

The *frustration-aggression hypothesis*, formulated from a social learning point of view in the late 1930s (Dollard, Doob, Miller, Mowrer, & Sears, 1939), states that aggressive behavior is a logical and expected consequence of frustration. Frustration—any condition that blocks attainment of a desired goal—tends to be followed by aggression—behavior that is meant to destroy or remove the frustrating block. If conditions prohibit destruction or removal of the frustration, the aggression may be directed toward other objects (displaced aggression). Many kinds of social behavior have been interpreted within this framework, including ethnic and racial prejudices and the displacement of hostility toward members of alien groups.

Whatever its source, the expression of aggression in our culture is influenced by socialization. Some forms of aggression are stringently forbidden, such as murder; others are consistently, though less vigorously, forbidden, such as property destruction. Both these taboos, however, may be suspended in time of war—at least so long as the property and lives destroyed are those of a collective enemy. In our culture, boys are encouraged to be more aggressive than girls, and overt display of aggression is progressively less socially acceptable as the individual grows older. Like dependency, however, a few specified forms of aggression are socially acceptable even in adulthood. Persistence, renewed striving, and continued efforts in overcoming obstacles to one's success are regarded as desirable traits. In fact, we often use the adjective "aggressive" to describe the kind of person who displays intensity, perseverance, and initiative in pursuing his personal goals (Henry, 1949).

Aggression, like altruism, is influenced by the norm of reciprocity and the assumption that behavioral acts are likely to be returned in kind. If kindness will bring kindness, likewise violence will bring violence. The reciprocity norm encourages altruism but deters aggression (Geen, 1968).

In addition, the presence of models who set an example of violent behavior also tends to increase the likelihood that aggression will occur (Bandura, Ross, & Ross, 1961; Berkowitz, 1964). Whether this effect is due to imitation and identification is difficult to establish; it is equally plausible that observation of an aggressive person merely implies a norm of acceptability, suggesting that such behavior is condoned and approved in that situation (Baron & Kepner, 1970).

The psychological study of *violence* is most seriously handicapped by the lack of adequate definitions of violent behavior. The word is used loosely in popular discussions of the blood and gore not only of the entertainment media but of everyday life as well. Violent behavior includes aggression, but the term carries further connotations of uncontrolled (or at least unrestrained) behavior, as well as implications of extremeness of actions. Although violence is a popular topic of discussion these days, social psychology can offer little toward its understanding until we adopt a meaningful definition of the idea.

VIOLENCE IN THE MOVIES

A series of studies was designed to test the hypothesis that angered individuals will not show aggressive behavior toward safe and readily available targets unless aggressive cues (external stimuli related to aggression) are present. In what appeared to the subject as a learning situation, pairs of subjects could punish each other by means of electric shock when proper learning failed to take place. One member of the pair was an experimental confederate whose task was to provoke the subject to anger. The number and intensity of shocks delivered by the subject to his partner subsequent to the provocation served as a measure of aggressive behavior. The presence and intensity of aggressive cues were also manipulated. In one study some subjects were shown a brutal fight scene from the motion picture *Champion,* starring Kirk Douglas. Other subjects were angered by receiving an undue number of shocks from a confederate introduced to them as either *Kirk* Anderson or Bob Anderson. Some subjects were presented with both aggressive cues, others with none. In another study some subjects were told that a gun lying on an adjacent table belonged to their tormentor (the target person), and some were told it belonged to the experimenter. Others were exposed to nonaggressive cues such as a badminton racquet, and still others were not exposed to any particular cues. Aggressive behavior in all cases increased significantly with the number of aggressive cues present, especially if they could be associated with the target person.

BERKOWITZ AND GEEN (1966)
BERKOWITZ AND LEPAGE (1967)

"VIOLENCE" BEHIND THE WHEEL

When a person's car is blocked by another car at a signal-controlled intersection, he usually vents his anger by honking his horn impatiently. This typical response can be considered as an aggressive act because its primary aim is to bombard the offending driver with unpleasant stimuli and thus make him feel uncomfortable. A study was conducted at six intersections in Palo Alto, California, with the blocking car being either a shiny 1966 Chrysler Imperial hardtop or an unobtrusive gray 1961 Rambler sedan. At the end of each trial, observers noted the frequency, latency, and length of each honk by drivers behind them. These observations were combined into a measure of aggression. There was significantly more display of aggression by drivers who were blocked by the Rambler (low status) than by the Chrysler (high status).

DOOB AND GROSS (1968)

SOCIAL POWER AND COMPLIANCE

Social power is a particular kind of reciprocal interaction involving interpersonal control or manipulation. It involves a dominance-submission relationship in the diad, whether or not this relationship is intentionally sought by the persons involved. *Social power* includes all kinds of situations involving the ability of one person to influence or control the behavior of another.

A useful overall scheme for distinguishing several different bases of social power has been described by Raven and French (1958). This scheme describes five common kinds of interpersonal power. Two of these resemble what Thibaut and Kelley (1959) called *fate control* because they involve the power of one person to manipulate the fate of another rather than to control his actions directly.

Reward power occurs when one person is in a position that permits him to deliver rewards to another who complies with his influence; similarly, *coercive power* occurs when one can deliver punishments to another who fails to comply. These two forms of social power are more or less determined by the circumstances of the relationship between two people. The powerful person achieves his power by being in a particular position. Reward power and coercive power are thus external to the voluntary choice of the influenced person. The power relationship involved is one of controlling the consequences of behavior rather than the behavior itself; however, by controlling the outcome of another's actions, a powerful person can obviously control the other's selection of particular actions.

Two others resemble what Thibaut and Kelley (1959) labeled *behavior control* because they involve one's capacity for direct manipulation of the actions of another, apart from the consequences or outcome of these actions. They depend on the voluntary acquiescence or granting of power by one person to another. *Referent power* occurs when one person has power over another because the latter wishes to emulate him, identify with him, or be accepted by him. (The concept of referent power applies to the kind of social influence described in Chapter 10 as normative social influence.) *Expert power* (which is analogous to informational social influence) occurs when one person regards another as possessing knowledge or abilities that are potentially useful to him. Both referent and expert power are voluntarily granted because they occur only when the influenced person willingly allows another to exert power over him.

A fifth form of power described by Raven and French, *legitimate power,* is derived from formal relationships between the positions occupied by two people. When one person perceives another as externally empowered (by virtue of his formal position) to influence him, a relationship of legitimate power is said to exist. In this case one person allows another to influence him simply because he feels that things are supposed to be that way. Formalized group structures frequently generate legitimate power relationships. The "legitimate" does not imply that other kinds of social power are "illegitimate." It merely describes the fact that the power relationship is accepted by members of the group as a legitimate part of the group's formal organization.

These five bases of social power are theoretically distinguishable, but in actual situations they often occur in combination. For example, legitimate power may characterize the influence relationships that occur within a military system and permit one person to influence another purely because of rank. However, military relationships also involve capacities for men of higher rank to reward and punish men of lower rank (reward and coercive power), and seniority may be associated with both personal respect (referent power) and differences in ability or expertise (expert power).

Because leadership is generally conceived as a composite of power functions arising from several origins, the ability of a leader to influence others within his group may be derived from any combination of the kinds of power described. The importance of each component in contributing to a leader's power may vary considerably from one situation to another. This is one of the reasons that the prediction of leadership ability from knowledge of an individual's personality characteristics alone often is only moderately successful. Different kinds of individual ability may contribute to the attainment of different kinds of power, depending on the structural and circumstantial characteristics of the particular group in which the power or leadership relation occurs (Raven & French, 1958; French & Raven, 1959; Evan & Zelditch, 1961; Elder, 1963).

Compliance is the submissive end of a diadic power relationship. In social psychology the behavior we commonly call acquiescence, obedience, and submission can be subsumed under the general label of compliance to social power.

The development of sociometry as a method of measuring interpersonal relationships during the 1930s provided a boost to the study of social power. Several investigations explored perceived leadership and power within natural groups, but the first important experimental studies of social power were carried out during the 1940s to explore actual manifestations of interpersonal control in organized groups (Lippitt, Polansky, Redl, & Rosen, 1952). "Attributed power" was defined as a set of perceptions and expectations held by people about each other. Accordingly, leadership and power were defined in this sense as role expectations. Another concept, "manifest power," was defined as the actual overt display of successful interpersonal control and influence. Field studies of preadolescent boys in summer camps used these concepts to analyze the circumstances under which social power was most likely and most effective. Boys who were perceived by others as holding high-status positions attempted more often to influence others, and when they did, they were actually more successful. Moreover, they were more direct and open in their control attempts. On the other hand, boys in lower-status positions tried less frequently to influence others; they were less successful when they did try; and they were more devious and circuitous in these attempts. Both perceived power and actually manifested power were associated with high levels of ability in areas pertinent to the situation—in this case, athletic ability and general knowledge of campcraft.

Like altruism, compliance is subject to circumstances. The presence of models who comply with the power attempts of another will increase the likelihood that an observer will also comply (Milgram, 1963). Especially when the powerful person is viewed as taking the responsibility for the actions, the submissive member of the power relationship is likely to comply (Opton, 1970). This is plain and simple buckpassing. The cop-out is an important aspect of compliance when submission offers an escape from responsibility. This accounts for the behavior of submissive soldiers under such crises as the Mi Lai incident in the Viet Nam War, or the Nazi effort to exterminate Jews during World War II. The same kind of compliance happened within

---

THAT'S AN ORDER!

About forty males between the ages of 40 and 50, drawn from various communities surrounding Yale University, participated in an experiment that presumably studied memory and learning. Each naive subject ("the teacher") was required to administer increasingly more punishment to another subject ("the learner"), who in reality was an experimental confederate. The rationale offered for the administration of punishment was that it would increase the learner's ability to remember words from a list provided to the teacher. Punishment was administered by means of a shock generator with thirty switches ranging from Slight Shock to Danger: Severe Shock. Each subject was introduced to the learner, both received sample shocks of low intensity, and then both student and learner were put into separate booths out of each other's sight. The subject was seated near the switchboard panel and could communicate with the learner via loudspeaker. The subject was ordered to increase shock severity every time a light in an answer box indicated that the learner had given a wrong response (predetermined by the experimenter). During the administration of shocks the subject heard what appeared to be the learner's agonized cries of pain, pounding on the walls, and pleas for ending his ordeal. The primary measure was the maximum shock each subject was willing to administer before he refused to continue further. Fourteen subjects refused the order at some point after hearing the learner's plight, but twenty-six subjects obeyed the experimental command fully and went all the way in administering the highest shock on the generator. The subjects' behavior was marked by profuse sweating, trembling, seizures, stuttering, and nervous laughter.

S. MILGRAM (1963)

DOCTOR'S ORDERS

An experimental study in nurse-physician relationships was conducted in twenty-two wards in a public and a private hospital. Pill boxes bearing identical hospital labels were placed in each ward. The pills (harmless placebos filled with glucose) were labeled as 5 mg. capsules of "Astroten," of which the prescribed safe maximum daily dosage was 10 mg. An experimental confederate would telephone the nurse on duty, curtly identify himself as Dr. Smith of the hospital staff, and instruct her to give 20 mg. to one of the patients at once because he (the physician) was in a hurry and could only come in later. Observers stationed near the medicine supply cabinets who subsequently interviewed the nurses reported that in twenty-one out of the twenty-two cases there was little or no conscious delay in carrying out the order after the conclusion of the call. Yet when graduate nurses were presented with a hypothetical situation identical to the real experiment, twenty-one out of twenty-two said that they would have refused to administer the medicine without written orders from the physician, especially in view of the dosage discrepancy. In the real experiment, eleven nurses denied being aware of such a discrepancy. The overwhelming majority of the nurses did, however, make pointed references to the displeasure of doctors when nurses offer resistance to what they consider improper instructions.

HOFLING, BROTZMAN, DALRYMPLE, GRAVES, AND PIERCE (1966)

the Nixon administration and the Committee to Re-elect the President in the Watergate catastrophe of 1972 and 1973.

Factors within the individual, in his personality makeup and value systems, may also contribute to compliant behavior and the exertion of social power. The motives behind dependent help-seeking or attention-seeking behavior (described earlier) often induce a person to enter into a submissive relationship with a more powerful person. Similarly, the notion of Machiavellianism (described in Chapter 7) accounts for individual differences in both the desire and the ability to manipulate other people and to exert social power.

"WHO? ME?"

(From Rat Publications, 241 East 14 Street, New York, New York.)

THE FOOT IN THE DOOR

How to obtain compliance without pressure by means of the-foot-in-the-door technique was demonstrated in two separate studies involving over 200 residents of Palo Alto, California. In the first study, subjects were solicited by telephone to first comply with a small request and then 3 days later with a larger, related request. The small request consisted of having subjects answer a series of questions about their use of household goods. The larger request consisted of asking the subjects to have six men come to their houses to do the actual classification of the household goods. About a third of the people approached refused any request, but among those approached with the larger request, there was more compliance if they had previously complied with the small request than when they were directly approached. Similar results were obtained in the second study, even though the requests were unrelated and made by different experimenters on each occasion. The small request in the second study consisted of asking the subjects either to put up a small sign or sign a petition to keep California beautiful; the large request was to have them install on their front lawns a large sign that said "Drive Carefully."

FREEDMAN AND FRASER (1966)

NEGOTIATION AND BARGAINING

Under some circumstances two people may become engaged in activities that present conflicts of interest. In these cases, unless the situation is abandoned completely or unless one person completely overcomes the other in some way, interpersonal negotiation and bargaining become necessary. Many aspects of cooperation and competition come into play when people confront one another over conflicting goals or interests. A variety of procedures, ranging from naturalistic studies of human conflict to laboratory experiments, have been used to study negotiations and bargaining for individual or mutual advantage. Gaming procedures (described in Chapter 3) are especially useful for this kind of research. One game, the Prisoner's Dilemma, affords a player the opportunity to choose either cooperative or competitive strategies. Usually the situation is arranged so that a logical and rational solution can permit both players to cooperate to mutual advantage. But often people will abandon rational conservative strategies of cooperation in favor of more risky competitive strategies (Guetzkow et al., 1963; Wallach, Kogan, & Bem, 1962, 1964, 1965). This paradox, called the "risky shift," is described in detail in Chapter 10.

The strategies adopted in these games are influenced by a number of factors, including the context in which the game is presented experimentally (Evans & Crumbaugh, 1964, 1966) and the magnitude of the actual payoff amounts associated with each strategy (Steele, 1966). When conditions permit players to communicate freely, they are more likely to enter cooperative strategies (Loomis, 1959). When people are led to believe that the game will terminate at a given time, with a reckoning of each player's accumulated winnings, people often tend to "go for broke" by playing the more reckless and irrational high-risk competitive strategies (Bixenstein & Wilson, 1963). Rapoport (1964) and others have found that the strategy adopted by a player on a particular trial in such games is influenced to some extent by what happened on the preceding trial. Simultaneous confession may be viewed as treachery, resulting sometimes in subsequent attempts to gain vengeance by continuing high-risk temptation strategies to get even with the opponent. Simultaneous cooperation in holding out against the captors in the prisoner's dilemma game may lead one player to perceive the other as trustworthy, thereby giving rise to expectations that the status quo of rational cooperation is likely to be retained by the other player on future occa-

THE TRUCKING GAME

Female personnel of a telephone company were asked to play a simulated trucking game that involved bargaining between pairs of players. Each player guided a truck to a given destination, with the payoff being a fixed amount of imaginary money per trial paid in direct proportion to the speed of the truck's arrival. Because of one-way sections of the road, each player had the choice of taking an alternate, but longer, road to the destination. Using the alternate road represented a loss for the player. In addition, players were sometimes provided with "controls" by which they could block each other's way. Bilateral controls allowed both players to threaten each other's pathways, whereas unilateral controls allowed this privilege only to one player. As a rule bargaining occurred because both players realized that cooperative situations were better in the long run, or no worse, than competitive coexistence; and that cooperation was "safer" because it involved less risky decisions. When the fortune of the game led one player to have strong control, safety decreased markedly due to the controlling player's increased risk-taking, especially when bilateral controls were used. Communication channels provided no guarantee for better bargaining, and in competitive situations actually became superfluous. The conclusion was that the availability of threat makes it more difficult for bargainers to reach a mutually profitable agreement.

DEUTSCH AND KRAUSS (1960)

sions. Prior familiarity with the other player or an initial favorable impression of him tends to make a player more likely to attempt cooperative strategies in playing such games. However, the role of personality factors within the individual that induce him to play a particular strategy in these games has not yet been fully investigated.

In general, cooperative negotiation in game situations is associated with older males, younger females, upper-class adults, lower-class children, strong needs for

PRISONERS OF OUR OWN DILEMMA?

Philip S. Gallo, an experimenter who has used the prisoner's dilemma game in his research, questioned the generalization of findings in game research to everyday conflict situations. He suggested that the tendency of game research to consider the games as analogous to real-life conflicts such as husband-wife interactions, labor-management negotiations, or various aspects of the cold war is clearly unwarranted. The major weakness of game research during the 1960s, according to Gallo, was that it failed to make the necessary distinction between tangible payoffs (money, fringe benefits, control of land, etc.) and symbolic payoffs (maintaining face, self-respect, prestige, honor, etc.). It is even doubtful whether players in typical game research experience real pressure or conflict. Many of them evidently are bored by consistent cooperative responses for little or no money.

Gallo criticizes those who generalize game research findings to international conflict situations, pointing out that "the introduction of $16 in real money solved seemingly intractable conflicts in a trucking game, but it seems unlikely that the leaders of the United States and North Vietnam could resolve the Vietnam War for $16." Gallo suggested that "based upon our laboratory experiments to date, the best advice we can give to real-world decision makers is to be extremely careful in the choice of language to describe conflict. The temptation is always present to rally support by overemphasizing the value of the symbolic payoffs at stake. By so doing, they may be digging their own graves, and ours along with them."

GALLO (1966, 1968)
GALLO AND SHEPOSH (1971)

affiliation and achievement, bureaucratic family backgrounds, political internationalism, tolerance for ambiguity, cognitive complexity, and freedom from rigidity. In contrast, more competitive strategies in game bargaining are associated with older females, younger males, upper-class children, lower-class adults, entrepreneurial family backgrounds, political isolationism, cognitive rigidity, authoritarianism, Machiavellianism, power and dominance needs, intelligence, risk-taking, and strong self-esteem (Vinacke, 1969; Wrightsman, O'Connor, & Baker, 1972).

Despite numerous studies during the past decade on negotiation and bargaining, particularly those involving the prisoner's dilemma game, the question of how relevant game playing in the laboratory is has remained largely unanswered. Some investigators have concluded that game research can be extended to real-life interpersonal, intergroup, and even international relations (e.g., Deutsch, 1969), but others, realizing the limiting "as if" qualities of laboratory research, have warned fellow psychologists not to become "prisoners of our own dilemma" (Gallo, 1966, 1968; Gallo & Sheposh, 1971).

IMITATIVE BEHAVIOR

Imitation is a special kind of interpersonal influence in which one person provides a model for another to copy. In the earliest speculations of social psychology it was often assumed that certain animals (including human beings) were instinctively bound to emulate the actions of others. In fact it was so common to assume that imitation was characteristic of the ape family that the term "aping" has become a synonym for it. Interestingly, though, the empirical laboratory study of imitation has made little use of apes and monkeys because early investigators found it difficult to get apes to show imitation in the laboratory. Human beings, especially young children, are much better subjects for the study of this kind of interpersonal behavior.

Behavioral Contagion

The spontaneous imitation of one person by another (including the radiation of ripples of imitation through a group) has been called *behavioral contagion.* This is an unintentional kind of imitation in which the person copied need have neither awareness nor intention of being imitated. Such contagion is often observed in crowds and audiences, especially under stress and excitement (see Chapter 13). In an early laboratory study, behavioral contagion was observed with high school students playing a competitive dart-throwing game. At one point the game was interrupted by instructions to leave the interesting game and begin a dull noncompetitive activity involving manipulation of pencils. Later, a confederate of the experimenter began a progression of violations of the experimenter's instructions. First he abandoned the dull pencil activity; then he began a set of finger, arm, and body movements; and he finally returned to playing darts. All along the way, the other subjects showed some degree of contagion of these actions. With no overt attempt to exert power, the confederate induced 30 to 60 percent of the other students to copy his behavior (Lippitt, Polansky, Redl, & Rosen, 1952).

Observational Learning

There are important differences between *blind imitation* (as represented by behavioral contagion) and *observational learning.* In blind imitation a person matches his behavior to that of a model purely for the sake of duplicating him; in observational learning one approximates his behavior to that of a model in order to learn behavior appropriate to the situation.

WHO IMITATES?

College students were given a three-choice learning discrimination problem, and took turns with another subject who had been preinstructed. Subjects could either settle for imitating the other person blindly, or persist in attempts to discover cues that led to the other person's success. More imitation occurred in people whose achievement needs were low, had strong feelings of benevolence toward others, displayed less emotional stability, and showed more cognitive rigidity.

McDAVID (1966)

WHO IS IMITATED?

Various pairs of college students were asked to play a game in which they were to place bets on a number of imaginary horse races. Members of the pairs were out of each other's sight, so each subject could be led to believe that he was person B playing after person A. After every response, each member was informed about the payoff. The experimenter, who programmed A's responses and provided him with a high level of competence (winning 75 percent of the time) or low level of competence (winning 25 percent of the time), was thus in the position to see to what degree person A was imitated. Models who were perceived as attractive were only imitated when they were also competent; when they were incompetent, imitation dropped sharply.

BARON (1970)

A series of experimental investigations by Miller and Dollard (1941) provided the greatest impetus for later research on imitation and observational learning in human beings. In defining imitation they excluded coincidental matching of behavior (which they called "same behavior"). For example, when two automobile drivers approach a traffic light and stop, one has not imitated the other. Both have responded independently to the same cue (the red light) because they have learned that the appropriate response to red lights is to stop. As simpleminded as this distinction may sound, one frequently encounters discussions in which such coincidental parallels and uniformities in behavior are mislabeled as imitation or social influence. When masses of individuals have learned or have been taught the same patterns of response and behavior during the course of parallel socialization experiences, they may continue to exhibit uniformities of behavior apart from the operation of direct social influences among them.

Miller and Dollard confined their interest primarily to a form of blind imitation, which they called *matched-dependent behavior*. This occurs when one organism learns to match or duplicate the behavior of another. Thus matched-dependent behavior represents a "dead-end" sort of imitation, involving simple matching of actions, which remains dependent on the model, who defines what should be matched. In the absence of a model, one who has learned merely to match his behavior to that of the model remains empty-handed; once the model is taken away, no independent learning has occurred, and the imitator is back where he started. Thus Miller and Dollard essentially investigated situations in which laboratory rats and kindergarten children learned *to imitate* (blind imitation), and not situations in which they learned *by imitating* (observational learning). Their studies did, however, contribute an important shift in the direction of research on imitation by bringing this form of behavior within the domain of general applicability of basic principles of motivation, learning, and reinforcement. They demonstrated that both rats and children can readily be taught, by systematic administration of rewards, to match their behavior to that of others who provide models or examples for them, and that they can be trained to differentiate one model from another, imitating one but not the other. These findings provide a useful framework for understanding an important process in social learning. For example, in socialization, young individuals may be taught by use of systematic rewards to copy the behavior demonstrated to them by adult agents of the society; they may learn to differentiate the appropriateness of copying male adults as compared to female adults; they may eventually learn to adopt the styles, conventions, and even beliefs of their peers and associates.

Only one of the series of important experiments done by Miller and Dollard directly raised the question of observational learning through imitation. In one study with children, they demonstrated that under some circumstances imitation of the behavior of a model might serve as a means of guiding the imitator toward exposure to significant cues or signal conditions in the environment that determined the exemplary model's choice of actions. Thus when the imitator responds not merely by blindly matching his behavior to that of a model, but by searching the environment to determine which cue conditions the model is responding to, independent learning may occur. In several subsequent studies designed to extend those of Miller and Dollard, other investigators found that independent learning in situations in which blind matching of behavior was systematically rewarded could occur occasionally, though not in all cases (Church, 1957; W. C. Wilson, 1958; Rosenblith, 1959).

A number of investigations of learning in subhuman animals have shown that cats and monkeys learn readily by observing the actions of others (Riopelle, 1960). Similarly, studies of both imitation as well as conformity to group norms have shown that human beings may also learn independently when they are socially influenced by other people or groups. Although there are still many unanswered questions about the factors that govern the extent to which an individual will learn independently when given the opportunity to match his behavior to that of models and examples, several studies have shown that individuals differ in their tendency to settle for copying others blindly when given a chance to imitate or to attempt to search out the determinants of their model's actions. Those inclined to attempt to learn independently are likely to show personality characteristics such as strong achievement needs, emotional stability, and objectivity, whereas those who imitate blindly are likely to show characteristics such as strong affiliation and nurturance needs, values for conformity and benevolence toward others, and cognitive rigidity (McDavid, 1966a). Among children, the tendency to imitate blindly without attempting to learn through observation has been found to be associated with maternal rejection and strictness in controlling the child, as well as with maternal indulgence and overprotection (McDavid, 1959b). Thus it appears that the conditions of parent-child interaction that tend generally to stifle the child's independent exploration of his world, either through restriction of his freedom to explore or through overindulgence that satisfies his needs without requiring independent exploration, tend to inhibit his inclination to learn by observing others. Furthermore, the strict parent who demands blind allegiance and allows no give-and-take in discipline and control probably systematically rewards the child's blind and unquestioning acquiescence to the guidance of others.

Imitation and observational learning can be successfully analyzed merely as special kinds of learning in which the cues controlling the selection of particular actions in behavior are social rather than impersonal. That is, when an individual finds himself in a particular situation, his actions may be steered either by impersonal aspects of the situation, or by the behavior of others in the same situation, or by a combination of both. The behavior of an exemplary model in a particular set of circumstances presents a complex cue pattern, and the imitator may respond either to selected parts of this pattern (for example, by responding only to the observed behavior of the model and ignoring other situational conditions, and thus blindly imitating), or he may respond to the overall pattern of relationships between the model's behavior and the circumstances surrounding it, leading to independent learning by observation. Several experimental studies that have analyzed observational learning in this fashion suggest that basic principles of learning in complex situations are applicable to this as a special form of learning (McDavid, 1962a, 1964).

Social learning through observation provides an extremely important means of abbreviating the learning process. An individual may shorten his search for appropriate actions in a particular situation by emulating the successful behavior of others more experienced than he. Thus long and arduous searches for the most effective action to accomplish a goal can be eliminated. Such abbreviation becomes especially important in the process of socialization, providing a means of transmission of culturally evolved habits from one generation to the next rapidly and efficiently.

RELEVANCE AND APPLICATION

The entire domain of social psychology is the study of social interaction; the simplest form occurs in face-to-face encounters of two people. Consequently the kinds of interpersonal transactions examined in this chapter are the basic building blocks from which more complex kinds of social interaction are derived.

In an overpopulated world where people crowd into a limited number of population centers, the need for cooperation and prosocial behavior is self-evident. Human beings are forced from birth to be at least partially dependent on others, and the decision to live collaboratively involves an implied pact of cooperation and mutual benevolence. No longer can each man meet his own needs; an urban society demands mutual dependence. The psychological exploration of dependency and altruism, then, affords a working basis for addressing urban problems and the psychological adjustment of the individual to crowded living and the complexity of a network of mutual dependencies. To some extent psychology has studied the roots of help-seeking more thoroughly than the roots of help-giving. Knowledge of the origins and conditions of dependency is considerably more extensive than understanding of the origins and conditions of the benevolent nurturance required to satisfy dependency needs.

Recognition of the progressive growth and modification of forms of dependent behavior as the child grows from infancy to maturity is a critical part of the educational process. In order to optimize their role in the socialization of the child, teachers must be trained to recognize and confront their role in handling the independence training of the child as he grows toward productive autonomy in adulthood.

In our culture the elaborate array of sex- and age-related differential codes concerning dependent behavior often generate problems of personal adjustment. Dependency conflicts are especially pronounced for males because this aspect of behavior is considered to be traditionally nonmasculine and therefore unacceptable. Increased awareness of the roots of dependency conflicts in early socialization experiences and their relation to cultural pronouncements and restraints facilitates the development of both preventive and remedial mental health measures related to such conflicts.

The exercise of social power and the manipulation of people by one another are basic to the stability and development of our society. Leadership is a derivative of social power relationships, and the basic processes of interpersonal social power described here are fundamental to understanding and controlling social leadership. Compliance, or followership, is the reciprocal of leadership power. Expanded understanding of these processes affords a basis for cultivating effective and productive social leaders as well as for strengthening the resistance of followers to the attempted power of socially threatening leaders. The effective management of social power relationships is critical to the maintenance of stability in a society.

Blind imitation is a nonproductive form of behavior, whereas observational learning (following the examples of appropriate models) is a critical and important shortcut in the learning process. Especially through identification, youngsters and newcomers to a society are rapidly assimilated into a culture. Without the capacity to profit by observing others and to learn through observation and imitation, the long and tedious route of individual trial-and-error learning would severely restrict the individual's capacities for social learning.

Analysis of the psychological economics of interpersonal negotiation to resolve conflicts of interest provides a promising route toward understanding the origins of war and possible alternatives to the resolutions of interpersonal and international conflicts of interest. Moreover, the control and management of interpersonal conflicts is an integral part of the social order in a complex urban society. The closer people live, the more frequent their encounters over conflicting interests or goals. Increased understanding of the psychology of conflict and negotiation offers some promise for more peaceful coexistence in a crowded world.

The study of aggressive and violent behavior—and means of controlling or inhibiting its display in socially disruptive ways—also promises applicability to the handling of interpersonal and intergroup conflicts.

In general, the utility of psychological exploration of basic forms of diadic interpersonal exchange is not limited to one-to-one human encounters. These diadic interactions are the building blocks of complex social organization, and they represent a starting point for almost all applied social psychology.

REVIEW

1. *Diadic* social behavior involves two people in face-to-face reciprocal social interaction.

2. The *norm of reciprocity* assumes others will respond to one's actions with like actions, or that "you will do unto me as I do unto you."

3. *Prosocial* behavior involves a benevolent exchange of help and goodwill. *Dependent* behavior is care-seeking behavior, including help-seeking, attention-seeking, and affection-seeking. *Nurturant* behavior is care-giving behavior, including help-giving, attention-giving, and affection-giving.

4. *Instrumental* dependency is a means of satisfying needs or desires; *emotional* dependency is an end in itself. Generally instrumental dependency involves help-seeking, whereas emotional dependency involves affection-seeking.

5. *Aggression* is behavior that is intended to injure or destroy. Aggression may be either a means to an end (to overcome obstacles in one's pursuit toward goals) or an end in itself (motivated by sheer hatred and malevolence). The *frustration-aggression hypothesis* states that aggressive behavior is a logical and expected consequence of frustration.

6. *Violence* is difficult to study psychologically because it is inadequately defined. Violent behavior includes aggression, but the term carries further connotations of uncontrolled and extreme action.

7. *Social power* involves interpersonal control or manipulation, regardless of whether this relationship is sought by the persons involved.

8. *Fate control* involves the power of one person to manipulate another's fate by manipulating his rewards and punishments; *behavior control* involves one's capacity

for direct manipulation of the actions of another, apart from the consequences or outcome of those actions.

9. *Reward* power occurs when one person is able to deliver rewards to another for complying with his influence. *Coercive* power occurs when one can deliver punishments to another for failure to comply. *Referent* power occurs when one person influences another because the latter wishes to emulate him, identify with him, or be accepted by him. *Expert* power occurs when one person influences another because the latter regards him as possessing useful knowledge or abilities. Another form of *legitimate* social power occurs when formal external circumstances are recognized and accepted as imposing the right of one person to control or influence another.

10. *Compliance* is the submissive end of a diadic power relationship, and it includes acquiescence, obedience, and submission.

11. When two people confront each other over conflicting goals or interests, *negotiation* or *bargaining* may be required to resolve those conflicts. *Cooperation* includes negotiated options that have mutual benefit, whereas *competition* includes negotiated options that benefit only one party involved.

12. *Imitation* includes all kinds of interaction in which one person provides a model for another to copy in his behavior. *Behavioral contagion* is an unintentional kind of imitation in which the person imitated has neither awareness nor intention of being copied. *Observational learning* is a special form of imitation in which one approximates his behavior to that of a model in order to learn behavior appropriate to the situation.

ORGANIZED SOCIAL BEHAVIOR

In attempting to understand man's experience and behavior in social surroundings, social psychologists are especially interested in *organized* social systems. The term *group* has a specific definition in social psychology: it refers not simply to a number of people, but particularly to a set of people who are participating in an *organized system.*

Most of what we know about organized social systems is derived from research on fairly small groups, but larger groups and organizations are assumed to operate in essentially the same way, and societies may be analyzed as complex systems made up of many interrelated groups. Practical considerations make it difficult for the social scientist to investigate large and complex systems precisely or in detail, so there has evolved a branch of experimental social psychology known as *group dynamics*. This area of study concerns itself with systems that have come to be known glibly as "small groups." However, it is not easy to answer directly the question, "How large is a 'small group'?" A half facetious answer is perhaps the most appropriate: the number of people who comprise a small group is "greater than the graces" (three) and "fewer than the muses" (nine). At least this is a fair description of the research commonly called "small groups studies."

The question of how many individuals are required for the emergence of a group may be answered in several ways. Even two individuals may develop an organized mode of relationship, as in the case of a marriage. Such two-person groups are called *diads*. However, systems with three or more participants have several added dimensions. A third party affords an audience for interactions between the other two. Each person may be not only directly but also indirectly related to each of the others because the third party can be a mediator between the first two. Among three people, factions are possible. Thus there are several reasons for differentiating diads from groups of three or more. In general the kinds of organized social systems that are the major focus of group dynamics are those involving at least three people.

Three essential properties of organization define a social group: a set of standard "rules of conduct" (*norms*) that regulate both the group and its individual members (Chapter 10); a *structure,* made up of relationships among the behavioral roles of individual members (Chapter 11); and *performance* as a unitary system (Chapter 12). The working definition of a group for social psychology can be stated this way: *a social-psychological group is an organized system of two or more individuals who are interrelated so that the system performs some function, has a standard set of role relationships among its members, and has a set of norms that regulate the function of the group and each of its members.*

10

REFERENCE GROUPS AND CONFORMITY

When a person is a member of a social system, usually he accepts and adheres to the standards of behavior set by that system. If he refuses to do so, he may find himself a part of the group or society in name and body, but not psychologically. This distinction between being physically present in an aggregate of people and being a psychological member of a social group is a very important issue in the study of group dynamics. In social psychology, one is not regarded as truly a member of a group unless he is fully participating in the group's systematic organization. There are many ways in which social psychology has explored these powerful effects of the group system upon the behavior of individual group members.

REFERENCE GROUPS

During the 1930s Theodore Newcomb investigated the function of psychological reference groups in influencing an individual's attitudes and opinions, and demonstrated the crucial importance of the distinction between psychological *reference* groups and mere nominal *membership* groups (Newcomb, 1950). Most people develop somewhat more liberal political and economic perspectives as they become better educated

---

REFERENCE GROUPS AND ATTITUDES

Between 1935 and 1939 more than 600 women (the entire student body at Bennington College, Vermont) were studied with respect to relationships between their behavior and attitudes, and their assimilation into the college community. The essential facts about the Bennington membership group were

1. It was small: data could be obtained from every member.
2. It was insulated: college facilities included a post office, beauty parlor, cooperative store, and a wide range of recreational opportunities, so that the average student visited the 4-mile distant village about once a week.
3. It was self-conscious and enthusiastic, in part because it was new.
4. It was unusually active and concerned about public issues: the faculty felt that its educational duties included the familiarizing of an oversheltered student body with the implications of a depression-torn America and a war-threatened world.
5. It was relatively homogeneous with respect to the students' home backgrounds: tuition was expensive, and a majority of students came from urban, economically privileged families whose sociopolitical attitudes were conservative.

Attitude toward public affairs were selected as the criterion for adaptation to the college community. Observations and various self-report measures showed a consistent shift from conservatism during the students' freshman year to nonconservatism during the senior year. For example, during the 1936 presidential election, 62 percent of the freshmen and only 14 percent of the juniors and seniors "voted" for the Republican candidate, 29 percent of the freshmen and 54 percent of the juniors and seniors for Roosevelt, and 9 percent of the freshmen as compared to 30 percent of the juniors and seniors for the Socialist or Communist candidates. The major device for the assessment of conservatism, which consistently showed that seniors were less conservative than freshmen, was the specially designed scale of Political and Economic Progressivism (PEP), which dealt with issues made prominent by the New Deal, such as unemployment, public relief, and the rights of organized labor.

Sociometric choice data ("name five students most worthy to represent the college") and PEP scores showed that *individual prestige was associated with nonconservatism* in each of the three classes (freshman, junior, and senior). It was assumed that the conspicuously displayed attitudes of nonconservatism by leaders of the community (teachers and students) and the majority of the student body would serve as a point of reference for the acquisition of political and economic attitudes in students. To explore this point of reference, students' reputations among their colleagues for citizenship in the college community were used to classify them as *highly identified* ("absorbed in college community affairs"), *indifferent* ("indifferent to activities of student committees"), or *resistant* ("resistant to community expectations"). These measures, along with information about students' awareness of differences between their own attitudes and those of their fellow students, afforded determination of the students' reference to both the home and the college community with respect to their political attitudes. Some students reacted to a membership group as a *positive reference group* (their attitudes were directly influenced); others reacted to a membership group as a *negative reference group* (their attitudes were inversely influenced); and others did not use the membership group as a reference group at all (their attitudes were independent of reference group influences). Table 10–1 (adapted from data in Newcomb [1947]) summarizes some typical comments of students in each of these categories.

Table 10–1 Summary of Reactions to Reference Groups

Reference Group Value of the Home and Family	Reference Group Value of the College Community		
	Positive Reference Group	*No Reference Group*	*Negative Reference Group*
Positive Reference Group	"It was really wonderful that I could agree with all the people I respected here and at the same time move in the direction that my home friends were going."	"All that's really important that has happened to me occurred outside of college, so I never became very susceptible to college influences."	"I wanted to disagree with all the noisy liberals . . . so I built up a wall inside me against what they said. . . . I decided to stick to my father's ideas."
No Reference Group	"I had been allowed so much independence by my parents that I needed desperately to identify myself with an institution with which I could conform conscientiously. Bennington was perfect."	"I'm not rebelling against anything. . . . I'm just doing what I had to do to stand on my own feet intellectually."	"Probably the feeling that [my] instructors didn't accept me led me to reject their opinions."
Negative Reference Group	"I started rebelling against my pretty stuffy family. . . . I took sides with the faculty immediately. . . . It provided just what I needed by way of family rebellion."	"I accepted liberal attitudes here because I had always secretly felt that my family was narrow and intolerant."	"All my life I have resented the protection of governesses and parents. . . . The easy superficiality with which so many prestige-hounds here go 'liberal' only forced me to think it out more intensely."

A follow-up study over 20 years later revealed a remarkable consistency of political attitudes among the women who had graduated from Bennington College. The single factor that contributed most to these women's maintenance of either liberal or conservative attitudes throughout the years was the selection of husbands, friends, and a general social environment supportive of their existing political beliefs.

NEWCOMB (1950, 1957)

(see Chapter 4), and Newcomb was especially interested in factors leading to changes in political and economic opinions when an individual became involved in the social organization of a college student body. In his now-classic "Bennington study," Newcomb studied patterns of change in political and economic attitudes of a population of girls enrolled at a small, relatively isolated women's college in Vermont. Bennington College was established as a seat of liberal and progressive political thought, and Newcomb thought it paradoxical that most of its students came from conservative upper-middle-class business and professional families. His investigations showed that, indeed, the Bennington student body gradually came to function as a reference group for girls who enrolled there. As freshmen the girls remained fairly conservative in their political and economic views, but as they progressed to upper-class status, their views became increasingly progressive or liberal. Interviews revealed that as freshmen they tended to remain psychologically members of the old reference groups from which they had come (their Wall Street families or conservative suburban or preparatory school societies) even though they were nominally members of the Bennington student body. As seniors their nominal membership had grown into genuine psychological participation in the student body, accompanied by increasing acceptance of its values and attitudes. Of course not all of the girls accepted the student body as an appropriate reference group: some rejected it actively. For some the student body provided a negative reference group, a point of contrast for personal attitudes and opinions. But the central significance of Newcomb's investigation is the lucid distinction between *psychological* membership and *nominal* membership in a group. Participation in an organized group brings changes in an individual's attitudes, values, opinions, and behavior in the direction of the group's norms.

SOCIAL NORMS

Perhaps the most evident characteristic of any organized group is the set of devices through which it attempts to maintain uniformity among its members. Even the Senate of the United States is an organization characterized by the operation of strict informal norms. Back in the 1950s, at the height of extreme McCarthyism and paranoid witch-hunting for communists in the United States Government, W. S. White (1956) described the Senate hearings on Senator McCarthy as constituting more than just a trial—they involved the determination of "the degree that a member had transgressed the rules, written or not, and the spirit of the club to which he belonged." In a way, the ambivalence and controversy over the guilt of William Calley in connection with the military massacre at Mi Lai in Vietnam also involved debate over the validity of the informal norms and codes of conduct in the military organization. In connection with the McCarthy episode, White further pointed out that after the hearings had been completed, "when McCarthy rose to speak there was in the chamber that rarest of all demonstrations, a demonstration of conscious disorder and inattention." Even the Senate could tolerate only a limited amount of deviation within its ranks.

The term *norm* as used in group dynamics refers to standardized rules of conduct that are accepted by participants in the group as legitimate specifications of the expected function of the group as a system as well as of each member within the system. Group norms regulate the performance of the group as an organized unit, keeping it on the course of its pursuit of particular objectives. Norms also regulate the differentiated but interrelated functions of individual members of the group, in which case they are often called "role expectations." Like other aspects of a group's organization, norms may be either *formal* (as in the case of a written constitution or by-

OLD NORMS NEVER DIE, THEY JUST FADE AWAY

The stability of norms was studied in a laboratory experiment on conformity. Experimental confederates in a group of subjects helped to establish a new group norm (consensual agreement to judge a line as 15.5 inches long instead of previous judgments averaging 3.8 inches). The confederates were then progressively replaced by new members who stayed in the group from two to four blocks of trials, or "generations." The previously established normative "tradition" persisted through four to five generations after the last confederate was replaced, before dissipating (returning to the original average judgment) by the sixth generation.

JACOBS AND CAMPBELL (1961)

laws) or *informal* (as in the case of unstated, more or less "intuitively" accepted conventions).

Group norms are generally conservative mechanisms that tend to maintain the status quo. They have considerable functional value in maintaining the organization of a group, preserving the stability of its structure, and holding it on the course toward its objectives. However, changed conditions or the occurrence of unexpected events may necessitate reorganization within the group and revisions of its structure and functioning. When changes are required, sometimes the established group norms impede the adjustment of the group to new conditions. It is possible for strong group norms to introduce a kind of conservative rigidity, which eventually interferes with, rather than facilitates, its overall performance.

It is easy to overlook the fact that group norms define not only *prescribed rules of conduct* but also *ranges of acceptable variation* around that prescription. The norms and standards that a group evolves rarely involve complete and inflexible demands that every individual must "toe the line" and completely adhere to every norm.

Group norms regulate both diversity and uniformity within the group by prescribing rules of conduct for individual members. Uniformity of individual behavior within a group may stem from a variety of sources. For one thing, the group environment provides some influence. Furthermore, members usually are exposed simultaneously to the same general patterns of stimulation from events that confront the group. Members of a Boy Scout troop, for example, tend to be influenced by the same agents of socialization, by the same kinds of activities, and by the same kinds of presentation of information about the world. Homogeneity of behavior among members of the troop develops in part because each member is individually influenced by the same kinds of forces surrounding the group, and not necessarily because of factors within the group.

There are at least two important ways in which group norms induce uniformity of behavior. First, group standards provide information and guidance to the individual about matters he cannot handle independently. One may act like others in a group simply because he is uncertain as to how he should otherwise behave; he may merely look to others for *information* about possible actions that will be effective in meeting the circumstances. Second, group norms may be a key to acceptance by others in the group. One may adhere to group norms because he feels that some kind of advantage is to be gained by behaving as others expect or wish him to. This advantage may satisfy his own personal goals, or it may simply be the reward of social acceptance in the group with interpersonal approval and nurturance. Thus the influence of group norms on the individual may stem from the quest for *agreement*. A large amount of research has suggested that both processes operate in all kinds of interpersonal social influence. Some formally organized groups have formal mechanisms for exclu-

COMMUNICATION, DEVIATION, REJECTION

Experimental groups were given a human relations problem in which the delinquent behavior of a boy was described with a series of suggested reactions ranging from extremely mild to extremely severe condemnation. The group's task was to decide which penalty should be applied. In every group, one experimental confederate attempted to voice the general attitude of the group ("norm-voicer"), another took the opposite role, but after a while weakened and joined the group in its decision (the "slider"), and a third (the "deviator") opposed the group's opinion and did not change his mind. Initially there was a sharp increase in communication toward the deviator, primarily in the form of attempts to persuade him to join the group's decision. Toward the end of the hour, there was a considerable drop of communication toward the deviator, implying the loss of psychological membership in the group. For some reason the slider occupied an enviable position, perhaps because he had shown his "reasonableness." Repetition of this study in Holland, Sweden, France, Norway, Belgium, and Germany showed similar results.

SCHACHTER (1951)
SCHACHTER, NUTTIN, DEMONCHAUX, MAUCORPS, OSMER, DUIJKER, ROMMETVEIT, AND ISRAEL
(1954)

sion of deviates who violate group norms: one may be excommunicated from the Roman Catholic Church for heresy, or one may be deported from a nation for violation of its laws. In informal groups, however, exclusion of a deviate is much more subtle. He may not be denied physical membership in the group, but he can nevertheless be denied psychological membership by "freezing him out" of a role within the organized structure and by excluding him from communication within it.

During the early stages of group organization, as norms are being crystallized and structure stabilized, excessive communication is directed toward deviates, apparently to bring them into greater concordance with the group's norms. Refusal to accept and abide by group norms, however, eventually reduces the amount of communication addressed to the deviate. Eventually the deviate may be virtually excluded from communication within the group. Psychologically he becomes an isolate, with no effective position in the group. Among factory employees who are paid a base rate according to the average output of the work group, both overproduction (which threatens to elevate the base line) and underproduction (which means that some get paid for work they do not do) are discouraged forms of deviation.

Scientific exploration of the processes involved in the formation and change of individual attitudes has consistently accentuated the importance of group norms and standards in producing uniform attitudes and values among members who belong to the same psychological groups. Newcomb's Bennington study, described earlier in this chapter, showed how a social group provides a frame of reference (both to com-

HOW TO BING A RATEBUSTER

Prevailing norms for production in informal work groups in industrial plants showed that individual members were expected to produce within a limited range, and that the "ratebuster" who exceeded that norm was viewed with disfavor. Among the various corrective attempts to reduce the ratebuster's output were disapproval, ridicule, scorn, warnings, and "binging"—striking him lightly on the upper arm.

ROETHLISBERGER AND DICKSON (1939)

REFERENCE GROUP BLUES

Groups of Jewish and groups of Protestant college women were individually tested
for pain endurance by means of a blood-pressure measuring apparatus. In the
experimental condition each member was casually told that her ability to bear pain
was generally lower than the ability displayed by outgroup members. Upon retest,
the "tolerable pain limit" displayed by both groups was higher.

LAMBERT, LIBMAN, AND POSER (1960)

municate information and to set standards for social approval) in determining political attitudes.

A frequently overlooked but vitally important function of group norms is the regulation of diversity within the group. Differentiation of roles and stabilization of relationships among roles are possible only because norms regulate the patterns of interaction among members. Role expectations involve pressures toward uniformity of
behavior (as in dedicated pursuit of the common objective), but they also involve
normative pressures that maintain differences among roles. For example, groups often
evolve informal norms about both the nature and extent of communication between
individuals in high and low positions. One member may be bound by expectations to
behave in one way, and another in a different way. An individual who violates the
expectations for his unique behavior in his own role may be punished as severely by
the group (in terms of rejection and disapproval) as one who violates the general
norms (Roethlisberger & Dickson, 1939).

Under certain conditions, however, a kind of immunity may be granted to one with
good past performance. By functioning in accord with the group's norms, a member
gains status, prestige, and respect. By behaving consistently in valued ways that contribute to the effective performance of the group, he may ascend to a position of high
status. He may then be granted extra latitude for occasional deviation from norms.
Hollander (1960) has termed this latitude *idiosyncrasy credit.* The high-status member accumulates "credits" that allow him freedom for occasional idiosyncratic deviations from the norms of the group without threat of rejection. This allowance affords
the member an important kind of power to influence the overall operation of the
group. It enables him to introduce innovations and to change the direction of the
group in ways that would otherwise not be permitted. This phenomenon of idiosyncrasy credit does not necessarily represent a suspension of the group's norms with
respect to certain members; instead, it represents merely a change in the latitude of
acceptable variation around the group norm. The normative standards for expected
behavior remain the same for the group as a whole, but for the high-status member,
deviance is temporarily permitted because his past record of congruence has earned
him a reputation of eventual return to congruence with the major standards of the
group.

Group norms often influence the goals an individual sets for himself, and the direction and level of his aspirations and hopes (Coffin, 1941). Under some circumstances
an individual may lack sufficient information to permit him to set his goals and anticipate his level of performance realistically; in such cases he may look to the standards
of performance of a reference group with which he can identify psychologically in
order to estimate his probability of success. Furthermore one may sometimes express certain goals and aspirations publicly merely because he wishes to be congruent with the aspirations and goals of his group.

Group norms often influence behavior not merely with respect to activity within the
group, but even extending into other areas. Lewin (1947), in a series of related
studies during World War II, demonstrated several ways in which group discussion

---

IDIOSYNCRASY CREDIT?

A group member's "idiosyncrasy credit" is the positive relationship between his rise in status (by showing competence and by conforming to expectancies of others) and the accumulation of positive impressions ("credits") that allow him to deviate with increasingly greater impunity. Four-person groups of college students were given a choice task that required fifteen trials. A confederate subject in each group contrived to be correct on all but four trials, thus reflecting considerable task competence. His competence, however, was achieved through methods that violated conformity procedures agreed upon by each group in pretrial discussions. Nevertheless, subsequent ratings designed to assess the confederate's influence showed increasingly higher positive ratings of the confederate by the others (as "credit" accrued), despite his lack of conformity.

HOLLANDER (1960)

---

and decision influenced the subsequent behavior of those who participated, even though the group never met again. When pressures were exerted to influence someone to change his behavior in some prescribed way, a direct request (even when made by a supposed expert authority) was less effective in inducing the change than was participation in a group discussion of the proposed change. Thus it appears that group discussion permits the operation of some additional highly persuasive source of influence. This persuasive resource within the group stems from the operation of normative influences. During discussion the group evolves a set of standards that prescribe the change, and these norms appear to be more effective in influencing behavior than the advice of an authority.

These studies were somewhat primitive and subject to several kinds of criticism. Because there was some likelihood that the very fact of group discussion led the individuals to expect that they might later be questioned about their behavior, Levine and Butler (1932) ruled aside this differential factor and found that group discussion still remained a more effective means of inducing change. Unfortunately, in some of the early studies people were merely asked to express willingness to make a prescribed change, rather than observed directly to see if they actually did. To circumvent some of these critical flaws and to be more precise about specific factors in group discussion responsible for influencing the individual, Bennett (1955) conducted an investigation that allowed her to conclude that group discussion encourages the individual to make a decision in his own mind as to whether he will carry out the prescribed action, forces the individual to make public his decision as a commitment to action, and conveys the impression that the group has adopted the recommended action as a norm or standard for expected behavior. A number of related investigations in industrial and laboratory settings show that even indirect or vicarious participation in group discussion by means of representative agents produces similar influences on the individual (Coch & French, 1948; French, Israel, & As, 1960). Such factors as very strong initial commitments counter to the recommended action may, however, suppress the effectiveness of group discussion in inducing individual change (Willerman, 1943; see also Chapter 4).

SOCIAL CONFORMITY

One major problem in studying conformity to social norms has been the lack of precise and clear-cut definitions. Different labels have been used inconsistently to designate several similar kinds of social influences on an individual's behavior.

DECISION, ACTION, AND NORMS

During World War II a group of psychologists headed by Kurt Lewin conducted a series of studies of the influence of decisions made by groups upon an individual's readiness to change his behavior. Most of the studies dealt with changes in established food habits, but their design and theoretical prediction allowed for further generalization of findings.

Culturally influenced food preferences and aversions are deep-seated and particularly resistant to change. Because wartime conditions had caused certain food shortages, an attempt was made to convince housewives to use such "unpalatable" food items as beef hearts, sweetbreads, and kidneys. The experimental situation involved six Red Cross groups of volunteers ranging in size from thirteen to seventeen members. Only 45 minutes was available to the experimenter to achieve his purpose. In one condition, three groups attended lectures by expert nutritionists in an attractive setting, with mimeographed material including a variety of recipes adding to the lecturers' emphasis on the palatability and healthful aspects of these kinds of meat. The other three groups participated in discussions about "housewives like themselves" and the effect of introducing food changes in general, the husband's possible reaction, the smell of cooking and manner of preparation of sweetbreads, beef hearts, and kidneys. In the early part of the experiment a census was taken of how many women had served any of these foods in the past, and at the end of the meeting they were asked to indicate by show of hands how many were willing to try one of these foods within the next week. A follow-up study showed that only 3 percent of the women who had heard the lectures served one of the "unpalatable" meats, whereas after the group decision 32 percent served one of them (see Figure 10–1).

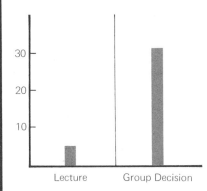

Figure 10–1 Percentage of individuals serving type of food never served before, after lecture and after group decision. (Redrawn from "Group Decision and Social Change" by Kurt Lewin from *Readings in Social Psychology* edited by Theodore M. Newcomb and Eugene L. Hartley. Copyright 1947 by Holt, Rinehart and Winston, Inc. Reproduced by permission of Holt, Rinehart and Winston, Inc.)

The demonstrated effectiveness of *group decision* over *individual decision* could have involved several factors. Group discussion (if initiated and conducted correctly) allows for greater *involvement* and *freedom of decision* for the individual participant than does lecturing. Increased involvement may in turn lead to increased *motivation*. The fact-to-face group situation tends to make the individual unwilling to depart from *group standards*. Expectations concerning subsequent follow-up monitoring of individual behavior may vary. Finally, because the lectures were conducted by expert nutritionists, and the groups by an experienced group leader, the problem of *leader personality* should be taken into consideration. Subsequent studies revealed that expectations about follow-ups, as well as the personality of the leader, were negligible factors in accounting for the original findings. These effects were not limited to the three kinds of foods originally discussed, nor to tightly knit groups. The effectiveness of group decision was found to persist even after 4 weeks.

Of particular interest was one study in which subjects were mothers who had had their first child and were leaving the hospital. Prior to leaving, these women met *individually* with expert nutritionists who gave them specific advice as to what kinds of food their babies should be fed. Despite the individual attention given to the

(Continued on p. 262)

women, a follow-up check showed that among another group of mothers, with whom the group decision method was employed, the nutritionists' advice was more frequently followed (Figure 10–2). The effect seemed to be increasingly persistent over time.

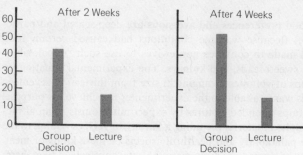

Figure 10–2 Percentage of mothers reporting an increase in the consumption of fresh milk, after 2 weeks and after 4 weeks. (Redrawn from "Group Decision and Social Change" by Kurt Lewin from *Readings in Social Psychology* edited by Theodore M. Newcomb and Eugene L. Hartley. Copyright 1947 by Holt, Rinehart and Winston. Reproduced by permission of Holt, Rinehart and Winston, Inc.)

If the necessary leadership skills and appropriate situational conditions are provided, it appears that group discussion can have useful and important implications for decision-making processes in industry, medicine, and other areas of social management.

LEWIN (1947)

(These include conformity, suggestion, compliance, persuasion, acquiescence, submission, and imitation.) Once it was common to think of socially influenced behavior as motivated by instincts to conform or to imitate, but these simplified notions of socially influenced behavior have been discarded.

Suggestion (or suggestibility) has been very poorly defined in psychology. In the beginnings of clinical psychology, Charcot (1894), Sidis (1898), and other French physicians conceived of hysteria as a form of behavioral disorder characterized by heightened suggestibility, related to Mesmer's notions of "animal magnetism." But this early concept included much more than susceptibility to the influences of other individuals and groups; it also embraced a notion of generally increased sensitivity or responsivity to *any* kind of stimulation. This broad concept of suggestion has persisted. For example, Hollingworth (1920), Titchener (1910), Binet (1900), and others studied suggestibility by measuring response to a variety of kinds of minimal stimulation from either social or nonsocial sources. In social psychology, however, a more restrictive definition of social suggestibility is required.

Demonstrations of normative pressures on the individual were reported in the early literature of social psychology. H. Clark (1916) brought a small stoppered bottle into a classroom and asked the students to indicate when they smelled the liquid. A few seconds after he removed the stopper someone in the first row smelled it; shortly thereafter, students in the second row indicated that they smelled it; after 3 minutes, a total of 33 of the 168 students (predominantly seated in front on one side of the classroom) had indicated that they had smelled the liquid. At that point, Clark informed the class that the bottle contained only pure, odorless, distilled water. Thus, the students had responded not only to Clark's initial suggestion that an odor would be detected, but also to the normative influences of other students around them. Similarly, several early studies of the phenomenon of *social facilitation* (Munsterberg, 1914; F. H. Allport, 1924; Jenness, 1932) demonstrated "bandwagon" effects in which members of groups influenced the judgments and actions of one another. Extensive experimental investigation of the influence of group norms on the individual in laboratory settings did not occur, however, until the 1930s. F. H. Allport (1934) reported a series of field investigations of individual conformity to institutionalized social norms such as customs and traditions. From observing the adherence of people to such conventions as stopping at traffic signs, punching a time clock at work at a prescribed time, or performing ritualistic acts upon entering a church, Allport concluded that people as a whole were remarkably subject to group pressures even in casual everyday behavior.

During the 1930s Sherif (1966) initiated an important set of laboratory studies of social norms. He made clever use of an unusual optical phenomenon, the *autokinetic effect,* which occurs when one views a tiny source of light in an otherwise totally dark visual field. Under such conditions a stationary point of light appears to move about, sometimes jerking, sometimes vibrating, or sometimes moving in long sweeps. Most people with normal vision experience this illusion readily, and it is particularly difficult to try to estimate the distance of the apparent movement. When judgments are expressed individually, most people report some movement, with varying distance estimates, and their estimates tend to gradually stabilize with repeated exposure to the illusion. But Sherif wished to study how social influences affect such judgments, so he arranged for his subjects to hear the reported judgments of other people in the same situation. Under these conditions individual estimates were profoundly influenced by the overheard judgments of others. In very ambiguous and unstructured situations (which afford no stable frame of reference for judgment), people often refer to group norms for informational guidance in making judgments. Further extensions of these studies have suggested many ways in which instability of external frames of reference enhance one's susceptibility to social influences.

A different kind of experimental study of group norms and individual judgment was carried out by S. E. Asch (1956). Sherif had explored conformity to norms in judgments of very ambiguous and ill-defined phenomena, whereas Asch looked at conformity in highly structured and unambiguous situations. He arranged a set of simple perceptual judgments that were very easy for the average person. He established this fact prior to beginning his experiments by showing that most subjects had no trouble making the judgments correctly and confidently when they performed the task independently. But in the experimental studies, he arranged for the subject to confront a unanimous majority of colleagues while they all reported erroneous judgments. Asch found that under such conditions his subjects could be induced to report wildly incorrect judgments. Thus his investigations demonstrate the influence of group norms on the individual's behavior even when he has clearly defined standards for determining appropriate behavior in the situation. In this context the influential effect of the group on the individual's judgments stems primarily from efforts to seek agreement with the group and avoid embarrassing consequences attached to deviation.

Both Asch's and Sherif's investigations demonstrate the potent influence of group norms on behavior as one interacts with others. Although sharply contrasted in method as well as in the kind of social influence observed, both investigations describe the operation of group norms in producing uniformity of behavior. These important early programs of investigation steered the course of a great deal of psychological research concerning conformity to group norms.

CONFORMITY TO SOCIAL NORMS

An important series of studies of the influence of group attitudes and norms on the judgments of individuals was conducted by Muzafer Sherif during the 1930s. Male college students were asked to observe the apparent movement of a tiny point of light at a distance of about 20 feet. In reality the light was not moving at all: the subjects unknowingly reacted to the perceptual phenomenon of *autokinesis,* an illusory movement of a stationary point of light in the dark. The subjects pressed a key linked to the experimenter when they perceived movement, and the experimenter controlled the opening of a shutter over the hole in the box. After the light was thus made to disappear, each subject reported orally his estimate of the distance in inches through which the light had "moved."

The responses of subjects working alone were recorded. They showed great individual differences, but on repetition individual norms and ranges of estimates *peculiar to each* individual were rapidly established. Similarly, when subjects responded in two- or three-man *groups* in varying order, a group norm and range were also rapidly established. When subjects moved from one experimental condition (being alone) to another (being in a group), there was a tendency for the responses of the individuals in each group to converge around the group norm. This occurred more slowly for subjects who had worked alone prior to working in a group than for subjects who made their first set of judgments in a group. Subjects who worked alone *after* having first been in a group continued to adhere to the group norm, although to a lesser degree than when they were actually with the group. Either way, Sherif conceived this pattern of convergence of individual norms around the group norm as a reflection of *suggestibility* of individual members to the social influence generated by the entire group.

Such suggestibility was apparent in the *majority* of subjects, although they were unaware of such behavior. The social influence effects were independent of contrived manipulations by the experimenter, unlike the experiments conducted by S. E. Asch (1956) in different settings. In subsequent experiments Sherif demonstrated that by "planting" confederate subjects in the group, the judgment of individual members could be influenced toward almost any norm or range.

Despite the consistency in Sherif's findings, the experimental situation is, according to Sherif himself, "simply one unstable, *unstructured* situation that is new for the subject," rather than a "pressing social situation as found in the reality of everyday life." An indispensable aspect of daily life is the feedback information that a perceiver obtains from the situation itself, as well as from the other individuals with whom he interacts, before making a judgment. Inasmuch as the experimental situation in the Sherif study was so unstructured as to practically eliminate any feedback properties, it is possible that the social influence observed was a function of *information-seeking* (rather than norm-seeking): failing to get information from the situation, subjects tried to obtain it from each other. Presumably, if proper feedback is available, social influence effects are much reduced. Subsequent research has tended to support this contention: discrediting information about other group members, advance information that the stimulus light would "move" intermittently, information of the subject's success or failure after each trial experience with a moving light immediately preceding autokinesis, and disorientation of the individual's frame of reference—all of these affect the extent of social influence effects on judgments of autokinetic movement.

SHERIF (1966)

A MINORITY OF ONE

Independence and submission to group pressure in judgmental tasks concerning a simple, clear matter of fact were studied by Solomon Asch in the early 1950s. The experimental task was ostensibly labeled as an experiment in visual perception. Seven-, eight-, and nine-man groups of male college students were seated around a table and asked to state publicly, one after another, which of three lines on various cards matched a standard line on another card. Figure 10–3 shows a typical pair

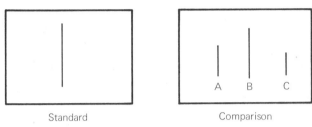

Standard   Comparison

Figure 10–3 A pair of stimulus cards typical of those used by Asch (1956).

of stimulus cards. Except for one naive or "critical" subject, all other members in a given group were preinstructed confederate subjects. The naive subject was maneuvered into sitting either at the end of the table or next to the end. The confederate subjects were instructed to be unanimous (upon experimenter's cues) in their pronouncement of an inaccurate judgment, which they were to deliver in a detached and impersonal manner.

When the judgment of the confederate subjects was *unanimously* incorrect, about 37 percent of the 123 naive subjects erred by compromising, or *yielding* to the group's incorrect judgment. Thus, unlike Sherif's findings, the majority of subjects displayed nonyielding or independent behavior. Yielding was maximized with an 8-inch standard line and minimized with a 3-inch standard line, but in general, as the discrepancy between the standard and comparison lines increased, yielding decreased. However, those who displayed yielding did so consistently, from the very start. Neither repetitive accurate nor repetitive inaccurate majority judgment succeeded in bringing about subsequent changes in the overall judgment pattern. However, yielding decreased sharply when the naive subject was allowed to respond in writing, presumably because private commitment tends to alleviate group pressure. Yielding rate approached a ceiling with majorities of three persons. Unanimous majorities of four, eight, or fifteen produced no more yielding than did a unanimous majority of three.

The effect of *nonunanimous* majorities on the behavior of the typical subject was quite different. The early introduction of a dissenting confederate subject drastically reduced yielding, but if the dissenter later "deserted" the naive subject and joined the incorrect majority, yielding was restored to its full force. A complete reversal of the experimental design—that is, one confederate subject voicing incorrect judgments in the presence of a naive majority—caused amusement and derisive comments among the naive subjects.

During postexperimental interviews, many subjects (yielders *and* independents) tended, perhaps defensively, to underestimate the frequency of their committed errors. Two kinds of independent behavior occurred—one of *strength* or one *without confidence*. Independence of strength was accompanied by a high degree of self-confidence, distrust of the group, and strong efforts to remain independent. Independence without confidence was accompanied by a feeling that the group's judgment was correct, but because of the subject's sense of obligation to adhere to the instructions to report what he saw, he ignored the group. Yielding at the *perceptual level* occurred when the subject seemed to have convinced himself that he

(Continued on
p. 266)

actually saw the lines the way the group members stated their judgments. Yielding at the perceptual level occurred rarely, primarily in subjects who displayed a lack of trust in themselves and unawareness of having yielded. Yielding at the *judgmental level* occurred frequently, either because the subject was simply not sure that he understood the task set for him or because he did not wish to spoil the experiment (akin to independence without confidence). Yielding at the *action level* occurred in subjects who were very much aware of their yielding behavior and uncomfortable about it, but persisted in it for fear of being excluded, ostracized, or considered eccentric.

Asch's interviews were exploratory and were not designed to measure specifically defined variables in a precise manner. His experimental design was rather rigid, and it restricted normal communication and feedback within the group. The role played by his instructed confederates was a difficult one, which may have varied slightly from one subject to the next. Nevertheless, his experimental situation represents a face-to-face confrontation with pressures to conform. This kind of situation is presumably more conducive to the elicitation of *norm-seeking* behavior (conformity for its own sake) than the experimental situations studied by Sherif. On the whole, Asch's findings do reflect everyday characteristics of conformity: most subjects did not yield; practically all subjects were aware of the type of behavior they consciously chose to display; and both independence and yielding were motivated by a variety of considerations.

S. E. ASCH (1956)

Normative and Informational Conformity

Early concepts of conformity tended to regard socially influenced behavior as having a single set of motivations in which conformity to norms was an end in itself. More recently, however, accumulating evidence has led to reformulation of the concept, with a more functional concern with means-end relationships and the purposive aspects of behavior. Conformity is now generally viewed as a mode (or set of modes) of behavior that may occur in connection with a variety of motivational bases.

A particularly useful distinction was proposed in 1955 by Deutsch and Gerard (1955), who described differences between *normative social influence* and *informational social influence.* The former occurs when one is influenced by others because he aspires to agree with them and to avoid violating their expectations of him; this kind of behavior represents an end in itself. The latter occurs when one is influenced by others because their influence is useful; this kind of conformity represents a means to some other end, and agreement is merely incidental to the utilization of other people as sources of useful guidance or information.

Other investigators still use different labels to describe forms of conforming behavior, but the labels proposed by Deutsch and Gerard are useful and appropriate. They are consistent with the implications of other investigations and theories. For example, Festinger (1953) discussed "social reality" (information-seeking) and "group locomotion" (pressures toward homogeneity within a group for its own sake) as two kinds of forces inducing uniformity within groups. Asch, describing various modes of yielding to unanimous group pressure on perceptual judgments, noted similar differences among incentives that operate in social influence. His descriptions of yielding at the "perceptual" and "judgment" levels suggest the operation of information-seeking motives to conform, and his discussion of yielding at the "action" level suggests the operation of agreement-seeking motives. A comparative psychologist, Riopelle (1960), has criticized students of human social psychology for having been slower to evolve differentiations of conforming behavior than their colleagues studying animal behavior, and has suggested a distinction between duplicative or blindly imitative behavior (agreement-seeking) and observational learning (information-seeking). Thibaut and Kelley (1959) and Kelman (1958) have distinguished three forms of social influence: *compliance, identification,* and *internalization.* The compliant type of influence emphasizes external conditions that induce one individual to accept the influence of another; identification is described as an influence process based on agreement-seeking or identity-seeking; and internalization is described as a process based on information-seeking.

In the overall picture, then, although contemporary theorists have used different kinds of language to describe the differentiated processes that induce a person to accept the influence of others around him, there is general consensus that at least two broad categories of social influence must be differentiated: normative influence, which involves motivation to seek agreement with others as an end in itself, and informational influence, which involves motivation to accept the influence of others as an instrumentally useful means of attaining the individual's own ends or objectives.

Conformity, Independence, and Rebellion

Another kind of distinction among various forms of socially influenced behavior is also useful. Early research on conformity to group norms focused on acceptance of social influence and conforming behavior. The other side of the coin, the rejection of the influence of others, was left aside. But nonconformity has recently become a target of research. Psychologists recognize the importance of distinguishing true independence (indifference to the normative expectations of other people or groups) from rebellion (direct rejection of those expectations). Although both independence and rebellion represent nonconforming behavior, they are by no means identical. *Conformity* occurs when one is sensitive to group norms and the expectations of others and adheres to the norms and meets the expectations. *Rebellion* occurs when one is likewise aware of such norms and expectations, but rejects the norms and acts contrary to expectations. True *independence* is very different from either of these because it represents indifference to the norms and expectations of others. This kind of rebellious behavior has also been named *counterformity* (Krech, Crutchfield, & Ballachey, 1962) or *anticonformity* (Willis & Hollander, 1964). Everyone has experienced both of these in himself and others.

Sometimes a particular kind of behavior within a different social context may represent any or all of these kinds of response to social norms. During the 1960s, for example, hair length came to be a very important personal symbol for many young men. Conventional norms in most Western cultures for nearly a century dictated that males should wear their hair short enough to expose the ears, so young people used hair as a means of expressing rejection of the dominant "establishment" culture. Blond or dark, straight or curly, silky or wiry, Anglo or Afro, young men avoided barbers and nourished their hair in every way possible to grow blatantly long tresses. As this symbolic rebellion took hold, the youth "counterculture" emerged as a coherent social system with norms of its own. Other young people, desiring to establish their indentity with the youth movement, adopted this norm and conformed to it eagerly. This visible rejection of a norm recognized so clearly by both the establishment and the counterculture led to countless controversies—from parent-child conflicts to school and community conflicts. Eventually the dominant culture began to accept new standards of hair length, absorbing them as establishment norms. When this happened, the symbolic rebellion lost its visibility. Now, in the 1970s, hair length no longer visibly identifies one as either with or against the establishment. Instead, people more or less independently decide, for their own reasons, how they wish to wear their hair. The musical comedy *"Hair,"* very popular in the 1960s, was a chronicle of

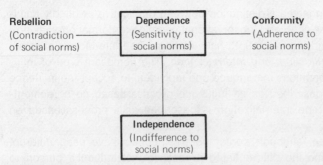

Figure 10–4 A model to distinguish conformity, rebellion and independence.

this symbolic importance of hair length to display rebellion (against the establishment) and conformity (to the counterculture).

Figure 10–4 shows how conformity, rebellion, and independence are related to one another. The axes of the T represent two underlying dimensions of response to social norms: sensitivity to the norms and expectations of others and decision to accept or reject those expectations. One can see from this that some kinds of rebellion are more closely related to conformity than to true independence. Independence and rebellion are alike because they both represent unconventional, nonconforming behavior. But they differ in other ways. Conformity and rebellion are alike because they both represent conditions when behavior is dependent on standards or expectations set by others; in one case, these expectations are accepted and met, but in the other they are rejected and defied. Often people who think of themselves as rebels are not at all independent. Their negative reactions may be highly dependent on being against some established norm, rather than for some independent and unorthodox alternative. Typically, adolescents are much more rebellious against their parents than independent of them. When one behaves truly independently, sometimes he is likely to be in accord with social norms, but sometimes at odds with them. Only a conformist is consistently in accord with social norms of all kinds; likewise, only a rebel is consistently in violation of them.

Situations of Conformity

Perhaps the most crucial single variable affecting the occurrence of social influence is the ambiguity of the behavioral situation in which influence is exerted. One of the most important differences between Sherif's (1966) early investigations of social conformity and S. E. Asch's (1956) studies is that Sherif made use of highly ambiguous and unstructured situations in which there was little or no basis to permit one to arrive at a proper judgment without utilizing the judgments of others as guideposts or reference points. Asch chose to study an unambiguous and well-structured situation in which each individual was expected to be able to arrive at a correct judgment that differed from judgments expressed by others around him. For this reason, the investigations of Deutsch and Gerard (1955) and others during the 1950s (calling attention to the distinction between normative and informational forms of social influence) are especially critical. Consistently, studies of both ambiguous and unambiguous situations have found that people are a great deal more likely to conform in ambiguous, unstructured situations and tasks they find difficult, than in unambiguous, well-structured situations and tasks they find relatively easy. Manipulations that disorient the subject and confuse his frame of reference make him more susceptible to social influences of group norms. These observations support the concept of informational social influence, which suggests that one basis of conforming behavior is simply

---

DISORIENTED CONFORMITY

Male college students were subjected to conditions of situational uncertainty, first alone and then in groups, as follows: (1) a small room with a brief glimpse at its spatial arrangement; (2) a huge theater in total darkness with the subject being led to his seat; and (3) a maze that the subject had to work his way through in total darkness. The *norm* (median judgment) and the *variability* of size estimates were highest in condition (3) and lowest in condition (1). As situational uncertainty increased from condition (1) to condition (3), variability decreased and norm convergence increased as the subjects passed from the alone condition into the group condition.

SHERIF AND HARVEY (1952)

---

willingness to use judgments of others and norms of groups in which one participates as guideposts or frames of reference for making decisions.

The context in which one is subjected to pressures toward conformity also influences the kind of motivation that dominates his behavior. Motivational "sets" may be established when circumstances lead the individual to orient his behavior toward the attainment of certain specified objectives. In some situations the individual may be led to assume a set in which he recognizes agreement with others and uniformity within his group as important goals; in order to attain them he may become more susceptible to pressures to conform to group norms (Harvey & Consalvi, 1960). In other situations, however, the individual may assume a set in which he values independence, and orient himself toward striving for personal excellence and achievement. In such cases one may conform only when he elects to utilize the judgments of others or the norms of his group as a means to personal success (informational social influence). Arousal of the individual's motivation to strive for personal achievement may make him more resistant to pressures to conform in structured, unambiguous tasks he can easily do with his own resources, but more susceptible to group pressures in unstructured, ambiguous, or difficult tasks (McDavid, 1966b; McDavid & Sistrunk, 1964).

The manner in which one expresses his judgment or behavior is also related to his susceptibility to social influence. One is more likely to conform when he must display his response to these pressures publicly than when his response is concealed from the group or person attempting to influence him. Of course public acquiescence or compliance to group pressures is not necessarily accompanied by private influence: one may conform overtly and superficially, but remain uninfluenced in his own judg-

---

NUMBER 2 TRIES HARDER

Groups of delinquent boys were asked to estimate the distance between two simultaneous flashes of light in a dark room. Unknown to the subjects, the leader and either the second highest-in-status member or the lowest-status member were exposed to two flashes 48 inches apart, as compared to the two 12-inches-apart flashes observed by the rest of the group. To increase motivation, group rewards for accuracy were promised to the subjects. Under the assumption that all were seeing the same light, verbal pressure against deviants' judgments occurred because the subjects made their judgments aloud. The second highest-in-status member's responses indicated greater conformity to judgments of the other members than did those of either the leader or the lowest-status member.

HARVEY AND CONSALVI (1960)

---

ment. This kind of superficial overt conformity was typical of many of the subjects in Asch's experiment, in which college men were subjected to pressures to express ridiculous wrong judgments of simple perceptual problems in the presence of eight or nine peers. The kind of conformity described earlier as normative social influence (in which agreement with others is an end in itself) is likely to occur more readily when one's response to social pressures is public than when private (Deutsch & Gerard, 1955). On the other hand, informational social influence (in which one accepts the influence of other people or groups as a means to his own personal ends) is likely to occur as readily in private situations as in public situations. S. Milgram (1964) also distinguished between the superficial kinds of conformity that occur when a person merely wants to display agreement with others on trivial and unimportant issues ("signal conformity") and the more considered kinds of response to group norms and social pressures when the consequences of one's action are more significant and irrevocable ("action conformity").

Models for Conformity

Particular characteristics of the group or individual exerting influence on one may determine the likelihood that he will accept their influence. In the case of informational social influence, one is more likely to accept the influence of others whom he regards as particularly able or qualified in the behavioral activity that is influenced (Willis & Hollander, 1964). Information that leads a person to believe that his influencers have previously been successful in a task makes him more likely to accept their influence, especially if the task is ambiguous or difficult.

When informational social influence occurs, the expertise or prior success of the influencer is an important determinant of the effectiveness of social influence. But when normative social influence occurs (as, for example, in connection with very easy and unambiguous tasks), whether the influencer is particularly able or successful may become irrelevant. There is some evidence to suggest further that when informational conformity occurs, compromises between the individual's own personal judgment and that of his influencers are likely to occur. In contrast, when normative conformity occurs, with agreement with the influencer being the objective attained by accepting social influence, conformity to the source of influence is more likely to be complete and uncompromised.

People are more likely to conform to influencers whom they like personally or to groups to which they would like to belong. Thus conformity is especially likely to occur when it is a prerequisite to the individual's gaining acceptance by the individual or group influencing him. This relationship between conformity and personal attraction to a source of social influence is especially important in the occurrence of normative conformity: an individual is not likely to be concerned about attaining

---

CONFORMITY AND COMPETENCE

Judgments of line length were made by pairs of subjects. Feedback about the performance of each partner was manipulated by the experimenter according to a predetermined schedule. When the perceived competency of the partner was *maximized*—the subject was told that his partner had been correct in 90 percent of his judgments—the subject's *conformity* increased significantly on subsequent trials. When the perceived competency of the partner was minimized—the subject was told that in 90 percent of all judgments the partner was wrong—the subject's *counterconformity* (deliberate antithetical behavior) increased significantly.

WILLIS AND HOLLANDER (1964)

CONFORMITY AND CHARACTER

During the 1950s Richard Crutchfield developed a mechanical device (commonly referred to as the Crutchfield apparatus) to study independence and submission to group pressure. Members of five-man groups were seated side by side in individual booths screened from one another. Speaking to the experimenter or to one another was not allowed. Instead, each subject had in front of him a switch by which he could illuminate signals to indicate to the experimenter and to the other group members whether he agreed or disagreed with various statements presented to the group. Each subject read from a panel of signal lights before him the purported responses of the other members of the group. On certain occasions he was made to believe that he was the last of the four to express judgment. These reported "responses" of others were actually manipulated by the experimenter, who thus could create a unanimous bogus majority of four or any other combination. In a typical 1-hour session as many as fifty statements (facts, opinions, and attitudes, varying in difficulty or complexity) were given to the subjects for judgment.

Most people *yielded* to the judgment of a unanimous majority (whether correct or incorrect) on some items and not on others. However, a few subjects yielded on almost all statements, whereas some asserted their *independence* by yielding on none. As expected, yielding was greater on difficult items than on easy ones. The average amount of yielding over an hour-long session remained constant because some individuals became increasingly more yielding, and others became less so.

Some of Crutchfield's findings closely resemble those of S. E. Asch (1956) even though both investigators employed different procedures. For example, postexperimental interviews revealed that the self-confidence of those who maintained independence throughout the testing session was severely affected. Individual retesting after a group session seemed to alleviate the effects of group pressure as witnessed by a drastic decline in yielding behavior. Yet the yielding effect was essentially consistent and persistent: whereas feedback information to the subject in the form of a repudiation of the bogus majority judgment by expert authority lowered yielding behavior by a mere 15 percent, an increase of 25 percent (from 45 to 70 percent) occurred when expert authority confirmed the bogus majority judgment. Moreover, yielding occurred even on items that presumably had high personal or social relevance to the subject. For example, the statement "I doubt whether I would make a good leader" was not endorsed independently by a single army officer, but under unanimous peer-group pressure 37 percent of the officers expressed agreement with the statement.

College students, under unanimous peer group pressure, sometimes expressed agreement to rather bizarre statements: that 60 to 70 percent of all Americans are over 65; that the average American male is about 8 to 9 inches taller than the average American female, but has a life expectancy of only 25 years; that the average American eats six meals a day but sleeps only 4 to 5 hours a night.

These investigations were not limited to college students. Members of ethnic and racial minorities were found to display great conformity when the composition of the group emphasized their minority status. Females generally yielded more frequently than did males; in fact, as the testing session proceeded, most females displayed increased yielding behavior, whereas most males displayed a decrease. Yielding in females was also related to acquiescence to the traditional female role, whereas independence seemed to be accompanied by feelings of frustration and conflict concerning that role. The traditional male role was not related to yielding or independence. Regardless of the subjects employed, there were always some initially independent subjects who suddenly "broke down" (joined the bogus majority) and then became extreme yielders. Finally, observational ratings by expert psychologists who were unaware of the subjects' performances in the experimental situation described yielders as more submissive, inhibited, indecisive, lacking insight into their own motivation and behavior, confused, unadaptive under stress, and

(Continued on p. 272)

exploitable; independents were described as more efficient, ascendant, resourceful, active, outgoing, unaffected, self-reliant, imaginative, masculine, and sensuous.

Postexperimental interviews also suggested that the subjects did not attribute their conformity to pressures of the norm, lack of clarity of instructions, difficulty of stimulus materials, or complexity of the apparatus. They blamed the discrepancy either on others or on themselves, or denied that any conflict had existed at all. A considerable number of subjects (17 percent) displayed insight into the experimental deception, but Crutchfield's studies do not clearly indicate how this affected the general findings.

CRUTCHFIELD (1955)
TUDDENHAM AND McBRIDE (1959)

agreement for its own sake with a group or an individual about whom he cares little to establish a close interpersonal relationship. On the other hand, personal attraction to the source of influence is more or less irrelevant to the occurrence of informational social influence. An individual may be influenced by the judgment of people or groups about which he cares very little personally if he is merely using them as sources of information or guidance. One's regard for the ability of his influencers would be more important than his personal attraction to them in the case of information conformity. But personal attraction to the influencer is more important than regard for the influencer's ability in the case of normative conformity.

The influence of group norms on an individual increases as the size of the group majority increases. However, this is not a simple linear relationship: after a certain point (when the majority is sufficiently large to establish the group's norms clearly and unequivocally), further increases in the size of the majority do not increase the effectiveness of the norms in influencing individual behavior.

The degree of concurrence of the majority that defines a group norm is an important determinant of the effectiveness of the norm. Especially when normative social influence occurs, unanimity may be required before a norm effectively influences people. For example, in Asch's studies conformity to the majority norms required the

WHO CONFORMS, TO WHOM, AND WHEN?

Statements about everyday issues of information and opinion were presented to large groups of college students with the request that they indicate agreement or disagreement. The students were informed of the supposed majority response of previous groups who had done the same task. In some cases the previous groups were identified as highly attractive campus organizations such as the varsity letter club or Phi Beta Kappa, but in others the previous groups were identified as corporation employees or prison inmates. From pretesting with other students, the statements could be sorted into "easy" or "difficult" judgments. It was possible to predict conforming behavior accurately only when both difficulty of the judgment and attractiveness of the conformity model were considered. When judgments were difficult, the attractiveness of the reference group did not matter much, and subjects would conform to social pressures from both kinds of groups. But when judgments were easy and unambiguous, students conformed only to the highly attractive reference groups, and very rarely to the unattractive groups. This is typical of studies of conforming behavior because both the *personality* a person brings with him and the *situation* in which he finds himself interact to determine what he will do in response to social pressures.

McDAVID (1966)

STATUS OF A JAYWALKER

Pedestrians violated the prohibition of an automatic traffic signal more often in the presence of a confederate subject serving as a model who violated the prohibition, than when the latter conformed or was absent. Significantly more violations occurred among pedestrians following the lead of a well-dressed (presumably high-status) nonconforming model than those following the lead of a poorly dressed (presumably low-status) nonconforming model.

LEFKOWITZ, BLAKE, AND MOUTON (1955)

individual to abandon his own personal standards for reasonable judgment. Under these circumstances, conformity to the experimental group norm occurred only when the majority was unanimous. When even one person other than the lone individual being observed violated the majority norm and expressed an independent judgment, the experimental subject rarely conformed to the ridiculous group norm. In fact, when the unanimity of the norm was broken, the situation became laughable and ridiculous to the experimental subjects. Clearly, unanimity increases the effective influence of a group norm (Blake, Rosenbaum & Duryea, 1955; Allen & Levine, 1968).

I GAVE AT THE OFFICE

An experimental study varied the conditions under which donations were solicited from staff and graduate students in the psychology department of a large university for a gift for a retiring secretary. Prior experience suggested that the average donation on such occasions was about 50 cents. When the prospective donors were told that everyone else gave 75 cents, the average amount donated was boosted to 64 cents; similarly, when told that everyone else gave 25 cents, the average donation was depressed to 27 cents. In other conditions, donors were told that the norm was more variable, implying that most people (but with some variation) gave 75 cents (in which case the average gift was about 62 cents) or that most gave about 25 cents (in which case the average gift was about 35 cents). Thus, to induce gift-giving, unanimous and specific norms were more effective than variable norms.

BLAKE, ROSENBAUM, AND DURYEA (1955)

Personality and Conformity

Every individual brings with him into a group situation a set of personality characteristics and past experiences. These personal attributes interact with the social situation he confronts (including characteristics of the behavioral activity in which he is involved as well as characteristics of the people or groups that influence him) to determine his susceptibility to social influences. There is insufficient empirical evidence at present to settle once and for all the argument about whether there is such a thing as "the conformity personality." From time to time, various investigations have shown stable and consistent personality correlates of individual tendencies to conform to social pressures in experimental situations. But there is little uniformity from one investigation to another in the kinds of personality correlates established. Personality factors associated with conforming behavior in one kind of situation are not always associated with conformity in other situations. The conceptual distinction between normative conformity and informational conformity certainly suggests that the personality variables associated with one kind of conformity are not the same as those associated with the other. A great deal of additional research, taking careful account of the situational circumstances in which conformity occurs and the characteristics of the persons or groups exerting social influence on an individual, must be accumulated before questions about the personal characteristics of the conformer can be fully answered.

Investigations of the relationship between emotional stability and conformity have also been made, yielding evidence that extreme consistency in conforming to group norms may be associated with neuroticism and chronic anxiety (DiVesta, 1958). These relationships are difficult to interpret, however, without taking careful account of many components that define neuroticism. For example, certain measures of chronic anxiety, such as the commonly used Taylor Manifest Anxiety Scale (J. A. Taylor, 1953), have been found to be highly correlated with measures of the need for social approval (see Chapter 4). Furthermore, because certain kinds of susceptibility to social influence may represent appropriately adaptive and useful forms of behavior, relationships between various measures of neuroticism and conforming behavior are likely to be quite dependent on the situation in which conformity occurs (see Chapter 5).

Several studies have demonstrated relationships between authoritarianism as measured by the California F scale and conforming behavior (Adorno et al., 1950). The authoritarian personality syndrome assessed by this scale is a composite of such variables as intolerance of ambiguity, ethnocentrism and suspicion of alien or unfamiliar people, and fascistic tendencies to prefer clearly delineated lines of authority and submission in interpersonal relationships. Thus it is reasonable to expect that such a measure should be related to the occurrence of both normative and informational forms of social influence. Unfortunately, however, these findings have to be qualified by recognition of an inherent flaw in the construction of the F scale itself: the scale is arranged so that high scores result from consistent agreement with items in the scale, whereas disagreement with an item reduces the score total. Because agreement with a printed statement itself represents a kind of conforming behavior, the scores derived from the F scale may be a product of the individual's tendency to conform. Thus artificial inflation of the relationships between this scale and other measures of conforming behavior is likely (Nadler, 1959; Malof & Lott, 1962).

Highly intelligent people are more resistant to pressures to conform than duller people, but this relationship has not been consistently established in all studies (DiVesta, 1958). Intelligence is probably more directly related to informational conformity than to normative conformity. Brighter individuals are perhaps less dependent on others for aid in making judgments and choosing ways of behaving. On the other hand, when subjected to pressures to adhere to group norms or expectations for the sake of agreement as such, intelligence becomes a less important variable in determining response to social pressures.

The extent to which one is confident of his abilities in a particular situation is an important determinant of conformity to social pressures: people who are confident of their judgment are more resistant to pressures to conform than people who are uncertain and insecure (Kelley & Lamb, 1957; McBride, 1958; Walker & Heyns, 1962). In fact, the relationships between intelligence and conforming behavior may in part be due to the fact that brighter people learn to trust their own judgment and abilities more than duller people.

In our culture females are typically more susceptible to pressures to conform than are males, perhaps because cultural prescriptions for docility, compliance, and submissiveness have been associated with the feminine role (DiVesta, 1958). Furthermore certain learned values and motives associated with conforming behavior (such as dependency and approval-seeking) are characteristically stronger in females than in males. Although most investigations have found women to be more conforming

> **PROFILE OF A CONFORMIST**
>
> A series of studies showed that conformity was *positively* related to self-perception of being modest, tactful, kind, mannerly, obliging, helpful, and patient; to personality measures of submissive-restrained, cautious-controlled, and theoretical-intellectual orientations; to information to subjects that their intelligence was being assessed; to anxiety and threat of shock; and to cooperation for group reward. Conformity was *negatively* related to self-perception of being moody, optimistic, logical, rational, demanding, humorous, and original; to personality measures of outgoing-sociable orientation and need for achievement; to age; to intellectual ability; to self-confidence; and to competition for individual reward. Conformity was not related to personality measures of hostility or to need for affiliation.
>
> DI VESTA (1958)

than men, these differences do not hold in all cases. A few studies in which such variables as achievement motivation and affiliation motivation were manipulated independently of the sex of the subject have revealed no sex differences in conforming behavior (McDavid & Sistrunk, 1964; Sistrunk & McDavid, 1971). Furthermore, the tendency of females to regard certain areas as essentially domains of masculine superiority may lead them to be more conforming in those activities than males. One investigation of areas of masculine superiority, feminine superiority, and "neutral" areas found that women conformed more than men only in areas they regarded as associated with masculine superiority, but not in areas that were neutral or associated with feminine superiority (Sistrunk & McDavid, 1971).

The intensity of the individual's original motivation toward independent actions or judgments may also affect his resistance to group pressures. A person strongly committed to a particular course, and highly motivated to continue in that direction, does not succumb to social pressures that attempt to sway him; but when one is uncommitted and unmotivated to begin with, he may be highly susceptible to pressures to conform.

A number of studies have investigated the relationship between affiliative motivation and tendencies to conform to social influences. However, affiliative motivation may be conceptualized in several different ways, leading to different methods of measuring this variable. Consequently research findings in this area are inconsistent. A more specific motivational variable, the need for social approval, has been found to be related to conforming behavior (Crowne & Marlowe, 1964). Individuals with strong motivation to gain and retain the approval of others (and behave in socially desirable ways) conform more readily to group pressures. This motivation, of course, is particularly relevant to the concept of normative influence, in which conformity is motivated by the direct desire to be in agreement with others. There are many conditions (such as pressures to conform in ambiguous situations about which the individual has relatively little knowledge) under which people with relatively low levels of motivation to gain approval may nevertheless readily conform to group norms.

Achievement motivation and the personal desire to be individually successful may also be related to the individual's susceptibility to pressures to conform under some circumstances. In relatively unambiguous situations, in which the individual's own abilities are adequate to manage the situation with which he is confronted, people with strong achievement needs tend to be resistant to group pressures. However, in ambiguous situations in which one may distrust his own abilities, the strongly achievement-motivated person may be particularly susceptible to social influence (McDavid & Sistrunk, 1964). This pattern of relationships between conformity and achievement motivation is consistent with the concept of informational conformity involving the

SEX OF THE CONFORMIST

Male and female college students were presented with statements about everyday opinions and matters of fact and asked to indicate individually whether they agreed, disagreed, or were undecided about the content of each statement. Others were asked to indicate whether each statement referred to a matter of fact or a matter of opinion. Still others were asked to judge each item as a matter likely to be of greater interest to males or to females, or to be of equal interest to both sexes. The subjects' responses served to standardize a set of items for an experiment in conformity to either *masculine, feminine,* or *neutral* issues. Males conformed about equally often on all three kinds of sex-related issues. Females conformed more often than males on masculine issues, but did not conform more often on feminine or neutral issues.

SISTRUNK & McDAVID (1971)

utilization of other people only as sources of information or guidance.

Developmental aspects of conforming behavior have not been well explored, but several investigations bear indirectly on this issue. Generally speaking, as a child grows older he becomes more self-sufficient and less dependent on his elders for guidance and control of his behavior. Tendencies toward blind and automatic conformity to others appear to decrease with age (Berenda, 1940; Tuddenham, 1961). On the other hand, conformity may also become an instrumental means of learning and achievement. In contrast to normative social influence, informational social influence represents an instrumental and adaptive form of behavior. This type of conformity may be less directly related to age than blindly dependent conformity, although there is no conclusive evidence to support this point. Among adults, the age variable, of course, has a completely different meaning. But it appears that age groups comprise different kinds of psychological reference groups for adults, so that people in their thirties, for example, are influenced more by their peers than by their parents; in reverse, it would appear that "senior citizens" are not readily influenced by the norms of younger adults in the society.

The complexity of interaction between personal characteristics of the individual and situational conditions associated with the exertion of social pressures makes it difficult if not impossible to specify certain isolated characteristics as always associated with tendencies toward conformity. Conformity is clearly not the simple phenomenon it is often thought to be when people speak globally of conformists and nonconformists. Conforming behavior assumes a variety of complexions, and its utility and practical purpose differs from one situation to another. The unfortunate tendency of many people to judge whether conformity is good or bad is incompatible with scientific efforts to understand social influence as a complex but basic aspect of human behavior. To summarize contemporary research evidence on the prediction of an individual's tendencies to conform in social situations, it is fair to say that prediction is possible only when the combinations of characteristics of the behavioral context in which conformity occurs, characteristics of the group or person exerting pressures toward conformity, and characteristics of the individual subjected to social pressures are simultaneously taken into account.

RELEVANCE AND APPLICATION

The study of group norms, reference groups, and conforming behavior is useful in understanding many kinds of everyday problems. For everyone, acculturation represents a process of becoming familiar with social norms and learning to accept and adhere to them (see Chapter 4). If one fails to do so, he loses his identity and membership in the group, often at great cost in terms of personal welfare and satisfaction (see Chapter 13). When one moves from one culture to another he may experience distress as he struggles to recognize and meet changed expectations of him. Norms may be either formal and explicit or informal and vague. Often we are not even fully aware of the important role they play in everyday behavior because we generally take them for granted.

For this reason it is sometimes very easy to manipulate large numbers of people by controlling the reference groups and norms that steer their behavior. Clever propagandists capitalize on this in planning persuasion campaigns (see Chapter 5). A good campaigner in a political election never admits that he is a loser; he must always consider himself a winner to establish a norm for voting in his favor. A good public relations man always strives to make visible the fact that his man or firm or product is held in favor by "most people like you and me." Much successful advertising manipulates consumer habits of the buying public by trying to establish prestigiously attractive reference groups as users of the advertised product.

Teaching may also be carried out by manipulating reference group norms. The desired outcome, especially if it involves cultivation of a value system or internalized attitude, may be achieved more readily if the learner is induced to believe and recognize that his reference groups hold the same desired value as a norm. In some ways educational psychology makes use of this knowledge to try to enable teachers to harness the power of group norms in the classroom so that they work in favor of the educational process rather than against it (D. W. Johnson, 1970).

In clinical psychology the force of group norms may also be harnessed to induce affective change within the individual toward more appropriate styles of everyday encounter with others. Recognition of the norms held by those who comprise one's reference group is a useful source for defining acceptable and unacceptable behavior, and for learning what one need or need not feel guilty about (Wechsler, Solomon, & Kramer, 1970).

In community and political psychology the key to understanding groundswells and social movements often rests on analysis of the standards of conformity that emerge among people and the forces and conditions that induce adherence to them. Disorientation in time of chaos, upheaval, accident, or disaster often leads people to revert to blind conformity, which may appear unintelligent, stupid, and self-defeating. People may sometimes seem to discard logic in exchange for love if they fear that logic would lead to rejection and isolation from the group. Unpopular causes become popular overnight, and popular ones unpopular, if group norms are perceived as shifting. The hypocrisy of the voting public, and the discrepancy between pre-election talk and election-day action may be understood only by taking into account the way people look to their reference groups for definition of what is good or proper. The public is fickle, and its points of reference change with the winds of group norms.

REVIEW

1. Nominal *membership* groups may become psychological *reference* groups only when a person participates fully in the norms, structure, and performance of the group. When he does, the reference group influences his goals, attitudes, values, and behavior.

2. Reference groups may provide *positive* reference (directly influencing the person) or *negative* reference (inversely influencing him).

3. Group norms, whether *formal* or *informal,* are rules of conduct for the group's members. These are highly effective controls over each member's behavior.

4. Deviation from group norms is usually met with social rejection and disapproval, although very high-status members may sometimes be granted special freedom, *idiosyncrasy credit,* to deviate from norms without penalty. Of course, very low-status members deviate relatively freely, for they have little to lose anyway if they are socially rejected or isolated.

5. *Normative* conformity occurs as an end in itself for one who seeks to gain agreement with his group's expectations and goals, even if they differ from his own, simply to avoid rejection or disapproval.

6. *Informational* conformity serves as a means to an end for one who merely uses the group and its standards as a source of information or guidance.

7. *Conformity* involves one's awareness of norms and choice to adhere to them; *rebellion* involves one's awareness of norms and choice to defy them; *independence* is distinguished from either of these because it represents indifference to social norms. It may occur either when one is unaware of social norms or when one purposely ignores them.

8. Clear and *unambiguous* situations that call for public compliance maximize *normative* conformity; *ambiguous* and unclear situations without demand for public compliance minimize *normative* conformity but maximize *informational* conformity.

9. The higher the status of the *model* for conformity, and the greater the unanimity or uniformity of the expressed model or norm, the greater the likelihood of conformity.

10. Conformity can be predicted only from knowledge of both the individual's personality and the situation in which he interacts with others, because these two interact. Sex, self-perception, expectations, values, and other personality attributes work in combination with stimulus and reward conditions in a particular group situation to determine conforming behavior.

11

ROLES, STRUCTURE, AND LEADERSHIP

The general definition of a social psychological group notes three essential properties of social organization: norms, roles, and collective performance. This chapter is concerned with the internal roles and structural organization of a social system.

ROLES

Structural properties of human groups have provoked the interest of social scientists for many years. Durkheim (1893), an early French sociologist, wrote at length on the significance of organized division of effort within groups and societies.

Virtually all social organizations are characterized by some means of dividing the total effort of the system so that each member's function is articulated with that of every other. Later experimental studies of human behavior in groups have consistently supported Durkheim's observations.

One of the most important properties of a group or society, then, is the stabilization of a set of mutual relationships among individual members and a set of functions associated with each member. Such stable patterns of individual behavior are called *roles.* They are interdependent, and the overall pattern of their relationships defines the group's structure. These structural properties are important to the group's attainment of its purposes and objectives. They are also closely related to the regulative norms within the group. The stability of the group's overall structure and of each member's role is maintained by norms that regulate both individual and collective behavior.

The concept of role links psychology with sociology and anthropology. Linton (1945), an anthropologist, Newcomb (1950), a psychologist, Parsons (1960), a sociologist, and Berne (1963), a psychiatrist, are all theorists who have made extensive use of the role concept in studying individual social behavior.

The functioning of any social organization depends on patterns of reciprocal behavior among individual members of the organized system. These patterns become institutionalized within the group or society. Each position within the overall structure of the group is associated with a common body of beliefs and expectations shared by all members of the organization. Thus the term *position* is used to designate the particular slot or niche within the structure occupied by a given individual, including the configuration of expectations that influence his behavior there. The term *role,* then, applies to the pattern of behavioral function displayed by someone occupying a given position—a product of the interaction between his own personality and the situational position he occupies.

Role Perception, Enactment, and Expectations

Many social scientists have criticized the vague and nebulous use of the term "role" by psychologists and sociologists, pointing out that the concept requires several definitions for each of several components. The term *enacted role* refers to the behavior displayed by an individual in a particular position within a social organization. *Perceived role* is defined as the perception of behavior associated with a certain position in a social organization. That is, each member of a group perceives and reacts to the behavior of each other member in his own unique fashion. The problems of interpersonal perception described in Chapter 8 show that everyone tends to be selective in perceiving the behavior of others. Furthermore everyone also perceives his own behavior as a member of the group. Chapter 7 described how self-perception is influenced by social interactions with others, and how people often do not perceive their own behavior with perfect accuracy. Thus role perception and role enactment do not always correspond perfectly. Within a family as an organized group, for example, the behavior of the man in the husband-father position may be perceived more or less objectively by a psychologist observing the family (enacted role) but in dramatically different ways by the man himself and by his wife (perceived roles). Hence the separation of the concepts of enacted role and perceived role aids in understanding individual behavior within a group.

A third concept is that of *expected role,* defined as the set of expectations held by group members for the behavior of one in a particular position in the group. Such role prescriptions provide regulative norms associated with each role position within the social system. Foa (1958) has suggested that even further delineation of concepts of role expectation is desirable. The term *predicted role* refers to expectations that are based simply on probabilities, derived from the expectation that a member will continue to behave as he has in the past. In contrast, the term *prescribed role* designates expectations related to the regulative norms of the group, representing expectations

---

ROLE CONFUSION IN THE SCHOOL SYSTEM

A study of school superintendents and their school boards showed how role expectations are related to personal satisfaction for people who participate in an organized institutional structure:

1. The motivation of school board members to achieve the stated goals of the school system was directly related to the expectations held by their school superintendents.
2. The greater the congruence of a superintendent's expectations and school board actions, the greater the satisfaction of the superintendent with his position and with his school board.
3. Discrepancies of both role perceptions and role expectations between the superintendent and the school board were associated with overt conflicts between superintendent and board.
4. Role conflicts and discrepancies were associated not only with low job satisfaction, but with broadly reduced career satisfaction for the school superintendent.
5. In 91 percent of cases of role discrepancies and conflicts, resolution occurred through either expediency (coercive compliance to school board expectations) or moralism (rationalized reduction of dissonance on the part of the superintendent).

GROSS, MASON, AND McEACHERN (1958)

ROLE CONFUSION IN THE HOSPITAL

Role confusion because of lack of clarity in role definition was observed in a group of psychiatric nurses in a mental hospital. Newly given instructions allowed extreme freedom to the patients ("chronic schizophrenics"), limited only by considerations of health and safety. These role definitions were in stark contrast to the nurses' norms and preferences, the normal institutional requirements, and the traditional role of the nurse. The result of both vague instructions and conflict of roles was lack of clear-cut expectations, leading to inconsistent and inappropriate role performance on the part of the nurses.

SCHWARTZ (1957)

ROLE CONFUSION IN THE ARMY

Role confusion in military chaplains was demonstrated in a study dealing with the conflicting expectations encountered toward religious leaders and military officers. On one hand, chaplains were found to be more aware of their officers' rank than any other officers' group (mainly because of their ambivalence toward it) and consequently worked very hard to "become as one of the fellows" among the officers. On the other hand, the social distance that is an integral part of the officer-enlisted man relationship, if maintained, led to ineffective fulfillment of the clergyman role.

BURCHARD (1954)

as to what one in a particular position "ought" to do. Role *predictions* and role *prescriptions* both involve *expectations* about behavior, but they are not identical. In the example of the family as a social group, a wife may be able to state clearly what she thinks her husband *ought to do* in a particular situation, and to differentiate this from what she thinks he *probably will do*.

Enacted roles gradually stabilize as a group becomes organized. That is, the patterns of behavior associated with particular positions in the group gradually come to be habitually displayed by occupants of each position. These enacted roles are partially shaped by role expectations (especially role prescriptions) held by other members of the group (Whyte, 1943; Lupfer, 1964). The correspondence between role perception and role enactment increases as a group becomes organized and as individual members become increasingly familiar with one another (E. E. Smith, 1957; Lupfer, 1964). Studies of self-perception (which represents one kind of role perception) show that one's perception of himself is dependent on others' perceptions and expectations of him (see Chapter 7). The stabilization of role expectations as organized groups evolve norms and standards has been demonstrated in studies of small groups in laboratory settings (Berkowitz et al., 1963, 1964), as well as through analysis of role relationships in natural groups under natural conditions (Whyte, 1943, 1955).

The Description of Roles

The concept of role is global, incorporating all of the dimensions that might describe one's pattern of behavior within a social organization. The content of a particular role may be described in terms of many different qualities.

The description of role content most useful to a social psychologist depends on his purpose in analyzing group structure. The clinician or counselor may describe roles in terms of their relationship to the ongoing therapeutic process in a group, using such terms as "facilitator," "encourager," "supporter," or "rescuer" to describe the function carried out habitually by particular members of the group. Focusing on the subjective perceptions of each member, this kind of description is used by the humanistic and Gestalt-transactional theorists (Bradford, Gibb, & Benne, 1964; Satir, 1968; Fagan & Shepherd, 1970). Industrial psychologists studying decision making in organizations and bureaucracies might use such terms as "norm-voicer," "deviate," or "slider," to describe the opinion position taken by a person in a group discussion (Schachter, 1951). An approach to role analysis that focuses attention on the value orientation of each member and its relationship to overall group function has been developed by Bales (1970), describing each role in terms of three dimensions: up-down, forward-backward, and positive-negative.

Attempts to reduce these different kinds of descriptive categories to a few underlying dimensions have converged upon identification of three main qualities in role

---

ROLES AND EXPECTATIONS

College students selected in terms of self-, interaction, and task orientation on the basis of a personality inventory were assigned to groups of three representing each of these orientations, to play a stock market game. At the end of each session all subjects predicted the others' behavior in the next session. Over 6 weeks, members' expectations influenced each other's behavior, and ability to predict each other's behavior became more accurate. There was no relationship between a subject's personality and his enacted role.

LUPFER (1964)

A DESCRIPTION OF GROUP ROLES

In order to better understand personality and interpersonal behavior, Robert Freed Bales has combined two methods of investigation—that of direct observation of social behavior through *interaction process analysis* (Bales, 1958; see Chapter 3 and Figure 11–1), and that of subjective self-report through the *value profile* (Bales & Couch, 1969). The former technique makes use of categorical codes to describe the content of interpersonal transactions during a sample of group activity, and the latter is a paper-and-pencil inventory of statements about behavior in social situations with which the testee may agree or disagree. Both may be scored in ways that can be converted to a common set of dimensions: *Upward-Downward, Positive-Negative,* and *Forward-Backward.*

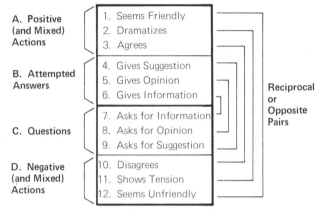

Fig. 11–1 Categories for Interaction Process Analysis. (From *Personality and Interpersonal Behavior* by Robert Freed Bales. Copyright © 1970 by Holt, Rinehart and Winston, Inc. Reprinted by permission of Holt, Rinehart and Winston, Inc.)

Upward-Downward (U-D). This dimension might be characterized as one of ascendancy. The upward-oriented *U* role is outgoing, extroverted, ascendant, and oriented toward upward status mobility with respect to others; its counterpart, the *D* role is more withdrawn, introverted, and downward-status-oriented.

Positive-Negative (P-N). This dimension is related to the nature of interpersonal affect. The positive-oriented *P* role shows warmth and positive effect toward others; its counterpart, *N,* shows indifference or hostility and negative affect.

Forward-Backward (F-B). This dimension is related to the task-oriented qualities associated with the role. The forward-oriented *F* role is task-directed, contributing to movement of the group toward its goals; its counterpart, *B,* involves distraction from group goals, contributing toward movement away from group objectives.

In a broad sense, then, the *U-D* dimension is a reflection of the quality of *individual* roles, the *P-N* dimension is related to the quality of group *maintenance* roles, and the *F-B* dimension to the quality of *task* roles, as described in the text. This descriptive system is applicable to the analysis of all kinds of interpersonal relations, particularly to those occurring in clinical, industrial, or educational organizational settings.

BALES (1950, 1970)

LADIES AND GENTLEMEN OF THE JURY . . .

Mock jury deliberations involved subjects drawn by lot from a regular jury pool, using protocols of twelve sessions concerning an auto negligence case. Male jurors tended to initiate acts directed at the solution of the task problem, whereas female jurors more often reacted to the contributions of others. Female jurors also tended to be less competent than males in discussing issues of negligence and damages; instead, they displayed social-emotional specialization aimed at maintaining harmonious group relations.

STRODTBECK AND MANN (1956)

content: *maintenance* or group-building functions, *task-oriented* goal-directed functions, and *individual* self-centered functions (Benne & Sheats, 1948; Bales, 1958). *Maintenance roles* include functions serving to maintain the organization of the group and interpersonal harmony within it (for example, the "harmonizer" or the "encourager"). *Task* roles are essentially directed toward solving the group's problems or achieving its objectives (for example, the "information seeker," the "initiator" of new ideas, or the "coordinator" of scattered contributions). *Individual* role functions serve the needs of the individual member rather than the collective needs of the group, and are thus irrelevant to either the organization or the performance of the group as a system. These include the "recognition-seeker" and the "playboy" (P. Slater, 1955; Bales, 1958, 1970; Berrien, 1961).

Bales (1958) found that most organized groups tend to evolve "specialist" roles, so that one person might concentrate on group-maintenance activities and another on task-related activities. In most cases, the "social specialist" evolves earlier in the group's life than the "task specialist." In some groups individuals adopted stable role patterns of self-aggrandizement, which Bales termed the role of the "overactive deviant." On occasion, but rarely, all three of these kinds of specialization were incorporated into the single role of the "great man." Differentiation of the general high activity level of the "overactive deviant" from the constructive activity of the "task specialist" may evolve relatively slowly and only after prolonged interaction in the group (Mann, 1961).

Generally these analytic studies provide useful leads toward understanding the basic qualities of role description, but they are still not regarded as conclusive. Many kinds of investigations imply that the content of roles displayed in a group remains highly dependent on such factors as group size, member qualities, and even the methods of investigation used to study the group (Borgatta et al., 1958, 1960).

Personality, Position, and Role

The pattern of behavior that constitutes a role is a product of the circumstances defining a position and the components of the *personality* of the individual occupying that position. The role displayed by one person in a particular position may differ considerably from that displayed by another in the same position. Furthermore, two members of a group with essentially the same personal makeup may show very different patterns of role behavior, depending on the position they occupy in the group. Several studies have investigated the question of whether personality or position makes the greater contribution in determining behavior in a group. But the two are interdependent, and group dynamicists have concluded that one cannot fully separate the effects of personality and of position as determinants of role behavior. It is almost impossible to ascertain whether teachers become stuffed shirts as a result of their

IT DEPENDS ON WHERE YOU SIT

Interaction patterns of five-person groups showed that seating arrangements and types of behavior were closely related. Several years of observation behind a one-way mirror (member 1 on the left side of the table near the door, members 2, 3, and 4 along the long side of the table opposite the mirror, and member 5 on the right side, farthest from the door) showed that members opposite each other (1 and 5) or in a central position (3) were recipients of most communications, and also seemed to do most of the talking. Members who chose seats 1 and 5 were more extroverted, dominant, and task-oriented than those who did not. Members who chose the central seat displayed a marked tendency toward social-emotional and group-maintenance behavior. Members with high levels of anxiety tended to prefer seats 2 and 4 (thus avoiding "high-talking" seats). In purely social situations there was a tendency for most interaction to occur between members in adjacent seats.

HARE AND BALES (1963)

professorial role, or whether stuffy and pompous people merely gravitate toward the teaching profession.

Bass (1962) has studied the interaction between personality and position in the group. Using a model suggested by many group dynamicists (e.g., Benne & Sheats, 1948; Cattell, 1951; Bales, 1958), Bass developed a psychological test called the *Orientation Inventory* designed to measure the extent to which one is predisposed to prefer self-centered roles (self-orientation), task-related roles (task orientation), or group-maintenance-related roles (interaction orientation) when he participates in organized groups. By selecting people according to their scores on this test, Bass investigated the patterns of behavior they displayed when brought into interaction with others in the laboratory. Generally these studies show that personal predispositions do contribute to (although they do not exclusively determine) one's behavior in social situations. Task-oriented people are particularly likely to exhibit perseverant task-oriented behavior, persistence in the face of problems, and other similar activities in the group. Interaction-oriented people are likely to be more susceptible to group pressures and to be passive but agreeable in groups. Self-oriented individuals are more likely to be disagreeable, sensitive, anxious, and self-centered (Bass, 1965a).

Status

At one level of analysis, roles may be described simply by characterizing different individual activities within the group, with no allusion to the value or significance of these functions for the group. But at another level, these role activities may be evaluated according to their utility to the group as a system. Roles involving functions that contribute significantly either to maintaining the group's existence as a system (the social specialist) or to achieving group goals (the task specialist) are usually regarded with greater respect and esteem by other participants in the group (Bales, 1953, 1958). Conversely, roles involving distracting functions that are detrimental to the group's welfare are held in low esteem. As a result, there is a vertical differentiation of roles within the group, according to their value. This is called *status*.

People in different status positions behave differently. Furthermore, other members of the group usually behave differently toward high- and low-status members. People in high-status positions are more likely to be targets of communication and interaction than people of low status (Katz et al., 1950; Kelley, 1951). As would be expected, people of high status are usually better satisfied with their positions (Berkowitz, 1956; Trow, 1957). High-status roles often involve greater freedom for expression of diver-

PECKING ORDER IN THE HOSPITAL

Role behavior of professionals in mental health institutions is strongly related to interdisciplinary squabbles. Social workers are at a double disadvantage: compared to the other professions, they have lower academic degrees; also, they work in public and thus are open to scrutiny by both patients and the other professionals. Psychologists zealously guard what they consider their own professional domain, psychotherapy and (especially) testing; and they try very hard to develop their own mystical professional jargon to differentiate them from the social workers who are increasingly employing standard psychological jargon. General physicians' initial prestige is high, but they must fight subsequent loss of status due to the fact that they are assigned routine jobs that most nurses can and do handle as well. Psychiatrists are on top of the ladder because of their great occupational and legal prestige. To maintain this high status, they tend to draw on the "secret magic" of both psychology and medicine, so that when challenged by an expert in one discipline they can always use counterarguments involving the jargon of the other discipline.

HARSHBARGER (1970)

STATUS AND COMMUNICATION

The communication output of members in positions of high and low status in experimental groups, with or without the possibility of mobility between different status levels, was measured. High-status members offered more negative comments about the group talk when downgrading was possible than when it was not possible, whereas low-status members made fewer negative comments when upward mobility was possible than when it was not possible. Low-status members addressed these communications primarily to members of high status, but the highs, when dissatisfied, communicated among themselves.

KELLEY (1951)

gent and nonconforming attitudes (Hollander, 1960). Leadership includes a particular set of functions associated with high-status roles that involve respect from other members of the group and power to influence their behavior. These power qualities were discussed in Chapter 9, and the leadership role as such is discussed later in this chapter.

GROUP STRUCTURE

Group Communication

Probably the most clearly evident aspect of structural organization within a group is the stabilization of lines of communication among members of the group. In an organized social system, even though each individual may be free to communicate with each other member of the group, the process of group organization involves systematic utilization of these communication channels. Each participant does not interact equally often with each other participant, and stabilized lines of interaction become apparent. In some groups, structure may be formalized, permitting communication only through specified channels connecting specific positions within the group (as, for example, in military organizations and certain businesses). In other groups, structure may be informal, but nevertheless stable. Even when there are no external restraints on communication, such factors as physical proximity may limit the use of available communication channels (Hare & Bales, 1963). As groups become organized, subgroup cleavages, individual compatibilities and similarities of interest, and other as-

CIRCLES, CHAINS, WHEELS, AND Ys

Five-man groups were assigned a task in one of four communication nets: circle, chain, wheel, and Y (see Figure 11–2). Group members occupied "cells" that

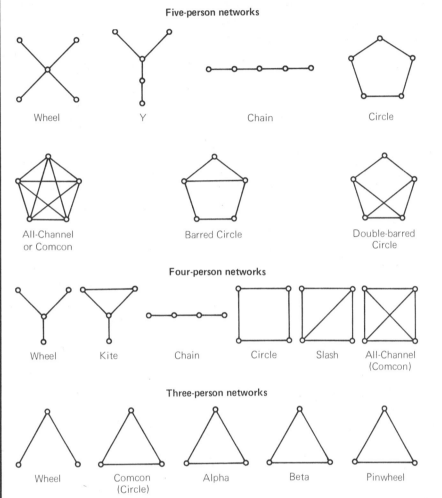

Figure 11–2 A sample of frequently studied communication networks. (Reprinted from *Group Performance* by James H. Davis by permission of Addison-Wesley Publishing Company.)

prevented them from seeing each other, and they were allowed to communicate only by means of written notes dropped into mail chutes. Each trial lasted until each of the group members indicated to the experimenter by means of an electrically operated signal light that he had made his choice. The results showed that the circle net used the largest amount of messages. More messages were made in the circle and the chain nets than in the Y or wheel nets. In the general sequence from circle to chain to Y to wheel nets, the circle extreme was related to activity, lack of leadership, least organization and direction, but also to more enjoyment by the members. The wheel at the other extreme showed the opposite characteristics. Centrality of position in nets was related to greater satisfaction (which increased over time), whereas the opposite held true for peripheral positions.

LEAVITT (1951)

pects of role relationship eventually tend to define a stable structure of channels of communication. This structure is called the *communication net.*

Precise and controlled investigations of communication nets in natural groups under natural conditions are difficult because of the many problems of making observations of all of the possible kinds of communication (words, gestures, facial expressions, etc.) that may occur. If a group is very large, the number of possible lines of communication between pairs of participants becomes unmanageable. To study communication patterns in groups, social psychologists often make use of laboratory conditions that limit the size of the group, the kind of communication that may occur, and the rapidity with which it takes place, thereby permitting the investigator to observe the communication. For example, by arranging that communication can take place only by telephone calls or written messages, the investigator can monitor the frequency with which messages are sent, their sources, and their recipients.

The investigations of Bavelas (1950), Leavitt (1951), Shaw (1954, 1956) and others are typical of this kind of experimentation. These studies involved groups whose members were permitted to communicate by message according to certain predefined lines. Several examples of fixed communication nets that have been studied in this manner are shown in Figure 11–2. The "all-channels-open" net (com con) permits each of the participants to communicate directly with the others. Under such conditions, however, each of the available channels is not used equally often, and the actual communication net evolved tends to be somewhat more simplified in structure. In the "circle" pattern, each participant can communicate with only two others, but the network circles back on itself. The "chain" is like a broken circle, with the result that the two participants can communicate with only one other person; they are thus said to occupy "peripheral" positions in the net. A "wheel" network concentrates the available channels of communication around one central "hub" position, placing the other participants in peripheral positions. The other pattern shown in Figure 11–2 represent nets intermediate between the wheel and the chain, and are somewhat more complex.

The structure of the communication net in small problem-solving groups is related both to the group's performance in achieving its goals and to its efficiency in satisfying its members. Patterns such as the circle are associated with slow and uneconomical performance, but such highly centralized patterns as the wheel expedite group achievement. In solving problems, the circle pattern requires transmission of a greater number of messages and produces more errors than the centralized structures. But the circle type of network affords a flexibility that is lacking in highly centralized structures. Leavitt found that the circle pattern allowed for internal correction of errors made by individual participants, whereas the wheel pattern tended to perpetuate errors.

The relationship between structure of the communication net and individual satisfaction in participating in the group is quite different. Centralized patterns, despite their effective performance, afford little satisfaction to their participants. Members in peripheral positions feel uninvolved, and get little satisfaction from their participation. Some structures that maximize group achievement may interfere with individual attraction to the group. When organization of the group must be maintained by continued attraction of individual members to the group, highly centralized structures may be unable to maintain group organization, despite the group's achievements.

Group Size

The organizational structure of a group is also related to the number of participants. The most essential difference between a dyad and groups of three or more is that in larger groups, subgroup cleavages and coalitions are possible. Even in a triad, two

TWO AGAINST ONE

A series of studies of triads (three-person groups) engaged in discussion tasks showed that the two most active members tended either to support or to be in conflict with each other. When conflict occurred, each active member began to attempt to form a coalition with the third (least active) member, but these maneuvers usually failed to bring about stability and solve the conflict. Eventually this was often achieved by a compromise coalition between the two active members with the low man permanently excluded.

Another experiment showed that the weakest member was chosen when the strength of the other two was about equal, because such coalitions were "cheap" (making least demands on its members).

In still another experiment, two confederate role players allowed the third member to form a coalition with one of them and then combined against him. Despite being overtly deserted by the original partner, the third member retained his liking for him.

MILLS (1953, 1954, 1956)
CAPLOW (1956, 1959)
MILLS et al. (1957)

members may enter a coalition against the third. In larger groups there appear to be differences in the organized function of groups comprised of an even number of members and those comprised of an odd number, especially with respect to the formation of majority coalitions. Whether people prefer to work in groups containing odd or even numbers of members appears to depend largely on the relative advantages of maintaining deadlocks (in even-numbered groups) or deriving majority coalitions against a minority (in odd-numbered groups).

There is some tendency in larger groups for organizational structures to become more formal and impersonal, especially with respect to lines of communication. However, because the communication nets become very complex in larger groups, precise investigation of their characteristics becomes awkward. More authoritarian styles of leadership typically emerge in larger groups (Blau, 1955), which suggests that they may be more hierarchically organized than smaller groups.

In larger groups, opportunity for direct interaction between all pairs of members becomes drastically reduced; thus clearly defined role perceptions and role expectations for each position may be impossible. In such cases, clusters of roles may be perceived in terms of a general constellation of "class" of positions, rather than as individually unique roles. In large groups and societies, individual members are more likely to react to and interact with other members in terms of their membership in a class rather than as individuals (see Chapter 13).

In general, group dynamicists believe that their scientific understanding of the structural organization of small groups can be extrapolated, at least in general terms, to understand the structural properties of large organizations. However, difficulties in conducting precise investigations of the structure of large organizations limits the social psychologist's ability to answer questions about large groups, at least until better empirical evidence becomes available.

Group Atmosphere

The concept of group climate or atmosphere is a global way of characterizing the structural properties of a group; it is not a single measurable dimension of group structure, but a descriptive summary of a number of attributes of a group's organization. Thus the concept has rather limited usefulness in a precise scientific sense, but it remains useful as a convenient way of describing various kinds of groups.

One general set of descriptive terms has been used by Bovard (1951, 1952) and others to describe the climate of various groups as either predominantly "group-centered" or "leader-centered." Group-centered climates involve a great deal of mutual attraction among members, strong adherence to collective group norms and standards, strong identification of individual members with the group as a system, and warm and enthusiastic interaction. In contrast, leader-centered climates involve looser organization of the group, with tendencies for individual members to orient their behavior toward the influence of a controlling leader rather than toward one another. Group-centered climates are associated with what might be called demo-

---

THREE SOCIAL CLIMATES

A series of studies designed to investigate group functioning under experimentally induced group atmospheres of "social climates" began as early as 1938 under the general direction of Kurt Lewin and continued throughout the 1950s. In one major study, four groups of 10-year-old boys operated in a natural setting; each group was a genuine hobby club that met after school and was comprised of five members roughly equated on patterns of interpersonal relationship; personality characteristics; and intellectual, physical, and socioeconomic status. Four adult leaders were trained to proficiency in the three leadership treatments (see Table 11–1) and shifted from club to club every 6 weeks. The clubs met in the same place and engaged in similar activities (arts and crafts, primarily the making of masks) with similar materials.

Table 11–1 Three Defined Styles of Leadership Role

Authoritarian	Democratic	Laissez-faire
All determination of policy by the leader	All policies a matter of group discussion and decision, encouraged and assisted by the leader	Complete freedom for group or individual decision, with a minimum of leader participation
Techniques and activity steps dictated by the authority, one at a time, so that future steps were always uncertain to a large degree	Activity perspective gained during discussion period. General steps to group goal sketched, and when technical advice was needed, the leader suggested two or more alternative procedures from which choice could be made	Various materials supplied by the leader, who made it clear that he would supply information when asked. He took no other part in work discussion
The leader usually dictated the particular work task and work companion of each member	The members were free to work with whomever they chose, and the division of tasks was left up to the group	Complete nonparticipation of the leader
The dominator tended to be "personal" in his praise and criticism of the work of each member; remained aloof from active group participation except when demonstrating	The leader was "objective" or "fact-minded" in his praise and criticism, and tried to be a regular group member in spirit without doing too much of the work	Infrequent spontaneous comments on member activities unless questioned, and no attempt to appraise or regulate the course of events

Source: Ralph K. White and Ronald O. Lippitt, *Autocracy and Democracy*, Harper & Row, 1960. Reprinted by permission of Harper & Row, Publishers.

The overall evidence supported the following generalizations:

Laissez-faire climates are not the same as democracy.
1. There was less work done, and it was poorer.
2. It was more characterized by play.
3. In interviews, the boys expressed preference for the democratic leader.

Democracy can be efficient.
1. The quantity of work done in autocracy was greater only when the leader was in the room.
2. Work motivation was stronger in democracy, as shown for instance, when the leader left the room.
3. Originality was greater in democracy.

Autocracy can create much hostility and aggression, as well as submissive behavior.
1. In one study the autocratic group showed more dominant ascendence (individual taking-over behavior), much more hostility (in a ratio of 30 to 1), more demands for attention, more destruction of own property, and more scapegoat behavior (aggression toward "innocent" and helpless members).
2. In another study, the typical reaction pattern to the autocratic leader was one of submissiveness.

Autocracy can create discontent that does not appear on the surface.
1. Four boys dropped out, and all of them did so during autocratic club periods in which overt rebellion did not occur.
2. Nineteen out of 20 boys preferred their democratic leader.
3. There was more discontent expressed in autocracy—even when the general reaction was submissive—than in democracy.
4. "Release" behavior on the day of transition to a freer atmosphere suggested the presence of previous frustration.

There was more dependence and less individuality in autocracy.
1. There was more submissive or dependent behavior.
2. Conversation was less varied—more confined to the immediate situation.
3. In the submission reaction to autocracy, there was an absolute (though not relative) reduction in statistical measures of individual differences.
4. The observers' impression was that in autocracy there is some loss of individuality.

There was more group-mindedness and more friendliness in democracy.
1. The pronoun "I" was used relatively less frequently in the democratic group.
2. Spontaneous subgroups were larger.
3. Group-minded remarks were more frequent.
4. Friendly remarks were more frequent.
5. Mutual praise was more frequent.
6. Friendly playfulness was more frequent.
7. Readiness to share group property was more frequent.

LIPPITT (1940)
WHITE AND LIPPITT (1960)

cratic organization within the group, whereas leader-centered climates are associated with autocratic organization.

In group dynamics, leadership refers to a particular set of role relationships that involve one member's ability to influence and manipulate the behavior of others. In the following studies of group atmosphere the adult advisor was not really a fully integrated member of the group, and his leadership functions remained somewhat external to the organization of roles among the boys themselves. The experimental manipulations in this study were designed to create three kinds of group atmosphere: an *autocratic* atmosphere (the adult remained aloof from the group and exerted maximal control over the activities of the boys), a *laissez-faire* atmosphere (the adult

> **SOCIAL CLIMATE IN INDIA**
>
> Six-person groups of preadolescent Hindu boys living in northern India worked for 6 weeks in a boys' club setting on various art projects. The study was closely modeled after the White and Lippitt (1960) experiment, except that it was limited to two social climates, authoritarian and democratic. Unlike the findings with American children, the authoritarian climate elicited greater productivity and satisfaction than did the democratic climate.
>
> MEADE (1967)

remained aloof and nondirective, exerting little control over the boys' activity), and a *democratic* atmosphere (the adult attempted to integrate himself into the group as much as possible without actually taking over important constructive activities and without exerting strong influence upon the group's decisions about its activities).

On the whole, however, four rather than three kinds of atmosphere were generated. The organizational pattern within all of the groups subjected to the democratic condition, as well as within all of those subjected to laissez-faire treatment, appeared to be homogeneous, but two noticeably different kinds of atmosphere evolved under the autocratic treatment. In some groups the boys openly resented and rebelled against the authoritarian control of the adult advisor ("aggressive autocracies"); but in other groups the boys passively accepted the autocratic control ("apathetic autocracies"). Evaluation of the performance of each kind of group by means of several different criteria showed generally that the authoritarian-autocratic groups were brittle and nonresilient in that they could not cope with threatened disruption of the group as readily as could the other atmospheres. Although the authoritarian adult advisor could drive his group to peaks of industrious performance in their constructive activities, both kinds of autocratic atmospheres were ill-equipped to cope with the absence of the adult advisor and to sustain themselves as effective groups when he was removed even temporarily. The laissez-faire atmosphere proved to be one that was relatively ineffective in its performance because it was slower to achieve any kind of organizational stability than either of the other kinds of treatment. Overall then, the democratic atmosphere proved to be the most adaptive and resilient kind of group structure. Furthermore, most of the boys who participated in these studies expressed a preference for it.

On several occasions, critics of these studies have raised the important question of whether a certain amount of cultural preconditioning might account for both the expressed preferences as well as the superior performance of the democratic atmosphere groups. Several psychologists (e.g., Fromm, 1941; Eriksen, 1950) suggest that the typical democratic structure of the American family may serve as a prototypical training ground that prepares American youth for participation in democratic organizations, whereas such family structures as the old stereotype of the Victorian European family as a paternal autocracy would perhaps better prepare European youths for participation in autocratic organizations. Yet replications of these studies of group atmosphere in western European countries produced no evidence to support the notion that the pattern of findings observed in the original studies was unique to midwestern American youths. Of course it must be conceded that the stereotype of the European family as an autocracy may be an outdated and inaccurate notion, especially because the overall political tone of western Europe underwent a great deal of democratization after World War II. It is not really possible, from available data, to answer definitively the question of whether these findings may be culturally conditioned; the most that can be said is that for a sample of midwestern American boys in the 1940s, the structural organization of groups showed clear and striking differences under each of these kinds of group atmosphere.

293

Roles,
Structure, and
Leadership

Group Cohesiveness

Like the concept of group atmosphere, the concept of *cohesiveness* is a multidimensional composite characteristic of a group's structure. A suitable general definition of cohesiveness is that it is the "resultant of all the forces acting on all the members to remain in the group" (Cartwright & Zander, 1960, p. 74). The specific dimensions that might contribute to this resultant include such factors as the attraction of individual members to one another, the attraction of individual members to the activities and functions of the group, and even the extent to which the individual is attracted to the group as a means of satisfying his own personal needs. Thus "cohesiveness" is a general term for a variety of specific dimensions of individual attraction to a group. Like many of the terms that Lewin and his colleagues coined in their early studies of group dynamics, as empirical studies of small groups have increased in number, scope, and precision, need has arisen for more precise definitions and clearer, more specific concepts. Festinger (1953, 1954) particularly has emphasized the importance of differentiating the individual's attraction to the group in terms of its organized movement toward some goal (group locomotion) from attraction based on the group's service of his own personal and individual needs, including validation of his cognitive understanding of the world around him (social reality).

Cohesiveness is a multidimensional concept that is difficult to define, but it has proven useful to characterize the degree of "we" feeling in a group. Lewin's (1939) early theoretical discussions of group characteristics pointed out that as a group becomes organized as a bounded social system, there are increasing internal attractions within it. The greater the cohesiveness of the group, the clearer the definition of its boundaries and the sharper the distinction between members of the group and nonmember outsiders. Cohesive groups with well-defined boundaries are more difficult to enter and leave than noncohesive groups. There is greater resistance to threat of disorganization in cohesive groups. The greater the difficulty in achieving entry into a group, the greater the value attached to belonging to it, and the greater the adherence to its norms. Lewin referred to this network of correlates of cohesiveness as *membership character* (Lewin, 1951).

One way to analyze cohesiveness is to assess the total amount of diadic interpersonal attraction among member pairs within the group (as described in Chapter 8). Another approach involves examination of the attraction of each member to the group as an organized system. Similarities of interests, values, and attitudes are important aspects of one's attraction to a group (Hartley, 1960; Walster & Walster, 1963). One

---

ROADBLOCKS THAT ATTRACT

College women who volunteered to participate in discussion groups underwent three kinds of "initiation." One group (severe initiation) was required to read some embarrassing material before joining the group; another (mild initiation) read some material that was not embarrassing; a third group (control) was not required to read anything. Each subject then listened to a tape recording of the group she was to join, and then evaluated the group and its discussants. The women who underwent severe initiation judged their respective groups as significantly more attractive than did those who underwent mild initiation or no initiation, presumably to "justify" the pain and effort they had undergone.

ARONSON AND MILLS (1959)

LIKING TO BE LIKED

Each person in a group of 160 college students was told that he had been assigned (as the only outsider) to another group engaged in dream research. The other group was described as either similar to the subject's own group or as dissimilar. Three experimental conditions were established:

1. *concerned about being liked,* when no further information was given to the subject;
2. *assured of being liked,* when the subject was told that, for plausible reasons, he would be introduced to the other group in a favorable manner; and
3. *assured of being disliked,* when the subject was told that, for plausible reasons, he would be introduced to the other group in an unfavorable manner.

    Under conditions 1 and 3 the subjects expressed a preference to join a group similar to their own, but under condition 2 they expressed a preference for a dissimilar group.

WALSTER AND WALSTER (1963)

is likely to join groups whose interests and norms are congruent with his own values, or at least groups where he can expect to be accepted and liked.

Instrumental need satisfaction may also provide a basis for one's attraction to a group (Kelley, 1951; Ross & Zander, 1957; Jackson, 1959). People usually prefer to join groups that have been successful and competent rather than ones that have been incompetent (Shelley, 1950; Jackson, 1959). Schachter's (1958) studies of the bases of affiliation show that anxiety reduction, for example, can provide a basis of attraction to a group because affiliation with others may indeed be very comforting and reassuring.

A circular reciprocal relationship exists between group cohesiveness and group performance: as in the old chicken-and-egg riddle, one cannot say whether groups become more cohesive because they perform successfully and include happy members, or whether they perform more successfully and make their members happier be-

NOTHING ATTRACTS LIKE (GROUP) SUCCESS

Three-person groups consisting of previously unacquainted members of the U.S. Air Force were given several intellectual and nonintellectual tasks under varying conditions of motivation (probabilities to get monetary rewards for successful task completion). Attraction to one's group was highest when a member had experienced success rather than failure with his group, and when he perceived others as favorable rather than unfavorable in their participation in the group task.

DEUTSCH (1959)

COHESION, THREAT, AND FRUSTRATION

Young boys in a summer camp were studied for the effects of threat and frustration on group cohesiveness. Threat and frustration were experimentally manipulated by means of verbal predictions of wins or losses in athletic events. Within-group choices to such questions as "Who would you like to go with you on an overnight hike?" served as measures for group cohesiveness: the greater the number of such choices, the greater the group's cohesiveness. Threat reduction increased cohesiveness, but frustration reduction did not. Strong frustration produced withdrawal in the form of reduced intergroup competition and increased cooperation within groups.

PEPITONE AND KLEINER (1957)

cause they are cohesive. It is simply true that cohesiveness and level of performance in the group are associated directly.

LEADERSHIP

Scientific interest in understanding the behavior of people in organized social systems has directed attention to those who display particular abilities to influence others and to steer the course of group action. This ability—*leadership*—has been a consistent focus of research in group dynamics.

Leadership involves the execution of a particular kind of role, defined essentially in terms of power or the ability to influence others. Like any other role, leadership involves both overt actions as well as certain patterns of interpersonal perception and certain expectations about behavior. In some groups leadership may be concentrated in one individual; in others, it may be shared by a number of people. As a role, leadership may be more or less specific to the structure of the group: a leader in one group may not necessarily be a leader in another. As group membership changes, the leadership functions of a given individual may change. Likewise, as the purpose and activities of a group change, individual manifestations of leadership within that group may change. The leadership role articulates with other roles within the group. That is, leadership directly implies "followership" on the part of others in the group. For every occurrence of social power, one person *exerts* influence and others *submit* to influence. This conception of a role involving power relationships, then, defines leadership as *the frequency with which an individual may be identified as one who influences or directs the behavior of others within the group.*

Once, the idea of "born leaders" was widely accepted. It was assumed that men of genius appeared from time to time, destined to exert profound influence on their society. This theory persists even into contemporary group dynamics. Sir Francis Galton, an early student of psychological measurement, believed that individuals with outstanding talents emerged as leaders to shape crucial changes in the social organizations in which they participated. Galton's early notions led to the assumption that proper psychological assessment could evaluate these capacities and predict the emergence of leadership in groups and societies. The fact that certain families (such as the Mill, Adams, or Bach families) produced more than their share of eminent men gave general support to the idea that genetic inheritance of exceptional capacities might be associated with leadership.

An alternative idea came into popularity in the early twentieth century when social scientists (e.g., Simmel, 1902; Pigors, 1935) reconsidered leadership as a product of situational conditions. Leadership was viewed not as a set of properties associated only with the individual, but as a way of behaving derived from the leader's relationship to others in the group. The leader was not conceived of as endowed with powers enabling him to influence others. Instead, he is granted these powers by his followers as his role evolves within the structural organization of the group. With the development of sociometric techniques for measuring *interpersonal* relationships as a supplement to the psychological measurement of *individual* personality variables (see Chapter 3, Sociometric Assessment), this interpersonal conception of leadership became increasingly accepted. For example, Jennings (1943) (a student of J. L. Moreno closely identified with the early development of sociometry as a method for measuring interpersonal relationships) called attention to the situational definition of leadership by pointing out that in studying individual leadership one should ask, "Leadership in what respect? For whom? In what sort of group?"

In contemporary group dynamics, leadership is conceived largely from the situational point of view, as a particular kind of role within the group. However, there is some evidence that particular personal attributes enhance the likelihood that certain people will assume roles of leadership consistently in many groups in which they participate.

It is important to make a distinction between formal, or *titular,* leadership and informal, or *emergent,* leadership. The position of leader in a group may be formally designated as a structural position to which a particular member is assigned. Certain formal privileges and duties may be arbitrarily attached to this position, and there are certain expectations about the behavior of individuals who occupy it. However, under some conditions it is possible that someone in the titular position of leader may not influence other members of the group as effectively as some other emergent leader within the group. Emergent leadership, then, describes the actual role behaviors that involve effective power and influence over others. Emergent leadership may not always corrspond to titular leadership. In group dynamics, interest in titular leadership is essentially restricted to questions concerning the extent to which formal labels of position within the group contribute to emergent leadership functions on the part of occupants of those positions.

As a role, leadership may be enhanced by *charisma,* a mystical "aura of greatness." Concepts of leadership in community, national, or world affairs often are extrapolated far beyond the basic power relationships that define leadership in the psychological study of small groups. An important element in the power of political leaders is the fact that a certain amount of their power may reside in the office they occupy. In formal organizations, the position occupied by a person may account for much of his power and influence over others. The influence of one who occupies a position of legitimate power may be independent of his personality. Even imbeciles who have inherited the crowns of royal nations have exerted power and influence over masses of people. Furthermore, leadership and power generate their own increase. The legend of greatness that comes to surround one in a position of power may distort the impression he makes on others. The notion of so-called charismatic leaders, endowed with gifts of greatness, does not necessarily imply the possession of singularly distinctive abilities; often the "gift" (charisma) is given by his followers as much as by the gods. It is a gift of expectations and self-fulfilling prophecies. Once the legend of greatness is widely accepted, an otherwise ordinary mortal may maintain power over many followers—so long as no one dares challenge the legend.

The status of leader affords both duties and privileges. The occupant of such a position is ascribed certain role expectations by other members of the group, in some ways placing greater responsibility on him (as spokesman, decision maker, or pathfinder for the group). But in other ways his position affords him greater freedom. For example, high-status positions are associated with relaxation of demands for conformity to the group's norms. Having arrived at a position of power, respect, and liking within a group, the leader may then maintain his acceptance by others even when he deviates slightly from prescribed group norms. Hollander has termed this freedom "idiosyncrasy credit" (see Chapter 11). Behavior that earns high status (much of which, of course, involves conformity to group norms) also earns credit that later allows one to deviate from norms without direct penalty. Harvey and Consalvi (1960) have shown that it is the number-two status position in a group that is associated with greatest conformity. Neither the low-status members nor the occupant of the top position display as great adherence to group norms.

Leadership Styles

Many frameworks have been used to describe the variety of forms of leadership that occur within organized groups. Kinds of emotional relationships among members of a group that may contribute to leadership and power relationships have been described from many points of view (Lippitt, 1940; Redl, 1948; Bales, 1950). As men-

LEGITIMACY AND LEADERSHIP

Artificially created laboratory groups elected (by means of experimental manipulation) leaders who actually were preinstructed confederate subjects. In one condition, the "elected" leaders, presumably representing "legitimate" power, were allowed to function; in another, they were replaced by appointed substitutes, who thus represented "coercive" power. Conditional manipulations included requests for "slowing down" productivity made by either type of "leader." Leaders with legitimate power were more frequently accepted and induced greater productivity than did leaders with coercive power.

FRENCH AND RAVEN (1959)

tioned earlier, on the basis of empirical investigations, Bales (1950) has shown that two components of leadership may be defined according to two major areas of group function: task-related functions and group-maintenance functions. The social specialist contributes to maintaining organization and internal harmony among group members; the task specialist contributes to successful attainment of group aims and objectives. In many groups these two kinds of leadership reside in different roles, so that the overall leadership of the group is shared by two or more people. In such cases the role of the social specialist tends to stabilize more quickly than that of the task specialist. Occasionally, both functions are combined into a single "great man" role. However, this role is an overactive one that occurs rarely. The differentiation of two or more specialized kinds of leadership implies, of course, that different sets of personal characteristics may be associated with success in different kinds of leadership roles.

Leadership may be analyzed globally as a particular set of role relationships involving lines of social influence, but the specific ways individuals carry out these functions vary considerably. Power and influence may be exerted in an essentially autocratic style (through coercion and authoritative manipulation) or in a more democratic style (through cajoling, seduction, and persuasion). Among Americans and western Europeans, democratic styles of leadership are not only preferred by most people, but they also tend to facilitate effective performance of the group. These findings do not necessarily prove that democratic leadership is inherently superior to other styles because it is conceivable that the socialization experiences of Americans and western Europeans condition them toward such preferences (Meade, 1967). In educational settings, American students prefer and perform better in learner-centered classes than in teacher-centered ones (B. O. Smith, 1971), and several investigations

WHEN THE BOSS MINGLES

Discussion groups with supervisory and participatory leaders were compared to one another on a variety of measures. Supervisory leadership occurred when the preinstructed leader did not take part in the discussion and limited his function by seeing that the discussions were finished on time. Participatory leadership occurred when the preinstructed leader not only took part in the discussion but also insured equal participation to all group members. In general, participatory leadership resulted in more group agreement, greater and more permanent influence by the leader on the members, and greater satisfaction and enjoyment for both leader and group members.

PRESTON AND HEINTZ (1949)

have found that participants in discussion groups are often better satisfied and perform better with democratic, participatory leaders than with autocratic, supervisory leaders.

Several factors influence the style of leadership adopted by an individual in a group. His own personality and needs, as well as the particular circumstances in which he must operate, may predispose him toward the adoption of a particular style of leadership (Merei, 1949; Hare, 1957). Characteristics of other members, and even the pattern of communication linkages among them, may also affect leadership style (French & Snyder, 1959). In highly centralized networks that channel information into a single position within the group, leadership is more autocratic than in groups whose communication networks are more open and evenly distributed. Generally, the style of leadership becomes increasingly autocratic and authoritarian as the size of the group increases (Carter et al., 1951). In larger groups, hierarchical chains of command become increasingly necessary to maintain and preserve the complex organizational structures. This in turn requires that power relationships become more formalized. Leadership may be shared by a number of individuals in larger groups, but such sharing of leadership tends to be ordered into hierarchical levels and areas of specialization. Stress or crisis in the group may also demand formalization of power relationships. In some cases a crisis creates demands for rapid adjustment in group function, resulting in sudden reorganization of the group's power structure (Whyte, 1943).

Leadership Stability

Leadership involves role relationships among members of a group, so one person cannot display leadership unless others display the reciprocal role of followership. Social power is not an attribute *within* the individual, but a relationship *between* the individual and others. The extent to which one displays leadership behavior may vary considerably as he moves from group to group, or as the activities of these groups change from time to time.

In general, there is some consistency in leadership as an individual moves from one group to another, so long as each group performs similar kinds of activities. For example, factory foremen who are successful with one group of workers also tend to be successful with other groups of men as long as their work activities are essentially the same. However, when the characteristics of various groups differ, the sta-

---

LEADERS IN CRISIS

Three-person groups of college students were asked to play a shuffleboard-type game without knowing its rules, but were encouraged to attempt various procedures. A red light flashed whenever a rule of the game was violated, and a green light flashed whenever a score was made. Leadership behavior was assessed by outside observers on the basis of the subjects' influence attempts (to introduce a procedure) and the degree that such attempts were successful. After the subjects had learned the game, twelve groups were subjected to a "crisis" in the form of continuously changing rules, which made a newly learned rule illegal the moment it was accepted. During the last three sessions the members failed to make a single score. A comparison between the groups who continued to play under the original rules and the groups under "crisis" showed that with increasing crisis the influence of the leaders gradually began to diminish. In fact, when the established leader did not meet the crisis promptly and efficiently, he was immediately replaced.

HAMBLIN (1958)

LEADERSHIP STABILITY

The Office of Strategic Services (OSS) developed tests during World War II to assess leadership potential. In one test, leaderless groups were presented a controversial topic for discussion while observers rated members on exhibited leadership behavior. The ratings were then compared to successful leadership in real-life situations based on ratings by supervisors and/or peers. Among the real-life subjects under observation were administrative trainees, ROTC cadets, fraternity members, sorority members, foremen in federal shipyards, and Civil Service administrators. All comparisons yielded moderate but significantly positive relationships, suggesting some generality of leadership potential across a variety of situations, tasks, and groups.

BASS (1960)

bility of individual leadership function may decrease considerably. Some people may be successful as leaders of small groups, but unsuccessful in leading larger groups (Borg, 1957; Havron & McGrath, 1961). A leader who is effective with authoritarian followers may be ineffective with nonauthoritarian followers, and vice versa (Blau, 1955). Changes in the communication network or other aspects of structural organization within the group may contribute to instability of an individual's leadership function (Barlund, 1955).

Changes in the activities of a group may disrupt individual leadership. Different kinds of activities may require different abilities for leadership. But within the same group of people, there is some degree of consistency of individual leadership despite changes in their activity (Bass & Wurster, 1953; Bass, 1960). But the greater the change, the less the stability of leadership. When a group shifts from one activity to a highly dissimilar one, some rearrangement of leadership and power roles is likely to occur.

It is difficult to evaluate the effects of changed activities or other circumstances on stability of leadership and power because once a leader has established his role, a certain amount of inertia follows. Regulative group norms tend to maintain organizational stability within the group. The stabilization of behavioral activity and the expectations of members for each other discourage dramatic reshuffling of the group's internal structure. When structure and leadership roles have been externally imposed and arbitrarily defined, the group's organizational structure is likely to be less stable than when leadership roles have emerged spontaneously as a by-product of emergent

WHO'LL TAKE OVER?

A series of studies on small military groups tried to answer the question, "What is the optimal number of men that one leader, unassisted, can control and supervise?" For small rifle squads, the optimum size for effective leadership was about six members (one leader and five men). Another study showed that when army squads specially trained in leadership behavior were compared to conventionally trained army squads on a tactical test problem of what to do on a mission where the leader and his assistant had been "killed," there was no overlap in performance scores between the two groups: the army-trained squads who depended entirely on the leader's initiative failed to solve the problem, whereas in the specially trained group there was always someone who could substitute for the leader, and inevitably did so.

HAVRON AND McGRATH (1961)

organization. The leadership structure of groups initially organized under autocratic atmospheres and authoritarian control reshuffled considerably when these groups were later democratized (McCandless, 1942). But in democratically organized groups, even the formal appointment of a new titular leader may fail to bring about an actual rearrangement of emergent leadership functions (Borg, 1957).

There is generally some stability of leadership within the same group as activities and circumstances are changed, as well as across groups when their activities remain similar. The most severe test of the great-man theory (which implies that leadership is basically an inherent quality of the individual) can be achieved by gauging the consistency of individual leadership across different groups performing different tasks. Few experimental studies have assessed leadership consistency in this way. The correlations among measures of individual leadership status in changing groups and changing activities are very low, but they are statistically significant. Thus there is a seed of evidence that a set of not yet precisely defined personal attributes may be associated with individual predispositions toward emergence as leaders of groups.

Personality and Leadership

Because leadership is an *inter*personal, rather than an *intra*personal, attribute, it is not surprising that research attempts to define specific personality characteristics associated with emergent leadership have been inconclusive. It is difficult to predict the likelihood that a particular person will achieve leadership in a group without having information about the group and its activities as well as about the individual himself.

There is surprisingly little agreement among many studies of personality attributes of people who emerge as leaders. Although interest in predicting leadership ability during World War II led to the rapid accumulation of data on leadership and personality, there is very little consistency of research findings (Stogdill, 1948; Gouldner, 1950; C. A. Gibb, 1954; Campbell, 1955; Mann, 1961). Comprehensive reviews of research in this area have particularly criticized failure to recognize the importance of specific group activities and specific membership characteristics in determining emergent leadership.

Berelson and Steiner (1964), however, are less pessimistic in their conclusions from an evaluation of research findings. Reinterpreting the variety of labels applied to particular measures of personality characteristics (thus combining variables measured by different investigators into categorical clusters), they concluded that leadership reliably relates to physical size; physical appearance and dress; self-confidence and self-assurance; sociability and friendliness; will, determination, and energy; and intelligence. However, C. A. Gibb (1954) cautioned that large discrepancies between the intelligence of leaders and followers may interfere with effective leadership by establishing a gulf that cannot be bridged readily. Stogdill (1948) also noted some consistency in findings that leaders are likely to be people who are academically successful, active in their groups, and perceived by others as reliable and dependable. One characteristic that all of these "stable" correlates of leadership have in common besides physical size (most of these are studies of leadership among groups of men) is *social desirability*. Thus, just as popularity status is generally correlated with any measure of socially desirable behavior (Chapter 8), these research findings imply that leadership behavior tends to be accompanied by the display of many kinds of socially attractive behavior (Partridge, 1934; Zeleny, 1939).

Conceding to evidence that leadership is determined largely by situational conditions within the group, it might nevertheless be suggested that certain personality attributes may be stably associated with particularly *successful* and *effective* leadership. A few investigations have implied that effective leaders are likely to be particularly sensitive to the feelings, attitudes, and needs of other members of their group (Trapp, 1955; Berrien, 1961). However, findings on this issue are inconsistent and subject to the criticism that statistical artifacts lead to improper interpretations of this relationship (Campbell, 1955).

The conception of leadership as a set of role relationships identifies the study of leader behavior as a problem in interpersonal perception. Fiedler's (1963, 1967) *leadership contingency* model analyzes the emergence of leadership, as well as its style and quality, in terms of the contingent circumstances of the situation in which it occurs. Three such circumstances particularly influence the nature and effectiveness of leadership behavior: affective relationships (liking) between the leader and his followers; task structure (or ambiguity) in the activities of the group; and position power—the legitimacy of power associated with a given nominal position within the group. The level of these factors in a particular group will govern the kind of leadership likely to emerge, and therefore who is likely to become a leader, as well as how effective his leadership will prove.

In general (at least with air force bomber crews) effective leaders seem to maintain a moderate degree of interpersonal distance between themselves and their followers. Bomber crews are rather highly task-oriented, and leadership style tends to be relatively directive and controlling, especially in more successful and effective crews (Fiedler, 1963). The most effective leaders are leaders who are admired, liked, and trusted by their followers, so that they are predictable and reliable (Partridge, 1934; Clifford & Cohn, 1964). However, Fiedler's data suggest that in well-structured and task-oriented groups, extreme transparency and closeness between leader and followers may make the leader's position more vulnerable by exposing his weaknesses and "feet of clay." Even the Wizard of Oz preserved his social power through maintenance of a legend of greatness, concealing himself and keeping himself distant and inaccessible. Many political leaders attempt to follow the same philosophy.

Leadership is so highly contingent upon the specific circumstances of a group situ-

---

THE EFFECTIVE LEADER

A specific technique allowed the derivation of LPC (least preferred co-worker) scores on the basis of a leader's description of the members of his group. Leaders who described their least preferred co-worker relatively favorably tended to be relatively permissive, considerate of others, and encouraging of good interpersonal relations.

A series of investigations on the effectiveness of bomber crews, tank crews, infantry squads, steel shops, company management, church leadership, sales display teams, high school basketball teams, and service station management showed a rather consistent pattern: although in most cases leaders of successful task-oriented groups received relatively high sociometric rankings on liking, competency, and so on, they tended to put a certain amount of interpersonal distance between themselves and other group members (low LPC scores). Eventually, it was found that both the high- and the low-LPC leadership styles are effective, but under different conditions. When things are going well for the group, *and* when things do not go well, the task-oriented low-LPC leader is most effective: in the first case because there is no reason to reject him, and in the second because his directive leadership saves the group from falling apart. However, when the group situation is moderately favorable (things are going neither very well nor very badly), the group expects to be treated with more consideration, and the permissive, socially oriented, high-LPC leader becomes the most effective one.

FIEDLER (1963, 1967)

ation that it is difficult to predict which people will become effective leaders or to train people for that role. During World War II the Office of Strategic Services operated an elaborate assessment program on the prediction of military leadership, but their studies proved disappointing. The best predictor of a man's leadership effectiveness in military missions was his performance in prior similar situations (OSS, Office of Strategic Services, 1948).

To state any summary of the implications of research on the qualities of an effective leader, it is necessary to refer to very broad and general qualities that cut across situational contingencies, rather than to define specific behavioral traits. The most evident of these are: *sensitivity* (to the needs and demands confronting the group and its members); *flexibility* (in adapting one's abilities to changing demands from moment to moment); and *responsibility* (willingness to exert initiative as the first to do whatever is required for the group's success).

Leadership Training

A question of practical interest in the study of leadership concerns the possibility of training people to become effective leaders. Unfortunately, in the absence of conclusive evidence about what kinds of personal attributes are associated with leadership, it becomes difficult to define the kind of training necessary. Moreover, the situational contingency of leadership makes it highly situation-specific. Research findings show only scattered and inconsistent success in attempts to train people to be effective in leading others (Bavelas, 1942; Barlund, 1955; Levi, 1956). In fact, the training programs that are most successful in producing effective leaders are those in which training focuses on the development of specific kinds of skills applicable to a particular kind of activity. The increased effectiveness of leaders subsequent to training might be due to training in skills valued by their group, not necessarily to training in general leadership ability as such. Even with such training, however, certain individuals may still lack the capacity to be effective in leading others. As Fiedler (1958) has commented, some people couldn't even lead a troop of Girl Scouts across the street.

HOUSE-BREAKING THE LEADER

Students rated by their peers as ineffective leaders were divided into small discussion groups in which the average leadership qualities of the members as rated by their classmates was about equal. Sixteen subjects were rated on leadership behavior by observers prior to and after being given a 2-week leadership training course. The trained leaders showed a significant increase in initiating discussion, regulating the amount of participation, and resolving conflict.

BARLUND (1955)

RELEVANCE AND APPLICATION

All of the social sciences have long made use of the concept of role for descriptive purposes. The general fact that almost all social systems show some kind of division of labor makes this a useful approach to understanding and describing them. Even in history and political science, the progress of civilization is often described and interpreted in terms of the roles played by the actions of key figures in the community of mankind.

Psychologically speaking, the analysis of roles is especially useful to understand how the individual fits into and is affected by social systems. Industrial organizations may be analyzed in terms of their formal and nominal structures by examining each position within the institutional framework and the expectations associated with it. In turn, then, the role behavior, perceptions, expectations, and satisfactions of the particular people who occupy these positions becomes more readily understood This kind of analysis comprises a large portion of the branch of modern industrial psychology called organizational psychology (Bass, 1965b).

Other institutions, such as the educational system in a school district, may also be analyzed as large organized social structures and broken down into their component role relationships. At the classroom level, social organization and role relationships involving teachers and pupils may also be analyzed. Modern educational psychology often makes use of this approach to facilitate the teaching process, especially in terms of affective growth and development of the learner.

Studies of social structure and communication within groups may be used to gain insight to permit more effective management and manipulation of a social system. For example, in industrial settings the output or productivity of an organization may be facilitated through effective management of the formal aspects of structural organization through control of communication channels. This kind of reasoning is behind the concept of military organization, structure, and communication; however, one may wonder whether the formality of structure in modern armies may be outdated and no longer effective in the technologically advanced world of the 1970s.

Studies of leaders in all kinds of social organizations hold the key to understanding social movements at all levels. To be able to predict effectively the emergence of leadership roles in a group (not to mention being able to manipulate their emergence) would vastly facilitate the economy of operation of social systems in industry, education, the military, and even community and neighborhood contexts. But leadership is an elusive variable. Despite an appreciable accumulation of research evidence, specific leadership effectiveness can be predicted only crudely. The training and cultivation of effective leaders is equally difficult because the particular skills or attributes needed for effective leadership vary so widely from one social organization to another.

The structure and functioning of groups are also relevant to many issues facing clinical psychology. The primary aim of various approaches to group psychotherapy is to reeducate the disturbed individual toward more successful adaptation to his social context. But there are differences of opinion among psychotherapists and social psychologists as to exactly which factors of group organization and functioning contribute most effectively toward these aims. For example, Slavson (1955) has argued that the emergence of group norms and goal values may be detrimental to the therapeutic process, and Bion (1961) has warned particularly of the danger of normative forces that induce conformity within the group to nonbeneficial standards for behavior. However, others stress the acquisition of collective group values and the formation of constructive norms as essential to success in psychotherapy (Dreikurs, 1960; Luchins, Aumack, & Dickman, 1960). The differentiation of roles within the group, as well as the generation of role expectations on the part of group members about one another's behavior, is clearly recognized as an important component in the therapeutic process (Moreno, 1946; Frank & Powdermaker, 1953; Fagan & Shepherd, 1971).

The function of the therapist in the role of group leader may also be analyzed as contributing to the group's movement toward its therapeutic goals. In most therapeutic groups the psychotherapist is recognized by his patients from the outset as possessing some degree of legitimate power to manipulate their actions. Furthermore, he has expert power as a recognized authority on human relations, as well as referent power, through virtue of the fact that the patient tends to view him as an object of identification whose behavior and reactions are worthy of emulation (Rosenbaum, 1965; Harari, 1971, 1972). In didactic directive approaches to group therapy, the psychotherapist may assume a relatively autocratic style of leadership, but in the more nondirective approaches, his role is usually one of inhibited democratic leadership. In the sense that the therapist himself becomes something of a participant in the group, some psychologists have even recommended the use of multiple therapists to provide diffused leadership (Dreikurs, 1960).

Because the effectiveness of group psychotherapy depends largely on rich social interaction among participants, the size and physical arrangements of the group may prove critical to the therapeutic process. Groups containing fewer than six members tend to be encumbered with inertia and complacency, but groups of more than ten do not permit extensive interaction among members and allow passive members to become lost in the crowd (Slavson, 1943; Hinckley & Hermann, 1951; Luchins, 1964). In order to facilitate interpersonal communication, a circular seating arrangement appears to be best (McCann & Almada, 1950). Homogeneity of background of the members (in terms of sex, age, intelligence, and the like) appears to facilitate the therapeutic process, perhaps largely because it enhances cohesiveness and maximizes identification of each member with the group as a system (Hinckley & Hermann, 1951; Luchins, 1964).

The pragmatic approach to group psychotherapy as an efficient means of permitting one therapist to deal with many patients gives rise to didactic "audience-approach" types of psychotherapy in which the therapist merely "lectures" his patients. Although such approaches are probably better than no therapy at all, they are of relatively little benefit to patients (Singer & Goldman, 1954; Zimet & Fine, 1955). However, just as group discussions facilitate changes in individual attitudes and actions, combination lecture-discussion approaches in group therapy have proved effective (Chapell et al., 1937; Snowden, 1940; Klapman, 1946, 1950; Luchins, 1964). In general, the most effective approaches to group psychotherapy have been those that fully exploit the operation of group forces to expedite the attainment of therapeutic goals. In such techniques the therapist plays a retiring and inconspicuous role and allows the group to generate full properties of an organized social system (that is, to become a group rather than an audience). The group charts its own course, unrestricted by the therapist unless there is evidence of impending conflict beyond the capacity of the group to handle (Hobbs, 1951; Bion, 1961). Often the individual members are first prepared through several sessions of individual therapy before they become participants in the group (Wolf, 1950).

A variety of devices may be used in conjunction with group psychotherapy: puppet shows, paintings done by the patients, or even taped transcripts of relevant discussions may be used to initiate group discussion along particular lines (Bach, 1950; Hartley & Gondor, 1956; Luchins, 1964). But perhaps the most effective means of instigating pertinent action in a group is through role playing. With this approach, the therapist induces one or more members of the group to assume a particular kind of behavioral role. Moreno (1946) developed an elaborate approach to role playing in group therapy, which he called *psychodrama*. With this technique, the group becomes a party to a theatrical production. The therapist has the role of director, producer, counselor, and sometimes interpreter and critic of the action that takes place on the stage. A group-member may assume a given role, either derived from his past experience or in anticipation of his future behavior. Other members assume the roles of significant figures in the central figure's life, and in some cases they may assume the role of "alter ego" or shadow or conscience to the central figure. In some contexts it is possible to conduct group therapy along these lines with the actual participation of several members of a natural group such as a family. In clinical work with children and adolescents, bringing together the entire family for therapeutic interaction under supervision of a psychotherapist is especially effective (Jackson, 1959).

REVIEW

1. *Position* refers to a particular location in the structural framework of a social group.

2. *Role* refers to the behavior displayed by a person occupying a certain position.

3. *Status* refers to the value attached by the group to particular role behaviors.

4. The overall system of integrated position, role, and status relationships is called *group structure.*

5. The overt behavior displayed by a person in a given position is called *enacted role* or *role enactment.*

6. The way other members of the group perceive that behavior is called the *perceived role* or *role perception.*

7. The expectations held by other members for each other's behavior define *expected roles* or *role expectation.*

8. Role expectations include both *role-predictions* (probability estimates of the likelihood that a person will behave in some expected way, based largely on his past performance) and *role-prescriptions* (obligations and expectations that a person ought to behave in some expected way, based largely on the group's norms and ideals).

9. *Group task roles* represent behaviors that contribute to the group's attainment of its goals and objectives.

10. *Group maintenance roles* represent behaviors that contribute to the organization of the group and harmony among its members.

11. *Individual roles* represent behaviors that primarily serve each individual's private needs and have little or no relevance to the group as a social system.

12. Stabilized lines of interpersonal role relationship and interaction within the group define its *communication net.*

13. Common organized communication networks include wheels, circles, chains, Ys, and variations of these. A network that places one person at the center of a pattern of communication is said to show high *centrality;* the member in the center occupies a *central* position, and others around the rim occupy *peripheral* positions. A network that distributes everyone in equally peripheral positions is said to have low *centrality.*

14. The degree of centrality of a group's structure influences both its productivity and satisfaction within the group. The centrality of the position occupied by a group member influences his own personal productivity and satisfaction.

15. The structure of a group is directly affected by the number of members in it. In large groups, *coalitions* of subgroups are possible. The formation of such coalitions is in turn related to group performance, member satisfaction, and role behaviors within the group, including leadership.

16. Social *climate* or *atmosphere* is a way of describing the overall character of a group according to the nature of its structure of internal role relationships. At least among Americans, a *democratic* atmosphere promotes greater group productivity and member satisfaction than an *autocratic* or *laissez-faire* climate.

17. Group *cohesiveness* is a multidimensional description of the amount of "we" feeling in a group, defined in terms of both the total mutual attraction among pairs in the

group as well as the attraction of each member to the group as a social organization. Cohesive groups are characterized by high morale, greater productivity, internal stability, sharp delineation of boundaries separating members from nonmembers, pronounced effectiveness of norms and standards, and rites of passage for entering or leaving the group.

18. *Leadership* is a role defined by the frequency with which a person influences or directs the behavior of other members of the group.

19. *Titular* leadership is defined by one's nominal position in the group; *emergent* leadership is defined by one's enacted role in the group.

20. *Leadership style,* the way one plays the leader role, may be described in a variety of ways, such as autocratic/democratic; task-oriented/group-oriented; supervisory/participatory. The style adopted by a person as leader is a result of both his personality and the needs and circumstances of the group.

21. There is moderate but limited stability of leadership roles within the same group as its activities and circumstances change. There is also limited stability of one person's leadership behavior in different groups of people, so long as their activities remain similar.

22. The ability and effectiveness of a person as leader in a group are difficult to predict reliably because personality factors and situational conditions interact to define leadership. The emergence, style, and quality of leadership in a particular group are *contingent* upon situational conditions, especially the *affective relationship* of the leader to his followers, the *structure* or ambiguity of the group's task, and *power associated with a particular position* in the group.

23. Because the particular behavioral traits associated with effective leadership are specific to particular situations, one can speak only in broad generalizations about general qualities of good leaders. These include *sensitivity, flexibility,* and *responsibility.*

24. There is little evidence that general leadership ability can be readily trained or cultivated; however, training may develop specific skills needed by a particular group for a particular purpose, and thus facilitate leadership in a specific case.

12

GROUP PERFORMANCE

An essential characteristic of a social psychological group (in addition to norms and roles) is that of performance as an integrated unit. It performs some function as a system, such as attaining an objective goal, or escaping some kind of threat. Group goals direct the activity of the system toward particular ends and objectives in the same way that individual motivational goals direct an individual's behavior. In an organized social system group goals are interwoven with group norms and roles, so that all three are interdependent.

Modern psychologists and sociologists are interested in the collective performance of the group as well as the individual performance of members within the organized system. However, early research and theory in group dynamics often failed to recognize the importance of *organization* itself. These early investigations often involved speculations about the effect of the presence of other people upon one's activities, treating all collections of people the same, regardless of whether or not they actually constituted organized groups, or whether they were merely audiences to one another. Thus some false leads were developed in the early study of performance in groups.

SOCIAL FACILITATION

Early sociologists and psychologists took note of the apparent fact that individual behavior is "facilitated" in several ways when people act in the presence of others. For example, Munsterberg (1914) found that when he presented two cards containing almost equal numbers of dots in a circular field and asked individuals to judge which card contained the greater number of dots, more accurate judgments were expressed in groups than by individuals judging alone. Similarly, Jenness (1932) conducted studies of the ability of people to guess the number of beans contained in a jar and found that when people had opportunity to discuss their estimates with others, more accurate judgments were expressed. Because both of these investigators ignored the "bandwagon" effects that occur when people go along with the majority, the notion of group mind lent itself readily as a way of describing these observations. It was assumed that in groups individual function is enhanced by a superordinate "group mind." It is true that the presence of other people brings about marked changes in an individual's performance of various activities, but the fiction of a "group mind" does not explain these differences. One must explore the effect of others as social stimulus forces in order to understand such changes in behavior.

Extending some early investigations by Moede (1920) and Triplett (1897), F. H. Allport (1920, 1924) conducted a series of studies in which he compared solitary performance with performance of the same tasks in the presence of others. The latter condition did not provide for true organization of the group as a system because the other people merely comprised an audience watching while one performed individual tasks; such nonorganized sets of people have sometimes been termed *coacting* groups, to distinguish them from genuinely organized interacting groups. With very simple rote tasks such as cancellation of particular vowels or digits from a printed series of letters or numbers, Allport found that individuals performed faster in the presence of others than when alone, but that some people made a greater number of errors in the presence of others. Similarly, in solving simple arithmetic problems, although individuals solved more problems in the presence of others than when alone, the proportion of wrong answers was greater for many people when performing with others than when performing alone. This increase in quantity of output (even though often accompanied by a decrease in the quality or accuracy of the product) was interpreted as evidence of the facilitative effect of the presence of other people upon individual performance. Allport also found that there were differences in the kinds of judgments expressed alone. For example, in preparing rebuttals to arguments, individuals working in the presence of others produced less original refutations than individuals working alone. Furthermore, when asked to judge odors along an absolute scale from "very pleasant" to "very unpleasant," or to judge weights along a scale from "very heavy" to "very light," there was a tendency for judgments made in the presence of others to converge around the middle categories, with relatively infrequent use of extreme ones.

In other studies (F. H. Allport, 1920) people were asked to associate as many words as they could think of with each of a set of stimulus words. In the presence of other people, these word associations were more commonplace and trite than associations made alone. It appeared in general that a kind of conservatism, in terms of tendencies toward moderation in judgment, was typical of individuals performing in the presence of others. From these findings, Allport concluded that the presence of other people generally exerted a facilitative effect on individual performance with respect to simple motor performance, but he recognized somewhat deleterious effects on individual reasoning and judgment. Similar studies by other investigators (e.g., Triplett, 1897; Whittemore, 1924) generally corroborated Allport's findings.

Somewhat later Dashiell (1935) reconsidered Allport's findings and suggested that the effects of competition with others might partially account for the observed differences. He reviewed several studies, adding empirical findings of his own, to separate the effects of competition from other effects of the presence of an audience. He found that even when people were merely told that others were performing the same tasks (that is, presumably exciting competition, but without having others actually present), the same kinds of "facilitative" effects were observed. Similarly, when other people were actually present, the reduction of competition reduced the magnitude of these effects. Thus Dashiell's conclusion was that competition among individuals provides at least one basis for the observed increases in output and decreases in quality of the product of individuals performing tasks together. However, his explorations still noted a residual difference suggestive of facilitative effects of the sheer presence of others.

Other experiments have attempted to isolate and define the specific factors in social

---

STAGE FRIGHT

A study showed that low degrees of stage fright ("audience anxiety") in children were associated with frequent parental reward, infrequent parental punishment, and a generally favorable parental view of the child's social development. High degrees of stage fright were associated with frequent punishment for failure to meet parental standards and with unfavorable parental evaluation of the child's social behavior and achievement. Willingness to perform before others was associated with exhibitionism; unwillingness was associated with self-consciousness and audience anxiety.

In another study preadolescents were asked individually to tell a story to either of two audiences: the experimenter or a group of six adults. Audience anxiety was evident with the larger audience; that is, children who were high in both exhibitionism and self-consciousness (to whom the audience was, respectively, a source of attraction and fear), made more errors than their counterparts. Children low in exhibitionism and high in self-consciousness tended to speak for less time before the larger audience than did their counterparts, presumably because of the inhibiting effects of audience stress.

PAIVIO, BALDWIN, AND BERGER (1959, 1961)
LEVIN, BALDWIN, GALLWEY, AND PAIVIO (1960)

situations that affect a person's performance of various tasks. The typical pattern of performance under any kind of stress is one of increased quantity in effort and output, accompanied by decreased quality or accuracy. High levels of motivational drive, frustration, and even pain and physical discomfort produce the same pattern of effects (J. S. Brown, 1961). And there is considerable evidence that, at least for some people, the presence of other people watching one's performance has the same kind of stressful effect (Paivio et al., 1959, 1961). In other words, there is little doubt that at least one factor in the pattern of so-called social facilitation is nothing other than stage fright or audience anxiety.

However, this kind of audience stress effect has little or nothing to do with one's participation in *organized* groups. To the extent that social facilitation is merely a form of stress derived from being watched, it is independent of questions raised about organized interaction and group performance. Being watched by an audience is not the same thing as participating in an integral way in an organized group (Zajonc & Sales, 1966; Martens, 1969).

Another facet of "social facilitation" can also be explained by a simple social phenomenon. The fact that people working together report more accurate estimates or judgments of difficult and ambiguous matters (as compared to people working alone) probably represents nothing other than a case of social conformity (see Chapter 10). In collective situations people are likely to go along with the judgments of the majority. As long as the majority is correct, such influence leads to greater accuracy and the kind of social facilitation observed by Dashiell, Allport, and others. However, should the majority be in error at the outset, conformity to the judgment of the majority would, of course, lead to "nonfacilitative" effects on judgment.

The fact that early studies of social facilitation also observed tendencies toward conservatism in the expression of individual judgments in the presence of other people may also be ascribed to group norms and conformity. Regulative mechanisms maintaining a group's stability usually discourage deviation among its members (see Chapter 10). Thus people working in the presence of others are somewhat inhibited and less likely to express extreme judgments, to generate innovations or novel ideas, or to voice highly personal or unusual notions. This is merely a reflection of conservatism about the risk of being called upon to defend one's unorthodox judgments. Social motivation to behave in socially acceptable ways probably underlies this aspect of social influence.

A paradoxical parallel concerning conservatism and risk in the expression of ideas and choices in public situations has been observed in studies of gambling and other kinds of venturesome behavior. Just as people are *less* willing to express unorthodox *individual* or personal ideas in a group, so are people *more* willing to express risky and unorthodox ideas *collectively* in the name of the group. That is, when the judgment or idea is viewed as one of *individual* responsibility, there is a shift toward conservatism and cowardice; but when the idea or judgment is viewed as one of

---

THE COWARDLY SHIFT

Audiences ranging from one to ninety-six members were asked to volunteer ideas for the solution of a problem. With increments in group size there were progressively smaller increments in the number of ideas produced. With increasing group size there were corresponding increases of reported feelings of inhibition about participating in the task. It was suggested that feelings of threat as the group increases in size may reduce individual participation, thereby creating an obstacle to the completion of tasks in very large groups.

J. R. GIBB (1951)

collective responsibility, there is a shift toward greater risk. Thus, the "cowardly shift" of the individual-before-an-audience, and the "risky shift" of the collective group performing as an organized system operate in opposite directions.

311

Group
Performance

THE RISKY SHIFT: SHORTCUTS TO RELEVANCE

Recently psychologists have focused intensively on studies of risk taking in individuals and groups. In one series of experiments college students were faced with a problem-solving task in which increased risk associated with selecting a more difficult task was compensated by monetary gain. Comparison between the performance of groups and individuals showed that group decision by consensus tended to be more "risky" than individual decisions. Groups selected more difficult problems with possible higher payoffs, even when the actual problem solving was done by a single member. This shift toward greater risk was interpreted as a characteristic of groups to diffuse responsibility among their members. To preclude alternative explanations, an experiment was designed to emphasize physical pain and loss of money. Subjects were told either that their decisions would be publicly discussed or that they would be able to make them in the presence of like-minded peers. The first condition implied the possibility that greater risk taking in groups was related to social desirability (virility, showing off), whereas the second condition assumed anxiety alleviation (misery loving miserable company). Under both conditions, risk taking occurred less than under conditions of consensual group decision. This has been called "responsibility diffusion" (Wallach, Kogan, & Bem, 1962, 1964, 1965).

Much recent research on this "risky shift" (from individuals to groups, or in individuals after group discussion) has used the Choice Dilemma Questionnaire (CDQ). The CDQ includes twelve items, each describing a choice situation varying in riskiness and degree of reward, as seen in the following item:

Mr. A, an electrical engineer who is married and has one child, has been working for a large electronics corporation since graduating from college 5 years ago. He is assured of a lifetime job with a modest, although adequate, salary, and liberal pension benefits upon retirement. It is very unlikely that his salary will increase much before he retires. While attending a convention, Mr. A is offered a job with a small, new company that has a highly uncertain future. The new job would pay more to start and would offer the possibility of a share in the ownership if the company survived the competition of the larger firms.

Imagine that you are advising Mr. A. Listed below are several probabilities or odds of the new company's proving financially sound. Please decide the *lowest* probability that you would consider acceptable to make it worthwhile for Mr. A to take the new job.

1. The chances are 1 in 10 that the company will prove financially sound.
2. The chances are 3 in 10 that the company will prove financially sound.
3. The chances are 5 in 10 that the company will prove financially sound.
4. The chances are 7 in 10 that the company will prove financially sound.
5. The chances are 9 in 10 that the company will prove financially sound.
6. Mr. A should not take the new job no matter what the probabilities.

Obviously the subject who regards the new job acceptable under condition (1) is more of a risk-taker than the one who chooses (2) or even more so than the one who chooses (3) and so on. For those who refuse to take *any* risk, choice (6) is provided to advise against taking the new job, regardless of the odds.

The consistency of the research findings has led to generalizations to relevant real-life situations. The implication that decision-making groups are prone to take greater risks than their individual members would can scarcely be ignored at times when world leaders and their advisors gather to make vital decisions under the shadow of nuclear threat. Newer findings, however, raise serious uncertainty about what exactly transpires in group decision. For example, although the total CDQ score consistently indicates a risky shift in group decision, on at least two specific items the shift was toward greater caution (whether to build an industrial plant in

(Continued on p. 312)

the United States or to build it abroad, with both greater anticipated risks and profits; and whether to accept a marital counselor's optimistic predictions regarding a marriage beset by difficulties). Frequent criticism that the CDQ's hypothetical choice situations are not valid approximations of real-life situations receives support from the discovery of a "Walter Mitty" effect. Like James Thurber's fictional hero who lived a sedate life but pretended to engage in risky adventures, CDQ respondents perceive themselves as high risk-takers, but act rather cautiously when faced with actual decisions (Pruitt, 1969). As Higbee (1971) demonstrated, the CDQ is a more appropriate measure of how risky a person *thinks* he will be than of how risky he *actually* will be. Critics also point out that most risky shift studies involve the same subjects moving from individual decision making to group decision making. It may therefore be more appropriate to speak of shifts in *choices,* than of *differences* between individuals who are considering the problems for the first time (Cartwright, 1971).

Can psychologists generalize research findings on choice shifts in group decisions to the real world, when so many of their findings have been contradictory? According to Cartwright the only feasible way is through the arduous search of theoretical formulations about the nature of these choice shifts, because "there would appear no shortcut to relevance." Among the formulations reviewed by Pruitt (1971), risky shift is explained by diffusion of responsibility, familiarization (group discussion reduces uncertainty), leader's ability to persuade, social comparison (to be as risky as the other fellow), pluralistic ignorance (erroneously having assumed others are cautious), and commitment by the individual to irrevocable initial positions.

This series of studies and theoretical speculations affords an intriguing glimpse into the microculture of psychological research. First, someone postulates an interesting hypothesis and substantiates it by experimental proof. Then follows a rash of generalizations to real-life situations, some of which are tenuous at best. Other studies cast doubts on the validity of the original findings. The phenomenon undoubtedly exists, despite conflicting findings, so strenuous efforts are made to find encompassing theoretical formulations to account for it. If the attempt is successful, subsequent findings and generalizations have greater utility and relevance; if the attempts are unsuccessful, the topic fades into limbo. Whether choice shifts in group decision are destined to be a fad or a landmark in psychological research on group dynamics remains to be seen.

PRUITT (1969, 1971)
CARTWRIGHT (1971)
HIGBEE (1971)

GROUP GOALS AND THE INDIVIDUAL

Experimental studies of individual performance in collective situations have often shown an apparent superiority of collective performance over individual performance. But the kind of activity in which a group engages is an important factor determining the degree of benefit gained from collective action.

Group goals represent collective commitments that guide the performance of a group as a unitary system. In some situations the primary performance objective may be to arrive at one proper solution to a soluble problem (such as decoding a message, assembling a puzzle, solving a riddle, or producing a manufactured article): in this case the activity is said to be *convergent,* because the efforts and actions of the group converge on one objective. In other situations, however, the objective may be to generate innovative ideas, plans, or policies and strategies in situations that afford more than one reasonable approach (such as in planning boards, "brainstorming" sessions, creative conferences, or consideration of alternatives and implications): in this case, the activity is said to be *divergent,* because the efforts and actions of the group fan outward to consider and explore in all directions. In some cases, both processes may be involved at different stages of the group's activities: for example, a jury in its deliberations may first air all possible alternatives and implications of various bits of information (divergent), but eventually develop these into a consensual decision on the part of the group (convergent). In any case, the performance goals and objectives of the group are related to the degree of superiority of collective over individual action.

In a convergent task, when any single member of the group happens to attain the one correct solution, the group as a whole would be credited with having solved the problem. Thus a kind of artifact may be introduced when group performance is compared to individual performance, reflecting nothing other than the fact that there is greater statistical probability that *some one* out of ten people working together will arrive at a correct solution than that *each and every one* of these ten working individually would arrive at the correct solution. To attempt to control this artifact and pursue comparisons of individual versus collective performance, comparisons may be made among individuals, "real" groups, and artificial "statisticized" groups. The latter are concocted by pooling observations of a number of people who actually work alone, treating them *as if* they had worked in a group, and crediting the entire set of people with having solved a problem if any one of them actually solved it. Findings from such investigations suggest strongly that at least part of the observed superiority of groups over individuals must be ascribed to such probabalistic artifacts (Tuckman & Lorge, 1962; Ryack, 1965).

Group goals may be either *formal* and explicit (as in the case of a committee charged with arriving at a decision on a specified issue) or *informal* and implicit (as in the case of a group of children who get together regularly as neighborhood playmates). Often the formal and publicly stated objectives of a group may be only nominal and inaccurate reflections of the real purposes of the group. For example, men's "service" clubs, ladies' "literary" societies—even college fraternities and sororities—all exist largely for the mutual entertainment and pleasure of their members, regardless of their more nobly stated platitudes about goals and functions. In fact, many informal groups, such as neighborhood play groups or a clique of students who get together regularly to have a few beers, may exist almost altogether for purposes of mutual enjoyment.

In many cases, groups commit themselves to certain *nonoperational* goals at one level, but function more directly in terms of short-range immediate *operational* goals

---

ARE FOUR HEADS BETTER THAN ONE?

Four-person groups drawn from research scientists and advertising personnel in a mining company worked on various problem-solving tasks—the Thumbs Problem (what would happen if everyone had an extra thumb on each hand?), the Tourist Problem (what can we do to get more European tourists to come to America?), the People Problem (what would happen if due to dietary changes the height of the average American increased to 80 inches and his weight doubled?); and the Education Problem (what to do to alleviate a hypothetical future teacher shortage?). Some of the groups consisted of as-if members (i.e., they worked individually but their productivity was subsequently pooled). A quality comparison between solutions of the real and as-if groups showed the latter to be superior. It was concluded that the pooled effort of four persons attacking a problem produced an average of 30 percent more ideas than problem solving in an actual four-person group session.

DUNNETTE, CAMPBELL, AND JAASTAD (1963)

(March & Simon, 1958). A ladies' literary society may formally endorse the nonoperational goal of "uplifting the cultural level of the community," but function as a group in terms of more immediate operational goals such as planning a spring dinner-dance to raise funds for a scholarship. Similarly, an informal group of playmates may adopt a sequence of transitory operational goals, such as "let's build a fort," or "let's play baseball." The operational goals of a group are likely to be somewhat more transitory and shorter in range than its nonoperational goals. Thus many groups that endure nominally for a long period of time under a set of formally stated nonoperational goals may actually move from time to time through a sequence of operational goals. Because it is the immediate operational goals that characterize the true effective organization of a group, one might argue accurately (although with a certain amount of hairsplitting) that a "new" group is generated every time a new operational goal is adopted. There is no question that the adoption of new operational goals often brings about a new structure, a new set of individual behavioral roles, and even a new set of regulative norms and standards within the group. For this reason, groups may sometimes become unpredictable when they undergo a shift in operational purpose, even though they remain comprised of exactly the same people.

The term *syntality* designates the total performance of a group as a unitary system, and the term *synergy* has been coined to describe the total amount of energy available for expenditure by the group as an organized system (Cattell, 1951). By means of a factor analytic study of a wide array of measures of group performance, group structure, and characteristics of individual members, Cattell arrived at the conclusion that there are two general categories of energy expenditure in group performance: *maintenance synergy,* which is energy expended to maintain the group and to sustain the attraction of individual members to remain in the group, and *task synergy,* which is energy expended to execute the group's task and to pursue attainment of group goals and objectives.

Groups tend to move simultaneously toward two kinds of general objectives: the execution of some purposeful function and the maintenance of the group as an organized system. Kurt Lewin suggested the term *group locomotion* to describe the movement of the group toward attainment of these objectives. Both are crucial to the sustained organization of a group as a social system. *Maintenance* functions are displayed in mechanisms that encourage harmony and discourage conflict among members, or that enhance the interest of each member in the group's activities and his attraction to other members of the group, or that reward members for contributions to the organized system and punish them for interference with the operation of the group as a system. A large proportion of the resources of some groups must be addressed to this objective, especially if there are no external contraints to hold individuals within the group. On the other hand, some groups are composed of members who are more-or-less coerced into remaining in the group, either by personal necessity, or by obstacles that prevent their leaving. In such cases, relatively less energy may be required for maintenance of the group as a system.

Task functions include activities that move the group toward completion of its task and direct attainment of its functional objectives, and they include the exchange of information and ideas and individual contributions pertaining to the job at hand. Some groups are highly task-oriented, so that the majority of their efforts are addressed toward task functions; others are less task-oriented and may concentrate on making the group remain attractive to its members. By analyzing the structure and role relationships within various groups (see Chapter 11), Robert Freed Bales and others have been able to evaluate various kinds of groups in terms of their performance of each of these functions.

Ordinarily, group goals, as objectives of the organized social system, are adopted by each member as his own personal goals. Of course when group and individual goals coincide, the individual experiences maximum personal satisfaction in the group's success.

The close relationship between collective goals and individual goals in organized groups has been demonstrated in several ways. Some time ago Zeigarnik (1927) conducted experiments in which subjects were given various tasks to perform but were interrupted before they could be completed. When these people were later asked to recall what tasks they had performed, they remembered the interrupted tasks considerably better than those that had been completed. This phenomenon of better memory for interrupted than for completed tasks is commonly called the *Zeigarnik effect,* and it is usually interpreted as evidence that residual motivational tension is left when one's goals are not achieved. Later, Lewis and others (Lewis & Franklin, 1944) investigated the Zeigarnik effect in connection with group tasks, and found that when pairs of people performed tasks cooperatively, even if only one of them succeeded in completing the task, no Zeigarnik effect occurred for the other partner. Horwitz (1954) pursued this curiosity further in studies of five-person groups, and found that the Zeigarnik effect could be eliminated by allowing the group to choose whether or not it would like to complete the task. In Horwitz's studies, the Zeigarnik effect of superior recall for uncompleted tasks occurred only when the group had voted to complete a task but had been subsequently interrupted. These studies show the interdependence of group goals and individual goals. They demonstrate that group success functions for the individual as though it were his own success when he is personally committed to group goals. Conversely, group failure leaves each committed member of the group with unresolved motivational tension.

THEY WIN—I WIN; THEY LOSE—I LOSE

Groups were given five trials on a mechanical task and then asked to jointly set up group goals. The task consisted of all the group members grasping a long pole and collectively striking a ball toward a series of targets. Goal setting was done by having the members jointly predicting, after each trial, how well they expected to do on the next trial. When the preceding attempt was successful, goals were set higher for the subsequent attempt. When the preceding attempt was not successful, the groups lowered their goal. It was concluded that a group's level of aspiration (degree of goal setting) follows essentially the same dynamics as that of individuals.

ZANDER AND MEDOW (1963)

EVALUATION OF GROUP EFFECTIVENESS AND SATISFACTION

The adequacy of a group in performing its functions as an organized system can be evaluated along two dimensions. These generally parallel the two kinds of functions described: one is concerned with evaluation of the extent to which a group is successful in attaining its task-related objectives (*effectiveness*), and the other is concerned with evaluating the extent to which a group satisfies the needs of its individual members (*satisfaction*).

Such measures as quantity or quality of articles produced by a group of factory workers, the number of puzzles solved by a problem-solving group in a laboratory study, the practical value of policies or strategies adopted by a corporate planning board, and the ingenuity of new ideas produced in a brainstorming session—all would constitute measures of group effectiveness. In essence, effectiveness is an index of the amount of return on a group's investment of task synergy.

The second concept, satisfaction, is a broad notion of the degree to which the group is successful in maintaining itself. Such measures as the extent to which the needs of each individual person are satisfied through his participation in the group and each member's liking for other members reflect this dimension.

A variety of personal goals may be served by a person's participation in a group: he may gain prestige from his identification with the group (Willerman & Swanson, 1953) or he may find security and relief from anxiety (Schachter, 1959). Many other kinds of personal goals that are more or less independent of collective group goals may provide the initial incentive that attracts a person to enter a group. Several group dynamics experts (Lewin, 1947; Festinger, 1953; Cartwright & Zander, 1960) have emphasized that group performance involves not only *group locomotion* (movement of the group as a system toward the attainment of objectives), but also *group satisfaction* (the instrumental provision of means whereby individual members may use the group to satisfy their own needs). This latter issue is discussed further later in this chapter.

In examining the question of why people join and remain in groups, Cartwright and Zander (1960) identify two sources of attraction: the group itself may be the object of some motivational desire, such as a quest for approval and recognition; and being in the group may represent a means of satisfying some motivational desire arising elsewhere, such as dependence on the help of others to achieve a personal goal, utilization of the group as a teacher or source of information, or reassurance from others to relieve fears or anxieties.

Festinger (1954) proposed that one function of the group is to provide each member with evidence about "social reality." In his *theory of social comparison processes,* Festinger suggests that people may utilize feedback from groups in which they are participating as a basis for understanding the world around them. They compare their cognitive interpretations of the world with those of others. They use the group as a means of "socially evaluating and determining appropriate and proper reactions."

The alleviation of anxiety may be a particularly important source of attraction to groups. Grinker and Spiegel (1945) investigated fear, anxiety, and insecurity in military personnel during World War II, and found that men in bomber crews were especially reassured and less anxious when they were in the company of other members of their crew. Later, Schachter (1959) extended this hypothesis into a series of experimental studies of the basis of affiliative motivation, and generated convincing evidence that the reduction of anxiety is indeed an important motivator in affiliative behavior.

Of course similarities of interests, values, and attitudes are important aspects of an individual's attraction to any group of people (see Chapter 8). One is likely to join and participate in groups with whose interests he has much in common and whose norms and values are congruent with his own. It is far less likely that a person would be attracted to a group whose members differ considerably from himself and whose activities are incompatible with his own purposes, goals, or desires.

Unfortunately, it is clear from studies of stereotyping that people often judge an entire group by generalizing from contacts with a limited number of members. Inasmuch as members of a group are indeed likely to share attitudes, values, and interests, there may be some validity to such generalizations. But it is limited, and overgeneralized stereotypes often lead to inaccurate judgments.

Aronson and Mills (1959) suggest another basis of one's attraction to a group, one that is particularly pertinent to continued participation in a group once it has been joined. They propose that the more difficult one's entry into a group (that is, through severe initiation, rigid selection, or arduous effort to gain membership), the greater will be one's estimate of the value of belonging to that group. This hypothesis, then, actually suggests a kind of rationalization that affords a means of maintaining cogni-

JOB SATISFACTION AND PERFORMANCE

A study of over 10,000 managerial-supervisory, salaried, and hourly employees in a large manufacturing concern showed considerable overlap in the importance attributed to job characteristics. Managerial-supervisory employees considered the performance of subordinates and cooperation among fellow workers as of greatest importance. Among the salaried employees, future pay, satisfaction from work, company reputation, and their own contribution to the organization, was considered to be of greatest importance. The hourly employees considered of greatest importance the overall quality of the work place, with an emphasis on facilities, equipment, supplies, and materials. These stated attitudes, however, were not necessarily related to subsequent behavior on the job. Job satisfaction and dissatisfaction in terms of production per unit, tardiness, sick calls, absenteeism, and so on showed that expressed attitudes and corresponding behavior occurred only when the type of direct supervision of the worker was of critical importance.

RONAN (1970a,b)

tive order, consonance, and closure: overestimation of the value of belonging to the group "justifies" the uncomfortable passage into membership. Lewin (1951) discussed a similar notion, which he called "membership character," but at a theoretical level without empirical documentation.

Processes of interpersonal perception and attraction among members of highly organized social systems may be very complex. Distinctions may be drawn between members of one's own group whose goals are compatible with one's personal goals (the "ingroup") and members of alien groups whose goals are antagonistic or incompatible (the "outgroup"). Such complexities of attraction within groups and hostilities between groups within complex organizations, bureaucracies, or even societies have important implications for understanding sociopolitical behavior. These are discussed further in Chapter 13.

Group Performance and Group Goals

The performance of a group as a collective system is generally limited by the clarity of the group's collective objectives and the correspondence between the collective goals of the group and the individual goals of its members. When collective goals are vague or ambiguous, or if for some reason they are not communicated clearly to members, disruptive effects on group performance occur (Raven & Reitsma, 1957). Discrepancies or conflicts between individual goals and group goals also interfere with the organization of a group and thus impede its performance (Deutsch, 1949; Fiedler, 1958). In a general sense, the greater the extent of individual competitive conflict within a group, the less effective is the overall performance of the group as a collective system.

There is a mutual relationship between the success of a group in attaining its collective goals and its success in meeting the personal needs of its individual members. On one hand, individuals ordinarily find relatively little satisfaction in participating in groups that persistently fail to reach collective goals (Deutsch, 1959). On the other hand, groups that fail to satisfy the personal needs of individuals participating in the group usually tend to be relatively ineffective in attaining their collective objectives (Schutz, 1955). Thus maximally effective performance of a group occurs when the group succeeds both in satisfying personal individual needs of each member and in achieving its collective goals.

GOAL CLARITY AND PERFORMANCE

College students were assigned to groups and then individually asked to cut out geometrical figures for the purported use of the other members of their group, who supposedly were engaged in a construction task. While involved in the task, each subject heard a tape recording that told him what his group was doing with the pieces he had been providing. In one experimental condition, perceived goal clarity was maximized by means of clear and understandable information, whereas in another the information was obscure and vague. Individual productivity was measured by the subject's response rate to requests for accelerated productivity by the others (in the form of fictitious notes delivered by a messenger). A comparison between experimental conditions showed a positive relationship between perceived goal clarity, lack of hostility, and productivity.

RAVEN AND RIETSMA (1957)

GOAL CONFLICT AND PERFORMANCE

The effectiveness of basketball teams in Illinois was evaluated by examination of their season records of wins and losses. At the same time, the internal structure of these teams as social organizations was examined. Teams that included an outstanding "star" who was visibly different from the rest of the team and recognized by all as a candidate for "high-scorer" or other singular distinction, had poorer overall season records than teams whose membership was more even and undifferentiated. The effort to achieve solo distinction seems not always compatible with the effort to achieve team success, and the conflict of these two is disruptive of the team's performance.

FIEDLER (1967)

Group Performance and Group Norms

Group norms and standards afford regulation of both the structure and function of organized groups. But just as the effective and efficient performance of a group is dependent on its structural properties, so also are these qualities dependent on the adequacy of effective regulative mechanisms within the group. These regulative mechanisms normally are derived from values that are in accord with the movement of the group toward its goals and with maintenance of structural organization within the group. Unclear norms or standards impede the effectiveness of the group in attaining its goals (Coch & French, 1948). Conflicting norms tend also to reduce the satisfactions that the group offers to its members. Individual deviation from group norms and standards is disruptive to the group, both in detracting from its collective performance as well as in interfering with its organizational structure. To some extent, specific norms may be evolved within a group in the form of expectations about the function of each individual in performing his own assigned functions. When an

HAPPY GROUPS DELIVER

Five-man groups of naval trainees competed against one another in a series of experimental tasks. The groups were composed of either "personal" members (who preferred close and intimate relations with others), "counterpersonal" members (who preferred to keep others at a distance), or mixed types. Groups compatible in terms of member-needs (all of the same type) were more productive than were incompatible groups (mixed type).

SCHUTZ (1955)

THE WORKER AS BOSS

A field experiment designed to study workers' resistance to industrial change in a Virginia pajama factory employed three groups of workers prior to the transfer of their members to similar settings where the advocated change was already in force. A control group involved no participation of its members with management in planning and deciding on the advocated change; one experimental group involved participation through representation of the workers; the other experimental group involved the total participation of its members. Participation of workers in planning the advocated change, especially if participation was total, was related to greater group cohesiveness and productivity in the new setting, whereas nonparticipation in such planning resulted in less cohesiveness and a decline in productivity.

COCH AND FRENCH (1948)

---

individual violates these expectations, the consequence is a disruption of both the group's organizational efficiency and its effective performance (Whyte, 1943). In general, the success of a group, both in its efforts as a system as well as in satisfactions to its individual members, is highly dependent on the adequacy of its regulative norms and standards. The way these regulative mechanisms operate was discussed more fully in Chapter 10.

STREET-CORNER SOCIETY

Street-corner gangs of juveniles in an urban area were studied by a participant-observer. Examples of the development and maintenance of group structure were displayed clearly in these adolescent groups. Although systems of mutual obligation existed, high-status members refrained from accepting money from low-status members so as not to be obligated to them. Conflict among high-status members resulted in leadership changes rather than in an "uprising from the bottom." Seating positions at tables during social events were based on status differences. Low-status members rarely obtained a hearing in a discussion unless their suggestions were picked up by high-status members. Even the bowling scores of members reflected their status. When the observer bowled with only the boy lowest in status the latter tended to make respectable scores, but in the group (presumably in line with members' expectations) his score dropped considerably. When his score rose momentarily out of line, merciless heckling that shook the confidence of the low-status member brought it back to the expected low level of performance.

WHYTE (1943)

Group Performance and Group Size

Relationships between the performance of a group and the number of members participating are rather complex. For one thing, it is important to distinguish between *coactive* group tasks, in which people work parallel to one another but do not interact, from *interactive* tasks, in which people interact with one another in an organized way to produce a single product, decision, or judgment. In cases of parallel coaction, the relationship between the number of participants and their performance of a task is usually a simple linear one: performance quality and output go up directly as the number of workers increases. If one man can shovel a pile of coal in 10 hours, then ten men can shovel the same pile of coal in 1 hour. But any kind of interaction among parallel coacting workers will alter this linear relationship. If coworkers begin to interact, in some cases it may distract from their individual work and interfere with overall total performance. In other cases, interaction may increase total output.

Another important factor affecting the relationship between group size and group performance is the nature of the group's goals and objectives. If the group's task demands *convergent* activity (to arrive at one single correct solution), a relatively small number of people may be required to reach optimum productivity, especially if the task requires only a limited set of resources, skills, or abilities. On the other hand, if the task demands *divergent* activity (such as "brainstorming" for ideas; see page 321), the optimum size to maximize performance may be considerably larger because a larger number of people will represent a wider array of viewpoints and perspectives.

When group products require systematic cooperation and integration of efforts on the part of each member, the performance of the group is not a mere summation of the individual performance of its members. In cases of group problem-solving (such as solving puzzles in experimental groups or the analysis of a soluble industrial problem by a trouble-shooting committee), the relationship between group size and performance is more frequently curvilinear. There is a function of diminishing returns: the addition of individual members to the group provides decreasing increments in group performance as the size of the group increases. For example, if one man can solve a problem in 50 minutes, two men may require 20 minutes rather than 25, and three men may require 15 minutes rather than 10. Eventually a point of no further gain may be reached, so that addition of even an infinite number of members may produce no further increment in group performance. In fact, under some circumstances the group may become large and unwieldy and require so much investment of energy in communication and maintenance that its efforts are distracted from the task, thus requiring even greater time for solution of the problem. It may turn out that four men still require 15 minutes to solve the problem described.

In terms of economics, this point of no further return may come even earlier. If one had to pay each man a dollar a minute to solve the problem, a one-man committee would cost $50, and a two-man committee would cost only $40. However, a three-man committee would cost $45, and a four-man committee would cost $60. In this case, the point at which no further absolute gain is realized would be at three members, but the point of no further overall economic gain would be at two members. The decision of optimum size for setting up such a group, then, would rest on an evaluation of the relative importance of time and money.

Several experimental studies have demonstrated this curvilinear relationship between group size and group performance in interactive problem solving (Thelen, 1949; Taylor & Faust, 1952). However, the specific size at which optimum gains are realized depends on the nature of the task. In general, so long as additional members contribute additional skills and resources, further gains in group performance are realized. However, there is some redundancy of contribution as the number of members increases, and eventually all of the skills and resources required for solution of the problem are available within the group, so that additional members contribute nothing more. Because the kinds of resources required by different kinds of problems vary, no single absolute statement about optimum group size can be made. Evidence has consistently shown that the kind of curvilinear relationship between size and performance is generally the same for problem-solving groups, although the shape of the curve varies according to the task. It is difficult to evaluate the performance and product of policy-planning and decision-making groups, so it is more difficult to make definitive statements about relationships between performance and size in such cases. In brainstorming and creative groups, the quality of innovative products may be used as a criterion for gauging performance, and the relationship between size and performance is generally similar to that for problem-solving groups.

BRAINSTORMING

As a problem-solving procedure, "brainstorming" in this study called for the expression of ideas without regard to quality and no evaluation of ideas until all of them were expressed. The problem called for listing of unusual uses of an ordinary clothes hanger and a broom. The number of "creative" ideas per subject using brainstorming procedures was 7.94 during a 5-minute period, whereas nonbrainstorming subjects averaged only 3.88.

MEADOW, PARNES, AND REESE (1959)

Thelen (1949) summarized these relationships under the "principle of least group size," which states that the optimum group size for performance of an interactive task is the minimum number of individuals required to make available to the group all of the resources required for execution of its task. Thus both of two rather different old adages are paradoxically true: "Two heads are better than one," but nevertheless, "Too many cooks spoil the broth."

HOW MANY COOKS SPOIL THE BROTH?

College students were assigned to either two-person or four-person groups or were individual subjects. For 4 days in succession they were given four problem words from the twenty questions game, in which the subject is required to identify an object (word) by a series of questions that can be answered only by yes or no, with only the initial clue that the object is mineral, animal, or vegetable. The most economic solution started with high-order conceptualizations, which gradually became more specific. On the fifth day, all subjects worked on four other problem objects. Over time, both groups and individuals showed greater efficiency (economy) in problem solving, but group performance excelled that of individuals in terms of number of questions (fewer), number of failures, and time per problem. Groups of four were not superior to groups of two except in terms of number of failures to reach solution of the problem. In terms of man-minutes needed per problem, the performance of individuals excelled that of groups of two, and groups of two excelled groups of four.

TAYLOR AND FAUST (1952)

Group Performance and Group Structure

The effectiveness of a group's performance as an organized system also depends on certain structural properties. Chapter 11 described some of the most important aspects of group structure. The concept of cohesiveness is used to describe the extent to which a group holds together coherently as a system. In general, any factors or conditions that facilitate coherent structural organization in a group will also enhance its performance as a system. As mentioned in the preceding paragraph, when a group provides satisfaction of the individual needs of its members, these members tend to remain in the group. This attraction to the group facilitates cohesive organization, in turn affording greater effectiveness in task-related performance (Schutz, 1955; Cervin, 1956; Deutsch, 1959). Under some conditions, however, group organization may be maintained by external factors that compel individual members to remain rather than by internal individual attractions. Under these conditions, the satisfaction of individual personal needs may be unrelated to the level of performance of the group.

In general, the stability of the organizational structure of a group is directly related

WHEELS, CIRCLES, AND STAR PERFORMANCE

Studies of three-person groups placed in various communication nets and given either a simple or complex computational task showed the following major findings:

1. Groups working on simple problems reached solutions more quickly, communicated more, and showed higher morale than groups working on complex problems.
2. Overall amount of communication was equal for circle nets and wheel nets, but circle nets solved complex problems faster and more accurately.
3. Central subjects in circle, wheel, or star nets showed greater satisfaction and productivity than other members of each net.
4. Distributed relevant information in concom nets (open channels) resulted in most efficient problem solving.

SHAW (1954, 1956, 1958)

to the effectiveness of its performance as a system. The emergence of stable differentiations of function (roles), providing for the organized division of effort, enhances the group's effectiveness. When roles are vague, ambiguous, or unstable, the group tends to be less successful in attaining its collective objectives (Shaw, 1954, 1956, 1958; Guetzkow et al., 1955, 1957, 1960). On the other hand, excessive rigidity in role differentiation may interfere with effective performance. When the organizational structure is highly fixed, so that in an emergency the role functions of one member cannot be assumed by others, disruption of the group's overall performance may follow (Shaw, 1954, 1956, 1958). Such conditions are analogous to "feather bedding" in the division of function by labor unions so that one category of workers is prohibited from carrying out the functions of another.

In some cases the differentiation of functional roles assigned to each member of the group may prove incompatible with the individual's own personality and abilities. Under such conditions individuals may be unable to carry out their expected functions effectively, and thus the collective performance of the group as a system may be impeded.

In most groups, the lines of interaction among members become stabilized either

SEX AND GROUP PERFORMANCE

Same-sex and mixed-sex groups were presented with a series of problems involving logistics (getting a group of people across a mined road), finances (distributing $3000 to a group of students), and human relations (settling an argument between two group members). The quality of problem solution was scored for all-male groups, groups composed of three males and one female, and groups composed of two or three females and one or two males. On all three problems, mixed-sex groups performed better than same-sex groups.

HOFFMAN AND MAIER (1961)

INTELLIGENCE AND GROUP PERFORMANCE

On the basis of their scores on a standard intelligence test, respondents were divided into three categories: high (H), medium (M), and low (L) intelligence. Three-person groups based on combinations of homogeneity (e.g., MMM, LLL) and heterogeneity (e.g., HML) were then administered the test for a second time. With the exception of the HHH group (which had the highest average score), heterogeneous groups were superior to homogeneous groups in their average scores on the second test.

LAUGHLIN, BRANCH, AND JOHNSON (1969)

as a by-product of the adoption of particular roles or by organizational rules imposed

from outside, as in the case of military ranks or flow-charts of authority in business organizations. Some patterns, especially those that involve high degrees of centralization of authority in funneling interactions toward one member of the group, are associated with effective task performance, but with little satisfaction to the peripheral participants. Patterns that involve more even distribution of interaction patterns tend to be associated with lower levels of task performance but with greater satisfaction to individual participants (Leavitt, 1951; Shaw, 1954, 1956, 1958).

Group Performance and Cooperation-Competition

Although collective group goals are ordinarily adopted by each member of a group as his own personal goals, it does not necessarily follow that an organized group will always evolve when a set of people commit themselves simultaneously to the same goal. For example, three young men, each of whom wishes to marry the same woman, would not ordinarily constitute an organized group, at least not in a monogamous society. The way commonly adopted goals are defined is critical to the organization of a psychological group. *Competitive* goals are those toward which a number of individuals aspire, but they are defined so that one can attain his goal only if others do not. A timed distance race represents such a competitive goal situation. In contrast, *cooperative* goals are those that are defined so that each individual can attain his goal only if other members of the group also attain their goals. A relay race represents such a cooperative goal situation. In general, competitive goals tend to discourage the organization of purpose that characterizes a psychological group. Individuals who are committed to competitive goals do not ordinarily develop unity of purpose as a system, articulated mutual role relationships, or commonly adopted regulative norms that generate social organization among them. Instead, competition breeds conflict among individuals and works counter to the maintained organization of the group. Cooperative goals, on the other hand, tend to foster organization within a group. Deutsch (1949) has pointed out that cooperative goal commitments tend to produce attractions among members of a group, because each contributes to the other's progress toward the goal; readiness to substitute one member's activities for another's, because the activity of each is evaluated in terms of its contribution to goal attainment; and willingness of individuals to accept influence from one another, because each is helping the other. Thus cooperative definition of goals contributes directly to the emergence of mutually interrelated roles and commonly adopted regulative norms. Deutsch and others have studied the performance of groups of individuals under commitment to cooperative and competitive goals, showing clearly that group organization and performance are facilitated by cooperative goals (Deutsch, 1949; Deutsch & Krauss, 1960). In a study with children, however, Stendler, Damrin, and Haines (1951) found that within organized groups, competitive situations may occur in connection with specific activities of the group, disrupting group performance of that particular activity, without generalizing into other areas of the group's activity. The disruptive effects of competition within groups therefore appear perhaps restricted to the activities of the group only in pursuit of the competitive goals. Organized groups that pursue superordinate cooperative goals may thus tolerate a limited amount of competition in pursuit of transitory intermediate goals without destroying the overall organization of the group as a system (Smith, Madden & Sobol, 1957).

RELEVANCE AND APPLICATION

Long before scientific analysis approached detailed understanding of the processes operating within an organized social group, man recognized the social significance

---

COOPERATION, COMPETITION, AND GROUP PERFORMANCE

Five-person groups were given the task of solving human-relations problems and puzzles at each of several meetings. Groups that were told that they would be collectively rewarded for the best solution were labeled as cooperative, whereas rewards for individual excellence in groups labeled the latter as competitive. Observers' ratings and subjects' self-reports showed that members of cooperative groups were better oriented toward the task, more coordinated and orderly, readier to accept one another's ideas, and more friendly than were members of the competitive groups. They also paid more attention to one another, worked together more frequently, showed less desire to excel others, agreed more often with their fellow members, perceived other members as more cooperative, contributed more to discussions, and displayed overall greater productivity. The main concern of the typical member of a cooperative group was to have the group excel, rather than to please the experimenter.

DEUTSCH (1949)

---

of the powerful productive forces operating in groups. Possibly it would be fair to say that this same recognition is at the very roots of political structure and social organization in a civilized world. As Hobbes, Rousseau, and others suggested, men made their first primitive entries into social contracts with one another as a result of their recognition of the advantages of collective action over individual action. Out of these social contracts evolved the complex governmental structures in our modern civilized world—structures that attempt, through law, custom, tradition, and socialization to control and order these forces to maximize productive output and satisfaction for each participant in the society.

Even before the Industrial Revolution, men worked in groups to produce the articles needed for collective living, exchanging goods among themselves rather than requiring each individual to work alone to produce the articles needed. As factories grew, machinery became more complex, and industrial output increased rapidly in the nineteenth century. Large industrial organizations evolved, most of which centered upon the productive output of small work groups. The profit motive initially swamped any concern for the welfare of the worker, and the criterion of group effectiveness was simply one of output quality and quantity, with little or no concern for worker satisfaction.

With the industrial reforms of the twentieth century came a new kind of applied social science—group dynamics. Among the earliest efforts along these lines were those of Mayo and others at the Harvard School of Business (Mayo, 1933; Roethlisberger & Dickson, 1939; Homans, 1950), who conducted research on the production and satisfaction of workers in organized groups in industrial settings. Although the typical American worker appears to be highly task-oriented (rather than the stereotyped "social American") while he is on the job (Smuts, 1953; Bass, 1962), there is evidence that his production rate and task performance are very much influenced by group norms and conventions and by the expectations of his co-workers. For example, the overproducing worker in a factory where wages are based on standardized rates of expected production is called a "rate-buster" and is not viewed with great esteem by his co-workers. His overproduction threatens possible reevaluation and elevation of the expected production rate, and he is regarded by his colleagues as a social deviate. Similarly, the underproducer, who is paid at full base-line rate but fails to carry his share of the production load, is called a "chiseler," and he is also treated as a disapproved deviate (Homans, 1950).

Production rates of industrial workers have been found to be closely related to their morale and job satisfaction. Managerial practices that cultivate identification of the worker with the business as a social community generally tend not only to make the worker better satisfied, but also to increase his productivity (Stagner, 1958; Bass, 1965b). For example, procedures that allowed factory workers to have a voice in decisions concerning changes in policy and practice produced better morale during and after the changes, and their production rates recovered more rapidly following the changes (Coch & French, 1948; French, Israel, & As, 1960). The individual self-oriented goals of workers may be readily superseded by collective company goals, provided the workers exercise relatively high levels of personal involvement and see their role as one that is an integral part of the factory community (Slater, 1959).

The origins of modern industrial social psychology stem from a time when industrial production was centered in modest-sized factories, in which workers functioned in small groups. However, modern industrial production is highly automated, and machines have in large measure replaced the hand-workers of a half-century ago. Modern industry involves large and complex bureaucratic organizations made up of men who operate and manage the machines. Yet these organizations are made up of men in groups, ranging from production workers on an assembly line to administrative boards and committees at the managerial level. In a way, modern business firms represent miniature societies comprised of many interdependent subgroups. They tend to evolve company "cultures," including norms, standards, belief systems, laws, and values. This culture is transmitted to new employees as they are "socialized" into the system. Thus the applicability of psychological research to both the socialization process (Chapter 6) and group dynamics (Chapters 10, 11, 12) has given rise to what is today called *organizational psychology*.

Education is another area of significant application of our understanding of group dynamics and group performance. The American public educational system is one that through practical necessity requires each teacher to deal with an audience of many students at the same time rather than on a one-to-one basis. Because their interaction is continued over extended periods of time through a succession of purposes and activities, classroom groups eventually show many properties of organized groups. Thus educational research has directed its attention to the psychological study of group dynamics.

The style of behavior of a classroom teacher in the leadership role in the classroom tends to establish a well-defined group atmosphere. Practical circumstances require that the teacher exert some control over students, with firm maintenance of disciplinary norms; consequently, most classroom atmospheres tend to be somewhat autocratic. This tendency is augmented by the fact that public school teachers have been found to be people who are likely to show authoritarian tendencies (McCandless, 1961). However, several experimental investigations have compared such autocratic (teacher-centered) atmospheres with more democratic (learner-centered) ones. In general these studies suggest the superiority of nondirective, democratic, student-centered classroom atmospheres because they are associated with greater productivity as well as with greater satisfaction and higher morale among the students (Thelen & Withal, 1949; Bovard, 1951; Flanders, 1954). However, there are exceptions to every rule; *some* students prefer more autocratic schoolroom atmospheres, and *some* teaching situations bog down under democratic atmospheres (M. J. Asch, 1951; Wispe, 1951; Johnson & Smith, 1953).

A particularly significant area of application of knowledge about group dynamics has evolved in connection with clinical psychology and mental health services. Many of the applications of ideas from basic social psychology to problems of personal adjustment, preventive psychiatry, and remedial psychotherapy are described in Chapter 7. Included among these are several movements (such as gestalt therapy and transactional analysis) that particularly attempt to enlist the forces of group dynamics to contribute to the therapeutic process. Pioneering attempts in group psychotherapy initially met with hostile resistance from hospitals, clinics, and private psychotherapists (Schildre, 1940; Moreno, 1945). However, the growing demand for professional psychotherapeutic service to large numbers of patients eventually brought about a change of attitude toward group techniques.

During and after World War II, the military, the Veterans Administration, and community mental health and child guidance clinics faced increasing pressure from waiting lists of clients in need of professional treatment. Thus the rapid development of group psychotherapy during the past 20 years in one sense occurred for very poor (but nevertheless important) reasons: group psychotherapy was conceived merely as a stop-gap measure aimed at attaining better patient-therapist ratios in the face of an extreme shortage of trained psychotherapists. On the other hand, a number of clinical psychologists and psychotherapists have argued persistently for the expansion of group therapeutic techniques on the more logical premise that group forces may contribute directly to the therapeutic process itself. That is, the therapeutic group may be seen as a miniature society in which the patient may enact new roles on a trial basis to gauge the reactions of others to his new behavior patterns. The therapeutic group may become a source of collective reward and punishment through acceptance or rejection of each member's actions; the group may erect norms that guide and control the actions of each of its members; and quite importantly, the group may provide a shelter of collective support for the insecure patient as he works his way toward better adjustment to the less sensitive social world. This latter argument in support of group therapy is, of course, a more defensible one in terms of basic scientific psychology. It is not merely a *cheaper* way, but a genuinely *better* way of accomplishing certain of the goals of psychotherapy.

Perhaps the most significant effort to use principles of social psychology for the betterment of community and industrial organizations is represented by the program of the National Training Laboratories since its inception at Bethel, Maine, in 1947. Through workshops designed to train key leaders in the community toward increased sensitivity to interpersonal relationships and awareness of the nature of groups and social systems, this program has had wide-reaching effects in both industrial and civic affairs. These workshops make use of a set of ideas and methods that have come to be called T-group (training-group) approaches (Bradford, Gibb, & Benne, 1964). Many industrial organizations have sent their key personnel to N.T.L. workshops for training in procedures of the sort described in the preceding pages, to enhance the operation of the industrial organization. In the same manner, individuals who have attended N.T.L. workshops have returned to their communities to serve in positions of leadership in handling such social problems as racial desegregation, anti-Semitism, and relationships among ethnic minority groups.

Although the problem of crime and juvenile delinquency is still met socially by traditional arguments for stringent police authority and punitive treatment of offenders, alternative approaches have been considered increasingly since World War II. The fact that adolescents are especially prone to be "joiners" who participate in closely knit peer groups tends to insulate them from effective relationships with adult authorities. Especially in urban communities, juvenile delinquency is likely to occur in organized gangs that erect norms that override the individual youth's own personal standards of conduct. The identification of social status and acceptance within the peer group with such socially unacceptable acts as theft, rape, or excessive aggression induces widespread delinquent offense against organized society. Procedures patterned along the lines of group psychotherapy may be utilized to realign these adolescent group forces so that they are more in accord with recognized dominant social standards. One such approach is that of the street club worker, who gains the acceptance of an already organized adolescent group, permitting him to enter the group as an inconspicuous therapeutic force. Instead of "coming on strong" as a crusading reformer from outside, he gains access to the group from within and allows the group to utilize its own dynamics and gradually reorient itself into more constructive channels. Through effective work, significant gains in relieving community pressures from organized juvenile crime have been achieved (Salisbury, 1958).

REVIEW

1. Organized social groups function as a system to produce, perform, or achieve some objective.

2. Generally, there are advantages to collective performance as compared to individual performance. However, these are complex, and the early observations of *social facilitation* were superficial and misleading. Group performance usually is characterized by increased output and decreased quality (as compared to individual performance), but there are many exceptions.

3. One component in apparent "social facilitation" is social conformity. *Individual* behavior in the presence of other people tends to be conservative, inhibited, and cautious.

4. In contrast to individual behavior in the group, *collective* action within a group tends to be more venturesome. This shift has been called *the risky shift.*

5. Group goals, like personal goals, steer the course of action of the group as a system. These may be either *formal* or *informal.* Sometimes the formal and explicitly stated goals of a group may be *nonoperational* (operating in name only), whereas informal, implicit goals provide the true *operational* goal-direction of the group.

6. Group *synergy* (energy expended by the collective group system) may be channeled into either *task-related* or *group-maintenance* activities. The former contribute more directly to group output and performance; the latter contribute more to individual member satisfaction.

7. Group performance may be evaluated in terms of two independent sets of criteria: one is related to the productive output of the group (group *effectiveness*), and the other is related to the satisfaction provided for individual participants in the group (group *satisfaction*).

8. Group performance is enhanced by clarity of group goals, freedom from ambiguity and conflict in group goals, and strong commitment of individual group members to the purposes and goals of the collective group.

9. Group performance is enhanced by clarity of norms and standards within the group, and is fostered by mechanisms that maintain and enforce its norms and standards for behavior.

10. Group performance is often, but not always, enhanced by increases in group size. In *convergent* tasks (aiming at a single solution to a problem and requiring a limited set of skills or resources), the optimum size for effective performance is usually smaller than in a *divergent* task (aiming at the production of multiple and varied ideas or strategies and thriving on a wide array of varied resources). There is no absolute optimum size for group performance, and the most workable rule of thumb is the principle of least group size, which holds that the best group size for optimum performance is the smallest number of people representing all of the needed skills or resources required by the group's task.

11. Group performance is enhanced by organized structure within the group, with clear definition of roles and division of labor. However, if this internal organization becomes exaggerated and rigid, it may even reach a point of interfering with group performance.

12. Group performance is enhanced by cooperative endeavor within the group, when group members are strongly committed to joint action rather than individual excellence; competition within the group usually interferes with group performance.

COLLECTIVE SOCIAL BEHAVIOR

The most diffuse level of man's social behavior occurs at the *collective* level. Collective social behavior involves far more people than the simple diadic relationships described in Section III and lacks the properties of systematic organization that characterize the groups described in Section IV. Hence the analysis of behavior in collective situations requires different approaches and different concepts. The unorganized social aggregates to be considered at this level of examination of social behavior are sometimes referred to as *masses,* and the study of them has been called *mass psychology.*

Despite the fact that the earliest kinds of social psychology began with curiosity about collective behavior, this remains a very underdeveloped area. There are few theories of collective behavior, and even attempts to bridge other kinds of psychological theories and models to account for collective behavior have had only limited success. Consequently our science of mass behavior remains primitive and limited. It is hardly more than descriptive. Several dimensions for describing and categorizing different kinds of collective behavior have been examined, and it is possible to develop a taxonomy for labeling different kinds of collective situations. But theoretical analysis of these situations is limited, and our application of such analysis to practical problems is extremely primitive. In the United States recent upsurges in the frequency and intensity of collective action (in mobs, crowds, riots, demonstrations, and social movements) have drawn attention to the inadequacy of knowledge of crowds and mass collective action. Furthermore, we have been unable to apply our knowledge to effective means of crowd control when collective behavior gets out of hand and threatens destruction of life and property.

Using the descriptive knowledge that is available from scientific studies of collective behavior, Chapter 13 differentiates several categories of collective social aggregates. The most diffuse level of man's social behavior—collective behavior—is examined here.

13

MASSES: FROM CROWDS TO COMMUNITIES

There are many kinds of social aggregates, but only those that show properties of systematic organization are called groups. Those that lack these properties and remain essentially unorganized, or at best only very loosely organized, are sometimes called *masses.*

There are several ways in which masses may differ significantly from one another. They may vary in *size:* some may be small enough to be contained within a room, others so large that they can be contained only in a stadium or a public plaza, and still others (such as TV audiences or newspaper readers) so large and diffuse that they could never be contained in one place at one time. Gigantic audiences have become possible only as a consequence of the development of mass media of communication. Until the development of radio and television, such extremely large audiences did not even exist; now they comprise a very significant force in the life of every civilized human being—especially in the United States.

The term *polarization* may be used to describe the extent to which the attention of each participant in a mass is simultaneously oriented in the same direction. In mob activities, for example, there is usually some singular driving force that focuses the attention of the participants and impels their action. Similarly, audiences usually direct their attention toward a performer of some kind. In the case of mass media audiences, complete polarization occurs because the audiences are unassembled and communication is possible in only one direction.

Masses also differ with respect to activity—the extent to which they involve active behavior (as contrasted with merely passive reaction) among the participants. Mobs and congregated crowds are usually characterized by mobility and activity on the part of each participant: each does things actively that affect other participants and the mass as a whole. On the other hand, audiences (especially very large ones and mass media audiences) typically involve only passive attention and responsiveness of the participants. For example, one is likely to laugh openly and applaud at a play in a theater; in contrast, one rarely laughs aloud and almost never applauds when he views the same play alone at home on television.

Masses may differ in congregation—how often (if ever) they assemble in one place. Some may never congregate (TV viewers). Others may gather once and only once (bystanders and onlookers at a hotel fire); others may convene regularly (season subscribers to a symphony).

Combining the dimensions of activity and congregation, Table 13–1 is a classification of four broad kinds of collective social situations. Although both of these dimensions are best considered as continua ranging from one extreme to the other with shades of gray between, the table simplifies them into broad dichotomies. Aggregates that are ordinarily assembled in one congregation, and whose participants are overtly engaged in some common kind of activity, are called mobs, and these include riots, panics, and demonstrations. Similar aggregates that are characterized by passive reaction on the part of participants are called crowds or congregated audiences. In contrast to these, uncongregated passive-responsive aggregates are called *mass media audiences,* and these include radio-listeners, TV-viewers, and readers of mass-produced printed material. Finally, *social movements* include those collective aggregates that are rarely if ever gathered together but that involve simultaneous parallel activity on the part of all their participants. These include cult movements, protest movements, and institutionalized behavior. Ultimately, social movements usually generate an emergent kind of primitive social organization that may be called a *community.* This semiorganized product of a social movement may be more accurately described as intermediate between a collective situation and a group. Consequently, communities are described separately in this chapter, and they include Utopias (experimental minisocieties), bureaucracies, neighborhood communities, and—at the largest and most complex level—nations.

Degree of Activity	Degree of Congregation	
	Uncongregated	Congregated
Passive-Reactive	*Mass Media Audiences* (Radio, TV, readers)	*Crowds* (Congregated audiences)
Casual	TV viewers who witnessed Lee H. Oswald's murder by Jack Ruby on network news in November 1963	Bystanders and onlookers watching a downtown hotel fire in progress
Intentional Informative Entertaining	Classroom lecture audience Movie theater audience	TV news program viewers TV comedy-program viewers
Active-Interactive	*Social Movements* (Cults and protests)	*Mobs* (Riots, panics, demonstrations)
Goal-directed Acquisitive	Petitioners, crusaders, charity campaign volunteers	Guerilla raid, looters, department store sale stampede
Defensive	Protest movements	Panic in disaster
Expressive	Religious cult, nonviolent demonstrations	Political rally, pep rally, "power" movement parade
Aggressive	Hate movement, violent demonstrations	Lynch mobs, riots

CROWDS AND AUDIENCES

The term "crowd" is used loosely in the social sciences to refer to any kind of congregation of human beings gathered together for any purpose. The word has been defined in many ways, but never very specifically. Hence it has no precise scientific meaning. Likewise, the term "audience" is used loosely to refer broadly to spectators or watchers of any event, whether or not they are located in the same place and are in contact with one another.

In the present context of describing different kinds of collective social behavior, "crowd" and "audience" are used to denote two particular kinds of collective social situations. The term *audience* refers to any mass of people, whether congregated or not, whose attention is polarized toward some person or event to which they are responding passively and reactively. The term *crowd* is used more narrowly to specify a congregated audience—an aggregate of people gathered in one place, responding passively with attention polarized upon a person or event.

The polarized attention that characterizes crowds and audiences may occur accidentally and by coincidence, leading to what LaPiere (1938) called a casual audience. Or it may be directly *intentional,* when attention is polarized for the express purpose of being informed or entertained. As long as the focal person or event holds the responsive attention of the audience, certain common properties are displayed. But once this polarity is lost—as when a speaker becomes boring or a performer becomes inept—the audience may change its characteristics. Its members may interact among themselves and move into overt activity. If they are a congregated crowd, they may even begin to show some of the properties of a mob. Eventually, if conditions are appropriate, an audience may generate an active social movement, and even ultimately an organized group. Thus in many cases audiences and crowds are merely early transitional phases of what later can become social organization.

Congregated Crowds

Casual audiences occur by chance when a number of people happen to be in a certain place and witness some event that draws their attention simultaneously. An automobile crash may turn the heads of fifty people who drop whatever they are doing and polarize their attention upon the accident. Yet none of the bystanders could say that they came to that place at that time for the purpose of watching an automobile accident. After the novelty of the crash passes, the audience may begin to move into other forms of social behavior. If the accident is sufficiently disturbing, some participants may move into a state of panic and mob action. If people are more rational and level-headed, they may begin to organize for the purpose of seeing that victims are cared for, that the accident is reported to the police, and that traffic is directed around the debris.

Because the polarized focus of attention of participants in an intentional audience is directly motivated, intentional audiences may be longer-lived than casual audiences. In some cases the audience may intentionally reconvene at specified intervals, just as members of a college class reassemble several times weekly for several months for the same purpose. The intent that brings an audience together may be either predominantly *information*-seeking or predominantly *entertainment*-seeking. Often the intent is mixed. Although most students ostensibly attend classes in order to be informed, they may often choose their instructors according to their ability to entertain and amuse them and to make the dose of instruction less distasteful. Similarly, people may go to the theater to be entertained, but they may also acquire important and useful information about human relations, social problems, or literary style and dramatic construction.

CROWD CONTAGION

The subjects in this study were 1424 pedestrians on a busy New York City street who passed along a 50-foot length of sidewalk. At a signal flashed from the sixth floor of an office building, confederates of the experimenter gazed up at the window from where the signal was given for a period of 60 seconds. The confederates were designated as a stimulus crowd, and the number of pedestrians who stopped and looked up, or who merely looked up, was recorded at various times. The stimulus crowd consisted of one, two, three, five, ten, or fifteen persons. As the stimulus crowd increased in size so did its drawing power. One person induced 42 percent of the passersby to look up (4 percent stopped), a stimulus crowd of fifteen persons induced 86 percent of the passersby to look up (40 percent stopped).

MILGRAM, BICKMAN, AND BERKOWITZ (1969)

Audiences of the Mass Media

The term *mass media* is a cliché abbreviation of "mass media of communication," a phrase that refers to the entire family of technological devices that permit communication among masses. Mass media have, in principle, existed ever since man carved hieroglyphics on stone or clay tablets, permitting the communication of ideas over both time and space. From that time, the significant changes in mass media have been essentially ones of mobility and immediacy. From stone tablets, to the printing press, to daily newspapers, to telephone and telegraph, to radio, and ultimately to TV, the mass media have evolved toward permitting increasingly immediate and close communication to mass audiences.

Although mass communication is limitless in the technological sense, it may remain incomplete for economic and practical reasons. During the 1930s, radio sets were a luxury and this medium had not yet saturated the public; during the early 1950s, television was similarly confined to higher socioeconomic classes. By the 1960s, however, most of the economic barriers to saturation of the public as a mass audience were removed. TV, radio, and newspapers are almost equally available to everyone, regardless of his socioeconomic standing. Exposure to mass media is largely a matter of choice and habit.

Audiences of the mass media are normally intentional, and their intentions govern selection of particular channels of communication. Only occasionally do the mass media reach casual audiences whose attention is accidental. Watchers of a televised auto race may accidentally witness a hideous crash, or a reader may encounter an unexpected item in a newspaper.

Mass media audiences vary considerably in their voluntary attention to particular kinds of media. Several investigations have identified the readership of particular magazines or newspapers according to demographic and psychological characteristics (Lazersfeld, Berelson, & Gaudet, 1944; Bogart, 1957). Others have evaluated the opinions of mass audiences about the credibility of various media (Tebbel, 1962).

A considerable amount of research has explored the content of mass media communications. Not only is the American society often judged by its literature, its movies, and its television and radio programs, but even the characteristics of particular subgroups within the society may sometimes be inferred from their tastes in mass media content (Lazarsfeld, Berelson, & Gaudet, 1944; Shannon, 1954; Bogart, 1957; Merrill & Lowenstein, 1971).

As cultural products, mass communications sometimes become highly institutionalized and stereotyped. To many Americans, *Punch* is a British institution as enduring as Parliament, and the blank-stare eyes of Little Orphan Annie (even though she should by now be middle-aged) have been familiar to three generations of Americans.

Questions have been raised about the impact of television and movie heroes as identification models in the socialization process. The violence and terror, blood and gore, of American movies and TV are sources of much criticism by Europeans and some American parents, who argue that this content in mass media products is an inappropriate reflection of American life, and that it provides undesirable models for the values and behavior of young audiences (Maccoby, 1966; Eron, et al., 1972). Evidence has shown that, indeed, television and movie performers may become objects of identification that influence children's behavior (Bandura, 1963; Berkowitz & Daniels, 1964), but as yet there is no unequivocal evidence that the models of TV

WAR OF THE WORLDS

On Halloween of 1938, Orson Wells produced a convincing broadcast of H. G. Wells' science fiction story *The War of the Worlds* in the form of a simulated special news broadcast. The presentation proved so convincing to radio listeners who tuned in late that an estimated million people were disturbed to the brink of panic. Subsequent interviews comparing relatively unfrightened listeners with highly frightened ones showed the latter to be more poorly educated, less able to evaluate the credibility and reliability of information sources, and generally susceptible to mass suggestion. Although the broadcast produced no mob action or panic in the streets, a wave of fright passed through an unassembled audience of thousands of gullible and suggestible people, mobilizing them into readiness for action.

CANTRIL, GAUDET, AND HERTZOG (1940)

and movies are more influential than the live models of parents and other authority figures. In fact, some psychologists have suggested that the as-if quality of television is recognized by children as a fantasy world more readily than many parents realize. Even so, typical TV and movie fare of the 1970s implies that violent and aggressive behavior is usually condoned and acceptable.

The mass media have provided a significant force toward homogenization of the society. With common immediate communication of information, tastes, and values throughout the population, regional and social class differences have been reduced. No longer is the Kansas farmer a stranger to the Broadway theater. Differences in the tastes and buying habits of rural and urban consumers have diminished. False stereotypes based on limited information have tended to fade as the mass media provide knowledge and sophistication about the entire world to audiences of millions. Americans are familiar with the manner and bearing of the French president and the British queen; white southerners are exposed to educated and accomplished blacks. Although regional pockets of ignorance are obliterated by the pervasive communication of the mass media, ignorance may nevertheless become standardized when the mass media disseminate inaccurate or incomplete images.

The mass media represent a new force in the socialization process. Newspapers, radio, movies, and television have partially supplanted parents, teachers, and other direct authority figures, and performers enter the lives of even very young children. The traditional primary importance of parents and teachers in relaying the culture to young people has been vastly diluted by the rapid expansion of mass media of communication.

MASS MEDIA AUDIENCES

A classification of mass media audiences in the United States yielded the following population estimates:

1. "Intellectuals." The quotes indicate that the people thus categorized can read, but are not inclined to do so. They constitute about 60 percent of all mass media consumers. Their primary exposure is to picture publications, movies, TV, and radio. Their consumption of mass media is for entertainment and excitement. Their typical fare is TV or movies dealing with sex and adventure, or various comic strips. They are neither idea-oriented, nor are they involved in the larger social world outside their families or neighborhoods. They are overrepresented at the poverty or near-poverty level.

2. Pragmatists. They constitute about 30 percent of all mass media consumers. They read publications such as the *Reader's Digest, Time,* and the *Wall Street Journal.* They are active, ambitious, mobile, and consumer-oriented. They expect the mass media to provide them with information on how to advance, how to get along with others, and how to be socially useful. They are not idea-oriented, however, and if they do gather ideas from the mass media, it is only because it is socially "expected" or potentially useful. This population exercises the largest amount of social power in the United States.

3. Intellectuals. This label does not necessarily denote "intelligent ones." The very term "mass" is disdainful to them, and they tend to focus their attention on relatively high-brow media such as the *Saturday Review* and *Harper's.* They are idea-oriented, but also clannish, introverted, and elitist. When they watch movies or TV it is not to be helped in a practical way, but for mental stimulation for its own sake. In this respect they differ from another type of intellectual, the ideologues, who are like missionaries trying to push their concepts on others.

MERRILL AND LOWENSTEIN (1971)

THE BUYING PUBLIC

In a study of buying habits, 596 supermarket shoppers were observed and subsequently interviewed. The major findings concerned unplanned, or "impulse" shopping. The greater the grocery bill, the greater the chance of people buying on impulse. The presence of a shopping list, especially with a large number of products (over fifteen) inhibits impulse buying. Couples married less than 10 years have the lowest rate of impulse buying, presumably because of their greater reliance on shopping lists (due to less shopping experience) and less need for quantity and variety of food. Impulse buying, however, is not associated with income of household, existence of food budgets, stores' manner of advertising, or shoppers' personality characteristics.

KOLLAT AND WILLET (1967)

The overwhelming impact of mass media advertising on the individual's economic behavior has become a very powerful force in our society. The presence of advertising messages in mass media is taken for granted, but in a way this represents a form of captive casual audience. Most people do not intentionally watch TV or listen to the radio in order to see or hear the commercials. (In some measure, however, newspaper readers do intentionally seek the newspaper as a source of advertising information.) This aspect of mass media communication has generated increasing awareness of the collective economic behavior of the buying public and its relationship to the overall social structure. The application of psychological knowledge to these kinds of problems is known as *consumer psychology.* This includes not only the exploration of behavioral manipulation through advertising (see Chapter 5), but also consideration of the rights and interests of the consumer as a member of these mass audiences as well as the social impact of advertising and economic manipulation on the society.

MOBS

Like other terms used to describe collective social behavior, the word "mob" has no precise scientific definition. In general use, however, it connotes disorganized activity and even violence. LeBon's (1895) early discussions of the psychology of "crowds" used that term broadly, obscuring differences between active and passive crowds, and particularly ignoring differences between the highly organized properties of groups and societies as compared to unorganized mobs, crowds, and social movements. But mobs and mass movements differ significantly from groups and societies because they lack properties of systematic order.

The term *mob* is used here to refer to a congregated, active, polarized aggregate of people. Its most salient features include homogeneity of thought and action among its participants and impulsive and irrational actions by its participants. Further differentiation of various kinds of mobs can be drawn according to the nature of the purpose of their polarized activity. The term *riot* describes a situation in which mob action is impelled primarily toward *acquisitive* ends—attempting to gain some object (raids) or person (kidnapping or lynching). *Panic* describes mob action that is *defensive,* seeking escape or avoidance of injury or threat. A new word—*demonstration*—recently has come into use to define another kind of active collective behavior the purpose of which is simply *expressive*—to display publicly an attitude or belief. Demonstrations are usually intentional, and in such cases they show limited amounts of organization and order. Other demonstrations, however, are spontaneous (and even some organized ones get out of hand and become uncontrolled)—and these more closely resemble typical mob behavior.

The concept of mass *suggestion* has been employed in a vague way to account for the homogeneity that characterizes mobs. Freud (1922), LeBon (1895), and others have interpreted these phenomena as manifestations of hypnotic suggestion. Tarde (1890) invoked the notion of an instinct of imitation to account for it, and McDougall (1908, 1925) elaborated the same notion into a concept that he called "primitive sympathy."

In a more behavioristic approach, Miller and Dollard (1941) pointed out the important role of repetitive stimulation in producing mob homogeneity. Apart from the hypnotic effects of repetition, they suggested that stimulation of the individual in the mob is intensified by the summated effects of repeated stimuli. One shout of "Boo" toward an unpopular speaker is compounded by successive repetitions, bringing the stimulation rapidly to peak intensity. Clapping, whistling, or stamping of feet in a crowd may produce similar summative effects. A snowballing effect may then follow: as the stimulation becomes more intense, each participant's reaction to it becomes intensified. In Chapter 1 considerable importance was attached to the capacity of social stimuli to change as a function of one's reaction to them. In the case of mob activation, as each participant's response intensifies, it becomes a more intense stimulus to others in the mob. The mob, then, becomes a catalytic medium that reverberates interpersonal stimulation to higher and higher levels of intensity. This successive intensification, described by Miller and Dollard as *circular reaction,* eventually amplifies certain specific kinds of stimulation and thereby fosters homogeneity within the mob.

The impulsive quality that characterizes human behavior in mobs has been described as both *emotional* and *irrational* (LeBon, 1895; R. W. Brown, 1954). The stimulation and excitation of an active mob tend to foster impulsive and uncontrolled behavior. Impulse is translated into action without the tempering filtration of logic and reason. The intensification of stimulation through repetition and circular reverberation, described by Miller and Dollard (1941), may produce conditions in which the individual is so urgently prodded by strong stimulus forces that he cannot control behavioral impulses that ordinarily would be repressed or blocked.

Phenomena of social influence may also account for impulsivity in mobs. In ambiguous situations, individuals are extremely susceptible to influence by the behavior of others (see Chapter 5), and the chaos and excited confusion of a mob certainly produce disorientation and cognitive ambiguity. A prestigious leader whose impulses break through uncontrolled is likely to influence others around him to follow suit (see Chapter 10). Behavioral contagion, the unintentional exertion of social power, is enhanced in mob activity. Often the initial instigators of mob action are themselves criminal and antisocial in the sense that they are motivated toward destructive ends, but participant followers in a mob may be well-controlled, law-abiding citizens. Miller and Dollard (1941) suggest that mob action implies a social norm that certain actions that are ordinarily restricted and socially unacceptable temporarily become acceptable. A large mob may carry the implication that its actions are right and justified, giving the individual participant the impression that so many people could not possibly be all wrong or evil.

Riots

The element of acquisitiveness, or directed efforts to obtain possession and control of some object, person, or territory, may sometimes characterize mob actions. This generates the kind of collective behavior usually called a *riot.* In guerrilla warfare, raids that are clearly not organized military sorties may take place to plunder a village or a post and secure equipment. Adolescent gangs in large cities sometimes erupt into mob action in order to assert control of a particular area (Salisbury, 1958). Frequently in times of natural disaster such as fires, floods, or hurricanes, mobs of plunderers raid the broken shopwindows, scooping up displayed goods. People who ordinarily would not consider direct theft, or even shoplifting, may be seduced into following the implied norms that natural chaos and broken windows make the goods public property, and that picking them up is justified and acceptable.

Perhaps the most graphic example of an acquisitive mob in action is the cartoon stereotype of women at a large department store sale as the store opens for business. Women who poured tea from silver services with elegantly lifted pinkies the afternoon before may be seen to scramble, shove, and grab in their efforts to gather in the choicest sale items. The norms and mores of the department store mob are not those of the Ladies' Aid Society. Likewise, the chivalry of the well-dressed executive in Manhattan is at least temporarily suspended as he scrambles for a seat in the subway.

A dangerous kind of mob action occurs when a crowd of people embrace the common purpose of injuring or destroying some person or object. The aggression may be relatively inconsequential, as when students seek to destroy the homecoming parade floats of an opposing school the night before a big football game. On the other hand, it may be brutal and savage, as when bands of rabid whites in the South once sought to take Negro prisoners from jails to mutilate and eventually kill them.

Although *lynch mob* usually connotes violence and lawlessness in current usage, the origin of the term is associated with rather mild and lawful collective actions. Colonel Charles Lynch was an American patriot of the revolutionary war period, who organized a band of citizens in Virginia to arrest and punish terrorist Tory conservatives who were harassing the revolutionary forces and impeding the war against England. Their action was essentially in the nature of a citizen's arrest. Because the nearest legal court was a considerable distance away, Lynch and his followers set up their own court for trying the offenders. They virtually never invoked a death penalty, and their action was intended simply as a substitute for legal arrest and conviction (Cutler, 1905). This original concept of lynching has come to be known as "Bourbon lynching," to differentiate a reasonably orderly kind of collective action from the violent and lawless "proletariat lynchings" (Raper, 1933; Cantril, 1941; Myrdal, 1944). The Bourbon lynching was presumably administered by community leaders in good conscience as a substitute for formal court action. Such lynch activities precipitated little internal conflict or guilt within individuals who participated in them, and they were easily rationalized as justifiable and proper.

The "proletariat lynching," characterized by violent aggression and inhumane actions, however, was more typical of lynch activities in the United States through the late nineteenth and early twentieth centuries. Although Bourbon lynchings tended to occur throughout frontier regions of the United States during that period, violent and lawless lynchings were more or less confined to the southeastern United States. These lynchings typically involved a band of economically insecure whites who sought to mutilate and kill a Negro accused of having raped a white woman. Psychological significance has been attached to all of the elements in this pattern. Economic insecurity appears to be a force inducing restlessness, frustration, and resentment. There is evidence that the poor whites of the South perceived the emancipation of Negro slaves as a threat to their jobs, and even the wealthier whites resented the loss of slaves as cash-value property (Raper, 1933). The aggressive action in the lynchings of the southern Black Belt was typically addressed against the Negro *race* rather than against a Negro *individual*. There was rarely any interest in clearly establishing the guilt of the accused, but in most cases there was considerable interest in demonstrating terror before the other Negroes of the community (an element of expression in mob action).

In some ways riot actions are analogous to lynch mobs, although in riots the aggressive actions of the mob are usually broadcast and diffused, rather than aimed toward a single individual. There is usually widespread property destruction and pointless violence. But their sources are often similar: discontent and restlessness, a sense of futility on the part of an underdog minority who resent mistreatment by an unfair dominant group, and the temporary suspension of organized social controls that normally inhibit impulsive eruption of hostile feelings. Riots may occur when students in a university cafeteria take exception to the menu, cost, or appearance of the food and precipitate a riot of food-throwing, brawls, and property destruction. Inmates in jails and prisons often riot in the same way. Even ordinarily well-mannered students at intellectually selective universities sometimes erupt into rioting mobs. For many years after World War II the "spring riot" at Princeton University became an almost traditional student affair. Its timing was variable, but to some degree predictable because it tended to coincide with the spring thaw (inducing restlessness and "spring fever") and the deluge of midsemester examinations (both threatening and frustrating). Its ostensible objectives varied from one year to the next, depending on the cause célèbre of the time, but its aggressive action was diffuse and without purpose. Nevertheless, even such presumably intelligent and mature young men more than once went so far as to tip railroad cars off their tracks, and one year even released a railroad car and allowed it to roll downhill at great speed from a spur line onto the mainline tracks of the Pennsylvania Railroad between New York and Philadelphia, threatening not only the lives of hundreds of passengers on other high-speed trains, but millions of dollars worth of railroad equipment.

Race riots, like lynchings, have been common in the stormy history of readjustment between Negroes and whites in the United States since 1956. In times of crisis, such as during the depression of the 1930s (economic threat), both world wars (insecurity and personal anxiety), and the recent period of active formal and informal pressures toward desegregation and clarification of the civil rights of Negroes (rapid social readjustment), race riots have occurred especially frequently. The lynching has tended to be associated with rural areas and small towns, whereas the riot as a form of mob expression and aggression is an urban phenomenon. Race riots have occurred in large cities in both the North and the South, and to some extent have been associated with concentrations of Negro population in cities with large white populations, where Negroes represent a sharply defined minority.

A particularly tragic riot in Detroit in 1943 has been the focus of several investigations and psychological analyses (Lee & Humphrey, 1943; R. W. Brown, 1954). Stemming from a fight between a Negro and a white man, and rampant rumors that white hoodlums had thrown a Negro child from a bridge (as well as rumors that reversed the racial roles), some 5000 people became involved in riotous disorder that lasted over 24 hours until federal troops reestablished a truce. It appeared that a minor fight precipitated the eruption of violent hostilities between the two groups. The wildfire spread of rumor augmented impulsive action, and the circular reverberations of interpersonal stimulation produced civil disorder almost immediately. The pattern of events in racial riots in Harlem in 1943 and in Watts, California, in 1965 was essentially parallel to that in Detroit. Although the similarities are immediately apparent, thorough investigations and analyses of the Watts situation have not yet been reported. In all of these cases it appears that certain lawless and criminal elements instigated and accelerated the riot actions, but that many ordinarily law-abiding citizens took part in the riots because of their inability to resist the seductive pressures of mob action: the intensification of stimulation with excitement and chaotic interaction, the spread of rumor, the impression of a collective norm that excused violence

RIOTS THAT HAPPENED

A study of seventy-six race riots in the United States from 1913 to 1963 showed the following immediate precipitants to rioting: interracial fighting (sixteen); killings, arrest, or search of black men by white policemen (fifteen); civil liberties and segregation issues in public facilities and housing (fourteen); interracial murder and shooting (eleven); rape, murder, attack, or hold-up of white women by black men (ten); other incidents (ten). A statistical comparison between cities marked by high incidence of riots and cities matched in size and region with low incidence of riots showed that in high-riot cities there was a smaller black-white difference in labor, domestic, and service occupations (indicating either black occupational threat to whites, increased black militancy as blacks moved out of their traditional niche, or both). High-riot cities had also fewer black policemen (per 1000 blacks) than low-riot cities, and larger election districts (possibly providing for less responsible government). High- and low-riot cities did not differ in amount of population increase, unemployment, or black-white income discrepancies.

LIEBERSON AND SILVERMAN (1965)

A RIOT THAT DID NOT HAPPEN

"The riot that did not happen" is a description of preventive measures taken by a collaborative unit of social scientists and law enforcement agencies preparing for an influx of 6000 visitors to a national motorcycle race at Upper Marlboro, Maryland. Similar races held earlier that summer in New Hampshire had resulted in bloody riots. The first strategy by the unit was aimed at avoiding polarization between the authorities and the motorcyclists. Joint meetings were arranged where each side was encouraged to give frank expression of its gripes and expectations concerning the other's position. The police were shown that the motorcyclists neither constituted a homogeneous class nor should they be treated as a breed apart from other citizens, and that harsh treatment would only confirm the motorcyclists' sense of persecution. Local motorcyclists were encouraged to exercise control over possible rowdiness. Potentially dangerous milling behavior was minimized by the provision of adequate camping facilities. Drag racing, stunt riding, and other crowd-pleasing activities that did not impinge on the nonmotorcycling citizenry, were permitted. All events were constantly monitored by the social scientists, especially in places where the police could not routinely go. Despite some minor conflict and lack of coordination between the social scientists and the various law enforcing agencies, the weekend passed without incident and the races took place as scheduled.

SHELLOW AND ROEMER (1966)

and aggression, and the opportunity for the expression of personal hostilities directed (or at least displaced) toward the other race.

Panic

Unlike acquisitive mobs, which pursue a common goal, defensive mobs are characterized by aversive behavior. That is, the activity within the mob is oriented by a defense *against* something or an escape *from* something. Defense against threat may often provide impetus for the evolution of a group, provided the defending participants interact in cooperative defensive effort and develop structured and interrelated roles and regulative norms to govern action. However, threat often precipitates unorganized defense with uncooperative action and disorderly mob activity. The term *panic* is used to describe such disorganized reactions to threat. When an army is threatened with defeat, it may withdraw its forces in an orderly cooperative retreat, or it may flee in panic. Whereas aggressive, acquisitive, and expressive mobs often (though not always) involve intentional congregation on the part of participating individuals, defensive mobs ordinarily take shape accidentally and unintentionally. When people congregate purposefully for defensive action, they usually (though again, not always) work cooperatively and generate an organized group. Because panic is unpredictable, it is, of course, difficult to study panic reactions under natural field conditions. There are, however, a few conflicting reports on panic in times of natural disaster such as floods, fires, or storms (Foy & Harlow, 1928; Killian, 1952; Turner & Killian, 1957; Fritz, 1961).

Disasters such as the Iroquois Theater fire in Chicago in 1903 (when 500 people were killed in less than 8 minutes, despite the fact that the theater suffered only superficial damage) and the almost equally disastrous Coconut Grove Nightclub fire in Boston in 1942, tend to produce irrational behavior. In both cases the severity of the fire was so slight that it was altogether unnecessary that any lives be lost; nevertheless, irrational mob action caused hundreds of deaths by trampling and asphyxiation. But as Fritz (1961) pointed out, when such disasters (and the panic that follows) occur naturally, only anecdotal reports are ordinarily available for use as data sources. Such reports, based on observations made in times of great excitement, of course suffer from distortions in perception and memory, and are therefore somewhat untrustworthy. Interviews conducted at later times also have limited value because victims of such tragedies are often unwilling to recall and discuss such unpleasant experiences.

Alternative approaches have been utilized with limited success to investigate the nature of panic and defensive mob action. In a limited series of studies, simulation of an air raid (with recorded sound effects and technically produced flashes of light) was carried out with enclosed audiences (Hudson, McDavid, & Roco, 1954). With such simulations, of course, ethical responsibility demands that the experiment be terminated at the onset of true panic and mob action; consequently, such approaches

---

PANIC AND DISASTER

A survey of human responses to peacetime disasters such as tornadoes, floods, or large explosions led to the following conclusions:

1. People who have previously experienced disaster respond in a more appropriate manner than those who have not.
2. There is little panic during and immediately after the disaster, and any such occurrences are grossly exaggerated.
3. There is generally more traffic toward the scene of disaster than away from it.
4. Informal but effective and highly unified social organization arises soon after the disaster to deal with the consequences; disorganization is temporary and it rarely occurs at the primary-group (e.g., family) level.
5. With the passage of time, social distinctions gradually reappear, as well as conflicts over alleged inequities in handling the consequences.
6. Concern for the safety of one's family and other intimates is predominant, even by people with community responsibilities.
7. Even though most people affected by disaster suffer some kind of emotional or physical upset (nausea, diarrhea, short temper, and the like) that continues even some time after the disaster, it is essentially transitory, does not affect realistic responses to the disaster, and rarely leads to chronic states of severe mental disturbance.
8. The disaster remains a major event in the lives of the victims (reference point for dating events or identifying fellow inhabitants in terms of the social role they occupied at the time of the disaster, and the like).

FRITZ (1961)

PANIC IN THE LAB

In a series of experimental studies, college women in groups were faced with danger (a threatened electric shock) and could either wait until the escape route became unjammed and then try to escape in cooperation with the rest of the group, or escape the danger immediately by sacrificing fellow group members to certain exposure to the shock. In general, between one-fourth and one-half of the subjects showed willingness to save themselves at the expense of their fellow members. No differences in the incidence of this panic response were observed in relation to group size, time pressures, penalties for escape failures, occurrence of panic in other members of the group, or anonymity of each subject. On a personality test, women who sacrificed others to save themselves were found to be more sensitive, feminine, dependent, anxious, and hypochondriacal. Women who were only children showed the panic response more often and sooner than did later-borns.

SCHULTZ (1969)

yield only limited data about the pre-panic reactions of individuals. In the laboratory several kinds of experiments have investigated behavior under conditions analogous to panic-producing threat situations (Mintz, 1951; Schultz, 1969).

The patterns of mob action in threat situations, whether they occur as disaster under natural conditions or in the laboratory, are very much the same. Without organized interaction and reciprocal interpersonal relationships, people tend to become bent on competitive self-protection, even at the expense of others. In the absence of strong identifications with a group, such selfish competition is quite likely to occur when an individual's life, security, or even comfort, is threatened. But under mob conditions, when unorganized masses of people are congregated, the conditions discussed earlier—such as circular reverberation and intensification of stimulation, cognitive disorientation, and massive interpersonal influence and suggestion—often produce panic and defensive mob action.

Demonstrations

The activity of many mobs simply involves diffuse demonstration of ideas, attitudes, or feelings. Unfortunately the catalytic exciting forces that result when people are physically congregated often turn what was initiated as an orderly and well-planned demonstration into an aggressive mob. Furthermore, expressive elements often occur in the background in mobs that are predominantly acquisitive, resulting in aggressive mob action. Riots are often justified as attempts to achieve a cause or purpose (such as "better food," or "fairer treatment of the minority"). Even though the initiators of demonstrating mobs are sometimes motivated solely by noble purposes, the followers are frequently instigated by less noble goals of personal gain or aggression. This, unfortunately, was the case in some of the civil rights demonstrations of the 1960s.

Both grief and joy many be expressed in collective behavior. In New Orleans, the death of a celebrated figure in the jazz world is customarily marked by street parades of jazz bands that follow the procession to the grave playing dirges, but return from the cemetery dancing in the streets and playing the most joyful kinds of Dixieland jazz to demonstrate their joy over the entry of the departed into the Promised Land. The carnival spirit, wherever it occurs, stimulates expressive mob activity. The Mardi Gras season in New Orleans, Rio de Janeiro, and other cities with large Catholic populations is accompanied by suspension of standard social conventions and restraints. Transvestism and promiscuity occur openly in the streets. At the end of World War II, strangers embraced and kissed indiscriminately in Times Square as the news was announced. In fact such orgies occur annually on New Year's Eve all over the world. As with other kinds of mob action, the ordinary control of impulse is suspended and the revelry becomes irresponsible, uninhibited, and irrational.

SOCIAL MOVEMENTS

Uncongregated collective behavior has several properties in common with congregated mobs. Mass movements involve widespread interpersonal stimulation, social influence, and suggestion, but the pace of stimulation is much slower than that of a mob. Mass movements usually occur with no physical congregation of participants at all. They often depend primarily upon communication through mass media or lengthy "grapevines" of word-of-mouth communication.

Mass movements, like other forms of unorganized collective behavior, tend especially to gain momentum under conditions of social ambiguity. A state of readiness to subscribe to some belief in order to interpret some poorly understood event or social crisis (for example, war or sudden social change) may occur among people and feed an emerging social movement. This kind of susceptibility to suggestion often appears as sheer gullibility. Participants in mass social movements often accept completely irrational and illogical ideas without critical evaluation. Beliefs are likely to be taken on faith, without demand for supportive documentation. In fact, sometimes logical arguments that contradict basic articles of faith subscribed to in the mass movement may be rejected and denied in the effort to maintain cognitive order and orientation (see Chapter 4, the theory of cognitive dissonance).

Cults

Most social movements begin as a polarization of thought around a single idea or person. When this polarization is protagonistic, or supportive, it can be termed a kind of "mass mania." A number of participants subscribe to common commitment to a cause or adoration of a person, and as momentum is gained, the collective behavior displayed by participants becomes more and more manic. Such movements are often called *cults*.

A dynamic leader or a central focal idea—either as a desired objective or as a feared threat—may induce polarized action within an uncongregated mass of people. Christianity represents an ideological cult that has endured nearly 2000 years since it was initiated by the dynamic leadership of Jesus Christ of Nazareth. A more recent movement oriented around a single person is the Kingdom of Father Divine (Cantril, 1941). The contemporary cult of UFOers, who believe that flying saucers do in fact exist and must be accounted for either as visitors from outer space or as highly secret projects of our own government, represents a mass movement polarized toward an idea, but not toward a particular person. People who joined in "bank runs" by withdrawing their accounts upon rumor of bank failure in the 1930s, and those who began to hoard silver coins when the U.S. government began minting "sandwich" coins with reduced silver content during 1965, are also representative of such "idea-based" mass movements.

These mass movements may be classified, like mobs, according to the nature of the impetus for their development. Acquisitive goal-pursuit or defensive avoidance and escape may give rise to *acquisitive* or *defensive* movements. Intense shared feelings or attitudes may generate *expressive* movements; or a combination of expressive and purposive elements may produce *aggressive* movements.

Purposive or acquisitive or defensive movements are sometimes ineffective in their efforts. They generate a lot of noise but little action. In order for purposive mass movements to achieve success, some degree of organized action is usually required. Participants may eventually band together for mob assertion and action, or organize into a group or a society (a *sect*) whose systematic efforts become more effective.

Defensive movements, like acquisitive ones, remain ineffective so far as action is concerned unless they resort to mob action or unless they evolve some degree of systematic organized cohesiveness. Even with direct action, the efforts of defensive mobs are not always effective: the panic of defensive escape mobs, even though it involves direct action, is usually nonadaptive unless some organized cooperation occurs (Mintz, 1951; Schultz, 1969). Like acquisitive cults, defensive cults offer satisfaction to the participant through his sense of identification with a movement. Even in the absence of direct action against a threat, identification with a collective movement may offer a sense of protection and security. Gullible acceptance of the beliefs of a cult may resolve cognitive conflicts, account for unexplained events, or otherwise reduce anxiety. Several situations have been reported in which waves of rumor and collective endorsement of certain ideas have occurred in response to disorienting and unaccountable events (Mackay, 1932; Cantril, Gaudet, & Hertzog, 1940; D. M. Johnson, 1945).

TULIPOMANIA

In 1634, a widespread craze often referred to as "Tulipomania" spread through Holland. The rage to own tulip bulbs became so great that fantastic sums of money were invested in rare bulbs, and certain kinds of bulbs were bought and hoarded in such great numbers that their owners could not possibly have cultivated them all. Eventually, as in any economic panic, the bubble burst, resulting in almost tragic economic depression. Similar "stampedes" have occurred throughout the world in various contexts: the land boom in Florida during the 1920s eventually burst, almost simultaneously with the occurrence of a severe hurricane, leaving the area severely economically depressed for several years.

MACKAY (1932)

MASS MANIA IN MATTOON

In September of 1944 a woman in the small city of Mattoon, Illinois, reported that someone had opened her bedroom window and sprayed with a sickish-sweet-smelling gas that partially paralyzed her legs and made her ill. During the 10 days that followed, dozens of cases with similar symptoms were reported, and police exerted full effort to catch the "gasser," who had become known in newspapers throughout the nation as the phantom anesthetist of Mattoon. Although the story died away within 2 weeks, an investigation through interviews with "victims" and police revealed that the episode was based on hysteria and a wave of mass suggestion. Rumor was rampant, people became apprehensive and disoriented, and they were gullible and suggestible. Those most susceptible were women below average in educational and economic level. Following the wave of hysterical suggestion came a successive wave of "contrasuggestion," with critical public attitudes toward hysterical suggestion and low ebbs in police records of prowler reports. Without mob congregation, a cultish wave had united a collection of "victims," and subsequently a collection of "critics" of these victims.

D. M. JOHNSON (1945)

ENCOUNTER BOOM

The rapid increase in encounter groups and the so-called growth centers across the nation reflects a vigorous social movement to meet pressing needs in our culture. Its popular incubating location, California (e.g., 200 encounter groups and 75 growth centers in the Palo Alto area alone) offers a milieu that exaggerates certain characteristics of contemporary American society, such as geographic and social mobility. The rapid disappearance of stable and intimacy-fostering environmental factors such as the primary family, the neighborhood merchant, and the family doctor have made it increasingly difficult for people to maintain facades of adequacy, competence, and self-sufficiency. Encounter groups (either in cooperation or direct competition with churches) offer a social oasis that meets needs for communion, intimacy, and nurturance.

LIEBERMAN, YALOM, AND MILES (1972)

Often, participants in an uncongregated collective movement simply feel better with reassurance that others share their insecurity; there may be a vague sense that somebody somewhere will do something about the threat. Cultish movements of this type often develop in the wake of a dynamic public figure. Adherents of "McCarthyism" in the 1950s seemed to be reassured simply by the fact that they had a champion to defend against the "internal communist conspiracy" in the State Department. Thousands of Americans troubled by inability to account for frequent reports of "flying saucers" find solace in adherence to UFO groups that reassure them that Major Donald Kehoe leads the fight to wring from the United States government a confession that the explanation of the saucers is indeed known but kept secret from the population.

Expressive movements are typified by religious cults. For example, in its day the Kingdom of Father Divine was a cult whose major activities involved the expression of feelings and attitudes, although like most cults, it also offered a sense of security, protection, and cognitive consonance to its participants (Cantril, 1941). To some extent the politically oriented John Birch Society may be thought of as an expressive movement. In fact, most citizens who call themselves Democrats or Republicans are simply labeling their identification with a collective movement, unless they are genuinely active in the political activities of a party organization.

Examples of aggressive movements include hate cults that endorse injury or violence against others as well as rebellious social movements that advocate the undoing of established order. The "massive resistance" movement led by the Byrd family and others in Virginia following the 1954 Supreme Court School Desegregation Order represented a passive movement whose aggressive intent was subordinated to its expressive intent. Almost the entire population of Salem, Massachusetts, at the peak of a wave of witch-burning hysteria, participated in a hate-based aggressive collective movement. Aggressive movements, like aggressive mobs, usually synthesize elements of purposive intent with elements of expressive demonstration. Acquisitive and defensive movements are sometimes inclined to adopt aggressive tactics.

Cultish social movements involving fads or crazes attract participants on the basis of a sense of identity and belonging. Such movements might be seen as defensive in that they provide protection for the insecure individual against a sense of alienation and isolation (Mackay, 1932). Of course, cultish sects serve different purposes for different individuals. For many, participation in a social movement is a defense against anxiety; for others it may be merely a vehicle for satisfying selfish motivation under the shelter of collective diffusion of responsibility (for example, orgies), or a channel through which personal peeves or hostilities may be expressed (Toch, 1965). The rather strange fashions of the Carnaby Street "Mod" fad in England and the United States during the late 1960s, for example, were attributed in England primarily to the expression of hostile alienation of young people from adults, but in the United States primarily to faddism. A British youth accounted for his clothing tastes as a throwback to the revolt of Edward VII against his "hypocrite of a mother, Queen Victoria," commenting that "Edward revolted against the hyprocrisy of his times, and so are we." In contrast, an American youth said simply, "The kids wear the clothes because it's the 'in' thing to wear; it's the fashion fad of the moment" (Shearer, 1966). In fact, by 1973, the "Carnaby look" was 'out,' replaced by Edwardian coats, baggy pleated pants, and high-heeled shoes for men.

Protests

Protest movements are often quicker to emerge visibly than protagonistic movements —simply because it is usually easier to know what one is "against" than to know what one is "for." The genesis of a social movement often lies within personal discontent and frustration, and the compelling motivation that polarizes people into parallel action is often the desire to express a defensive protest. Thus protest movements are like other cultish movements, but their distinguishing feature is the commitment to voice protest against some threatening or frustrating condition.

Some protest movements are essentially expressive in nature, aimed only at displaying publicly the sentiments of the protesting movement. Many of the early activities of the Student Nonviolent Coordinating Committee and the Southern Christian Leadership Conference under the direction of Rev. Martin Luther King were expressive protest movements. They did not seek violent or aggressive immediate action, but merely to call public attention to practices unfair to black Americans. Other movements, such as the Black Panther movement, are overtly aggressive, threatening both life and property in pursuit of their goals.

Protest movements, although negative and antagonistic in their origins, often eventually transform into positive protagonistic movements. Following the phase of expressing protest and action against some threat or frustration, the movement may eventually generate positive goals and programs of action to achieve a more desirable situation than the one that inspired the protest. A truly effective protest movement does not cease with destroying the old order, but continues to create and achieve a new order that is more acceptable.

STRANGE BEDFELLOWS

A comparison between a sample of 1063 students from 61 colleges across the nation and a standard sample of U.S. adult population showed that even though students lean slightly more to the political left, both groups tend to reject extremists from the far left and the far right by an overwhelming margin (95 percent). Of particular interest was the finding that extremism apparently has an appeal for its own sake; a significant portion of sympathizers with far right organizations such as the John Birch Society and the Ku Klux Klan gave favorable ratings to far left organizations such as the Students for Democratic Society, the Weathermen, and the Black Panthers; and vice versa.

AMERICAN INSTITUTE FOR PUBLIC OPINION (1971)

Seven Lively Powers

BLACK POWER

Black consciousness is the cornerstone for a social movement that transcends the diverse goals of the many black organizations currently in existence. Overt personal and subtle institutionalized racism accounts for the facts that 29 percent of all black families in the United States still exist below the poverty level as compared to 8 percent of all whites, and that a college-educated black man's median income was $7154 in 1970 compared to $8754 for the white high school graduate. Increasing unemployment and economic depression in black communities, and the realization that racial integration often co-opts the black into inactivity and loss of identity, have led to a new awakening among blacks. The results are reflected in a reformulation of the old concepts of Garvey, DuBois, and other black intellectuals of the past—cultural independence, community control, and the expression of the dignity and beauty of Blackness and Soul.

CARMICHAEL AND HAMILTON (1967)
BUCKHOUT (1971)

CHICANO POWER

The stereotype of the Mexican-American is an individual lacking in ambition and energy, hopelessly engaged in joining the dynamic Anglo culture. Throughout the Southwest, where 90 percent of the Chicanos live, a third are below the official poverty line of $3000 annual income; their life expectancy is about 10 years less than that of whites; their children are steered to "realistic" vocational school programs; and they are subject to frequent police brutality. But Tío Taco (Uncle Taco —the equivalent of Uncle Tom for blacks) is no more the sole representative for the 5.6 million Mexican-Americans in the United States. Increasing ethnic consciousness, cultural pride, and political militancy have emerged during the last few years. Caesar Chavez unionized California grape-pickers and successfully initiated a nationwide boycott of grapes until his demands were met. Political pressure resulted in the elimination of early IQ-test administration by school authorities to Chicano children struggling with the English language. There is a trend toward greater community control over schools. *La Raza Unida* attempts to field independent candidates to gain control in areas where Chicanos are the majority. It also represents 200 Chicano organizations attempting to organize a common political front with blacks and other minorities.

NEWSWEEK (1970)

NATIVE-AMERICAN POWER

There are about 600,000 Native-Americans (Indians) in the United States, on which the government spends about half a billion dollars annually—enough to give each Indian family a direct income of $6,000. Yet three times as many Indians as whites still die prematurely, and ten times as many adults cannot find work. They live in substandard conditions on a deficient diet of pinto beans, tortillas, and potatoes (the bulk of the Indian menu is starch, resulting in obesity, which disguises malnutrition). Young Indians, however, are beginning to resent Uncle Tomahawk, the stereotype of the Native-American succumbing to paternal white handouts until he gradually fades away in an alcoholic stupor. In 1969 they dramatized their plight by invading the bleak island of Alcatraz, offering to buy it from the U.S. government for $24 in glass beads and cloth, in order to turn it into a cultural center. (In 1972 they temporarily occupied the Federal Bureau of Indian Affairs in Washington, D.C., and in 1973 they publicly "seceded" the town of Wounded Knee, South Dakota, from the United States.) The major thrust of the militants is to advocate

Pan-Indian nationalism, that is, to think of themselves as Indians rather than as Sioux, Crow, or Navajo.

HEDGEPETH (1970)
MANGEL (1970)
MAXEY (1970)

ASIAN-AMERICAN POWER

Asian-Americans constitute about 1 percent of the U.S. population, and are congregated mostly on the West Coast. Very large masses of Asians in the United States (e.g., 70 percent of the population in San Francisco's Chinatown) speak no English; they earn as little as 70 cents an hour for a 12-hour day; and they have the highest suicide and tuberculosis rate in the nation. Those Asians who somehow have gained access to the dominant Anglo culture are often "marginal people," accepted by neither culture. Attempts are currently under way to reawaken interest in the positive aspects of Asian culture, such as the fostering of family ties and the curbing of juvenile delinquency. At the same time, political alignment with other minorities is advocated by organizations such as the Asian-American Political Alliance (AAPA), the Intercollegiate Chinese for Social Action (ICSA), and the Filipino-American Collegiate Endeavor (FACE).

HING (1970)
WONG (1971)

WOMAN POWER

The Women's Liberation movement to fight long-term oppression institutionalized in a male-dominated society has gathered considerable momentum across the United States during the past decade. Female consciousness is a concept embraced by many women, even though they may not belong to any of the organizations promoting it. The two major women's organizations are the National Organization of Women (NOW), and the National Women's Political Caucus (NWPC), which wield considerably greater influence than their estimated 40,000 paid membership would indicate. NOW concerns itself primarily with economic discrimination on the basis of sex. NWPC is more politically oriented, attempting to field election candidates espousing its cause. Both organizations point out that over one half of the 63 million women in the United States between the ages of 18 and 64 are working. Only one-third of this population, however, are married to men who theoretically could support a family. The majority are either married to men whose annual income is $7000 or less, or they are separated, widowed, or divorced (many of them with children). In full-time jobs that pay $5000 or less annually, there are three times as many women as there are men. Women occupying the same jobs as men are usually given different titles and lower pay, and their professional skills are generally underutilized. On the political front, even though 51 percent of the eligible electorate in the United States are women, there is one woman in the Senate, there are twelve in the House of Representatives, there are no female governors, and there are only a few women mayors, who serve more or less nominally. In order to increase women's political and economic power, a National Women's Action Alliance has been formed recently in order to coordinate the many loosely knit organizations that comprise the Women's Liberation movement.

CENTER FOR WOMENS STUDIES AND SERVICES (1971)
FLEXNER (1971)

GAY POWER

Since June 1969, when New York City police raided a landmark homosexual bar in Greenwich Village and met with unexpected resistance, the homosexual's timid and browbeaten history has undergone a dramatic change. Increasingly militant tactics by homosexuals have included "trashing" (wrecking) places of business that

(*Continued on* p. 350)

discriminate against them, "dumping on" (heckling) unsympathetic religious leaders such as Billy Graham, and "zapping" (confronting) politicians on issues such as equal housing and employment rights. There are about 100,000 members of various homosexual organizations in the United States, a small number compared to the estimated number of homosexuals in the nation (4 million according to the National Institute of Mental Health, over 10 million according to various homosexual sources). Their influence, however, has become increasingly potent. Major homosexual organizations, New York's Gay Activist Alliance (GAA), San Francisco's Society for Individual Rights (SIR), the Mattachine Society, Daughters of Bilitis, and the Metropolitan Community Church, combine with many smaller organizations to promote, via 200 newsletters and publications, gay consciousness and pride. Their representatives are now accepted as speakers in Rotary clubs, Chambers of Commerce, various TV talk shows, and government hearings. In Washington, a representative of the Mattachine Society gathered a respectable number of votes (twice as many as a black-power advocate) for a seat in the House of Representatives, and a 28-year-old homosexual who had publicly applied for a license to marry his male lover was elected overwhelmingly as the president of the 43,000-member student body of the University of Minnesota. Federal courts have ruled that homosexuals can no longer be regarded automatically as security risks. Many segments of the psychiatric and religious establishments recognize that homosexuality is not necessarily a mental nor a genetic pathology. Respectable voices call for the abolition of criminal penalties for homosexual practices among consenting adults (following the lead of Colorado, Connecticut, Illinois, and Idaho).

MARLOWE (1965)
NEWSWEEK (1971)
BOWERS (1972)

SENIOR CITIZEN POWER

The social movement dedicated to the needs of the elderly had its roots in the Townsend movement in the 1930s. At that time about 5 million followers of a California physician, Dr. Francis Townsend, endorsed his plan to fight economic depression by simply allocating $200 monthly to everyone over 60. The subsequent initiation of Social Security by President Roosevelt took the steam out of Townsend's plan (which would have cost about half the national budget). During the past decade, however, there has been an increased awakening among the 20 million senior citizens (age 65 and over) in the United States, of whom 1 out of 4 live in extreme poverty. The National Council of Senior Citizens and the American Association of Retired Persons have a combined membership of over 6 million. In the past most of their efforts were geared toward economic and recreational issues such as increased Social Security payments, better and less expensive medical care, inspection of nursing homes, elimination of job discrimination, and travel and recreational facilities for the elderly. Lately, however, there has been an increased emphasis on political power by the elderly through block voting in order to meet their needs. Despite the newly enfranchised youth vote in 1972, as a rule twice as many voters over 50 than under 25 turn out to vote. Political pressure has also been instrumental in the goals for "action in the 70s" provided in position papers delivered at the White House National Conference on Aging.

SMELSER (1962)
NCOA POSITION PAPER (1970)
SENIOR CITIZENS NEWS (1971)
AARP NEWS BULLETIN (1972)

COMMUNITIES

The kinds of collective social behavior described up to this point are alike in lacking properties of systematic order and social organization. As already mentioned, however, they are often transitional states that are superseded by various forms of social organization. There are semiorganized social situations (in transition from unorganized collective behavior to organized behavior in groups and societies) that may best be called *communities.* These are quasi-groups: they do not show all the properties of social order described in Section IV, but they are outgrowths of collective social situations that begin to show some systematic order.

Utopias and Sects

Some collective movements that originate as cults may eventually evolve into organized minisocieties called *sects.* (If they become more or less completely organized, they become groups or societies as described in Chapters 10, 11, 12.) Many religious cults have evolved into complex organizations. The Christian church, which began as a cult 20 centuries ago, now constitutes a worldwide movement embracing many interrelated organized social systems.

Under some circumstances social movements evolve into planned and intentional miniature societies. The term *Utopia* (coined by Sir Thomas More in 1516 to describe

Table 13–2   Utopias in Western Literature

Author	Time	Work	Brief Description
Plato	4th century B.C.	*The Republic*	Plato envisioned an ideal society with a hierarchy of classes, each having its particular obligations. Philosophers would rule, poets would be excluded.
Sir Thomas More	1516	*Utopia*	In coining the word "Utopia," More anticipated an order in which natural virtues would be unhindered.
Sir Francis Bacon	1627	*The New Atlantis*	Bacon placed primary emphasis on technological productivity.
Edward Bellamy	1888	*Looking Backward*	Bellamy's utopia was a socialist work, containing scathing critiques of his contemporary world. The work sold tremendously in the United States.
H. G. Wells	1905	*A Modern Utopia*	In this work Wells describes a future paradise; in others he outlined the destruction of the world.
Aldous Huxley	1932	*Brave New World*	A satirical account of a frightening future world in which individuality is sacrificed for the community ideals. Humans are produced in test tubes and graded according to intelligence.
George Orwell	1948	*1984*	Orwell predicted the rise of Big Brother and the loss of freedom in this negative utopian prediction. Three world powers exist, two of which are always warring against the third.
B. F. Skinner	1948	*Walden Two*	Skinner applied the principles of learning theory in an effort to produce a population rich in idealism and devoid of negative impulses.

Source: Copyright © 1970 by International Textbook Company. Reprinted from *Man and Men: Social Psychology as Social Science* by Martin Grossack and Howard Gardner by permission of Chandler Publishing Company.

HARE KRISHNA

The International Society for Krishna Consciousness was formed in 1966 by Prabhupada A. C. Bhaktivendanta, Swami of India. Krishna consciousness involves the dovetailing of one's interest to the Supreme Enjoyer, the Lord, Sri Krishna. For example, the writer writes about Krishna, the publisher publishes about Krishna, the businessman establishes temples for Krishna, and the householder raises children in the science of Krishna. The society is especially geared to bring Krishna's message to the Western world. It publishes books, pamphlets, and records to induce ecstatic Krishna consciousness by congregational chanting in public schools, parks, streets, or via mass media.

KRIYANDA (1970)

his concept of the ideal state) has come to be applied broadly to experimental societies. Table 13–2 summarizes several of the more widely known Utopian plans that have been outlined in the literature of the Western world. Few of these have actually been implemented, but there have been many social movements organized to achieve manifestation of such Utopian societies.

During the nineteenth century a number of social movements in the United States originated as cults but intentionally attempted to transform themselves into experimental Utopian societies. The Mormon movement eventually led to the establishment of the Church of Jesus Christ of Latter Day Saints as a society that now dominates the state of Utah and extends around the world. Other experimental societies were created on a smaller scale in the Oneida Community in New York, the Amana Colonies in Iowa, and the New Harmony Community in Indiana. Even today there exists a movement whose participants hope to transform the ideas of a Utopian community described by psychologist B. F. Skinner in his novel *Walden Two* (1948) into actuality. And although their efforts are concentrated primarily upon development of a physical city rather than a social community, the developers of planned communities such as Columbia, Maryland, and Reston, Virginia aspire to create Utopian cities in the 1970s.

Applied group dynamics was, of course, unknown to the planners of nineteenth-century experimental societies in the United States. Nevertheless the congruence between the organizing principles outlined in connection with these microsocieties and contemporary group dynamics is remarkable. The founding constitutions and bylaws of these societies tend to direct explicit attention toward commitment of participants toward a common set of goals or purposes, usually religious or ethical in nature, but often with defensive overtones; the clear-cut differentiation of roles within the structure of the society; and the generation of binding norms to govern the conduct of members of the society. Thus the essential properties of systematic social organization seem to have been recognized implicitly in planning these societies. Most have been short-lived in that they have eventually been assimilated into the social and political organization of the government.

Bureaucracies

Another kind of semiorganized social behavior occurs under the conditions of loose social organization that we sometimes call *bureaucracy*. A bureaucracy is an organized social system that usually does not encompass the total life of its participants as does a society or a group. That is, bureaucracies usually affect only one segment of a person's existence, or a portion of his day, or only one of the many behavioral roles he may play. The bureaucracy itself may be highly organized (with respect to

UP THE ORGANIZATION

A "survival manual for successful corporate guerillas" written in a somewhat tongue-in-cheek style by a corporate executive provides numerous suggestions for avoiding the stifling effects of inefficient bureaucracies. Among the observations and recommendations:

1. Professional campus recruiters should be fired and be replaced by the most efficient chiefs within the organization.
2. Institutionalized management consultants are worthless and should only be mentioned to organizational personnel as a prodding-to-action threat.
3. Organizational charts produce organizational rigor mortis.
4. The computer mystique can be put in better perspective if one remembers that computers are no more than "dumb adding-machines—typewriters."
5. A person with the title "Chairman of the Executive Committee" (or the like) has better chances to mollify customers than "Head of the Complaint Department."
6. The usual 3-weeks upper-echelon decisions can be made at a lower level within 3 seconds.
7. A perennial snooper and "bad guy" executive who stirs matters up can avoid the hardening of bureaucratic arteries.
8. Reserved parking spaces, special-quality stationery, company plane for executives are sure to lower morale.
9. Board of directors' meetings (if composed of meddling people from outside the organization) following cocktails and a heavy lunch are guaranteed to put the directors (literally) to sleep.
10. If bonus checks are handed out personally by a supervisor and are accompanied by conversation, incentive effectiveness will be ensured (i.e., a bonus is not something the recipient can "count on" automatically).

TOWNSEND (1970)

role differentiation, channels of communication, codes of desirability and acceptability, and pressures toward uniformity of behavior). Yet the individual participant may shed all of these when he moves beyond the scope of the bureaucratic organization and into another facet of his life.

Large businesses are usually characterized by bureaucratic organizations. The "worker society" is sometimes forced to operate within rules and standards imposed from outside by the power of management; but in other cases, that society is an emergent product of the voluntary behavior of the workers and the implicit norms and standards they generate themselves. The study of bureaucratic organizations and their effects on the individual's behavior comprise a large portion of what is known as *organizational psychology*. Most governmental structures evolve bureaucracies among their employees in exactly the same way large businesses do. Schools and universities usually evolve the same kind of bureaucracies. In all of these cases, the social organization produced is a by-product rather than the purpose of the collection of people who generate it. The business of an industrial firm is to produce goods or services efficiently; the purpose of a government is to make and enforce laws; the purpose of a school or university is to facilitate learning. But in the process of organizing aggregates of people into a system to achieve these purposes, miniature societies tend to emerge. The evolution of bureaucracies, in this sense, is more or less inescapable. An efficient bureaucracy, of course, is one that gets its job done and at the same time provides satisfactions to its members. Under such circumstances few participants in the bureaucracy even object or complain. In fact many never stop to recognize that they are participants in a bureaucratic organization. It is only when bureaucratic organizations break down, become wastefully inefficient, fail to satisfy the needs of their participants, and otherwise misfunction, that one complains about them.

Communities

The customary usage of the word *community* refers to emergent loose social organizations from such natural collective units as neighborhoods, housing projects, geographical areas, or other bases of common interest among people. Normally such collective units have little or no extensive social organization; yet from time to time they may evolve temporary organization in the face of a crisis or collective purpose. Sometimes the organization is loose and informal, becoming active and formalized only when called up for a specific objective.

The simplest kind of community is the result of physical proximity and common interests or values. Residential units (buildings, projects, neighborhoods) usually suggest the physical boundaries of a community. Under some circumstances, however, communality of interests and values may be sufficient to define a community without any reference to physical proximity or direct contact. Members of a particular profession, for example, usually recognize their membership in a community even though their direct contact and interaction may be limited. People of particular political inclinations usually feel themselves members of a common community, as do black, gay, or socioeconomically disadvantaged Americans.

Members of a particular socioeconomic class in our society can be thought of as members of an uncongregated community. The quasi-organized state of such "class" communities has some important effects on the behavior of the individual. The degree of systematic organization within social class communities within a broader society is not nearly as specific and complete as in smaller and more intimate groups that meet face-to-face. Yet the consequences for the individual are generally similar.

In some societies very formal delineation of membership in class communities is defined at birth according to one's parentage. Such formal social class communities are known as *castes*. In India, for example, the Brahman caste is "superior" to the

---

THE SCHOOL COMMUNITY AS MELTING POT

Sociometric measures were administered to a sample of 1360 students in a Seattle high school composed of non-Jewish whites (55 percent), Jews (15 percent), Japanese (10 percent), Chinese (10 percent), Blacks (9 percent), and Filipinos, Hawaiians, and Indians (1 percent). Assessed were the dimensions of *leadership* (subjects were asked to nominate school representatives to a big national meeting), *work* (subjects chose co-workers for a school picnic), *dating* (subjects were asked to choose dates from the school population), and *friendship* (subjects indicated who were their friends in school). Also measured was the degree of expressed *ethnocentrism* (in-group choices).

Overall, the lowest degree of ethnocentrism was displayed by Jews choosing leaders; the highest degree was displayed by blacks' choice of friends. High ethnocentrism was also displayed by the Chinese and blacks, respectively, in their working and dating choices, and by the non-Jewish whites' choice of leaders. Next to themselves, the following ethnic groups were liked best on all dimensions in the following order: non-Jewish whites, Jews, Japanese, and Chinese. A marked antipathy, presumably because of scholastic competition, was evident between Jews and Japanese. The non-Jewish white majority showed significant in-group choices in leadership, work, and dating, but not in friendship. Nevertheless they were rebuffed in their friendship choices by the minorities (whose friendship choices were strictly in-group), presumably as a response by the latter to the majority's rejection of minorities on all dimensions other than friendship. Progressively, ethnocentrism among non-Jewish whites went from leadership/work to dating, while among the minorities it went from work to friendship.

LUNDBERG AND DICKSON (1965)

Table 13–3 Caste and Class

355

Masses: From
Crowds to
Communities

Upper-Upper Class

"OLD ARISTOCRACY"	UU
"Aristocracy," but not "old"	LU
"Nice, respectable people"	UM
"Good people, but 'nobody' "	LM
——— "Po' whites" ———	UL LL

Lower-Upper Class

"Old aristocracy"
"ARISTOCRACY, BUT NOT OLD"
"Nice, respectable people"
"Good people, but 'nobody' "
——— "Po' whites" ———

Upper-Middle Class

"Society" { "Old families"	UU
"Society," but not "old families"	LU
"PEOPLE WHO SHOULD BE UPPER CLASS"	UM
"People who don't have much money"	LM
	UL
"No 'count lot"	LL

Lower-Middle Class

"Old aristocracy": (older)   "Broken-down aristocracy" (younger)
"People who think they are somebody"
"WE POOR FOLKS"
"People poorer than us"
"No 'count lot"

Upper-Lower Class

——— ———	UU
	LU
"Society" or the "folks with money"	UM
"People who are up because they have a little money"	LM
"POOR BUT HONEST FOLK"	UL
"Shiftless people"	LL

Lower-Lower Class

———   ———
"Society" or the "folks with money"
"Way-high-ups," but not "Society"
"Snobs trying to push up"
"PEOPLE JUST AS GOOD AS ANYBODY"

CAPITALS = descriptions of one's own class.   ——— = sharp class differentiations.
Lower Case = descriptions of other classes.   ·········· = indefinite class differentiations.

Note: In a study of the "white caste" class system in "Old City," a medium-sized town in the Deep South area of the United States, "class" was defined as "the largest group of people whose members have intimate access to one another." A large number of informants drawn from various occupational, associational, and other status groups "placed" individuals' social position according to the informant's conception of class criteria. The descriptions in the table demonstrate that the way in which people conceive of class division (including their own class) varies with their social position.

Source: Abstracted from A. Davis, B. B. Gardner, and M. R. Gardner, *Deep South: A Social Anthropological Study of Caste and Class* (Chicago: University of Chicago Press, 1941). Chart reprinted by permission of the publisher.

other castes. Our own society claims to be free of formal caste distinctions, yet blacks and females can certainly point to the discriminatory treatment as evidence of residual caste distinctions. Moreover, even this relative freedom from caste distinctions does not generate a "classless" society at all. Indeed, the very fact of role differentiation and differentiation of the function of subclasses (by sex, age, skills, etc.)

WHO SPEAKS FOR THE COMMUNITY?

A survey was conducted in an unincorporated area adjoining the city of Seattle, Washington, with an estimated population of 80,000. The representative sample of 561 households ranged from high-income groups of engineers and professionals through salesclerks and semiprofessionals to poorly paid unskilled workers and the unemployed. Community leaders were identified through nominations and reputational methods. There was a large divergence of concerns expressed by the members of the community and their leaders. The community leaders' primary concern was with roads, highways, recreational facilities, and political harmony. The members of the community were more interested in the breakdown of morality, crime, and traffic fatalities. An even more startling finding was that on practically all issues of concern to the community members, they did not know who in the community could act as a spokesman and problem solver.

FIEDLER, FIEDLER, AND CAMPF (1971)

suggests that in principle no society is ever completely classless. However, our society is a very fluid one that permits the individual to migrate more or less freely from one social class to another according to his merits and achievements. Of course this would not be possible in a caste-based society. Freedom for such migration is known as *social mobility*. In some cases this freedom can generate problems of a disorientation for the person who moves rapidly from one social role to another. The problems of being "caught between" with poorly defined or conflicting expectations about one's role in his group or community result in *marginality* and *anomie.* These issues were discussed in Chapter 7.

In our society the most appropriate bases for defining social class membership empirically are occupation, level of education, or income. For purposes of broad classification, the American social class structure is frequently dichotomized at the middle into "working class" (a euphemism for the lower half of the distribution, which includes occupational levels from unemployment through unskilled and semiskilled labor) and the "middle class" (which includes the upper half of the distribution, represented by such groups as highly skilled labor, so-called white-collar workers, managerial and professional occupations, and the aristocracy of the "landed gentry"). Stable differences in the typical behavior of members of each of these classes have

ACCULTURATION INTO THE COMMUNITY

A sample of college students, all of whom were Cuban refugees in the United States during the regime of Fidel Castro, took a specially constructed measure designed to assess attitudes toward assimilation (into another culture), a measure of dogmatism (Rokeach E scale), a measure of rigidity (Wesley Rigidity scale), and various other personality measures. Dogmatism was found to be inversely related to positive attitudes toward assimilation. Subjects who wanted to assimilate into American culture (speak the language, join groups, and identify with the majority) were less dogmatic than the subjects who showed strong ingroup feelings with little desire to assimilate. Attitudinal rigidity and positive assimilation attitudes were also inversely related, as were behavioral rigidity (involving a routine, well-organized approach to daily life) and positive assimilation attitudes. Age was positively related to assimilation attitudes, but years in the United States was not. Males tended to have more favorable attitudes toward assimilation than did females.

FINEMAN (1966)

been observed in several contexts. Ordinarily the objective definition of one's social class membership by criteria such as occupation, education, and income coincides with the individual's own subjective appraisal of his social class identification (Warner, Meeker, & Eels, 1949). However, when there is some discrepancy, the individual's behavior usually resembles the class with which he is subjectively psychologically identified rather than the class to which he would objectively be assigned (Merton & Kitt, 1950). In other words, the social class to which a person *thinks* he belongs defines his psychological reference group more accurately than objective criteria. Table 13–3 describes the composite of social classes of American society (in a particular geographical area) and their perception of one another.

Suburban neighborhoods, housing projects, rural communities, and other geographically bounded population units often evolve a sense of community that generates some degree of social organization. From a sociological point of view, in order to understand one's involvement and participation in various levels of social organization, one may proceed outward from the isolated individual to the widest range of social organization in which he participates. For most people the most intimate social structure is the *family,* bounded within the physical household. Beyond this, the neighborhood comprises an expanded community. The next level is a municipality, followed by county, state, and other regional political units, and finally at the broadest levels, the national community. A few individuals are sufficiently farsighted to consider their membership in the greater world and universal communities, but for most people these are too remote to exert much influence on their behavior. The degree to which a person participates actively in the informal structure of his community is reciprocally related to the degree of influence it exerts on his behavior (Form & Sauer, 1960; S. Greer, 1960; Yinger, 1960; Fiedler, Fiedler, & Campf, 1971).

Community Relations

Sometimes communities come into direct conflict with one another. A by-product of the emergent social organization that makes one identify with his community is a sense of alienation from other communities—especially those that may threaten one's own. This is an important contributor to racial and ethnic prejudices and ethnocentrism (see Chapter 8). The term *ingroup* is used to designate the relationship between two individuals who are participants in the same organizational system; all nonparticipants of that system are then said to constitute the *outgroup.* In Chapter 12, the effect of intragroup cooperation (which enhances cohesive attraction within the group) on intergroup competition and conflict between groups was described. One important consequence of high levels of cohesiveness within a group is the tendency to maximize ingroup-outgroup distinctions. Among a set of interrelated groups, high levels of within-group cohesion are associated with high levels of intergroup conflict. In an organized group, sanctions normally are evolved in the form of norms that inhibit the open expression of hostility among ingroup members. When occasional interpersonal frustrations occur within the group as one member blocks another from attainment of his own personal goals, effective group organization tends to discourage one member from direct retaliation against another. Instead, he may be encouraged to displace his hostility and redirect it toward some target outside the group. Thus the suppression of hostility among the ingroup often contributes an important basis for the phenomenon of *scapegoating,* in which aggression toward a frustrator is suppressed and displaced upon some nonparticipant bystander.

In turn, such scapegoating further aggravates the development of intergroup hostility. There are important consequences in this fact for the coexistence of sharply defined and cohesive subgroups within a complex society of interrelated groups. Intense regionalism and regional loyalties tend to breed distrust and contempt for

"COMMUNITIES" IN CONFLICT: THE ROBBERS' CAVE STUDIES OF INTERGROUP RELATIONS

The subjects in these experiments were preadolescent boys in summer camps, who were told that they were attending camps set up to study camping methods. They were normal boys without previous relationships as friends or members of existing groups, and they were homogeneous with respect to age, sex, and general background. The camps, isolated from outside influences, allowed opportunity for a varity of activities and for manipulation of conditions and circumstances of social interaction. The experimental design was arranged sequentially to maximize coordinated activity within each group around goals of high value in order to achieve ingroup cohesiveness, to induce intergroup conflict by selecting activities embodying goals in which success by one group led to frustration in the other, and to reduce intergroup friction. Data were collected without the subjects' knowledge, by using hidden microphones and cameras. These were augmented by direct observation, sociometric tests, interpersonal ratings, and manipulated events.

Experiment 1. Experimental Production of Intergroup Friction (1949)

Two established ingroups in a summer camp in Connecticut, the Bulldogs and the Red Devils, participated in a 5-day contest of competitive games and contests for prizes allotted on the basis of the individual's contributions within his own group. Referees' decisions were intentionally slanted to favor the Bulldogs. Good sportsmanship, which prevailed at first, gradually deteriorated into hostility between the two groups. The contest was followed by a party proposed by the staff to "let bygones be bygones." At the party, half of the refreshments spread on a table were whole and delectable, whereas the other half were crushed and unappetizing. The Red Devils were allowed to appear first and take the good half of the refreshments. From this point on, intergroup hostilities reached a high pitch. For two days, the boys were allowed to ventilate their feelings of aggression by means of name-calling, threatening posters, and food-throwing ("catharsis"). At this point the experiment was terminated, and no further experimental induction of intergroup friction was attempted. Nevertheless the two groups continued to function with extreme hostility toward each other.

Thus democracy and cooperation within a group do not necessarily extend to the outgroup if the interests of the outgroup are in conflict with those of the ingroup. Intergroup hostilities persist even after the need for actual hostility is past, and cathartic ventilation of aggression seems only to increase intergroup hostility.

Experiment 2. Production of Intergroup Conflict and Its Reduction (1954)

A second experiment was conducted in an experimental summer camp at Robbers' Cave State Park in Oklahoma. The subjects were twenty-two 11-year-old boys from homogeneous backgrounds who were divided into two equal groups, the Rattlers and the Eagles. Ingroup solidarity and intergroup conflict were generated according to the procedures used in the earlier experiment.

The first attempt to reduce intergroup friction through mere contact, even in pleasant situations, was unsuccessful. In fact, hostile and aggressive behavior even showed some increase. In a second attempt, arrangements were made to require interaction between the hostile groups in achieving focal and urgent superordinate goals, which could be attained only through the pooled resources of both groups: inspecting pipes and tanks to see why the camp was out of water, pooling money to rent a highly desired movie, and towing in a broken-down supply truck on an overnight hike. Following situations that required cooperative interaction between the groups, ingroup-outgroup delineations became blurred, the tendency to stereotype outgroup members was reduced, and intergroup hostility largely disappeared.

SHERIF, HARVEY, WHITE, HOOD, AND SHERIF (1954)
SHERIF AND SHERIF (1956)

outsiders, and thus to make difficult cohesive national organization; similarly, intense national loyalties tend to make difficult cohesive international organization. For example, one of the greatest deterrents to effective international organizations such as the League of Nations and the United Nations has been intense national loyalty. In fact, in the 1960s, regional loyalties and cohesiveness among citizens of the southern bloc of the United States tended to breed distrust of other regions and suspicion and distaste for strong federal governmental organization.

Another by-product of the delineation of ingroup and outgroup that results when group cohesiveness is maximized is the likelihood of coalitions among members of the outgroup. When a highly organized ingroup threatens isolated outsiders, pressures may be generated to induce a coalescence among them to form a protective organization. Such phenomena occur from time to time at the level of social and political movements. For example, the relatively tight ingroup loyalties of the dominant "WASP" majority in our American society have tended to generate coalitions among blacks, Jews, and Catholics in their quest for protection of the rights of minorities. Perception of common threat from another group, then, may provide the common cause or purpose that initiates organization of a group among otherwise unrelated members of an outgroup.

Nations

Nations are actually greater communities. "Nation" and "society" are not synonymous. The term *society* is a descriptive label for the social scientist's conception of a common culture (i.e., related languages or dialects, religious systems, socialization practices, beliefs and values, and the like) shared by a broad population of people. In contrast, the term *nation* refers to a specific geopolitical unit, bounded in some way that defines membership characteristics (citizenship) for its participants, with formal laws and some form of semiorganized social structure within it. In this sense a nation may be considered a community that simply operates at a more remote level from the individual than his family, neighborhood, or municipality.

The study of collective international behavior has attracted increasing attention since World War II. Especially during the prolonged period of the Vietnam War and the domestic discontents it engendered among citizens of the United States, social psychologists turned their attention and research to examination of the dynamics of community, national, and international relations. One approach to the study of international affairs emphasized the psychology of the individual and such variables as aggression, fear, trust, and distrust (Klineberg, 1964). Others protested that this individualistic aproach was an inadequate "argument by analogy" and proposed instead the examination of nations as semiorganized communities or social structures (Kelman, 1965).

At the level of "individual psychology," many investigations have proved useful in understanding international affairs. For example, there have been investigations of attitudes toward internationalism and the personality characteristics that accompany them (Christiansen, 1959; Hermann, 1963); studies of chauvinism and ethnocentric national loyalties (Adorno et al., 1950; Guetzkow & Simon, 1955); studies of images and stereotypes of other nations (Klineberg, 1959; Duikejr & Frijda, 1960; Feierabend, Feierabend, & Gurr, 1972); and studies of cross-national contacts of individuals (Kelman, 1965).

At the broader level of examination of the social structures of nations, there have also been many productive investigations. At this level, research has explored the role of public opinion in shaping international policies (Almond, 1950; Bauer, Pool, & Dexter, 1963), the importance of individual actors as agent representatives in international negotiation and bargaining (Snyder, Bruck, & Sapin, 1962), and processes of

PSYCHOPOLITICAL DIAGNOSIS OF NATIONS

A rather novel approach to cross-cultural research has drawn on the resources of two disciplines, political science and psychology. Ivo Feierabend (a political scientist) and Rosalind Feierabend (a psychologist) have conducted extensive statistical analyses of diverse information such as a country's gross national product (GNP), number of telephones, incidents of political assassinations, and infant mortality rate. The analyses allowed for the establishment of national profiles in which countries are viewed as psychopolitical entities (e.g., West Germany, East Germany, Ireland, etc., rather than the Germans, the Irish, etc.). Moreover, it was feasible to apply psychological concepts derived from individual circumstances to social circumstances. For example, the classic frustration-aggression hypothesis (Dollard et al., 1939) predicts that the thwarting of individual goals, aspirations, and expectations induces aggression. According to the Feierabends, frustration induced by the social system creates the social strain and discontent that are the precursors of instability and violence.

Psychopolitical Diagnosis of a Healthy Nation

The study lists a series of empirical threshold values. If above them, countries are predominantly stable; if below them, countries are predominantly unstable. From these empirical thresholds, a composite picture of the stable country emerges at mid-twentieth century:

a GNP of $300 or more per person per year
45 percent or more of the population living in urban centers
90 percent or more literacy
2 percent or more of the population having telephones
65 or more radios and 120 or more newspapers per 1000 population
2525 or more calories per day per person
not more than 1900 persons per physician

Psychopolitical Diagnosis of Violence

To measure political violence, the Feierabends performed a series of statistical analyses on reports of mass demonstrations, riots, palace revolts (*coup d'etats*), purges, violations of civil rights, and external aggression (ranging from antiforeign demonstrations to military action and war). They also studied various ecological indicators (degree of literacy; degree of urbanization; GNP; and the number per person of newspapers, radios, telephones, physicians, and calories) that eventually served as a "satisfaction index" of each nation's needs.

The most significant correlate to political violence was *socioeconomic frustration* (the discrepancy between need formation and satisfaction). This was particularly evident in underdeveloped nations trying to achieve high levels of modernity: high development in science, technology, specialized skills, and education. Unfortunately the acquisition of modern goals is not synonymous with their attainment. The lag between the two tends to foster, in order, rising expectations, rising frustration, and finally violence and instability (see Table 13–4).

The relationship between the coerciveness of a country's regime and display of political violence also followed the predictions of the frustration-aggression hypothesis. Low levels of punishment do not serve as inhibitors, and high levels induce anxiety and withdrawal. Punishment at mid-levels of intensity are most apt to produce frustration without inhibiting the overt expression of violence. Consequently permissive regimes such as those in Australia or Denmark, *or* highly coercive regimes such as those in Taiwan or Saudi Arabia, show a high degree of stability. Mid-level coercive regimes such as those in Bolivia or Iraq are most prone to experience internal turmoil and violence.

FEIERABEND, FEIERABEND AND GURR (1972)

Table 13–4 Political Instability Profiles of 84 Countries (1948–1965) (Stability Score Shown for Each Country Is Grouped Score, Averaged)

1	2	3	4	5	6
Netherlands 04021	U.K. 07112	Belgium 10162	France 13435	Argentina 16445	Indonesia 18416
Luxembg. 03012	Ghana 07106	Chile 10156	U. of So. Africa 13422	Bolivia 16318	
	Austria 07057	Mexico 10111	Brazil 13209	Cuba 16283	
	Denmark 07030	Uruguay 10100	Morocco 13194	Iraq 16274	
	Iceland 07026	Israel 10064	Portugal 13190	Colombia 16244	
	W. Germany 06087	Liberia 10036	Turkey 13189	Burma 16213	
	Finland 06056	Ethiopia 10034	Poland 13179	Venezuela 15429	
	Taiwan 06039	Italy 09192	Thailand 13152	Syria 15329	
	Australia 06026	Libya 09069	Jordan 13145	Korea 15291	
	Sweden 06020	Romania 09060	Cyprus 13123	Haiti 15205	
	Ireland 05031	Costa Rica 09058	Hungary 13113	Peru 15196	
	S. Arabia 05018	Afghan. 09029	Philipp. 13105	Greece 14236	
	N. Zealand 05015	Canada 08084	Czech. 13100	Guatem. 14234	
		Switzer. 08042	China (M) 13086	Lebanon 14212	
		Norway 08034	Cambodia 13071	Egypt 14152	
			India 12360	Paraguay 14141	
			Iran 12237	E. Germany 14138	
			Pakistan 12231	Laos 14129	
			Sudan 12189	Tunisia 14126	
			U.S.S.R. 12165	Honduras 14105	
			Ecuador 12117	Panama 14101	
			Nicaragua 12096	El Salvador 14079	
			U.S.A. 11318		
			Spain 11284		
			Dom. Rep. 11195		
			Ceylon 11152		
			Japan 11123		
			Malaya 11108		
			Yugosl. 11077		
			Bulgaria 11071		
			Albania 11067		
Stability					**Instability**

Source: Feierabend, I. K., Feierabend, R. L., and Gurr, T. R., *Anger, Violence, and Politics: Theories and Research* © 1972. Reprinted by permission of Prentice-Hall, Inc., Englewood Cliffs, New Jersey.

NATIONALISM AND INTERNATIONALISM IN THE CONGRESS

A content analysis of legislative speeches made in Congress revealed that

1. The greater a congressman's personal sense of insecurity, the more nationalistic his voting record; the greater his security, the more internationalistic his voting.
2. The greater a congressman's intolerance of ambiguity, the more nationalistic his voting record; the greater his tolerance for ambiguity, the more internationalistic his voting.
3. The more negative a congressman's orientation to or value for people, the more nationalistic his voting record; the more positive his orientation toward people, the more internationalistic his voting record.

HERMANN (1963)

intergroup interaction and conflict (Sherif et al., 1954; Deutsch & Krauss, 1960; Guetzkow et al., 1963).

Our scientific understanding of all of these complex processes involved in the individual's relation to his community and national contexts, and of relationships between and among these nations, is still incomplete. Yet much of the accumulated knowledge of social psychology is applicable to analysis of these problems, and it is likely that this will be one of the most active and significant areas of social psychology during the 1970s and 1980s. Public concern over war and its consequences has never been so great, nor the breakdown between public sentiment and official national policy and action so severe.

INTERNATIONAL GAMES

One type of experimental study of international relations was conducted by Guetzkow (1963) by using the "Inter-Nation Simulation." This is an ambitious attempt to simulate a complete international system in the laboratory—"nations" with varying characteristics, with different individuals playing the roles of national decision makers within each nation. Subjects in the Inter-Nation Simulation do not behave as individuals (as in most small group studies), but they are constrained to play the roles imposed by their nations. Public opinion (feedback from constituents) enters the system in preprogrammed ways, and responsibility must be assumed for the international consequences of national decisions, which are also preprogrammed. In experiments using this "laboratory game," it is possible to explore a variety of foreign-policy moves: armament-disarmament problems, trade, foreign aid, and alliances. Their consequences can be examined in terms of public tension levels, international cooperativeness, and even the outbreak of hypothetical limited or nuclear wars.

GUETZKOW, ALGER, BRODY, NOEL AND SNYDER (1963)

RELEVANCE AND APPLICATION

Almost from the inception of modern social psychology, the study of mass collective social behavior has been an area of especially significant application. The earliest precursors of modern social psychology were vague speculations about the nature of collective behavior in crowds and mobs, but as social psychology evolved its scientific footing, important distinctions were made between the systematic order that characterizes groups and the disorganization of most forms of collective behavior.

The manipulation of people in crowds and congregated audiences has traditionally been more an art than a science. Skilled showmen like Billy Sunday practiced better crowd control "intuitively" than most people could be trained to practice scientifically now. Our analytic knowledge of techniques of crowd control has much to offer to enable one to manipulate congregations of people effectively, but there are still people who are masters of crowd control without any explicit analytic knowledge or awareness of what they are doing. The magic of what is often called "charisma" (see Leadership in Chapter 11) in such people is in part a set of cultivated skills of crowd manipulation.

Since the 1930s the marketing arm of American industry has invested vast amounts of money and effort into the manipulation of the economic behavior of mass media audiences. Advertising represents a significant element in the total economy of the nation, and a large portion of the cost of any item bought by the consumer public reflects investment in the distribution of the item and the cultivation of a buying market for it. Even beyond the actual investment in market manipulation and the propaganda efforts of media advertising (see Propaganda, Chapter 5), this industry has also invested in research and development activities to generate and expand the knowledge base upon which advertising is built. In economic impact this is possibly the greatest area of application of any part of social psychology.

The upsurge of the consumer public's appetite for violence and aggression in the entertainment media—and the corresponding adjustment of producers of entertainment to satisfy this appetite—is increasingly apparent. The popularity of such violently aggressive movies as *Straw Dogs, A Clockwork Orange, The Godfather,* and *The Getaway* during the early 1970s brought widespread public reaction. These movies were not only popular with the typical consumers of cheap low-budget "crap" movies, but they were received with equal enthusiasm by well-educated and sophisticated people. In this context, many professionals voiced increasing concern about the impact of the content of mass media entertainment productions upon children and adults with respect to instigation to violent aggression, deviant or excessive sexual behavior, and other asocial variations. The American Psychological Association lent enthusiastic cooperation to the U.S. Senate in its attempt to review psychological literature addressed to this question, concluding that there was indeed evidence of a linkage between the content of the entertainment media and the implied social acceptability of the behaviors represented in the media (Maccoby, 1966; Eron et al., 1972; Holden, 1972).

The apparent regression that characterizes disorganized collective behavior poses a critical social problem. When conditions instigate riots, panics, and other kinds of mob behavior, people regress to sheer animal behavior, shedding all the characteristics of control that normally make them "human." The damage to life and property that results is often a serious social problem. For example, the riots that grew out of political demonstrations at the Chicago convention of the Democratic Party in 1968 had serious social consequences. The immediate damage to property and injury of people was costly, and moreover, the extended litigation and trial of "the Chicago Seven" was costly and painful to the judicial system. Ultimately there was created an atmosphere in which residents of other cities, fearing repeated similar occurrences, no longer welcomed the political conventions to their cities. Strong protests were voiced in Miami against the Convention Bureau's invitation to the political parties in 1972, and protests in San Diego caused the Republicans to relocate their 1972 convention in Miami.

Social psychology is called upon to apply its knowledge of collective behavior not only to immediate crowd control in the crisis of an ongoing riot, but more importantly to apply this knowledge to effective riot prevention. Occasionally this has been possible, as in the case of "A Riot that Didn't Happen" (p. 341). It is difficult enough to train public officials and law enforcement personnel to apply psychological knowledge in crises, but even more difficult to persuade them to use this information in the "crunch." Without question, public awareness of the significance of social movements has increased recently. The social influence of grassroots movements—especially those that evolve some degree of quasi-organization—can be overwhelming. Probably the most significant and effective social movements in recent times have been those focused upon racial desegregation and civil rights. However, the humanistic values underlying the concern for civil rights have spun off an array of related movements addressed to the humanistic individual rights of other categories of people: females, homosexuals, elderly people, Oriental Americans, Latin Americans, and American Indians, among others. The organizers of such social movements strive to put into practice the full array of the knowledge accumulated by social psychology. But these efforts bring into focus the inadequacies and gaps in this knowledge and the need for further study in order to understand and control the currents of social movement in a complex society.

Communities represent semiorganized collective systems, and consequently border between unorganized collective behavior (Section V) and organized social behavior (Section IV). They show properties intermediate between crowds, mobs, and audiences on one hand, and organized social groups on the other. Consequently principles drawn from both group dynamics and mass psychology are applicable to social problems at the level of communities.

Although the earliest discussions of Utopian societies were more theoretical than actual, there have been many attempts to realize such societies experimentally. Probably the peak of such Utopian "action experiments" occurred in the United States in the late nineteenth and early twentieth centuries with the westward population migrations. But there has occurred a recent upsurge of similar interest on more limited levels. The kibbutzim (collective farms) of Israel have been approached as microsocieties seeking to apply psychological knowledge to limited-level social organization. Likewise, the extended "family" communes generated within the contemporary youth counterculture in the United States represent applied social psychology at the community level. Although the sociological approach to community organization and community planning is not new, there is increasing integration of psychological knowledge and sociological knowledge in contemporary social planning. Housing developments and relocation moves are planned carefully with attention to basic psychological information. As in many other areas of social action, the vast gulf between available knowledge and actual practice is great. Only in rare cases does the public action that really takes place truly live up to what might have been possible at ideal levels. In other words, here as in other areas, the knowledge base available far exceeds our ability to utilize it effectively.

Finally, at the level of national and international affairs, social psychology has much to offer. The acute awareness of the American public was focused upon the Vietnam War in the early 1970s, and out of this grew discontent with public policy, distrust of the national decision makers (the "credibility gap"), and concern about the mechanisms for reflecting public opinion in national policy, and in turn the mechanisms linking public policy to international action. The psychology of international relations that has grown out of this context as a specialty area within social psychology is a large and important area of applied social engineering.

Direct empirical research on international relationships is scarce, but a few attempts have been made to conduct research on issues related to individual psychological dynamics that would allow a "psychological profile" of nations (Feierabend, Feierabend, & Gurr, 1972). The personal communications of key decision makers in governments during the weeks preceding the outbreak of a war have also been analyzed by means of content analysis to ascertain the significance of individual psychodynamics of key national figures as a component in international relations (Zinnes, North, & Koch, 1961; Zinnes, 1962). In fact, because war represents aggressive behavior, it is often assumed that one has only to examine the etiology of individual aggressive behavior in order to understand war (see Chapter 9). Certainly war involves individual aggression, but personal motivations of fear, distrust, and competition may be equally pertinent. Oversimplified analogies between individual aggression and international war have led to drawing analogies between war and irrational (even psychotic) behavior. But such analogies may obscure other intra- and intersocietal dynamics that generate conflicts among nations. Herbert Kelman, a social psychologist actively interested in the development of research on international relations, has cautioned that "any attempt to conceptualize the causes of war and the conditions of peace that starts from individual psychology rather than from the analysis of the relation between nation states is of questionable relevance" (Kelman, 1965, p. 5).

Conflicts between nations generally arise out of conflicts in the pursuit of each nation's own goals, that is, out of situations of intergroup competition. The resolution of goal conflicts, whether between individuals or between groups, appears from research evidence to proceed most effectively when superordinate cooperative goals are introduced to require coalescence among the groups in conflict (LeVine, 1961; Krauss, 1963; Rabinowitch, 1964). Even when such superordinate goals occur, however, groups in conflict with one another tend to underestimate the congruence between their own goals and those of competitive groups. In one study, for example, two groups were led to develop competing alternative solutions to a problem in the laboratory. After members of each group indicated that they were thoroughly familiar with both their own proposed solution and that of the competing group, they were presented with a list of statements about the solutions, some of which were common to both groups, some of which occurred only in one group's solution, and some of which occurred in neither group's solution. Rather consistently, members of such competing groups identified statements common to both solutions as solely their own; in other words, they seriously underestimated agreement between the groups in pursuit of a common goal (Blake & Mouton, 1961). It appears now that the common goal shared by the United States and the Soviet Union with respect to the containment of China is rarely perceived as shared by both nations. Even when international coalitions in pursuit of common goals do occur, they often occur for reasons other than actual recognition of the need for cooperative action. The European Common Market was achieved less through the high ideals of European economic integration than through more specific and practical selfish considerations of each member nation (Schokking & Anderson, 1960). Osgood's analysis of political ends and military means in Europe since the seventeenth century suggests clearly that unlimited goal conflicts have tended to produce unlimited international violence (Osgood, 1963).

Unfortunately experimental negotiations between small groups in laboratory settings appear to proceed more smoothly and effectively than actual international negotiations and conferences. It took the delegates at the Peace of Westphalia Conference in 1648 a full 6 weeks to decide in what order they should enter and be seated at the conference table! At the Potsdam Conference in 1945, the same problem arose, but Churchill, Stalin, and Truman solved the problem by arranging to enter the room simultaneously from three separate doors. Even when such trivia are managed successfully, the agenda for negotiation conferences (such as the Paris Peace Talks on Vietnam) tend to be long and complicated, with unimportant and less controversial issues placed at the beginning of the agenda. Negotiators are often worn down and tired by the time the major issues arise. Even labor-management negotiations in connection with labor disputes proceed along the same patterns.

International negotiations in the middle of the twentieth century have come increase-ingly into the public arena, where even bilateral negotiations are often conducted in the presence of the world through mass media communication. This results in what former Secretary of State Dean Rusk has referred to as "football-stadium diplomacy," in which the negotiators become more interested in scoring points in international debate than in honest efforts to achieve resolution of the negotiated conflicts.

The forum of international affairs involves participation not only of a few dominant and powerful nations in varying degrees of conflict, but also of many minor and less powerful states. For example, Egypt made significant economic and political gains in the course of allowing the United States and Soviet Russia to vie for its support in order to prevent the U.A.R. from forming a coalition with the other "strong" nation. It appears that most of the new states in Africa are eager to follow similar routes.

Such arenas for negotiation as the United Nations provide opportunity for the reso-lution of international tensions without war, but they are not always used profitably. Just as within-group cooperation and cohesiveness tend to accentuate distinctions between the ingroup and outsiders, so also do regional, provincial, and national loyal-ties interfere with cooperation at federal and international levels. Intense ingroup loyalties often breed distrust and exaggerated hostility toward members of other groups. Similarly, regional loyalties within the United States have for years been the primary source of antifederalism and distrust of centralized government. The Missis-sippian tends to be slow to trust the purity of motives of the "Yankee" civil rights worker, and often assumes subterfuge and selfish dishonesty to be the source of any federal action that conflicts with his own local norms and values. Intense nationalism, particularly within the United States, eventually proved to be the downfall of Wood-row Wilson's dream of a League of Nations. But the chaos and horror of World War II and the threat of nuclear destruction, in combination with increased media of communication around the world, sufficiently reduced the intensity of such provincial nationalistic feelings to permit successful establishment of the United Nations. Even now, however, its stability is not yet certain, and there is still a hard core of isolation-istic opposition to it within certain segments of the American public.

Within the United Nations, however, a framework of situational circumstances de-termines the nature and extent of negotiations that are possible. A survey that compared diplomatic groups within the United Nations with similar groups who remained in their national capitals revealed that the UN at least provides for greatly increased contact and communication between "unfriendly" nations (Best, 1960). Nevertheless, such a simple matter as alphabetical seating arrangements tends to expedite communication between certain pairs of nations. For example, extensive conversations have been observed between Hungary and Honduras, between the Netherlands and Nepal, and between Afghanistan and Yugoslavia. What kind of com-munication could have occurred between the warring nations of Israel and Iraq had not their delegates to the UN been separated by the Irish delegation between them? Best's survey revealed that many delegates to the UN found themselves in contact with nations of which they had never even heard. Some of the African delegates were sur-prised to learn of similarities between the position of the United States and that of the Union of South Africa on key issues; likewise, Eastern European diplomats were sur-prised to learn that the Scandinavian countries were frequently aligned with colonial powers on colonial issues. In any case, regardless of its inability to achieve decisive resolution of international conflicts quickly and easily, the United Nations does appear to provide an important means of communication and contact among the many na-tions of the world.

Other means of achieving increased international contact may lead eventually to the reduction of provincial isolationism and increased awareness of the superordinate goals confronting all of mankind. Technological developments such as the communications satellites provide more immediate mass media communication around the world. Increased mobility and opportunity for travel allows individuals to escape the confines of their own culture-boundedness and to become aware of the cultural values and habits of other people. Arrangements for the exchange of students between the United States and other nations contribute significantly to this process. Unfortunately many of the requirements for eligibility for scholarships for education in the United States have tended to restrict such exchanges to somewhat elite groups. Students from other countries must still be relatively wealthy in order to study and travel in the United States, and even with governmental and institutional financial support, the requirement that one speak English fluently in order to secure a scholarship proves a handicap to citizens of the newly emerging African nations (Mishler, 1965). Even when students from other nations are able to come to the United States, they often meet disappointment in their reception by Americans. Although Europeans are generally warmly accepted, students from other nations are often accorded relatively low social status and are less likely to enjoy warm interaction with Americans (Selltiz, Christ, Havel, & Cook, 1963). Dark-skinned students from India or Africa are often mistreated in public restaurants and barbershops, especially in the anti-Negro belt of the southeastern United States. Indian students may react defensively to questions implying that Americans view their country as backward (Lambert & Bressler, 1956). Scandinavian students resent the fact that many Americans cannot differentiate among Norway, Sweden, Denmark, Finland, and even Holland but look upon these countries as one large blur in northern Europe (Mishler, 1965). The American "democratic way" that denies formal status distinctions often proves confusing to Japanese students (Bennet, Passin, & McKnight, 1958). And, of course, provinciality works both ways: non-Western visitors sometimes intentionally limit their contacts with Westerners for fear of becoming "too Westernized" and hence suffering unpleasant conflicts upon returning home (Bennet, Passin, & McKnight, 1958).

REVIEW

1. Aggregates of human beings that remain unorganized or only loosely organized are called *masses.*

2. Masses may vary in *size, polarization* (degree of parallel orientation of the attention of participants), *activity* (extent to which participants are active as contrasted to passive and reactive), and *congregation* (frequency with which the aggregate assembles physically in the same place).

3. An *audience* is a mass of people, whether congregated or not, whose attention is polarized toward some person or event to which they are responding passively and reactively.

4. A *crowd* is a congregated audience—an aggregate of people gathered together, responding passively with attention polarized on a person or event.

5. Crowds and audiences may be either *casual* (accidentally gathered and polarized) or *intentional* (purposely gathered and polarized). Intentional audiences may be gathered for purposes of either being *entertained* or being *informed.*

6. *Mass media audiences* are uncongregated masses of people whose attention is polarized and whose response is passive. Because the mass media afford only one-way communication, participants in these audiences usually do not interact directly with one another.

7. *Consumer psychology* is the study of the behavior and experience of the buying public, especially as they comprise a mass audience in marketing and advertising.

8. A *mob* is a congregated, active, polarized aggregate of people. Mobs include *riots* (mob action impelled toward acquisitive ends), *panics* (mob action that is defensive, seeking to escape or avoid injury or threat), and *demonstrations* (mob action whose purpose is to express an attitude or belief).

9. *Social movements* involve uncongregated mass behavior that is polarized and active. These include *cults* (protagonistic or supportive mass action) and *protest movements* (mass action that rejects or protests threat or frustration).

10. *Communities* are partially organized social systems that evolve in transition from unorganized collective behavior to organized behavior in groups and societies. They are "quasi-groups."

11. Collective social movements that originate as cults but emerge into organized minisocieties are called *sects.* Similar movements that are planned and intentional may be termed *Utopias* of experimental societies.

12. *Bureaucracy* is a special kind of community state that exists within many industrial, governmental, educational, and other organizations. A bureaucracy is a community that involves a portion of its participants' lives and that emerges as a by-product (rather than the main objective) of the organizational system within which it operates.

13. Neighborhoods, housing projects, geographical areas, subdivisions, and municipalities all define social *communities.*

14. Social classes also define a particular kind of uncongregated community. A *caste* system differentiates classes of participants according to their birth status; a *class* system differentiates participants by functional categories defined by their behavior within the social structure.

15. *Social mobility* is the freedom for people to move about within a class-differentiated society. When people move rapidly from one class to another, either horizontally or vertically, they are sometimes caught between, in a position of *marginality.* If their position becomes ambiguous or undefined, people become disoriented and experience *anomie.*

16. The study of *community relations* and intergroup conflict is a derivative of both group dynamics and the study of communities.

17. *Nations* represent extended communities that operate at levels that are more remote from the individual, but nevertheless influence his behavior.

BIBLIOGRAPHY
AND AUTHOR INDEX

The pages on which citations appear are given in brackets.

AAUP (American Association of University Professors) News Bulletin, 1972, **13,** 3. [350]

Abell, R. G., 1972, A look at modern techniques in group psychotherapy, Scientific Proceedings, American Psychiatric Convention, 239–241. [303–304]

Abelson, R. P., 1968, When the polls go wrong and why, Trans-action, **5,** 9, 20–27. [334–336]
See also Lesser, G. S.

Abrahams, D. See Walster, E.

Abramson, H. A. See Lennard, H.

Abravanel, E. A., 1962, A psychological analysis of the concept of role, unpublished Master's thesis, Swarthmore College, Swarthmore, Pa. [206]

Adams, J. S., 1963, Toward an understanding of inequity, Journal of Abnormal and Social Psychology, **67,** 422–436. [230]

Adams, J. S., and Rosenbaum, W. B., 1962, The relationship of worker productivity to cognitive dissonance about wage inequity, Journal of Applied Psychology, **46,** 161–164. [231]

Adams, M., 1971, The compassion trap, Psychology Today, November 1971. [346]

Adelson, J. See Douvan, E.

Adler, A., 1925, The practice and theory of individual psychology, New York: Harcourt Brace Jovanovich. [172]

Adorno, T. W., Frenkel-Brunswik, Else, Levinson, D. J., and Sanford, R. N., 1950, The authoritarian personality: studies in prejudice, New York: Harper & Row. [180, 183, 199, 274, 359]

Aichhorn, A., 1935, Wayward youth, New York: Viking. [120]

Aiello, J. R., and Jones, S. A., 1971, Field study of the proxemic behavior of young school children in three subcultural groups, Journal of Personality and Social Psychology, **19,** 351–356. [125, 127]

Ajzen, I., and Fishbein, M., 1970, The prediction of behavior from attitudinal and normative variables, Journal of Experimental Social Psychology, **6,** 466–487. [86]

Alexander, B. K. See Seay, B.

Alger, C. F. See Guetzkow, H.

Allen, K. E., Hart, B., Buell, J. S., Harris, F. R., and Wolf, M. M., 1964, Effects of social reinforcement on isolate behavior of nursery school children, Child Development, **35,** 511–518. [113]

Allen, V. L., and Levine, J. M., 1968, Consensus and conformity, Journal of Experimental Social Psychology, **5,** 389–399. [273]

Allport, F. H.
1920, The influence of the group upon association and thought, Journal of Experimental Psychology, **3,** 159–182. [308, 309]
1924, Social psychology, Boston: Houghton Mifflin. [263, 308, 309]
1934, The J-curve hypothesis of conforming behavior, Journal of Social Psychology, **5,** 141–183. [261, 263]

Allport, G. W.
1937, *Personality: a psychological interpretation,* New York: Holt, Rinehart and Winston. [198]
1958, *The nature of prejudice,* Garden City, N.Y.: Doubleday. [198]

Allport, G. W., and Kramer, B. M., 1946, Some roots of prejudice, *Journal of Psychology,* **22,** 9–39.

Allport, G. W., and Postman, L. H., 1947, *The basic psychology of rumor,* New York: Holt, Rinehart and Winston. [71, 78, 102, 103]

Allyn, J., and Festinger, L., 1961, The effectiveness of unanticipated persuasive communications, *Journal of Abnormal and Social Psychology,* **62,** 35–40. [95]

Allynsmith, W. *See* Rebelsky, F. G.

Almada, A. A. *See* McCann, W. H.

Almond, G. A., 1950, *The American people and foreign policy,* New York: Harcourt Brace Jovanovich. [359]

Alper, T. G. *See* Wapner, S.

Altman, I., and McGinnies, E., 1960, Interpersonal perception and communication in discussion groups of varied attitudinal composition, *Journal of Abnormal and Social Psychology,* **60,** 290–305. [207]

Altman, I., Taylor, D. A., and Wheeler, I., 1971, Ecological aspects of group behavior in social isolation, *Journal of Applied Social Psychology,* **1,** 76–100. [127]

Altman, I. *See also* McGrath, J. E.

Altrocchi, J., 1959, Dominance as a factor in interpersonal choice and perception, *Journal of Abnormal and Social Psychology,* **59,** 303–307. [224]

Altus, W. D., 1966, Birth order and its sequelae, *Science,* 7 January 1966, 151, 3706, 44–49. [115]

American Institute of Public Opinion, 1971, Princeton, N.J. (poll). [347]

Ames, A., 1946, Binocular vision as affected by relations between uniocular stimulus-patterns in commonplace environments, *American Journal of Psychology,* **59,** 333–357. [72]

Amidon, E. J., and Flanders, N. A., 1963, *The role of the teacher in the classroom,* Minneapolis: Amidon. [303]

Anderson, L. *See* Gronlund, W. E.

Anderson, N. H., 1968, A simple model for information integration. In R. P. Abelson, E. Aronson, W. J. McGuire, T. M. Newcomb, M. J. Rosenberg, and P. H. Tannenbaum (eds.) *Theories of cognitive consistency: a sourcebook,* Chicago: Rand-McNally. [200]
See also Hovland, C. I.; Schokking, J. J.

Andrews, R. E., 1955, *Leadership and supervision: a survey of research findings,* Personnel Management Series No. 9,

Washington, D.C.: U.S. Civil Service Commission. [294]

Anisfeld, M., Bogo, N., and Lambert, W. E., 1962, Evaluational reactions to accented English speech, *Journal of Abnormal and Social Psychology,* **65,** 223–231. [134–135]

Anisfeld, M., Munoz, S., and Lambert, W. E., 1963, The structure and dynamics of the ethnic attitude of Jewish adolescents, *Journal of Abnormal and Social Psychology,* **66,** 31–36. [149]

APA (American Psychological Association), *Ethical principles in the conduct of research with human participants,* Washington, D.C.: American Psychological Association. [22]

Applezweig, M. H. *See* Moeller, G.

Aramoni, A., 1972, Machismo, *Psychology Today,* January, 1972. [348]

Arenberg, D. *See* Lazarus, R. S.

Argyle, M. [152]
1957, Social pressure in public and private situations, *Journal of Abnormal and Social Psychology,* **54,** 172–175. [272]
1959, The concepts of role and status. In P. Halmos and A. Alliffe (eds.), *Readings in general psychology,* New York: Philosophical Library. [207]

Argyle, M., Gardner, G., and Cioffio, F., 1958, Supervisory methods related to productivity, absenteeism, and labor turnover, *Human Relations,* **11,** 23–42. [325]

Aronfreed, J., 1961, The nature, variety, and social patterning of internalized responses to transgression, *Journal of Abnormal and Social Psychology,* **63,** 223–240. [113]
1968, *Conduct and conscience,* New York: Academic. [88, 114, 169]

Aronson, E. *See* Walster, E.

Aronson, E., 1966, Avoidance of inter-subject communication, *Psychological Reports,* **19,** 238. [293]

Aronson, E., and Mills, J., 1959, The effect of severity of initiation on liking for a group, *Journal of Abnormal and Social Psychology,* **59,** 177–181. [102, 293, 316]

As, D. *See* French, J. R. P.

Asch, M. J., 1951, Nondirective teaching in psychology: an experimental study, *Psychology Monographs,* **6,** No. 4. [325]

Asch, S. E.
1946, Forming impressions of personality, *Journal of Abnormal and Social Psychology,* **41,** 258–299. [200]
1952, *Social psychology,* Englewood Cliffs, N.J.: Prentice-Hall. [263]
1956, Studies of independence and submission to group pressure: I. A minority of one against a unanimous majority, *Psychology Monographs,* **70,** No. 9 (Whole No. 416). [263, 265, 268, 271]

Ashley, W. R., Harper, R. S., and Runyon, D. L., 1951, The perceived size of coins in normal and hypnotically induced economic states, *American Journal Psychology,* **64,** 564–572. [72]

Atkinson, J. W. *See* McClelland, D. C.

Aumack, L. *See* Luchins, A. S.

Austrin, H. *See* Scodel, A.

Ausubel, D. P., 1968, *Educational psychology: a cognitive view,* New York: Holt, Rinehart and Winston. [176]

Ausubel, D. P., and Schiff, H. M., 1955, Some intrapersonal and interpersonal determinants of individual differences in socioempathic ability among adolescents, *Journal of Social Psychology,* **41,** 39–56. [165]

Bach, G. R., 1950, Dramatic play therapy with adult groups, *Journal of Psychology,* **29,** 225–246. [304]

1966, The marathon group: intensive practice of intimate interaction, *Psychological Reports,* **18,** 995–1002. [130]

Back, K. *See* Festinger, L., Hood, T. C.

Baer, D. M. *See* Gewirtz, J. L.

Baehr, R. F., 1965, Need achievement and dialect in lower-class adolescent Negroes, *American Psychologist,* **20,** 483 (abstract). [130, 150, 176]

Baker, B. O., and Block, J., 1957, Accuracy of interpersonal prediction as a function of judge and object characteristics, *Journal of Abnormal and Social Psychology,* **54,** 37–43. [205]

Baker, J. M. *See* Canning, R. R.

Baldwin, A. L. *See* Levin, H.; Paivio A.

Bales, R. F.

1950, *Interaction Process Analysis: a method for the study of small groups,* Cambridge, Mass.: Addison-Wesley. [39, 202, 282, 283, 284, 296, 297]

1953, A theoretical framework for interaction process analysis. In D. Cartwright and A. Zander (eds.), *Group dynamics: research and theory,* New York: Harper & Row. [286]

1958, Task roles and social roles in problem solving groups. In E. E. Maccoby, T. M. Newcomb, and E. L. Hartley (eds.), *Readings in social psychology,* 3rd ed., New York: Holt, Rinehart and Winston. [283, 284, 286]

1970, *Personality and interpersonal behavior,* New York: Holt, Rinehart and Winston. [282, 283, 284]

See also Borgatta, E. F.; Hare, A. P.; Heinecke, C.

Bales, R. F., and Borgatta, E. F., 1955, Size of group as a factor in the interaction profile. In A. P. Hare, E. F. Borgatta, and R. F. Bales (eds.), *Small groups: studies in social interaction,* New York: Knopf.

Ballachey, E. L. *See* Krech, D.

Bandura, A., Ross, D., and Ross, S. A.

1961, Transmission of aggression through imitation of aggressive models, *Journal of Abnormal and Social Psychology,* **93,** 575–582. [118, 237]

1963, Vicarious reinforcement and imitative learning, *Journal of Abnormal and Social Psychology,* **67,** 601–607. [118]

Bandura, A., and Walters, R.

1959, *Adolescent Aggression,* New York: Ronald Press.

1963, *Social Learning and Personality Development,* New York: Holt, Rinehart and Winston. [118, 120, 335]

Banta, T. J., and Hetherington, M., 1963, Relations between needs of friends and fiancés, *Journal of Abnormal and Social Psychology,* **66,** 401–404. [224]

Barbe, W. B., 1954, Peer relationship of children of different intelligence levels, *School Sociology,* **80,** 60–62. [212]

Barber, T. X., Caverley, D. S., Forgione, A., McPeake, J. D., Chaves, J. F., and Brown, B., 1969, Five attempts to replicate the experimenter bias effect, *Journal of Consulting and Clinical Psychology,* **33,** 1–6. [20]

Barber, T. X., and Silver, M. J., 1968, Fact, fiction, and the experimenter bias effect, *Psychological Bulletin Monographs,* **70,** 1–29, 48–62. [20]

Barker, R. G., and Wright, H. F., 1954, *The midwest and its children: the psychological ecology of an American town,* New York: Harper & Row. [24, 125]

Barlund, D. C., 1955, Experiments in leadership training for decision making groups, *Speech Monographs,* **22,** 1–14. [299, 302]

Barnard, C. I., 1938, *The functions of the executive,* Cambridge, Mass.: Harvard University Press. [314]

Baron, R. A., 1970, Attraction toward the model and model's competence as determinants of adult imitative behavior, *Journal of Personality and Social Psychology,* **14,** 345–351 [244]

Baron, R. A., and Kepner, C. R., 1970, Models' behavior and attraction toward the model as determinants of adult aggressive behavior, *Journal of Personality and Social Psychology,* **14,** 335–344. [237]

Baron, R. A., and Liebert, R. M., 1971, *Human social behavior: a contemporary view of experimental research,* Homewood, Ill.: Dorsey. [118]

Bartlett, F. C., 1932, *Remembering: a study in experimental and social psychology,*

Cambridge, Mass.: Harvard University Press. [28, 78]

Bass, B. M.
1955, Authoritarianism or acquiescence? *Journal of Abnormal and Social Psychology,* **51,** 616–623.
1960, *Leadership, psychology and organizational behavior,* New York: Harper & Row. [299]
1962, *The orientation inventory,* Palo Alto, Calif.: Consulting Psychologists Press. [285, 324]
1965a, *Social behavior and the orientation inventory: a review,* Technical Reports G, Contract NONR-624(14), November 1965. [285]
1965b, *Organizational psychology,* Boston: Allyn & Bacon. [303, 325]
See also Berg, I.; Klubeck, S.

Bass, B. M., and Wurster, C. R., 1953, Effects of the nature of the problem of LGD performance, *Journal of Applied Psychology,* **37,** 96–99. [299]

Bateson, N., 1966, Familiarization, group discussion, and risk taking, *Journal of Experimental Social Psychology,* **2,** 119–129.

Battle, E. S., and Rotter, J. B., 1963, Children's feelings of personal control as related to social class and ethnic group, *Journal of Personality,* **31,** 4, 482–490.

Bauer, R. A., Pool, I. deS., and Dexter, L. A., 1963, *American business and public policy: the politics of foreign trade,* New York: Atherton. [359]

Baughman, E. E., 1971, *Black Americans,* New York: Academic.

Baumrind, D., 1964, Some thoughts of ethics of research: After reading Milgram's study of obedience, *American Psychologist,* **19,** 421–423.

Bavelas, A.
1942, Morale and the training of leaders. In G. Watson (ed.), *Civilian morale,* New York: Harcourt Brace Jovanovich. [302]
1950, Communication patterns in task-oriented groups, *Journal of the Acoustical Society of America,* **22,** 725–730.

Beach, F. A. *See* Ford, C. S.

Beaty, W. E., and Shaw, M. E., 1965, Some effects of social interaction on probability learning, *Journal of Psychology,* **59,** 299–306.

Beier, H. *See* Inkeles, A.

Bem, D. J., 1970, *Beliefs, attitudes, and human affairs,* Belmont, Calif.: Brooks/Cole. [91]
See also Wallach, M. A.

Benjamin, L. *See* Katz, I.

Benne, K., and Sheats, P., 1948, Functional roles of group members, *Journal of Social Issues,* **4,** 41–49. [207, 284, 285]

Bennet, J. W., Passin, H., and McKnight, R. K., 1958, *In search of identity: the Japanese scholar in America and Japan,* Minneapolis: University of Minnesota Press. [367]

Bennett, E. B., 1955. Discussion, decision, commitment, and consensus in "group decision," *Human Relations,* **8,** 251–274. [280]

Bennett, E. M., and Cohen, L. R., 1959, Men and women: personality patterns and contrasts, *Genetic Psychology Monographs,* **59,** 101–155.

Bennis, W. G., and Shepard, H. A., 1956, A theory of group development, *Human Relations,* **9,** 415–537.

Bensley, M. *See* Heidbreder, E.

Berelson, B.
1952, *Content analysis in communication research,* New York: Free Press. [41]
1954, Content analysis. In G. Lindzey (ed.), *Handbook of social psychology,* vol. 1, Cambridge, Mass.: Addison-Wesley. [40]
See also Lazarsfeld, P. F.

Berelson, B., and Salter, P. J., 1946, Majority and minority Americans: an analysis of magazine fiction, *Public Opinion Quarterly,* **10,** 168–190.

Berelson, B., and Steiner, G. A., 1964, *Human behavior: an inventory of scientific findings,* New York: Harcourt Brace Jovanovich. [300]

Berenda, R. W., 1940, *The influence of the group on the judgments of children,* New York: King's Crown Press, Columbia University Press. [276]

Berg, I., and Bass, B. M. (eds.), 1961, *Conformity and deviation,* New York: Harper & Row. [43]

Berger, S. N. *See* Paivio, A.

Berkowitz, L.
1956, Personality and group position, *Biometry,* **19,** 210–222. [286]
1957, Effects of perceived dependency relationship upon conformity to group expectations, *Journal of Abnormal and Social Psychology,* **55,** 350–354. [286]
1959, Anti-Semitism and the displacement of aggression, *Journal of Abnormal and Social Psychology,* **59,** 182–187.
1964, Aggressive cues in aggressive behavior and hostility catharsis, *Psychological Review,* **71,** 104–122. [237]

Berkowitz, L., and Daniels, L. R.
1963, Responsibility and dependency, *Journal of Abnormal and Social Psychology,* **66,** 627–636. [282]
1964, Affecting the salience of social desirability norms, *Journal of Abnormal and Social Psychology,* **68,** 275–281 [282, 335]

Berkowitz, L., and Geen, R. G., 1966, Film violence and the cue properties of available targets, *Journal of Personality and Social Psychology, 3,* 525–530. [238]

Berkowitz, L., and LePage, A., 1967, Weapons as aggression-eliciting stimuli, *Journal of Personality and Social Psychology, 7,* 202–207. [238]

Berkowitz, L., and Macaulay, J. R., 1961, Some effects of differences in status level and status stability, *Human Relations, 14,* 135–148. [215]

Berlyne, D. E.
1955, The arousal and satiation of perceptual curiosity in the rat, *Journal of Comparative and Physiological Psychology, 48,* 238–246. [172, 175]
1958, The influence of the albedo and complexity of stimuli on visual fixation in the human infant, *British Journal of Psychology, 49,* 315–318. [172]

Berne, Eric, 1963, The structure and dynamics of organizations and groups, Philadelphia: Lippincott. [280]

Bernstein, B., 1959, A public language: some sociological implications of linguistic form, *British Journal of Sociology, 10,* 311–326. [131]

Berrien, K. F., 1961, Homeostasis theory of group implications for leadership. In L. Petrullo and B. M. Bass (eds.), *Leadership and interpersonal behavior,* New York: Holt, Rinehart and Winston. [284, 301]

Best, G., 1960, Diplomacy in the United Nations, Ph.D. dissertation, Northwestern University, Evanston, Ill. [366]

Bettelheim, B.
1950, *Love is not enough,* New York: Free Press. [120]
1952, Individual and mass behavior in extreme situations. In G. E. Swanson, T. M. Newcomb, and E. L. Hartley (eds.), *Readings in social psychology,* rev. ed., New York: Holt, Rinehart and Winston.

Bickman, L., 1971, The effect of social status on the honesty of others. *Journal of Social Psychology, 85,* 87–92. [171]

Bieri, J., 1953, Changes in interpersonal perception following social interaction, *Journal of Abnormal and Social Psychology, 48,* 61–66. [176, 207]

Biller, H. B., 1971, *Father, child, and sex role.* Lexington, Mass.: Heath-Lexington Books.

Binet, A., 1900, *La suggestibilite,* Paris: Schleicher Frères. [262]

Bion, W. R., 1961, *Experiences in groups,* New York: Basic Books. [303, 304]

Birdsell, J. B. *See* Coon, C. S.

Bitterman, M. E., and Kniffin, C. W., 1953, Manifest anxiety and "perceptual de-fense," *Journal of Abnormal and Social Psychology, 49,* 248–252.

Bixenstein, V. E., and Wilson, K. V., 1963, Effects of level of cooperative choice by the other player on choices in a Prisoner's Dilemma Game: Part II, *Journal of Abnormal and Social Psychology, 67,* 139–147. [242]

Black, H., 1969, Race and sex factors influencing the correct and erroneous perception of emotion, *Proceedings,* 77th Annual Convention, APA, 363–364. [203]

Blackwood, B., 1935, *Both sides of Buka Passage: an ethnographic study of social, sexual and economic questions in the northwestern Solomon Islands,* Oxford: Clarendon. [140, 142]

Blake, R. R., and Mouton, J. S., 1961, *Group dynamics: key to decision making,* Houston: Gulf. [365]

Blake, R. R., Rosenbaum, M., and Duryea, R. A., 1955, Gift-giving as a function of group standards, *Human Relations, 8,* 73–81. [273]

Blake, R. R. *See also* Coleman, J. F.; Freed, A. M.; Helson, H.; Kimbrell, D. L.; Lefkowitz, M.; Mouton, J. S.; Olmstead, J. A.; Rosenbaum, M.

Blau, P. M.
1955, *The dynamics of bureaucracy,* Chicago: University of Chicago Press. [289, 299]
1962, Patterns of choice in interpersonal relations, *American Sociological Review, 27,* 41–55. [211, 214, 223, 224]

Bleuler, M., and Bleuler, R., 1935, Rorschach inkblot tests and social psychology, *Character and Personality, 4,* 99–114. [28]

Bleuler, R. *See* Bleuler, M.

Boas, F., Efron, D., and Foley, J. P., Jr., 1936, A comparative investigation of gestural behavior in "racial" groups living under different as well as similar environmental conditions, *Psychological Bulletin, 33,* 760. [129]

Bogardus, E. S., 1925, Measuring social distance, *Journal of Applied Sociology, 9,* 299–308. [193, 198]

Bogart, L., 1957, Comic strips and their adult readers. In B. Rosenberg, and D. M. White (eds.), *Mass culture: the popular arts in America,* New York: Free Press. [335]

Bonney, M. E.
1946, A sociometric study of the relationship of some factors to mutual friendships of elementary, secondary, and college levels, *Sociometry, 9,* 21–47. [215]
1955, Social behavior differences between second-grade children of high and low sociometric status, *Journal of Education Research, 48,* 481–495. [212, 215]

Bonney, M. E., Hoblit, R. E., and Dreyer, A. H., 1953, A study of some factors related to sociometric status in a men's dormitory, *Sociometry*, **16**, 287–301. [212]

Borg, W. R., 1957, The behavior of emergent and designated leaders in situational tests, *Sociometry*, **20**, 95–104. [299, 300]

Borgatta, E. F., 1960, Rankings and self-assessments: some behavioral characteristics replication studies, *Journal of Social Psychology*, **52**, 279–307.

Borgatta, E. F., Cottrell, L. S., and Mann, J. H., 1958, The spectrum of individual interaction characteristics: an interdimensional analysis, *Psychological Reports*, **4**, 279–306. [284]

Bossom, J., and Maslow, A. H., 1957, Security of judges as a factor in impression of warmth of others, *Journal of Abnormal and Social Psychology*, **55**, 147–148. [205]

Bovard, E. W., Jr.
1951, Group structure and perception, *Journal of Abnormal and Social Psychology*, **46**, 398–405. [290, 325]
1952, Clinical insight as a function of group processes, *Journal of Abnormal and Social Psychology*, **47**, 534–539. [290]

Bowditch, J. L., and King, D. C., 1970, Relationship between biographical similarity and interpersonal choice, *Proceedings, 78th Annual Convention, American Psychological Association*, 381–382. [216]

Bowers, F., 1972, Homosex: Liking the life, *Saturday Review*, February 12, 1972. [350]

Bradford, L. P., Gibb, J. R., and Benne, K. D. (eds.), 1964, *T-group theory and laboratory method*, New York: Wiley. [282, 326]

Braly, D. W. *See* Katz, D.

Bracht, G. H., 1970, Experimental factors related to aptitude-treatment interactions, *Review of Educational Research*, **40**, 627–645. [184]

Brandon, A. C. *See* Sampson, E. E.

Brandt, R. M., 1958, The accuracy of self-estimate: a measure of self-concept, *Genetic Psychology Monographs*, **58**, 55–99. [165]

Brassard, E. I., 1964, Social desirability and self-concept description, *Dissertation Abstracts*, **8**, 3240. [183]

Breck, S. J., 1950, A sociometric measurement of status in physical education classes, *Research Quarterly of the American Association of Health, Physical Education, and Recreation*, **21**, 75–82. [213]

Brehm, J. W.
1959, Increasing cognitive dissonance by a fait-accompli, *Journal of Abnormal and Social Psychology*, **58**, 379–382. [102]

1966, *A theory of psychological reactance*, New York: Academic. [75]
1972, *A response to loss of freedom: a theory of psychological reactance*, Morristown, N.J.: General Press. [75]

Brehm, J. W., and Cohen, A. R., 1962, *Explorations in cognitive dissonance*, New York: Wiley. [102]

Bressler, N. *See* Lambert, R. D.

Bretsch, H. S., 1952, Social skills and activities of socially accepted and unaccepted adolescents, *Journal of Educational Psychology*, **43**, 449–504. [213]
See also Kuhlen, R. G.

Brigham, J. C., 1971, Ethnic stereotypes, *Psychological Bulletin*, **76**, 15–38. [193]

Brock, T. C., 1965, Communicator-recipient similarity and decision change, *Journal of Personality and Social Psychology*, **1**, 650–653. [97]

Bronfenbrenner, U.
1953, Personality. In C. P. Stone (ed.), *Annual review of psychology*, vol. 4, Stanford, Calif.: Annual Reviews. [32]
1958, Socialization and social class through time and space. In Eleanor Maccoby, T. M. Newcomb, and E. L. Hartley (eds.), *Readings in social psychology*, 3rd ed., New York: Holt, Rinehart and Winston. [146]
1961, The changing American child: a speculative analysis, *Journal of Social Issues*, **17**, 6–18.

Broverman, I., Broverman, D., Clarkson, F., Rosenkrantz, P., and Vogel, S, 1970, Sex-role stereotypes and clinical judgments of mental health. *Journal of Consulting Psychology*, **34**, 1–7. [153, 197]

Brown, C. T. *See* Eriksen, C. W.

Brown, J. S., 1961, *The motivation of behavior*, New York: McGraw-Hill. [310]

Brown, R. W.
1954, Mass phenomena. In G. Lindzey (ed.), *Handbook of social psychology*, Cambridge, Mass.: Addison-Wesley. [212, 338, 340]
1958, What shall a thing be called? *Psychological Review*, **65**, 14–22. [132, 133]
1965, *Social psychology*, New York: Free Press. [221]

Brown, R. W., Black, A. H., and Horowitz, A. E., 1955, Phonetic symbolism in natural languages, *Journal of Abnormal and Social Psychology*, **50**, 388–393.

Brown, R. W., and Lenneberg, E. H., 1954, A study in language and cognition, *Journal of Abnormal and Social Psychology*, **49**, 454–462. [128, 133]

Bruner, J. S., 1957, On perceptual readiness, *Psychological Review*, **64**, 123–152. [70]

Bruner, J. S., and Goodman, C. C., 1947, Value and need as organizing factors in perception, *Journal of Abnormal and Social Psychology,* **42,** 33–44. [70]

Bryan, J. H., and Test, A. T., 1967, Models and helping: naturalistic studies in aiding behavior, *Journal of Personality and Social Psychology,* **6,** 400–407. [234]

Bryson, J. B., 1974, Factor analysis of impression formation processes, *Journal of Personality and Social Psychology,* in press. [201]

Buckhout, R., 1971, *Toward social change,* New York: Harper & Row. [348]

Buell, J. S. *See* Allen, K. E.

Burchard, W. W., 1954, Role conflicts in military chaplains, *American Sociological Review,* **19,** 528–535. [281]

Burdick, H. A., and Burnes, A. J., 1958, A test of "strain toward symmetry" theories, *Journal of Abnormal and Social Psychology,* **57,** 367–370. [223]

Burks, F. W., 1937, The relation of social intelligence test scores to ratings of social traits, *Journal of Social Psychology,* **8,** 146–153. [211]

Buros, Q. K. (ed.), 1959, *Mental measurements yearbook,* Vol. 5, New Brunswick, N.J.: Rutgers University Press. [28]

Butler, J. *See* Levine, J.

Butler, R. A., 1953, Discrimination learning by rhesus monkeys to visual-exploration motivation, *Journal of Comparative and Physiological Psychology,* **46,** 95–98. [172]

Byrne, D.
1959, The effect of a subliminal food stimulus on verbal response, *Journal of Applied Psychology,* **43,** 249–252. [90]
1961, Interpersonal attraction and attitude similarity, *Journal of Abnormal and Social Psychology,* **62,** 713–715. [216]

Byrne, D., and Nelson, D., 1964, Attraction as a function of attitude similarity-dissimilarity: the effect of topic importance, *Psychonomic Science,* **1,** 93–94. [216]

California Folklore Society Newsletter, 1968. [134]

Call, H., 1972, Gloria Steinem on "Lib," *San Diego Union,* May 6. [153]

Calvin, A. D., and Holtzman, W. H., 1953, Adjustment and the discrepancies between self-concept and inferred-self, *Journal of Consulting Psychology,* **17,** 39–44. [183]

Cameron, P., Robertson, D., and Zaks, J., 1972, Sound pollution, noise pollution, and health: community parameters, *Journal of Applied Psychology,* **56,** 67–74. [121]

Campbell, D. T.
1953, *A study of leadership among submarine officers,* Columbus: Ohio State University, Personnel Research Board.

1955, An error in some demonstrations of the superior social perceptiveness of leaders, *Journal of Abnormal and Social Psychology,* **51,** 694–695. [300, 301]

Campbell, J. P., and Dunnette, N. D., 1968, Effectiveness of T-group experiences in managerial training and development, *Psychological Bulletin,* **70,** 73–104.

Cantril, H.
1941, *The psychology of social movements,* New York: Wiley. [339, 344, 345]
1947, *Understanding man's social behavior,* Princeton, N.J.: Office of Public Opinion Research. [344]
1950, *The "why" of man's experience,* New York: Macmillan. [339]
1960, *Soviet leaders and mastery over man,* New Brunswick, N.J.: Rutgers University Press. [345]

Cantril, H., Gaudet, H., and Hertzog, H., 1940, *The invasion from Mars,* Princeton, N.J.: Princeton University Press. [335, 345]

Caplow, T. A.
1956, A theory of coalitions in the triad, *American Sociological Review,* **19,** 23–29.
1959, Further development of a theory of coalitions in the triad, *American Journal of Sociology,* **64,** 488–493.

Capra, P. C., and Dittes, J. E., 1962, Birth order as a selective factor among volunteer subjects, *Journal of Abnormal and Social Psychology,* **64,** 302. [218]

Carkhuff, R. R.
1969, *Helping and human relations: a primer for lay and professional helpers,* New York: Holt, Rinehart & Winston. [204]
1971, *The development of human resources: education, psychology, and social change,* New York: Holt, Rinehart & Winston.

Carkhuff, R. R., and Berenson, B. H., 1967, *Beyond counseling and therapy,* New York: Holt, Rinehart & Winston. [204]

Carlsmith, J. M. *See* Festinger, L.

Carmet, D., Miles, C., and Cervin, V., 1965, Persuasiveness and persuasibility as related to intelligence and extraversion, *British Journal of Social and Clinical Psychology,* **4,** 1–7. [163]

Carmichael, L., Hogan, H. P., and Walter, A. A., 1932, An experimental study of the effect of language on the reproduction of visually perceived form, *Journal of Experimental Psychology,* **15,** 73–86. [78, 132]

Carmichael, S., and Hamilton, C. V., 1967, *Black power,* New York: Random House. [348]

Carpenter, G. R. *See* Christenson, H. T.

Carter, L. F., Haythorn, W., Meirowitz, B., and Lanzetta, J. W., 1951, The relations of categorizations and ratings in the observation of group behavior, *Human Relations*, **4**, 239–254. *See also* Haythorn, W. [298]

Cartwright, D. R., 1971, Risk taking by individuals and groups: an assessment of research employing choice dilemmas, *Journal of Personality and Social Psychology*, **20**, 361–378. [312]

Cartwright, D. R., and Zander, A. F. (eds.) 1960, *Group dynamics: research and theory*, 2nd ed., New York: Harper & Row. [293, 318]

1968, *Group dynamics: research and theory*, 3rd ed., New York: Harper & Row.

Casler, L., 1961, Maternal deprivation: a critical review of the literature, *Monographs of the Society for Research in Child Development*, **26**, 2, Serial No. 80. [232]

Cattell, R. B., 1951, New concepts for measuring leadership in terms of group syntality, *Human Relations*, **4**, 161–184. [285, 314]

Caudill, W., and Lin, T., 1967, *Mental health research in Asia and the Pacific*. Honolulu: East-West Center Press. [176]

Center for Women's Studies and Services, 1971, California State University at San Diego (Bulletin). [349]

Cervin, V., 1956, Individual behavior in social situations: its relation to anxiety, neuroticism, and group solidarity, *Journal of Experimental Psychology*, **51**, 161–168. *See also* Carmet, D. [321]

Chance, J., 1965, *Independence training and children's achievement*, presented at Society for Research in Child Development meetings, March 1965, Minneapolis, NIMH Research Grant MH-5298. [165, 176]

Chapanis, N. N., and Chapanis, A., 1964, Cognitive dissonance: five years later, *Psychological Bulletin*, **61**, 1–22. [75]

Chapman, D. W., and Volkman, I., 1939, A social determinant of the level of aspiration, *Journal of Abnormal and Social Psychology*, **34**, 225–238. [162]

Chappell, M. N., Stefano, J. S., Rogerson, J. S., and Pike, F. H., 1937, Values of group psychological procedures in treatment of peptic ulcers, *American Journal of Digestion, Dietetics, and Nutrition*, **3**, 813–817. [304]

Chapple, E. D., 1940, Measuring human relations: an introduction to the study of the interaction of individuals, *Genetic Psychology Monographs*, **22**, 1–147. [39]

Charcot, J. M., 1894, *Oeuvres complètes*, 9 vols., Paris: Bureaux du Progrès Médical, 1888–1894. [262]

Chave, E. J. *See* Thurstone, L. L.

Chomsky, N., 1965, *Aspects of the theory of syntax*, Cambridge: Massachusetts Institute of Technology Press.

Chowdry, K., and Newcomb, T. M., 1952, The relative abilities of leaders and nonleaders to estimate opinions of their own groups, *Journal of Abnormal and Social Psychology*, **47**, 51–57. [207]

Christenson, H. T., and Carpenter, G. R., 1962, Value behavior discrepancies regarding premarital coitus in three Western cultures, *American Sociological Review*, **27**, 66–74. [143]

Christiansen, B., 1959, *Attitudes towards foreign affairs as a function of personality*, Oslo, Norway: Oslo University Press. [359]

Christie, R., 1970, The Machiavellis among us, *Psychology Today*, **4**, 82–86. [173, 174]

Christie, R., and Geis, F. L., 1970, *Studies in Machiavellianism*, New York: Academic. [173, 174]

Church, R. M., 1957, Transmission of learned behavior between rats, *Journal of Abnormal and Social Psychology*, **54**, 163–165. [246]

Clark, E. L., 1949, Motivation of Jewish students, *Journal of Social Psychology*, **29**, 113–117. [149, 195]

Clark, H., 1916, The crowd, *Psychological Monographs*, **21**, 26–36. [262]

Clark, K. B., and Clark, M. P., 1957, Racial identification and preference in Negro children, in T. M. Newcomb and E. L. Hartley (eds.), *Readings in social psychology*, New York: Holt, Rinehart & Winston. [161]

Clark, M. P. *See* Clark, K. B.

Clark, R. A., Teevan, R., and Ricciuti, H. N., 1956, Hope of success and fear of failure as aspects of need for achievement, *Journal of Abnormal Social Psychology*, **53**, 182–186. [175]

Clark, R. A. *See also* McClelland, D. C.

Clifford, C., and Cohn, T. S., 1964, The relationship between leadership and personality attributes perceived by followers, *Journal of Social Psychology*, **64**, 57–64. [301]

Cline, V. B., and Richards, J. M., Jr., 1960, Accuracy of interpersonal perception—a general trait? *Journal of Abnormal and Social Psychology*, **60**, 1–7. [204]

Coch, L., and French, J. R. P., 1948, Overcoming resistance to change, *Human Relations*, **1**, 512–513. [26, 280, 318, 319, 325]

Coffin, T. E., 1941, Some conditions of suggestion and suggestibility, *Psychology Monographs*, **53**, No. 4. [259]

Cohen, A. R.
1957, Need for cognition and order of communication as determinants of opinion change. In C. I. Hovland (ed.), *The order of presentation in persuasion,*

New Haven, Conn.: Yale University Press.

1958, Upward communication in experimentally created hierarchies, *Human Relations,* **11,** 41–56.

See also Brehm, J. W.; Hovland, C. I.; Stotland, E.

Cohn, T. S., Yee, W., and Brown, V., 1961, Attitude change and interpersonal attraction, *Journal of Social Psychology,* **55,** 207–211. [97]

Cohn, T. S. *See also* Clifford, C.

Collins, B. E., 1969, Attribution theory analysis of forced compliance, *Proceedings,* 77th Annual Convention, APA, 309–310. [192, 201]

Consalvi, C. *See* Harvey, O. J.

Cooley, C. H., 1902, *Human nature and the social order,* New York: Scribner. [157, 159]

Coon, C. S., Garn, C. M., and Birdsell, J. B., 1950, *Races: a study of problems in race formation,* Springfield, Ill.: C. C Thomas. [148]

Cottrell, L. S. *See* Borgatta, E. F.

Cottrell, N. B. Performance in the presence of other human beings. In E. C. Simmel, R. A. Hoppe, and G. A. Milton (eds.), 1968, *Social facilitation and imitative behavior,* Boston: Allyn & Bacon.

Couch, A. S. *See* Borgatta, E. F.; Haythorn, W.

Cowan, G. The machiavellian: manipulator or failure in self-presentation, *Proceedings,* 77th Annual Convention, APA, 1969, 357–358.

Criswell, E., and Peterson, S., 1972, The whole soul catalog, *Psychology Today,* April. [184]

Criswell, J. H., 1939, Social structure revealed in a sociometric retest, *Sociometry,* **2,** 69–75. [215]

Crow, W. J., 1957, The effect of training upon accuracy and variability in interpersonal perception, *Journal of Abnormal and Social Psychology,* **55,** 355–359. [205]

Crowne, D. P., and Marlowe, D., 1964, *The approval motive,* New York: Wiley. [114, 167, 275]

Crumbaugh, C. M. *See* Evans, G. W.

Crutchfield, R. S., 1955, Conformity and character, *American Psychologist,* **10,** 191–198. [272]

See also Krech, D.; Postman, L. J.

Cutler, J. E., 1905, *Lynch-law,* London: Longmans. [339]

Dabbs, J. W., Jr., 1964, Self-esteem, communicator characteristics, and attitude change, *Journal of Abnormal and Social Psychology,* **69,** 173–181. [97]

Damrin, D. *See* Stendler, C. B.

Darley, J., and Latané, B., 1968, Bystander intervention in emergencies: diffusion of responsibility, *Journal of Personality and Social Psychology,* **8,** 377–383. [235]

Dashiell, J. F., 1935, Experimental studies of the influence of social situations on the behavior of individual human adults. In C. Murchison (ed.), *Handbook of social psychology,* Worcester, Mass.: Clark University Press. [309]

Davis, F., 1967, Why all of us may be hippies some day, *Trans-action,* December.

Davis, J. A., 1957, Correlates of sociometric status among peers, *Journal of Educational Research,* **50,** 561–569. [131, 212, 215]

Davis, K., 1947, Final note on a case of extreme isolation, *American Journal of Sociology,* **52,** 432–437. [109]

Davitz, J. R., 1955, Social perception and sociometric choice of children, *Journal of Abnormal and Social Psychology,* **50,** 173–176. [216, 223]

Dean, D. G., 1961, Alienation: its meaning and measurement, *American Sociological Review,* 26, 753–758. [177–178]

de Beauvoir, Simone, 1953, *The second sex,* New York: Knopf. [173]

DeMonchaux, C. *See* Schachter, S.

Dennis, W., 1957, Use of common objects as indicators of cultural orientations, *Journal of Abnormal and Social Psychology,* **55,** 21–28.

deNuoy, L., 1947, *Human destiny,* New York: McKay.

Dertke, M. C., Penner, L. A., and Ulrich, K., 1972, ''Ripping off'' the college bookstore: Race, sex, and the reporting of shoplifters, Paper presented at Southeastern Psychological Association, Atlanta. [171]

Deutsch, M.

1949, An experimental study of the effects of cooperation and competition upon group processes, *Human Relations,* **2,** 199–232. [318, 323]

1959, Some factors affecting membership motivation and achievement motivation in a group, *Human Relations,* **12,** 81–95. [294, 317, 321]

1960, The pathetic fallacy: an observer error in social perception, *Journal of Personality,* **28,** 317–332. [323]

1969, Happenings on the way back to the forum, *Harvard Educational Review,* **39,** 523–557. [243]

Deutsch, M., and Gerard, H. B., 1955, A study of normative and informational social influences upon individual judgment, *Journal of Abnormal and Social Psychology,* **51,** 629–636. [266, 268, 270]

Deutsch, M., and Krauss, R. M., 1960, The effect of threat on interpersonal bargaining, *Journal of Abnormal and Social Psychology,* **61,** 181–189. [243, 323, 359]

DeVault, M. U., 1957, Classroom sociometric mutual pairs and residential proximity, *Journal of Educational Research,* **50,** 605–610. [215]

DeVos, G., 1961, Symbolic analysis in the cross-cultural study of personality. In B. Kaplan (ed.), *Studying personality crossculturally,* New York: Harper & Row, 599–634. [176]

Dickman, H. *See* Luchins, A. S.

Dickson, L. *See* Lundberg, G. A.

Dickson, W. J. *See* Roethlisberger, F. J.

Dill, W. R. *See* Guetzkow, H.

Dillehay, R. L., and Jernigan, L. R., 1970, The biased questionnaire method, *Journal of Personality and Social Psychology,* **15,** 144–150.

DiVesta, F. J., 1958, *Susceptibility to pressures toward uniformity of behavior in social situations: a study of task, motivational and personality factors in conformity behavior,* Syracuse University, June. [274, 275]

Dollard, J., Doob, L. W., Miller, N. E., Mowrer, O. H., and Sears, R. R., 1939, *Frustration and aggression,* New Haven: Yale University Press. [237, 360]

Dollard, J., and Miller, N. E., 1950, *Personality and psychotherapy: an analysis in terms of learning, thinking and culture,* New York: McGraw-Hill. [31, 76, 87, 88, 231]

Dollard, J. *See also* Miller, N. E.

Doob, A. N., Carlsmith, J. M., Freedman, J. L., Landauer, T. K., and Tom, S., 1969, Effect of initial selling price on subsequent sales, *Journal of Personality and Social Psychology,* **4,** 345–350. [238]

Doob, A. N., and Gross, A. E. 1968, Status of frustrator as an inhibitor of horn-honking responses, *Journal of Social Psychology,* **76,** 213–218. [238]

Dorr, M. J. *See* Havighurst, R. J.

Douvan, E., and Adelson, J., 1958, The psychodynamics of social mobility in adolescent boys, *Journal of Abnormal and Social Psychology,* **56,** 31–44.

Dove, A., 1968, The soul-folk-chitling test, reported in *Time,* February 5. [151]

Dozier, E. P., 1956, Two examples of linguistic acculturation, *Language,* **32,** 146–157. [133]

Drabell, T. E., and Stephenson, J. C. 1971, When disaster strikes, *Journal of Social Psychology,* **1,** 187–203.

Dreger, R. M., and Miller, K. S.
1960, Comparative psychological studies of Negroes and whites in the United States, *Psychological Bulletin,* **57,** 361–402.

1968, Comparative psychological studies of Negroes and whites in the United States, 1959–1965, *Psychological Bulletin Monograph Supplement,* **70**(3), Part 2, 1–58. [149]

Dreikers, R., 1960, *Group psychotherapy and group approaches* (collected papers of Rudolph Dreikers), Chicago: Alfred Adler Institute. [303]

Dreyer, A. H. *See* Bonney, M. E.

Driscoll, R., Davis, K. E., and Lipetz, M. E., 1972, Parental interference and romantic love: the Romeo and Juliet effect, *Journal of Personality and Social Psychology,* **24,** 1–10. [76]

Duijker, H. *See* Schachter, S.

Dunnette, M. D., Campbell, J., and Jaastad, K., 1963, The effect of group participation on brainstorming effectiveness for two industrial samples, *Journal of Applied Psychology,* **47,** 30–37. [313]

Durkheim, E., 1893, *The division of labor in society (De la division du travail social),* Paris: Alcan. [280]

Duryea, R. A. *See* Blake, R. R.

Dworkin, R. S. *See* Helson, H.

Edwards, A. L.
1954, *Manual: Edwards personal preference schedule,* New York: Psychol. Corp. [167, 175]

1957, *The social desirability variable in personality assessment and research,* New York: Dryden. [167, 212]

Eels, K. *See* Warner, W. L.

Efron, D. *See* Boas, F.

Ehrlich, D., Guttman, I., Schonbach, P., and Mills, J., 1957, Post-decision exposure to relevant information, *Journal of Abnormal and Social Psychology,* **54,** 98–102. [102]

Ekman, P., and Friesen, W. V., 1971, Constants across cultures in the face and emotions, *Journal of Personality and Social Psychology,* **17,** 124–129.

Elder, G. H., 1963, Parental power legitimation and its effect on the adolescent, *Sociometry,* **26,** 50–65. [239]

Elkin, F., 1945, The soldier's language, *American Journal of Sociology,* **51,** 414–422. [130, 133]

Elkind, D., and Flavell, J. H., 1969, *Studies in cognitive development: essays in honor of Jean Piaget,* New York: Oxford University Press. [173]

Ellertson, N. *See* Schachter, S.

Emerson, P. E. *See* Schafer, H. R.

Engels, F. *See* Marx, K.

Eriksen, C. W., and Brown, C. T., 1956, An experimental and theoretical analysis of perceptual defense, *Journal of Abnormal and Social Psychology,* **52,** 224–230.

Erikson, E. H., 1950, *Childhood and society,* New York: Norton. [292]

Eron, L. D., Huesmann, L. R., Lefkowitz, M. M., and Walder, L. O., 1972, Does television violence cause aggression?, *American Psychologist,* **27,** 4, 253–263. [118, 335, 363]

Ervin, S. M. *See* Landar, H. J.

Evan W. M., and Zelditch, M. H., 1961, A laboratory experiment on bureaucratic authority, *American Sociological Review,* **26,** 883–893. [239]

Evans, G. W., 1964, Effect of unilateral promise and value of reward upon cooperation and trust, *Journal of Abnormal and Social Psychology,* **69,** 587–590.

Evans, G. W., and Crumbaugh, C. M., 1966, Effects of prisoner's dilemma format on cooperative behavior, *Journal of Personality and Social Psychology,* **3,** 486–488. [242]

Fagan, J., and Shepherd, I. (eds.), 1970, *Gestalt therapy now: techniques, applications,* Palo Alto, Calif.: Science and Behavior. [183, 204, 282, 303]

Faust, W. L. *See* Taylor, D. W.

Feierabend, I. K., Feierabend, R. L., & Gurr, T. R., 1972, *Anger, Violence, and Politics,* Englewood Cliffs, N.J.: Prentice-Hall. [360, 361, 364]

Feldman, R. E., 1968, Response to compatriot and foreigner who seek assistance, *Journal of Personality and Social Psychology,* **10,** 202–214.

Feldman, S., 1968, What do you think of a *cruel, wise* man? The integrative response to a stimulus manifold. In R. P. Abelson, E. Aronson, W. J. McGuire, T. M. Newcomb, M. J. Rosenberg, and P. H. Tannenbaum (eds.), *Theories of cognitive consistency: a sourcebook.* Chicago: Rand-McNally. [200, 208]

Felipe, N. J., and Sommer, R., 1966, Invasion of personal space, *Social Problems,* **14,** 206–214. [125, 127]

Fendrich, J. M., 1967, A study of the association among verbal attitudes, commitment, and overt behavior in different experimental situations, *Social Forces,* **45,** 347–355. [87]

Feshback, S. *See* Janis, I. L.

Festinger, L.
1942, Wish expectation and group standards as factors influencing level of aspiration, *Journal of Abnormal and Social Psychology,* **37,** 184–200

1953, An analysis of compliant behavior. In M. Sherif and M. O. Wilson (eds.), *Group relations at the crossroad,* New York: Harper & Row. [266, 293, 318]

1954, A theory of social comparison processes, *Human Relations,* 7, 117–140. [31, 162, 164, 293, 316]

1957, *A theory of cognitive dissonance,* New York: Harper & Row. [31, 73, 74, 87, 102]

See also Allyn, J.

Festinger, L., and Carlsmith, J. M., 1959, Cognitive consequences of forced compliance, *Journal of Abnormal and Social Psychology,* **58,** 203–210. [101, 102]

Festinger, L., and Maccoby, N., 1964, On resistance to persuasive communications, *Journal of Abnormal and Social Psychology,* **68,** 359–366. [90]

Festinger, L., Schachter, S., and Back, K., 1950, *Social pressures in informal groups: a study of human factors in housing,* New York: Harper & Row. [25, 215]

Fey, F., 1955, Acceptance of others and its relation to acceptance of self and others: a re-evaluation, *Journal of Abnormal and Social Psychology,* **50,** 274–276. [163]

Fiedler, F. E.
1958, *Leader attitudes and group effectiveness,* Urbana: University of Illinois Press. [302, 317]

1963, A contingency model for the prediction of leadership effectiveness, Office of Naval Research Contract NR-177-472, Nonr-1834 (36), Technical Report No. 10. [301]

1967, *A theory of leadership effectiveness.* New York: McGraw-Hill. [301, 318]

See also Julian, J. W.

Fiedler, F. E., Fiedler, J., and Campf, S., 1971, Who speaks for the community? *Journal of Applied Social Psychology,* **1,** 324–333. [356]

Field, P. B. *See* Janis, I. L.

Fillenbaum, S., 1966, Prior deception and subsequent experimental performance: the "faithful" subject, *Journal of Personality and Social Psychology,* **4,** 532–537. [21]

Fine, B., 1957, Conclusion-drawing, communicator credibility and anxiety as factors in opinion change, *Journal of Abnormal and Social Psychology,* **54,** 369–374. [93]

Fine, H. J. *See* Zimet, C. N.

Fineman, C. A., 1966, Attitude toward assimilation: its relationship to dogmatism and rigidity in the Cuban refugee, unpublished Master's thesis, University of Miami, Coral Gables, Florida. [356]

Fishbein, M., 1963, An investigation of the relationship between beliefs about an object and the attitude toward that object. *Human Relations,* **16,** 233–239. [86, 200]

1972, The prediction of behavior from attitudinal variables. In K. K. Sereno and C. C. Mortensen (eds.), *Advances in communication research,* New York: Harper & Row.

Flanders, N. A., 1954, *Teaching with groups,* Minneapolis: Burgess. [325]

1970, *Analyzing teaching behavior,* Reading, Mass.: Addison-Wesley. [40]

Flavell, J. H., 1963, *The developmental psychology of Jean Piaget,* New York: Van Nostrand Reinhold.

Flexner, E., 1971, *Women's rights—unfinished business.* New York: Public Affairs Committee, 381 Park Avenue South, 10016. [349]

Foa, U. G., 1958, The contiguity principle in the structure of interpersonal relations, *Human Relations,* **11,** 229–237. [281]

Foley, J. P., Jr. *See* Boas, F.

Ford, C. S., and Beach, F. A., 1951, *Patterns of sexual behavior,* New York: Harper & Row. [143]

Form, W. H., & Sauer, W. L., 1960, Community power structure, *Social Forces,* **38,** 332–341. [357]

Foy, E., and Harlow, A. F., 1928, *Clowning through life,* New York: Dutton. [342]

Frank, J. D., and Powdermaker, F., 1953, *Group psychotherapy,* Cambridge, Mass.: Commonwealth Fund and Harvard University Press. [303]

Franklin, M. *See* Lewis, H. B.

Freedman, J. L. Role playing: psychology by consensus, *Journal of Personality and Social Psychology,* 1969, **13,** 107–114.

1971, The crowd—maybe not so maddening after all, *Psychology Today,* **5,** 58–61, 86. [125, 127]

Freedman, J. L., and Doob, A. N., 1968, *Deviancy: the psychology of being different,* New York: Academic. [164, 165]

Freedman, J. L., and Fraser, S. C., 1966, Compliance without pressure: the foot-in-the-door technique, *Journal of Personality and Social Psychology,* **4,** 195–202. [242]

Freedman, J. L., Klevansky, S., and Ehrlich, P. R., 1971, The effect of crowding in human task performance, *Journal of Applied Social Psychology,* **1,** 7–25. [127]

Freedman, J. L., Wallington, S. A., Bless, E., 1967, Compliance without pressure: the effect of guilt, *Journal of Personality and Social Psychology,* **7,** 117–124.

French, J. R. P., Israel, J., and As, D., 1960, An experiment of participation in a Norwegian factory: interpersonal dimension of decision making, *Human Relations,* **13,** 349. [260, 325]

French, J. R. P., and Raven, B., 1959, The bases of social power. In D. Cartwright (ed.), *Studies in social power,* Ann Arbor: University of Michigan Institute for Social Research. [239, 297]

French, J. R. P., and Snyder, R., 1959, Leadership and interpersonal power. In D. R. Cartwright (ed.), *Studies in social power,* Ann Arbor: University of Michigan Institute for Social Research. [298]

French, J. R. P. *See also* Coch, L.; Raven, B. H.

French, R. L., 1951, Sociometric status and individual adjustment among naval recruits, *Journal of Abnormal and Social Psychology,* **46,** 64–72. [212]

Frenkel-Brunswik, E. *See* Adorno, T. W.

Freud, S.

1913, *The interpretation of dreams,* London: Hogarth. [79, 87]

1918, *Totem and taboo,* New York: Moffat, Yard.

1922, *Group psychology and the analysis of the ego,* London: International Psychoanalytic Press. [338]

1930, *Civilization and its discontents,* London: Hogarth.

1933, *New introductory lectures,* New York: Knopf. [159]

1939, *Moses and monotheism,* New York: Knopf.

Friedan, B., 1963, *The feminine mystique,* New York: Norton. [153, 173]

Fritz, C. E., 1961, Disaster. In R. K. Merton and R. A. Nisbet (eds.), *Contemporary social problems,* New York: Harcourt Brace Jovanovich. [342]

Fromm, E.

1941, *Escape from freedom,* New York: Holt, Rinehart and Winston. [120, 233, 292]

1947, *Man for himself,* New York: Holt, Rinehart and Winston. [225]

1955, *The sane society,* New York: Holt, Rinehart and Winston.

1964, *The heart of man: its genius for good and evil,* New York: Harper & Row.

1968, *The revolution of hope, toward a humanized technology,* New York: Harper & Row.

1970, *The crisis of psychoanalysis,* New York: Holt, Rinehart and Winston.

Gaertner, S. L., 1970, A "call" for help: helping behavior extended to black and white victims by New York City liberal and conservative party members, *Proceedings,* 78th Annual Convention, American Psychological Association, 441–442. [49, 235, 236]

Gage, N. L., 1952, Judging interests from expressive behavior, *Psychological Monographs,* **66,** No. 18 (whole no. 350). [207]

Gage, N. L., and Charters, W. W., 1963, *Readings in the social psychology of education,* New York: Society for the Psychological Study of Social Issues.

Galbraith, J. K., 1961, *The affluent society,* London: Readers Union and H. Hamilton.

Gallo, P. S.

1966, Effects of increased incentives upon the use of threat in bargaining, *Journal of Personality and Social Psychology*, **1**, 14–20. [243]

1968, *Prisoners of our own dilemma?* Paper presented at Western Psychological Association, San Diego. [243]

Gallo, P. S., and Sheposh, J. P., 1971, Effects of incentive magnitude on cooperation in the prisoner's dilemma game: a reply to Deutsch, Gumpert, and Epstein, *Journal of Personality and Social Psychology*, **19**, 42–46. [243]

Gallwey, M. *See* Levin, H.

Gardner, R. C. *See* Lambert, W. E.

Gaudet, H. *See* Cantril, H.; Lazarsfeld, P. F.

Geen, R. G., 1968, Effects of frustration, attach, and prior training in aggressiveness upon aggressive behavior, *Journal of Personality and Social Psychology*, **9**, 316–321. [237]

Geis, F., and Christie, R., 1970, *Machiavellianism and the manipulation of one's fellow man,* in Marlowe, D., and Gergen, K. J. (eds.), *Personality and social behavior,* Reading, Mass.: Addison-Wesley. [173, 174]

Gerard, H. B., and Mathewson, J. C., 1966, The effects of severity of initiation on liking for a group: a replication, *Journal of Experimental Social Psychology*, **2**, 278–287. [102]

See also Deutsch, M.

Gergen, K., 1969, *The psychology of behavior exchange,* Reading, Mass.: Addison-Wesley.

Getzels, J. W., 1969, A social psychology of education, in G. Lindzey and E. Aronson (eds.), *The handbook of social psychology,* Vol. 5, Reading, Mass.: Addison-Wesley. [104]

Getzels, J. W., and Guba, E. G., 1954, Role conflict and effectiveness: an empirical study, *American Sociological Review*, **19**, 164–175.

Getzels, J. W., and Jackson, P. W., 1962, *Creativity and intelligence,* New York: Wiley. [173]

Gibb, C. A., 1954, Leadership. In G. Lindzey (ed.), *Handbook of social psychology,* Reading, Mass.: Addison-Wesley. [300]

Gibb, J. R., 1951, The effects of group size and of threat reduction upon creativity in a problem-solving situation, *American Psychologist*, **6**, 324 (Abstract). [310]

See also Bradford, L. P.

Gilbert, C. M., 1951, Stereotype persistence and change among college students, *Journal of Abnormal and Social Psychology*, **46**, 245–254. [194]

Glass, D. C., Singer, J. E., and Friedman, L. C., 1969, Psychic cost of adaption to an environmental stressor, *Journal of personality and social psychology*, **12**, 200–210. [127]

Glinski, R. J., Glinski, B. C., and Slatin, G. T., 1970, Nonnaivety contamination in conformity experiments: sources, effects, and implications for control, *Journal of Personality and Social Psychology*, **16**, 475–478.

Glucksberg, S. *See* Katz, I.

Goi, F. J. *See* Wells, W. D.

Gold, A. R., Friedman, L. N., and Christie, R., 1971, The anatomy of revolutionists, *Journal of Applied Social Psychology*, **1**, 26–43.

Goldberg, P. A., 1968, Are women prejudiced against women? *Trans-action*, **5**, 28–30. [153, 197]

Golding, S. L., and Lichtenstein, E., 1970, Confession and awareness and prior knowledge of deception as a function of interview set and approval motivation, *Journal of Personality and Social Psychology*, **14**, 213–223.

Goldman, G. D. *See* Singer, J. L.

Gollin, E. S., 1954, Forming impressions of personality, *Journal of Personality*, **23**, 65–76. [201]

Goodall, J., 1963, My life among wild chimpanzees, *National Geographic*, **124**, 272–308. [80, 128]

Goodenough, F. L., 1942, The use of free association in objective measurements of personality. In *Studies in personality,* New York: McGraw-Hill.

Goodman, C. C. *See* Bruner, J. S.

Goodnow, R. E., and Tagiuri, R., 1952, Religious ethnocentrism and its recognition among adolescent boys, *Journal of Abnormal and Social Psychology*, **47**, 316–320. [215]

Gouldner, A. W., 1950, *Studies in leadership,* New York: Harper & Row. [300]

1960, The norm of reciprocity: a preliminary statement, *American Sociological Review*, **25**, 161–179. [230]

Grant, D. A., 1951, Perceptual versus analytical responses to the number concept of a Weigl-type card sorting test, *Journal of Experimental Psychology*, **41**, 23–29. [79]

Green, B. F., 1954, Attitude measurement. In G. Lindzey (ed.), *Handbook of social psychology,* vol. 1, Reading, Mass.: Addison-Wesley. [52]

Green, J. A., 1969, Attitudinal and situational determinants of intended behavior to Negroes. Paper presented at the Western Psychological Association, Vancouver. [87, 237]

Greenberg, C., 1946, Avant-garde and kitsch, *The partisan reader,* New York: Dial, 378–389. [124]

Greenberg, M. S., 1967, Role playing: an alternative to deception? *Journal of Personality and Social Psychology,* **7,** 152–157.

Greenspoon, J., 1955, The reinforcing effort of two spoken sounds on the frequency of two responses, *American Journal of Psychology,* **50,** 409–416.

Greer, G., 1971, *The female eunuch,* New York: McGraw-Hill.

Greer, S., 1960, The social structure and political process of suburbia, *American Sociological Review,* **25,** 514–526. [355]

Gregory, D. *See* Schachter, S.

Grinker, R., and Spiegel, J., 1945, *Men Under Stress,* New York: McGraw-Hill-Blakiston. [316]

Gronlund, N. E., and Anderson, L., 1957, Personality characteristics of socially rejected junior high school pupils, *Educational Administration and Supervision,* **43,** 329–338. [212]

Gross, N., Mason, W. S., and McEachern, A. W., 1958, *Explorations in role analysis,* New York: Wiley. [281]

Grossack, M., and Gardner, H., 1970, *Man and men.* New York: International Textbook Co. [351]

Grossman, B., and Wrighter, J., 1948, The relationship between selection-rejection and intelligence, social status, and personality among sixth-grade children, *Sociometry,* **11,** 346–355. [212]

Guetzkow, H.
1957, Isolation and collaboration: a partial theory of inter-nation relations, *Journal of Conflict Resol.,* **1,** 48–68.

1959, Use of simulation in the study of inter-nation relations, *Behavioral Science,* **4,** 183–191.

1960, Differation in roles in task-oriented groups. In D. Cartwright and A. Zander (eds.), *Group dynamics: research and theory,* New York: Harper & Row. [322]

Guetzkow, H., Alger, C. F., Brody, R. A., Noel, R. C., and Snyder, R. C., 1963, *Simulation in international relations,* Englewood Cliffs, N.J.: Prentice-Hall. [63, 242, 362]

Guetzkow, H., and Dill, W. R., 1957, Factors in the organizational development of task-oriented groups, *Sociometry,* **20,** 175–204. [322]

Guetzkow, H., and Simon, H. A., 1955, The impact of certain communication nets upon organization and performance in task-oriented groups, *Management Science,* **1,** 233–250. [322, 359]

Guilford, J. P., 1931, Racial preferences of a thousand American university students, *Journal of Social Psychology,* **2,** 179–204. [193]

Guttman, I. *See* Ehrlich, D.

Guttman, L.
1944, A Basis for scaling qualitative data, *American Sociological Review,* **9,** 139–150. [51]

1950, The third component of scalable attitudes, *International Journal of Opinion and Attitude Research,* **4,** 285–287. [51]

Haffner, D. *See* Haythorn, W.

Haggstrom, W. C., 1963, Self-esteem and other characteristics of residentially desegregated Negroes, *Dissertation Abstracts,* **7,** 3007 [163]

Haines, A. C. *See* Stendler, C. B.

Hall, C., 1960, The language of space, *Landscape,* Autumn, 41–44. [125, 127]

Hamachek, D. E., 1971, *Encounters with the self,* New York: Holt, Rinehart and Winston. [171, 183]

Hamblin, R. L., 1958, Leadership and crisis, *Sociometry,* **21,** 322–335. [298]

Hamme, R., 1969, Role playing: a judge is a con, a con is a judge, *New York Times Magazine,* September 14.

Hammond, K. R., 1948, Measuring attitudes by error-choice: an indirect method, *Journal of Abnormal Social Psychology,* **43,** 38–48. [48]

Hanfmann, E. *See* Inkeles, A.

Harari, H., 1967, An experimental evaluation of Heider's balance theory with respect to situational and predispositional variables, *Journal of Social Psychology,* **78,** 177–189. [223]

1971, Interpersonal models in psychotherapy and counseling, *Journal of Abnormal Psychology,* **78,** 127–133 [120, 121, 304]

1972, Cognitive manipulations with delinquent adolescents in group therapy, *Psychotherapy: Theory, Practice and Research,* **2,** 303–307. [304]

See also McDavid, J. W.

Harari, H., Boujarski, R., Houlne, S., and Wullner, K., 1972, Student power or cop out, unpublished manuscript, San Diego: California State University.

Harari, H., and McDavid, J. W., 1966, Cultural influences on retention of logical and symbolic material, *Journal of Educational Psychology,* **57,** 18–22.

1969, Situational influence on moral justice: a study of "finking," *Journal of Personality and Social Psychology,* **11,** 240–244. [164]

1973, Teachers' expectations and name stereotypes, *Journal of Educational Psychology,* 65, 222–225. [195, 196]

Hardyck, J. A. *See* Stein, D. D.

Hare, A. P., 1957, Situational differences in leader behavior, *Journal of Abnormal and Social Psychology,* **55,** 132–134. [298]

Hare, A. P., and Bales, R. F., 1963, Seating position and small group interaction, *Sociometry,* **26,** 480–486. [285, 286]

Hare, A. P., Borgatta, E. F., and Bales, R. F. (eds.), 1955, *Small groups: studies in social interaction* (rev. ed., 1965), New York: Knopf. [125]

Harlow, A. F. *See* Foy, E.

Harlow, H. F., 1958, The nature of love, *American Psychologist,* **13,** 673–685. [232] *See also* Seay, B.

Harlow, H. F., Harlow, M. K., and Meyer, D. R., 1950, Learning motivated by a manipulation drive, *Journal of Experimental Psychology,* **40,** 228–234. [172]

Harlow, H. F., and Zimmerman, R. R., 1959, Affectional responses in the infant monkey, *Science,* **130,** 421–432. [232]

Harlow, M. K. *See* Harlow, H. F.

Harrington, M., 1962, *The other America,* New York: Macmillan. [177]

Harris, F. R. *See* Allen, K. E.

Harris, T. A., 1967, *I'm O.K., You're O.K.,* New York: Harper and Row

Harshbarger, D., 1970, High priests of hospitaldom, *Hospital and Community Psychiatry,* May, 156–159. [286]

Hart, B. *See* Allen, K. E.

Hart, M., 1971, Women sit in the back of the bus, *Psychology Today,* October. [153, 197]

Hartley, R. E., 1960, Relationship between perceived values and acceptance of a new reference group, *Journal of Social Psychology,* **51,** 181–190. [293]

Hartley, R. E., and Gondor, E. I., 1956, The use of art in therapy. In *Progress in clinical psychology,* New York: Grune & Stratton. [304]

Hartman, G. W., 1936, A field experiment on the comparative effectiveness of "emotional" and "rational" political leaflets in determining election results, *Journal of Abnormal and Social Psychology,* **31,** 99–114.

Harvey, O. J.
1956, An experimental investigation of negative and positive relations between small groups through judgmental indices, *Sociometry,* **19,** 201–209. [206]
1963, *Motivation and social interaction,* New York: Ronald. [87]
See also Hovland, C. I.; Sherif, M.; Wright, J. M.

Harvey, O. J., and Consalvi, C., 1960, Status and conformity to pressures in informal groups, *Journal of Abnormal Social Psychology,* **60,** 182–187. [269,296]

Harvey, O. J., Hunt, D. E., & Schroder, H. M., 1961, *Conceptual systems and personality organization,* New York: Wiley. [76, 205]

Haskins, J., 1966, Factual recall as a measure of advertising effectiveness, *Journal of Advertising Research,* **6,** 2–8. [93]

Hastorf, A. H., Schneider, D. J., and Polefka, J., 1970, *Person perception,* Reading, Mass.: Addison-Wesley.

Havemann, E., 1969, Alternatives to analysis, *Playboy,* November.

Havighurst, R. J., and Davis, A., 1955, A comparison of the Chicago and Harvard studies of social class differences in child rearing, *American Sociological Review,* **20,** 438–442.

Havighurst, R. J., Robinson, M. Z., and Dorr, M. J., 1946, The development of the ideal self in childhood and adolescence, *Journal of Educational Research,* **40,** 241–257. [146]

Havron, M. D., and McGrath, J. E., 1961, The contribution of the leader to the effectiveness of small military groups. In L. Petrullo, and B. M. Bass (eds.), *Leadership and interpersonal behavior,* New York: Holt, Rinehart and Winston. [299]

Haythorn, W., Couch, A. S., Haffner, D., Langham, P., and Carter, L. F., 1956, The effects of varying combinations of authoritarian and equalitarian leaders and followers, *Journal of Abnormal and Social Psychology,* **53,** 210–219. [180]

Haythorn, W. *See also* Carter, L. F.

Hearn, L., 1894, The Japanese smile. In *Glimpses of unfamiliar Japan,* 2 vols., London: Cape. [211]

Hebb, D. O., 1955, Drives and the conceptual nervous system, *Psychological Review,* **62,** 243–254. [173]

Hedgepeth, W., 1970, America's Indians: reawakening of a conquered people, *Look,* June 2, p. 23. [349]

Heidbreder, E., Bensley, M., and Ivy, M., 1948, The attainment of concepts: IV. Regularities and levels, *Journal of Psychology,* **25,** 299–329. [79]

Heider, F.
1944, Social perception and phenomenal causality, *Psychological Review,* **51,** 358–374. [191]
1958, *The psychology of interpersonal relations,* New York: Wiley. [31, 75, 218, 221]

Heider, F., and Simmel, M., 1944, An experimental study of apparent behavior, *American Journal of Psychology,* **57,** 243–259. [191]

Heinicke, C., and Bales, R. F., 1953, Developmental trends in the structure of small groups, *Sociometry,* **16,** 7–38.

Helson, H.
1947, Adaptation-level as a frame of reference for prediction of psychophysical data, *American Journal of Psychology,* **60,** 1–29. [31, 72]
1948, Adaptation-level as a basis for a quantitative theory of frames of reference, *Psychological Review,* **55,** 297–313. [72]

Helson, H. (*Cont.*)

1959, Adaptation level theory. In S. Koch (ed.), *Psychology: a study of a science. vol. 1, Sensory, perceptual and physiological formulations,* New York: McGraw-Hill. [72]

Helson, H., Dworkin, R. S., and Michels, W. C., 1956, Quantitative denotations of common words as a function of background, *American Journal of Psychology,* **69,** 194–208.

Henry, W. F., 1949, The business executive: the psychodynamics of a social role, *American Journal of Sociology,* **54,** 286–291. [176, 237]

Hermann, L. *See* Hinckley, R. G.

Heron, W. *See* Becton, W. H.

Hertzler, V. B. *See* Lundberg, G. A.

Hertzog, H. *See* Cantril, H. [149]

Herman, M. G., 1963, Some personal characteristics related to foreign aid voting of Congressmen, mimeographed Master's thesis, Northwestern University, Evanston, Ill. [359, 360]

Herzberg, F., 1966, *Work and the nature of man,* Cleveland: World.

Herzog, E., and Lewis, H., 1970, Children in poor families; myths and realities, *American Journal of Orthopsychiatry,* **40,** 375–387.

Hess, R. D., and Shipman, V., 1965, Early experiences and the socialization of cognitive modes in children, *Child Development,* **36,** 869–886. [130, 136]

Heyns, R. W. *See* Walker, E. L.

Higbee, K. L., 1971, Expression of "Walter Mitty-ness" in actual behavior, *Journal of Personality and Social Psychology,* **20,** 416–422. [312]

Hilgard, E. R.

1942, Success in relation to level of aspiration, *School and Society,* **55,** 423–428.

1962, *Introduction to psychology,* New York: Harcourt Brace Jovanovich. [28]

Himmelfarb, S., 1972, Integration and attribution theories in personality impression formation, *Journal of Personality and Social Psychology,* **23,** 309–313. [192]

Himmelstein, P., and Kimbrough, W. W., 1963, A study of self-disclosure in the classroom, *Journal of Psychology,* **55,** 437–440. [206]

Himmelweit, H. T., 1955, Socio-economic background and personality, *International Social Science Bulletin,* **7,** 29–35. [163]

Hinckley, E. D., and Rethlingshafer, D., 1951, Value judgments of heights of men by college students, *Journal of Psychology,* **31,** 257–262. [72, 73]

Hinckley, R. G., and Hermann, L., 1951, *Group treatment in psychotherapy,* Minneapolis: University of Minnesota Press. [304]

Hing, A., 1970, The need for a united Asian-American front, *AION,* Spring, 9–11; reprinted in Buckhout, R. (ed.), *Toward social change,* New York: Harper & Row, p. 115. [349]

Hobbs, N., 1951, *Group centered psychotherapy in client centered therapy,* Boston: Houghton Mifflin. [304]

Hoblit, R. E. *See* Bonney, M. E.

Hodgson, R. C. *See* Lambert, W. E.

Hoffman, L. R., and Maier, N. R. F., 1961, Quality and acceptance of problem solutions by members of homogeneous and heterogeneous groups, *Journal of Abnormal and Social Psychology,* **62,** 401–407. [322]

Hofling, K. C., Brotzman, E., Dalrymple, S., Graves, N., and Pierce, C. M., 1966, An experimental study in nurse-physician relationship, *Journal of Nervous and Mental Disease,* **143,** 171–180. [241]

Hogan, H. P. *See* Carmichael, L.

Holden, C., 1972, TV violence: government study yields more evidence, no verdict, *Science,* **175,** 608–611. [118, 363]

Hollander, E. P.

1960, Competence and conformity in the acceptance of influence, *Journal of Abnormal and Social Psychology,* **61,** 365–370. [259, 260, 286]

See also Willis, R. H.

Hollingshead, A. B., 1949, *Elmtown's youth,* New York: Wiley. [215, 216]

Hollingshead, A. B., and Redlich, F. C., 1958, *Social class and mental illness: a community study,* New York: Wiley. [177]

Hollingworth, H. L., 1920, The psychology of functional neuroses, New York: Appleton. [262]

Holtzman, W. H. *See* Calvin, A. D.

Homans, G. C.

1950, *The human group,* New York: Harcourt Brace Jovanovich. [104, 324]

1961, *Social behavior: its elementary forms,* New York: Harcourt Brace Jovanovich. [230]

Hood, T. C., and Back, K. W., 1971, Self-disclosure and the volunteer: a source of bias in laboratory experiments, *Journal of Personality and Social Psychology,* **17,** 130–136. [21]

Horner, M. S., 1969, Woman's will to fail, *Psychology Today,* November. [152, 153, 176, 197]

Horney, Karen

1937, *The neurotic personality of our time,* New York: Norton.

1939, *New ways in psychoanalysis,* New York: Norton. [173]

1942, *Self-analysis,* New York: Norton.

1945, *Our inner conflicts,* New York: Norton.

1950, *Neurosis and human growth,* New York: Norton. [162]

Horowitz, A. E. *See* Brown, R. W.; Landar, H. J.

Horwitz, M., 1954, The recall of interrupted group tasks: an experimental study of individual motivation in relation to group goals, *Human Relations,* **7,** 3–38. [315]

Hosken, B. *See* Kagan, J.

Hovland, C. I., Campbell, E., and Brock, B. T., 1957, The effects of "commitment" on opinion change following communication. In C. I. Hovland (ed.), *The order of presentation in persuasion,* New Haven, Conn.: Yale University Press. [94]

Hovland, C. I., Harvey, O. J., and Sherif, M., 1957, Assimilation and contrast effects in reactions to communication and attitude changes, *Journal of Abnormal and Social Psychology,* **55,** 244–252.

Hovland, C. I., Lumsdaine, A. A., and Sheffield, F. D., 1949, *Experiments on mass communication,* Princeton, N.J.: Princeton University Press. [94]

Hovland, C. I., and Mandell, W., 1952, An experimental comparison of conclusion-drawing by the communicator and by the audience, *Journal of Abnormal and Social Psychology,* **47,** 581–588. [93]

Hovland, C. I., and Pritzker, H. A., 1957, Extent of opinion change as a function of amount of change advocated, *Journal of Abnormal and Social Psychology,* **54,** 257–261. [98]

Hovland, C. I., and Sherif, M., 1952, Judgmental phenomena and scales of attitude measurement: item displacement in Thurstone scales, *Journal of Abnormal and Social Psychology,* **47,** 822–832. [52]

Hovland, C. I., and Weiss, W., 1951, The influence of source credibility on communication effectiveness, *Public Opinion Quarterly,* **15,** 635–650. [96, 99]

Hovland, C. I. *See also* Hunt, D. E.; Janis, I. L.

Hoyt, M. F., Henley, M. D., and Collins, B. E., 1972, Studies in forced compliance: confluence of choice and consequent attitude change, *Journal of Personality and Social Psychology,* **23,** 205–210. [101]

Hraba, J., and Grant, G., 1970, Black is beautiful: a reexamination of racial preference and identification, *Journal of Personality and Social Psychology,* **16,** 398–402. [161]

Hudson, B. B., McDavid, J. W., and Roco, M., 1954, Response to the perception of threat. In symposium on human behavior in natural disasters, *American Psychologist,* **8,** 503. [342]

Hulin, W. S., and Katz, D., 1935, The Frois-Wittman pictures of facial expression, *Journal of Experimental Psychology,* **18,** 482–498. [210]

Hull, C. L.
1943, *Principles of behavior: an introduction to behavior theory,* New York: Appleton. [87]
1952, *A behavior system: an introduction to behavior theory concerning the individual organism,* New Haven, Conn.: Yale University Press. [87]

Humphrey, G., 1951, *Thinking, an introduction to its experimental psychology,* New York: Wiley. [79]

Humphrey, N. D. *See* Lee, A. McC.

Hunt, D. E., and Hovland, C. I., 1960, Order of consideration of different types of concepts, *Journal of Experimental Psychology,* **59,** 220–225. [79, 149]

Hunt, J. McV., 1961, *Intelligence and experience,* New York: Ronald.

Huntington, M. J., 1957, The development of professional self-image. In R. K. Merton, G. G. Render, and P. Kendall (eds.), *The student physician,* Cambridge, Mass.: Harvard University Press, 179–187. [161]

Hurwitz, J. I., Zander, A. F., and Hymowitch, B., 1960, Some effects of power and the relations among group members. In D. Cartwright and A. Zander (eds.), *Group dynamics,* New York: Harper & Row, 800–809. [164]

Inhelder, B., and Piaget, J., 1958, *The growth of logical thinking,* New York: Basic Books. [135]

Inkeles, A., Hanfmann, E., and Beier, H., 1958, Modal personality and adjustment to the Soviet socio-political system, *Human Relations,* **11,** 3–22. [137]

Insko, C. A.
1965, Verbal reinforcement of attitude, *Journal of Personality and Social Psychology,* **2,** 621–623. [91]
1967, *Theories of attitude change,* New York: Appleton.
See also Sampson, E. E.

Irwin, O. C., 1960, Infant speech: effect of systematic readings of stories, *Journal of Speech and Hearing Research,* **3,** 187–190. [136]

Israel, J. *See* French, J. R. P.; Schachter, S.

Ivy, M. *See* Heidbreder, Edna.

Jackson, J. M., 1959, Reference group processes in a formal organization, *Sociometry,* **22,** 307–327. [294, 304]

Jacobs, R. C., and Campbell, D. T., 1961, The perpetuation of an arbitrary tradition through several generations of laboratory microculture, *Journal of Abnormal and Social Psychology,* **62,** 649–658. [257]

Jacobs, R. L. *See* Leventhal, H.

Jacobsen, A. *See* Ruesch, J.

James, W.

1890, *Principles of psychology,* New York: Holt, Rinehart and Winston. [157, 164]

1902, *The varieties of religious experience,* London: Longmans. [159]

Janis, I. L.

1954, Personality correlates of susceptibility to persuasion, *Journal of Personality,* **22,** 504–518.

1955, Anxiety indices related to susceptibility to persuasion, *Journal of Abnormal and Social Psychology,* **51,** 663–667.

Janis, I. L., and Feshback, S.

1953, Effects of fear-arousing communications, *Journal of Abnormal and Social Psychology,* **48,** 78–92. [92]

1954, Personality differences associated with responsiveness to fear-arousing communications, *Journal of Personality,* **23,** 154–166.

See also Hovland, C. I.; King, B. T.; Lumsdaine, A. A.

Janis, I. L., and Field, P. B., 1959, Sex differences and personality factors related to persuasibility. In C. I. Hovland and I. L. Janis (eds.), *Personality and persuasibility,* New Haven, Conn.: Yale University Press. [103]

Janis, I. L., Kaye, D., and Kirschner, P., 1965, Facilitating effects of eating-while-reading on response to persuasive communication, *Journal of Personality and Social Psychology,* **1,** 17–27. [90]

Janis, I. L., and King, B. T., 1954, The influence of role-playing on opinion change, *Journal of Abnormal and Social Psychology,* **49,** 211–218. [100, 101, 103]

Janis, I. L., and Terwillinger, R. T., 1962, An experimental study of psychological resistance to fear arousing communications, *Journal of Abnormal and Social Psychology,* **65,** 403–410. [92]

Jenness, A., 1932, The role of discussion in changing opinion regarding a matter of fact, *Journal of Abnormal and Social Psychology,* **27,** 279–286. [263, 308]

Jennings, H. H., 1943, *Leadership and isolation: a study of personality in interpersonal relations,* New York: McKay. [58, 295]

Jensen, A. R., 1969, How much can we boost IQ and scholastic achievement? *Harvard Educational Review,* **39,** 1–123. [150]

Johnson, D. A., Porter, R. J., and Mateljan, P. A., 1971, Racial discrimination in apartment rentals, *Journal of Applied Social Psychology,* **1,** 364–377. [199]

Johnson, D. M., 1945, The "phantom anesthetist" of Mattoon: a field study of mass hysteria, *Journal of Abnormal and Social Psychology,* **40,** 175–186. [345]

Johnson, D. M., and Smith, H. C., 1953, Democratic leadership in the college classroom, *Psychology Monograph,* **67,** 361. [325]

Johnson, D. W., 1970, *The social psychology of education,* New York: Holt, Rinehart and Winston. [277]

Jones, E. E., and Davis, K. E., 1966, From acts to dispositions: the attribution process in person perception. In *Advances in experimental social psychology,* Vol. 2, 219–266, New York: Academic. [191]

Jones, E. E., Davis, K. E., and Gergen, K. J., 1961, Role playing variations and their informal value for person perception, *Journal of Abnormal and Social Psychology,* **63,** 302–310.

Jones, E. E., and Thibaut, J. W., 1958, Interaction goals as bases of inference in interpersonal perception. In R. Tagiuri and L. Petrullo (eds.), *Person perception and interpersonal behavior,* Stanford, Calif.: Stanford University Press. [223, 224]

Jones, M. C., and Mussen, P. H., 1958, Self conception, motivation, and interpersonal attitudes of early and late maturing girls, *Child Development,* **29,** 491–501. [163]

See also Mussen, P. H.

Jones, R. A., 1969, Choice, degree of dependence, and possibility of future dependence as determinants of helping behavior, *Proceedings,* 77th Annual Convention, APA, 381–382. [191]

Jordan, N., 1953, Behavioral forces that are a function of attitudes and cognitive organization, *Human Relations,* **6,** 273–278. [223]

Jospe, A., 1964, Jewish college students in the United States. In *American Jewish Yearbook,* vol. 65, The American Jewish Committee and the Jewish Publication Society of America. [148, 176, 195]

Jourard, S. M., 1964, *The transparent self,* New York: Van Nostrand Reinhold. [206]

Jung, C. G.

1923, *Psychological types,* New York: Harcourt Brace Jovanovich. [79]

1939, *The integration of the personality* (trans.), New York: Holt, Rinehart and Winston. [129]

Jung, J., 1971, *The experimenter's dilemma,* New York: Harper & Row. [20, 21]

Kagan, J., 1965, Individual differences in the resolution of response uncertainty, *Journal of Personality and Social Psychology,* **2,** 154–160. [76]

1970, The determinants of attention in the infant, *American Scientist,* **58,** 298–306.

1971, *Changes and continuity in infancy,* New York: Wiley.

Kagan, J., Hosken, B., and Watson, S., 1961, The child's symbolic conceptualization of the parents, *Child Development, 32,* 625–636.

Kagan, J., and Moss, H. A.
1960, The stability of positive and dependent behavior from childhood through adulthood, *Child Development, 31,* 577–591. [114, 152, 231, 234]
1962, *Birth to maturity,* New York: Wiley. [116]

Kagan, J., and Talbot, N. B., 1971, *Behavioral science in pediatric medicine,* Philadelphia: Saunders. [153, 161]

Kardiner, A., 1939, *The individual and his society,* New York: Columbia University Press. [137]

Karling, M., Coffman, T. L., and Walters, G., 1969, On the fading of social stereotypes: studies in three generations of college students, *Journal of Personality and Social Psychology, 13,* 1–16. [194]

Katz, D., 1951, Survey Research Center: an overview of the Human Relations Program. In H. Guetzkow (ed.), *Groups, leadership, and men,* Pittsburgh: Carnegie Press Publishers.

Katz, D., and Braly, K. W., 1933, Racial stereotypes of 100 college students, *Journal of Abnormal and Social Psychology, 28,* 280–290. [193]
See also Hulin, W. S.

Katz, D., and Stotland, E., 1959, A preliminary statement to a theory of attitude structure and change. In S. Koch (ed.), *Psychology: a study of a science, vol. 3, Formulations of the person and the social context,* New York: McGraw-Hill. [31]

Katz, E., and Lazersfeld, P. F., 1955. *Personal influence: the part played by people in the flow of mass communication,* New York: Free Press. [97]

Katz, I., Glucksberg, S., and Krauss, R., 1960, Need satisfaction and EPPS scores in married couples, *Journal of Consulting Psychology, 24,* 205–208. [224]

Katz, I., Goldstone, J., and Benjamin, L., 1958, Behavior and productivity in biracial work groups, *Human Relations, 11,* 123–141.

Katz, K., Maccoby, N., and Morse, E., 1950, *Productivity, supervision, and morale in an office situation,* Ann Arbor: University of Michigan Institute for Social Research. [286]

Kelley, H. H.
1950, The warm-cold variable in first impressions of persons, *Journal of Personality, 18,* 431–439.
1951, Communication in experiment created hierarchies, *Human Relations, 4,* 39–56. [286, 294]
1971, Moral evaluation, *American Psychologist, 26,* 293–300. [192]
1972a, Attribution theory in social psychology. In D. Levine (ed.), *Nebraska Symposium on Motivation,* Lincoln: University of Nebraska Press. [191]
1972b, Causal schemata and the attribution process. Morristown, N.J.: General Learning Press. [191]
See also Dittes, J. E.; Thibaut, J. W.

Kelley, H. H., and Lamb, T. W., 1957, Certainty of judgment and resistance to social influence, *Journal of Abnormal and Social Psychology, 55,* 137–139. [274]

Kelley, H. H., and Woodruff, C. L., 1956, Member's reaction to apparent group approval of a counter-norm communication, *Journal of Abnormal and Social Psychology, 52,* 67–74.

Kelly, G. A., 1955, *The psychology of personal constructs,* 2 vols., New York: Norton. [101]

Kelman, H. C.
1958, Compliance, identification, and internalization, *Journal of Conflict Resolution, 2,* 51–60. [267]
1965, (ed.), *International behavior,* New York: Holt, Rinehart and Winston. [359, 365]
1967, Human use of human subjects: the problem of deception in social psychological experiments, *Psychological Bulletin, 67,* 1–11. [22]

Kendler, T. S., 1962, Development of mediating responses in children. In J. C. Wright and J. Kagan (eds.), Basic cognitive processes in children, *Monograph, Society for Research in Child Development, 28,* No. 2, 33–52. [79]

Kent, G. H., and Rosanoff, A. J., 1910, A study of association in insanity, *American Journal of Insanity, 67,* 37–96. [80]

Kerckhoff, A. C., and Davis, K. E., 1962, Value consensus and need complementarity in mate selection, *American Sociological Review, 27,* 295–303. [224]

Kerr, W. *See* Speroff, B.

Kiesler, C. A., and Kiesler, S. A., 1964, Role of forewarning in persuasive communication, *Journal of Abnormal and Social Psychology, 68,* 547–549. [95]

Kiesler, S. A. *See* Kiesler, C. A.

Killian, L. M.
1952, The significance of multiple group membership in disaster, *American Journal of Sociology, 57,* 309–314. [342]
See also Turner, R. H.

King, B. T., 1959, Relationships between susceptibility to opinion change and child-rearing practices. In C. I. Hovland and I. L. Janis (eds.), *Personality and persuasibility,* New Haven, Conn.: Yale University Press. [103]

See also Janis, I. L.

King, B. T., and Janis, I. L., 1956, Comparison of the effectiveness of improvised versus non-improvised role playing in producing opinion changes, *Human Relations,* **9,** 177–186.

Kinsey, A. C., Pomeroy, W. B., and Martin, C. E., 1948, *Sexual behavior in the human male,* Philadelphia: Saunders. [143, 225]

Kinsey, A. C., Pomeroy, W. B., Martin, C. E., and Gebhard, P. H., 1953, *Sexual behavior in the human female,* Philadelphia: Saunders. [225]

Kitt, A. S. *See* Merton, R. K.

Klapman, J. W.
1946, *Group psychotherapy: theory and practice,* New York: Grune & Stratton. [304]
1950, The case for didactic group psychotherapy, *Diseases of the Nervous System,* **9,** 35–41. [304]

Klein, S. D., 1970, Psychologist at City Hall —a problem of identity, *American Psychologist,* **25,** 195–199.

Kleiner, A. *See* Pepitone, A.

Kleitman, N., 1952, Sleep, *Scientific American,* **187,** 34–38. [141]

Klineberg, O., 1964, *The human dimension in international relations,* New York: Holt, Rinehart and Winston. [28, 130, 131, 132, 359]

Kluckhohn, C., and Leighton, D., 1946, *The Navajo,* Cambridge, Mass.: Harvard University Press. [132]

Kniffin, C. W. *See* Bitterman, M. E.

Knight, R. C., Sheposh, J. P., and Bryson, R. B., 1974, College student marijuana use and societal alienation, *Journal of Health and Social Behavior,* in press.

Knox, R. E., and Inkster, J. A., 1968, Postdecision dissonance at post time, *Journal of Personality and Social Psychology,* **8,** 319–323. [102]

Koch, S., 1971, *Psychology as science.* Invited address, University of Canterbury, England, September, 1971.

Kogan, N. *See* Tagiuri, R.; Wallach, M. A.

Kohlberg, L., 1966, Moral education in the schools: a developmental view. *School Review,* **74,** 1–30.
1969, The cognitive-developmental approach to socialization. In D. A. Goslin (ed.), *Handbook of socialization research and theory,* Chicago: Rand-McNally, 347–480. [169]

Kollat, D. T., and Willet, R. P., 1967, Customer impulse purchasing behavior, *Journal of Marketing Research,* **4,** 21–31. [337]

Komarovsky, M., 1946, Cultural contradictions and sex roles, *American Journal of Sociology,* **52,** 184–189. [173]

Krauss, R. *See* Katz, I.

Krauss, R. M., 1963, Motivational and attitudinal factors in interpersonal bargaining, *American Psychologist,* **18,** 392 [abstract]. [365]

Krech, D., Crutchfield, R. S., and Ballachey, E. L., 1962, *Individual in society,* New York: McGraw-Hill. [267]

Kremers, J., 1960, *Scientific psychology and naïve psychology,* Nijmegen, Netherlands: Drukkerij Gebrakt Janssen N. V. [204]

Kriyanda, 1970, Cooperative communities: how to start them and why. San Francisco: Ananda Publications. [352]

Ktsanes, T., 1955, Mate selection on the basis of personality types: a study utilizing empirical typology of personality, *American Sociol. Review,* **20,** 547–551. [223, 224]

See also Winch, R. F.

Ktsanes, V. *See* Winch, R. F.

Kudirka, M. Z. *See* Leventhal, H.

Kuhlen, R. G., and Bretsch, H. S., 1947, Sociometric status and personal problems of adolescents, *Sociometry,* **10,** 122–132. [212]

Kukla, A., 1972, Attribution and achievement, *Journal of Personality and Social Psychology,* **21,** 166–174.

LaBarre, W.
1946, *Some observations on character structure in the Orient: the Chinese, Psychiatry,* **9,** 375–395. [137]
1947, The cultural basis of emotions and gestures, *Journal of Personality,* **16,** 49–68. [129]

L'Abate, L., and L'Abate, B., 1973, *Love in marital and familial therapy,* Atlanta: Georgia State University Institute for Psychological Services (mimeographed). [173, 225]

Labov, W., 1964, Stages in the acquisition of standard English, in Shuy, R. (ed.), *Social dialects and language learning,* Champaign, Ill.: National Council of Teachers of English.

Lamb, T. W. *See* Kelley, H. H.

Lambert, P., Miller, D. M., Wiley, D. E., 1962, Experimental folklore and experimentation: the study of programmed learning in the Wanwatosa Public Schools, *Journal of Educational Research,* **55,** 485–494.

Lambert, R. D., and Bressler, N., 1956, *Indian students on an American campus,* Minneapolis: University of Minnesota Press. [367]

Lambert, W. E., Hodgson, R. C., Gardner, R.C., and Fillenbaum, S., 1960, Evaluational reaction to spoken languages, *Journal of Abnormal and Social Psychology,* **60,** 44–51. [196]

Lambert, W. E., Libman, E., and Poser, E. G., 1960, The effect of increased saliency of membership group on pain tolerance, *Journal of Personality,* **28,** 350–357. [259]

Lambert, W. W., Triandis, L. M., and Wolf, M. M., 1959, Some correlates of beliefs in the malevolence and benevolence of supernatural beings: a cross-societal study, *Journal of Abnormal and Social Psychology,* **58,** 162–169. [117]

Landar, H. J., Ervin, S. M., and Horowitz, A. E., 1960, Navaho color categories, *Language,* **36,** 368–382. [132]

Landis, C., 1924, Studies of emotional reactions, II, General behavior and facial expression, *Journal of Comparative Psychology,* **4,** 447–509. [41, 210]

Langham, P. *See* Haythorn, W.

Lantz, D., and Stefflre, V., 1964, Language and cognition revisited, *Journal of Abnormal and Social Psychology,* **69,** 471–481. [128]

LaPiere, R. T., 1938, *Collective behavior,* New York: McGraw-Hill. [333]

Latané, B., and Darley, J. M., 1968, Group inhibition of bystander intervention in emergencies, *Journal of Personality and Social Psychology,* **10,** 215–221. [235]

Latané, B., and Rodin, J., 1969, A lady in distress: Inhibiting effects of friends and strangers on bystander intervention, *Journal of Experimental Social Psychology,* **5,** 189–202. [235]

Laughlin, P. R., Branch, L. G., and Johnson, H. H., 1969, Individual versus triadic performance on a unidimensional complementary task as a function of initial ability level, *Journal of Personality and Social Psychology,* **12,** 144–150. [322]

Lawler, E. E., 1968, Equity theory as a predictor of productivity and work quality, *Psychological Bulletin,* **70,** 596–610. [231]

Lazarsfeld, P. F., Berelson, B., and Gaudet, H., 1944, *The people's choice,* New York: Meredith. [89, 335]

Lazarsfeld, P. F. *See also* Katz, E.

Leavitt, H. J., 1951, Some effects of certain communication patterns on group performance, *Journal of Abnormal and Social Psychology,* **46,** 38–50. [287, 288, 323]

LeBon, G., 1895, *Psychologie des foules,* Paris: Odeon (trans., *The Crowd,* London: Unwin). [337, 338]

Lee, A. McC., and Humphrey, N. D., 1943, *Race riot,* New York: Dryden. [340]

Lefkowitz, M., Blake, R. R., and Mouton, J. S., 1955, Status factors in pedestrian violation of traffic signals, *Journal of Abnormal and Social Psychology,* **51,** 706–708. [273]

Leichty, M. M., 1963, Family attitudes and self-concept in Vietnamese and U.S. children. *American Journal of Orthopsychiatry,* **33,** 38–50. [163]

Leighton, D. *See* Kluckhohn, C.

Lenneberg, E. H. *See* Brown, R. W.

Lesser, G. S., and Abelson, R. P., 1959, Personality correlates of persausibility in children. In C. I. Hovland and I. L. Janis (eds.), *Personality and persuasibility,* New Haven, Conn.: Yale University Press, 187–206. [103]

Lessing, E. E., and Zagorin, S. W., 1972, Black power ideology and college students' attitudes toward their own and other racial groups, *Journal of Personality and Social Psychology,* **21,** 61–73. [163]

Leventhal, G. S., and Anderson, D., 1970, Self-interest and the maintenance of equity, *Journal of Personality and Social Psychology,* **1,** 57–62.

Leventhal, G. S., and Bergman, J. T., 1969, Self-depriving behavior as a response to unprofitable inequity, *Journal of Experimental Social Psychology,* **5,** 153–171. [230, 231]

Leventhal, G. S., Weiss, T., and Long, G., 1969, Equity, reciprocity, and reallocating rewards in the dyad, *Journal of Personality and Social Psychology,* **13,** 300–305.

Leventhal, G. S., and Whiteside, H. D., 1973, Equity and the use of reward to elicit high performance, *Journal of Personality and Social Psychology,* **25,** 75–83. [230]

Leventhal, H.

1957, Cognitive processes in interpersonal predictions, *Journal of Abnormal and Social Psychology,* **55,** 176–180. [205]

1967, Fear—for your health, *Psychology Today,* **1,** 54–58. [92]

Leventhal, H., and Singer, R., 1966, Affect arousal and positioning of recommendations in persuasive communication, *Journal of Personality and Social Psychology,* **4,** 137–146 [92]

Levi, M., 1956, *"Group atmosphere" and completion of survival instructor training,* Reno, Nev.: Stead Air Force Base, Crew Research Laboratory, February. [302]

Levin, H., Baldwin, A. L., Gallwey, M., and Paivio, A., 1960, Audience stress, personality and speech, *Journal of Abnormal and Social Psychology,* **61,** 469–473. [309]

Levine, J., and Butler, J., 1952, Lecture versus group decision in changing behavior, *Journal of Applied Psychology,* **36,** 29–33. [260]

LeVine, R. A., 1961, Anthropology and the study of conflict: introduction, *Journal of Conflict Resolution,* **5,** 3–15. [365]

Levinson, C., 1963, Mood, perceived similarity, and the judgment of mood of others, *Journal of Social Psychology,* **61,** 99–110.

Levinson, D. J. *See* Adorno, T. W.

Lewin, K., 1936, *Principles of topological psychology,* New York: McGraw-Hill.

Lewin, K. (*Cont.*)

1939, Field theory and experiment in social psychology: concepts and methods, *American Journal of Sociology,* **44,** 868–897. [293]

1947, Group decision and social change. In T. M. Newcomb, and E. L. Hartley (eds.), *Readings in social psychology,* New York: Holt, Rinehart and Winston. [259, 262, 318]

1951, *Field theory in social science,* New York: Harper & Row. [26, 317]

Lewis, H. B., and Franklin, M., 1944, An experimental study of the role of the ego in work, II, The significance of task orientation in work, *Journal of Experimental Psychology,* **33,** 195–215. [315]

Libman, E. See Lambert, W. E.

Lieberman, B., 1960, Human behavior in a strictly determined 3 × 3 matrix game, *Behavioral Science,* **5,** 317–322.

1962, Experimental studies of conflict in some two-person and three-person games. In J. H. Criswell, H. Solomon, and P. Suppes (eds.), *Mathematical models in small group processes,* Stanford, Calif.: Stanford University Press, [62]

Lieberman, M. A., Yalom, I. D., and Miles, M., 1972, *Encounter: confrontations in self and interpersonal awareness,* New York: Macmillan. [346]

Lieberman, S., 1956, The effects of changes in roles on the attitudes of role occupants, *Human Relations,* **9,** 385–402. [25]

Lieberson, S., and Silverman, A. R., 1965, The precipitants and underlying conditions of race riots, *American Sociological Review,* **30,** 887–898. [341]

Liebert, R. M. and Baron, R. A., 1971, Short term effects of televised aggression on children's aggressive behavior. In R. A. Baron and R. M. Liebert, *Human social behavior,* Homewood, Ill.: Dorsey. [118]

Likert, R. A.

1932, A technique for the measurement of attitudes, *Archives of Psychology,* No. 140. [52]

1961, *Organization theory,* New York: McGraw-Hill.

Linton, R., 1945, *The cultural background of personality,* New York: Appleton. [206, 280]

Lippitt, R. O., 1940, An experimental study of the effect of democratic and authoritarian group atmosphere, *University of Iowa studies in child welfare,* **16,** 43–195. [291, 296]

See also Bradford, L. P.: Lewin, K.; White, R. K.

Lippitt, R. O., Polansky, N., Redl, F., and Rosen, S., 1952, The dynamics of power, *Human Relations,* **5,** 37–64. [240, 244]

Loeb, M. B. See Ruesch, J.

Loomis, C. P., and Proctor, C., 1950, The relationship between choice status and economic status in social systems, *Sociometry,* **13,** 307–313. [212]

Loomis, C. P. See also Proctor, C. H.

Loomis, J. L., 1959, Communication, the development of trust, and cooperative behavior, *Human Relations,* **12,** 305–315. [242]

Lorge, I. See Tuckman, J.

Lott, A. J., Aponte, J. F., Lott, B. E., and McGinley, W. H., 1969, The effect of delayed reward on the development of positive attitudes toward persons, *Journal of Experimental Social Psychology,* **5,** 101–113.

Lott, A. J. See also Malof, M.

Lowell, E. L. See McClelland, D. C.

Luce, R. D., and Raiffa, H., 1957, *Games and decisions,* New York: Wiley. [62]

Luchins, A. S.

1944, On agreement with another's judgment, *Journal of Abnormal and Social Psychology,* **39,** 97–111.

1945, Social influences on perception of complex drawings, *Journal of Social Psychology,* **21,** 257–263.

1957a, Experimental attempts to minimize the impact of first impressions. In C. I. Hovland et al. (eds.), *The order of presentation in persuasion,* New Haven, Conn.: Yale University Press. [202]

1957b, Primacy-recency in impression formation. In C. I. Hovland et al. (eds.), *The order of presentation in persuasion,* New Haven, Conn.: Yale University Press. [202]

1964, *Group therapy: a guide,* New York: Random House. [30, 304]

Luchins, A. S., Aumack, L., and Dickman, H., 1960, *A manual in group psychotherapy,* Roseburg, Ore.: Veterans Hospital. [353]

Lumsdaine, A. A., and Janis, I. L., 1953, Resistance to "counterpropaganda" produced by one-sided and two-sided "propaganda" presentations, *Public Opinion Quarterly,* **17,** 311–318. [94]

Lumsdaine, A. A. See also Hovland, C. I.

Lund, F. H., 1925, The psychology of belief, *Journal of abnormal and social Psychology,* **20,** 174–196. [94]

Lundberg, G. A., and Dickson, L. 1965, Selective Association of ethnic groups in a high school. New York: International Association for Advancement of Ethnology and Eugenics. [354]

Lundberg, G. A., Hertzler, V. B., and Dickson, L., 1949, Attraction patterns in a university, *Sociometry,* **12,** 158–169. [215]

Lupfer, Michael B., 1964, Role enactment as a function of orientation, expectations, and duration of interaction, Ph.D. dissertation,

Coral Gables: University of Miami. [63, 282]

McBride, D., *See* Schachter, S.
McBride, P. D., 1958, Studies in conformity and yielding, IX, The influence of confidence upon resistance of perceptual judgment to group pressure. Office of Naval Research Contract NR-159-170, University of California, Berkeley, Technical Report No. 10. *See also* Tuddenham, R. D. [274]
McCandless, B. R.
  1942, Changing relationships between dominance and social acceptability during group democratization, *American Journal of Orthopsychiatry*, **12**, 529–535. [300]
  1961, *Children and adolescents.* New York: Holt, Rinehart and Winston. [145, 325]
  1967, *Children: behavior and development,* 2nd ed., New York: Holt, Rinehart and Winston. [176]
McCann, W. H., and Almada, A. A., 1950, Roundtable psychotherapy: a technique in group psychotherapy, *Journal of Consulting Psychology*, **14**, 431–435. [304]
McCarthy, D., 1954, Language development in children. In L. Carmichael [ed.], *Manual of child psychology*, 2nd ed., New York: Wiley. [135, 136]
McClelland, D. C.
  1951, *Personality,* New York: Holt, Rinehart and Winston.
  1961, *The achieving society,* New York: Van Nostrand Reinhold. [125]
McClelland, D. C., and Watson, R. I., 1973, Power motivation and risk-taking, *Journal of Personality*, **41**, 121–139.
McClelland, D. C., Atkinson, J. W., Clark, R. A., and Lowell, E. L., 1953, *The achievement motive,* New York: Appleton. [175]
McCord, J., and McCord, W., 1958, The effect of parental role model on criminality, *Journal of Social Issues,* **3**, 66–75. [122]
McCord, W. *See* McCord, J.
McDavid, J. W.
  1959a, Some relationships between social reinforcement and scholastic achievement, *Journal of Consulting Psychology*, **23**, 151–154. [114]
  1959b, Imitative behavior in preschool children, *Psychological Monographs,* **73**, 16 (whole number 486). [246]
  1959c, Personality and situational determinants of conformity, *Journal of Abnormal and Social Psychology*, **58**, 241–246.
  1962a, Effects of ambiguity of environmental cues upon learning to imitate, *Journal of Abnormal and Social Psychology*, **65**, 381–386. [247]

1962b, The incentive and reward value of social approval and disapproval, Office of Naval Research Contract ONR-840 (22), Technical Report No. 2, Coral Gables: University of Miami.
  1964, Effects of ambiguity of imitative cues upon learning by observation, *Journal of Social Psychology*, **62**, 165–174.
  1965a, Approval-seeking motivation and the volunteer subject, *Journal of Personality and Social Psychology*, **2**, 115–117. [21, 114]
  1965b, The sex variable in conforming behavior, Office of Naval Research Contract ONR-400(08), Technical Report No. 8.
  1966a, Personality factors in blind imitation and observational learning, unpublished manuscript, Coral Gables: University of Miami. [246]
  1966b, Conforming behavior as a function of respect and attraction for the source of influence (abstract), Office of Naval Research Contract 400(08), final report, Coral Gables: University of Miami. *See also* Harari, H.; Hudson, B. B.; Sistrunk, F. [269]
McDavid, J. W., and Harari, H., 1966, Stereotyping of names and popularity in grade school children, *Child Development*, **37**, 453–459. [196, 214, 244, 272]
McDavid, J. W., and Harari, H., 1968, *Social psychology: individuals, groups, societies,* New York: Harper & Row.
McDavid, J. W., and McCandless, B. R., 1962, Psychological theory, research, and juvenile delinquency, *Journal of Criminal Law, Criminology, and Police Science*, **53**, 1–14.
McDavid, J. W., and Sistrunk, F., 1964, Personality correlates of two kinds of conforming behavior, *Journal of Personality*, **32**, 421–435. [247, 269, 275]
McDougall, W.
  1908, *Introduction to social psychology,* London: Methuen. [30, 338]
  1925, *The indestructible union: rudiments of political science for the American citizen.* Boston: Little, Brown. [338]
McEachern, A. W. *See* Gross, N.
McEvoy, J., Chesler, M., and Schmuck, R., 1967, Content analysis of a superpatriot protest, *Social Problems*, **14**, 455–463.
McGarvey, H., 1943, Anchoring effects in absolute judgment of verbal material, *Archives of Psychology,* Number 281. [72]
McGinnies, E. *See* Altman, I.; Mitnick, L. I.; Postman, L. J.
McGranahan, D. V., and Wayne, I., 1948, German and American traits reflected in popular drama, *Human Relations*, **1**, 429–455. [124]

McGrath, J. E. *See* Havron, M. D.

McGrew, J. M., 1967, How "open" are multiple-dwelling units? *Journal of Social Psychology,* **72,** 223–226. [199]

McGuire, W. J., 1966, Attitudes and opinions, *Annual Review of Psychology,* **17,** 475–514.

1969, Suspiciousness of experimenter's intent. In R. Rosenthal and R. L. Rosnow (eds.), *Artifact in behavioral research,* New York: Academic. [22]

McGuire, W. J., and Papageorgis, D., 1961, The relative efficacy of various types of prior belief-defense in producing immunity against persuasion, *Journal of Abnormal and Social Psychology,* **62,** 327–337. [94, 95]

1962, Effectiveness of forewarning in developing resistance to persuasion, *Public Opinion Quarterly,* **26,** 24–34. [90, 94, 95]

Mackay, C., 1932, *Extraordinary popular delusions and the madness of crowds,* New York: Farrar, Strauss. [345, 346]

McKinney, J. C., 1948, An educational application of a two-dimensional sociometric test, *Sociometry,* **11,** 356–367. [58]

McKnight, R. K. *See* Bennet, J. W.

McMillen, D. L., 1971, Transgression, self-image, and compliant behavior, *Journal of Personality and Social Psychology,* **20,** 176–179. [235, 236]

Maccoby, E., 1966, *The development of sex differences,* Stanford, Calif.: Stanford University Press. [152, 176, 335, 363]
See also Sears, R. R.

Maccoby, E., and Maccoby, N., 1954, The interview. In G. Lindzey (ed.), *Handbook of social psychology,* Reading, Mass.: Addison-Wesley. [45]

Maccoby, E., and Wilson, W. C., 1957, Identification and observational learning from films, *Journal of Abnormal and Social Psychology,* **55,** 76–87. [119]

MacDonald, A. P., 1970, Anxiety, affiliation, and social isolation, *Developmental Psychology,* **3,** 242–254. [218]

Malinowski, B., 1927, *Sex and repression in savage society,* New York: Harcourt Brace Jovanovich. [27]

Malof, M., and Lott, A. J., 1962, Ethnocentrism and the acceptance of Negro support in a group pressure situation, *Journal of Abnormal and Social Psychology,* **65,** 254–258. [274]

Mandell, W. *See* Hovland, C. I.

Mangel, C., 1970, Sometimes we feel we're already dead, *Look,* June 2, pp. 38–43. [349]

Manis, M., 1955, Social interaction and the self concept, *Journal of Abnormal and Social Psychology,* **51,** 362–370. [159, 160]

Mann, R. D., 1961, Dimensions of individual performance in small groups under task and social-emotional conditions, *Journal of Abnormal and Social Psychology,* **62,** 674–682.
See also Strodtbeck, F. L. [284, 300]

March, J. G., and Simon, H. A., 1958, *Organization,* New York: Wiley. [314]

Markle, S. M., 1969, *Good frames and bad: a grammar of frame writing,* New York: Wiley. [41]

Marlowe, D. *See* Crowne, D. P.; Minas, J. S.

Marlowe, K., 1965, *The male homosexual,* Los Angeles: Sherbourne. [350]

Marquis, D. P., 1941, Learning in the neonate: the modification of behavior under three feeding schedules, *Journal of Experimental Psychology,* **29,** 263–281. [141]

Martens, R., 1969, Effect of an audience on learning and performance of a complex motor skill, *Journal of Personality and Social Psychology,* **12,** 252–260. [310]

Martin, J. G., 1964, Racial ethnocentrism and judgment of beauty, *Journal of Social Psychology,* **63,** 59–63. [214]

Marx, K., and Engels, F., 1847, *The Communist manifesto,* Samuel H. Beer, ed., New York: Appleton. [175]

Maslow, A. H.

1943, A theory of human motivation, *Psychological Review,* **50,** 370–396. [172]

1954, *Motivation and personality,* New York: Harper & Row. [31, 87, 172, 235]

1968, *Toward a psychology of being,* 2nd ed., New York: Van Nostrand Reinhold. [31, 171, 172, 235]

Mason, W. S. *See* Gross, N.

Masters, R., and Johnson, V., 1966, *Human sexual response,* Boston: Little, Brown. [143, 225]

Maucorps, P. H. *See* Schachter, S.

Maw, W. H., and Maw, E. W., 1965, *Personal and social variables differentiating children with high and low curiosity,* ED 003 274, Cooperative Research Project No. 1511, Newark: University of Delaware. [175]

Maxey, D. R., 1970, America's colonial service, *Look,* June 2, p. 35. [349]

May, R.

1953, *Man's search for himself,* New York: Norton. [171, 225, 235]

1969a, *Existential psychology* (2nd ed.), New York: Random House. [31, 235]

1969b, *Love and will,* New York: Norton. [31, 225, 235]

Mayo, E., 1933, *The human problems of an industrial organization,* New York: Macmillan. [104, 324]

Mead, G. H., 1934, *Mind, self, and society: from the standpoint of a social behaviorist,* Chicago: University of Chicago Press. [157, 159]

Mead, M.

1935, *Sex and temperament,* New York: Morrow. [234]

1951, The study of national character, in D. Turner and H. D. Lasswell (eds.), *The policy sciences,* Stanford, Calif.: Stanford University Press.

Meade, R. D., 1967, An experimental study of leadership in India, *Journal of Social Psychology,* **72,** 35–43. [292, 297]

Meade, R. D., and Whittaker, J. O., 1967, A cross-cultural study of authoritarianism, *Journal of Social Psychology,* **72,** 3–7.

Meadow, A., Parnes, S. J., and Reese, H. W., 1959, Influence of brainstorming instruction and problem sequence on a creative problem-solving test, *Journal of Applied Psychology,* **43,** 413–416. [321]

Medley, D. M., 1969, OSCAR goes to nursery school: a new technique for recording pupil behavior, paper presented at annual meetings of American Educational Research Association. [40]

Medley, D. M., Quirk, T., Schluck, C. G., and Ames, N. P., 1971, *The personal record of school experience: a manual for PROSE records,* Princeton, N.J.: Educational Testing Service.

Meeker, M. *See* Warner, W. L.

Mehrabian, A., and Diamond, S. G., 1971, Effects of furniture arrangement, props, and personality on social interaction, *Journal of Personality and Social Psychology,* **20,** 18–30. [127]

Meirowitz, B. *See* Carter, L. F.

Merei, F., 1949, Group leadership and institutionalization, *Human Relations,* **2,** 23–39. [298]

Merrill, J. C., and Lowenstein, R. L., 1971, *Media, messages, and men,* New York: McKay. [335, 336]

Merker, F., 1904, *Die Masai,* Leipzig: Phillipp Recalm. [133]

Merton, R. K., and Kitt, A. S., 1950, Contributions to the theory of reference group behavior. In R. K. Merton and P. F. Lazarsfeld (eds.), *Continuities in social research: studies in the scope and method of the "American Soldier,"* New York: Free Press. [177, 357]

Michels, W. C. *See* Nelson, H.

Michotte, A., 1954, *La perception de la causalité,* 2nd ed., Louvain, France: Publications Universitaires de Louvain. [191]

Milgram, N. A., and Helper, M., 1961, The social desirability set in individual and grouped self-ratings, *Journal of Consulting Psychology,* **25,** 91.

Milgram, S., 1963, Behavioral study of obedience, *Journal of Abnormal and Social Psychology,* **67,** 371–378. [240]

1964a, Group pressure and action against a person, *Journal of Abnormal and Social Psychology,* **69,** 137–143. [270]

1964b, Issues in the study of obedience: a reply to Baumrind, *American Psychologist,* **19,** 848–852.

1969, Lost-letter technique, *Psychology Today,* **2,** 30–33.

1970, The experience of living in cities, *Science,* **167,** No. 3934, 1461–68. [49, 59, 127, 235, 237]

Milgram, S., Bickman, L., and Berkowitz, L., 1969, Note on the drawing power of crowds of different size, *Journal of Personality and Social Psychology,* **13,** 79–82. [334]

Miller, D. R., and Swanson, G. E.

1958, *The changing American parent: a study in the Detroit area,* New York: Wiley.

1960, *Inner conflict and defense,* New York: Holt, Rinehart and Winston.

Miller, G. A., 1951, *Language and communication,* New York: McGraw-Hill. [77]

Miller, N. E., 1948, Studies of fear as an acquirable drive, I, Fear as motivation and fear-reduction as reinforcement in the learning of new responses, *Journal of Experimental Psychology,* **38,** 89–101. *See also* Dollard, J.

Miller, N. E., and Dollard, J., 1941, *Social learning and imitation,* New Haven, Conn.: Yale University Press. [31, 118, 245, 338]

Millett, K., 1970, *Sexual politics,* Garden City, N.Y.: Doubleday. [153]

Mills, J., Aronson, E., and Robinson, J., 1959, Selectivity in exposure to information, *Journal of Abnormal and Social Psychology,* **59,** 250–253. [102]

Mills, J., and Jellison, J. M., 1967, Effect on opinion change of how desirable the communication is to the audience the communicator addressed, *Journal of Personality and Social Psychology,* **5,** 459–463. [96, 97]

1968, Effect on opinion change of similarity between the communicator and the audience he addressed, *Journal of Personality and Social Psychology,* **9,** 153–156.

Mills, J. *See also* Aronson, E.; Ehrlich, D.

Mills, T. M.

1953, Power relations in three person groups, *American Sociological Review,* **18,** 351–357. [289]

1954, The coalition pattern in three person groups, *American Sociological Review,* **19,** 657–667. [289]

1956, Developmental processes in three person groups, *Human Relations,* **9,** 343–354. [289]

Mills, T. M., et al., 1957, Group structure and the newcomer: an experimental study of group expansion, *Univer. Oslo Inst. Sociol. Stud. in Sociol.,* No. 1. [289]

Mintz, A., 1951, Non-adaptive group behavior, *Journal of Abnormal Social Psychology,* **46,** 150–159. [343, 345]

Mischel, W., 1958, Preference for delayed reinforcement: an experimental study of a cultural observation, *Journal of Abnormal and Social Psychology,* **56,** 57–61. [88]
1968, *Personality and assessment,* New York: Wiley.

Mishler, A. L., 1965, Personal contact in international exchanges. In H. C. Kelman (ed.), *International behavior,* New York: Holt, Rinehart and Winston. [366]

Moede, W., 1920, *Experimentelle Massenpsychologie,* Leipzig: Hirzel. [308]

Moore, L. M., and Baron, R. A., 1969, Effects of wage inequity on work attitudes and performance, *Proceedings,* 77th Annual Convention, APA, 361–362.

Moreno, J. L.
1934, *Who shall survive?* Washington, D.C.: Nervous and Mental Disease Publishing Co. [12, 58]
1945 (ed.), *Group psychotherapy,* Beacon, N.Y.: Beacon House. [326]
1946, *Psychodrama,* Beacon, N.Y.: Beacon House. [303, 304]

Morse, S. J., and Gergen, K. J., 1970, Social comparison, self-consistency, and the concept of self, *Journal of Personality and Social Psychology,* **16,** 148–156.

Moss, H. A. *See* Kagan, J.

Mouton, J. S. *See* Blake, R. R.; Coleman, J. F.; Freed, A. M.; Helson, H.; Lefkowitz, M.

Mowrer, O. H., 1950, *Learning theory and personality dynamics: selected papers,* New York: Ronald. [89]

Munn, N. L., 1940, The effect of the knowledge of the situation upon judgments of emotion from facial expression, *Journal of Abnormal and Social Psychology,* **35,** 324–338. [210, 211]

Munsterberg, G., 1914, *Psychology and social parity,* New York: Doubleday. [263, 308]

Murstein, B. I., 1961, The complementary need hypothesis in newlyweds and middle-aged married couples, *Journal of Abnormal and Social Psychology,* **63,** 194–197. [224]

Mussen, P. H., 1950, Some personality and social factors related to changes in children's attitudes toward Negroes, *Journal of Abnormal and Social Psychol.,* **45,** 423–441. [98]
See also Jones, M. C.; Scodel, A.

Mussen, P. H., and Jones, M. C., 1957, Self conception, motivation, and interpersonal attitudes of early- and late-maturing boys, *Child Development,* **28,** 243–256. [163]

Myrdal, G., 1944, *An American dilemma,* New York: Harper & Row. [339]

Nadler, E. B., 1959, Yielding, authoritarianism, and authoritarian ideology regarding groups, *Journal of Abnormal and Social Psychology,* **58,** 408–410. [180, 274]

Naegele, K. D., 1958, Friends and acquaintances: an exploration of some social distinctions, *Harvard Educational Review,* **28,** 232–252. [211, 214]

NCOA, 1970, Position paper; *Recommendations for action in the 70's,* The National Council of the Aging, Washington, D.C. 20036. [350]

Nelson, D. *See* Byrne, D.

Newcomb, T. M.
1950, *Social psychology,* New York: Dryden. [31, 206, 254, 255, 280]
1953, An approach to the study of communicative acts, *Psychological Review,* **60,** 393–404. [75]
1956, The prediction of interpersonal attraction, *American Psychologist,* **11,** 575–586.
1957, *Personality and social change: attitude formation in a student community,* New York: Holt, Rinehart and Winston. [255]
1961, *The acquaintance process,* New York: Holt, Rinehart and Winston. [216, 218, 220]
1963, Persistence and regression of changed attitudes: long-range studies, *Journal of Social Issues,* **19,** 3–14. [31, 97, 164, 215, 216, 218]
See also Chowdhry, K.; Maccoby, E.; Swanson, G. E.

Newcomb, T. M., and Hartley, E. L. (eds.), 1947, *Readings in social psychology,* New York: Holt, Rinehart and Winston. [255, 261]

Newcomb, T. M., Turner, R. H., and Converse, P. E., 1965, *Social psychology,* New York: Holt, Rinehart and Winston.

Newsweek, 1970, Tío Taco is dead!, June 27. [348]
1971, The militant homosexual, August 23. [350]

Niles, P., 1964, The relationship of susceptibility and anxiety to acceptance of fear arousing communications, unpublished Ph.D. dissertation, Yale University, New Haven, Conn. [92]

Nisbett, R. E., and Kanouse, D. E., 1969, Obesity, food deprivation, and supermarket shopping behavior, *Journal of Personality and Social Psychology,* **12,** 289–294.

Norman, R. D., 1953, The interrelationships among acceptance-rejection, self-other identity, insight into self, and realistic perception of others, *Journal of Social Psychology,* **37,** 205–235. [205]

North, R. C. *See* Zinnes, D. A.

Northway, M. L., 1940, A method for depicting social relationships obtained by sociometric testing, *Sociometry,* **3,** 144–150. [57]

Nunally, J. C., and Bobren, H. M., 1959, The variables governing the willingness to receive communications on mental health, *Journal of Personality,* **27,** 38–46. [92]

Nunn, C. Z., 1964, Child control through a "coalition with God," *Child Development,* **35,** 417–432. [117]

Nuttin, J. *See* Schachter, S.

Ober, R. L., Bentley, E. L., and Miller, E. A., 1971, *Systematic observation of teaching,* Englewood, N.J.: Prentice-Hall. [40]

Office of Strategic Services Assessment Staff (eds.), 1948, *Assessment of men,* New York: Holt, Rinehart and Winston. [302]

Ogden, C. K., and Richards, I. A., 1947, *The meaning of meaning,* New York: Harcourt Brace Jovanovich. [133]

Omwake, K. T., 1954, The relations between acceptance of self and acceptance of others shown by three personality inventories, *J. Consulting Psychology,* **18,** 443–446. [205]

Opton, E. M., 1970, Lessons of My Lai. In N. Sanford and C. Comstock (eds.), *Sanctions for evil,* San Francisco: Jossey Bass, 1970. [240]

Ora J. P., Jr., 1965, Characteristics of the volunteer for psychological investigations, Office of Naval Research Contract 214(03), Technical Report No. 27. [21]

Orne, M. T., 1962, On the social psychology of the psychological experiment: with particular reference to demand characteristics and their implications, *American Psychologist,* **17,** 776–783. [21]

Osgood, C. E.
  1952, The nature and measurement of meaning, *Psychological Bulletin,* **49,** 197–237. [53, 79, 80, 81]
  1953, *Method and theory in experimental psychology,* New York: Oxford University Press.
  1960, The cross-cultural generality of visual-verbal synesthetic tendencies, *Behavioral Science,* **5,** 146–169. [129]
  1963, *An alternative to war or surrender,* Urbana, Ill.: University of Illinois Press. [365]

Osgood, C. E., and Tannenbaum, P. H., 1955, The principles of congruity in the prediction of attitude changes, *Psychological Review,* **62,** 42–55. [75, 79, 80]

Osgood, C. E., Tannenbaum, P. H., and Suci, G. J., 1957, *The measurement meaning,* Urbana, Ill.: University of Illinois Press.

Osmaer, O. *See* Schachter, S.

Packard, V., 1957, *The hidden persuaders,* New York: McKay. [104, 175]

Paivio, A., Baldwin A. L., and Berger, S. N. 1959, Measures and correlates of audience anxiety or "stage fright," *Journal of Personality,* **27,** 1–17. [309, 310]
  1961, Measurement of children's sensitivity to audiences, *Child Development,* **32,** 721–730. [309, 310]

Paivio, A. *See also* Levin, H.

Parker, J. H., 1968, The interaction of Negroes and whites in an integrated church setting, *Social Forces,* **46,** 359–366. [198]

Parsons, T., 1959, An approach to psychological theory in terms of the theory of action. In S. Koch (ed.), *Psychology: a study of a science,* vol. 3, New York: McGraw-Hill.
  1960, *Structure and process in modern societies,* New York: Free Press. [280]

Partridge, E. D., 1934, Leadership among adolescent boys, *Teachers College, Columbia University Contributions to Education,* No. 608. [300, 301]

Passin, H. *See* Bennet, J. W.

Peil, G. *See* Schnierla, T. C.

Pepitone, A., and Kleiner, A., 1957, The effects of threat and frustration on group cohesiveness, *Journal of Abnormal and Social Psychology,* **54.** 192–199 [295]

Perlman, D., 1970, The encounter group versus psychiatrists, *San Francisco Chronicle,* May 18.

Perls, F. S., 1966, Address to APA convention, New York, 1966. [225]
  1969a, *In and out of the garbage pail,* Lafayette, Calif.: Real People Press. [204]
  1969b, *Gestalt therapy verbatim,* compiled and edited by J. O. Stevens, Lafayette, Calif.: Real People Press.

Pervin, L. A., and Yatko, R. J., 1965, Cigarette smoking and alternative methods of reducing dissonance, *Journal of Experimental Social Psychology,* **1,** 30–36. [102]

Pettifor, J. L., 1964, The role of language in development of abstract thinking: a comparison of hard-of-hearing and normal hearing on levels of conceptual thinking, Center for Study of Cognitive Processes, Detroit: Wayne State University. [136]

Pettigrew, T. F.
  1958, Personality and sociocultural factors in intergroup attitudes: a cross-national comparison, *Journal of Conflict Resolution,* **2,** 29–42. [198, 200]
  1964, *A profile of the Negro American,* New York: Van Nostrand. [176, 195]

Pheterson, G. I., Kiesler, S. B., and Goldberg, P., 1971, Evaluation of the performance of women as a function of their sex, achievement, and personal history, *Journal of Personality and Social Psychology,* **19,** 114–118. [153, 197]

Piaget, Jean

1926, *The language and thought of the child,* New York: Harcourt Brace Jovanovich. [135]

1932, *The moral judgment of the child,* London: Routledge & Kegan Paul.

1951, *Play, dreams, and imitation in childhood,* New York: Norton. [173]

1952, *The origins of intelligence in children,* New York: International Universities Press. [71, 75, 135, 169, 173]

See also Inhelder, B.

Pigors, P., 1935, *Leadership or domination,* Boston: Houghton Mifflin. [295]

Pike, F. H. *See* Chappell, M. N.

Piliavin, I. M., Rodin, J., and Piliavin, J. A., 1969, Good samaritanism: an underground phenomenon? *Journal of Personality and Social Psychology,* **4,** 289–299. [236]

Pope, B., 1953, Socioeconomic contrasts in children's peer culture prestige values, *Genetic Psychology Monographs,* **48,** 157–220. [152, 153, 213]

Porter, L. W., 1962, Job attitudes in management, I, *Journal of Applied Psychology,* **46,** 375–384.

1963, Job attitudes in management, IV, *Journal of Applied Psychology,* **47,** 386–397.

Poser, E. G. *See* Lambert, W. E.

Postman, L. J., and Schneider, B., 1951, Personal values, visual recognition and recall, *Psychological Review,* **58,** 271–284.

Postman, L. J. *See also* Allport, G. W.; Bruner, J. S.

Powdermaker, F. *See* Frank, J. D.

Preston, M. G., and Heinz, R. K., 1949, Effects of participatory versus supervisory leadership on group judgment, *Journal of Abnormal and Social Psychology,* **44,** 345–355. [297]

Pritzker, H. A. *See* Hovland, C. I.

Proctor, C. H., and Loomis, C. P., 1951, Analysis of sociometric data. In M. Jahoda, M. Dutch, and S. W. Cook (eds.), *Research methods in social relations: with especial reference to prejudice,* New York: Dryden. [58]

Proshansky, H. M., 1943, A projective method for the study of attitudes, *Journal of Abnormal and Social Psychology,* **38,** 393–395. [48]

Pruitt, D. G.

1969, "Walter Mitty" effect in individual and group risk taking, *Proceedings, 77th Annual Convention,* APA, 425–426. [312]

1971, Choice shifts in group discussion: an introduction review, *Journal of Personality and Social Psychology,* **20,** 339–360. [312]

Pudovkin, V. I., 1954, *Film technique and film acting,* London: Vision. [129, 210, 211]

Rabinowitch, E., 1964, *The dawn of a new age: reflections on science and human affairs,* Chicago: University of Chicago Press. [365]

Raiffa, H. *See* Luce, R. D.

Rakstis, T. J., 1970, Sensitivity training: fad, fraud, or new frontier? *Today's Health,* January.

Ransford, O., 1968, *Livingston's lake: the drama of Nyasa.* London: Murray. [178]

Raper, A., 1933, *The tragedy of lynching,* U.S. No. 614.35, Chapel Hill: University of North Carolina Press. [339]

Rapoport, A.

1963, Formal games as probing tools for investigating behavior motivated by trust and suspicion, *Journal of Conflict Resolution,* **7,** 570–579.

1964, *Strategy and conscience,* New York: Harper & Row. [242]

Raths, L., and Schweikert, E. F., 1946, Social acceptance within inter-racial school groups, *Educational Research Bulletin,* 85–90. [214]

Raven, B. H., and French, J. R. P., 1958, Group support, legitimate power, and social influence, *Journal of Personality,* **26,** 400–409. [238, 239]

Raven, B. H., and Rietsma, J., 1957, The effects of varied clarity of group goal and group path upon the individual and his relation to his group, *Human Relations,* **10,** 29–45. [318]

Razran, G.

1939, A quantitative study of meaning by a conditioned salivary technique (semantic conditioning), *Science,* **90,** 89–90. [78]

1950, Ethnic dislikes and stereotypes, *Journal of Abnormal and Social Psychology,* **45,** 7–27. [195, 196]

Reader's Digest, 1948, Highly irregular, September, **53,** 112. [131]

Redl, F., 1948, Resistance in therapy groups, *Human Relations,* **1,** 307–313. [296]

Redl, F., and Wineman, D., 1951, *Children who hate,* New York: Free press. [120]

Reese, H. W., 1961, Relationships between self-acceptance and sociometric choices, *Journal of Abnormal and Social Psychology,* **62,** 472–474. [163, 212, 213]

Reim, B., Glass, D. C., and Singer, J. E., 1971, Behavioral consequences of exposure to uncontrollable and unpredictable noise, *Journal of Applied Social Psychology,* **1,** 44–56. [127]

Reiss, A., 1951, Delinquency as the failure of personal and social controls, *American Sociological Review,* **16,** 196–207.

Reitsma, J. *See* Raven, G. H.

Rethlingshafer, D. *See* Hinckley, E. D.

Reuveni, U., and Speck, R. V., 1969, Using encounter group techniques in the treatment of the social network of schizophrenics, *International Journal of Group Psychotherapy,* October.

Rheingold, J., 1964, *The fear of being a woman: a theory of maternal destructiveness,* New York: Grune & Stratton.

Ricciuti, H. N. *See* Clark, R. A.

Richards, I. A. *See* Ogden, C. K.

Richards, J. M., Jr. *See* Cline, V. B.

Richardson, H. M., 1940, Community of values as a factor in friendship in college and adult women, *Journal of Social Psychology,* **11,** 303–312. [215]

Riesman, D., 1950, *The lonely crowd,* New Haven, Conn.: Yale University Press. [120, 165, 167]

Ring, K., 1963, Experimental social psychology: some sober reflections about some frivolous values. *Journal of Experimental Social Psychology,* **3,** 113–123. [22]

Ring, K., Lipinski, C. E., and Braginski, D., 1965, The relationship of birth order to self-evaluation, anxiety-reduction, and susceptibility to emotional contagion, *Psychology Monographs,* **79,** 10 (whole number 603). [218]

Riopelle, A. J., 1960, Complex processes, Chapter 8 in R. H. Waters, D. A. Rethlingshafer, and W. E. Caldwell (eds.), *Principles of comparative psychology,* New York: McGraw-Hill. [246, 266]

Robinson, M. Z. *See* Havighurst, R. J.

Roco, M. *See* Hudson, B. B.

Roethlisberger, F. J., and Dickson, W. J., 1939, *Management and the worker,* Cambridge, Mass.: Harvard University Press. [24, 258, 324]

Rogers, C. R., 1951, *Client-centered therapy,* Boston: Houghton Mifflin. [183]
1959, A theory of therapy personality, and interpersonal relationships, as developed in the client-centered framework. In S. Koch (ed.), *Psychology: a study of a science,* vol. 3, New York: McGraw-Hill. [87]

Rogerson, J. S. *See* Chappell, M. N.

Rokeach, M., 1960, *The open and closed mind,* New York: Basic Books. [179, 180]

Rommetveit, R. *See* Schachter, S.

Ronan, W. W., 1970a, Individual and situational variables relating to job satisfaction, *Journal of Applied Psychology Monographs,* vol. 54, no. 1. [317]
1970b, Importance of job characteristics, *Journal of Applied Psychology,* **54,** 192–200. [318]

Rosanoff, A. J. *See* Kent, G. H.

Rosen, B. 1956, The achievement syndrome, *American Sociological Review,* **21,** 203–211.

Rosen, B. C., 1955, Conflicting group membership: a study of parent-peer group cross-pressures, *American Sociological Review,* **20,** 155–161. [176]

Rosenbaum, M., 1956, The effect of stimulus and background factors on the volunteering response, *Journal of Abnormal and Social Psychology,* **53,** 118–121.
1965, *Group psychotherapy and psychodrama,* New York: McGraw-Hill. [303]
See also Blake, R. R.; Hartley, E. D.

Rosenbaum, M., and Blake, R. R., 1955, Volunteering as a function of field structure, *Journal of Abnormal and Social Psychology,* **50,** 193–196.

Rosenberg, L. A., 1963, Conformity as a function of confidence in self and confidence in partner, *Human Relations,* **16,** 131–139.

Rosenberg, M. J., 1965, When dissonance fails: on eliminating evaluation apprehension from attitude measurement, *Journal of Personality and Social Psychology,* **1,** 18–42. [21]
1969, The conditions and consequences of evaluation apprehension. In R. Rosenthal and R. L. Rosnow (eds.), *Artifact in behavioral research,* New York: Academic.

Rosenblith, J. F., 1959, *Learning by imitation in kindergarten children, Child Development,* **30,** 69–80. [246]

Rosenthal, R.
1958, Note on the fallible E, *Psychological Reports,* **4,** 662.
1963, Experimenter attributes as determinants of subjects' responses, *Journal of Projective Techniques and Personality Assessment,* **27,** 234–331. [20]
1964, Experimenter outcome-orientation and the results of the psychological experiment, *Psychological Bulletin,* **61,** 405–412.
1966, *Experimenter effects in behavioral research,* New York: Appleton. [20, 21]

Rosenthal, R., and Jacobson, L., 1968, *Pygmalion in the classroom: teacher expectation and pupils' intellectual development,* New York: Holt, Rinehart and Winston.

Rosenthal, R., and Rosnow, R. L., 1969, The volunteer subject. In R. Rosenthal and R. L. Rosnow (eds.), *Artifact and behavioral research,* New York: Academic. [21]

Rosnow, R., and Robinson, E. (eds.), 1967, *Experiments in persuasion,* New York: Academic. [94]

Rosnow, R. L., and Rosenthal, R., 1970, Volunteer effects in behavioral research. In T. M. Newcomb (ed.), *New directions in psychology, IV,* New York: Holt, Rinehart and Winston. [21]

Ross, I., and Zander, A., 1957, Need satisfaction and employee turnover, *Personnel Psychology,* **10,** 327–338. [294]

Rotter, J. B., 1966, Generalized expectancies for internal versus external control of reinforcement, *Psychology Monographs* 80 (whole number 609). [165, 167]

1967, A new scale for the measurement of interpersonal trust, *Journal of Personality,* **35,** 651–665. [21, 165, 167, 206]

1971, Locus of control, *Psychology Today,* **4,** June, 49–52. [166]

Rotter, J. B., and Mulray, R. C., 1965, Internal versus external locus of control of reinforcement and decision time, *Journal of Personality and Social Psychology,* **2,** 598–604.

Rubin, Z., 1970, Measurement of romantic love, *Journal of Personality and Social Psychology,* **16,** 265–273.

Rubovits, P. C., and Maehr, M. L., 1973, Pygmalion: black and white, *Journal of Personality and Social Psychology,* **25,** 210–218. [196]

Ruesch, J., Jacobsen, A., and Loeb, M. B., 1948, Acculturation and illness, *Psychology Monographs,* **62,** 1–40.

Ryack, B. L., 1965, A comparison of individual and group learning of nonsense syllables, *Journal of Personality and Social Psychology,* **2,** 296–299. [313]

Salisbury, H. E., 1958, *The shook-up generation,* New York: Harper & Row. [326, 339]

Sales, S. M. *See* Zajonc, R. B.

Sampson, E. E., and Insko, C. A., 1964, Cognitive consistency and performance in the autokinetic, *Journal of Abnormal and Social Psychology,* **53,** 118–121. [223]

Sanford, R. N. *See* Adorno, T. W.

Sanford, R. P., 1936, The effects of abstinence from food upon marginal processes: a preliminary report, *Journal of Psychology,* **13,** 283–293.

Satir, V., 1968, *Conjoint family therapy,* Palo Alto, Calif.: Science and Behavior Books. [183, 282]

1972, *Peoplemaking,* Palo Alto, Calif.: Science and Behavior Books.

Sattler, J., 1970, Racial "experimenter effects" in experimentation, testing, interviewing, and psychotherapy, *Psychological Bulletin,* **73,** 137–160. [20, 208]

Schachter, S.

1951, Communication, deviation, and rejection, *Journal of Abnormal and Social Psychology,* **46,** 190–207. [258, 282]

1959, *The psychology of affiliation: experimental studies of the sources of gregariousness,* Stanford, Calif.: Stanford University Press. [216, 218, 294, 316, 318]

1963, Birth order, eminence and higher education, *American Sociological Review,* **28,** 757–768. [176, 218]

See also Festinger, L.

Schachter, S., Ellertson, N., McBride, D., and Gregory, D., 1951, An experimental study of cohesiveness and productivity, *Human Relations,* **4,** 229–238.

Schachter, S., Nuttin, J., DeMonchaux, C., Maucorps, P. H., Osmer, O., Duijker, H., Rommetveit, R., and Israel, J., 1954, Cross-cultural experiments on threat and rejection, *Human Relations,* **7,** 405–440. [258]

Schafer, H. R., and Emerson, P. E., 1964, The development of social attachments in infancy, *Monographs, Society for Research in Child Development,* **29,** No. 3, 94. [232]

Scheidel, T., 1963, Sex and persuasibility, *Speech Monographs,* **30,** 353–358. [103]

Schein, E. H., 1957, Reaction patterns to severe chronic stress in American army prisoners of war of the Chinese, *Journal of Social Issues,* **13,** 21–30. [103]

Schiff, H. M. *See* Ausubel, D. P.

Schilder, P., 1940, Introductory remarks on group therapy, *Journal of Social Psychology,* **12,** 83–100. [326]

Schmitt, R. C., 1966, Density, health, and social disorganization, *Journal of American Institute of Planners,* **32,** 38–40. [127]

Schneider, B. *See* Postman, L. J.

Schneider, D. M., 1957, Political organization, supernatural sanctions, and the punishment for incest on Yap, *American Anthropologist,* **59,** 791–800. [117]

Schneirla, T. C., and Piel, G., 1948, The army ant, *Scientific American,* **413,** 2–9. [128]

Schoggen, M., Barker, L. S., and Barker, R. G., 1963, Structure of the behavior of American and English children. In R. G. Barker (ed.), *The stream of behavior,* New York: Appleton.

Schoggen, P., 1951, A study in psychological ecology: a description of the behavioral objects which entered the psychological habitat of an eight-year-old girl during the course of one day, unpublished Master's thesis, University of Kansas, Lawrence. [24]

Schokking, J. J., and Anderson, N., 1960, Observations on the European integration process, *Journal of Conflict Resolution,* **4,** 385–410. [365]

Schonbach, P. *See* Ehrlich, D.

Schultz, D. P., 1969, The human subject in psychological research, *Psychological Bulletin,* **72,** 214–228. [343, 345]

Schutz, W. C., 1955, What makes a group productive? *Human Relations,* **8,** 429–465. [317, 321]

Schwartz, C. G., 1957, Problems for psychiatric nurses in playing a new role in a mental hospital ward. In M. Greenbalt, D. J. Levinson, and R. H. Williams (eds.), *The patient and the mental hospital,* New York: Free Press, 402–406. [281]

Schwartz, H. A. *See* Stiller, A.

Schweikert, E. F. *See* Raths, L.

Scodel, A., and Austrin, H., 1957, The perception of Jewish photographs by non-Jews and Jews, *Journal of Abnormal Social Psychology,* **54,** 278–280. [196]

Scotch, N. A., 1960, A preliminary report on the relation of sociocultural factors of hypertension among the Zulus, *Annals of the New York Academy of Sciences,* **84,** 1000–1009. [127, 177]

Scott, W. A., 1957, Attitude change through reward of verbal behavior, *Journal of Abnormal and Social Psychology,* **55,** 72–75. [91, 101]

1959, Cognitive consistency, response reinforcement, and attitude change, *Sociometry,* **22,** 219–229. [91]

Seader, S. *See* Wells, W. D.

Sears, R. R.

1936, Experimental studies of projection, I, Attribution of traits, *Journal of Social Psychology,* **7,** 151–163. [205]

1944, Experimental analysis of psychoanalytic phenomena. In J. McV. Hunt (ed.), *Personality and the behavior disorders,* vol. 1, New York: Ronald, 306–332. [31]

Sears, R. R., Maccoby, E., and Levin, H., 1957, *Patterns of child-rearing,* New York: Harper & Row. [114, 146, 152, 164, 169, 231]

Seay, B., Alexander, B. K., and Harlow, H. F., 1964, Maternal behavior of socially deprived monkeys, *Journal of Abnormal and Social Psychology,* **69,** 345–354. [232]

Seeman, I., 1969, Deception in psychological research, *American Psychologist,* **24,** 1025–1028. [22]

Selltiz, C., Christ, J. R., Havel, J., and Cook, S. W., 1963, *Attitudes and social relations of foreign students in the United States,* Minneapolis: University of Minnesota Press. [367]

Senior Citizens News, 1971, **3,** 115. 1627 K St. NW, Washington, D.C. 20006. [350]

Shannon, L. W., 1954, The opinions of Little Orphan Annie and her friends, *Public Opinion Quarterly,* **18,** 167–179. [124, 335]

Shaw, M. E.

1954, Some effects of problem solving complexity upon problem solution efficiency in different communication nets, *Journal of Experimental Psychology,* **48,** 211–217. [288, 322, 323]

1956, Random versus systematic distribution of information in communication nets, *Journal of Personality,* **25,** 59–69. [288, 322, 323]

1958, Some effect of irrelevant information upon problem solving in small groups, *Journal of Social Psychology,* **47,** 33–37. [322, 323]

Shearer, Lloyd, 1966, Why they dress this way, *Parade Magazine,* October 16, 30–31. [347]

Sheats, P. *See* Benne, K.

Sheatsley, P. B. *See* Hyman, H. H.

Sheffield, F. D. *See* Hovland, C. I.

Shelley, H. P., 1950. The role of success and failure in determining attitude toward the group as a means to member goals, *Conference Research,* Ann Arbor: University of Michigan. [294]

Shellow, R. S., and Roemer, D. V., 1966, The riot that did not happen. *Social problems,* **14,** 221–233. [341]

Shepherd, I., *See* Fagan, J.

Sherif, M.

1948, *An outline of social psychology,* New York: Harper & Row.

1966, *The psychology of social norms,* New York: Harper & Row. [264, 268]

See also Hovland, C. I.

Sherif, M., and Harvey, O. J., 1952, A study in ego functioning: eliminating of stable anchorages in individual and group situations, *Sociometry,* **15,** 272–307. [269]

Sherif, M., Harvey, O. J., White, B. J., Hood, W. R., and Sherif, C. W., 1954, *Experimental study of positive and negative intergroup attitudes between experimentally produced groups: robbers cave study,* Norman: University of Oklahoma Press. [358, 359]

Sherif, M., and Sherif, C. W.

1948, The standardization of names, unpublished manuscript, cited in M. Sherif and C. W. Sherif, *An outline of social psychology,* New York: Harper & Row, 477–481.

1956, *An outline of social psychology,* rev. ed., New York: Harper & Row. [358]

Sherwood, J., and Nataupsky, M., 1968, Predicting the conclusions of Negro-white intelligence research from biographical characteristics of the investigator, *Journal of Personality and Social Psychology,* **8,** 53–58. [152]

Shipman, V. *See* Hess, R. D.

Shostrum, E. L., 1969, Group therapy: let the buyer beware, *Psychology Today,* May.

Shuey, A. M.

1958, *The testing of Negro intelligence,* Lynchburg, Va.: Bell.

1966, *The testing of Negro intelligence,* 2nd ed., New York: Social Science Press. [150]

Shuy, R., 1964, *Social dialects and language learning,* Champaign, Ill.: National Council of Teachers of English.

Sidis, B., 1898, *The psychology of suggestion*, New York: Appleton. [262]

Sigall, R., Aronson, E., and Van Hoose, T., 1970, The cooperative subject: myth or reality, *Journal of Experimental Social Psychology*, **6**, 1–10. [21]

Sikes, M. P., and Cleveland, S. E., 1968, Human relations training for police and community, *American Psychologist*, **23**, 766–769.

Silverman, I., 1970, The psychological subject in the land of make-believe, *Contemporary Psychology*, **12**, 718–721. [22]

Silverman, I., Shulman, A., and Weisenthal, D. L., 1970, Effects of deceiving and debriefing psychological subjects on performance in later experiments, *Journal of Personality and Social Psychology*, **14**, 203–212.

Simmel, G., 1902, The number of members as determining the sociological form of the group, *American Journal of Sociology*, **8**, 1–46. [299]

Simmel, M. *See* Heider, F.

Simon, H. A. *See* March, J. G.

Simons, C. W., and Piliavin, J. A., 1972, Effect of deception on reactions to a victim, *Journal of Personality and Social Psychology*, **21**, 56–60.

Singer, J. L., and Goldman, G. D., 1954, Experimentally contrasted social atmospheres in group psychotherapy with chronic schizophrenics, *Journal of Social Psychology*, **40**, 23–37. [304]

Singer, J. L., and Schonbar, R., 1961, Correlates of day dreaming: a dimension of self-awareness, *Journal of Consulting Psychology*, **25**, 1–6.

Singer, J. L. *See also* Feshbach, S.

Sistrunk, F., and McDavid, J. W., 1971, Sex variable in conforming behavior, *Journal of Personality and Social Psychology*, **2**, 200–207. [275, 276]

Skeels, H. M., 1966, Adult status of children with contrasting early life experiences, *Monographs, Society for Research in Child Development*, **31**, No. 105.

Skinner, B. F.
1938, *The behavior of organisms: an experimental approach*, New York: Appleton.
1948, *Walden Two*, New York: Macmillan. [352]
1953, *Science and human behavior*, New York: Macmillan. [118]
1957, *Verbal behavior*, New York: Appleton. [136]
1971, *Beyond freedom and dignity*, New York: Knopf. [87]

Slater, C. W., 1959, Some factors associated with internalization of motivation towards occupational role performance, Ph.D. dissertation, University of Michigan, Ann Arbor. [325]

Slater, P., 1955, Role differentiation in small groups, *American Sociological Review*, **20**, 300–310. [207, 284]

Slavson, S. R.
1943, *An introduction to group therapy*, New York: Commonwealth Fund. [304]
1955, Criteria for selection and rejection of patients for various types of group psychotherapy, *International Journal of Group Psychotherapy*, **5**, 3–30. [303]

Smelser, N., 1962, *Theory of collective behavior*, New York: Free Press. [350]

Smith, A. J., Madden, H. E., and Sobol, R., 1957, Productivity and recall in cooperative and competitive discussion groups, *Journal of Psychology*, **43**, 193–204. [323]

Smith, B. O. (ed.), 1971, *Research on teacher education: a symposium*, Englewood Cliffs, N.J.: Prentice-Hall. [297]

Smith, D. A., 1967, A speaker's model project to enhance pupils' self-esteem, *Journal of Negro Education*, **36**, 177–180. [118]

Smith, E. E., 1957, Effects of clear and unclear role expectations on group productivity, *Journal of Abnormal and Social Psychology*, **55**, 213–217. [282]

Smith, M. B. *See* Stein, D. D.

Smith, R., 1967, Behind the riots, *American Education*, **10**, 2–3. [118]

Smith, R. J., Ramsey, C. E., and Castillo, G., 1963, Parental authority and job choices: sex differences in three cultures, *American Journal of Sociology*, **69**, 143–149.

Smucker, L. L., 1960, Human encounter, personality types, and implicit theory of personality, *Dissertation Abstracts*, **20**, 3873. [216]

Smuts, R. W., 1953, *European impression of the American workers*, New York: King's Crown. [324]

Snow, R. E., 1969, Unfinished business: review of "Pygmalion in the Classroom," *Contemporary Psychology*, **14**, 197–199.

Snowden, E. N., 1940, Mass psychotherapy, *Lancet*, **11**, 759–770. [304]

Snyder, R. *See* French, J. R. P.

Snyder, R. C., Bruck, H. W., and Sapin, B., 1962, *Foreign policy decision-making: an approach to the study of international politics*, New York: Free Press. [359]

Sommer, R., 1969, *Personal space*, Englewood Cliffs, N.J.: Prentice-Hall. [125, 127]

Sommer, R., and Becker, F. D., 1969, Territorial defense and the good neighbor, *Journal of Personality and Social Psychology*, **11**, 85–92. [125, 127]

Spence, K. W.
1948, The methods and postulates of "Behaviorism," *Psychological Review*, **55**, 67–78. [32]

1956, *Behavior theory and conditioning,* New Haven, Conn.: Yale University Press.

1958, A theory of emotionally based drive (D) and its relation to performance in simple learning situations, *American Psychologist,* **13,** 131–141.

Spencer, H., 1855, *Principles of psychology,* London: Williams & Norgate.

Speroff, B., and Kerr, W., 1952, Steelmill "hot strip" accidents and interpersonal desirability values, *Journal of Clinical Psychology,* **8,** 89–91. [213]

Spiegel, J. *See* Grinker, R.

Spiro, M. E., 1958, *Children of the kibbutz,* Cambridge, Mass.: Harvard University Press. [175]

Spitz, R. A.

1945, Hospitalism: an inquiry into the genesis of psychiatric conditions in early childhood, in A. Freud et al. (eds.), *The psychoanalytic study of the child,* vol. 1, pp. 53–74, New York: International Universities Press. [232]

1946, Hospitalism: a follow-up report on investigations described in vol. 1, 1945. In A. Freud et al. (eds.), *The psychoanalytic study of the child,* vol. 2, pp. 113–117, New York: International Universities Press, 1946. [232]

Spitz, R. A., and Wolf, K. M., 1946, Anaclitic depression: an inquiry into the genesis of psychiatric conditions in early childhood, II. In A. Freud, et al. (eds.), *The psychoanalytic study of the child,* vol. 2, pp. 313–342, New York: International Universities Press.

Stagner, R., 1958, Motivational aspects of industrial morale, *Personnel Psychology,* **11,** 64–70. [325]

Steele, M. B., 1966, *Matrix indices and behavior in mixed-motive games,* Ph.D. dissertation, University of Miami, Coral Gables. [63, 241]

Stefano, J. S. *See* Chappell, M. N.

Stefflre, V. *See* Lantz, D.

Stein, D. D., Hardyck, J. A., and Smith, M. B., 1965, Race and belief: an open and shut case, *Journal of Personality and Social Psychology,* **1,** 281–289. [198]

Steiner, G. A. *See* Berelson, B.

Stendler, C. B., Damrin, D., and Haines, A. C., 1951, Studies in cooperation and competition, I, The effects of working for group and individual rewards on the social climate of children's groups, *Journal of Genetic Psychology,* **21,** 241–260. [323]

Stern, C., and Kiesler, E. W., 1968, *OSCI: Observational system for classroom interaction,* Southwestern Regional Laboratory, 11300 LaCienega Boulevard, Inglewood, Calif., 90304.

Stevenson, H. W.

1961, Social reinforcement with children as a function of CA, sex of E, and sex of S, *Journal of Abnormal and Social Psychology,* **62,** 147–154. [114]

1965, Address of the President of Division 7, American Psychological Association, Chicago, III., 1965, *A.P.A. Division Seven Newsletter,* Winter.

Stiller, A., Schwartz, H. A., and Cowen, E. L., 1965, The social desirability of trait-descriptive terms among high school students, *Child Development,* **36,** 981–1001. [167]

Stogdill, R. M., 1948, Personal factors associated with leadership, *Journal of Psychology,* **25,** 35–71. [300]

Stonequist, E. V., 1937, *The marginal man,* New York: Scribner. [178]

Storms, M. D., and Nisbett, R. E., 1970, Insomnia and the attribution process, *Journal of Personality and Social Psychology,* **16,** 319–328. [192]

Stotland, E., Zander, A., and Natsoulas, T., 1961, Generalization of interpersonal similarity, *Journal of Abnormal and Social Psychology,* **62,** 265–274. [97]

Stotland, E. *See also* Katz, D.

Streufert, S., Clardy, M., Driver, M. J., Karlins, M., Schroder, H. M., and Suedfeld, P., 1965, A tactical game for the analysis of complex decision making in individuals and groups, *Psychological Reports,* **17,** 723–729. [63]

Stricker, L. J., 1967, The true deceiver, *Psychological Bulletin,* **68,** 13–20.

Stricker, L. J., Messick, S., and Jackson, D. N., 1959, Evaluating deception in psychological research, *Psychological Bulletin,* **71,** 343–351.

1970, Models of conformity, *Journal of Personality and Social Psychology,* **16,** 494–507.

Strickland, B. E., 1972, Delay of gratification as a function of race of the experimenter, *Journal of Personality and Social Psychology,* **22,** 108–112. [20]

Strodtbeck, F. L., and Mann, R. D., 1956, Sex role differentiation in jury deliberations, *Sociometry,* **19,** 3–11. [284]

Stroebe, W., Insko, C. A., Thompson, V. D., and Layton, B. D., 1971, Effects of physical attractiveness, attitude similarity, and sex on various aspects of interpersonal attraction, *Journal of Personality and Social Psychology,* **18,** 79–81. [226]

Sundberg, N. D., Rohila, P. K., and Tyler, L. E., 1970, Values of Indian and American adolescents, *Journal of Personality and Social Psychology,* **16,** 374–397. [137]

Swanson, G. E. *See* Miller, D. R.

Swanson, L. *See* Willerman, B.

Symonds, P. M., 1925, Notes on rating, *Journal of Applied Psychology,* **7,** 188–195. [201]

Taft, R., 1955, The ability to judge people, *Psychological Bulletin,* **52,** 1–28. [205]

Tagiuri, R.
1952, Relational analysis: an extension of sociometric method with emphasis upon social perception, *Sociometry,* **15,** 91–104. [59]
1957, The perception of feeling among members of small groups, *Journal of Social Psychology,* **46,** 219–227. [164]
See also Goodnow, R. E.

Tagiuri, R., Kogan, N., and Bruner, J. S., 1955, The transparency of interpersonal choice, *Sociometry,* **18,** 624–635. [206]

Tannenbaum, A. S., Wechsler, I. R., and Massarik, F., 1961, *Leadership and organization: a behavioral science approach.* New York: McGraw-Hill.

Tannenbaum, P. H., 1956, Initial attitude toward source and concept as factors in attitude change through communication, *Public Opinion Quarterly,* **20,** 413–425. *See also* Osgood, C. E. [97, 98]

Tarde, G., 1890, *The laws of imitation* (original French ed., 1890), trans., New York: Holt, Rinehart and Winston, 1903. [338]

Taylor, D. W., and Faust, W. L., 1952, Twenty questions: efficiency in problem solving as a function of size of group, *Journal of Experimental Psychology,* **44,** 360–368. [274, 320, 321]

Taylor, I. K.
1956, Awareness of one's social appeal, *Human Relations,* **9,** 47–56. [164]
1963, Phonetic symbolism re-examined, *Psychological Bulletin,* **60,** 200–209. [131]

Taylor, J. A., 1953, A personality scale of manifest anxiety, *Journal of Abnormal and Social Psychology,* **48,** 285–290. [274]

Tebbel, J., 1972, Credibility of news sources among the mass media, *Saturday Review,* January 8, 48–49. [335]

Teevan, R. *See* Clark, R. A.

Tessler, R. C., and Schwartz, S. H., 1972, Help seeking, self-esteem, and achievement motivation: an attributional analysis, *Journal of Personality and Social Psychology,* **3,** 318–326. [233]

Thelen, H., 1949, Group dynamics in instruction: principle of least group size, *School Review,* **57,** 139–148. [320, 321, 325]

Thelen, H., and Withal, J., 1949, Three frames of reference: a description of climate, *Human Relations,* **2,** 159–176. [325]

Thibaut, J. W., and Kelley, H. H., 1959, *The social psychology of groups,* New York: Wiley. [230, 239, 267]

Thistlethwaite, D., 1950, Attitude and structure as factors in the distortion of reasoning, *Journal of Abnormal and Social Psychology,* **45,** 442–458. [48]

Thomas, W. I., 1937, *Primitive behavior,* New York: McGraw-Hill. [133]

Thornton, G. R., 1944, The effect of wearing glasses upon judgments of personality traits of persons seen briefly, *Journal of Applied Psychology,* **28,** 203–207. [200]

Thurstone, L. L.
1928, Attitudes can be measured, *American Journal of Sociology,* **33,** 529–554. [193]
1929, Theory of attitude measurement, *Psychological Bulletin,* **36,** 222–241. [51]
1931, The measurement of social attitudes, *Journal of Abnormal and Social Psychology,* **26,** 249–269. [51]

Thurstone, L. L., and Chave, E. J., 1929, *The measurement of attitudes,* Chicago: University of Chicago Press. [51]

Time, 1970, Human potential: the revolution in feeling, November 9, 54–58.

Titchener, E. B., 1910, *A textbook of psychology,* New York: Macmillan. [262]

Toch, Hans, 1965, *The social psychology of social movements,* Indianapolis: Bobbs-Merrill. [347]

Townsend, C. W., 1928, Food prejudices, *Scientific Monthly,* **26,** 65–66. [140]

Townsend, R., 1970, *Up the Organization,* New York: Knopf. [353]

Trapp, P., 1955, Leadership and popularity as a function of behavioral predictions, *Journal of Abnormal and Social Psychology,* **51,** 452–457. [301]

Trent, R. D., 1957, The relation between expressed self-acceptance and expressed attitudes toward Negroes and whites among Negro children, *Journal of Genetic Psychology,* 91, 25–31. [163]

Triandis, H. C., 1971, *Attitude and attitude change,* New York: Wiley.

Triandis, H. C., and Triandis, L. M., 1962, A cross-cultural study of social distance, *Psychological Monographs,* **76,** 21, whole number 540.

Triandis, L. M. *See* Lambert, W. W.; Triandis, H. C.

Triplett, N., 1897, The dynamogenic factors in pacemaking and competition, *American Journal of Psychology,* **9,** 507–533. [308, 309]

Trow, D. D., 1957, Autonomy and job satisfaction in task-oriented groups, *Journal of Abnormal and Social Psychology,* **54,** 204–209. [286]

Truax, C. W., and Carkhuff, R. R., 1967, *Toward effective counseling and psychotherapy: training and practice,* Chicago: Aldine-Atherton. [204]

Tuckman, B., 1963, Personality structure, group composition, and group functioning, doctoral dissertation, Princeton University, Princeton, N.J.

Tuckman, J., and Lorge, I., 1962, Individual ability as a determinant of group superiority, *Human Relations*, **15**, 45–51. [27, 313]

Tuddenham, R. D.

1958, The influence of a distorted group norm upon individual judgment. *Journal of Psychology*, **46**, 227–241.

1961, *Studies in conformity and yielding: a summary and interpretation*, final report, Office of Naval Research Contract NR 170–159, Berkeley: University of California. [276]

Tuddenham, R. D., and McBride, P. D., 1959, The yielding experiment from the subject's point of view, *Journal of Personality*, **27**, 259–271.

Tuddenham, R. D., McBride, P. D., and Zahn, V., 1958, The influence of the sex composition of the group upon yielding to a distorted norm, *Journal of Psychology*, **46**, 243–251. [272]

Turner, R. H., and Killian, L. M., 1957, *Collective behavior*, Englewood Cliffs, N.J.: Prentice-Hall. [342]

Udry, J. R., 1960, The importance of social class in a suburban school, *Journal of Educational Sociology*, **33**, 307–310. [215, 216]

Veblen, T. B., 1899, *The theory of the leisure class: an economic study of institutions*, New York: Viking, 1931 (original edition, 1899). [174]

Vinacke, W. E., 1969, Variables in experimental games: toward a field theory, *Psychological Bulletin*, **71**, 293–318. [244]

Volkman, I. See Chapman, D. W.

von Frisch, K., 1950, *Bees: their vision, chemical senses, and languages*, Ithaca, N.Y.: Cornell University Press. [128]

Vreeland, R. S., 1972, Is it true what they say about Harvard boys? *Psychology Today*, **5**, January, 65–68. [226]

Wagner, C., and Wheeler, L., 1969, Model, need, and cost effects in helping behavior, *Journal of Personality and Social Psychology*, **12**, 11–116.

Walker, E. L., and Heyns, R. W., 1962, *An anatomy for conformity*, Englewood Cliffs, N.J.: Prentice-Hall. [274]

Wallach, A. M., Kogan, N., and Bem, D. J.

1962, Group influence of individual risk taking, *Journal of Abnormal and Social Psychology*, **65**, 75–86. [241, 312]

1964, Diffusion of responsibility and level of risk-taking in groups, *Journal of Abnormal and Social Psychology*, **68**, 265–279. [312]

1965, Group decision making under risk of aversive consequences, *Journal of Personality and Social Psychology*, **1**, 453–460. [312]

Walster, B. See Walster, E.

Walster, E., Aronson, E., and Abrahams, D., 1966, On increasing the persuasiveness of a low-prestige communicator, *Journal of Experimental Social Psychology*, **2**, 325–342. [96]

Walster, E., Aronson, V., Abrahams, D., and Rottman, L., 1966, Importance of physical attractiveness in dating behavior, *Journal of Personality and Social Psychology*, **4**, 508–516. [226]

Walster, E., and Walster, B., 1963, Effect of expecting to be liked on choice of associates, *Journal of Abnormal and Social Psychology*, **67**, 402–404. [216, 293, 294]

Walster, E., Walster, G. W., Piliavin, J., and Schmidt, L., 1973, "Playing hard to get": understanding an elusive phenomenon, *Journal of Personality and Social Psychology*, **26**, 113–121. [227]

Walter, A. A. See Carmichael, L.

Walters, R. See Bandura, A.

Warner, W. L., Meeker, M., and Eels, K., 1949, *Social class in America*, Chicago: Science Research. [357]

Watson, S. See Kagan, J.

Wayne, I. See McGranahan, D. V.

Wechsler, H., Solomon, L., and Kramer, B. M., 1970, *Social psychology and mental health*, New York: Holt, Rinehart and Winston. [277]

Weiss, W., and Steenbock, S., 1965, The influence on communication effectiveness of explicitly urging action and policy consequences, *Journal of Experimental Social Psychology*, **1**, 396–406. [93]

Weiss, W. See also Hovland, C. I.

Weisstein, N., 1969, Woman as nigger, *Psychology Today*, **3**, 20–27.

Wells, W. D., Goi, F. J., and Seader, S., 1958, A change in a product image, *Journal of Applied Psychology*, **42**, 120–121. [194]

Wever, E. G., and Zener, K. E., 1928, The method of absolute judgment in psychophysics, *Psychological Review*, **35**, 466–493. [72]

White, R. K., and Lippitt, R. O., 1960, *Autocracy and democracy*, New York: Harper & Row. [291]

White, T. M., 1960, *The making of a president: 1960*, New York: Harper & Row. [104]

1973, *The making of a president: 1972*, New York: Atheneum. [104]

White, W. S., 1956, Who really runs the Senate? *Harper's Magazine*, **213**, 35–40. [256]

Whiting, B., and Whiting, J. W. M., 1966, *Six cultures, rev. ed.,* New York: Wiley. [139]

Whiting, J. W. M.

1944, The frustration complex in Kwoma society, *Man,* **44,** 140–144.

1959, Sorcery, sin, and the superego: a cross-cultural study of some mechanisms of social control, *Nebraska Symposium on Motivation,* M. R. Jones (ed.), Lincoln: University of Nebraska Press. [117]

Whittaker, J. O.

1965a, Sex differences and susceptibility to interpersonal persuasion, *Journal of Social Psychology,* **66,** 91–96.

1965b, Attitude change and communication-attitude discrepancy, *Journal of Social Psychology,* **65,** 141–148. [99]

Whittemore, I. C., 1924, The influence of competition on performance: an experimental study, *Journal of Abnormal and Social Psychology,* **19,** 236–253. [309]

Whorf, B. L., 1940, Science and linguistics, *Technology Review,* **34,** 229–231, 247–248. [132]

Whyte, W. F.

1943, *Street corner society: the social structure of an Italian slum,* Chicago: University of Chicago Press. [282, 298, 319]

1948, *Human relations in the restaurant industry,* New York: McGraw-Hill.

1955, *Money and motivation: an analysis of incentives in industry,* New York: Harper & Row. [282]

1956, *The organization man,* New York: Simon & Schuster. [120]

Wicker, A. W., 1969, Attitudes versus actions: The relationship of verbal and overt behavioral responses to attitude objects, *Journal of Social Issues,* **25**(4), 41–78. [86]

Wicker, A. W., 1971, An examination of the "other variables" explanation of attitude-behavior inconsistency, *Journal of Personality and Social Psychology,* **19,** 18–30. [86]

Willerman, B., 1943, Group decision and request as means of changing food habits, Washington, D.C.: Committee on Food Habits, N.R.C. [260]

Willerman, B., and Swanson, L., 1953, Group prestige in voluntary organizations, *Human Relations,* **6,** 57–77 [316]

Williams, G. G., 1935, *Creative writing,* New York: Harper & Row. [131]

Willis, R. H., and Hollander, E. P., 1964, An experimental study of three response modes in social influence situation, *Journal of Abnormal and Social Psychology,* **69,** 150–156. [267, 270]

Wilson, K. W., *See* Bixenstein, V. E.

Wilson, P. R., 1968, Perceptual distortion of height as a function of ascribed academic status, *Journal of Social Psychology,* **74,** 97–102. [207]

Wilson, W. C., 1958, Imitation and the learning of incidental cues by preschool children, *Child Development,* **29,** 393–398. [246]

See also Maccoby, E.

Winch, R. F., Ktsanes, T., and Ktsanes, V., 1954, The theory of complementary needs in mate selection: an analytic and descriptive study, *American Sociological Review,* **19,** 214–249. [224–225]

Wineman, D. *See* Redl, F.

Winnick, C., 1964, Taboo and disapproved colors and symbols in the various foreign countries, *Journal of Social Psychology,* **59,** 361–368. [129]

Wispe, L. G., 1951, Evaluating section teaching methods in the introductory course, *Journal of Educational Research,* **45,** 161–186. [325]

Withal, I. *See* Thelen, H.

Witkin, H. A., Dyk, R. B., Faterson, H. F., Goodenough, D. R., and Karp, S. A., 1962, *Psychological differentiation: studies of mental development,* New York: Wiley. [76]

Wittreich, W. J., 1952, The Honi phenomenon: a case of selective perceptual distortion, *Journal of Abnormal and Social Psychotherapy,* **4,** 1–68. [304]

Wolf, M. M. *See* Allen, K. E.; Lambert, W. W. groups, Part 2, *American Journal of Psychotherapy,* 4, 1–68. [304]

Wolf, M. M. *See* Allen, K. E.; Lambert, W. W.

Wolfe, J. B., 1970, Some psychological characteristics of American policemen: a critical review of the literature, *Proceedings,* 78th Convention, APA, 453–454.

Wolin, L. R., 1956, An analysis of the content of interpersonal perception, *Dissertation Abstracts,* **16,** 396–397.

Wong, A. S., 1971, Encounter and the marginal man—a search for identity: the psychological aspects. In Buckhout, R. (ed.), *Toward social change,* New York: Harper & Row. [349]

Woodworth, R. S., 1938, *Experimental psychology,* New York: Holt, Rinehart and Winston. [80]

Worthy, M., and Markle, A., 1970, Racial differences in reactive versus self-paced activities, *Journal of Personality and Social Psychology,* **16,** 439–443. [150]

Wright, H. F. *See* Barker, R. G.

Wright, J. M., and Harvey, O. J., 1965, Attitude change as a function of authoritarianism and punitiveness, *Journal of Personality and Social Psychology,* **1,** 177–181. [180]

Wrightsman, L. S., 1960, Effects of waiting with others in felt levels of anxiety, *Journal of Abnormal and Social Psychology,* **61,** 216–222. [218]

1968, *Contemporary issues in social psychology,* Belmont, Calif.: Brooks-Cole.

Wrightsman, L. S., 1969, Wallace supporters and adherence to "law and order," *Journal of Personality and Social Psychology,* **13,** 17–22. [87]

Wrightsman, L. S., O'Connor, J., and Baker, N. J., 1972, *Cooperation and competition: readings on mixed motive games,* Belmont, Calif.: Brooks-Cole. [244]

Wuebben, P. L., 1967, Honesty of subjects and birth order, *Journal of Personality and Social Psychology,* **5,** 350–352.

Wurster, C. R. *See* Bass, B. M.

Wyer, R. S., 1970, Information redundancy, inconsistency, and novelty and their role in impression formation, *Journal of Experimental Social Psychology,* **6,** 11–127. [200]

Yatko, R. J. *See* Pervin, L. A.

Yinger, J. M., 1960, Contraculture and subculture, *American Sociological Review,* **25,** 625–635. [357]

Zagora, S., and Harter, M., 1966, Credibility of source and recipient's attitude: factors in the perception and retention of information on smoking behavior, *Perceptual and Motor Skills,* **23,** 155–168. [96]

Zajonc, R. B., and Sales, S. M., 1966, Social facilitation of dominant and subordinate responses, *Journal of Experimental Social Psychology,* **2,** 160–168. [310]

Zander, A. F. *See* Cartwright, D. R.; Hurwitz, J. I.; Ross, I.; Stotland, E.

Zander, A. F., and Medow, H., 1963, Individual and group levels of aspiration, *Human Relations,* **16,** 89–105. [315]

Zazzo, R., 1960, *Les jumeaux, le couple, et la personne,* Paris: Presses des Universités de France.

Zeigarnik, B., 1927, Das Behalten erledgiter und unerledgiter Handliegen (The memory of completed and uncompleted actions), *Psychologische Forschung,* 1–85. [315]

Zeleny, L. D., 1939, Characteristics of group leaders, *Sociological Research,* **24,** 140–149. [300]

Zillig, K., 1928, Einstellung und Aussage, *Zeitung Für Psychologie,* **106,** 58–106. [191]

Zimet, C. N., and Fine, H. J., 1955, A quantitative method of scoring picture story tests, *Journal of Clinical Psychology,* **11,** 24–28. [304]

Zimbardo, P., Ebbesen, E., and Fraser, S., 1968, Emotional persuasion: arousal state as a distractor, unpublished manuscript, Stanford University, Stanford, Calif. [90]

Zimbardo, P. G., and Formica, R., 1963, Emotional comparison and self-esteem as determinants of affiliation, *Journal of Personality,* **31,** 141–162. [218]

Zimbardo, P. G., Weisenberg, M., Firestone, I., and Levy, B., 1965, Communicator effectiveness in producing public conformity and private attitude change, *Journal of Personality,* **33,** 233–256. [92]

Zimmerman, R. R. *See* Harlow, H. F.

Zinnes, D. A., 1962, Hostility in international decision-making, *Journal of Conflict Resolution,* **6,** 236–243. [364]

Zinnes, D. A., North, R. C., and Koch, H. E., 1961, Capability, threat, and the outbreak of war. In J. N. Rosenau (ed.), *International politics and foreign policy,* New York: Free Press. [364]

SUBJECT INDEX